TOWARDS VERY LARGE KNOWLEDGE BASES

Towards Very Large Knowledge Bases

Knowledge Building & Knowledge Sharing 1995

Edited by

N.J.I. Mars

University of Twente, Enschede, The Netherlands

1995

IOS
Press

Ohmsha

Amsterdam, Oxford, Tokyo, Washington, DC

ISBN 90 5199 217 3 (IOS Press)
ISBN 4 274 90049 5 C3000 (Ohmsha)
Library of Congress Catalogue Card Number 95-075767

Publisher
IOS Press
Van Diemenstraat 94
1013 CN Amsterdam
Netherlands

Distributor in the UK and Ireland
IOS Press/Lavis Marketing
73 Lime Walk
Headington
Oxford OX3 7AD
England

Distributor in the USA and Canada
IOS Press, Inc.
P.O. Box 10558
Burke, VA 22009-0558
USA

Distributor in Japan
Ohmsha, Ltd.
3-1 Kanda Nishiki - Cho
Chiyoda - Ku
Tokyo 101
Japan

PRINTED IN THE NETHERLANDS

Preface

In the early days of Artificial Intelligence, up to the 1970's, it was widely believed that future powerful computers would enable mankind to solve many real-world problems through the use of very general inference procedures and very little domain-specific knowledge. With the benefit of hindsight, this view can now be called quite naive. The field of Expert Systems, which got its start around 1970, embraced the paradigm that *Knowledge is Power:* even very fast computers require very large amounts of very specific knowledge to solve non-trivial problems. Thus, the field of Large Knowledge Bases has emerged.

The First International Conference on Building and Sharing Very Large-Scale Knowledge Bases, held in December 1993 in Tokyo, Japan, offered the first opportunity for researchers and practitioners in this field to meet. The papers in the present book reflect the progress made since that first meeting. All papers in this volume were presented at the Second International Conference on Building and Sharing Very Large-Scale Knowledge Bases, held in April 1995 at the University of Twente, Enschede, The Netherlands.

It is remarkable that even in the short time since the first conference, considerable progress has been achieved. Two large-scale projects, EDR and CYC, have been (almost) completed; their results now await commercial exploitation. In specific scientific domains, progress has been even more formidable: in molecular biology, for instance, large knowledge bases have become (part of the) essential tools for researchers in that domain, as reported in this volume.

Another development, already visible at the first conference, and quite evident in this book, is the attention being paid to structuring large knowledge bases. Here, the use of a carefully developed set of concepts, called an ontology, is becoming almost standard practice.

I hope that, like its predecessor, this book will be a guide to the current state of the art in building and sharing very large knowledge bases, and a catalyst to future research, development and applications.

Nicolaas J.I. Mars
Chair, KB&KS'95
April 1995

Contents

Preface   v

Part 1. Towards Large Knowledge Bases   1
Steps to Sharing Knowledge, *D.B. Lenat*   3
Knowledge Bases and Computational Molecular Biology, *F. Rechenmann*   7
The Impact of the EDR Electronic Dictionary on Very Large Knowledge Bases, *T. Yokoi*   13

Part 2. The Role of Ontologies   23
Ontologies and Knowledge Bases Towards a Terminological Clarification, *N. Guarino and
   P. Giaretta*   25
Ontological Commitment and Domain-Specific Architectures: Experience with Comet and
   Cosmos, *W. Mark, J. Dukes-Schlossberg and R. Kerber*   33
Task Ontology for Reuse of Problem Solving Knowledge, *R. Mizoguchi, J. Vanwelkenhuysen
   and M. Ikeda*   46
The Generalized Upper Model Knowledge Base: Organization and Use, *J. Bateman,
   B. Magnini and G. Fabris*   60
Ontologies for Very Large Knowledge Bases in Materials Science: a Case Study,
   P.E. van der Vet, P.-H. Speel and N.J.I.Mars   73
A Knowledge Media Approach to Ontology Development, *T. Nishida, H. Takeda, K. Iino
   and M. Nishiki*   84

Part 3. Knowledge Acquisition   95
Steps Towards Automated Knowledge Acquisition, *Y. Wilks and S. Nirenberg*   97
Knowledge Acquisition from Natural Language Documents for Large Knowledge Bases,
   G.P. Zarri   103
Extracting Knowledge from Biological Descriptions, *A. Taylor*   114

Part 4. Large-Scale Applications   121
A Very Large-Scale Knowledge Base for the Knowledge Intensive Engineering Framework,
   M. Ishii, T. Sekiya and T. Tomiyama   123
A Scientific Knowledge Base for Extracting and Justifying Scientific Hypotheses in
   Atmospheric Research, *E. Kapetanios*   132
Building Consensual Knowledge Bases: Context and Architecture, *J. Euzenat*   143
A Case Study in the Use of Large-Scale Knowledge-Based Technology for an Environmental
   Application, *N.B. Pinto, L.M. Stephens and R.D. Bonnell*   156

Part 5. Scaling Issues   163
On the Integration of Specialized and General Reasoning, *G. Wickler*   165
Scalability of the Performance of Knowledge Representation Systems, *P.-H. Speel,
   F. van Raalte, P.E. van der Vet and N.J.I. Mars*   173

Part 6. Supporting Technology   185
Structuring Methods for Nonmonotonic Knowledge Bases, *G. Antoniou*   187
Exceptions in Composition Graphs, *M. Magnan and C. Oussalah*   194
COLOR-X: Object Modeling Profits from Linguistics, *J.F.M. Burg and R.P. van de Riet*   204

Part 7. Knowledge Bases and Data Bases   215
OSIRIS: an Object-Oriented System Unifying Databases and Knowledge Bases, *A. Simonet and M. Simonet*   217
Interfacing of Object-Oriented Databases and Knowledge-Based Engineering Systems Using Views, *K. Tanskanen, A. Aaltonen, P. Paasiala and A. Riitahuhta*   228
Why and How to Define a Similarity Measure for Object-Based Representation Systems, *G. Bisson*   236
Intelligent Caching in Heterogeneous Reasoning and Mediator Systems, *S. Adali and V.S. Subrahmanian*   247

Part 8. Knowledge Sharing and Reuse   257
An Agent Based Approach to Spacecraft Mission Operations, *M. Jones, J. Wheadon, D. Whitgift, M. Niezette, R. Timmermans, I. Rodriguez and R. Romero*   259
Workplace-Adapted Behaviors: Lessons Learned for Knowledge Reuse, *J. Vanwelkenhuysen and R. Mizoguchi*   270
Knowledge Bases, Texts and Lexicon, *F. Lemaire*   281
Evaluation and Assessment of the Knowledge Sharing Technology, *A. Gómez-Pérez, N. Juristo and J. Pazos*   289
Knowledge Dissemination - Digital Libraries + Collaboration Technology, *S.-S. Chen*   279

Author Index   303

Addresses of Authors   304

Part 1: Towards Large Knowledge Bases

Invited presentations given at KB&KS'95

Towards Very Large Knowledge Bases
N.J.I. Mars, Ed.
IOS Press, 1995

Steps to Sharing Knowledge

Douglas B. Lenat
Cycorp, Inc.
USA
doug@Cyc.com

ABSTRACT

It's so easy for people to share knowledge that we do it unconsciously. Unfortunately, that makes it all the more difficult for us to build programs that share their knowledge. Many of the prerequisite steps and skills have been "compiled out" by cultural and biological evolution and by early childhood experiences. Before machines can share knowledge as flexibly as do people, those prerequisites need to somehow be recapitulated by and/or for the machines. Building Cyc, over the past decade, has taught us some interesting things about this process.

1 PEOPLE DO IT

Raj Reddy once gave a talk with the marvelous title "How to Wreck a Nice Beach." His point was that when he utters that string of phonemes out loud, and you don't see the written title in front of you, you have no trouble interpreting the acoustic waveform properly, namely as the true topic of his talk that day: "how to recognize speech."

The same phenomenon happens when you see written sentences which involve

- polysemous words (which meaning of "pen" is meant in "The box is in the pen." versus "The pen is in the box."?)

- pronouns (what is the referent of "they" in "The police arrested the demonstrators because they feared violence." versus "The police arrested the demonstrators because they advocated violence."?)

- translation from one natural language to another. Consider "Mary poured the water into the teakettle, and after it whistled she poured the water into

the teacup." In translating this to japanese, you must translate the first "water" as "cold water" and the second as "hot water." In translating from italian to english, whenever you see the word "horologia" you decide without consciously thinking about it whether to translate it as "wristwatch" or "clock."

A third modality in which this occurs is the visual one. If I show you a photo of a room, you have no trouble disambiguating whether a particular object is a normal-sized telephone mounted on the back wall versus a tiny telephone hanging in mid-air near the camera lens.

A fourth modality, which lies halfway between the photo interpretation and the typed sentence examples is the following: reading someone else's handwritten script. The very same shape might be interpreted as an "a" in one place and an "o" in another. Even entire words (which appear as identical when compared side by side) can be effortlessly read as different words, in context, effortlessly.

That last word, "effortlessly," is the key. In the aural and typed and visual and handwritten examples, we resolve the ambiguities so easily that we rarely if ever consciously perceive them. I could give you many more examples, from these and other modalities, but you get the idea.

So, what does all this have to do with knowledge sharing? It leads us into a trap: the trap that it will be easy to get programs to share their knowledge. The next section addresses this in detail. It's the same trap that led AI pioneers to make unrealistic predictions 30 years ago about how soon human-level performance would be achieved in machine translation, image and speech understanding, etc. I.e., these are tasks for which it's so easy for people to perform them that we can't easily introspect on how we do it [8].

2 SO WHAT'S THE BIG DEAL?

When we first began building knowledge-based programs in earnest [1], we were optimistic about connecting them up together to form a sort of patchwork quilt of ever-expanding competence and coverage.

That hasn't happened, and much of the enthusiasm of the 1970's has soured into drastically scaled-back expectations, dovetailing with scaled-back funding (which in turn is caused by funders' dissatisfaction with AI's claims and promises and predictions that never came true.)

So what's the big deal? That is, why *can't* we just hook up our expert systems together?

One obvious problem is lack of shared vocabulary. For instance, let's consider the following question, which appears to be quite straightforward: How do you refer to a medical patient x being feverish? In some expert systems, this is represented by asserting FEVERISH(X). In others, it's SYMP(X, FEVER). In others, it's TEMPERATURE(X) > 98.6. In others, it's TEMP(X,HIGH), or TEMP(X,HIGH, "9:34am 3/4/95"), or FEELS(X, FOREHEAD) = HOT, or ABNORMAL(X,BODY-TEMP). In others, where the patient's identity is "understood" from context, it could be any of the previous ways, with X absent; e.g., TEMPERATURE > 98.6 .

Even if the vocabulary is standardized, there's still the issue of agreeing on the meaning of the terms. In medicine, such terms as "recent," "high," "severe," "frequent," etc. appear all the time, and yet their meaning varies from situation to situation.

Next there is the problem of all the implicit (hidden) assumptions that each system makes, assumptions about time, space, clinical situation, and so on. For instance, some programs assume that there is just one patient they're being told about, the patient has undergone a battery of tests at more or less the same time, and all of those were recently performed; such programs don't even have "time" or "patient" appear as a variable in their rules and data structures. By contrast, other programs might be tracking groups of patients involved in studies or regimens lasting months or years, and their rules will of course refer to distinct patients differently, and will tag data temporally. Each program also makes assumptions about what level of training the user has had, what type of medical tests and equipment are available, and so on.

We've used medical expert systems as our source of examples here, but the same comments apply to any community of knowledge-based programs trying to share their knowledge. To wit: Sometimes programs will use different terms to represent the same concept, in which case it does no good at all to add one's rules to the other. Sometimes they employ the same terms to mean (slightly) different things, and that leads to downright *worse* behavior if the rules get unioned. And

sometimes, even if they "agree" on the meaning of a rule which is present in program 1, it is quite possible that program 2 will give worse results, not better ones, if that rule were added to it, because of conflicting assumptions each program is implicitly making about the context of its use.

3 SO WHAT'S THE SOLUTION?

To resolve this dilemma, we need to go back and consider how it is that people manage to integrate information so easily, to recognize speech so easily, to disambiguate pronoun referents so easily, etc.

If you think about it for a moment, you'll realize that partly we do this by standing on the shoulders of our forebears, who evolved parsimonious brains (specialized hardware) and parsimonious natural languages (specialized software) that make these more doable.

And partly the answer lies in the shared substrate of "general world knowledge" that each of us assumes that everyone knows. We're not talking here about when the battle of Waterloo was fought, or who the current President of the United States is, or what the atomic number of Lithium is, or what inflation rates were in Mexico in 1994. Not so much factual knowledge as common wisdom: birds fly and live in nests in trees; writing pens are a few inches long and contain no foreign objects (other than ink, if you consider that not to be "part" of the pen); police try to prevent or quell outbreaks of civil violence; teakettles contain water while it's being heated; unsupported objects fall; (nonportable) telephones are usually either mounted on walls or sitting on tables or desks; etc.

This is the sort of knowledge which enables us to disambiguate the telephone on-the-wall versus in-mid-air image; to pick the correct meaning of "pen" in the box-in-the-pen sentence; to disambiguate the pronoun "they" in the police versus demonstrator sentences; and so on.

It is knowledge most of which we humans acquire at a very early age (with, to be sure, continual refinement and accretion throughout our lives.) We acquire much of it through generalization of our observations and our first-hand experiences and stories we're told; i.e., we do not acquire very much of it by being explicitly told it or reading it in some book. E.g., consider: when and how did you learn that telephones rarely float in mid-air?

For this reason, it is rare that such knowledge consciously comes to our minds, even more rarely does it explicitly get codified and articulated to another person, and virtually never is it recorded in some (non-biological) physical symbol system such as a book or article.

In the early 1980's, we came to the conclusion that having this large knowledge base of common sense was not a luxury but a necessity. We weren't the first to advocate this (see, e.g., [5]), but we were the first to bite the bullet and set out to manually construct it.

Why *manually* construct it, rule by rule, rather than drawing on one or both of the obvious methods for building it up automatically and painlessly: machine learning (discovering new information automatically) and/or natural language understanding (gleaning information from already-written texts)? Very reluctantly, we concluded that in each case it would be premature to rely on those techniques, because they themselves required this selfsame large KB (knowledge base) in order to succeed. In the case of natural language understanding, the examples given earlier are illustrative of why an NL system needs a common sense KB underneath it, to draw on for semantic disambiguation purposes. In the case of machine learning [4], it occurs at the fringe of what is already known, often by analogy to superficially far-flung facts and experiences, and thus it too requires a broad KB underneath it.

So, we gritted our teeth and embarked on the Cyc project, to prime the pump by manually assembling the first million or two rules. Our project has spanned the ensuing ten years, consuming over a person-century of effort. For details of its progress and results, see [2], [3], and [6].

The 1984 hope, and now the 1995 expectation, is that the 1995 Cyc KB will be sufficient to start the two positively-reinforcing "reactions" mentioned above, knowledge acquisition by natural language understanding and theory-guided discovery. In 1984 we hoped that these would be the foci of our work in the 1995–2005 and 2005–2015 decades, respectively, and we are excited about being more or less on track for these.[1]

4 HYPOTHESES

Usually the final section of an article is called "Conclusions," but it's too soon and too presumptuous for us to do much in the way of drawing definite conclusions, hence the title of this section.

Our hypotheses for what it takes for programs to share knowledge are few and simple:

- share terms

- share most of the meaning of most of those terms [7]

- be able to discuss and resolve conflicts when they do occur [3]

---

[1] Albeit due to a large number of errors cancelling each other out, over the past decade. These were errors in our expectations versus the reality of building Cyc; e.g., we underestimated the precision with which knowledge would have to be stated, and the amount to axiomatize in that fashion, but we also underestimated how rapidly an experienced knowledge enterer could write those axioms.

- to do the latter requires mastery of an adequately broad substrate of real-world "theories" — common sense [2]

Each of the above 4 items can be done by the human programmers to some extent, discussing and agreeing on term meanings, drawing on their own world knowledge and natural language abilities, etc. But one can never fully decontextualize pieces of knowledge, and hence continued sharing will require repeated and neverending interaction among the systems' builders, unless the systems themselves can do the adjucations necessary to resolve semantically conflicting use of terms. And that means the systems themselves, not just their builders, need to have common sense.

We're very excited about how much the Cyc project has built over the last decade, and even more excited about Cyc's prospects for the future. [2] focuses on current and future applications of Cyc, but we're also excited about its promise to qualitatively boost automated natural language understanding and automated knowledge discovery, and thereby knowledge sharing, in the future. To that end, we are doing something concrete to promote knowledge sharing:

In January, 1995, the MCC Cyc project was "spun off" from MCC as a separate company, Cycorp. Its mission is to commercialize the Cyc technology and to continue developing and improving that technology (growing the Cyc KB, augmenting the CycL inference engine, building better interfaces, working on natural language and machine learning, etc.) To foster the above bulleted items, we intend to release to the general public the entire Cyc ontology of about 10^5 terms, along with various basic hierarchical predicates interrelating them (subsetOf, elementOf, partOf), a very general "is-related-to-somehow-semantically" relation (computed from the Cyc KB as: x and y co-occur in the same axiom) and, importantly, an english description of the intended meaning of each term. Of course the final bullets will require access to the rest of the content of the Cyc KB, but releasing the Cyc ontology will be the first step toward enabling the global community to build programs that more readily share their knowledge.

ACKNOWLEDGMENT

I would like to take this opportunity to thank the dozens of individuals who have worked on the Cyc project in the last ten years, including at MCC, at our Member Companies, and as academic collaborators. Without your ideas, and your hard work, Cyc would not have become what it is today.

REFERENCES

1. Edward A. Feigenbaum, "The Art of Artificial Intelligence," *Proceedings of IJCAI-77*, Morgan Kaufmann, Palo Alto, 1977.

6

2. R. V. Guha and D. B. Lenat, "Cyc: enabling agents to work together," *Communications of the ACM*, July 1994.

3. Douglas B. Lenat *et al.*, "Cyc: toward programs with common sense," *Communications of the ACM*, August, 1990.

4. Douglas B. Lenat and John Seely Brown, "Why AM and Eurisko appear to work," *Artificial Intelligence Journal*, 23:269–294, 1984.

5. John McCarthy, "Programs with common sense," in (H. Levesque and R. Brachman, editors) *Readings In Knowledge Representation*, Morgan Kaufmann, Los Altos, CA, 1986.

6. Karen Pittman and Douglas B. Lenat, "Representing Knowledge in Cyc-9," MCC Technical Report Cyc-175-93P. December, 1993.

7. W. V. Quine, "Natural kinds," in *Ontological Relativity and other essays*, Columbia University Press, New York, 1969.

8. William A. Woods and J. Makhoul, "Mechanical Inference Problems in Continuous Speech Understanding," *Proceedings of IJCAI-73*, SRI Publications, Menlo Park, Ca., 1973.

Towards Very Large Knowledge Bases
N.J.I. Mars, Ed.
IOS Press, 1995

Knowledge Bases and Computational Molecular Biology

François Rechenmann
INRIA Rhône-Alpes
Grenoble, France
Francois.Rechenmann@inria.fr

ABSTRACT

Scientific knowledge bases aim at modeling a domain of scientific investigation. Molecular biology constitutes an excellent example of such a domain, where new objects are being discovered at an ever increasing rate. Knowledge bases in molecular biology must capture three types of knowledge : descriptive knowledge on the entities, such as genes or operons, and on the relationships between these entities; behavioral knowledge on the dynamic processes involved, such as the regulation of gene expression; methodological knowledge on the methods which can be used to identify the entities and their relationships. The links between pieces of formalized knowledge and the sources which support them must be kept. The sources are essentially on a textual form, so that terminological knowledge must be added at the frontier of the knowledge bases. Molecular biology thus states several challenges regarding knowledge modeling and knowledge management.

1 Introduction

Knowledge bases have been mostly viewed as components of the so-called "expert systems", i.e. problem-solving systems the efficiency of which relies on specialized knowledge. The large amounts of knowledge involved in these systems are expressed through a knowledge representation language : rules, objects, or a combination of both. The basic principle of such knowledge-based systems is thus to separate explicitly knowledge expression from its exploitation mechanisms. This organization presents several advantages : the knowledge base is easier to read and thus to update, and the inference mechanisms can be more easily traced. The trace is obtained in terms of the knowledge pieces as expressed in the representation language and may be transformed and used by adequate explanation modules. As compared with other problem-solving systems, such as neural networks, the knowledge-based systems are therefore essentially appreciated for their capacity to make the contents of the knowledge base and the problem-solving process understandable. They are better adapted than conventional procedural systems to capture non-consensual knowledge and to solve problems the solutions of which must be explained and justified.

"Expert" knowledge-based systems are known to be brittle. Their performances may drop suddenly when confronted with new problems or when a single piece of information is lacking during the problem solving process. To overcome this brittleness, it has been argued that common sense knowledge should also be encoded in the knowledge bases. The Cyc project [12] is certainly the most advanced example of such a large common sense knowledge base which can be used in a large range of situations, possibly in cooperation with specialized problem-solving systems in order to overcome some of their limitations.

Scientific knowledge bases constitute a third category. Their aim is to be a model of a domain of scientific investigation. They are constantly updated and they are expected to converge towards a consensus among the research community involved. If the term "expert" qualifies a piece of knowledge which results from personal experience, then, for its most part, the knowledge these bases gather cannot be said to be expert, even if it may, for some time, be accepted by only a part of the community. They do require common sense knowledge to be understood, but they do not intend to capture it. They are built to help understanding the objects of the domain and their relationships. They may constitute an exchange medium among researchers and may accelerate the scientific discovery process.

Molecular biology is a very good example of such a scientific domain which can highly benefit from knowledge base building. It involves very large volumes of raw data, as genomic and proteic sequences. The analysis of these data, together with concrete experiments, leads to the identification of numerous objects which participate in complex interaction mechanisms.

2 Objects and relationships in molecular biology

The DNA macro-molecule is the physical support of heredity (for an introduction to molecular biology, see [5] or [7]). Located in every cell, it encodes the information on which any living organism relies for its growth and its maintenance : the genome of the organism. It can be abstracted as a linear sequence of characters in a four-letter alphabet : A, C, G and T. A genome of a typical bacterium, such as *E. coli*, is 4.2×10^6 letters long; the human genome is 3.3×10^9 letters long.

The genetic code associates to every set of three DNA letters an amino acid, a basic component of proteins. Any protein can indeed be seen as a sequence of characters in a twenty-letter alphabet, the twenty amino acids which are used by living organisms. Thus, portions of DNA may be translated into proteins, through a complex process which implies other macro-molecules, which are themselves products of DNA translation. "Translation" is actually the name of the last phase of the whole process which implies an intermediary information support, RNA, into which DNA is first transcribed.

The transcription and translation processes are regulated so that proteins are produced only when required and in the right quantity, according to the needs and the role of the cell. These regulation mechanisms rely on the presence or the absence of proteins on some locations around the protein coding region. These proteins can themselves result from other translation processes, so that complex networks of interactions can be identified.

A gene is made up of the portions of DNA which contain the coding region together with the various signals involved in the regulation of its expression into a protein. It thus constitutes a basic example of the modeling challenges for knowledge bases in molecular biology. Its description should indeed contain its properties, its structure as a composite object, its relationships with other objects, in particular with other genes, and some behavioral knowledge on the regulation of its expression.

The majority of databases in molecular biology put the emphasis on the sequences, and therefore more on the objects than on the relationships between these objects.

3 From sequence databases to knowledge bases

Since the mid-seventies, the increasing flow of new genomic and proteic sequences led the biologists to store them into data banks [3]. Ever since, the improvements in the sequencing technology has led to a steadily increasing flow of data : the size of sequence data banks, such as GenBank or EMBL, doubles every year. Sequences are submitted to the banks directly from the sequencing projects, through the computer networks. They happen to be redundant or erroneous. Moreover, the information available is limited to the sequence itself, together with comments in plain text and some preliminary analysis results. For instance, the existence of coding or regulating regions may be indicated.

Thus, specialized databases are developed, partly relying on the contents of the data banks. They focus on an organism or on the comparative study of some specific mechanisms over several organisms. The sequences they contain are checked for errors and redundancy. The volume of information attached to the sequences is more important and structured.

Most of these so-called "databases" are still mere flat files. The relational model is used, but it is obviously not adapted to the description and the management of such large unstructured data. The object-oriented model is certainly much more convenient, and it begins to be used for the development of specialized databases [20]. It must be underlined that the volume of already stored data, together with the incoming flow of sequences, make the adoption of a new data model a very tedious process. Under the pressure of data, the biologists have not had, and still not have, the time to wait for the design of adapted computer tools.

The sequence databases essentially describe the basic objects which can be identified on the genomes. As more and more data are being produced by the large scale sequencing projects, the objective of which is to obtain the complete sequence of the genomes of model organisms, such as Man, but also the bacteria (*E. coli, B. subtilis,*...), the baker yeast (*S. cerevisae*), or the nematode (*C. elegans*), there is a growing need to organize and to structure the accompanying knowledge, and thus to shift the emphasis from the objects to their relationships.

4 Knowledge modeling in molecular biology

Three types of knowledge can be identified in molecular biology : descriptive knowledge on the various entities involved, behavioral knowledge on the dynamic processes implying these entities, and methodological knowledge on the methods to identify these entities and to complete their descriptions.

4.1 Descriptive knowledge

Genes are complex entities. Syntactically, they can be associated to the portions of the genome which contribute to the making of a protein : not only the coding region, but also the various signals which are used during the transcription and translation processes. In eukaryotic organisms, the cells of which include a nucleus, the coding zone itself may be structured into coding (exons) and non coding (introns) regions. Genes can be organized in higher order structures, such as operons in the bacterial genome. Representing these interrelated structured entities requires high-level knowledge models.

Semantic networks, and their implementation as object-oriented models, appear to be very well adapted, as exemplified by the Molgen project [5], one of the earliest attempts to represent knowledge in molecular genetics, and by GeneSys [14], or ColiGene [15, 21] which contains the description of more than 1500 genes of *E. coli*.

4.2 Behavioral knowledge

Multiple dynamic processes take place in the cells:

- as explained previously, gene expression is regulated according to the evolution of the cell environment. Since the early sixties, when Jacob and Monod have described the regulation of the lactose operon, numerous other examples of such regulation mechanisms have been studied.

- products of the gene expression, the proteins strongly interact with the metabolism of the cell.

- complex interactions take place during the development of the organisms, when undifferentiated cells evolve toward specialized cells and when forms emerge. These interactions involve DNA, RNA and proteins.

A knowledge base can gather the knowledge on these various dynamic processes. A first step in knowledge modeling consists in listing all the known interactions and to allow requests to be expressed on the database. The answers to these requests often come in a graphic form displaying the network of interactions. But simulating the behavior which results from the interactions is the next step. Since data on the nature of the interactions are often lacking, quantitative models, for instance as systems of differential equations, cannot be built and qualitative modeling is required.

One of the modeling experiments of the Molgen project [5] consisted indeed in modeling the behavior of the tryptophan operon. This operon operates through attenuation : when tryptophan is lacking, the genes of the operon are translated into enzymes which intervene in the synthesis pathways of the tryptophan. P.D.

Karp [9] describes a qualitative model of this dynamic system.

The EcoCyc database [10, 25] gathers the information about the genes and the metabolic pathways in the *E. coli* bacterium. It contains 1000 metabolic compounds, 40 pathways, and 160 reactions and enzymes. MetalGen [19] is another example of a similar modeling attempt.

A note on the term "behavior"

The need to model not only the properties and the relationships of the entities, but also their behavior in the real word (of the cell, in this context), helps clarifying the fundamental difference between the objects in programming languages and objects in knowledge modeling. The very general term "object" can indeed denote either an object of the real word, or an object which is internal to the computer implementation. The distinction becomes obvious when the notion of behavior is introduced.

In object-oriented programming languages, and in object-oriented database management systems, the term "behavior" refers to the set of executable methods which are part of the class description. Every instance of the class "behaves" according to these methods, which are executed in response to messages which come from the environment. For instance, a window of a man-machine interface is an object which behaves through methods for moving or resizing.

In object-oriented knowledge models, the objects directly denote the entities of the real world. Their behavior should thus be a model of the behavior of these entities in the real world, and not the behavior of the object which is the support of the representation.

If an operon were directly modeled as a class in some object-oriented language, methods could certainly be written to represent its behavior. But they would be mixed up with the methods which describe the behavior of the object itself, i.e. the instance of the class, for instance printing methods. Thus, two distinct levels of modeling would be confused.

¿From an operational point of view, this confusion does not have severe consequences, especially when abstract objects such as matrices or interface widgets are dealt with. It does have, however, when the knowledge bases are built as explicative models of reality. It is striking that most object-oriented knowledge models are extensions of object-oriented programming languages and are used as such. On the other hand, some of them do not include methods at all (see for example the terminological languages) and thus do not allow the modeling of any behavior. It is not surprising in this context that the distinction between objects which denote real world entities and objects which denote instances in a programming language is nearly never acknowledged.

4.3 Methodological knowledge

Molecular genetics relies on an important set of methods to analyse sequences and to identify pertinent objects on them :

- the recognition of coding regions, and of the intron-exon junctions, relies on various techniques, including machine learning and neural networks;

- the prediction of 2D and 3D spatial configurations of RNA and proteins from their sequences constitutes another important class of methods;

- distances between homologous sequences are used to construct phylogenetic trees, which display the filiation of species over time resulting from the evolution process.

To use these methods correctly and to interpret their results require some expertise. The problem becomes more and more accurate with the accumulation of specific knowledge on genomes of well studied organisms. Specialized methods, which exploit the specificities of these genomes, begin to appear.

As already experimented in scientific computing [6, 24], it is possible to describe methodological knowledge to help biologists in selecting these methods according to the class of problems they want to solve. Part of this knowledge is purely syntactic : if a method is known through the types of its input and output arguments, adequate hierarchical classification mechanisms are able to search for the methods which fit some input data or some expected results. But, as types become more and more specific, expertise is progressively encoded. Expert knowledge is particularly necessary in order to help the user in chaining up several methods to deal with a complex problem which cannot be directly solved through the choice and the execution of a single method. Task models can be used for that purpose as explained in [16, 13, 22].

A task is associated with a problem and is, like a method, modeled as an object class. To solve the task then amounts to solving the problem :

- An elementary task is solved by directly executing one of the attached methods. The selection of the adequate method among the set of available methods results from a classification process. For instance, the execution of the task *Multivariate analysis* triggers the execution of one of the three methods *Multiple Correspondence Analysis*, *Principal Component Analysis* or *Factorial Correspondence Analysis*.

- A complex task must be recursively decomposed into sub-tasks, down to elementary tasks. This decomposition is described by an operator (sequence, selection, etc.) and the list of tasks on which this operator applies. For example, the class *Search for REPs* (Repetitive Extragenic Palindromic units) is decomposed into the sequence : *Extract REPs*, then *Search for REP sub-classes*, then *Predict REP 2nd structure*.

- In order that the decomposition of a task into sub-tasks be dependent on the type of its input data, the decomposition step is preceded by a classification step, during which the current task is first characterised according to its known input values. For instance, the very generic task *Search for patterns in DNA sequences* is specialised through the sub-classes (Search) *Palindromic units*, *Translation signals* and *Transcription promoters*, and further decomposed into sub-tasks down to elementary tasks, and then methods, such as *Multiple Correspondence Analysis*.

5   The knowledge base as a model

Scientific knowledge bases support some problem-solving processes:

- hierarchical organisation of object classes allows characterization of partially known entities through classification : an entity which is known to belong to a class is recursively matched with its sub-classes;

- missing slot values may be computed using attached procedures or default values.

- qualitative simulation methods may be applied on the object relationships in order to understand the behavior of a sub-system.

But the first role of a scientific knowledge base is to be a model which helps the researchers to structure their knowledge into a consistent consensual form. It must therefore offers good browsing facilities and allows to formulate complex requests. Answers to these requests are often produced in some graphical form. For instance, in the EcoCyc knowledge base [10], metabolic pathways are drawn on the user screen from the data stored. HoverMap [4] displays the cytogenetic maps of chromosomes with their banding structure.

As any model, a scientific knowledge base is built on hypotheses, which are formulated from data and experiments. It is therefore highly important that the links between pieces of formalized knowledge, hypothesis formulations, data and experimental results be maintained in order for the scientist to evaluate the degree of validity of the knowledge base and to criticize its contents. Around a kernel of formalized knowledge, contextual knowledge must be made available.

A large part of this contextual knowledge exists in textual form in the scientific literature, including doctoral theses. Bibliographical databases have been built [23], but the problem is to link the object descriptions with the pieces of text which comment and justify them. The links may be of a terminological nature : from the names used by the object descriptions (names of classes, of properties and relationships, of instances) to the words used in the texts. As advocated by J. van de Riet [18], a lexicon can play the role of an interface between names and words and thus between natural language, which is used by the literature and by the users, and the formal knowledge base. Relations between terms, such as synonyms and hyponyms, can also be included, so that the user can navigate inside the lexicon before entering the knowledge base itself. The pieces of text themselves may be organized into an hypertext structure, thus supporting also a navigation process.

6 Conclusion

The ever increasing flow of data from genome sequencing projects led the biologists to use computers essentially for their capacity to store large volumes of data and to make intensive computations. Sequence databases and sequence analysis packages are the visible part of this investment in computer science. In very few years from now, whole genomes of "model" living organisms will have been completely sequenced. Accordingly, the emphasis would shift from data to knowledge : how computers can help in discovering new objects, new relationships between objects, new mechanisms ? This shift has already initiated as shown by the increasing complexity of sequence databases and the use of ever more descriptive data models.

It is highly necessary however to anticipate this incoming shift. The anarchic development of data banks under the pressure of the flow of sequences has led to the present situation where a large gap is being maintained between the real biological needs, which could be satisfied by advanced computer technologies, and the computer tools which are actually used.

Very interesting challenges are therefore proposed to the computer scientists, especially regarding knowledge modeling and knowledge management.

Managing large volumes of data and knowledge

First of all, the volume of knowledge, as evaluated as the number of object classes, is tremendous. The bacterial (*E. coli*) genome is estimated to contain 2350 genes; the human genome, 125 000 genes. These figures do not take into account the polymorphism : among the same species, the genome slightly differs from an individual to another. Moreover, as seen before, the genes are made up of other objects. All these objects interact in complex processes to produce objects of other classes : the proteins, which include the enzymes which play the role of catalysers in many reactions. These volumes clearly require adapted object management systems.

Incremental and concurrent knowledge base building

An important characteristic of molecular genetics is that new types of objects are still being discovered. The structure of the knowledge bases cannot therefore be fixed. New classes have to be added, or updated, and thus moved within the class/subclass hierarchy, without losing the contents of their instances. The management of this dynamics constitutes a fundamental and theoretical problem.

But the amount of knowledge to be described also requires new methodologies in knowledge acquisition. Sources of knowledge are indeed scattered among the numerous research laboratories involved. Even if a knowledge base is designed around a specific living organism, or some functional or evolutionary aspects through several organisms, it would be inefficient to ask a single researcher to gather and to formalize the various pieces of knowledge involved. Distributed and concurrent knowledge base building is the answer [17] : researchers in their own laboratories would contribute to the building of a consensual knowledge base, which would thus play the role of a knowledge exchange and confrontation medium.

Distributed problem-solving environments

As more information and data are being gathered on some living organisms, methods will tend to specialize by using these specific data. As an example, in the case of *E. coli* bacterium, the tRNA cellular frequencies are known, thus allowing for an efficient, but very specific, coding region identification method. More examples of such specialized methods have to be expected. A distributed sequence analysis environment can therefore be envisioned. Research laboratories would locally develop and maintain sequence analysis methods. These local methodological knowledge bases would together form a unique, but virtual, environment to which sequences could be sent for analysis. The processing of these sequences would thus be distributed over the different knowledge bases, according to the class of analysis requested and relying on the task descriptions.

Advanced knowledge models

In order to represent the three categories of knowledge – descriptive, behavioral and methodological – knowledge models have to be extended. Since most object-based knowledge models have been designed and implemented over an object-oriented programming language, they allow behavioral knowledge to be modeled as procedures only. Moreover, as explained before, behavior of the real world entity and behavior of the computer entity are mixed up. An adequate knowledge model should allow to use object slots to represent dynamic relationships between objects and to support qualitative or quantitative simulation methods.

ACKNOWLEDGEMENTS

This research is being supported by GIP GREG (Groupement de Recherches et d'Etudes sur les Génomes), and by CNRS (Centre National de la

Recherche Scientifique) – GdR 1029 "Informatique et génomes".

REFERENCES

The proceedings of ISMB (Intelligent Systems for Molecular Biology) international conferences, held in Bethesda in 1993 [8], Standford in 1994 [1] and Cambridge (UK) in 1995, contain several papers on data and knowledge modeling in molecular biology.

In the framework of the Hawaii International Conference on System Sciences (HICSS), several "minitracks" on the same questions have been organized; see for instance the minitrack on Data and Knowledge Issues on Genomics (proc. 27th HICSS, vol. V: "Biotechnology Computing", L. Hunter ed., IEEE Computer society Press, Los Alamitos, CA, 1994).

1. R. Altman, D. Brutlag, P. Karp, R. Lathrop, D. Searls, eds., Proceedings of the Second International Conference on Intelligent Systems for Molecular Biology, Stanford University, CA, AAAI Press, 1994

2. G. Bell, Th. Marr, Eds., "Computers and DNA", Addison-Wesley Publishing Company, 1990

3. C. Burks, "The Flow of Nucleotide Sequence Data into Data Banks: Role and Impact of Large-Scale Sequencing Projects", in [2], p. 35-45

4. F. Dorkeld, G. Perrière, C. Gautier, "Object-oriented modelling in molecular biology", in Proc. *Artificial Intelligence and Genome*, p. 99-106, Workshop 26, IJCAI, Chambry (FR), August 1993

5. P. Friedland, L. Kedes, "Discovering the secrets of DNA", Computer, November 1985, p. 49-69, 1985

6. E.N. Houstis, J.R. Rice (eds), IMACS *Second International Conference on Expert Systems for Numerical Computing*, (Purdue University, West-Lafayette, Indiana, USA, 24-26 avril 1990), Elsevier Science Publishers, Amsterdam, 1992

7. L. Hunter, "Molecular Biology for Computer Scientists", in Artificial Intelligence and Molecular Biology, L. Hunter ed., AAAI Press/The MIT Press, 1993

8. L. Hunter, D. Searls, and J. Shavlik, eds., Proceedings of the First International Conference on Intelligent Systems for Molecular Biology, Bethesda, MD, AAAI Press, 1993

9. P. D. Karp, "A Qualitative Biochemistry and Its Application to the Regulation of the Tryptophan Operon", in Artificial Intelligence and Molecular Biology, chapter 8, L. Hunter ed., p. 289-324, AAAI Press/The MIT Press, 1993

10. P.D. Karp and M. L. Mavrovouniotis, "Representing, Analysing, and Synthesizing Biochemical Pathways", IEEE Expert, p. 11-21, April 1994

11. K. Koile and G. C. Overton, "A Qualitative Model for Gene Expression", in Proc. of the 1989 Summer Computer Simulation Conference, p. 415-421, Society for Computer Simulation, July 1989

12. D. B. Lenat, R. V. Guha, K. Pittman, D. Pratt, M. Shepherd, "CYC: Toward Programs With Common Sense", Communication of the ACM, vol. 33(8), p. 30-49

13. C. Médigue, J. Willamowski, O. Schmeltzer, P. Uvietta, F. Rechenmann, F. Chevenet, G. Perrière, C. Gautier, "Modeling Tasks for Problem Solving in Molecular Biology", in Proc. *Artificial Intelligence and Genome*, p. 67-76, Workshop 26, IJCAI, Chambry (FR), August 1993

14. C.G. Overton, K. Koile, J.A. Pastor, "GeneSys: a knowledge management system for molecular biology", in [2]

15. G. Perrière, C. Gautier, "ColiGene: object-centered representation for the study of *E. coli* gene expressivity by sequence analysis", Biochimie, vol. 75, n° 5, p. 415-422, 1993

16. F. Rechenmann, "Modelling mathematical objects in knowledge-based systems for scientific computing", in J. Johnson, S. McKee, A. Vella (eds.), *Artificial intelligence in mathematics*, Clarendon Press, Oxford (GB), p. 183-194, 1994

17. F. Rechenmann, "Building and sharing large knowledge bases in molecular biology", in K. Fuchi, T. Yokoi (eds.), *Knowledge building and knowledge sharing*, IOS Press, Amsterdam (NL), 1994

18. R. van de Riet, "Linguistic Instruments in Knowledge Engineering, A Research Proposal and some Experiments", in K. Fuchi, T. Yokoi (eds.), *Knowledge building and knowledge sharing*, IOS Press, Amsterdam, 1994

19. T. Rouxel, A. Danchin and A. Hénaut, "METALGEN.DB: metabolism linked to the genome of *Escherichia coli*, a graphics oriented database", CABIOS vol. 9, n° 3, p. 315-324, June 1993

20. D.G. Shin, C. Lee, J. Zhang, K.E. Rudd, C.M. Berg, "Redesigning, implementing and integrating *Escherichia Coli* genome software tools with object-oriented database system", CABIOS, vol. 8, n° 3, p. 227-238, 1992

21. O. Schmeltzer, C. Médigue, P. Uvietta, F. Rechenmann, F. Dorfeld, G. Perrière, C. Gautier, "Building large knowledge bases in molecular biology", in [8] p.345-353

22. J. Willamowski, F. Chevenet, F. Jean-Marie, "A development shell for cooperative problem-solving environments", Mathematics and Computers in Simulation, vol. 36, 1994, p. 361-379

23. ACM Workshop on Information Retrieval and Genomics, National Library of Medicine, Bethesda, MD, May 2-4, 1994. Workshop notes are available at the URL: http://info.cs.vt.edu/WIRG/WIRG.html

24. Third International Conference on Expert Systems for Scientific Computing, Mathematics and Computers in Simulation, Special Issue, Guest Editors: E. Houstis, J. Rice and R. Vichnevetsky, vol. 36, n° 4-6, october 1994

25. http://www.ai.sri.com/ecocyc/ecocyc.html

The Impact of the EDR Electronic Dictionary on Very Large Knowledge Bases

Toshio Yokoi

Japan Electronic Dictionary Research Institute, Ltd. (EDR)

Tokyo, Japan

yokoi@edr.co.jp

ABSTRACT

The EDR Electronic Dictionary is a very large knowledge base of linguistic knowledge, that is, of knowledge relating to language. This electronic dictionary will have a substantial impact on very large knowledge bases of more general knowledge of the world, namely world knowledge. This is because, first, the EDR Electronic Dictionary is a representative prototype for very large knowledge bases of world knowledge; and second, the knowledge representation medium of natural language plays a crucial role in the description of world knowledge. This paper discusses the creation of a very large knowledge base of world knowledge through a generalized electronic dictionary.

1   INTRODUCTION

The EDR Electronic Dictionary [1] is a very large knowledge base of knowledge relating to language (linguistic knowledge). This electronic dictionary will have a major impact on research and development of very large knowledge bases of more general knowledge of the world, or world knowledge. There are two reasons for this. First, the EDR Electronic Dictionary is itself a representative prototype for very large knowledge bases of world knowledge. And second, the natural language, as a medium of knowledge representation, plays an essential role in the description of world knowledge.

The first of these points is discussed in Section 3. In that section, a generalized electronic dictionary (an information structure of linguistic knowledge) is proposed as a foundation for general linguistic knowledge, drawing on the results of the EDR Electronic Dictionary. This generalized electronic dictionary would be a very large knowledge base of world knowledge, with the simplest possible knowledge structure. The second of the two points is discussed in Section 4, where the connection between linguistic knowledge and world knowledge is elucidated. As an aid in considering this connection, the attributes of other very large knowledge bases such as CYC [2], [3] and WordNet [4] are briefly discussed as well.

2   WHAT IS REQUIRED FOR A VERY LARGE KNOWLEDGE BASE?

To review the requirements for a very large knowledge base, it is useful to refer to excerpts of two sections from the author's keynote speech [5] at the KB & KS '93 conference:

2.1   Basic requirements

A very large knowledge base should satisfy the following basic requirements:

Open system structuring: A very large knowledge base should have open system structuring rather than closed system structuring. Unlike a closed system structure which requires or expects little or no human involvement, an open system structure assumes cooperation between both human and computer. In this way, the knowledge (intelligence) system of a very large knowledge base must mesh with the knowledge (intelligence) system of the human brain. The representation media of the knowledge must have some degree of commonality between both human and computer. Because of the link between human knowledge space and computer knowledge space, a human will be able to understand in a certain context whatever knowledge the computer presents, if necessary, modify it, and then use the information in an appropriate way.

Applicable to various domains: The basic knowledge structures, knowledge base organization, and system functions of a very large knowledge base must be applicable to a wide range of knowledge domains. The design principle must be simple and widely applicable rather than complex and specialized.

Adaptable to various representation methods: A very large knowledge base should support a variety of languages and models for representing and processing knowledge. This does not mean that all languages and models must be integrated into a single knowledge representation method. Rather, standardized methods should be invented for representation of external specifications of the various languages as well as standardized frameworks usable for cross-conversion (translation).

Able to progress: A very large knowledge base must first and foremost be structured in such a way that it allows for a gradual increase in both quality and volume. That is, the system is designed such that when knowledge is added, the entire system does not have to be changed in order to accommodate the new information. Secondly, it must be supported by automated learning and self-organizing functions so that the growth and improvement speed is accelerated.

Able to acquire very large knowledge: The area of knowledge selected for research should be one that will yield large amounts of knowledge that meet the above mentioned requirements. The accumulated knowledge must also be sufficiently useful to warrant ongoing R&D.

2.2 Knowledge representation media

Knowledge representation media can be divided into "human (oriented) media" (media recognized and understood by people) and "computer (oriented) media" (media that can be processed by computer).

Human media have evolved throughout the history of the human species to represent, store, use, and transmit knowledge. In this context, people can be regarded as the systems that process, infer, and understand knowledge. Natural language, which is the most universal language and the most appropriate for symbolic representation, is used for general-purpose knowledge representation. Other knowledge representation languages include formal languages (algebraic formulas, logical formulas, computer media, etc.) and picture languages (architectural design drawings, electrical circuit diagrams, musical scores, etc.). In addition, images (static images, dynamic images, and animation) and sounds (speech, music, etc.) are used for

representing information or knowledge effectively and directly. Each medium has a specific and unique purpose. Used in combination, human media can be used to represent knowledge at a sophisticated level.

Computer media are for representing knowledge when computers are the processing, inference (and understanding) systems. Such media include many types of artificial languages, such as programming languages, database languages, and the knowledge representation languages used in AI. Each language is suited to a particular purpose, according to its area of application, capacity for representing knowledge objects, and processing efficiency. In areas such as neuro-computing and fuzzy logic, there is ongoing research into ways of enhancing the still limited ability of these developing technologies to represent knowledge.

An important consideration is the respective roles that the human and computer media can play in a very large knowledge base. The knowledge engineering approach favors computer media for representing very large-scale knowledge, whereas the hypermedia approach has mostly relied on human media. The following conclusions can be drawn from current R&D:

- Quite some time will be needed before computer media are able to fully represent human knowledge, even within a restricted range of knowledge domains. Recent developments in the computer media have been very limited in effect.

- Even with computer media, computers are only capable of reliably processing (understanding) knowledge insofar as they can execute representations as object codes. When it comes to processing at a meta level — for example, validation, deciding equivalence, and creating representations — computers are able to understand very little and most such tasks require human intervention.

Despite these limitations, some progress has been achieved in media technology, as shown by the following two examples:

- Multimedia techniques have made it possible to handle quite a wide range of knowledge represented in the human media at least as machine-readable data. Within this limited area, the gap between human and computer media is definitely closing. Furthermore, the integration of various human media on the computer has generated new functions.

- There has also been gradual progress towards enabling computers to understand human media to a level above that of multimedia. Definite results can be expected for natural language in particular. Processing capabilities have advanced considerably from the level of multimedia-type character strings.

The ability of computers to process syntax and morphemes is becoming fairly reliable and applicable to a wide range of texts. Semantic processing has also reached a promising stage, although at a low level of computer understanding, and similar efforts are now underway to enable context processing within a limited scope. Nevertheless, it must be conceded that the time when computers can process texts written freely in natural language is still in the distant future.

Returning to the question of the respective roles that human and computer media play in a very large knowledge base, the developments discussed above suggest that knowledge should be represented for systems integrating human and computer. That is, the proper starting point is to take the view that people bear the primary role in understanding knowledge and that computers should be developed to a level of understanding and functionality that would lend appropriate support to the human effort.

3 THE EDR ELECTRONIC DICTIONARY AS A VERY LARGE KNOWLEDGE BASE PROTOTYPE

In order to clarify the status of the EDR Electronic Dictionary as a representative prototype for a very large knowledge base, an extended and general electronic dictionary, which will be referred to as a generalized electronic dictionary is considered.

3.1 The generalized electronic dictionary

An integrated collection of data and knowledge pertaining to language, prepared for use in future research and development of language processing, will be referred to as a generalized electronic dictionary. In addition to being a dictionary, it also incorporates thesauri, corpora and text data. The EDR Electronic Dictionary is an attempt to realize an electronic dictionary based on integrated language data; but it represents only the first step toward a generalized electronic dictionary.

The EDR Electronic Dictionary has accumulated much knowledge and experience, and that, along with its research, constitutes a major foundation for studies towards a generalized electronic dictionary. Similar endeavors are underway at other organizations both within Japan and overseas. In Europe, electronic dictionaries such as Acquilex, Genelex and Multilex have been prepared; and the British National Corpus is an example of a general corpus. In the U.S., Comlex, WordNet and the Penn Tree Bank are machine oriented examples of a dictionary, a thesaurus and a corpus, respectively. In Japan, the dictionary used in the ALT (Automatic Language Translator) system, the JICST (The Japan Information Center of Science and Technology) Correspondence Dictionary, and the IPAL (Information-Technology Promotion Agency Lexicon) of the Japanese Language for Computers are also examples of large-scale data collection.

The generalized electronic dictionary is an initial form of a very large knowledge base of world knowledge. Its knowledge base and structure is derived from integrated words, sentences, text, and documents. By comparison, electronic dictionaries proceed from words toward documents, whereas world knowledge proceeds from documents toward individual words. Documents are regarded as world knowledge expressed in natural language.

3.2 Basic structure of the generalized electronic dictionary

Figure 1 illustrates a schematic diagram of the basic information structure of a generalized electronic dictionary. The information structure is divided into three different axes: descriptive unit, description level and type of language.

Figures 2 and 3 show where the content of the EDR Electronic Dictionary is situated in the basic information structure when viewed from the language axis.

(1) The characteristics of the information content

The information contained in the various subdictionaries can be characterized in the following three ways:

(a) **Descriptive unit:** Each subdictionary is composed of units such as words, phrases, sentences, etc.

(b) **Description level:** These descriptive units can be situated at various description levels, extending from the surface level to deeper levels of semantic description, or the concept level.

(c) **Type of language:** The natural language used for the structural units can vary, for example, Japanese, English, etc.

(2) The relations between the information content

The subdictionaries are collections of records, but these records are related in three ways. The information with records is defined through interrelations between records.

(a) Descriptive unit
Two basic relations are defined along this axis:

16

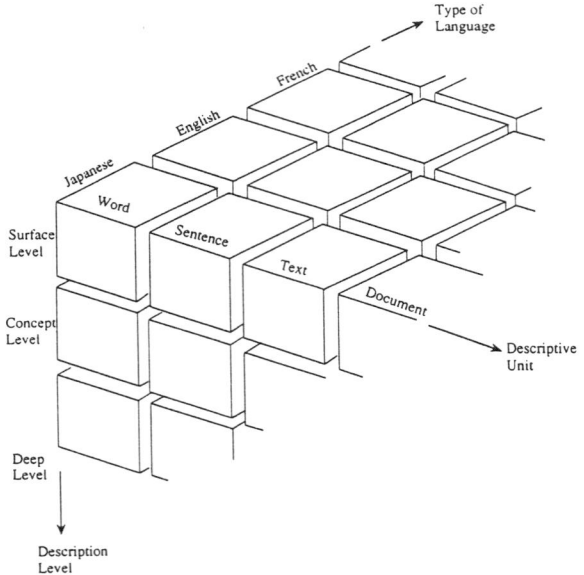

Figure 1: Basic structure of the generalized electronic dictionary

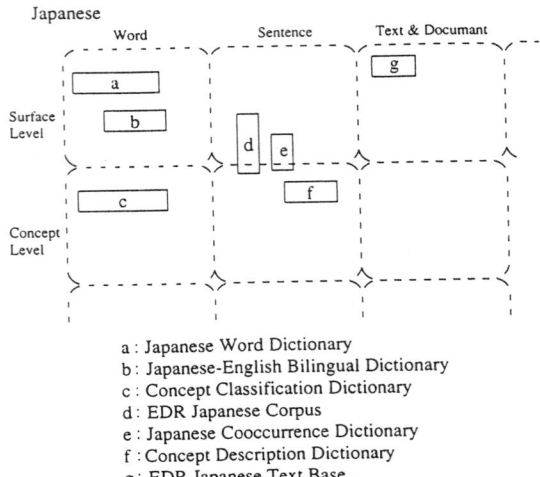

a : Japanese Word Dictionary
b : Japanese-English Bilingual Dictionary
c : Concept Classification Dictionary
d : EDR Japanese Corpus
e : Japanese Cooccurrence Dictionary
f : Concept Description Dictionary
g : EDR Japanese Text Base

Figure 2: EDR Electronic Dictionary (Japanese) in the generalized electronic dictionary

Contextual relations: A relation can be identified between a descriptive unit and the larger descriptive unit from which it derives. In other words, the larger descriptive unit sets the context for the smaller descriptive units that belong inside it. This relation can bridge across two different subdictionaries.

Explanatory relations: There is a relation between a descriptive unit and its explanation, or other related unit information, within a subdictionary. For example, there is a relation between a word and it explanatory word, phrase or sentence; a relation between a document and its abstract (written text); a relation between a document and its title (written in a phrase or sentence); and a relation between a document and its keywords.

(b) Description level

Semantic representation relations: There is a correspondence relation between a unit from the surface level, represented in natural language at this level, and a unit from the deeper level, represented in a different way, such as in code. There are also correlations between units with same meaning, but from different levels.

(c) Type of language

Correspondence relations between lan-

guages: There is a correspondence between a descriptive unit represented in a natural language and a descriptive unit in a separate natural language, that is, synonymy (or near-synonymy). As a rule, there are corresponding links between the same descriptive units from the separate languages. Correspondence relations are also identified between units from deeper levels of different languages.

3.3 Requirements to be satisfied by a generalized electronic dictionary

In keeping with the requirements necessary for a very large knowledge base (Section 2.1), the conditions that must be met for a generalized electronic dictionary are as follows:

(1) Usefulness

The dictionary should be designed to be useful with respect to future technical trends in natural language processing. In other words, it should be compatible with such trends as the achievement of processing robustness, higher-level semantic and context processing, language processing based on large corpora and large text data, and natural language processing in the form of document processing.

(2) Flexibility and universality

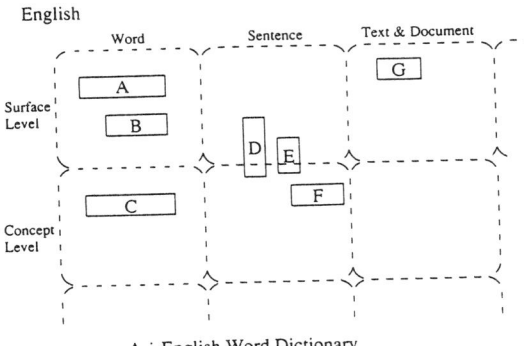

English

A : English Word Dictionary
B : English-Japanese Bilingual Dictionary
C : Concept Classification Dictionary
D : EDR English Corpus
E : English Cooccurrence Dictionary
F : Concept Description Dictionary
G : EDR English Text Base

Figure 3: EDR Electronic Dictionary (English) in the generalized electronic dictionary

The dictionary should have a flexible structure, enabling it to be adapted to circumstances as appropriate. Its scope should encompass the entirety of language processing. It should be neutral insofar as possible with respect to linguistic theory and processing methods. The ability to adapt to future changes in technology which cannot be foreseen is highly desirable. It should be freely modifiable to suit a given purpose. It should be able to serve as a representative example of a very large knowledge base.

(3) Feasibility

It should be possible to realize the production of a high precision large-scale dictionary at low cost. The dictionary data once produced must be precise enough for the computer to be able to process it. In terms of the actual development, a modular progression should be used in order to allow for gradual development. Once a certain scale and precision have been achieved, the dictionary should be of a level in which it can be utilized sufficiently. The development of powerful development support tools is also of importance. As the scale of the dictionary is expanded and the precision of the data is raised, the development support functions of the dictionary should also become more sophisticated. Also necessary in the development of a large-scale dictionary is the participation of non-specialists in the field.

3.4 The relationship between language processing (document processing) and the generalized electronic dictionary

In this section, the relationship between the basic processes of language processing (document processing) and the basic structure of the generalized electronic dictionary is discussed. This will serve to clarify the nature of use and application of the generalized electronic dictionary, as well as to verify the adequacy of the generalized electronic dictionary with respect to requirements (1) and (2).

Language processing is one type of problem solving. The most general procedure for solving problems is to divide a given problem into sub-problems which are as nearly independent as possible, obtain solutions for each of the sub-problems, then synthesize the solutions appropriately to arrive at a solution to the problem in question. In actuality, it is rare for sub-problems to be independent. In language processing, sub-problems are often interrelated in fairly complex way. From an engineering perspective, achieving an approximation of independence is a key issue. Practical applications will drive from those areas in which such an approximate independence is achieved.

(1) Problems in language processing

Checking problems: A unit of information written in one language can be analyzed to determine whether it is correct or meets certain conditions. The degree to which accuracy is met involves checking for morphological, syntactical or semantic correctness (or near-correctness), evaluation regarding readability, etc. Checking problems covers spell checking, style checking, and readability evaluation.

Comparing problems: Two separate units of information written in one language can be compared and analyzed to determine whether they meet certain conditions, such as being identical, or being analogous. The computation of the degree of comparison between the units of information is also included. Keyword retrieval (word and word), full text retrieval (word and document), similar word retrieval (word and document), similar sentence retrieval (sentence and document), and associative retrieval are all concerned with issues of comparison.

Transforming problems: A unit of information written in one language can be converted into an equivalent unit of information in the same language (system). Such transformations include Kana-kanji conversion, Braille conversion, and sentence analysis and generation.

Translating problems: A unit of information written in one language can be converted into an equivalent unit of information in a different language (system). Machine translation between two different languages, natural language interfaces (to a formal language), and natural language understanding (translation into a formal language) are example of such translation problems.

Summarizing problems: A unit of information written in one language can be converted into a condensed form in the same language (system). Exmanples of summarizing issues are keyword extraction, category extraction, knowledge frame extraction and abstract generation.

(2) Basic processes

Rule-based processes in a number of stages and example-based processes are appropriately combined to form a basic problem solving process so that the issues of each of the various problems are treated.

Rule-based processes

Step 1: Generation of an analytical structure from elements serving as structural units (descriptive units); that is, generation of structural elements and structure information

Step 2: Generation of a solution through adjustment of a collection of structural element solutions according to changes in the information on the structure

Example-based processes

Step 1: Search for an instance of a solution similar to a structural unit

Step 2: Generation of solutions by modifying solution instances

In generalized electronic dictionaries, the role a descriptive unit plays in the larger descriptive unit of which it is a part, as well as the smaller elements into which the descriptive unit can be analyzed is included. Normally, the manner in which this information is coded and applied to algorithms is left to the application of the electonic dicitonary.

(3) Correspondence with basic structure

Descriptive units: Basic division into sub-problems is performed along this axis.

Description level: As the levels become deeper, the processes become less ambiguous, more compact and in some cases more precise. The processing load however, is increased.

Type of language: Utilized in translating problems.

3.5 Correspondence with development processes

A correspondence is established between the basic processes of development and the basic structure of the generalized electronic dictionary. This is done in order to verify the feasibility of the dictionary, in keeping with the aforementioned requirement (3).

Basic procedures are determined with reference to the basic structure, such as the order in which to proceed, the items in sub-dictionary records from which to begin descriptions, and so on. In addition, the basic process for enlarging the scale of the dictionary and raising its precision is determined on the basis of mutual dependency and constraint relations of the contents. Factors influencing the basic development process include the stability of the description, the breadth of coverage of the description and the succinctness of the description. The description is more stable as it reaches the surface levels. Conversely, the breadth of coverage becomes broader as the descriptive units becomes smaller. As the language employed in the development of the generalized electronic dictionary nears one's native language, it becomes easier to secure workers and to utilize existing accumulated resources.

The basic processes necessary for the expansion of the scale of the generalized electronic dictionary includes both the cooperation of workers who have high linguistic ability as well as the support systems employed to check dependency and constraints in the data. In essence, in order to generate the descriptive contents necessary to realize a given language-processing function (a problem of language processing), a system which realizes that function itself is necessary. In order to resolve this dilemma, a gradual, self-organizing mechanism is needed.

4 FROM LINGUISTIC KNOWLEDGE TO WORLD KNOWLEDGE

In order to demonstrate that the medium of natural language plays an important role in the description of world knowledge, the relation between linguistic knowledge and world knowledge is explained.

4.1 Linguistic knowledge and world knowledge

The general connections between these two types of knowledge are summarized as follows:

(1) Expansion of the scale of linguistic knowledge
An electronic dictionary is a very large knowledge base in which is collected common knowledge about the use of language. The language used for knowledge representation is a combination of natural language and a simple artificial language. In any event, frequent use is made of natural language. For instance, explanations of the meanings of words, and the many examples of usage, are all texts and sentences in natural language. This is an important source of information for use in the improvement and expansion or enlargement of the scale of an electronic dictionary.

This improvement and expansion is a joint task for humans and computer programs with functions for acquisition of linguistic knowledge. A variety of different computer dictionaries can be produced for use by diverse natural-language processing programs, by using an electronic dictionary as the master dictionary. As the electronic dictionary is improved and expanded, the precision, performance and robustness of these natural-language processing programs will also be enhanced. Functions for linguistic knowledge acquisition will be provided by the natural-language processing programs. As the electronic dictionary is improved and expanded, the functions for linguistic knowledge acquisition will grow more powerful. In this way, a very large linguistic knowledge base will materialize.

(2) Larger-scale world knowledge
The next challenge is the realization of a very large knowledge base of world knowledge. This knowledge can be divided into knowledge specific to certain fields and knowledge common among these fields. Knowledge representation languages to be used for a very large knowledge base will be a combination of natural languages and artificial languages. The artificial language will be more complex than that used in electronic dictionaries, and will be devised so that it can be reused. Natural language is used because a means for making a computer understand all the knowledge possessed by humans has not yet been discovered. First, we should consider the effective representation of knowledge via human media, such as pictures, diagrams, voice, natural language, and so on. Of these human media, the most general-purpose is natural language. Knowledge represented in natural language includes knowledge drawn directly from textbooks, encyclopedias and glossaries, as well as knowledge newly written by editors for this

knowledge base. It constitutes an important knowledge source (information source) for the expansion and improvement of the knowledge base and thus enlargement of areas understandable by computers.

Again, the improvement and expansion of the knowledge base will be a joint effort carried out by humans and by computer programs with world knowledge acquisition functions. By processing knowledge represented in natural language in various ways, knowledge can be extracted in a variety of forms. Functions for acquisition of world knowledge will depend heavily on natural language processing functions. Enhancement of functions for acquisition of linguistic knowledge will lead to the enhancement of functions for acquisition of world knowledge.

This knowledge base of world knowledge may be used as it stands, but is primarily intended for use as a master knowledge base in generating knowledge bases specific to different areas of application.

(3) Relation of linguistic knowledge to world knowledge
Linguistic knowledge includes both knowledge of the organization of natural language as a medium, and also knowledge of the world which it tries to represent. Knowledge relating to the organization of language is concerned with the morphological and syntactic aspects of language. In addition, many regularities can be seen in this knowledge. On the other hand, knowledge relating to the world represented by language is concerned with semantics and pragmatics. Regularities and integration are partial and localized. Much of this corresponds to what in linguistics is called extra-linguistic knowledge. World knowledge is also included in this extra-linguistic knowledge. That is, knowledge related to the world expressed by language is connected to world knowledge, and corresponds to the most universally shared part of human knowledge.

4.2 The EDR Electronic Dictionary, WordNet, and CYC

Discussion on the specific connections between linguistic knowledge and world knowledge is valuable. In order to elucidate the current state of these connections, we compare three representative very large knowledge bases: the EDR Electronic Dictionary, WordNet, and CYC. WordNet is a knowledge base of English-language concepts developed by a group at Princeton University (U.S.A.) led by G.A. Miller. Initially a psycholinguistic approach was taken, but today utilization in natural language processing is included as a goal of WordNet.

The EDR Electronic Dictionary project, the WordNet project, and the CYC project share a common understanding; that is, that natural language is an important key when organizing general knowledge or world sense.

These three projects, however, each focus on different ways to handle knowledge. Knowledge, discussed in this context, includes knowledge about natural language and how it is used, as well as knowledge about what natural language represents. If knowledge as it defined here is divided into three levels - the surface level, the concept level and the knowledge level - the difference between each project's main focus is as follows:

The EDR Electronic Dictionary considers the surface level and the concept level, with only synonymy, hyponymy, and entailment being examined.

WordNet considers the concept level, with antonymy, meronymy and troponomy, in addition to the above, being examined.

CYC is mostly concerned with the knowledge level.

The products of the three projects as knowledge bases need to be further improved, expanded and developed. In order to make such improvement, expansion and development possible, it is necessary to clarify the following three points:

(1) The breadth of knowledge required (the necessary amount and type of knowledge, as well as knowledge collection methods) needs to be examined.

(2) The functions that may be realized through using such accumulated knowledge in various ways also requires thought.

(3) And, lastly the application systems which may be developed utilizing such functions also need consideration.

The EDR Electronic Dictionary aims broadly at realizing the following two functions:

(a) To judge sentences syntactically right or wrong (the syntactic processing function).

(b) To take each component word of a sentence and specify its corresponding meaning (the concept), and decide how deeply the components relate (the semantic processing function).

Functions (a) and (b) of the EDR Electronic Dictionary are yet to be completed. As for (a), efforts to expand and enrich the dictionary's vocabulary and refine its accompanying information will have to be continued to be made; and as for (b), continuous improvement and expansion will be necessary. On the whole, the quality of the English section of the Dictionary is still lower than that of the Japanese section.

Functions more advanced than (a) and (b) that are yet to be considered:

(c) A function that completes incomplete sentences in a text through context processing that includes processing of ellipsis, anaphora resolution, etc.

(d) A function that verifies the basic proposition expressed in a simple sentence.

(e) A function that verifies the compound proposition expressed in a compound sentence.

The efforts that WordNet has made to define a concept through various conceptual relationships move knowledge bases closer to the realization of function (c). The activities of CYC work toward the realization of functions (d) and (e).

A future research objective is to clarify the connections of (a), (b) and (c) to (d) and (e), and to establish a methodology for realizing knowledge on the levels (d) and (e) with the further development of a knowledge base.

5 CONCLUSION

At present the preparation of a national information infrastructure is being discussed in various fields, and is regarded as the most urgent problem in the fields of information and communication. Discussions have started from preparation of a network to serve as a foundation; following this are discussions of the preparation of an information environment on the network. Language, language processing technology, and the linguistic data supporting the former, form the framework of the information environment. The initiation of the EDR Electronic Dictionary was inspired by a desire to develop a machine translation system, but presently the project results are being viewed as linguistic data to serve as a shared basis for long-term R&D on a wider range of technologies. Improvements and extensions as well as cooperation with similar overseas activities, will be on the basis of such a status. There is an urgent demand for the initiation of projects to research and develop new technology suited to an information-originated society. The EDR Electronic Dictionary is expected to play a major role in such projects as well.

REFERENCES

1. EDR, "EDR Electronic Dictionary Technical Guide", http:// www.iijnet.or.jp/edr, 1995.

2. Lenat, D. B., "The Impact of CYC on Natural Language Analysis by Computer", KB & KS '95, (invited lecture), 1995.

3. Guha, R. V. and Lenat, D. B., "Enabling Agents to Work Together" Comm. ACM, Vol.37, No. 7, pp.123-142, 1994.

4. Miller, G. A., Beckwith, R., Fellbaum, C., Gross, D., Miller, K. and Tengi, R., "Five Papers on WordNet" Revised CSL Report 43, Cognitive Science Lab. Princeton Univ., 1993.

5. Yokoi, T., "Very Large-Scale Knowledge Bases Embodying Intelligence Space" in Kazuhiro Fuchi and Toshio Yokoi (Eds.), "Knowledge Building and Knowledge Sharing", Ohmsha and IOS Press, 1994.

Part 2: The Role of Ontologies

Ontologies and Knowledge Bases
Towards a Terminological Clarification

Nicola Guarino
National Research Council, LADSEB-CNR
Padova, Italy
guarino@ladseb.pd.cnr.it

Pierdaniele Giaretta
University of Padova
Padova, Italy

ABSTRACT

The word "ontology" has recently gained a good popularity within the knowledge engineering community. However, its meaning tends to remain a bit vague, as the term is used in very different ways. Limiting our attention to the various proposals made in the current debate in AI, we isolate a number of interpretations, which in our opinion deserve a suitable clarification. We elucidate the implications of such various interpretations, arguing for the need of clear terminological choices regarding the technical use of terms like "ontology", "conceptualization" and "ontological commitment". After some comments on the use "Ontology" (with the capital "o") as a term which denotes a philosophical discipline, we analyse the possible confusion between an ontology intended as a particular conceptual framework at the knowledge level and an ontology intended as a concrete artifact at the symbol level, to be used for a given purpose. A crucial point in this clarification effort is the careful analysis of Gruber' s definition of an ontology as a specification of a conceptualization.

1. Ontology as a philosophical discipline

2. Ontology as a an informal conceptual system

3. Ontology as a formal semantic account

4. Ontology as a specification of a "conceptualization"

5. Ontology as a representation of a conceptual system via a logical theory

   5.1 characterized by specific formal properties
   5.2 characterized only by its specific purposes

6. Ontology as the vocabulary used by a logical theory

7. Ontology as a (meta-level) specification of a logical theory

Figure 1: Possible interpretations of the term "ontology".

1 INTRODUCTION

The word "ontology" has recently gained a good popularity within the knowledge engineering community, especially in relation with the recent ARPA knowledge sharing initiative [1, 3, 2, 5, 4, 8, 7]. However, its meaning tends to remain a bit vague, as the term is used in very different ways. Limiting our attention to the various proposals made in the current debate within the knowledge sharing community, we can isolate the different interpretations reported in Fig. 1 below, which in our opinion deserve a suitable clarification.

The interpretation 1 is radically different from all the others, and its implications are discussed in the next section. The current debate regards the interpretations 2-7: 2 and 3 conceive an ontology as a conceptual "semantic" entity, either formal or informal, while according to the interpretations 5-7 an ontology is a specific "syntactic" object. The interpretation 4, which has been recently proposed as a *definition* of what an ontology is for the AI community [5, 6], is one of the more problematic, and it will be discussed in detail in the present paper. It may be classified as "syntactic" but its precise meaning depends on the understanding of the terms "specification" and "conceptualization".

According to interpretation 2, an ontology is the (unspecified) conceptual system which we may assume to underly a particular knowledge base: under this interpretation, we may say "the ontology of KB1 is different from that of KB2". Under interpretation 3, instead, the "ontology" which underlies a knowledge base is expressed in terms of suitable formal structures at the semantic level, like for instance those described in [9, 11].

Under interpretation 5, an ontology is nothing else than a logical theory. The issue is whether such a theory needs to have particular formal properties in order to be an ontology (for instance, we may impose it must be a "Tbox") or, rather, it is the intended purpose which lets us consider a logical theory as an ontology. The latter position is being supported for instance by Pat Hayes, which in recent e-mail discussions argued that an ontology is an annotated and indexed set of formal assertions about something. "Leaving off the annotations and indexing, this is a collection of assertions: what in logic is called a *theory*".

According to interpretation 6, an ontology is not viewed as a logical theory, but just as the vocabulary used by a logical theory. Such an interpretation collapses into 5.1 if an ontology is thought of as a *specification* of a vocabulary consisting of a set of logical definitions. We may anticipate that interpretation 4 collapses into 5.1, too, when a conceptualization is intended as a vocabulary; we shall see however that the problem is how to make clear the meaning of the term "conceptualization".

Finally, under interpretation 7, an ontology is seen as a (meta-level) specification of a logical theory, in the sense that it specifies the "architectural components" (or "primitives") used within a particular domain theory. This point of view is maintained in [12] and, in slightly different form, in [13]. Wielinga and colleagues argue that it is the ontology which specifies, for a theory where some formulas have the form of mathematical constraints, what a constraint is and how it differs from a formula of another kind; Mark argues that an ontology is "a representation of components and their

allowed interactions, with the purpose of providing an explicit framework in which to elaborate the rest of the system..."

We shall try to elucidate in this paper the implications of such various interpretations, arguing for the need of clear terminological choices regarding the *technical* use of terms like "ontology", "conceptualization" and "ontological commitment" within the knowledge engineering community. First we propose to use "Ontology" (with the capital "o") as a term denoting a philosophical discipline, then we analyse a number of possible senses of the term "ontology" (with the lowercase "o") where the term is somehow related to specific knowledge bases (or logical theories) designed with the purpose of expressing shared (or sharable) knowledge.

A starting point in this clarification effort will be the careful analysis of the interpretation 4 adopted by Gruber. The main problem with such an interpretation is that it is based on a notion of conceptualization (introduced in [14]) which doesn't fit our intuitions, as has been noticed in [9]: according to Genesereth and Nilsson, a conceptualization is a set of *extensional* relations describing a particular *state of affairs*, while the notion we have in mind is an intensional one, namely something like a conceptual grid which we superimpose to various possible states of affairs. We propose in this paper a revised definition of a conceptualization which captures this intensional aspect, while allowing us to give a satisfactory interpretation to Gruber's definition.

2   ONTOLOGY AND ONTOLOGIES

The first important distinction in the list of interpretations given in the previous section is between interpretation 1 and all the others. We stipulate that when we refer to *an* ontology (with the indeterminate article and the lowercase initial) we refer to a particular determinate object (whose nature may vary in dependence of the choice among interpretations 2-7), while speaking of Ontology (without the indeterminate article and with the uppercase initial) we refer to a philosophical discipline, namely that branch of philosophy which deals with the nature and the organisation of reality. Ontology as such is usually contrasted with Epistemology, which deals with the nature and sources of our knowledge[1].

Aristotle defined Ontology as the science of being as such: unlike the special sciences, each of which investigates a class of beings and their determinations, Ontology regards "all the species of being *qua* being and the attributes which belong to it *qua* being" (Aristo-

---

[1] This definition of "epistemology" is taken from Shapiro's "Encyclopedia of Artificial Intelligence" [15]. Regrettably, the entry "ontology" does not appear there. The philosophical community prefers to use the term "theory of knowledge" for what is here called "epistemology".

tle, *Metaphysics*, IV, 1). In this sense Ontology tries to answer to the question: *What is being?* or, in a meaningful reformulation: *What are the features common to all beings?*

This is what nowadays one would call *General* Ontology, in contrast with the various *Special* or *Regional* Ontologies (of the Biological, the Social, etc.). This distinction corresponds to the Husserlian one between Formal Ontology and Material Ontology [16]. But the Husserlian notion of "formal" does not involve only generality. For Husserl, the task of Formal Ontology is to determinate the conditions of the possibility of the object in general and the individuation of the requirements that every object's constitution has to satisfy.

Recently, Nino Cocchiarella defined Formal Ontology as "the systematic, formal, axiomatic development of the logic of all forms and modes of being" [17]. The connection of Cocchiarella's definition with the Husserlian notion is not clear, and, in general, the genuine interpretation of the term "formal ontology" is still a matter of debate [18]. However, Cocchiarella's definition is in our opinion particularly pregnant, as it takes into account *both* meanings of the adjective "formal": on one side, this is synonymous of "rigorous", while on the other side it means "related to the *forms* of being". Therefore, what Formal Ontology is concerned in is not so much the bare existence of certain objects, but rather the rigorous description of their *forms of being*, i.e. of their structural features. In practice, Formal Ontology can be intended as the theory of the distinctions, which can be applied independently of the state of the world, i.e. the distinctions:

- among the entities of the world (physical objects, events, regions, quantities of matter...);

- among the meta-level categories used to model the world (concept, property, quality, state, role, part...).

In this sense, Formal Ontology, as a discipline, may be relevant to both Knowledge Representation and Knowledge Acquisition [8].

3 KINDS OF ONTOLOGIES

Let us now refine the technical meaning of the word "ontology" when — within the knowledge engineering community — it is used to denote a particular object rather than a discipline. Here a possible confusion arises between an ontology intended as a particular conceptual framework at the semantic level (interpretations 2-3) and an ontology intended as a concrete artifact at the syntactic level, to be used for a given purpose (interpretations 4-7). This is an important distinction, and it is evident that we cannot use the same *technical* term to denote both things. In the current practice, however, the term "ontology" is used

1. Ontological engineering is a branch of knowledge engineering which uses Ontology to build ontologies.

2. Ontologies are special kinds of knowledge bases.

3. Any ontology has its underlying conceptualization.

4. The same conceptualization may underlie different ontologies.

5. Two different knowledge bases may commit to the same ontology.

Figure 2: Different statements making use of the term "ontology".

ambiguously with both meanings, either to refer to (various kinds of) symbol-level artifacts, or to their conceptual (or semantical) counterparts[2]. Therefore, rather than insisting on a unique precise meaning for such a term, what we propose is to adopt different technical terms to refer explicitly to the two levels, while tolerating an ambiguity in the interpretation of the term "ontology" (with the lowercase initial). We shall use the term *conceptualization* to denote a semantic structure which reflects a particular conceptual system (interpretation 3 in Fig. 1), and *ontological theory* to denote a logical theory intended to express ontological knowledge (interpretation 5). The underlying intuition is that ontological theories are designed artifacts, knowledge bases of a special kind which can be read, sold or physically shared. Conceptualizations, on the other hand, are the semantical counterpart of ontological theories. The same ontological theory may *commit* to different conceptualizations, as well as the same conceptualization may underlie different ontological theories. The term "ontology" will be used ambiguously, either as synonym of "ontological theory" or as synonym of "conceptualization". We need only to be consistent to the choice made within the same statement.

The details of the definitions mentioned above are the subject of the subsequent sections; for the time being, the meaning of statements like those listed in Fig 2 should however be clear enough under the assumptions we have made. In 1-4, the term "ontology" has a clear syntactic interpretations; the interpretation of statement 5 will be discussed later.

4 KINDS OF CONCEPTUALIZATIONS

Let us notice first that the use of the term "ontology" as related to an ontological theory is compatible with Tom Gruber's definition of an ontology as "an explicit

---

[2]The most common use is however the former one.

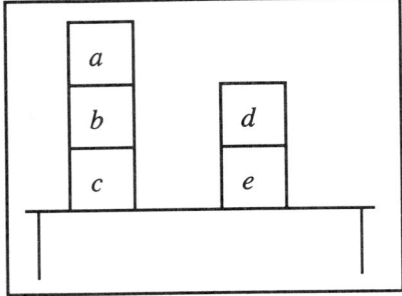

Figure 3: Blocks on a table. From [14].

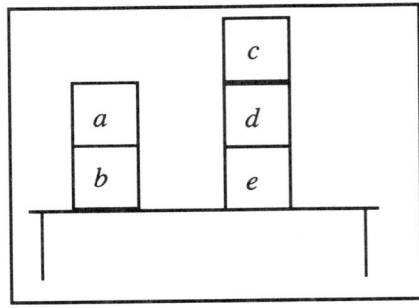

Figure 4: A different arrangement of blocks. A different conceptualization?

specification of a conceptualization", since it should be clear that an "explicit" object is a concrete, symbol-level object. The problem with Gruber's definition, however, is that it relies on an extensional notion of "conceptualization" [14] which, while being compatible with the preliminary characterization given in the previous section, does not fit our purposes of defining what an ontology is. We have already pointed to this problem in [10] ; we shall discuss it here in detail, proposing an alternative, intensional definition of "conceptualization" which satisfies our needs.

Let us consider the example given by Genesereth and Nilsson. They take into account a situation where two piles of blocks are resting on a table (Fig 3). According to the authors, a possible conceptualization of this scene is given by the following structure:

$$\langle \{a, b, c, d, e\}, \{on,\ above,\ clear,\ table\} \rangle$$

where $\{a, b, c, d, e\}$ is a set called the *universe of discourse*, consisting of the five blocks we are interested in, and $\{on,\ above,\ clear,\ table\}$ is the set of the relevant relations among these blocks, of which the first two, *on* and *above*, are binary and the other two, *clear* and *table*, are unary[3]. The authors make clear that objects and relations are extensional entities. For instance, the *table* relation, which is understood as holding of a block if and only if that block is resting on the table, is but the set $\{c, e\}$. It is exactly such an extensional interpretation which originates our troubles.

Let us notice first that the authors used natural language terms (like *on, above*) in the metalanguage chosen to describe a conceptualization. This could perhaps be seen as nothing more than a didactical device.

---

[3]In the original example also a function is considered, but for simplicity reasons we omit here to mention functions as a further element in the characterization of a conceptualization.

But such linguistic terms do convey essential information in order to understand the criteria used to consider some sets of tuples as the *relevant* relations. Such an extra information cannot be accounted for by the conceptualization itself.

Referring to the example given, consider a different arrangement of blocks, where c is on the top of d, while a and b together form a separate stack standing on the table (Fig. 4). The corresponding structure would be different from the previous one, generating therefore a different conceptualization. Of course there is nothing wrong in such a view, if one is only interested in isolated snapshots of the block world. But the meanings of the terms used to denote the relevant relations are still the same, since they are invariant with respect to the possible configurations of blocks. In fact, in the metalanguage adopted in their book, Genesereth and Nilsson would use the same terms (*on, above, clear, table*) to denote the new conceptualization. We prefer to say in this case that the states of affairs are different, but the conceptualization is the same. The structure proposed by Genesereth and Nilsson seems to be more apt to represent a *state of affairs* rather than a conceptualization.

In order to capture such intuitions, the linguistic terms we have used to denote the relevant relations cannot be thought of as mere comments, informal extra-information. Rather, the formal structure used for a conceptualization should somehow account for their *meaning*. As the logico-philosophical literature teaches us, such a meaning cannot coincide with an extensional relation.

Sticking to a set-theoretical framework, a standard way to approximate such meaning is to conceive it as an intension (*intensional relation*), taking inspiration from Montague semantics. This means that a single extensional relation is always relative to a possible world[4].

Formally, an intensional relation of arity n on a domain D is a function from a set W of possible worlds to the set 2^{D^n} of all possible n-ary relations on D. Such a function specifies a set of admissible extensions, relative to the domain and the set of possible worlds considered. This means that not only the extension in the actual world, but also those relative to the other possible worlds are specified. We can therefore represent a conceptualization by the following *intensional structure*:

$$\langle W, D, R \rangle$$

where W is a set of possible worlds, D is a domain of objects, and R is a set of intensional relations on D.

According to this intensional interpretation, a conceptualization accounts for the intended meanings of the terms used to denote the relevant relations. Such meanings are supposed to remain the same if the actual extensions of the relations change due to different states of affairs. This means that, for instance, the actual extensions of the relation *on* in the two examples of Fig. 3 and 4 belong to the image of the *same* intensional relation, applied to different worlds. Intuitively, we can see a conceptualization as given by a set of informal rules which constrain the structure of a piece of reality, which an agent uses in order to isolate and organize relevant objects and relevant relations: the rules which tell us whether a certain block is *on* another one remain the same, independently of the particular arrangement of the blocks. These rules can be viewed as conceptual links which put together different extensions belonging to the same intensional relation.

Notice that, given a set of relevant relations specified by linguistic terms like those of our example, there will be in general many conceptualizations of the form given above which satisfy the natural constraints we can attach to the meaning of such expressions. As shown in [9] , a convenient modal theory can be used to give an *approximate characterization* of such intended meaning, with the aim of excluding deviant extensions. For example, we can express the intuitive constraint that a tuple like $< a, a >$ should never belong to the extension of the relation specified by the word "*on*" by stating[5]

$$\text{nec } \forall x. \neg on(x, x)$$

Another interesting constraint which may be useful to characterize a unary relation like *block* (not mentioned by Genesereth and Nilsson) is that such a relation can be never "lost" by its instances, i.e. if it holds of an object, it holds of that object in all possible worlds:

$$\text{nec } (\forall x. block(x) \supset \text{nec } block(x))$$

Such a constraint has been called "ontological rigidity" in [9], and has been used to discriminate among various ontological categories of unary relations.

A set of formal constraints like those above, expressed in a suitable modal language, can therefore be used to (partially) *characterize* a conceptualization, in the sense of excluding unintended extensions of the relevant relations even for possible "worlds" different from the one considered. Notice that in general we cannot identify a *single* conceptualization by means of a set of formal constraints, since such a set may have many models. The set of such models is exactly what in [10] we defined as *ontological commitment*[6].

According to these considerations, we cannot see a particular theory as a *specification* of a conceptualization, since conceptualizations can be only partially characterized. What we can specify is a *set* of conceptualizations, i.e. an ontological commitment.

5 A SIMPLE EXAMPLE

Having discussed in detail the various implications underlying the notion of conceptualization, let us now use a simple example to see how such a semantic notion can be related to syntactic objects like logical theories. Consider the following logical theory:

$T1$:

$$\forall x. apple(x) \supset fruit(x).$$
$$\forall x. pear(x) \supset fruit(x).$$

$$apple(a1).$$
$$red(a1)$$

If we want to isolate the ontological content of such a theory, we can try to individuate, among its axioms, those which we consider to be more strictly related to the intrinsic intended meanings of the predicates used in the language. For example, the following axioms (which are usually related to what is called the *Tbox*) may be intended as capturing part of the meaning of *apple, pear* and *fruit* :

$T2$:

$$\forall x. apple(x) \supset fruit(x).$$
$$\forall x. pear(x) \supset fruit(x).$$

---

[4]Roughly, we can think of possible worlds like states of affairs or situations.

[5]For typographic reasons, we use the symbols **nec** and **pos** to stand for, respectively, the usual "box" and "diamond" operators.

[6]In that paper we did not introduce intensions as ingredients of our semantical structures, adopting instead standard modal models. Here we choose a different approach which seems to be better suited to the perspective we want to present.

We shall call a set of such axioms an *ontological theory*. An ontological theory contains formulas which are considered to be always true (and therefore *sharable* among multiple agents), independently of particular states of affairs. Formally, we can say that such formulas must be true in every possible world.

An ontological theory like the one above characterizes very roughly the ontological content of the theory from which it is extracted. To better grasp such a content, we should look at the intended conceptualization underlying both T1 and T2, which models (in a much finer way) the ontologically relevant aspects of the *language* used by our initial theory. According to the discussion made in the previous section, such a conceptualization can be *characterized* (in an approximate way) by a suitable modal theory T3. The formulas (theorems) of T2 will be true in every possible world belonging to the intended conceptualization, and therefore will appear as necessary formulas in T3; furthermore, T3 may contain other formulas capturing necessary facts not captured by T2. For the present example, we choose a very simple theory like the following:

$T3$:

$\mathbf{nec}(\forall x.apple(x) \supset fruit(x)).$

$\mathbf{nec}(\forall x.pear(x) \supset fruit(x)).$

$\mathbf{nec}(\forall x.apple(x) \supset \mathbf{nec}\ apple(x)).$

$\mathbf{nec}(\forall x.pear(x) \supset \mathbf{nec}\ pear(x)).$

$\mathbf{nec}(\forall x.fruit(x) \supset \mathbf{nec}\ fruit(x)).$

$\neg\mathbf{nec}(\forall x.red(x) \supset \mathbf{nec}\ red(x)).$

Such a theory expresses some very general constraints on the meaning of our predicates, namely the fact that *apple, pear* and *fruit* form a hierarchy, and that they are "rigid", differently from *red*. We say that T3 is the *specification of the ontological commitment* of T1.

Notice that the same information carried by T3 can be expressed by a meta-level theory, whose domain is given by the nonlogical symbols used in T1. For instance, we can write:

$T4$:

$apple \le fruit.$

$pear \le fruit.$

$rigid(apple).$

$rigid(pear).$

$rigid(fruit).$

$\neg rigid(red).$

Such a theory can be usefully adopted as an alternate specification of an ontological commitment, assuming of course that the meaning of predicates like $\le$ and *rigid* is such that T4 can be immediately converted into T3 by means of suitable translation rules.

6   WHAT IS AN ONTOLOGY?

Let us now go back to our original problem of clarifying the meaning of "ontology". Our goal is to propose a choice among the interpretations 2-7 of Fig. 1, and to give a precise sense to at least some of the statements listed in Fig 2. In the light of the discussion developed so far, we shall restrict our choice to three possible technical senses of the word "ontology".

In sense a), "ontology" is a synonym of "ontological theory". In this case statements 1-4 in Fig 2 have a unique interpretation, while statement 5 means that the two knowledge bases may have a common subtheory, which is an ontological theory. This choice is consistent with interpretation 5 in Fig. 1. As discussed in the previous section, an ontological theory differs from an arbitrary logical theory (or knowledge base) by its semantics, since all its axioms must be true in every possible world of the underlying conceptualization. This means that while an arbitrary logical theory (containing for instance a statement like $apple(a) \wedge pear(a)$, expressing uncertainty about the object a) may represent a particular epistemic state, an ontological theory can be only used to represent common knowledge independent from single epistemic states. Due to this formal difference between an ontological theory and an arbitrary logical theory, interpretation 5.2 is therefore discarded in favour of 5.1. T2 is an ontology according to such an interpretation.

In sense b), "ontology" is a synonym of "specification of an ontological commitment". This choice is still consistent with interpretation 5.1. In this case, statements 1-4 still get a unique meaning, while statement 5 has no sense, and it should be substituted by "The ontological commitment of two different knowledge bases may be specified by the same theory". T3 is an ontology according to this interpretation. The language used by T3 is in general richer than the one used by T1: as discussed in [9], the purposes are different, since the purpose of T3 is to convey meaning by using a very expressive language, while the language of T1 is the result of a tradeoff choice between expressivity and computational efficiency. Notice that T3 is an ontological theory like T2, since its formulas are always true.

In sense c), "ontology" is a synonym of "conceptualization". This choice is consistent with interpretation 3 in Fig. 1. In this case statements 1-4 in Fig 2 have no sense, while the occurrence of "ontology" in statement 5 gets a semantic interpretation. In this case, statement 5 is equivalent to "Two different knowledge bases may have the same conceptualization". None of the theories shown in the previous section is an ontology according to this choice.

Let us now see what the meaning of Gruber's definition "an ontology is a specification of a conceptualization" may be. First of all, it is evident that sense c) is incompatible with such a definition. Since we believe we have good reasons to keep the latter, we suggest to avoid the use of "ontology" in a semantic sense unless it is clear from the context.

Let us now consider senses a) and b), which assign the tag "ontology" to T2 and T3, respectively. Strictly speaking, none of them can be considered as a *specification* of a conceptualization, and hence Gruber's definition cannot apply. If we want to mantain its original (good) intuitions, we must weaken Gruber's definition, claiming that an ontology is only a *partial account* of a conceptualization. According to this choice, both T2 and T3 may be called "ontologies".

In fact, such a weakened definition leaves space both for senses a) and b), and this is exactly what we want: the *degree of specification* of the conceptualization which underlies the language used by a particular knowledge base varies in dependence of our purposes: an ontology of kind b) gets closer to specifying the indended conceptualization (and therefore may be used to establish consensus about the utility of *sharing* a particular knowledge base), but it pays the price of a richer language (and therefore, in general, undecidabile and inefficient). An ontology of kind a), on the other side, is developed with particular inferences in mind, designed to be shared among users which *already* agree on the underlying conceptualization.

There are still a couple of senses of "ontology", among those reported in Fig. 1, which are to be discussed, namely senses 6 and 7. The approach which seems to adopt such interpretations is the one followed in the KAKTUS project [12]; here an ontology is defined as "a metalevel viewpoint on a set of possible domain theories". In general, such a viewpoint is a set of metalevel definitions of the syntactic categories used in a knowledge base. The form of such definitions is not clear. What is interesting is that the description of a particular knowledge base according to such metalevel categories may have the form of a theory like T4. There is however an important difference: T4 uses meta-level semantic categories, defined in the language of T3, while Wielinga and Schreiber want to avoid any explicit semantic notion.

In conclusion, we hope to have given a clarification of the notion of "ontology" based on a notion of "conceptualization" defined in a rigorous semantic way; such a framework allowed us to underline the difference between an ontology and an arbitrary knowledge base, and to distinguish among various senses of "ontology" used in the current debate.

7   A SIMPLE GLOSSARY

We report below the informal definitions which we suggest to use as the preferred interpretations of the terms discussed in the present paper.

conceptualization: an intensional semantic structure which encodes the implicit rules constraining the structure of a piece of reality.

Formal Ontology: the systematic, formal, axiomatic development of the logic of all forms and modes of being.

ontological commitment: a partial semantic account of the intended *conceptualization* of a logical theory.

ontological engineering: the branch of knowledge engineering which exploits the principles of (formal) *Ontology* to build ontologies.

ontological theory: a set of formulas intended to be always true according to a certain *conceptualization*.

Ontology: that branch of philosophy which deals with the nature and the organisation of reality.

ontology: (sense 1) a logical theory which gives an explicit, partial account of a *conceptualization*; (sense 2) synonym of *conceptualization*.

ACKNOWLEDGMENT

This work has been made within the CNR project "Ontological and Linguistic Tools for Conceptual Modelling". We are grateful to Mike Uschold, Massimiliano Carrara and Alessandro Artale for their contribute to the final version of this paper.

REFERENCES

References

[1] Neches, R. and Fikes, R. and Finin, T. and Gruber, T. and Patil, R. and Senator, T. and Swartout, W.R. Enabling Technology for Knowledge Sharing. In *AI Magazine*, 1991.

[2] Musen, Mark A. Dimensions of Knowledge Sharing and Reuse. In *Computers and Biomedical Research*, vol. 25, pp. 435-467, 1992.

[3] Mars, N.J.I. *ECAI Workshop on Knowledge Sharing and Reuse: Ways and Means.* European Coordinating Committee for Artificial Intelligence (ECCAI), Vienna, Austria, 1992.

[4] Guarino, Nicola and Poli, Roberto. In Guarino, Nicola and Poli, Roberto, (eds.), *Formal Ontology in Conceptual Analysis and Knowledge Representation*, Kluwer (to appear).

[5] Gruber, Thomas R. Model Formulation as a Problem-Solving Task: Computer-Assisted Engineering Modeling. In *International Journal of Intelligent Systems*, vol. 8, pp. 105-127, 1993.

[6] Gruber, Thomas R. Toward Principles for the Design of Ontologies Used for Knowledge Sharing In Guarino, Nicola and Poli, Roberto, editors, *Formal Ontology in Conceptual Analysis and Knowledge Representation*, Kluwer (to appear).

[7] Mars, N.J.I. *ECAI Workshop on Comparison of Implemented Ontologies*. European Coordinating Comitee for Artificial Intelligence (ECCAI), Amsterdam, The Netherlands, 1994.

[8] Guarino, Nicola. Formal Ontology, Knowledge Acquisition and Knowledge Representation. In Guarino, Nicola and Poli, Roberto, (eds.), *Formal Ontology in Conceptual Analysis and Knowledge Representation*, Kluwer (to appear).

[9] Guarino, Nicola and Carrara, Massimiliano and Giaretta, Pierdaniele Formalizing Ontological Commitment. In Proc. of the *National Conference on Artificial Intelligence* (AAAI-94), Seattle, Morgan Kaufmann, 1994.

[10] Guarino, N. and Carrara, M. and Giaretta, P. An Ontology of Meta-Level Categories In J., Doyle and Sandewall, E. and Torasso, P., (eds.), Proc. of the Fourth International Conference *Principles of Knowledge Representation and Reasoning* (KR94), Morgan Kaufmann, San Mateo, CA pp. 270-280, 1994.

[11] van der Vet, P.E. and Speel, P.H. and Mars, N.J.I. Ontologies for very large knowledge bases in material science: a case study. In Proc. of the *Second international conference on building and sharing of very large-scale knowledge bases* (KB&KS '95), Twente, (to be appered).

[12] Wielinga, B. and Schreiber, A.Th. and Jansweijer, W. and Anjewierden, A. and van Harmelen, F. Framework and formalism for expressing ontologies. *ESPRIT Project 8145 KACTUS*, Free University of Amsterdam, deliverable DO1b.1, 1994.

[13] Mark, W. Ontology as Knowledge Base Architecture In Proc. of the *Banff Knowledge Acquisition Workshop*, 1995, (to appear).

[14] Genesereth, M.R. and Nilsson, N.J. Logical Foundation of Artificial Intelligence Morgan Kaufmann, Los Altos, California, 1987.

[15] Nutter, J.T. Epistemology In Shapiro, Stuart, editor, *Encyclopedia of Artificial Intelligence*, John Wyley, 1987.

[16] Bunge, M. Treatise on basic philosophy. Ontology I: the furniture of the world, Dordrecht, Reidel, 1977.

[17] Cocchiarella, N.B. Formal Ontology In Burkhardt, H and Smith, B, editors, *Handbook of Metaphysics and Ontology*. Philosophia Verlag, Munich, pp. 640-647, 1991.

[18] Poli, Roberto. Bimodality of Formal Ontology and Mereology In Guarino, Nicola and Poli, Roberto, (eds.), *Formal Ontology in Conceptual Analysis and Knowledge Representation*, Kluwer (to appear).

Ontological Commitment and Domain-Specific Architectures: Experience with Comet and Cosmos

William Mark, **Jon Dukes-Schlossberg** and **Randy Kerber**
Lockheed Artificial Intelligence Center
Palo Alto, CA, USA
mark@sumex.stanford.edu

ABSTRACT

Large knowledge bases are complex pieces of software that require development processes and tools for design, debugging, and maintenance. Task-specific architectures and taxonomic design methodologies offer part of the answer, but still do not address the need to ensure that all additions and modifications to the knowledge base preserve its core assumptions and its "contract of expectations" with the external world. We describe a knowledge base development process based on capturing the set of ontological commitments that define the interdependencies among key terms in the ontology. These commitments are explicitly represented and conceived as a domain-specific architecture that is enforced during knowledge base development. We have experimented with this process in two systems, Comet and Cosmos.

1 INTRODUCTION

Since the beginning of large scale knowledge base construction, knowledge bases have been viewed as complex pieces of software that must be carefully designed, debugged, and maintained over time. Any system has a "contract of expectations" with its outside world of users and other software systems. These expectations about how the system will behave – what functions it performs, what it is and is not capable of doing – are based on a combination of external knowledge about the domain of the system, explicit specifications of the system, and actual experience with the system. Thus, we have a set of expectations for word processors based on our knowledge about the domain of word processors; these expectations are refined through specific documentation and actual experience for the word processors we happen to use. The contract of expectations is that the system will always act like a word

processor throughout its entire range of behavior, in future releases, etc. Violations of the contract are considered to be bugs. This contract of expectations is inevitably implicit. No complex software system can be fully specified, fully tested, or completely understood.

In knowledge based systems, the knowledge base to a large extent determines system behavior. It should therefore be possible to create and enforce the contract of expectations in terms of the knowledge base. Indeed, the whole idea of knowledge based systems is to represent the information that determines their behavior in a form that is explicit and understandable (at least to knowledge representation experts).

As we were building systems that performed services for their users based on fairly sophisticated inferences over large, intricate knowledge bases, we were concerned about how to ensure that the knowledge base development process itself always worked to maintain the contract of expectations. How could we make sure that each addition or modification of the knowledge base would lead to system behavior that was in line with user expectations? Furthermore, in the systems we were building, after initial design the knowledge bases grew as a by-product of user interaction with the systems, not through knowledge acquisition by knowledge engineers. How could we construct knowledge bases such that the growth processes would always maintain the core assumptions about the domain?

We have been working with a knowledge base development approach based on the following tenets:

- a system's contract of expectations is embodied in the ontological commitments of the knowledge base;

- these commitments can be most effectively represented as explicit interdependencies among complex terms;

- all knowledge base development and growth processes must be constrained by inference over and

34

propagation of these interdependencies.

Our experiments with this approach have involved systems in two different domains: Comet [Mark, *et al.* 92] supports the design of software systems, specialized in the area of radar trackers (i.e., air traffic control systems and the like); Cosmos [Mark, *et al.* 94] supports engineering negotiation, specialized in the area of actively controlled gimbals (e.g., spacecraft components). Both systems give design feedback to their users. When a Comet user makes a change to a software module, the system provides feedback on which other modules are affected and will require modification. Cosmos provides hardware designers with analyses that indicate the impact of a proposed design change.

Both systems use domain-independent inference algorithms. The quality and accuracy of the advice they provide to their users depends on the extent to which the essential characteristics of their domains are embodied in their knowledge base. In both Comet and Cosmos, the knowledge base starts from a hand-built core that is meant to embody these essential characteristics. In both systems, the users' normal working interaction with the system causes the generation of new concepts that are automatically incorporated into the knowledge base. The users are not knowledge engineers; concepts are created and incorporated behind the scenes.

Our requirement, then, is to build the knowledge bases in a way that ensures that as new knowledge is added to the system (by knowledge engineers or automatically), users are still receiving advice according to the principles of the domain they think they are operating in. Comet's feedback must be based on the design principles that are known to result in *trackers*, not some other kind of software accidentally introduced during knowledge base development. Similarly, Cosmos needs to provide impact analyses based on the laws that govern actively controlled gimbals, or its advice will be misleading. Knowledge base design and development must maintain the system's contract of expectations.

2 KNOWLEDGE BASE DEVELOPMENT METHODLOGIES

There is a considerable amount of research and practice aimed at systematizing and improving the quality of knowledge base design and construction. In this section we discuss the existing work that informs, and in some cases forms the basis of, our approach.

2.1 Architecture-Based Approaches

A software architecture specifies the interdependency of modules at a given level of abstraction. The purpose of the architecture is to provide an explicit framework to guide the development process: any change

in a module must be accounted for – in the ways defined by the architecture – in the other modules at that level. In a conventional software system, the key interdependencies are data and control flows. Thus, if a change is made in the input/output specifications of a module, its interdependent "neighbors", as defined by the architecture for that level, must also be changed. The choice of architecture is not arbitrary – certain architectures have been found to lead to better system designs in given situations.

No modern developer would create a complex piece of software like a knowledge base without reference to an explicit architecture. If knowledge base development is to be treated as software development, the issues become (1) what constitutes the architecture of a knowledge base, and (2) what tools can be brought to bear on bringing the architecture into the knowledge base development process.

Since the mid-1980's, there has been a growing body of work in knowledge base construction using task-specific architectures [Chandrasekeran 86, 90] [Clancey 89] [Wielinga, *et al.* 92]. The fundamental insight is that problem-solving methods transcend application domains. Explicit representations of domain-independent but task-specific (or really "method-specific" as pointed out in [Musen and Tu 93]) problem-solving processes have been used to structure the design and construction of knowledge bases. Given a class of problems in a domain, an appropriate task-specific architecture is combined with domain-specific knowledge to create a knowledge base for solving that class of problems in that domain. Knowledge base construction tools embodying task-specific architectures have been created to partially automate this paradigm.

As with any architecture, these task-specific architectures specify interdependencies. In this case, the interdependencies deal with stages or aspects of a problem-solving process. These architectures are deliberately "meta" with respect to the interdependencies that define domain-specific terms. Therefore, while task-specific architectures provide valuable guidance for knowledge base construction, they cannot in themselves ensure that the knowledge base is constructed in accordance with the core assumptions of the domain. Their guidance is along a different dimension: they are not designed to determine whether an addition to the knowledge base violates the internal rules that make trackers trackers or gimbal gimbals.

2.2 Taxonomy-Based Approaches

On the other hand, taxonomic organization has been explicitly put forward as a mechanism to ensure that knowledge bases maintain the system's contract of expectations. Domain knowledge is structured as complex terms, and a generalization hierarchy of these terms is used as an organizational framework for the knowledge base. The idea is that abstract terms in the taxonomy are used to rigorously define the essential characteristics of the domain. These terms can only be specialized under strict system control, ensuring that the essential characteristics of the domain are rigorously enforced. This paradigm can be found as far back as Bill Woods's "conceptual coat rack" view of the taxonomy [Woods 75] (see also [Woods 91] for an in-depth discussion of this topic).

As with the task-specific architecture paradigm, tools have been created to automate knowledge base construction with this paradigm. Description logic representation systems [Brachman 92] have been specifically designed to manipulate structured terms, and, in particular, automatically maintain taxonomic relationships among these terms: "Because concepts have clear definitions, it is possible to have the system organize them into the subsumption hierarchy, rather than have the user specify their exact place" [Brachman, et al. 91]. In addition, description logic systems have codified certain system inferences such as contradiction detection and "completion reasoning", a set of inferences for determining the ramifications of certain interconceptual relationships.

Taxonomic organization and its representation in description logic are an important basis for knowledge base construction, but are not sufficient to ensure that the knowledge base maintains the system's contract of expectations. The reasons for this are twofold. First, within the bounds of the representation, taxonomic organization can only be partially enforced. Automated taxonomic reasoning works only on terms that are formed as structured compositions of existing terms; not on primitives (terms whose definition is either partially or completely unknown to the system). Even for compositional terms complete enforcement of the taxonomic organization is computationally infeasible (see [MacGregor 91] for one of several discussions of these points).

Second, the extent view of taxonomies and their representation in description logic does not adequately reflect crucial distinctions among terms. In particular, there is no way within the representation to distinguish terms that represent core concepts of the domain from terms that represent exogenous descriptions [Guarino 94]. Terms like *Single Hypothesis Tracker* and *Multi-Hypothesis Tracker* in Comet's domain are based on the intrinsic properties that make a piece of software a tracker. Any extension of Comet's knowledge base must be very clear on how the new knowledge relates to these terms, or the reasoning based on that extension would not necessarily pertain to trackers. On the other hand, relationships with terms like *Well Modularized Tracker* need not be clearly defined in extensions of the knowledge base, because it is perfectly plausible

to reason about trackers with or without the ability to address the quality of their modularization. Yet all of these terms are treated equally by description logic and other knowledge representation systems based on generalization hierarchies of complex terms. As Guarino points out, the crucial distinctions are *ontological* in nature, and knowledge base development must account for the ontological commitments that define the domain.

2.3 Shared Ontology Approaches

An approach to knowledge base development that has been gaining a great deal of interest is the creation of new knowledge bases by assembling or sharing existing ones. Shared ontologies are used to define the common terms that serve as the basis for sharing (e.g., see [Neches, et al. 91], [Walther, et al. 92], [Gruber 93], [Wielinga, et al. 94]). In this approach, ontologies are taken to be explicit specifications of the objects and relationships that make up some world (see [Gruber 93], *cf.* [Genesereth and Nilsson 87]). Ontologies, then, provide an explicit shared specification that enables all parties to use the same terms for the same conceptualizations.

But how far can an ontology can go in "ensuring" that the meaning of a term adequately reflects its underlying conceptualization? Both [Walther, et al. 92] and [Wielinga, et al. 94] discuss the problems inherent in mapping of terms from an ontology into an application setting: the specifications in the ontology may not adequately address key characteristics of the application domain, allowing misinterpretation when they are used in the application.

Recent work has attempted to clarify the role of ontological knowledge, including careful motivation for why such distinctions are important in building actual knowledge bases [Guarino 94], [Guarino, et al. 94]). Guarino and his colleagues argue for a formal representation of ontological commitments, and stress their importance as those aspects of the knowledge base that must remain invariant if the knowledge base is to embody the meaning of the domain. Ontologies must clearly express ontological commitments if the terms they specify are to be used without misinterpretation.

3 ONTOLOGICAL COMMITMENT AND DOMAIN-SPECIFIC ARCHITECTURE

The notion of ontological commitment precisely captures our requirement of expressing the system's contract of expectations at the knowledge base level. If Comet's knowledge base adequately represents the ontological commitments of the tracker domain, and if all changes to the knowledge base can be made to adhere to these commitments, Comet will fulfill its contract of expectations with its users. The question is how to operationalize ontological commitments so that they affect the knowledge base development process: how are ontological commitments identified, represented, and enforced?

In this section we describe our approach to knowledge base construction. It focuses on operationalizing one class of ontological commitments, using an architecture metaphor to express them. It uses subsumption reasoning and description logic to enforce the commitments as far as it can, and explores other reasoning mechanisms when description logic is inadequate.

3.1 A Class of Ontological Commitments

"Minimal ontological commitment" has been proposed as a design criterion for ontologies [Gruber 94]. In this context, "minimal" means that the ontology should specify as little as possible about a term so that it is easier for others to know what the term means and to see how it relates to their other terms. On the other hand, as Gruber points out, the ontology must specify enough to accurately embody the semantics of the term. In his example ontology of quantities and magnitudes, he notices that the specification of magnitudes should include a commitment to comparability: magnitudes of the same dimension (e.g., all distance magnitudes) are declared to be comparable. An ontology so "minimal" that it did not include the comparability commitment would not adequately express the meaning of magnitudes. Such an ontology would not satisfy the contract of expectations for the domain of quantities and magnitudes. For example, Gruber specifically notes that unit conversion for magnitudes is not possible without the comparability commitment.

The comparability commitment expresses the *interdependence* of terms, in this case among all magnitudes of the same dimension. In our effort to build large knowledge bases, we found that the "interesting" part of most terms was their interdependencies with other terms. As we were designing and building the knowledge bases, we were forced to look at terms in the design sense: *if we changed the specification of one term, which other terms in the knowledge base would have to change?*

To illustrate this point of view, we revisit Winston's description of the Blocks World arch (from the late 1960's, described again in [Winston 84]): an arch consists of two uprights and a lintel such that the uprights support the lintel and such that the uprights do not touch. Any extensions to the knowledge base must honor these ontological commitments. Looked at from our point of view, this means that any knowledge base extensions that specify uprights must be checked with respect to the specification of lintels. For example, someone or something must ensure that the *supportability* interdependence between lintels and uprights is being maintained: knowledge base extensions in which the lintels are things like megaliths are incompatible with extensions in which the uprights are things like playing cards. The ontology of Winston arches commits to this supportability interdependence among lintel and upright terms, just as Gruber's ontology commits to the comparability interdependence of magnitude terms. The knowledge base development process must take this interdependence into account as new terms are added.

In trying to account for these interdependencies in our knowledge base development process we needed to consider how the interdependencies would be selected and conceptualized in any domain, and also how they would be represented and enforced.

3.2 Domain-Specific Architectures

Turning first to the question of selection and conceptualization, it was clear that the ontologically important interdependencies would be domain-dependent. Ontologies describe the most useful (or at least the most well trodden) organization of knowledge in a given domain. We believed that, in many domains — including the engineering domains we were most interested in — the existing ontologies would clearly define the key interdependencies. The Blocks World has a well understood and well documented ontology of discrete solid objects with a small set of physical and spatial interdependency relationships (supports, on-top-of, etc.). Comet's domain of conventional software has a well understood ontology of modules with input/output, data access, and control interdependencies. Cosmos encompasses the mechanical domain (solids and fluids with physical linkages, spatial relationships, and functional interdependencies) and the electrical domain (components with connectivity, physical configuration, thermal, and radiation interdependencies).

In the engineering domains, these interdependencies are organized into and expressed as architectures (both software and hardware). Architectures express interdependencies at a given level of abstraction. As described above, there are only a few types of interdependency for any domain. Architectures are expressed in terms of levels, each level representing a configuration of specialized domain objects and concomittantly specialized interdependencies. This is precisely the notion of architecture found in the task-specific architecture community (e.g., see [Wielinga, et al. 94]). We have called our architectures *domain-specific* in order to emphasize the distinction (see Figures 5 and 8 for examples).

3.3 Using Description Logic

Systematizing our conceptualization of interdependencies in terms of architectures was only the beginning of our requirement to create a knowledge base development process that maintains the system's contract of expectations. Given our desire to create systems whose knowledge bases we saw evolving, in part automatically, over long periods of time, we knew that we needed the most help possible from our representation tools. We needed to represent these interdependencies as explicitly as possible, and we needed our knowledge representation system to automatically propagate and enforce them. When we changed the specification of a term, we wanted the system to tell us what else had to change.

The goal is to operationalize the interdependencies in a principled, generalizable way that the knowledge representation system can enforce. We understood from the beginning that this goal can only be accomplished to a degree in any real application. The supportability interdependency of the Winston arch can be arbitrarily hard to operationalize. Ideally, we would like a representation that completely covers supportability among any solid object classes, and that can be completely enforced at term specification time. It would cover friction (a sloping lintel is fine unless it is made out of a slippery material), load bearing (two weak uprights might be able to support a heavy lintel if the load were properly shared), etc. But complete representation of interdependencies that can be enforced solely by reasoning over specifications is not achievable because:

- creating such interdependencies may place a high burden on the specification process (it may be unreasonable to specify the load-bearing characteristics of uprights under all of the conditions that may arise in the domain);

- even complete specifications cannot be completely enforced in a computationally feasible way.

This representational inadequacy problem is well recognized; indeed one of the ontology design criteria in [Gruber 94] is natural language documentation of all terms — so that human knowledge base builders have a chance of understanding the terms, even if their knowledge representation systems cannot.

Nonetheless we felt that partial operationalization of the interdependencies could be very valuable, especially if it were tied to architectural levels. Within a level, the interdependency representation could be restricted to treat only the terms at that level. Also, knowledge representation systems do provide some mechanisms for representing and enforcing interdependencies among terms.

Description logic systems and their predecessors have been exploring representation of this kind of information for a long time (see discussions in [Woods and Schmolze 92] and [Schmolze and Mark 91]). We felt (and still feel) that description logic knowledge representation systems offer the most promising approach currently available. We therefore chose Loom [MacGregor 91] as the knowledge representation system for both Comet and Cosmos. Loom is a description logic-based system, and Comet and Cosmos particularly stress its description logic aspects. We were very conscious of both the benefits and limitations of description logic representation as embodied in Loom, and tried to use the representation so that we could benefit from the greatest possible automated enforcement of ontological commitments. Our experience is that description logic-based systems can provide substantial benefit if they are used carefully. But this is not an easy matter, and our use of Loom to represent ontological commitments developed considerably between Comet and Cosmos.

4 SYSTEMS

As mentioned earlier, both Comet and Cosmos are concerned with assessing the impact of (and providing users with feedback on) changes in their world. Users' changes are reflected in additions to the knowledge base, although the users have no direct awareness of this. Thus, creation of new software modules in Comet and new electromechanical design variations in Cosmos result in new Loom concepts being added to their knowledge bases. The users see the benefit of these additions via the reasoning that results in feedback about the software design in Comet and on the electromechanical artifact in Cosmos. From the development point of view, the importance of these additions is that they expand the knowledge base, adding to the stock of represented software designs or electromechanical components. In the following discussion, we adopt the knowledge base developers' point of view. Descriptions of the users' view can be found in [Mark, et al. 92] and [Mark, et al. 94].

It is essential in both Comet and Cosmos that the original hand-built core knowledge base encode the commitments that all additional knowledge must adhere to in order for the system's reasoning methods to act properly. Both Comet and Cosmos rely on indepth models, based on domain-specific architectures that reflect the ontological commitments of their respective domains. Comet's relevant ontology is software systems, specialized in the area of radar trackers. Cosmos has ontologies related to physical devices, specialized in the area of gimbals for use in spacecraft.

4.1 Comet

The top level (most abstract) Comet domain-specific architecture is a generic ontology of software systems. The abstract elements are software modules interrelated by input/output, data access requirements, and control commitments. Some of the information in the architecture is represented as a taxonomy to take full advantage of Loom's subsumption reasoning. Procedures are defined as specializations of the Loom con-

38

```
(defconcept ProcedureModule
    :is :primitive
    :constraints
(:and (:all submodule Module)
    /* every submodule must be a Module */
(:the parent ProcedureModule)
    /* the only parent is a ProcedureModule */
(:all input Datatype)
(:all output Datatype)
(:all submodule-interconnectivity Connection)
(:the performance-spec Behavior)))
```

Figure 1: Basic Loom module description definition

cept ProcedureModule (see Figure 1). The action performed by the procedure is represented in the Behavior specified via the performance-spec relation. For example, part of Comet's taxonomy of generic behaviors is shown in Figure 2[1].

Through this taxonomy, Comet establishes the accepted categories of behaviors in any domain: software procedures can perform Containment, Correspondence, and a few other operations. Correspondence is a behavior that establishes a relationship between a source Set and a target Set (Sets are collections of explicit elements). Containment is a behavior that applies some containment function to an element and a domain to determine whether the element is inside the domain. The domain may be a Set, or a Volume (a representation of a physical space whose elements need not be explicit). The containment function must be a kind of Filtering.

This taxonomy is useful for controlling the definition of new terms, but as discussed earlier, taxonomic reasoning as embodied in description logic is insufficient to enforce the ontological interdependency commitments inherent in any real domain-specific architecture. For example, Loom can determine whether a proposed BinarySearch term is subsumed by the Search term in the taxonomy by analyzing the roles and value restrictions of the Loom concepts. But, the domain-specific architecture of software systems includes an interdependency between BinarySearch and Sort: binary search procedures work only on sorted input. This interdependency must be represented and enforced if Comet is to give appropriate advice about the class of BinarySearch procedures.

The trouble is in representing this kind of interdependency in a way that allows automated subsumption. We at least want to represent something like "either the input to the binary search procedure is already sorted, or the binary search procedure must call

[1]Loom concepts are shown in ovals; double arrows show subsumption relationships; single arrows show roles.

```
(defconcept RequireSortCommit :is
(:and Commitment
(:the requirement
        SortedSource)))
(defconcept SortedSource :is
(:and Module
(:satisfies (?mod)
    (:or (:for-some (?datatype ?port)
            (:and (input-port-of ?mod ?port)
                (datatype ?port ?datatype)
                (Sorted ?datatype)))
        (:for-some (?behav)
            (:and (behavior-network-member*
                    (behavior-of ?mod)
                            ?behav)
                (Sort ?behav)))))))
```

Figure 3: Binary searches work only on sorted input

a sort procedure". A Loom representation for this interdependency is shown in Figure 3.

The representation in Figure 3 says that either one of the input data types must be known to be subsumed by Sorted, or there must be a procedure in the behavior network (i.e., in the control path) that is known to be subsumed by Sort. This representation is already well beyond the bounds of what can be handled by automated subsumption reasoning, and it still leaves open the question of how to determine subsumption by terms like Sorted.

One approach is to require the ontology of data objects to insist that data be declared to be "sorted" or not. This is plausible in modern strongly typed software languages for well known datatypes like sorted; but it is highly implausible for arbitrary datatypes. In Comet we pushed further in the representation of ontological commitments in order to handle the kind of data that are generated in the tracker domain.

Tracker systems take sensor data about vehicles moving through space and resolve the data into individual vehicle tracks. Tracking comprises a variety of functions, including accessing sensor data in the form of "contacts" (probable vehicle positions), checking volumes of space to see whether they could contain the contacts, etc. Again, part of the domain-specific ontological commitments of trackers can be represented taxonomically. Starting with the taxonomy in Figure 2, we created a Loom representation of the domain-specific taxonomy of the tracker domain. Figure 3[2] shows some of the specializtions created for the tracker domain.

Clusters, SceneGates, and TrackGates are all spe-

[2]Domain-specific concepts are shown in dotted ovals; double arrows connected by "looped lines" indicates a disjoint covering.

39

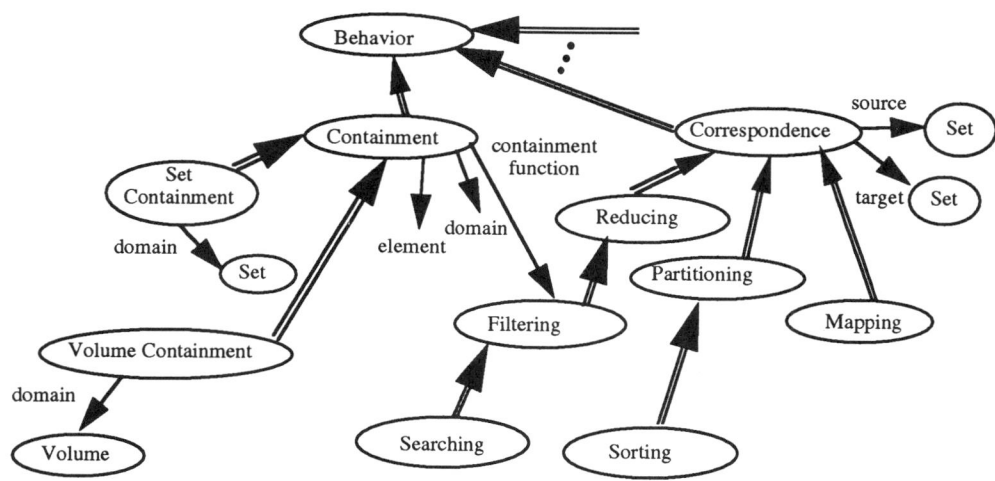

Figure 2: Part of the Comet generic ontology of behavior.

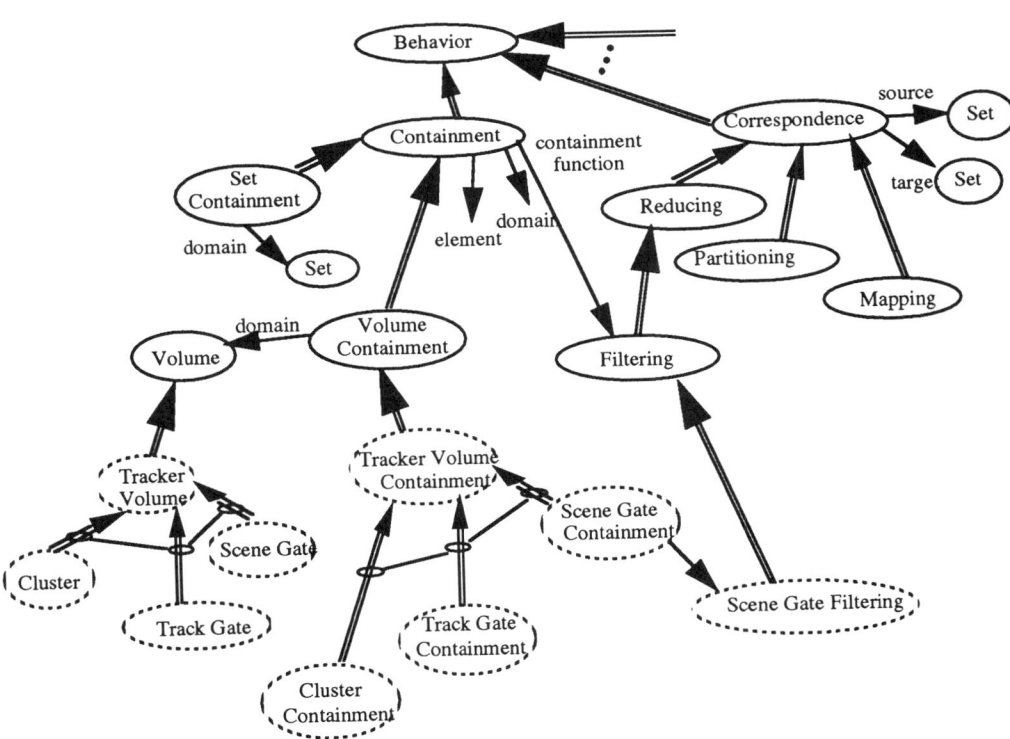

Figure 4: The Comet behavior ontology extended in the tracker domain.

cializations of the generic concept Volume; in fact they form a disjoint cover for that concept in the tracker domain. This rather esoteric terminology is part of the real ontology of trackers — and it has real impact on the design of real tracker systems. And, it should have real impact on the design of knowledge bases that purport to represent software in that domain.

Clusters, SceneGates, and TrackGates are reified in the tracker domain ontology in order to organize the procedures that determine whether a Contact is in one of these volumes, i.e., procedures with Containment behavior. In particular, there have to be three distinct kinds of VolumeContainment behavior, one for each kind of volume. Furthermore, each VolumeContainment behavior has to be associated with its own Filtering behavior. Taxonomic reasoning works well for this sort of ontological commitment. Once the tracker-specific Volumes have been created, Loom can automatically create the terms for the tracker-specific VolumeContainment behaviors. But as with binary searches, it is difficult to capture all of the ontologically important interdependencies. For example, how can the system determine that a new term is a valid description of a SceneGateContainment procedure?

Figure 5 shows, in architecture form, some of the other ontologically important interdependencies of SceneGateContainment. SceneGateContainment must include in its behavior network a Filtering behavior that works on SceneGates and Contacts. This behavior must check whether Scene Gates contain Contacts. In representing these interdependencies in Loom, we could use the same approach as we did for Sort, insisting that anything that purports to be a kind of SceneGateContainment produce an explicitly declared SceneGateAssociation datatype. The containment relationship between SceneGates and Contacts would be implicit in this declaration. But this is unrealistic in the domain: while there are explicitly declared Sorted datatyes, there are not SceneGateAssociation datatypes.

In our Comet representation, we decided to go one level deeper, requiring all specializations of SceneGate-Containment to include a specification of the kind of results their filtering behavior produces. The system can then check the interdependency in terms of that specification. Figure 6 shows the representation of the commitment in Loom. Given SceneGateContainment, Contact, and SceneGate terms, the *contains* relation explicitly checks whether the specification of SceneGateContainment includes the appropriate association of Contacts with SceneGates.

The purpose here is not to delve into the details of tracker software, but to indicate that ontologies have important things to say about the way knowledge bases should be put together. As shown above, these decisions are at different levels – the decision to

```
(defconcept SceneGateFilteringCommitment :is
  (:and
   (:satisfies (?mod)
  (:for-some (?behav)
     (:and (behavior-network-member*
            (behavior-of ?mod)
                      ?behav)
           (Filtering ?behav))))
  (:satisfies (?mod)
  (:for-some (?behav)
     (:for-all (?run)
       (:implies (test-run ?mod ?run)
       (:for-some (?scene-gate ?contact)
         (:and (test-output ?run
                       ?scene-gate)
               (SceneGate ?scene-gate)
               (test-output ?run ?contact)
           (Contact ?contact)
           (contains ?scene-gate
                      ?contact)))))))))
```

Figure 6: SceneGateContainment must associate contacts with scene gates

conceptualize and interrelate Containment and Filtering behaviors was quite removed from decisions about Clusters, SceneGates, and TrackGates. The decision as to what level of specification of SceneGateContainment the SceneGateFilteringCommitment should require was architectural in nature. The cumulative effect of these decisions is very hard for human knowledge base developers to handle manually. The partial enforcement of subsumption relationships through Loom helped, as did the additional reasoning mechanisms we implemented through individual interdependency commitments. However, the representation of these commitments in Comet was *ad hoc*, making enforcement of the domain-specific architecture unpredictable. One of our major goals for our next system, Cosmos, was to improve the representation of interdependency commitment relationships from an architectural point of view.

4.2 Cosmos

Cosmos is a "mediator" [Wiederhold 92] in a distributed design environment. Its task is to support the negotiation required to make a design modification fit into the existing design. To perform this task, Cosmos must maintain a model of the design as it evolves. Cosmos reasons about how changes in one element of the model affect other elements of the model, and delivers knowledge about these effects to the relevant designers. Cosmos's role for end-users is thus similar to Comet's, except that it works in a shared distributed environment. While Comet provides impact-of-change analy-

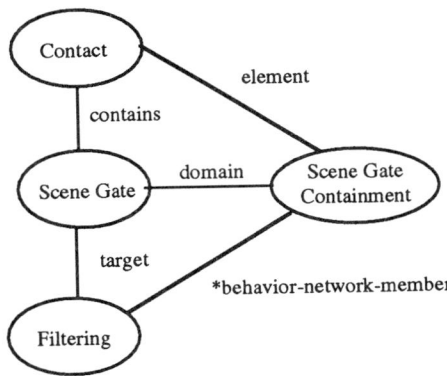

Figure 5: A part of one level of the domain-specific architecture in the tracker domain.

sis to individuals, Cosmos provides a shared impact-of-change analysis to be jointly explored by a group.

¿From a knowledge base development standpoint, Cosmos is more challenging than Comet. Cosmos is meant for large multi-disciplinary design efforts. The knowledge for these different areas (thermal analysis, structural analysis, etc.) is different in both terminology and structure. This means that a diverse set of ontologies is necessary to achieve coverage.

The Cosmos testbed is in the domain of satellite gimbals. Gimbals for satellites are complex electromechanical devices that play the critical role of preventing payloads from interfering with each other as they move independently. As in Comet, we began with a generic ontology, this time of Physical Components, Satellite Components, and so on (see Figure 7). Physical Components have, for example, mass; Satellite Components have, among other characteristics, a cost. Gimbals are Satellite Components that have subcomponents such as bearings, motors, and controllers, and characteristics such as inertia and structural stiffness. Bearings in turn have a diameter, running torque, dahl stiffness, etc. Since gimbals control the movement of very sensitive payloads (e.g., sensors pointing at the earth), a key problem in gimbal design is controlling jitter. Thus, some of the commitments among gimbal subcomponents deal with various kinds of jitter.

A domain-specific architecture view of the interdependencies that determine one kind of jitter, "pointing jitter", is shown in Figure 8. As in Comet, our Loom representation for these interdependencies had to be a compromise. The engineers wanted Cosmos to give them feedback based on approximations of jitter relationships. They already had detailed simulation software, but the simulations took too long to set up to be useful for supporting highly interactive design negotiation. Therefore, Cosmos's representation for jitter commitments could be approximate, but needed to account for the interdependencies of all of the key de-

sign variables in the engineers' ontologies. The Cosmos representation of the pointing-jitter approximation is shown in Loom in Figure 9.

Again, from the domain-specific architecture point of view, the challenge is to represent this commitment so that if a new specialization of Controller is introduced, its interdependency on Bearing is automatically enforced. In this case, this interdependency is based on a relationship of the proportional-gain property of Contoller and the dahl-stiffness of Bearing. In the representation in Figure 9, this relationship is expressed as an equation, taking it outside of the realm of automatic subsumption enforcement. However, the equation accurately reflects the ontological commitment between the two terms to the level required by the engineering community. Given current technology, any representation that allowed automated subsumption enforcement would be inadequate to express Cosmos's contract of expectations with its users: the system would give inappropriate advice about gimbals because it did not reflect the relationship of controllers and bearings.

Despite its shortcomings, the commitment representation is a major advance over Comet. Unlike Comet, Cosmos provides a common "language" within Loom for expressing commitments. All commitments in Cosmos are relations formed as compositions of other explicit Loom relations in the ontology, following the same form shown in Figure 9. The interdependency expressed by the commitment is always clearly defined (usually as an equation in this domain). Although we (and Loom) still need to improve the enforceability of commitments, the Cosmos representation is at least well-defined and consistent.

5 DISCUSSION

The knowledge base development approach used in Comet and refined in Cosmos is a first step toward ensuring that ontological interdependency commitments are consistently represented and enforced. Among the

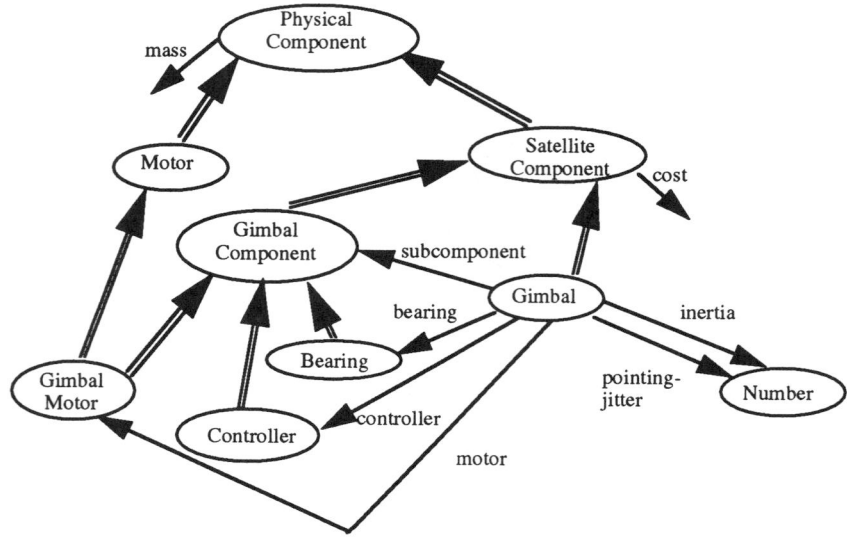

Figure 7: Part of the Cosmos generic ontology.

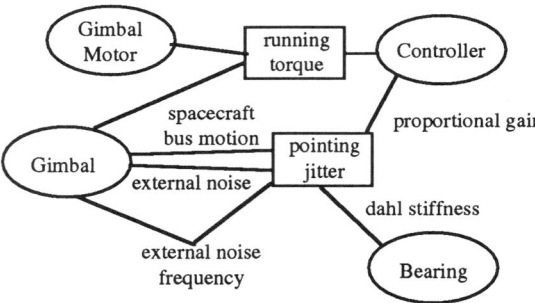

Figure 8: Part of the domain-specific architecture showing the interdependencies that determine pointing jitter.

many issues we continue to investigate are:

- Beyond description logic, how can ontological interdependency commitments be systematically represented and enforced?

- How does in-depth representation of term interdependency affect the sharability of the ontologies that contain them?

- Do domain-specific architectures exist in all domains?

- How do domain-specific architectures relate to task-specific architectures?

5.1 Representational Issues

Our goal is always to represent ontological interdependency commitments in the most general and extensible way possible. As mentioned above, it soon became clear during our work on Comet that our *ad hoc* commitment representation was too opaque to enable understandability and extensibility at large scale. In Cosmos, we represented the commitments as compositionally defined relations. While the language we allowed for these compositions cannot be automatically checked for subsumption by description logic systems, it does represent the beginning of a specialized constraint language for expressing commitments.

We believe that it is possible to create a constraint language that will adequately express interdependency commitments and still be computationally acceptable. The term specification language of the knowledge representation system will include a closed set of constructs for expressing classes of constraints that cover a broad class of interdependencies. The interdependencies we encountered in Comet and Cosmos could all be represented in terms of a few set membership and algebraic expressions. The language will not be subsumption testable (within the bounds of computational feasibility), but it will support a well-defined class of inferences to propagate and enforce the constraints.

5.2 Relationship to Portable Ontologies

There is general agreement that linkage at the ontology level is required to coordinate knowledge bases [Gruber 1993], but the mechanism for creating this linkage has not been described. The notion of minimal commitment described in [Gruber 1994] has been interpreted as a call for "light" ontologies. But as we discussed earlier, if the terms in the ontology are not to be misused in specific applications, what is "minimal" may not be very "light". That is, the specification of terms in portable ontologies will probably have to include in-depth interdependency commitments. If our experience with Comet and Cosmos generalizes, expression

```
(defrelation pointing-jitter
    :domain Gimbal
    :range Number
    :is (:satisfies
 (?g ?j)
 (:and (Gimbal ?g)
    (:forsome ?b ?c ?K_d ?K_p ?D_s
             ?N_e ?w_Ne ?w_np ?I_g)
    (:and (bearing ?g ?b)
    (controller ?g ?c)
    (dahl-stiffness ?b ?K_d)
    (proportional-gain ?c ?K_p)
    (spacecraft-bus-motion ?g ?D_s)
    (external-noise ?g ?N_e)
    (external-noise-frequency ?g ?w_Ne)
    (inertia ?g ?I_g)
    (= ?w_np
        (sqrt (/ (+ ?K_p ?K_d) ?I_g)))
    (= ?j
        (+ (* (/ ?K_d  (+ ?K_d ?K_p))
                ?D_s)
        (/ ?N_e
            (* ?K_p
        (sq (/ ?w_Ne ?w_np)))))))))))
    :characteristics :single-valued)
```

Figure 9: Loom approximation equation for determining pointing jitter

44

of these interdependencies adds to the burden of specifying the terms. We believe that anything lighter will be underspecified.

The architectural view of the ontological commitments offers at least some insight into the problem of linking ontologies. Domain-specific architectures define the interfaces of terms at a given level. If the interdependencies within the architecture are expressed in a well-defined constraint language, it should be possible to automatically propagate the constraints in mapping from one ontology to another.

5.3 Universality of Architectures

The Comet and Cosmos systems are both in engineering domains in which design architectures are natural constructs. These engineering design architectues map directly into our notion of domain-specific architectures, because they serve analogous purposes. Design architectures show key interdependencies among components; domain-specific architectures show key interdependencies among terms that represent components. It is reasonable to ask whether non-engineering domains also have domain-specific architectures of ontological interdependencies. We believe that domain-specific architectures, like task-specific architectures, are abstractions that apply regardless of domain. Even domains that do not have design architectures do have components and interdependencies. We have sketched domain-specific architectures in the medical domain and in the Blocks World, and believe that the idea generalizes.

5.4 Task-Specific and Domain-Specific Architectures

As with any complex software system, a large knowledge base will inevitably have different architectures representing different points of view. Just as modern conventional software systems often have a communications architecture, a process flow architecture, and a structured design architecture, knowledge bases can have domain-specific architectures, task-specific architectures, and maybe others. The interesting question for us is how these architectures interact. In the conventional software world, there has been much study in the interaction of architectures. This work has resulted in some tools that support the combination of architectural views. We believe that domain-specific architectures and task-specific architectures are complementary, and we are planning experiments with combining these architectures in a knowledge base development project.

REFERENCES

1. R. Brachman, "'Reducing' CLASSIC to Practice: Knowledge Representation Theory Meets Practice" in *Proceedings of KR '92*, Morgan Kaufmann, San Mateo, CA, 1992, pp. 247 - 258.

2. R. Brachman, *et al.*, "Living with CLASSIC: When and How to Use a Kl-ONE-Like Language", in J. Sowa [ed.], *Principles of Semantic Networks: Explorations in the Representation of Knowledge*, Morgan Kaufmann, San Mateo, CA, 1991.

3. B. Chandrasekeran, "Generic Tasks for Knowledge-Based Reasoning: High-Level Building Blocks for Expert System Design", *IEEE Expert*, Vol. 1, No. 3, 1986, pp. 23 - 30.

4. B. Chandrasekeran, "Generic Tasks for Knowledge-Based Reasoning: High-Level Building Blocks for Expert System Design", *AI Magazine*, Vol. 11, No. 4, 1990, pp. 59 - 71.

5. W. Clancey, "The Knowledge Level Reinterpreted: Modeling How Systems Interact", *Machine Learning*, Vol. 4, 1989, pp. 347 - 376.

6. M. Genesereth and N. Nilsson, *Logical Foundations of Artificial Intelligence*, Morgan Kaufmann, San Mateo, CA, 1987.

7. T. Gruber, "A Translation Approach to Portable Ontology Specifications", in *Knowledge Acquisition*, Vol. 5, 1993, pp. 199-220.

8. T. Gruber, "Toward Principles for the Design of Ontologies Used for Knowledge Sharing", in N. Guarino and R. Poli [ed.] *Formal Ontology in Conceptual Analysis and Knowledge Representation*, Kluwer Academic Publishers, 1994.

9. N. Guarino, *et al.* "Formalizing Ontological Commitments", in *Proceedings of AAAI 94*, MIT Press, Cambridge, MA, 1994, pp. 560-567.

10. N. Guarino, "The Ontological Level", in R. Casati, *et al.* [eds.] *Philosophy and the Cognitive Sciences*, Holder-Pichler-Tempsky, 1994.

11. R. MacGregor, "The Evolving Technology of Classification-Based Knowledge Representation Systems", in J. Sowa [ed.], *Principles of Semantic Networks: Explorations in the Representation of Knowledge*, Morgan Kaufmann, San Mateo, CA, 1991.

12. W. Mark, *et al.*, "Cosmos: A System for Supporting Engineering Negotiation", *Concurrent Engineering: Research and Applications*, Vol. 2, 1994, pp. 173 - 182.

13. W. Mark, *et al.*, "Commitment-Based Software Development", *IEEE Transactions on Software Engineering*, Vol. 18, No. 10, Oct, 1992, pp. 870 - 885.

14. M. Musen and S. Tu, "Problem-Solving Methods for Generation of Task-Specific Knowledge Acquisition Tools", in J. Cuena [ed] *Knowledge-Oriented Software Design* Elsevier, Amsterdam, 1993.

15. R. Neches, *et al.*, "Enabling Technology for Knowledge Sharing", *AI Magazine*, Vol. 12, No. 3, Fall, 1991, pp. 36 - 56.

16. J . Schmolze and W. Mark, "The NIKL Experience", *Computational Intelligence*, Vol. 7, 1991, pp. 134 - 159.

17. E. Walther, *et al.*, *Plug and Play: Construction of Task-Specific Expert System Shells Using Sharable Context Ontologies*, Technical Report KSL-92-40, Knowledge Systems Laboratory, Stanford University, 1992.

18. G. Wiederhold, "Mediators in the Architecture of Future Information Systems", *IEEE Computer*, Vol. 25, No. 3, Mar, 1992, pp. 38-49.

19. B. Wielinga, *et al.*, "KADS: A Modeling Approach to Knowledge Engineering", *Knowledge Acquisition*, Vol 4., pp 5 - 53, 1992.

20. B. Wielinga, *et al.*, "Framework and Formalism for Expressing Ontologies", *ESPRIT Project 8145 KACTUS Deliverable DO1b.1*, 1994.

21. P. Winston, *Artificial Intelligence*, Addison-Wesley, Reading, MA, 1984.

22. W. Woods, "Understanding Subsumption and Taxonomy", in J. Sowa [ed.], *Principles of Semantic Networks: Explorations in the Representation of Knowledge*, Morgan Kaufmann, San Mateo, CA, 1991.

23. W. Woods and J. Schmolze, "The KL-ONE Family", in F. Lehmann [ed.], *Semantic Networks in Artificial Intelligence*, Pergammon Press, Oxford, 1992.

Towards Very Large Knowledge Bases
N.J.I. Mars, Ed.
IOS Press, 1995

Task Ontology for Reuse of
Problem Solving Knowledge

Riichiro Mizoguchi, **Johan Vanwelkenhuysen**, and **Mitsuru Ikeda**
ISIR, Osaka University
Osaka, Japan
miz@ei.sanken.osaka-u.ac.jp

ABSTRACT

This paper presents a task ontology which plays a crucial role in reusing expertise. We first discuss a few basic issues concerning ontology for knowledge reuse. The first issue is typology of ontology stressing that there is more than one kind of ontology. The second topic is context. In order to enable knowledge sharing and reuse, knowledge should be decompiled into context-dependent and context-independent parts. In problem solving knowledge, the context is determined mainly by task structure. Based on this observation, we propose a task ontology which contributes to making the problem solving context explicit. After discussing these issues we show how to design task ontology. Finally, an overview of a task analysis interview system, MULTIS, based on task ontology is presented to illustrate how an implemented task ontology is used.

1 INTRODUCTION

Ontology is expected to play an important role in knowledge sharing and reuse[16]. However, it seems to the authors that there is no consensus on what an ontology is among the researchers. Although a number of discussions have been made on this topic, we can find difference between them. The first topic discussed in this paper is what an ontology is. The main point is that there is not only one kind of ontology. Typology of ontology is a crucial issue to discuss, though many people are ignorant of this very important point which helps make the discussion on ontology clearer.

The second issue is context. That is, what context should be taken into account when designing ontology. Does knowledge exist independently of any context? Is domain ontology or ontology of some object a candidate which can exist and be recognized independently of context? Our answer is no. There are several kinds of ontologies according to the context given. Explicit representation of the context is therefore critical to ontology design. After the context is made explicit, one can design ontology. From knowledge base technology perspective, knowledge should be considered in some context, that is, in problem solving situation. In contrast to a data base which is usually designed application-independent, a knowledge base is always application-specific in its nature.[1] Consequently, to the extent that we are interested in knowledge rather than data bases, the investigation of ontologies taking into account the context of knowledge application is a necessity.

Then, how to make the context explicit? Our claim is the context can be specified by making problem solving process and its environment explicit. This suggests the importance of task ontology which specifies problem solving process and workplace ontology[22] specifying the environment where the problem solving process is embedded. The former is discussed in this paper and the latter in the accompanying paper[23]

Another issue to discuss in connection with context is "whether sharing and reuse are the same or not". At least, there are two situations of sharing/reuse of knowledge. We do not care about the difference between the meaning of the terms: sharing and reuse, but think it is very important to distinguish the two situations: One concerned with multiple agents with own knowledge bases who ASK one another to solve some problems and the other concerned with a single agent(not necessarily multiple ones) who USEs knowledge in a knowledge base to BUILD another knowledge base. To investigate these two situations gives us stimulating thoughts useful for ontology design. After

---

[1]Knowledge bases in heuristics-based expert systems are full of knowledge specific to their application tasks.

does not necessarily represent its meaning and syntactic translation from one representation to another. Thus, a language like Ontolingua [2] works well for this purpose.

Before commitment, however, it is not the case, since designers and the potential users have to discuss the meaning of the ontology, otherwise people cannot commit to it. When the ontology is implemented in a computer, not only hierarchical relations but also meaning of each concept has to be represented. In order to represent the meaning of ontology, one needs procedural representation in addition to declarative one. Imagine one tries to build a qualitative model of some device by "reusing" several components, say, pipe, pump, water, etc., defined by another person. Needless to say, these are the basic concepts defined in an ontology of, say, plant domain. In this case, the specifications such as "water is a kind of liquid", "a pipe is a kind of conduit and connected to a pump" are of no use to him/her, since they can nothing to do with the qualitative simulation he/she wants to do. What he/she needs is procedural meaning of them, that is, how the components behave in the simulation. Therefore, when such an ontology is available, he/she does want to know procedural representation of them or procedural semantics of the interpreter which interprets their declarative representation. Thus, "before commitment ontologies" cannot be represented without procedural representation.

Apparently, we are now in the phase of "before commitment", since we have been struggling in designing ontologies to which many people commit. At this very period, to discuss "after commitment ontology" without making the assumption explicit makes the discussion misleading. In this paper, we would like to refer to "Before Commitment ontology" and "After Commitment ontology" as "BC ontology" and "AC ontology", respectively.

2.4 Knowledge level

Another issue to discuss is "knowledge level" which has been playing an important role in various discussions on knowledge representation[13]. The idea of knowledge level also applies to ontology discussion. The knowledge level model of communicating agents suggests that the participants already have made an ontological commitment if their communication is successful[3], in which "tell and ask" are major functions. This situation is depicted in Fig.1. Participants do not need a model of each other because they can communicate according to the protocol determined in advance based on the ontological commitment. This type of communication seems to be reasonable and typical one. However, we can imagine another type of communication among agents(humans) as shown in Fig. 2 where a domain expert and a knowledge engineer are involved in a knowledge acquisition interview.

In this case, ontological commitment is hard to make, since both are not familiar with the other's domain. Furthermore, knowledge engineers are responsible for making the interview fluently by building a model of the domain expert's conceptual representation of expertise. Thus, Communication 1 requires a communication ontology(tell&ask ontology), while Communication 2 requires a content ontology. The readers may notice the knowledge level of Communication 2 is viewed as the knowledge use level [15][21].

2.5 Is ontology like a conceptual schema?

Ontology is often explained by indicating an analogy to conceptual schema in a relational data base[2]. This analogy captures a portion of what ontology means, i.e., ontology can be partly viewed as a formal specification of conceptualization. But there is an ontology which has more implications than conceptual schema. That is, it gives not only specification of the content of knowledge but also defines meaning of the primitive concepts of knowledge. In the communication ontology, the specification ontology may be sufficient. However, content ontology has deeper implications.

In conceptual schema case, one does not have to define what a conceptual schema is or what a relational data base is or meaning of, say, "salary" and "name", since he/she already knows all of them. He/she can use the conceptual schema just using pattern matching. Therefore, one can say conceptual schema is portable. In this sense, however, conceptual schema analogy is somewhat misleading, since it only explains the communication ontology or AC ontology.

For another example, imagine a procedure of solving a set of linear equations. When one wants to share the procedure, specification of its input and output suffices. When one is involved in coding of the procedure, however, specification of input and output does not make sense for him/her. What he/she needs is the solution algorithm, that is, the content of the procedure.

2.6 Is ontology portable?

When one speaks of portable ontology[2], it implies computers can manipulate the ontology as a whole, but the reality is not so. What can computers do with ontology in the destination site? All the programs already existing there do not understand the ontology. It is true every program becomes portable when appropriate language translators are available. The usage of a program is understood just only knowing its function, that is, relations between input and output. In other words, users can use a ported program viewing it as a black box. Therefore, it is easy for users to use the ported program. However, this cannot apply to ontology, since ontology always requires HUMAN INTERPRETATION of its meaning. If one wants to discussing these general issues, we present an example of task ontology for scheduling tasks and the guidelines to ontology design. Finally, a task analysis interview system named MULTIS is described.

2 WHAT IS AN ONTOLOGY?

2.1 Definition

¿From the engineering perspective, ontology plays an important role in knowledge sharing and reuse. We have been involved in the design of ontology aiming at enabling knowledge reuse. Although we can find literature discussing several types of ontologies, many of the papers discuss it as if there exist only one type of ontology. Or, what kind of ontology is discussed is implicit. This makes the situation rather confusing. We have to be careful when we talk about ontology not to forget to specify what ontology we are discussing. In order to clarify what an ontology is, let us go back to its definition. There are several definitions of ontology. (1)From Philosophy, "Ontology is a systematic explanation of existence".
(2)From AI perspective,"Ontology is an explicit specification of conceptualization" [2]
(3)From knowledge base perspective, "Ontology is a system of concepts/vocabulary used as primitives for building artificial systems"[12]

In this paper, we adopt the third perspective. In other words, we are interested in knowledge for problem solving rather than knowledge in general.

2.2 What makes ontologies different from each other?

To consider how knowledge is used helps us understand what an ontology is. Let us enumerate what manners exist in using knowledge.
(1) Direct methods:
Imagine someone is trying to reuse knowledge in a knowledge base to build another knowledge base for a different purpose. In such a case, he/she has to investigate carefully the knowledge base to know what knowledge is reusable for his/her objective. The methods used in such cases could be called direct methods, since they directly manipulate knowledge.
(2) Indirect methods:
Indirect methods aim at sharing knowledge through communication among the owners of knowledge. An agent asks another agent to solve some problems according to a specified communication protocol. Therefore, these methods are not interested in what knowledge is used for solving a problem and how it is solved. Instead, they are interested only in which agent can solve the problem.
(3) Case-base methods:
This type of methods try to share knowledge through cases stored in case bases. This approach is based on the observation that sharing each piece of knowledge

in a very large knowledge is difficult. This matches new technologies such as case-based reasoning and memory-based reasoning.

The ontology problem is frequently discussed in the context of knowledge sharing and reuse. And sharability and reusability of knowledge are usually discussed at the same time. Because these two words share a lot, they prevent people from understanding the difference between the above first two uses of knowledge. However, discussion on the meaning of these words themselves is of no importance to our purpose. Rather, we would like to name the above three ways of knowledge use.

Although the first two methods are related to each other, they are very different. The former is interested in the details of knowledge in a knowledge base such as how it is organised and the goal and application condition of each piece of knowledge in it, that is, it treats a knowledge base as a "white box", while the latter considers one as a "black box" and is not interested in how the agent solves the problem but interested only in the answer to the problem. This difference affects very much the concept of ontology. We would like to call the former "REUSE" of knowledge, since it is just the same concept as "Program reuse" in software engineering and the latter "SHARING" knowledge.

Case-base methods do not require detailed analysis of cases but vocabulary for indexing them which determine another ontology. These three views on knowledge use and the role of knowledge bases cause differences in ontologies. Knowledge viewed from the direct methods perspective should be organized around how to use knowledge in what kinds of problem solving context. Viewing knowledge from the indirect method perspective, the ontologies should not be concerned with how to solve problems by each agent. The only thing of importance is how to ask a specific agent to get desirable information. So, the ontology is responsible for making the communication fluently. In a case base, how to retrieve appropriate cases is the main issue. So, ontology is necessary for appropriate characterization of cases as indices.

Thus, corresponding to the above three methods, we could list at least three kinds of ontologies which we could call
1)Content ontology for reusing knowledge,
2)Communication(tell&ask) ontology for sharing knowledge, and
3)Indexing ontology for case retrieval.

2.3 Before vs. after ontological commitment

One of the important issues concerning ontology is before/after ontological commitment. This has not been discussed seriously in spite of its importance. After commitment has been made to an ontology, what to do with the ontology is its formal representation which

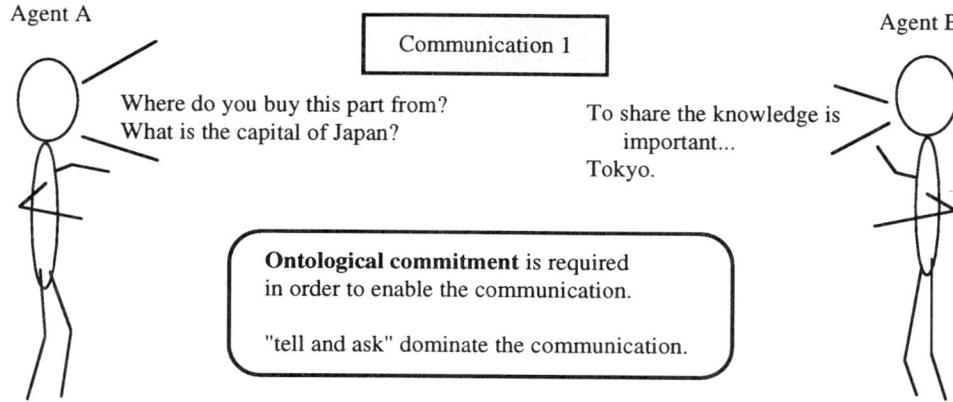

Figure 1: Communication 1(tell&ask).

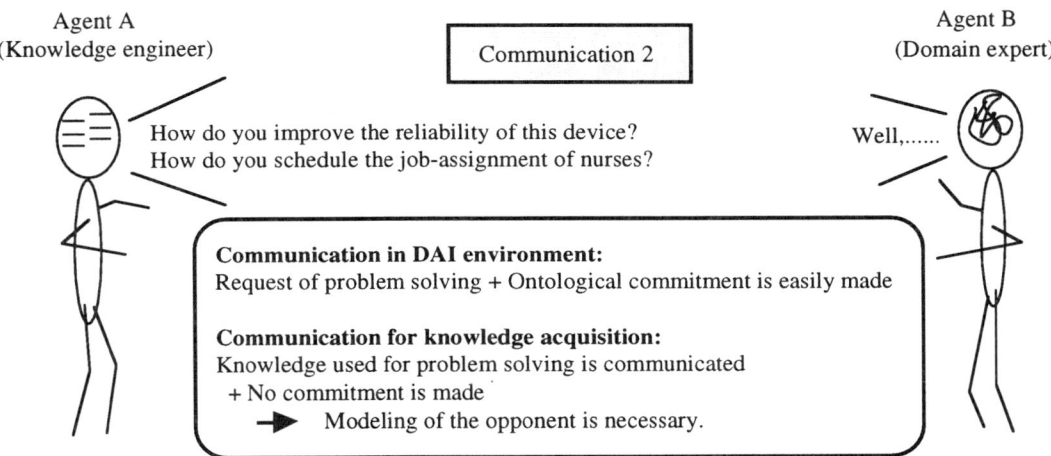

Figure 2: Communication 2(Knowledge acquisition).

use the ported ontology, he/she first understands it in depth, then he/she codes a new program for utilizing and manipulating the ontology. Thus, all the jobs to be done with ontology is performed not by computers but by humans. This is not the concept of portability.

In general, all the meaning lies in the primitive concepts, the relations and functions between them, and the methods utilizing them. And many of them cannot be represented declaratively. In conclusion, content ontology or BC ontology cannot be portable.

The above discussion is made from the content ontology point of view, that is, not "sharing" but "reuse" view point. How about the communication(tell&ask) ontology or AC ontology? If a user at the ported site knows the meaning of the ontology before hand, like the conceptual schema case, then some programs he/she has already coded could immediately use the ported ontology. Thus, communication ontology could be portable.

2.7 Data vs. Knowledge

There is considerable similarity between a data base and a knowledge base. However, if they are not completely the same, then what is the major difference between them. Among them, what we would like to point out is context-dependency. Data bases are designed so as to make the application-dependency as small as possible, while knowledge bases are application-specific in their nature. This difference is critical. Data in data bases are less context-sensitive than knowledge, in other words, data can be interpreted as the user wants more independently of any context than knowledge. When he/she applies knowledge in a knowledge base to a different problem, however, one has to pay close attention to the context of problem solving and check applicability of the knowledge(expertise).

Note here, however, there is knowledge which has characteristics similar to data, say, physical units and mathematical formulae[4][8]. These kinds of knowledge is "static" in the sense that it has the same meaning in any context. The other extreme is rules in a rule base which contains heuristic knowledge of a domain expert. They are highly context-dependent. Nevertheless both kinds of knowledge are referred to as "knowledge" which causes a serious confusion, since the former is very similar to data but the latter is not.

Let us show an example which highlights the difference between data and knowledge. Imagine a rule in a rule base. When one is retrieving rules appropriate for the current situation, the rule is viewed as not knowledge but data, since it is the same as data retrieval. After finding an appropriate one, he/she tries to execute the rule, then the rule becomes knowledge, since its execution affects the problem solving context. This shows a clear discrimination between data and knowledge. When one views knowledge from the point of view of communication 1 in Fig. 1, that is, tell&ask communication, it becomes data. When one views it from the communication 2 in Fig. 2 point of view, i.e., one is interested in the content of knowledge, on the other hand, he/she really discusses about "knowledge".

Therefore, one has to be very careful when he/she discusses knowledge in the context of tell&ask communication because if he/she does not make it explicit, readers understand "knowledge" is discussed in that discussion in spite of that not "knowledge" but "data" is discussed there.

2.8 How to use ontology

The last issue related to ontology is how to use it. Gruber states ontology is used for interface between multiple software agents[2]. This shows his standpoint from which he views ontology is one like conceptual schema. There are many researchers taking this view.

In a task analysis interview system, MULTIS, which will be discussed in the last section, we use ontology in two ways such as 1) to facilitate an interaction between domain experts and a computer interviewer for knowledge acquisition, that is, communication 2 by bridging the conceptual gap between the domain experts and computers, and 2) to reuse it to build a problem solving engine which simulates the problem solving behavior of the domain expert. Therefore, we do need content ontology.

2.9 Summary

We have thus far discussed the difference between ontologies and found out several dimensions which contribute to making the characteristics clear:

(1) Sharing vs. reuse
(2) Black box vs. white box.
(3) Communication 1(tell&ask) vs. communication

2(knowledge acquisition)
(4) After vs. before commitment
(5) Data vs. knowledge

Thus, research interests concerning ontology design largely differ from one another according to how he/she views ontology. When discussing ontology, therefore, we have to make it explicit which ontology we are talking about. As stated earlier, we will confine ourselves to content ontology and BC ontology for problem solving knowledge(expertise) reuse in the rest of this paper.

3 EXPLICATION OF PROBLEM SOLVING CONTEXT

3.1 The knowledge perspective

Knowledge cannot be viewed independently of the context determined by the problem solving process. From the definition of Ontology (1) in section 2 knowledge should be context-independent. But from (2), whether knowledge is independent of the context or not is implicit. From (3), one easily infers that it is dependent on the goal of the system built which apparently depends on the problem solving process the system is involved in. Especially, when we discuss the content ontology, we have to pay much attention to the context issue. That is, ontology design should begin by considering how to make problem solving context explicit.

A human problem solver is considered to be an expert if he can deal with and exploit effectively the many characteristics of his problem solving environment. The emergence of such a behavior is recognized to be the result of adaptation to a history of interactions with the problem solving environment.

Problem solving expertise, in particular, is a product of an on-going process in which a structure on knowledge emerges as an adaptation to the interactions with the problem solver's environment[22]. The knowledge being processed comes from various sources such as domain theory, objects being reasoned about, workplace environment, and so on. The structure allows for effective application of the knowledge in a problem solving situation. Expertise is thus tuned to the specific environment in which problem solving is carried out. Expertise is therefore often referred to as heuristic or compiled knowledge.

Because of the specificity of heuristic knowledge, reuse is limited. For enabling reuse of expertise, a technique of "knowledge decompilation" [11] is widely recognized as being useful. This technique decomposes expertise into several kinds of knowledge, making explicit and justifying the role this knowledge plays in the problem solving process. The importance of knowledge decompilation is that it unravels knowledge content issues (as opposed to representation). We argue that understanding knowledge content is a fundamental issue to allow for knowledge reuse and sharing.

Knowledge decompilation covers many aspects. In this article, we limit ourselves to task and domain decompositions and discuss their contributions to knowledge reuse and sharing.

Roughly speaking, problem solving knowledge can be decomposed into task-dependent and domain-dependent portions. We call the former task knowledge and the latter domain knowledge. Furthermore, task knowledge is deeply related to the environment, called workplace, in which the problem solving takes place. Careful study of workplace is necessary for us to discuss task knowledge which is sensitive to it. All the three kinds of knowledge require their own ontologies to make them reusable and sharable. Ontology for workplace is discussed in another paper[23].

Task knowledge is tightly related to problem solving structures specific to each task. There have been proposed several models for task structure description [1][9] [15][24] which contribute to providing reusable components for inference engines. Although they discuss their own views of problem solving structure in expert systems, they do not fully discuss "task ontology" which is required for task knowledge description. Task ontology provides us with a specification for what objects and relation among them are necessary for performing the task, which helps us design domain ontology.

3.2 Task ontology

"Task" is not the same as "problem" though some people consider contrary. This statement is justified by the fact that one can say "perform a task" but cannot "perform a problem", which shows their inherent difference. Here we consider "a task" as "a sequence of problem solving steps". Therefore, our task ontology necessarily includes "verbs" representing problem solving activities. Methods which is a concept similar to that of task consist of task structure with control. Because control structure has no task-specific concepts, we do not try to design ontology related to methods.

Task ontology[5][10][19] is a system of vocabulary for describing problem solving structure of all the existing tasks domain-independently. It is obtained by analyzing task structures of real world problems. Design of task ontology is done in order to overcome the shortcomings of generic tasks and half weak methods while preserving their basic philosophies. The ultimate goal of task ontology research includes to provide vocabulary necessary and sufficient for building a model of human problem solving processes.

When we view a problem solving process based on search as a sentence of natural language, task ontology is a system of semantic vocabulary for representing meaning of the sentence. The determination of the abstraction level of task ontology requires a close consideration on granularity and generality. Representa-

tions of two sentences with the same meaning in terms of task ontology should be the same. These observations suggest task ontology consists of the following four kinds of concepts:
(1) Generic nouns representing objects reflecting their roles appearing in the problem solving process,
(2) Generic verbs representing unit activities appearing in the problem solving process,
(3) Generic adjectives modifying the objects, and
(4) Other conceptsspecific to the task.

Task ontology for scheduling tasks which will be discussed in detail later, for example, looks as follows:

Nouns: "Schedule recipient", "Schedule resource", "Due date", "Schedule","Constraints", "Goal", "Priority", etc.
Verbs: "Assign", "Classify", "Pick up", "Select", "Relax", "Neglect", etc.
Adjectives: "Unassigned", "The last", "Idle" etc.
Others: "Strong constraint","Constraint predicates", "Constraint satisfaction","Attribute", etc.

Thus, task ontology provides primitives in terms of which we can describe problem solving context and makes it easy to put domain knowledge into problem solving context, since it provides us with abstract roles of various objects which could be instantiated to domain-specific objects. Domain knowledge organized without paying attention to its usage is difficult to find out how to incorporate what portion of it into a specific problem solving process. In the above examples, Schedule recipient and Schedule resource represent the two major objects in the scheduling task domain and its roles. Much of domain-dependent knowledge is incorporated into verbs which are formulated as operation and domain-dependent knowledge. For example, the verb "select" requires some criterion for evaluating objects to "select" appropriate one from them. This will be discussed again later.

4 TYPOLOGY OF ONTOLOGY

Domain ontology is a system of vocabulary for describing the domain. Although detailed discussion on it is omitted here because of space limitation, let us briefly discuss domain ontology. We believe domain ontology is divided into the following three categories:
(1) Object ontology related to objects under consideration in the task. This ontology covers the structure and components of the object.
(2) Activity ontology related to activities taking place in the domain. Verbs play important role in this ontology, however, they are different from those in task ontology. The subjects of the former verbs are objects, components, or humans involved in the activities of interest, while those of the latter are domain experts.
(3) Field ontology related to theories and principles which govern the domain. This ontology contains

primitive concepts appearing in the theories and relations and formulas constituting the theories and principles.

Content ontology includes another category, so called general ontology or common ontology used for representing common sense world discussed, say, in Cyc[7]. It consists of things, events, time, space, causality, behavior, function, etc. The authors have been investigating the last two topics, i.e., behavior and function for years and came up with a new ontology for them[14], though it is omitted here.

Ontology for representing ontology employed in, say, Ontolingua is called meta-ontology. Now, types of ontology are summarized in Fig. 3.

```
1. Content ontology
     Task ontology
          Generic noun
          Generic verb
          Generic adjective
          Others
     Workplace ontology[22]
          Domain ontology
          Object ontology
          Activity ontology
          Field ontology
     General/Common ontology
          Things
          Events
          Time
          Space
          Causality
          Behavior
          Function
          etc.
2. Tell&Ask ontology
3. Indexing ontology
4. Meta-ontology
```

Figure 3: Typology of ontology.

5   TASK ONTOLOGY DESIGN

This section presents an example of design process of task ontology.

5.1   What is task ontology design?

The purpose of task ontology design includes the following four issues:
(1) To understand in depth of how human experts solve problems.
(2) To extract and organize the vocabulary which characterizes the task.
(3) To identify knowledge for problem solving.
(4) To identify appropriate computational mechanisms.

Problem solving knowledge is tightly coupled with problem solving structure, that is, characteristics of task knowledge. Different knowledge is obtained by different formulations of task models. Thus, task ontology contributes to making problem solving knowledge explicit and extracting domain knowledge necessary for performing the task.

5.2   Guideline of task ontology design

A rough sketch of a procedure for designing task ontology is presented here. There are two methods for ontology design such as top-down and bottom-up methods. The former starts with analysis of existing expert systems, and come up with a set vocabulary which abstract the concepts obtained from the computational mechanisms found in the systems. The latter first analyses the domain experts behavior and come up with hierarchy of vocabulary with computational mechanisms. The following is a bottom-up one.

1) Identify task/subtask hierarchy.
2) Collect simple sentences stating unit problem solving activities in every subtask.
3) Discriminate between the domain-dependent knowledge and task-dependent knowledge by extracting verbs and identifying domain knowledge required by the verbs for its execution.
4) Refine verbs until obtaining those of appropriate grain sizes.
5) Refinement of the verbs is terminated when the domain knowledge required by each verb becomes homogeneous or the activity corresponding to an algorithm is reached. For example, a diagnostic task is viewed as "to identify the faulty part" or "to select the most plausible cause(s) from the sets of possible candidate causes" at the top level. Needless to say, grain size of "identify" and "select" of this example is too large. So, they need further refinement. But, as in nurse time shift scheduling, "to select the nurse of the heaviest load" is of the good grain size, since this "selection" is clearly defined by specifying a criterion function which calculates load of each nurse. When we are interested in the soybean disease diagnosis, on the other hand, the "identification" of the disease of the observed soybean can be interpreted as a classification task. Then, "classify" can be a candidate of task primitive verb, since the classification can be done using decision tree interpretation. The computation mechanism is an decision tree interpreter and domain knowledge is decision tree description of a specific problem.
6) Identify computational mechanism for each verb.

7) Identify nouns and other concepts as objects and components of the knowledge source of the verbs. Many of the nouns are identified as objects of verbs. Other nouns are obtained mainly by analyzing the knowledge sources associated with verbs. For example, knowledge required by "select" includes a criteria for evaluating various objects in which we find cost, precision, reliability, behavior, etc. Analysis of constraints also enables us to find other important concepts including many attributes of objects.

8) Abstract nouns to decrease domain-dependence and obtain task-general concepts which represent roles in the task/subtask.

9) Identify domain-independent adjectives which restrict or denote specific concepts/objects. Domain-dependent adjectives should be formalize as constraints.

The roles of task ontology is summarized as follows:

(1) To provide domain experts with human-readable conceptual primitives in terms of which they can express their way of problem solving.

(2) To enable a translation of the knowledge-level description of the problem solving process into symbol-level executable code.

(3) To specify the problem solving context which contributes to clarify domain knowledge.

(4) To enable us to build a task analysis interview system as will be shown in Section 6 where an overview of MULTIS is discussed as an example. Thus, task ontology is operationalized in such a system.

5.3 Task ontology for scheduling tasks

We have developed a task analysis interview system named MULTIS[10][18][19] which models the task structure of a domain expert based on task ontology. An ontology for scheduling tasks in MULTIS is shown as follows:

Generic nouns
  Schedule Recipient(RCP): (eg.) Job, Order, Driver, Nurse, etc.
  RCP-GRP: Group of RCPs
  Schedule Resource(RSC): (eg.) Line, Machine, Track, Duties, etc.
  RSC-GRP: Group of RSC
  Time slot: Slots of time RCP is assigned to. {These three are the basic terms in scheduling tasks, since solution is represented in terms of them.}
  Schedule: Solution of the task
    Schedule, Intermediate solution, Final solution, etc.
  Schedule representation
    Gantt chart[2], Time table, etc. {Solution and its representation are separated, since a solution can be

represented in several manners. Form of solution representation gives us very useful information because they have domain specific information such as terminology, types of problems, etc.}
  Constraint/condition: Constraints to be satisfied by the schedule
  Goal: Goal of the scheduling to optimize
  Priority
  Data/Information

Generic adjective
  Assigned/unassigned, Previous, Last, Next, Satisfying, Violating, etc.

Constraint-related vocabulary
  Constraint/Condition
    Strong constraint: Constraints which must be satisfied
    Weak constraint: Constraints which can be relaxed in some cases
  Constraint adjective:
    Maximal, Minimal, Earliest, Latest, Longest, Shortest, Largest, etc.
  Constraint-predicate:
    Equal to, Larger than, Smaller than, Include, Exclude, Overlap, etc.
  Attribute: Components of constraints/ attributes of objects
    Time interval
      Time available, Assigned time, etc.
    Time point
      Due date, Starting time, Ending time, etc.
    Frequency, Efficiency, Priority, Load, Cost, Tolerance, Amount, etc.

Goal: {Same as that appearing in generic noun}
  Status
    Maximum, Minimum, Uniform, Continuous, etc.
  Object
    Load balance, Rate of operation, Efficiency, Idle time, Operation time, etc.

RSC/RCP verb: {These verbs mainly take RSC or RCP as their objects. The subjects of them are domain experts.}
  Generate: Generates objects to process
    Assign: assign RCP to RSC and time
    Classify: classify objects into groups
    Combine: make tuples of objects
    Compute: obtain values of parameters
    Divide: divide objects into groups
    Insert: insert an object into a list
    Merge: merge some objects

Permute: generate a permutation
Pickup: take an object out of a list
Remove: remove objects from a list
Select: take objects satisfying a condition
out of a list
Sequence: arrange objects in order
Test: Test if an enumeration or search is exhaust
or not{This is used together with the
verb Pick-up}
Check: check object if it satisfies a
constraint/condition
Evaluate: evaluate an object to obtain score
Modify: Modify assignments and data
Reassign
Reassign
Exchange: exchange assignments
Shift left/right: shift assignment to
left/right
Pack-to-the-left
Update: update data

Constraint_verb: Verbs which take constraints as
their objects
Add
Delete
Neglect
Strengthen
Weaken/Relax

Several executable building blocks are associated
with every verb in MULTIS. Each building block is
defined as a combination of its main computational
mechanism and domain knowledge necessary for performing its function. Some examples of specifications
of typical building blocks are shown below

Classify: classify objects into some groups
input: list of objects
output: list of lists of object and its category
domain knowledge: decision tree, set of rules,
distance or similarity, etc.
ClassifyDT: classify objects using a decision tree
ClassifyAttr: classify objects of the same
attribute value
ClassifyDist: classify objects based on the
distances among them
ClassifyRule: classify objects by interpreting rules
Select: select object(s) satisfying constraint/condition
input: objects
output: list of object(s)
domain knowledge: condition, criterion function,
set of rules for evaluation
SelectMaxAll: make a list of all the objects of
maximum value calculated according to
the criterion function.

SelectMinAll, SelectMaxOne, SelectMinOne,
SelectMaxpAll, SelectMaxpOne, SelectSatisfyAll
SelectSatisfyOne: select an object satisfying
the constraint/condition
Sequence: arrange objects in order
input: list of objects with ordering information
output: list of ordered objects
domain knowledge: none
SequenceT: arrange objects according to values of
total ordering
SequenceP: arrange objects according to values of
partial ordering

Computational mechanisms of other verbs are omitted here due to the space limitation. Adjectives are
also omitted.

The authors had set up a consortium for developing and evaluating scheduling ontology in ASTEM/RI
in cooperation with eight companies. In the consortium, MULTIS has been evaluated by describing task
structures of several ESs which the members of the
consortium were involved in their development. The
evaluation shows our task ontology has sufficient expressive power for scheduling task structures. Scheduling systems used for evaluation include four job-shop
scheduling systems, three car-dispatching systems, two
production planning systems, two human resource allocation systems, and one configuration system.

In appendix, a portion of Ontolingua implementation of our scheduling ontology is shown. As stated
above, the implementation of our content ontology
in Ontolingua is not very satisfactory, but we think
it helps readers understand its formal representation.
The whole implementation will be available through
WWW soon.

6 MULTIS

6.1 Overview

In MULTIS, ontology is called a system of "generic
vocabulary" which consists of generic nouns, generic
verbs, generic adjectives, and other task specific concepts. A combination of generic verb and noun such
as "verb + noun" is referred to as "generic process".
A network of generic processes is called generic process network(GPN) which represents a skeleton of task
structure at the knowledge level.

Fig.4 shows the block diagram of MULTIS which
consists of seven modules such as CBR, generic
vocabulary/process library, building block library,
generic process network editor (GPNE), GPN com-
piler(GPNC), interview engine and interface. GPNE
builds a GPN through interaction with a domain expert. During the process, it retrieves several GPNs
from case DB and consults generic vocabulary(task ontology) library to translate the generic vocabulary contained in the cases(GPNs) into some domain-specific

---

[2]A gantt chart is a chart used for schedule representation of job-shop scheduling tasks.

concepts. After building a GPN, control is passed to GPNC which identifies building blocks necessary for implementing inference engine and eventually generates an executable code through interview.

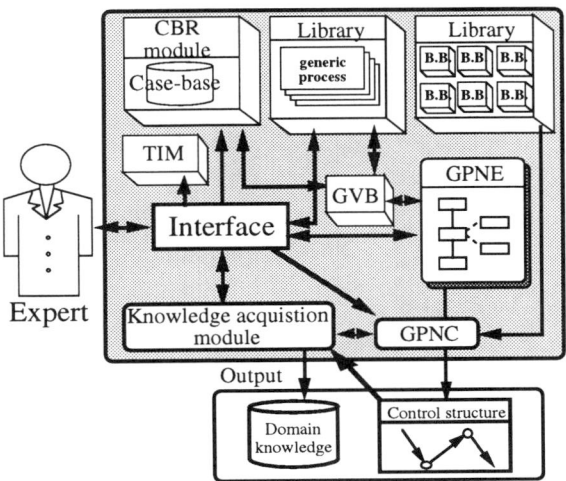

Figure 4: Block diagram of MULTIS

6.2   How it works

MULTIS first tries to obtain several basic concepts by using some templates of schedule representation. The rows, columns and entries of them correspond to time, schedule resources and schedule recipients, respectively. Thus, at least these three domain-specific concepts are easily obtained through a simple interaction.

One of the major issues in MULTIS research is how to enable domain experts to synthesize problem solving engines for their tasks. Generic vocabulary and generic processes are designed to this end. They are easy for domain experts to understand, so it becomes a relatively easy job to describe their problems in terms of generic vocabulary and generic processes.

Even if the vocabulary the interview system uses is intelligible to domain experts, however, it is not so easy for them to write a control structure from scratch. MULTIS employs CBR (Case-Based Reasoning) which presents the domain expert appropriate cases of several ESs' control structures described as GPNs. Domain experts can build their problem solving models by modifying the GPN retrieved. Thus, description of case data and retrieval of them are crucial issues in MULTIS. GPNs are stored in the case base with several kinds of indexes such as 1) domain, 2) solution representation, 3) goal, 4) group or dependencies between RCPs, and 5) time axis.

MULTIS can present the user the cases in several

ways one in terms of generic vocabulary, another one in terms of the domain concepts of the particular domain and yet another one in terms of the domain concepts under consideration since cases have correspondence between generic vocabulary and domain concepts. The translation between generic vocabulary and domain concepts is made very smoothly. This helps domain experts understand what the GPN is and how to modify cases to obtain their own network.

Fig. 5 shows an example of GPN obtained for a belt scheduling systems discussed in [19]. The upper part of each box includes representation of unit operation in domain terms and the lower part that in generic vocabulary. As described above, this GPN is configured mainly by cut&paste consulting the case base. The GPN shows main flow of the belt scheduling process and implicitly specifies domain knowledge required for each generic verb(see 5.3), which makes it easier to elicit domain knowledge.

After GPN design has been terminated, GPNC compiles it to generate Common lisp code by configuring building blocks during which GPNC asks the user several questions necessary for selecting appropriate building blocks associated with each verb and data flow among them. Backtrack information is also obtained through the interview. To enable this, MULTIS has an ontology for backtracking which is applicable to wide rage of backtracking phenomena observed in scheduling tasks.

6.3   Generality

Finally, we would like to discuss the generality of MULTIS. Note that MULTIS is designed in a highly modular structure. Content of the three libraries for generic vocabulary, GPN, and building blocks are dependent on the target task under analysis but they are passive data referred to by all the modules independent of the target task. This architecture makes MULTIS very general and applicable to analysis of other types of tasks such as design and diagnosis by replacing the three libraries with those of these tasks. The only exception to this generality is the interface module part of which is dependent on solution representation of scheduling, that is, gantt chart or time table. We have to modify this task-dependency in order to make MULTIS architecture task-independent.

7   CONCLUSIONS

Wielinga and Schreiber discuss ontological issues in knowledge base technology[25]. They take similar position as Ontolingua approach, that is, they consider ontology as a formal theory of conceptualization in knowledgeable agents. What makes their approach differ from that of Ontolingua is they introduce several types of ontologies reflecting the differences of applications, and hence, task structures. In this sense, we

56

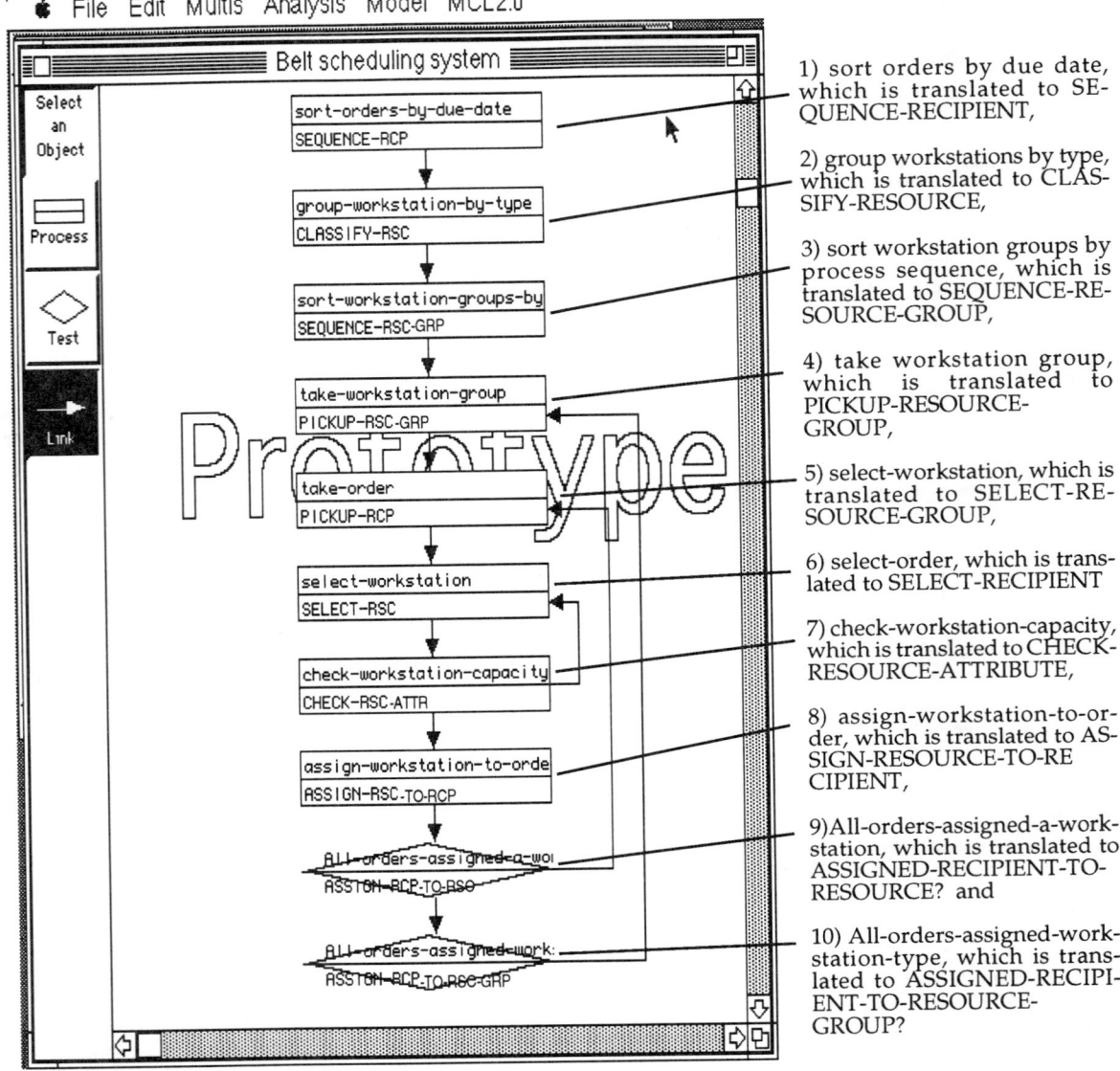

Figure 5: An example of GPN for a belt scheduling task.

1) sort orders by due date, which is translated to SEQUENCE-RECIPIENT,

2) group workstations by type, which is translated to CLASSIFY-RESOURCE,

3) sort workstation groups by process sequence, which is translated to SEQUENCE-RESOURCE-GROUP,

4) take workstation group, which is translated to PICKUP-RESOURCE-GROUP,

5) select-workstation, which is translated to SELECT-RESOURCE-GROUP,

6) select-order, which is translated to SELECT-RECIPIENT

7) check-workstation-capacity, which is translated to CHECK-RESOURCE-ATTRIBUTE,

8) assign-workstation-to-order, which is translated to ASSIGN-RESOURCE-TO-RECIPIENT,

9) All-orders-assigned-a-workstation, which is translated to ASSIGNED-RECIPIENT-TO-RESOURCE? and

10) All-orders-assigned-workstation-type, which is translated to ASSIGNED-RECIPIENT-TO-RESOURCE-GROUP?

share a lot with them. However, they weakly discuss task ontology which is one of the main issues in this paper. Although we adopt task-domain decomposition approach to knowledge modeling like them, we try to ontologize equally both domain-specific knowledge and task-specific knowledge.

We have discussed what an ontology is and pointed out several perspectives useful for understanding it in-depth. A task ontology is presented and task analysis interview system named MULTIS has been overviewed to show how task ontology is effectively operationalized. Although the usefulness of task ontology in task analysis interview is verified, how it helps acquire and organize domain knowledge is not fully evaluated. We plan to augment the expressiveness of task ontology in explaining the relations between organizational characteristics and problem solving process [22].

Acknowledgement

The authors are grateful to Mr. Seta for his contribution to Ontolingua implementation of the scheduling task ontology.

REFERENCES

[1] Chandrasekaran, B.: Generic tasks for knowledge-based reasoning: the right level of abstraction for knowledge acquisition, IEEE Expert, Vol.1, No.3, pp.23-30, 1986.

[2] Gruber, T.: A translation approach to portable ontology specifications, Proc. of JKAW'92, pp. 89-108, 1992.

[3] Gruber, T.: Toward principles for the design of ontologies used for knowledge sharing, TR KSL93-04, Stanford University, 1993.

[4] Gruber, T.: An ontology for engineering mathematics, Proc. of Comparison of implemented ontology, ECAI'94 Workshop, W13, pp.93-104, 1994.

[5] Hori, M., et al.: Methodology for configuring scheduling engines with task-specific components, Proc. of JKAW'92, pp.215-230, 1992.

[6] Karbach, W., M. Linster, A. Voss: Models, methods, roles and tasks: many labels – One idea?, Knowledge Acquisition, 2, pp.279-299, 1990.

[7] Lenat, D. and R. Guha: Building Large Knowledge-Based Systems, Addison-Wesley Publishing Company, Inc., 1990.

[8] Mars, N.: An ontology of measurement, Proc. of Comparison of implemented ontology, ECAI'94 Workshop, W13, pp.153-162, 1994.

[9] McDermott, J.: Using problem solving methods to impose structure on knowledge, Proc. of the Intl. Conf. on AI Applications, pp.7-11, 1988.

[10] Mizoguchi, R. et al.: Task ontology and its use in a task analysis interview systems – Two-level mediating representation in MULTIS –, Proc. of the JKAW'92, pp.185-198, 1992.

[11] Mizoguchi, R.: Expert systems and knowledge base technology, International J. of Computer and Engineering Management, Vol.1, No.2, pp.24-39, 1993.

[12] Mizoguchi, R.: Knowledge acquisition and ontology, Proc. of the KB&KS'93, Tokyo, pp. 121-128, 1993.

[13] Newell, A.: The knowledge level, Artificial Intelligence, Vol.18, No.1, pp.87-127, 1982.

[14] Sasajima, M., et al.: An investigation on domain ontology to represent functional models, Proc. of the Eighth International Workshop on Qualitative Reasoning about Physical Systems, pp.224-233, 1994.

[15] Steels, L. : Components of expertise, IEEE Expert, Vol.11, No.2, pp.28-49, 1990.

[16] Swartout, W. et al.: Knowledge sharing: Prospects and challenges, Proc. KB&KS, Tokyo, pp.95-102, 1993.

[17] Takaoka, Y. et al.: Towards re-use of knowledge - A study of methods regarding substation fault recovery operation support system -, Proc. of WCES'94, Lisbon, Paper-ID-336, 1994.

[18] Tijerino, A. Y. et al: A task analysis interview system that uses a problem solving model, Proc. of JKAW90, pp.331-344, 1990.

[19] Tijerino, A. Yuri, et al.: MULTIS II: Enabling end-users to design problem-solving engines via two-level task ontologies, Proc. of EKAW'93, 1993.

[20] Vanwelkenhuysen, Johan: Participative Conceptual system design of industrial knowledge systems, Technical Report 39-1, Artificial Intelligence Lab., Free University of Brussels, 1993.

[21] Van de Velde, W.: Issues in knowledge level modelling, Tech. Report, AI lab, Free University of Brussels, AI-Memo 93-09, 1993.

[22] Vanwelkenhuysen, Johan and R. Mizoguchi: Maintaining the workplace context in a knowledge level analysis, The Third Japanese Knowledge Acquisition for Knowledge-Based Systems Workshop, pp.33-47, 1994.

[23] Vanwelkenhuysen, Johan and R. Mizoguchi: Workplace-Adapted Behaviors: Lessons Learned for Knowledge Reuse, Proc. of KB&KS '95, 1995(Submitted).

[24] Wielinga, B. et al.: The KADS knowledge modelling approach, Proc. of JKAW'92, pp.23-42, 1992.

[25] Wielinga, B. et al.: Reusable and sharable knowledge bases: A European perspective,Proc. of KB&KS'93, Tokyo, pp.103-115, 1993.

Appendix: A portion of Ontolingua implementation of Scheduling task ontology
(define-class classify (?classify)
"Classify is one of the generic-verbs. It classifies a list of objects into some categories by using
domain knowledge.The domain knowledge is a relation between input objects and categories. Output is a list
of categories. Each category is a list of a category name and a list of its members"
   :def (exists (?input ?output ?dk)
     (and (verb.name ?classify classify)
       (verb.input ?classify ?input)
       (list ?input)
       (verb.output ?classify ?output)
       (category-list ?output)
       (verb.domain-knowledge ?classify ?dk)
       (constraint ?dk)
       (forall ?category
         (=> (and(member ?category ?output)
           (category ?category))
          (forall ?element
            (=> (member ?element(second ?category))
             (satisfies-constraint
              (listof ?element (first ?category))
                ?dk)))))))
   :axiom-def (subclass-of classify generic-verb))

;; generic-noun
(define-class rsc (?x)
"RSC is resource used in scheduling."
   :def (and(individual ?x)
      (value-type ?x rsc.attributes list))
   :axiom-def (and (subclass-of rsc generic-noun)
        (subclass-partition
          rsc
          (setof resource
            human-rsc
            material-rsc
            vehicle-rsc
            facility-rsc
            space-rsc
            duty-rsc
            ))))

;; generic-adjective
(define-relation un-assigned (?un-assigned)
   :axiom-def (subrelation-of un-assigned generic-adjective)
   :iff-def (not (assigned ?un-assigned)))

(define-relation assigned (?assigned)
"A kind of generic-adjective. Solution of scheduling is represented as a set of assignments in 'assignment-set'"
   :axiom-def (subrelation-of assigned generic-adjective)
   :iff-def (or
        (and (rsc ?assigned)
            (exists (?time ?rcp ?assignment-set)
              (and (assignment-set ?assignment-set)
                (member (listof ?assigned ?time ?rcp)
                  ?assignment-set))))
        (and (time-unit ?assigned)
            (exists (?rsc ?rcp ?assignment-set)
              (and (assignment-set ?assignment-set)
                (member (listof ?rsc ?assigned ?rcp)

```
                              ?assignment-set))))
(and      (rcp ?assigned)
          (exists (?rsc ?time ?assignment-set)
              (and (assignment-set ?assignment-set)
                  (member (listof ?rsc ?time ?assigned)
                      ?assignment-set)))))
```

Towards Very Large Knowledge Bases
N.J.I. Mars, Ed.
IOS Press, 1995

The Generalized Upper Model Knowledge Base: Organization and Use*

John Bateman
GMD/Institut für Integrierte Publikations-
und Informationssysteme (IPSI)
Darmstadt, Germany
bateman@gmd.de

Bernardo Magnini and **Giovanni Fabris**
Istituto per la Ricerca Scientifica
e Tecnologica (IRST)
Trento, Italy
{magnini,fabris}@irst.it

ABSTRACT

In this paper we discuss some issues in designing and re-using an abstract ontology for domain
modelling. We take our Generalized Upper Model
Knowledge Base (GUM)—an ontology being developed primarily for Natural Language Processing applications—as starting point. The GUM
knowledge base has been used in several contexts,
including multilingual generation projects and information retrieval projects, supporting different
knowledge domains. The motivations for this 'linguistically motivated' ontology are proving themselves to offer re-usability across domains, tasks,
and languages as well as the possibility of large
scaling-up. We describe the general principles underlying the organization of the knowledge base,
some steps towards extending its use, and some
examples of the content thus motivated.

1 MOTIVATIONS AND OVERVIEW

Experience with constructing general natural language
generation and analysis components has demonstrated
that interfacing such components with application systems or users is substantially simplified by the provision of general organizations of information that are
linguistically motivated (cf. Penman [36], XTRA [1],
LILOG [24], ALFresco [40] and many others— see [3]
for a comprehensive overview of positions. Moreover,

---
*Magnini is partially supported by the European Union
LRE (Language Research and Engineering) projects GIST
and TRANSTERM. Fabris is supported by a grant from the
Comune di Trento. Bateman is also a member of the Penman Project, USC/Information Sciences Institute, Marina
del Rey, Los Angeles. In addition to the authors of the
present paper, the current stage of development of the Generalized Upper Model has been significantly shaped by Re-
nate Henschel and Fabio Rinaldi.

in order to be effective, it is argued in [2] that such general organizations of information must aim to achieve
two potentially conflicting goals. On the one hand, the
organization must achieve a sufficient level of abstraction in the semantic types employed as to escape the
idiosyncracies of surface realization and ease interfacing with (possibly non-linguistically oriented) domain
knowledge. While on the other, the organization must
still maintain a sufficiently close relationship to surface regularities as to permit operationalisation and
interfacing with natural language surface components.
When the link with surface realization is broken, our
experiences shows that the modelling-style becomes
under-constrained and re-usability suffers.

Our starting point is the ongoing development work
on the design and use of *upper models* as originally proposed in the USC/ISI-BBN Janus collaboration [29, 30, 33]. An upper model is an abstract linguistically motivated ontology meeting both requirements stated above. In [6], we introduced our current work in which we are pursuing the development
of an upper model that is both sufficient for natural
language processing needs and re-usable and shareable across different languages as well as across different domains/tasks. This *Generalized Upper Model*
provides semantic distinctions appropriate and adequate for supporting natural language processing for
(at least) Italian, German and English. Hence, the
more specific designation of the ontology described:
the Generalized$_{English,\ German,\ Italian}$ Upper Model.

The design philosophy of this Generalized Upper
Model is that linguistically motivated concepts and
concept organizations are provided which are as far
as possible valid across distinct languages. However,
there is no theoretical requirement that all concepts
will be relevant for all languages. In this respect our
approach differs from standard conceptions of an 'interlingua'. Indeed, it is to be expected that languages

differ in the semantic organizations they require. However, it is also expected that the level of abstraction of the Generalized Upper Model is sufficient for substantial sharing and re-use across languages precisely because details of surface form have been left behind. The network as a whole, although multilingual in orientation, therefore makes no assumptions of universality. Rather the reverse is the case; that is, we assume that there will be differences between languages in the kinds of experiential semantic distinctions that they draw. To the extent, however, that different grammatical systems need to perform similar communicative functional tasks, they will induce similarities in the semantic organization. The motivation for this position is given in detail in [8, 7, 32, 9]. Our expectations have been strongly supported by our work so far, where extensions and alterations made on the basis of linguistic evidence from some particular language have most often proved equally applicable to the other languages covered. Examples of this for German and English have already been presented in [19]; additional discussion for Italian was presented in [6].

The general organization of information thus created offers many advantages for knowledge representation. The distinctions drawn tend to be finer and more broadly motivated than distinctions based on non-linguistic, or task or domain specific knowledge. Moreover, there is the additional functionality that whenever knowledge is organized in the manner described by the Upper Model, its expression in natural language is significantly simplified. This more fine grained set of categories brings its own problems however: it requires more effort for a knowledge engineer to use and more information in order to use it correctly. In this paper, our aim is to show some of the steps towards operationalization of the Generalized Upper Model that can be taken and to provide some examples of the kind of modelling it enables.

The paper begins with an outline of some of the criteria that have been established for including concepts and discriminations in such ontologies and their use for knowledge representation. We go on to present a detailed application of these criteria in one area of the conceptual hierarchy: that of communication processes. Finally, we briefly overview projects making use of versions of the Upper Model and describe ongoing work.

2 CRITERIA FOR BUILDING THE GUM ONTOLOGY

Upper Model types are proposed on the basis of two general considerations:

1. they are necessary in order to motivate sets of distinctions in their lexicogrammatical expression;

2. they capture differences in 'experiential' meaning and *not* differences due to textual variation (such as active-passive) or interpersonal alternations (such as question-assertion).

The first consideration is receiving increasing acknowledgement in linguistics generally, where it is now recognized that there are highly systematic relationships between surface patterns and their semantics (cf., e.g., [26] and the many references cited there). The second consideration is still largely restricted to functional linguistic approaches which differentiate among the distinct kinds of meaning that appear in languages (e.g., [16]). The restriction to one particular kind of variation in meaning for motivating upper model concepts is, however, very important for achieving operationalizable organizations that are nevertheless highly abstract. Furthermore, it is precisely their abstract nature that gives these organizations such a high degree of cross-linguistic viability, as well as domain and task independence. The most systematic and extensive theoretical statement of a position accepting both general considerations is that given in [17]; further motivations from a natural language processing perspective are given in [3].

The degree of abstraction achieved in an upper model rests on the nature and breadth of the evidence admitted. Whereas classification schemes for individual words are unlikely to show good re-usability characteristics, basing classification on systematic, re-occuring *grammatical* patternings is proving to be re-usable in the very broad sense mentioned above. An upper model is therefore essentially a classification of the kind of meanings that grammatical constructions themselves presuppose. Such meanings have a longer and more stable life than lexical meanings, as well as pervading the kind of structurings given in our general interpretations of the world. It is largely this property that lifts an upper model away from a discussion of word meanings (such as, for example, what a given 'verb' might mean) to a level of description that can be applied to non-linguistic modelling (such as, modelling classes of actions).

Although the design criteria for Upper Model construction are neatly summarized by the statement that *only* 'experiential' semantic information may be included and not 'textual', 'interpersonal', or 'logical' information (terms as defined in, e.g., [16]), in recent research we have attempted to construct more accessible operationalization strategies for upper model construction. These strategies are being applied for extensions to further languages and in domain modelling; they are summarized in Section 3. The improved principles set out should also allow for more effective evaluation of upper model content proposals, and will be applicable for any ontology where critieria are drawn from natural language usage. These principles in use are illustrated in the substantive extensions described in Section 4. The general design of the Generalized Upper Model is also undergoing refinement as our experiences with it increases; some of these changes are also motivated by considering a wider body of data (including considerations from further languages). Some refinements of this kind are reported below in Section 5.

3 OPERATIONALIZATIONS OF DESIGN PRINCIPLES

Some methodological refinement has been adopted relative to syntactical aspects that are particularly relevant for defining the portion of the conceptual hierarchy responsible for the representation of 'processes'/'states'—i.e., a semantic configuration possessing a 'time profile' (cf. [17]). In particular, generic indications about the correspondences between a verb subcategorization frame (i.e., the constellation of participants that necessarily co-occur syntactically with particular selections of verbs) and the concepts included within the Upper Model have been made more operative.[1] The following are the operative rules that have been adopted in the experimental work on Italian, and then reapplied to reassess the proposals for English and German.

- *Syntactic argument number*. We assume that for each element of the subcategorization frame (although see below on degrees of obligatoriness), a corresponding semantic participant has to be included in the Upper Model. From this hypothesis, we are led to a further hypothesis that verb classes with differing numbers of (strictly) subcategorized arguments will have different conceptual representations in the Upper Model.

- *Direct and Indirect syntactic arguments*. Direct arguments of the subcategorization frame show a stronger relation between the process and the participant than indirect arguments. This means that not all the participants to a process have the same status, both from a syntactic point of view (direct versus indirect arguments) and from a semantic point of view (a process can be "centered" around one participant). This rule has been applied, for example, in the **Verbal-Process** hierarchy. A verb like *inform* is classified as **Addressee-Oriented**, because the direct-object that the verb allows plays the semantic role of the addressee; a verb like *demonstrate* is classified as **Message-Oriented** because the direct object plays the semantic role of the message. This

subhierarchy is shown in detail in section 5.[2]

- *Necessary and optional syntactic arguments*. Much the same considerations of the previous point hold: necessary arguments show a participation relation stronger than optional arguments. If an element of the subcategorization frame is not lexically realized, this element is considered as a kind of semantic ellipsis (cf. principle 4 in [18]). For example in *"John told a story"* the indirect object is not superficially realized; however it is included in the semantic representation by means of the **Addressee** role.

- *Order of the syntactic arguments*. If the only syntactic variation concerns the order in which the elements of the subcategorization frame are realized (for example, the inversion between the direct and indirect object, or other textually motivated variation), this fact is not relevant for the Upper Model organization. For example, the two sentences *"John told a story to Mary"* and *"John told to Mary a story"* have a single corresponding concept in the Upper Model. A similar case concerns the passive form.

In addition to these syntactic criteria, there are also criteria motivated by distinctions in meaning that variations of the kind discussed in, for example, [26]. For example:

- *Semantic alternations*. Semantic alternations occur when the different patterns allow a shift of meaning. This is evident, for example, in the "locative" alternations [26, pp49-54], like the *spray/load* alternation, which allow for the so called "holistic effect"; here, the direct object is considered totally affected by the process, while the indirect object is considered partially affected (note that this is an additional evidence for the Direct/Indirect rule mentioned above). The usual examples are alternations such as: "He loaded the wagon with hay" *vs.* "He loaded hay onto the wagon".

Such alternations are relevant for the GUM organization in that the participation in an alternation typically shows a semantic feature of the process. For example, both in English and Italian, the verb *rake* participates in the "clean" alternation: *John raked the leaves off the garden [Giovanni ha rastrellato le foglie dal giardino]; John raked the garden [John ha rastrellato il giardino]*. The underlying semantic features typically constrain both the participants and the selectional restrictions over them. These kinds of rules have been applied to distinguish the English *tell*, which participates in the dative alternation, from *say*, which does not.

---

[1] Although sharing the general aim of operationalization with the account presented in [39], our intent differs in that we are seeking motivations for distinguishing between candidate Upper Model organizations, rather than presenting recognition criteria for an already established organization.

[2] There is a very interesting parallel here with the work on the semantic theory of 'Emphase' of Kunze [22, 23]; this needs to be investigated further.

Section 4.4 will show in more detail how such alternations can be represented in the Upper Model.

4 REPRESENTING KNOWLEDGE IN GUM

In this section we first describe the kinds of information specialization employed in the Upper Model and then move on to to focus on three representational issues which are crucial for NLP applications: we will describe how we represent in the GUM "relational opposites", "phrasal synonymity" and "semantic alternations". If an NLP application is using a grammatical component based on systemic-functional grammar (e.g., [36, 14, 4]) then the first two of these variations are properly included within the functionality of the component mapping semantic specifications into grammatical ones (as would be expected since both 'dependency' variation ('logical' in the terms of [16]) and textual constraints on the preferred allocation of semantic participants to surface constituents are explicitly excluded from that relevant for the Upper Model). If the natural language component does not support this functionality and require a more rigid relation between semantics and lexicogrammar, however, then the techniques described here can be considered as ways of providing it and, therefore, of correspondingly simplifying the task of the natural language component.[3]

4.1 Types of information specialization

According to the terminology established in [11] for the so-called *hybrid* approach to knowledge representation, an upper model occupies the Terminological Box (TBox) and may include intensional definitions of concepts and of the relations among them. The current version of the GUM Knowledge Base is fully implemented in LOOM [28], a knowledge representation language of the KL-ONE family. The definition contains the subsumption relations between the motivated concepts and role restrictions; further semantic specifications are being investigated.

Although the Generalized Upper Model is, like its predecessors, represented in terms of the concept and relation subsumption lattice definitions familiar from KL-ONE, there are in fact some rather different levels and kinds of specialization involved. Although at each level some information is added, generally speaking there can be four basic ways to further specialize information that can be used in the context of the Upper Model: (a) Dimensions and their Values, (b) Partitions, (c) Disjointness, and (d) Simple Specializations.

In the figures used in the paper, we adopt the following graphical conventions for these specialization types. Dimensions are represented by a shadow triangular area with pointers to the dimension values. The name of the dimension is indicated by a vertical write. Partitions are represented as dimensions. Disjointness is represented by diverging plain lines connected with a vertical line. Finally, simple specializations are represented by plain lines.

Dimensions and Values

In the Upper Model dimensions are used to describe different but compatible point of views on a certain entity. A dimension is equivalent to the use of a feature which admits a set of alternative values. Each specialization of the considered entity will be allowed to assume just one value for each of the dimensions. As an example, three dimensions are used for describing the `Material-World-Quality` structure, namely *Dynamic/Static*, *Polar/Taxonomic*, and *Scalability*. Each dimension allows a limited number of possible values; for example the *Scalability* dimension has two values, namely `Scalable-Quality` and `Non-Scalable-Quality`. Each entities classified as `Material-World-Quality` will typically assume a value for any dimension. Dimensions in the GUM are considered independent of each other; this means that the classification of one object under a certain dimension does not affect the classification of the same object under different dimensions. This kind of parallel classification has always played an important role in systemic-functional accounts of linguistic resources and has recently been foregrounded in work on constraint-based grammars and formalisms also (e.g., [13]). The GUM-organization for material world qualities is shown in Figure 1.

Partitions

A partition is used to represent mutually exclusive alternatives, with the additional constraint that all more specific entities have to be included within the partition. A partition is equivalent to a complete division into disjoint subsets of a set of elements. An example can be the top-level partition among `Process`, `Quality` and `Object`. This means that each domain concept has to be classified under one (and only one) of these alternatives.

Disjointness

A simple disjunction is used to represent mutually exclusive alternatives which do not cover all the possible specialization of a given entity. An example is the concept `Sense-And-Measure-Quality` (Figure 1), which has three specialized alternatives (i.e. `Size`, `Age` and `Color`) that are mutually exclusive. However the possibility of a generic classification under

---

[3]The price paid for this simplification is, of course, that the motivations for selecting one form rather than another—which is the critical information necessary, for example, in text generation—are obscured. Particular applications need to assess individually whether this is a price they can afford to pay.

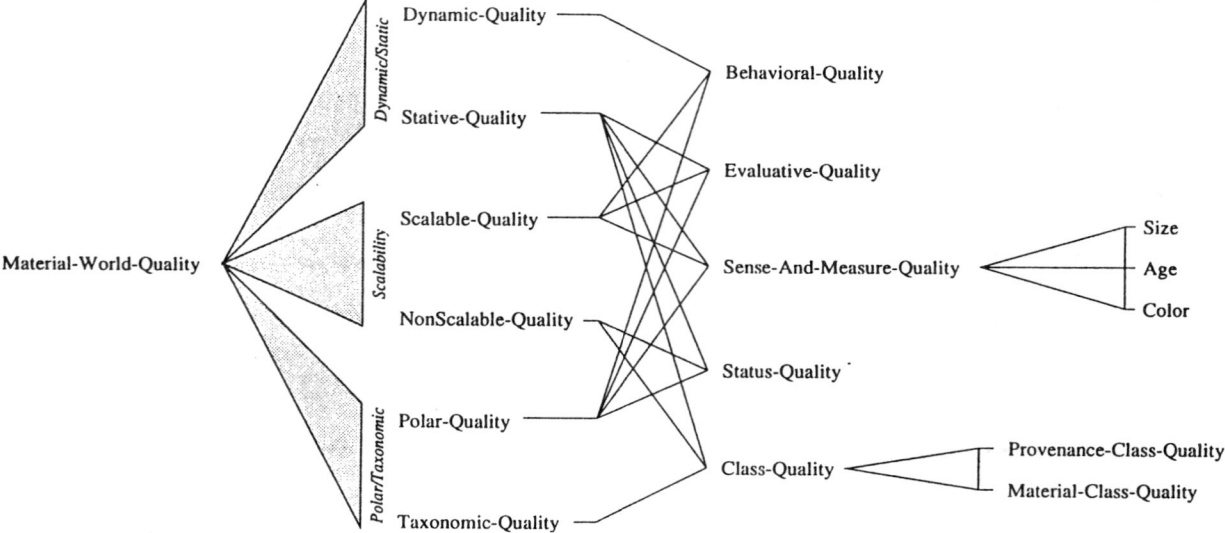

Figure 1: The `Material-World-Quality` subhierarchy.

`Sense-And-Measure-Quality` is left open in case a certain entity is not correctly positioned under any of the proposed alternatives (e.g., an instance of the `Taste` quality). This means that the Upper Model includes areas of incomplete knowledge, that are open to further specialization.

Simple Specialization

A specialization is used when nothing can be said about disjunctive properties of the elements being introduced. Simple specializations are typically used in GUM for defining intersections among values of different dimensions. Examples are the concepts `Behavioral-Quality`, `Evaluative-Quality`, `Sense-And-Measure-Quality`, `Status-Quality` and `Class-Quality`, all of them shown in Figure 1. Each of these concepts inherits information from all of the three dimensions which are used to describe `Material-World-Quality`. We call the level of the taxonomy in which values of different dimensions intersect the *intersection level*. This level is useful because it provides highly semantically motivated concepts, which usually can map directly into more specialized domain dependent concepts. As an example the concept of `Person` in GUM is defined as the intersection among `Concrete-Object`, `Individual`, `Conscious-Being` and `Decomposable-Object`.

4.2 Representing relational opposites

"Relational opposites" [12] occur when the relation between two objects can be expressed in two opposite ways. There are cases in which language provides specific words for the two relations (*below—above*) and there are cases in which we need to use some kind of paraphrase (*has part—part of*). In GUM we treat the two cases in the same way, relying on automatic inverse relation definitions. As long as the inverse relations are available, then these can be selected for capturing the

'perspectival' shift represented by the 'opposites'. The definition of inverses also begins to add more semantic information over and above the basic subsumption relations.

4.3 Representing phrasal synonymity

"Phrasal synonymity" occurs when the same 'content' is expressed using two different phrases. A frequent case involves the use of a possessive modifier (e.g., *John's house*) and a possessive verbal group (*The house owned by John*). Again, since it can be argued that there need be little difference in 'experiential meaning' (loosely: propositional content), in theory the GUM should represent these 'synonyms' similarly. This can be achieved, while still showing that there are some semantic distinctions, using the technique of *reification* as provided in LOOM as follows.

Knowledge representation languages of the KL-ONE family (among which LOOM) usually provide for definitions of *concepts*, meant to represent entities in the world, and *roles*, meant to represent relations among entities. In particular, to represent a relation $\mathcal{R}$ between two entities A and B, a role R is generally used, whose domain is A and whose range is B. However, the same information can be represented using a concept C with two participants associated and whose restrictions are A and B. The mappings between these two alternative configurations are captured by the reification schema shown in figure 2: a role-relation between two entities, and its inverse relation, are both conceptualized (i.e., reified) into a configuration that relates the two participants as domain and range of a 'concept'. This provides a means for freely expanding on the information associated with some relation, since for the concept C there is no *a priori* restrictions on the role-relations in which it can participate.

The use of reification allows us to draw a semantic similarity between structurally very distinct represen-

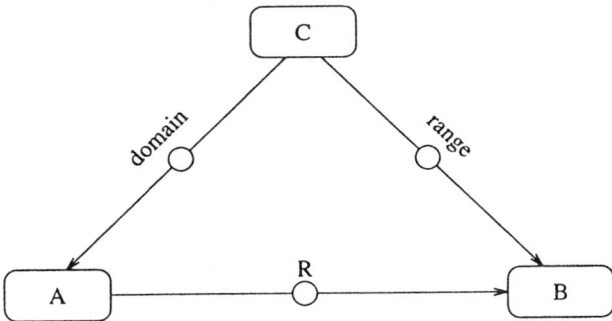

Figure 2: The reification schema.

tations and thus to preserve a similar assignment of propositional content even when a relatively rigid relation between the semantic representations and their surface realizations is maintained. Moreover, it provides a formalizeable path that brings together two candidate semantic representations that might otherwise have been proposed on the basis of diverging linguistic realizations.

As an example consider the possibility to express the location relation between an object and the place the object occupies:

(i) mod-np   *The picture in the museum*
(ii) inv-mod-rel   *The museum with the picture*
(iii) clause   *The picture is in the museum*

When a modified Noun Phrase is used, (i) and (ii), it can readily be mapped to a relational structure in which the NP subcategorized by the preposition is the range for a role, and the head NP is the domain of the same role. When a clause is used (iii) it more naturally maps into a conceptual (in opposition to 're-lational' in the LOOM-senses) structure in which the verb is a concept and the verb arguments are concepts that restrict participant verb roles. The latter structure seems necessary when additional verbal information (e.g., circumstances) are to be added (e.g., "*Today, the picture is in the museum*"); in this case a new role is quite naturally added to the conceptual structure. In fact, as argued in [6], an upper model will in general then prefer the latter representation on the basis that it contains more information. This 'verbal' orientation of the modelling is therefore in sharp contrast with the more typical nominal modelling style found in knowledge engineering.

4.4 Representing semantic alternations

"Semantic alternations" involve two participants of a process. In transitive alternations one pattern of the alternation allows one participant to be expressed as the direct object and the other as the indirect object of the process; the second pattern of the alternation usually allows for the inversion between the participants. For example, in the *spray/load* alternation we

have two patterns:

(i) NP1 V NP2 on NP3
     John loaded the hay on the wagon
(ii) NP1 V NP3 with NP2
     John loaded the wagon with hay

In pattern (i) NP2 is intended to be completely affected by the action (i.e., all the hay has been loaded on the wagon); in the second pattern it is the Location (NP3) which is the direct object and that is intended to be completely affected by the action (i.e., all of the wagon has been loaded).

We can represent this situation in the GUM using the expressivity of dimensions. Basically we allow one dimension for each participant of the process, except for the agent that is the external argument and usually does not participate in the alternation. Then each of the two dimensions admits two possible values: one value for the situation in which the participant is the direct object, and the other value for the situation in which the participant is the indirect object of the process. At this point we have four potentially possible intersections among the values, each intersection representing a potential pattern of one alternation. This situation, which is also reported in [34], is represented in figure 3. Usually one alternation selects just two of the intersections and in many cases these intersections correspond to semantically relevant classes.

Naturally, the dimensions must also receive some semantic interpretation and here there are, again, many interesting parallels to be drawn here with the work on *Emphase* Theory [22]. Essentially, the distinctions at issue can be viewed as presenting distinct *experiential perspectives* on some state of affairs or process. This captures both the intuition that some aspect of the meaning is shared, while also expressing the differences. In contrast to the former two example cases, there does appear to be a clear distinction even in experiential meaning between such alternations; this needs to find representation, therefore, in an upper model characterization. Indeed, in some cases the distinct perspectives are so engrained that it appears appropriate to 'hardwire' them into the hierarchy. This is the case shown in section 5, where we will see how this organization has been successfully applied to the

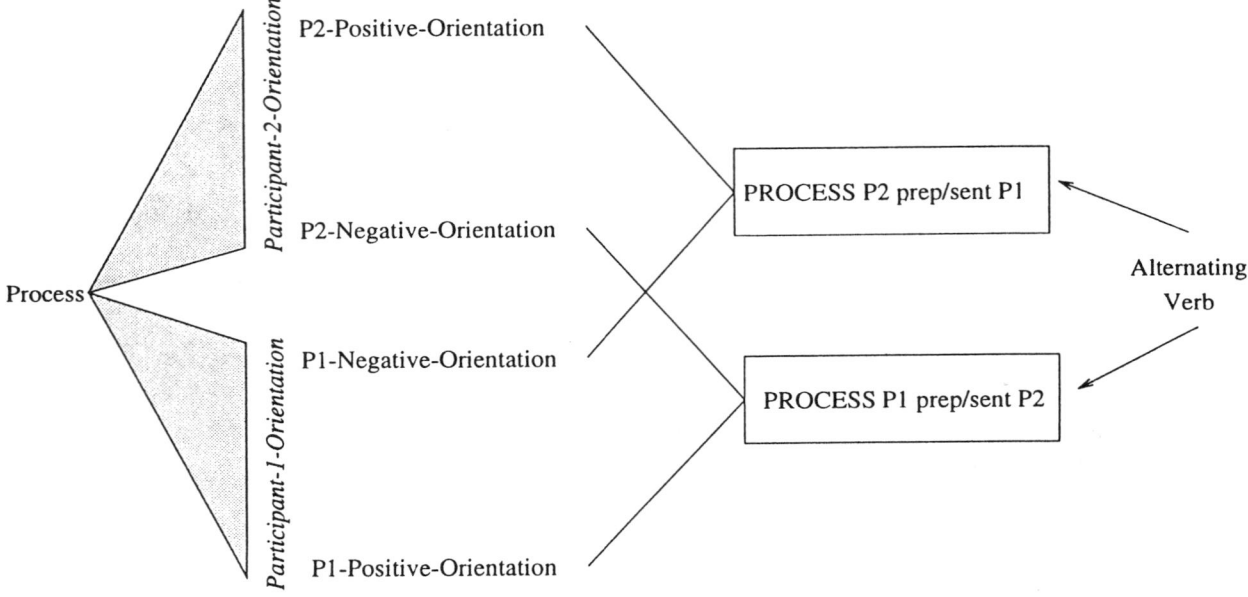

Figure 3: General schema for transitive alternations.

`Verbal-Process` subhierarchy.

5 AN EXAMPLE

In this section we present more detailed examples of the GUM knowledge base: first we introduce the kind of descriptions we use in the Upper Model as well as notational conventions; then we explore more closely the `Verbal-Process` hierarchy.

5.1 Linguistic descriptions and notations

Concepts in the GUM are generally described on the basis of their linguistic behavior rather than in terms of their intensional semantics. Thus, in deciding how to model a given concept, the essential question for an application is in what range of 'surface realizations' will the concept be required. The requirements of achieving a modelling that is adequate for supporting linguistic expression is typically sufficiently strong as to guarantee that the modelling will have a high degree of re-usability should further applications be considered.

For this reason, the specification of linguistic properties plays a central role in our definitions. We associate with each concept a linguistic description that includes relevant linguistic features. This dimension of description can be considered a proposal for enriching other current 'ontology' notations.

The full set of features used in the definition notation is open and currently includes:

- *Grammatical features* (tense:past, +/−dir-obj:(?), +/−addressee↘ind-obj, etc.) to indicate allowed or not allowed grammatical features, optional grammatical constituency, and linguistic expressions of concepts or roles respectively. Colons indicate features within one linguistic level (stratum), downward pointing arrows relations across strata (in this paper, always from semantics to lexicogrammar).

- *Linguistic realizations* (+/−pattern) to indicate allowed or not allowed lexicogrammatical realizations for a given concept. A lexicogrammatical pattern abstracts from particular realizations in one language and its function is to make the intended content of the concept being described clearer. A disjunction of the patterns allowed for a concept could be taken as a trivial generation or recognition specification for the concept concerned. There is a clear similarity to be drawn with, for example, the 'linking rules' discussed by [27] which could offer a candidate for a more formal notation.

- *Semantic selectional restrictions* (+/−participant-name:semantic-type) to indicate allowed or not allowed semantic restrictions over a certain participant role.

- *Definitional* to set up the subsumption lattice (subconcept < superconcept) and to introduce and name participant roles (+participant-name=Name).

- *Examples* (examples) to report commonly used sentences, phrases or words. These are further instantiated cases of the general realizations indicated in the 'pattern' slot. We report examples in two of the languages currently supported by GUM: English and Italian—although Italian will be the main language of illustration since this is new to the Upper Model specification; examples of German are given in [18] and of English in [5]. When a correct translation to English would require some changes in the linguistic description, the example is marked with a double question mark (??) indicating that a language dependent feature description is probably necessary.

In addition, we adopt the following typographical conventions: The `typewriter-font` is used to indicate objects in the Upper Model knowledge base. Examples occurring inside linguistic descriptions will be in normal text. Examples included in text will be in *italics*. Reference to words (as opposed to their denotation) will be included in "double-quote marks". The following specification is then part of the description for the concept `Part-Whole`.

`Part-Whole` < `Two-Place-Relation`
  +domain-name= `Part`
  +range-name= `Whole`
  +pattern= [(<`Part`> is a part of <`Whole`>]
             [<`Whole`> has <`Part`>)]
  +example=*A door handle is part of a door*
            A door has a door handle

Finally, although it is in the spirit of the GUM knowledge base trying to find as many possible intersections as possible among the languages we have considered, we allow a linguistic description to report a language dependent linguistic behavior. Language dependent features are introduced by a special language marker: #IT for Italian, #GE for German and #EN for English.

5.2   The Verbal Communication hierarchy

The principal functional characterizations of a verbal process are that it can 'project' a state of affairs or proposal (as in "*He says* [projecting] → *that he can't come* [projected]") and that it can have a receiver of the message (as in "*He told her* [`Receiver`] *a story*"). The former differentiates verbal processes from actions and relations, the latter differentiates verbal processes from mental processes (cf., the nonacceptability—disregarding telepathy—of "*He thought her that he would come*" and "*He thought to her that he would come*"). The combination of these defines the prototypical cases of verbal processes and can be used as the primary evidence for verbal process semantic distinctions (cf., for English, [16, §5.5.2: p129, §7.5: pp227-240], [31, §2.2.1.11: pp232-244]).

`Proper-Verbals` are then described in terms of two dimensions: *Addressee-Orientation* and *Message-Orientation*. Both addressee orientation and message orientation bring semi-independent realizational constraints with them; *Addressee-Orientation* brings constraints on the realization of the addressee; *Message-Orientation* on that of the message. Positive orientation along a dimension calls for a more 'direct' realization of the corresponding aspect of the verbal communication, i.e., realization as nominal phrases rather than prepositional phrases, realization as direct objects rather than indirect objects, obligatoriness rather than optionality, etc. Combining the two dimensions covers most of the observed variation for English, German and Italian. This is summarized in Figure 4.

5.2.1   Verbal-Process: the dimension level
`Proper-Verbals`
  +participant-name=**sayer**
  +participant-name=**addressee**
  +participant-name=**saying**
  +sayer:**signal-source**

This definition states that all the processes classified as `Proper-Verbals` will have three participants: the *sayer*, that is the entity which is responsible for the communication; the *saying*, that is the message of the communication; the *addressee*, that is the entity to which the message is addressed. In the following descriptions we assume that all the properties of the parent concepts in the hierarchy are inherited: we describe only the properties specific to each intersection concept.

Dimension: Message-Orientation. The *Message-Orientation* dimension admits two possible values: `Message-Oriented` and `Non-Message-Oriented`.

`Message-Oriented`
  +saying\dir-obj
  +examples= Giovanni dimostrò il teorema.
             John demonstrated the theorem.
  −saying\(?)
  −examples= *Giovanni dimostrò.
             *John demonstrated.
  −saying\indir-obj
  −examples= *Giovanni dimostrò al teorema.
             *John demonstrated to the theorem.

`Non-Message-Oriented`
  +saying\indir-obj
  +examples= Giovanni avvisò il conducente
             del problema.
             John informed the driver
             about the problem.
  +saying\(?)
  +examples= Giovanni avvisò il conducente.
             John informed the driver.
  −saying\dir-obj
  −examples= *Giovanni avvisò il problema.
             *John informed the problem.

Dimension: Addressee-Orientation. The *Addressee-Orientation* dimension admits two possible values: `Addressee-Oriented` and `Non-Addressee-Oriented`.

`Addressee-Oriented`
  +addressee\dir-obj
  +examples= Giovanni informò Maria
             John informed Mary
  −addressee\(?)
  −examples= *Giovanni informò

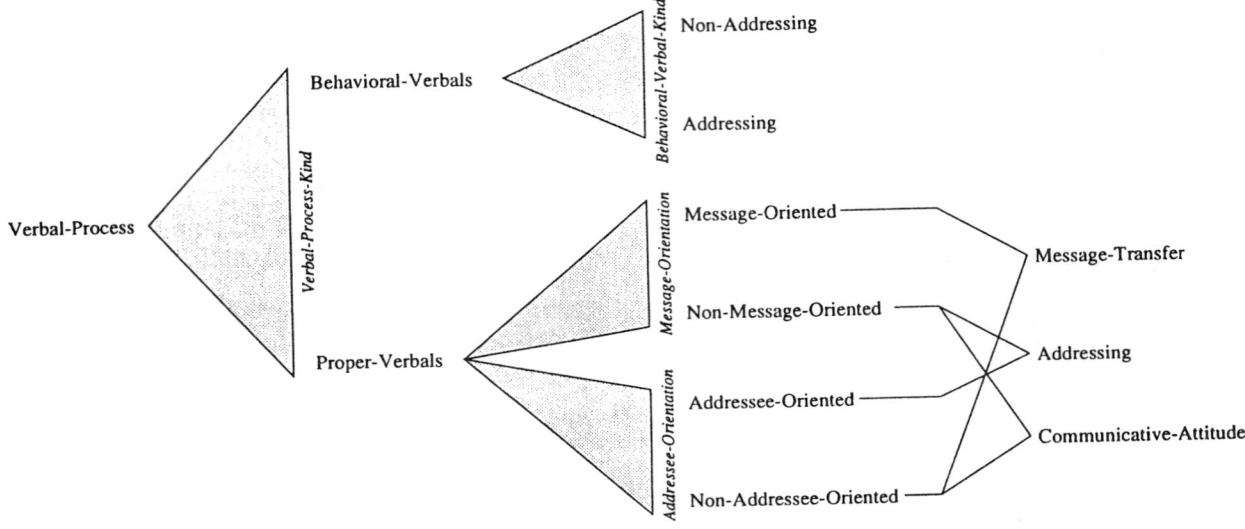

Figure 4: The Verbal-Process subhierarchy.

*John informed
−addressee\indir-obj
−examples= *Giovanni informò a Maria
　　　　　　*John informed to Mary

Non-Addressee-Oriented
　+addressee\indir-obj
　+examples= Giovanni confidò a Maria il segreto
　　　　　　John confided to Mary the secret
　+addressee\(?)
　+examples= Giovanni confidò il segreto
　　　　　　John confided the secret
　−addressee\dir-obj
　−examples= *Giovanni confidò Maria
　　　　　　*John confided Mary

5.2.2 The intersection level

According to the definitions of the two dimensions *Message-Orientation* and *Addressee-Orientation*, we can define four possible intersections among the values of the dimensions. We found that only three of them are meaningful for the three languages we considered. We defined these three classes (**Addressing**, **Message-Transfer** and **Communication-Attitude**) which actually group different kinds of verbs of verbal process: in the following descriptions we propose a number of examples for these classes. We will use data from a classification recently proposed in a study on Italian communication verbs [15]; in this study correspondences between syntactical behavior and meaning have been extensively applied to a large amount of data. This supports the classification motivated crosslinguistically and adopted in the GUM.

Addressing
　< **Addressee-Oriented, Non-Message-Oriented**
　#EN:examples=John implored Mary for a loan.
　#IT:examples= John ha implorato Maria
　　　　　　per un prestito.

According to the classification of [15] for Italian, this class includes, among others, verbs of manifesting consensus (*acclamare/acclaim*), verbs of manifesting disdain (*oltraggiare/outrage, insultare/insult, rimproverare/rebuke*), verbs of addressing the crowd (*arringare/harangue*), verbs of saying of doing or not doing (*esortare/urge, sollecitare/press for, supplicare/beseech, implorare/implore, consigliare/advise, diffidare/warm, convincere/convince, scoraggiare/discourage*), verbs of saying what one will do (*minacciare/threaten*), verbs of inducing moods (*illudere/deceive, offendere/offend*), verbs of greeting and thanking (*ringraziare/thank, salutare/greet*), verbs of advising (*ammonire/admonish*), verbs of asking for attention (*chiamare/call, interpellare/question*), verbs of speaking against (*contraddire/contradict*), verbs of interchange with one person (*interrogare/ask*), verbs of informing (*informare/inform, avvisare/warn*). This class include [26, §37.9], but some of the verbs are also reported as psychological verbs [26, §31.1]

Message-Transfer
　< **Non-Addressee-Oriented, Message-Oriented**
　#EN:examples=John listed his problems to Mary.
　#IT:examples= Giovanni elencò i suoi problemi
　　　　　　a Maria.

According to the classification of [15] for Italian, this class includes, among others, verbs of assertion (*dimostrare/dimonstrate, dire/say esporre/explain, affermare/affirm, confessare/confess, raccontare/tell, ammettere/admit, descrivere/describe*), verbs of negation (*negare/deny*), answering (*rispondere/answer, ricordare/remember*), ways of expression (*recitare/recite*), channel of communication (*telefonare/telephone*), saying of doing or not doing (*chiedere/ask, domandare/demand, pretendere/require*), authorization (*permettere/*allow*), group interchange (*contrattare/negotiate*), wide communication (*diffondere/spread*), verbs of foreseeing (*prevedere/foresee, pronosticare/predict*), verbs of listing (*elencare/list*), verbs of showing (*insegnare/teach*), verbs of promoting (*predicare/preach*), verbs of saying what one will do (*promettere/promise*), verbs of emitting words (*pronunciare/pronounce*), verbs of complaining (*lamentare/lament*), verbs of comparing (*paragonare/compare*). For this class about 200 verbs are listed. It includes [26, §37.7, §37.1, §37.4].

```
Communicative-Attitude
  < Non-Addressee-Oriented,
    Non-Message-Oriented
  #EN:examples=John is chatting with Mary
                about the weather.
  #IT:examples= Giovanni sta chiaccherando con
                Maria sul tempo.
```

Again according to the classification of [15] for Italian, this class includes, among the others, verbs of group interchange (*chiaccherare/chat, dialogare/converse, parlare/speak, scherzare/joke*), verbs of disdain (*spettegolare/gossip*), verbs of ways of expression (*imprecare/imprecate*), verbs of commenting upon (*dissentire/dissent, protestare/protest*), verbs of authorization (*acconsentire/acconsent*), verbs of performing (*rinunciare/renounce*). The class of `Communicative-Attitude` includes verbs reported in [26, §37.5, §37.6, §31.3].

In conclusion, we can see that the abstract categories introduced in the GUM on the basis of general patterns of lexicogrammatical realization found in English, German and Italian provide a semantically motivated, finely discriminating characterization for a wide range of verb classes in both Italian and English.

6 USING GUM

This section briefly reports our experiences in using the GUM for different Natural Language Processing applications. One of the main purposes of GUM is that of making easier the interfacing with other components of a NLP system. Particularly, the linguistic motivations underlying the Upper Model allow a direct interface to the linguistic modules of the system, such as the lexicon and the grammar; moreover, providing a high level of semantic knowledge, GUM is supposed to subsume specific knowledge of the application domain.[4] The basic idea of an Upper Model is to provide semantics for domain concepts and relations on the very general model that natural language grammars presuppose. This provides a very general ontological style that can be applied consistently when confronted with a new domain. The modelling choices are operationalized not only by rules found within the

knowledge representation tool but also by their consequences for natural language encoding as captured in the interface between grammars and upper model.

Additionally, the usability of GUM and its predesessors in different projects is a demonstration of the high level of portability that has been reached in successive refinements of the Upper Model. The following are some of the current projects that are using some version of the Upper Model.

Penman

The Penman text generation project has been using versions of the Upper Model since 1985 for generation in different domains. More recently, participation in the Pangloss machine translation project has resulted in an extensive semantic lexicon (several tens of thousands of items) being subordinated to a slightly modified version of the Upper Model [21, 20]. This demonstrates the potential for scaling up the concepts organized beneath the upper model portion of the hierarchy.

KOMET

The KOMET text generation project [10] has also built on top of the original Upper Model definition since 1989. A merge of a previous German Upper Model and the Penman English model is described in [18, 19]. Texts are being generated in various domains in English, German and Dutch.

TECHDOC

The TECHDOC project [38] aims at multilingual generation of technical documents; to this end several extensions of the original Penman Upper Model have been proposed and implemented. Exploratory studies of extensions for Russian have also been undertaken.

AlFresco

We now consider our experience in the use of GUM in the ALFresco Interactive System [40], developed at IRST. ALFresco is a system allowing the multimodal retrieval of information in the domain of Italian art history. The knowledge base of the system includes the Upper Model, the Domain Model Tbox and the Domain Model Abox, this last including the facts the system is supposed to retrieve. The DM is classified under GUM by means of ISA links, so allowing the inheritance of the information. A DM concept can be placed under several UM concepts, provided that they are compatible each other. The Lexicon provides the maps between words and objects (concepts and relations) of the knowledge base. This architecture has been described in detail in [25] and is currently used for supporting both lexical discrimination and semantic interpretation.

---

[4]Although this does raise some problems, see [10] for an alternative organization.

70

GIST

GIST (Generating multilingual In-Structional Texts) [35] is an EU founded project (LRE 062-09) which addresses the development of a multilingual generation system for the automatic production of texts describing bureaucratic procedures (e.g., the instructions that a citizen has to follow to apply for pension benefits) in three different languages: English, German, and Italian. The final prototype of GIST will integrate and adapt tools developed in the framework of numerous national and international projects. Apart from the domain-related advantages the system will provide (as, for example, the shortening of document production times), it will support also: (a) the parallel production of versions of the same document, avoiding the problems related to translation; (b) the accessibility of an abstract, non-linguistic representation of the documents' content; (c) the possibility of producing similar documents frequently (with respect to the representation/content—i.e., small changes in the knowledge base could imply larger changes in the final texts). The system, currently under development, will use the GUM knowledge base in the process of producing text in Italian, German and English. Relatively to the three languages concerned, GUM plays the role of an 'interlingua'; divergencies and mismatches among the languages are currently handled within the lexicon.

7 FUTURE DEVELOPMENTS AND CONCLUSIONS

Current work includes:

- the extension of the GUM further for languages including (in cooperation with ITRI, Brighton) French and (in cooperation with the University of Sydney) Chinese and Japanese;

- the preparation of automatic natural language analysis into the categories of the GUM;

- the use of the GUM for broader ranges of domain models.

Particular theoretical issues are also being investigated. In [6], for example, we focused on the problem of different structural organizations in GUM, which is mostly process centered, as opposed to Domain Models, which are usually object centered; we proposed a solution based on the extension of the reification mechanism. We are now addressing another crucial issue in the area, namely the problem of "incompatible classifications". This problem arises when the same Domain Model concept can be regarded under different and incompatible points of view which are triggered by different linguistic contexts. This suggests that classifications in the Upper Model have to be considered always in relation to a particular linguistic context in which the concept occurs. When we say that the concept

Milk is classified as a **Substance** we are saying that in the context of sentences like *"John drinks milk"* we consider **Milk** as a **Substance** and that, as far as this classification does not change, the linguistic behavior of **Milk** is that of a mass nouns. However **Milk** can be also considered as an **Artifact**, in which case it behaves as a numerable noun, as in the context of the sentence *"The milks of this zone are the best"*. Other examples involve the shift from the context in which an object is considered a **Concrete-Object** to a context in which the object is considered an **Abstract-Object**: this happens in the sentences *"John put the book on the table"* and *"John reads the book"*. These cases were the core of many studies in the area of the so called "logical polysemy", among which one of the most relevant is the *Generative Lexicon* approach [37]. However, there are no suggestions concerning the way this theory can be concretely realized in a knowledge based system: we think that the Upper Model might plays an important role in connecting lexical representations with conceptual representations.

Finally, we are looking for solutions to the problems of appropriate documentation and dissemination of versions of the GUM for effective evaluation through use. To this end, an extensive new documentation of the GUM based on sophisticated hyperdocument authoring tools will begin in March 1995 at IPSI for all of the languages currently under investigation.

REFERENCES

[1] J. Allgayer, K. Harbusch, A. Kobsa, C. Reddig, N. Reithinger, and D. Schmauks. XTRA: A Natural Language Access System to Expert Systems. *International Journal of Man-Machine Studies*, 31(2):161 – 195, 1989.

[2] J. A. Bateman. Upper modeling: organizing knowledge for natural language processing. In *5th. International Workshop on Natural Language Generation, 3-6 June 1990*, Pittsburgh, PA., 1990. Organized by Kathleen R. McKeown (Columbia University), Johanna D. Moore (University of Pittsburgh) and Sergei Nirenburg (Carnegie Mellon University).

[3] J. A. Bateman. The theoretical status of ontologies in natural language processing. In S. Preuß and B. Schmitz, editors, *Text Representation and Domain Modelling – ideas from linguistics and AI*, pages 50 – 99. KIT-Report 97, Technische Universität Berlin, May 1992. (Papers from KIT-FAST Workshop, Technical University Berlin, October 9th - 11th 1991).

[4] J. A. Bateman. KPML: The KOMET-Penman (Multilingual) Development Environment. Technical report, Institut für Integrierte Publikations- und Informationssysteme (IPSI), GMD, Darmstadt, January 1995. Release 0.7.

[5] J. A. Bateman, R. T. Kasper, J. D. Moore, and R. A. Whitney. A general organization of knowledge for natural language processing: the PENMAN upper model.

Technical report, USC/Information Sciences Institute, Marina del Rey, California, 1990.

[6] J. A. Bateman, B. Magnini, and F. Rinaldi. The Generalized{*Italian, German, English*} *Upper Model*. In *Proceedings of the ECAI94 Workshop: Comparison of Implemented Ontologies*, Amsterdam, 1994.

[7] J. A. Bateman, C. M. Matthiessen, K. Nanri, and L. Zeng. Multilingual text generation: an architecture based on functional typology. In *International Conference on Current Issues in Computational Linguistics*, Penang, Malaysia, 1991. Also available as technical report of the department of Linguistics, University of Sydney.

[8] J. A. Bateman, C. M. Matthiessen, K. Nanri, and L. Zeng. The re-use of linguistic resources across languages in multilingual generation components. In *Proceedings of the 1991 International Joint Conference on Artificial Intelligence, Sydney, Australia*, volume 2, pages 966 – 971. Morgan Kaufmann Publishers, 1991.

[9] J. A. Bateman, C. M. Matthiessen, and L. Zeng. A general architecture for multilinguality in natural language processing. Technical report, GMD/IPSI, Darmstadt and University of Sydney, in preparation.

[10] J. A. Bateman and E. Teich. Selective information presentation in an integrated publication system: an application of genre-driven text generation. *Information Processing and Management, Special Issue on Summarizing Text*, forthcoming.

[11] R. J. Brachman, V. P. Gilbert, and H. J. Levesque. An essential hybrid reasoning system: Knowledge and symbol level accounts of KRIPTON. In *Proceedings of the IJCAI-85*, pages 532–539, Los Angeles, CA, August 1985. IJCAI, Morgan Kaufmann Publishers Inc.

[12] D. Cruse. *Lexical Semantics*. Cambridge University Press, Cambridge, 1986.

[13] G. Erbach. Multi-dimensional inheritance. In H. Trost, editor, *KONVENS '94*, pages 102 – 111, Vienna, 1994.

[14] R. P. Fawcett and G. H. Tucker. Demonstration of GENESYS: a very large, semantically based systemic functional grammar. In *13th. International Conference on Computational Linguistics (COLING-90)*, volume I, pages 47 – 49, Helsinki, Finland, 1990.

[15] A. Goy and L. Lesmo. Representation of verb meaning: The case of Italian communication verbs. In *Proceedings of the Workshop: The Future of the Dictionaries*, Grenoble, October 17–19 1994.

[16] M. A. Halliday. *An Introduction to Functional Grammar*. Edward Arnold, London, 1985.

[17] M. A. Halliday and C. M. Matthiessen. *Construing experience through meaning: a language-based approach to cognition*. de Gruyter, Berlin, to appear.

[18] R. Henschel. Merging the English and the German Upper Model. Technical report, GMD/Institut für Integrierte Publikations- und Informationssysteme, Darmstadt, Germany, 1993.

[19] R. Henschel and J. Bateman. The merged upper model: a linguistic ontology for German and English. In *Proceedings of COLING '94*, Kyoto, Japan, August 1994.

[20] E. Hovy and K. Knight. Motivating shared knowledge resources: an example from the Pangloss collaboration. In *Proceedings of IJCAI Workshop on Knowledge Sharing and Information Interchange*. International Joint Conference on Artificial Intelligence, 1993.

[21] E. Hovy and S. Nirenburg. Approximating an interlingua in a principled way. In *Proceedings of the DARPA Speech and Natural Language Workshop*. Arden House, New York, 1992. Also available from USC/Information Sciences Institute (Marina del Rey, Los Angeles) as Technical Report ISI/RR-93-345, Febuary 1993.

[22] J. Kunze. *Sememstrukturen und Feldstrukturen*, volume XXXVI of *Studia Grammatica*. Akademie Verlag, Berlin, 1993.

[23] J. Kunze and B. Firzlaff. *Sememstrukturen und Feldstrukturen*, volume XXXVI of *Studia Grammatica*. Akademie Verlag, Berlin, 1993.

[24] E. Lang. The LILOG ontology from a linguistic point of view. In O. Herzog and C.-R. Rollinger, editors, *Text understanding in* LILOG: *integrating computational linguistics and artificial intelligence, Final report on the IBM Germany* LILOG-*Project*, pages 464 – 481. Springer-Verlag, Berlin, 1991. Lecture notes in artificial intelligence, 546.

[25] A. Lavelli, B. Magnini, and C. Strapparava. An approach to multilevel semantics for applied systems. In *Proceedings of the 3rd Conference on Applied Natural Language Processing*, pages 17 – 24, Trento, Italy, 31 March – 3 April 1992. Association for Computational Linguistics.

[26] B. Levin. *English Verb Classes and Alternations: a preliminary investigation*. University of Chicago Press, Chicago and London, 1993.

[27] L. Levin. Towards a linking theory of relation changing rules in lfg. Technical Report Report No. CSLI-87-115, Center for the Study of Language and Information, Stanford, California, 1987.

[28] R. MacGregor and R. Bates. The LOOM knowledge representation language. In *Proceedings of the Knowledge-Based Systems Workshop*, 1987. Held in St. Louis, Missouri, April 21-23, 1987. Also available as ISI reprint series report, RS-87-188, USC/Information Sciences Institute, Marina del Rey, CA.

[29] W. C. Mann. Janus abstraction structure – draft 1, 1985. An informal project technical memo of the Janus project at ISI.

[30] W. C. Mann, Y. Arens, C. M. Matthiessen, S. Naberschnig, and N. K. Sondheimer. Janus abstraction structure — draft 2. Technical report, USC/Information Sciences Institute, Marina del Rey, California, October 1985. (Circulated in draft form only.).

[31] C. M. Matthiessen. Lexicogrammatical cartography: English systems. Technical report, University of Sydney, Linguistics Department, 1992. Draft 5.

[32] C. M. Matthiessen, K. Nanri, and L. Zeng. Multilingual generation: dimensions of organization and forms of representation. In R. Dale, E. Hovy, D. Rösner, and O. Stock, editors, *Aspects of automated natural language generation: 6th International Workshop on Natural Language Generation, Trento, Italy, April 1992*, Lecture Notes in Artificial Intelligence No. 587, pages 300–302. Springer-Verlag, Berlin, 1992.

[33] J. D. Moore and Y. Arens. A hierarchy for entities, 1985. USC/Information Sciences Institute, Internal Draft.

[34] N. Nomura, D. A. Jones, and R. C. Berwick. An architecture for a universal lexicon. In *Proceedings of the 15th. International Conference on Computational Linguistics (COLING 94)*, volume I, pages 243 – 249, Kyoto, Japan, 1994.

[35] E. Not and O. Stock. Automatic generation of instructions for citizens in a multilingual community. In *Proceedings of the European Language Engineering Convention*, Paris, France, July 1994.

[36] Penman Project. PENMAN documentation: the Primer, the User Guide, the Reference Manual, and the Nigel manual. Technical report, USC/Information Sciences Institute, Marina del Rey, California, 1989.

[37] J. Pustejovsky. Towards a generative lexicon. *Computational Linguistics*, 17(4), 1991.

[38] D. Rösner and M. Stede. Generating multilingual documents from a knowledge base: the TECHDOC project. In *Proceedings of the 15th. International Conference on Computational Linguistics (COLING 94)*, volume I, pages 339 – 346, Kyoto, Japan, 1994.

[39] E. H. Steiner, U. Eckert, B. Weck, and J. Winter. The development of the EUROTRA-D system of semantic relations. In E. H. Steiner, P. Schmidt, and C. Zelinksy-Wibbelt, editors, *From Syntax to Semantics: insights from Machine Translation*. Frances Pinter, London, 1988.

[40] O. Stock. Natural language and exploration of an information space: The ALFresco interactive system. In *Proceedings of the 12th. International Joint Conference on Artificial Intelligence (IJCAI 91)*, volume 2, pages 972 – 978, Sydney, August 1991. IJCAI, Morgan Kaufmann Publishers Inc.

Ontologies for Very Large Knowledge Bases in Materials Science: a Case Study

Paul E. van der Vet, Piet-Hein Speel and **Nicolaas J.I. Mars**
University of Twente
Enschede, The Netherlands
{vet,speel,mars}@cs.utwente.nl

ABSTRACT

The present paper discusses issues in ontology design, where an illustration is provided by the Plinius ontology of ceramic materials and their properties. In our view, the primary function of an ontology is support for the design and development of possibly large knowledge bases. Other functions, such as that of promoting sharing and reuse, are secondary but in fact follow from careful design. The design issues identified by us (often in retrospect) are discussed with particular emphasis on their utility for developing large knowledge bases. The way these issues are addressed for the Plinius ontology and the ontology itself are discussed in some depth.

1 SETTING AND SCOPE

It has been submitted that ontologies play an important role in the development of large knowledge bases [17]. They enable disciplined development and better maintenance. In the present paper, we will identify ways in which an ontology may fulfill these functions. In a recent workshop on implemented ontologies [18], the participants in the final discussion agreed that there is currently no systematic way, let alone a recipe, for building ontologies. Ontology development can be called a craft rather than a science. We will present some design guidelines that have proven useful in our own research. We have gained practical experience with very large knowledge bases in a number of KL-ONE-like systems in the course of a Ph.D. research ([26,27]; for CLASSIC, see also section 5.3). Although the experience is limited, it supports the ideas set out in this paper.

A case study will serve as illustration throughout. This case study involves an ontology of ceramic materials and their properties. The ontology is still under development. It is part of the Plinius project which aims at building a system for semi-automatic knowledge acquisition from natural-language texts. More detailed information on the ontology itself [31,32,33] and on the Plinius project in general [20,21,30] is available elsewhere. In the discussion, we will sometimes have to address domain knowledge issues in some depth. Indeed, it is part of our standpoint on ontology development that such issues are essential for achieving useful ontologies. As a corollary, an ontology should not only be submitted to an AI audience, but also to workers in the relevant domain. The latter has been done for major parts of the Plinius ontology [31,32].

The paper first discusses the major design decisions we have identified (often in retrospect). Section 2 discusses design decisions that are relevant to ontologies for large knowledge bases in general, while section 3 details some of the general design decisions and introduces some others that are specific for Plinius. Section 4 then presents a summary of the Plinius ontology and section 5 discusses various representations and implementations of the ontology.

2 GENERAL DESIGN DECISIONS FOR ONTOLOGIES

2.1 Function

We approach the subject of ontologies from an engineering perspective. We regard the design of an ontology as an essential step in the design and actual implementation of knowledge bases and knowledge-based systems. The importance of the availability of an ontology is particularly evident when the knowledge base gets large [17].

The main point here is that of *surveyability*. An ontology offers a vocabulary of unambiguous domain-related concepts. The meaning of the concepts has to be anchored in consensus domain knowledge. The ontology has to be *limitative*: it has to embrace every concept that is needed. (This may necessitate intensional definitions.) Since the ontology is exhaustive, it tells what can be expected in the knowledge base in terms of scope (which domain) and granularity (which distinctions). We believe that the requirement of being exhaustive is essential: without it, the ontology's utility is impaired.

Genesereth and Nilsson ([8], Chapter 2) present an approach to designing knowledge-based systems that involves three stages: *conceptualization*, in which we identify the objects in our domain of interest and their interrelations; *formalization*, in which we write out the state of affairs in a formal language; and *implementation*, in which the system is implemented. The conceptualization can be regarded as a specification of the knowledge that in the course of the second step, formalization, is to be represented in some representation language. Genesereth and Nilsson provide a simple illustration in the form of yet another blocks world. The conceptualization here consists of (i) a set of names of blocks and (ii) sets of tuples that stand for the relations between the blocks.

We regard the ontology as being part of the conceptualization. The ontology only tells which concepts we choose to recognize and which relations may hold between them, but (in contrast to what is the case in the example of Genesereth and Nilsson) it does not describe any particular state of affairs. To arrive at a full conceptualization we will have to add a description of the state of affairs; and since we have an ontology, we will do so in terms derived from the ontology. For another and more intricate view on the relations between ontology, conceptualization, and formalization, see [12].

To pursue the blocks world example, an ontology for the blocks world would list the blocks (either as flat names or in a more intricate way) but it would not specify which relations hold between them. Instead, the ontology would define the relations that might hold between blocks. This only provides a language for talking about the blocks world. It is not a full conceptualization, because we have not yet specified which relations actually hold between the blocks. This is specified in the rest of the conceptualization, which makes use of the vocabulary given by the ontology.

For a simple world like the blocks world, separate development of an ontology does not pay. But for real applications the conceptualization is much more difficult. It is worth the trouble to develop the vocabulary separately, as a first step toward a full conceptualization. One advantage is that, in an ontology, we can specify general structural aspects of our domain as distinct from the specification of the actual state of affairs. This is already apparent if we make the blocks world a bit more complex, by allowing for sides and edges as extra objects. We will want to distinguish between blocks, sides, and edges, even if only by the simple expedient of introducing three sets of objects rather than a single set. We can then achieve further clarity by adding structure to the ontology, for instance by demanding that every side is a side of a block, that every edge is an edge between two sides, and so on. These demands hold no matter which side forms part of which block or which edge is an edge between which two sides.

In further steps in developing a knowledge-based system, the ontology can be used to govern further choices. As has been said above, the conceptualization can be regarded as a specification of the knowledge that in the course of the second step, formalization, is to be represented in some representation language. A representation language is required to be a logical language with well-defined syntax and semantics. Logical constants and their associated inferential properties can be treated as being given. The ontology is required to supply the meaning of *every* non-logical constant that occurs in the representation.

The ontology used this way also supports *modularization* of the knowledge base, another measure aimed at surveyability. The knowledge can be distributed over a number of knowledge bases and even be expressed in different representation languages because the ontology serves to unify the knowledge bases cooperating within a single system.

The function of an ontology implies that it has to be independent of any particular choice of knowledge representation language. One rather obvious reason is, that the ontology contains (incomplete) specifications of the knowledge base(s) to be built. The knowledge representation language has to be chosen so as to meet the specifications. Another advantage is the support of modularization, already mentioned above. More generally, an ontology supports sharing and reuse [9,23].

2.2 Implicit rather than explicit definitions of concepts

Large knowledge bases will contain very many concepts. Listing them all exhaustively in an ontology is not only a lot of work, it is also inefficient. Structure can be added in such a way that many concepts can be defined in terms of other concepts. The advantage is parsimonious design since most concepts can be defined implicitly rather than be enumerated explicitly. We call this the principle of conceptual construction kit. An ontology built according to this principle consists of atomic concepts, serving as primitives, and construction rules that define all other concepts. The non-atomic concepts are implicitly defined. Formally, the ontology is given as a tuple $\langle \mathcal{A}, \mathcal{C} \rangle$ with $\mathcal{A}$ the set of atomic concepts and $\mathcal{C}$ the set of construction rules. The tuple can be seen as a calculus with $\mathcal{A}$ the alphabet and $\mathcal{C}$ the transformation rules. The deductive closure of this calculus produces the explicit list of concepts.

2.3 Knowledge as assertions about entities

Scientific knowledge is the kind of knowledge primarily studied by us. In science, it is vital to be able to assess whether a new proposal is in conflict with what we already know. For a knowledge base with scientific knowledge, a similar requirement holds. In a first approximation, the problem is solved in science by distinguishing between defining and non-defining properties of entities. Well-known entities recognized or postulated by science include animal species, genes, molecules, elementary particles, planets, and much more. Brachman and Levesque seem to address this issue when they distinguish between terminological adequacy, which involves correct usage of the technical vocabulary, and assertional adequacy, which involves correct theories about the world [4]. They do not, however, address the issue of conflicts.

Knowledge can be viewed as consisting of assertions about entities. Two assertions can only conflict if they are about the same entity, and this can be found out by inspecting the defining properties of the entities. This strategy can be adopted for scientific knowledge bases, so that the detection of conflicts can be automated.

The principle of knowledge as assertions about entities requires decisions on the entities of interest in the domain, and on the properties deemed defining. This is a non-trivial matter. The biological species of elephant cannot be equated with the set of its instances. Rather, it is an abstraction. That is why Clyde can miss a leg and still be an elephant (compare [3]). Such abstractions have not been widely studied. Default logics, which are often discussed in this context, address situations involving incomplete information. In abstraction, however, the information is sufficient but we choose to use only a part of it. It appears that much research remains to be done. Meanwhile we can at least be aware of the fact that approaching concepts as corresponding to sets of instances is a coarse approximation.

3 DESIGN DECISIONS IN THE PLINIUS ONTOLOGY

3.1 Function

In Plinius, the ontology offers a limitative list of concepts dealing with ceramic materials, their properties, and the processes to make them. The knowledge contents of the various resources of the system (a lexicon with deep semantics and a background knowledge base) and the knowledge level format of the output of the process are required to be expressed in ontology concepts. Although Plinius is developed using a predetermined corpus, we have tried to steer away from *ad hoc* decisions that would become an obstacle if the process were upscaled to larger corpora. Our main

strategy has been to develop the ontology relatively independently of the particular corpus, anchoring it in more general, accepted domain knowledge instead. The domain knowledge has been taken from widely used textbooks such as [15]. Following this strategy takes a solid background in the relevant discipline.

The independence of particular representation languages has been achieved in the Plinius ontology by expressing it in the well-understood language of sets and tuples. Independence of particular representation languages is demonstrated by the fact that the Plinius ontology has been represented and implemented in a great variety of languages and systems for the Ph.D. research of one of us [26]. The version of Summer 1994 has been implemented in the KL-ONE systems CLASSIC, C-CLASSIC, BACK, BACK++, KRIS, and LOOM; and in Ontolingua version 4. A Prolog version is under development. An older version has been implemented in Ontolingua version 3, Prolog, LIFE, and three KL-ONE systems, the TAXON part of the COLAB system and, again, LOOM and CLASSIC. In addition, this older version has been represented but not implemented in Conceptual Graphs and L_{LILOG}. As far as we are aware no other ontology has been implemented in so many different ways.

3.2 The bottom-up conceptual construction kit

There are various ways to build a conceptual construction kit. KL-ONE-like systems seem to imply a modern variant of the Aristotelian *genus-species* approach, where the *species* are differentiated from the *genus* and from each other by means of *differentiae* (roles in KL-ONE). By contrast, our approach is based on *atomism*. Atomism proceeds bottom-up in that it builds objects out of smaller objects. Chemical elements, kinds of atoms, are among the more important atomic concepts. The construction rules construct concepts for more complex assemblies. Each construction rule is written as a definition that expresses constraints on the construction of every complex concept of the type in question.

Atomism implies a layered ontology, where the entities at each layer (save the lowest) are constituted of entities at one level lower. Thus, atoms compose molecules, collections of molecules compose substances, substances compose phases, and so on. The properties we ascribe to the entities can differ from one layer to the other, as in fact is the case for chemistry. We can ascribe an atomic number to atoms but not to molecules or substances; we can ascribe a melting point to substances but not to atoms or molecules, and so on. If, in the ontology, we include relations to express properties we will have to add constraints to ensure that the correct properties are ascribed.

An added advantage of the bottom-up approach is

that it allows for the definition of *all* relevant concepts of a given type in a single step. This is important for Plinius. Although we can easily assemble a list of all concepts occurring in our corpus, we do not want to re-design the whole ontology when we move to other corpora. Thus, we need a design that within the scope of the Plinius application in principle accommodates every concept of interest.

Consider, for an illustration, chemical concepts for pure substances. Pure substances, like table salt (NaCl) or water (H_2O) consist of chemical elements in whole number proportions. When chemical elements and natural numbers are given as atomic concepts, an appropriate construction rule defines every pure substance there is and many (technically, infinitely many) more besides. (Readers with a chemical background will note that isomerism poses some problems. These are, however, immaterial for the purposes of the present illustration.)

In Fregean terms, all concepts have sense but only some have reference. Since the concepts are defined implicitly, there is no burden on the system. The construction moreover anticipates new developments to some extent. Thus, 40 years ago chemists generally held that noble gases such as helium and xenon do not form compounds. This belief was shown unfounded by Bartlett's synthesis of $XePtF_6$ in 1962; other noble gas compounds soon followed. An ontology with explicit definitions of concepts for pure substances would have had to be rewritten in 1962, while a Plinius-like ontology would already have contained the concept implicitly.

3.3 Implicit definition of taxonomies

The bottom-up approach utilizing sets and tuples not only allows for parsimonious implicit definition of most concepts, but also for implicit definition of taxonomies. The logical basis is λ-abstraction over sets. We write `arbitrary`(X), where X is a set, to mean that for the concept that contains this term it is immaterial which element of X is substituted.

For a simple illustration, consider again concepts for pure substances. Starting with a concept for any amino acid, we can derive the concept for amino acid in general by substituting an appropriate `arbitrary`(X) for all parts of the specification save those that specify the NH_2- and COOH-parts of the molecule. The procedure can be repeated. Substitution of COOH by `arbitrary`(X) yields a concept for amino compounds, and substitution of the only remaining specific part, that for amino, finally yields the concept for pure substance in general.

3.4 What are the entities?

The principle of knowledge as assertions about entities poses problems for the conceptualization of the domain

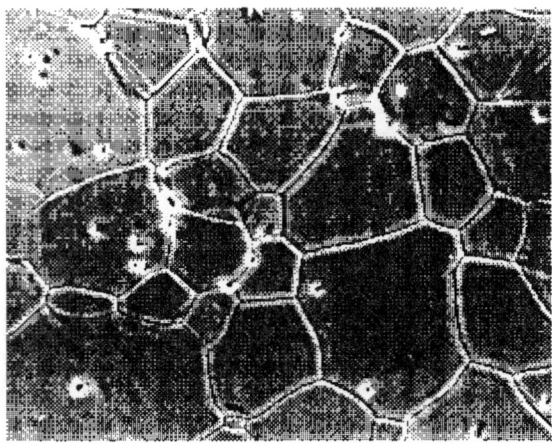

Figure 1: THE MICROSTRUCTURE OF A CERAMIC MATERIAL. This photograph shows a cross-cut of a typical ceramic sample, coarse-grained zirconia (ZrO_2) which is stabilized by 17 wt% Y_2O_3 and densified by heat treatment at 1550 °C. The average grain size of the present sample is 8 ± 2 μm, while abnormal grain growth has resulted in the presence of smaller grains (about 2 μm). The photograph also shows a number of included pores, visible as black spots surrounded by white. Photograph courtesy of the Inorganic Materials Science Group, University of Twente.

of ceramics. In the first approximation, the material's chemical composition is the primary defining property. But having only the chemical composition as defining property is too coarse-grained for materials science.

Ceramic materials come in two variants: glasses and polycrystalline materials. Polycrystalline materials consist of a large number of so-called grains. In between the grains and in the grains themselves there might be pores. The structure of the material at the scale of grains is called the *microstructure*, see figure 1. Since a great number of important properties of materials are determined not only by the chemical composition but also by the microstructure, the microstructure has to be added as the second defining property.

The scheme thus initially has ceramic materials for entities and chemical composition and microstructure as defining properties. Other choices would have been possible. For instance, Bachmann and Steffens [2], working in a top-down way, have an abbreviated specification of chemical composition and certain ranges of values of Young's modulus (determined under standard conditions) for defining properties. Our choice has been motivated by the consideration that, according to consensus knowledge in the domain, the properties called defining by us are held causally responsible for the values of all other properties. Thus, a materials scientist would attribute a particular value of Young's modulus to the material's chemical composition and microstructure (even though in the majority of cases Young's modulus cannot be actually predicted when chemical composition and microstructure are known).

Usage of the microstructure as defining property poses the difficult problem of choosing the right level of abstraction. The best possible description of the microstructure lists properties such as geometry, chemical composition, and aggregation state, of each and every grain in the sample and thus makes every sample unique. However, such a description is seldom, if ever, available. Worse, the level of detail is wrong. Materials science aims to generate assertions that can be used by others and therefore incorporate abstractions. The level of abstraction can be chosen anywhere in a continuum with the grain-for-grain description on one extreme and a bare specification of the chemical composition on the other. An ontology ideally provides the whole range, so that the appropriate level can be chosen depending on the application.

Since the microstructure is determined by the production process, one also finds materials specified by telling how they can be produced. The specification of the production process then serves as an indirect specification of the microstructure. Mixed specifications also occur. One attractive feature of specifying the production process is that it solves the problem of choosing the appropriate level of generalization. If the process is sufficiently controlled, the samples produced will exhibit a number of predictable properties. Some spread in microstructural detail will inevitably remain, but apparently it does not matter. For an ontology, this means that it has to accommodate specifications of materials involving production processes.

In the Plinius corpus, the texts typically specify microstructure only superficially. The caption of figure 1, although not taken from the corpus, gives a fair impression of the level of detail. What we have considered above can be paraphrased by saying that a whole range of different pictures would have been covered by the same caption. Since it is often unclear which microstructural changes affect particular properties of interest, any specification can turn out to be incomplete. This means that any specification of a microstructure at a level above that of the precise grain-for-grain specification covers a class of materials rather than a single material.

To accommodate the state of affairs, the Plinius ontology construes materials as abstractions from *samples*. Each sample is unique. In the analysis of input texts, Plinius initially interprets every reference to a material as reference to a sample and assigns a unique label to it. The label itself is interpreted as a sample characteristic and serves as shorthand for local production conditions.

The connection between sample and material can be made by means of two predicates, `said-to-consist-of` and `consists-of`. The `said-to-consist-of` predicate is used to express that the authors of a certain text claim that their sample consists of a particular material. Such an assertion is true no matter what the sample composition really is. The `consists-of` predicate expresses the quite different assertion that a sample consists of a particular material.

An alternative is presented in the context of the ALADIN project, which was concerned with knowledge-based support for the design of aluminium alloys [6, 13,14,25]. Microstructure is specified largely in qualitative terms. For our purposes, the ALADIN solution allows too few choices for representing microstructure and, moreover, does not address the issue of samples as distinct from materials.

4 THE PLINIUS ONTOLOGY

4.1 Overview

The complete Plinius ontology cannot be presented for lack of space. We will give a fairly comprehensive treatment of the ontology of chemical composition of ceramic materials, but more detailed considerations underlying the choices made had to be skipped. The ontologies of properties and of materials will be summarized only, while the ontology of processes is omitted.

The basic idea throughout is to apply the principle of bottom-up conceptual construction kit. We have atomic concepts, distributed over different sets for clarity, and a restricted number of construction rules to define the so-called complex concepts. The construction rules are expressed as definitions that impose constraints on the construction of concepts. Each construction rule implicitly defines a set of complex concepts of the same type. The concepts themselves appear as expressions involving sets and tuples that (within the context of this ontology) coincide with their definitions. Concepts can be given names for pragmatic reasons, but such names do not form part of the ontology itself. To avoid ambiguities, the expressions that define sets of complex concepts are written as fully formal intensional definitions of sets using first-order predicate logic with sets and equality. This must be regarded as a convenient way to express definitions rather than as an attempt to design a fully formal conceptualization.

The definitions are such that it is possible to determine the type of each concept automatically, provided that the concept is taken from the ontology. However, the definitions do not specify the relations between concepts of different types. The conclusion is, that complex concepts are defined to the extent that they can always be assigned to the correct type automatically and are primitive in the sense that there is no way to automatically reason about their relations if they are of different types. One way to solve the problem partly is to define special relations to hold between complex concepts of different types. An obvious candidate is the part-of relation (see also below).

In formalizing the complex concepts in some knowledge representation language, they might be expressed in a different manner. But let us suppose that we want to formalize in a way that preserves the conceptual structures defined by the ontology as much as possible. We would then use a language with complex terms that correspond to complex concepts and predicates that correspond to the relations between concepts. The language can be first-order since we do not need to quantify over predicates, but it has to provide the ability to make inferences utilizing the structure of complex terms and their constituents. For example, the Plinius ontology provides an implicit definition of taxonomies such that we can make a superconcept c_1 out of a concept c_2 (see section 3.3). An obvious predicate that makes the relation between c_1 and c_2 explicit is $\texttt{subconcept}(x, y)$, meaning that x is a subconcept of y. We require the language to be such that the truth of the assertion $\texttt{subconcept}(c_2, c_1)$ can be inferred on the basis of the structures and constituents of c_1 and c_2.

4.2 Chemical composition

In chemistry, glasses and polycrystalline materials are instances of *systems*. Systems come in two sorts according to whether there are macroscopic inhomogeneities (where "macroscopic" refers to a level above that of atoms and molecules). The grain boundaries visible in figure 1 are examples of such inhomogeneities. When no inhomogeneities are present, the system is called homogeneous.

Systems consist of one or more *phases*. The concept of phase is notoriously difficult and we will not attempt to elucidate it here (see, *e.g.*, [1], chapter 7). A phase is characterized by its chemical composition and by its aggregation state. Homogeneous systems by definition consist of a single phase. Systems with macroscopic inhomogeneities consist of one or more phases; in the latter case, they are called heterogeneous.

A phase, in turn, consists of one or more substances in certain proportions. Substances, finally, consist of chemical elements. The ontology is built up in the reverse order. For lack of space, we will not detail the ontology in full. Instead, we will give a flavor of what it is like by giving the construction rules for pure substance concepts, and then discuss the other constructs more summarily.

4.3 Atomic concepts

For an ontology of pure substances we need the following atomic concepts, distributed over different sets for clarity:

Chemical elements as characterized by atomic number and identified by their standardized chemical symbol. Examples include Na, H, O, Ca. The set of chemical elements is called E.

Natural numbers as defined in number theory (where 'natural number' is interpreted in the classical sense as an integer > 0); the set is called N.

It is allowed to single out specific subsets of these sets and give them names. For example, the set $Hal \subset E$, defined as $Hal =_{\text{Df}} \{\text{F}, \text{Cl}, \text{Br}, \text{I}\}$, is the set of halogens.

4.4 Construction rules for pure substances

Within the domain of ceramics, a substance is unambiguously specified by its so-called gross formula, which gives the constituent chemical elements and their proportions. We will not consider non-stoichiometric compounds here, so that the proportions are natural numbers. Such substances are called *pure substances*. Compared to the gross formula, we have added detail in the form of the introduction of the concept of *group*. A group corresponds to a molecular subunit of a pure substance (for ionic substances, each ion corresponds to a group). In this picture, groups are composed of chemical elements and pure substances of groups.

Groups are added for two reasons. (1) The unambiguous nature of the gross formula is a contingency. Adding detail anticipates the advent of certain ambiguities caused by isomerism. This is not sufficient for handling isomerism in general. Structural isomerism can be handled by expressing molecules as graphs. The idea to use graphs to conceptualize molecules is widely used in AI (*e.g.*, [7,16,22]) and for other computational purposes (*e.g.*, [24]). Groups can be considered abstractions of graphs since they list the nodes but omit the edges. For handling stereo-isomerism, the geometry of the molecule has to be specified. However, in ceramics science we do not expect cases of isomerism other than those that can be handled by groups. (2) Adding detail considerably facilitates the conversion of our concepts into systematic names or formulae and *vice versa*.

A group is expressed as a set of tuples $\langle e, n \rangle$ with $e \in E$ and $n \in N$. For chemical reasons, no chemical element can occur in more than one tuple in the same set. This gives rise to the following definition:

Definition 1 (Group) *A group is any member of the set GR defined as*

$$GR =_{\text{Df}} \{g \mid g \subset E \times N \ \wedge \ g \neq \emptyset \ \wedge$$
$$\forall vwxy[(\langle v, x \rangle \in g \wedge \langle w, y \rangle \in g \wedge x \neq y) \rightarrow v \neq w]\}$$

The last clause in the intensional specification of set GR rules out that a chemical element occurs in more than one tuple in the expression for a group g. g is a set of tuples. Consider the case that two tuples $\langle v, x\rangle$ and $\langle w, y\rangle$ form part of the same set g. v and w are chemical elements and x and y are natural numbers. For v and w we have two possibilities: either $v \neq w$ (which is always allowed) or $v = w$. The latter case is allowed only if also $x = y$, because then we have just listed the same tuple twice and from a set-theoretic viewpoint there is actually only one tuple.

The pattern is repeated for pure substances. Thus, a pure substance is expressed as a set of tuples $\langle g, n\rangle$ with $g \in GR$ and $n \in N$. For chemical reasons, no group can occur in more than one tuple in the same set. The set of pure substances is called PS. We obtain:

Definition 2 (Pure substance) *A pure substance is any member of the set PS defined as*

$$PS =_{\mathrm{Df}} \{s \mid s \subset GR \times N \ \wedge \ s \neq \emptyset \ \wedge$$
$$\forall vwxy[(\langle v, x\rangle \in s \wedge \langle w, y\rangle \in s \wedge x \neq y) \rightarrow v \neq w]\}$$

In these two definitions, part-of relations are implicitly present. Each concept is written as a set of tuples, and the first member of each tuple is a part of the whole defined by the set.

By way of a simple example, consider the concept for barium titanate $BaTiO_3$. We need two groups, $g_1 =_{\mathrm{Df}} \{\langle Ba, 1\rangle\}_{GR}$ and $g_2 =_{\mathrm{Df}} \{\langle Ti, 1\rangle, \langle O, 3\rangle\}_{GR}$ (where the subscript GR serves as a reminder of the kind of concept). The concept for barium titanate then is seen to be $\{\langle g_1, 1\rangle, \langle g_2, 1\rangle\}_{PS}$.

4.5 Toward an ontology of materials

The pattern of definitions 1 and 2 is repeated for the definitions of the composition of phases in terms of pure substances and of the composition of systems in terms of phases. As a complicating factor, a phase is not only characterized by its composition but also by its aggregation state. Therefore the proper definition of a phase consists of composition plus aggregation state. For systems, a marker is added to specify whether there are macroscopic boundary planes or not. This is sufficient for the ontology of the chemical composition of materials. The complete Ontolingua version of this ontology can be inspected through WWW at URL http://wwwis.cs.utwente.nl:8080/kbs/ontology/homepage.html. This is also the site where future versions and extensions will be made available.

4.6 Quantitative properties

We now turn to the ontology of quantitative properties. These properties, such as melting point, four-point bending strength, and Vickers hardness are often specified as a single quantity value. For a discussion about quantities, quantity values, and measurement

units, see [17] and [19]. Gruber and Olsen [11] have presented an interesting ontology of physical quantities. In a first approximation, a quantity value can be expressed as a tuple that consists of an absolute value and a unit. For Plinius, the canonical expression of a quantity value involves a unit taken from the *Système International*. Gruber and Olsen argue that quantity values cannot be expressed as tuples consisting of an absolute value and a unit. They state that the tuples $\langle 3, \text{feet}\rangle$ and $\langle 1, \text{yard}\rangle$ are different, even though they express the same quantity value since three feet is by definition equal to a yard. We miss their point. We agree that the tuples, as they stand, are not equal but we fail to see how that rules out the use of tuples. The existence of many systems of measurement units in fact makes use of tuples attractive because we have to know which units are used. Special procedures will have to be added to convert those tuples into some canonical form. Sameness of quantity value can be determined for canonical expressions directly and for other expressions through use of the conversion procedures.

The specification of a property as a single quantity value must be called a shorthand notation. A melting point is always determined at a particular pressure, and the pressure forms part of the property. This argument can be generalized. A melting point, including specification of the pressure, is itself a point taken from the p–T phase diagram (where p stands for pressure and T for thermodynamic temperature). A p–T phase diagram for a substance consists of a number of lines in the p–T plane, where each line corresponds to the set of values of p and T at which two aggregation states co-exist. At the melting points, one of the solid states and the liquid state co-exist. It is proper to say that the p–T phase diagram, rather than a single point on it, is the property at issue.

In the same vein, four-point bending strength and Vickers hardness are determined by complex tests. The outcome depends on many conditions (temperature, pressure, load, loading rate, ...) and the values found are expected to be different under different conditions. From a logical point of view, this means that a property is a relation between the quantity value at issue and the quantity values that specify all those conditions. The mathematical expression for a relation is a set of tuples.

In the Plinius ontology, a quantitative property is defined as a set of tuples of quantity values. For example, the p–T phase diagram for a substance can be expressed as a set Ph:

$$Ph = \{\langle p, t, a\rangle \mid p \in P \wedge t \in T \wedge a \in Ag\}$$

where P is a set of pressure values and T is a set of temperature values. It is understood that the members of P and T are themselves tuples involving (at least) a value and a unit. The set Ag contains all possible combinations of two different aggregation states:

$$Ag =_{\mathrm{Df}} \{\langle x,y \rangle \mid x \in A \wedge y \in A \wedge x \neq y\}$$

(where A is the set of aggregation states) so that a can be used to specify which two phases co-exist at the given p and t.

The set that corresponds to a property does not have to be specified completely. Often, it will include only a single tuple (as when only the melting point at standard pressure is known).

4.7 The ontology of materials

We are now in a position to outline the conceptualization of materials as found in the Plinius corpus. Materials are systems, so one ingredient of any concept of a material will be the specification of the system.

A second ingredient, the microstructure, has to be added for inhomogeneous systems. The microstructure can be specified as a set of properties that express microstructural quantities determined under certain conditions. For Plinius, typical microstructural properties are the average grain size and the porosity.

This conceptualization partitions the set of properties into two subsets: the set Mic of defining properties for materials (*i.e.*, microstructural properties) and the set Non of non-defining properties such as melting point, fracture toughness, and Young's modulus. The indirect way to specify microstructure, by specifying the production process of the material, will not be considered here.

The third ingredient is what we have called the material tag. Ceramics are made in a number of steps. The system at each step can be distinguished from the corresponding systems at other steps if sufficient microstructural information and background knowledge is given. The level of detail in the corpus does not support these distinctions. Moreover, the amount of background knowledge that has to be added to enable the distinctions is rather large. Within Plinius, this background knowledge would fulfill no other purpose. Therefore we have adopted a typical engineering solution by introducing a new set T of atomic concepts called material tags. The material tags correspond to stages in the production process; for now, the set comprises the labels `powder`, `greenling`, and `finished`.

5 REPRESENTATIONS AND IMPLEMENTATIONS OF THE PLINIUS ONTOLOGY

The Plinius ontology at various stages of maturity has been represented and implemented in a large number of representation languages and systems. To get a flavor of the problems encountered and the solutions chosen, a few issues will be addressed here. The languages chosen are: Ontolingua/KIF, CLASSIC, and Prolog.

5.1 Ontolingua

The Ontolingua language, written in KIF, is developed specifically for the purpose of portable ontology specifications. The system now comes with a syntax checker and a number of programs to translate an Ontolingua specification into other representations. The translations only cover the constructions that are specific for Ontolingua; KIF is so expressive that automatic translation into other languages is a long way off. Ontolingua and KIF are developed in the context of the Knowledge Sharing Effort [23]; for background information on Ontolingua, see [10]. Since Ontolingua is not designed as a language for operational use, an Ontolingua specification is a representation rather than an implementation of an ontology. Ontolingua is rapidly becoming a widely used language for representing ontologies. In the workshop on implemented ontologies [18], six out of the total of thirteen presented ontologies have been represented in Ontolingua.

The representation of extensionally defined sets of atomic concepts is easy in Ontolingua as it has a special construct for these cases. However, Ontolingua requires that additionally each member of an extensionally specified set is introduced separately. This is inconvenient but not problematic. The intensionally defined sets of atomic concepts in Plinius cover numbers. Complex numbers and certain subsets (real and natural numbers) are built in, so that no problems were encountered for those sets.

The Ontolingua representation however became problematic for the construction rules. Available Ontolingua constructs do cover sets of tuples, but there is no provision for constraints such as the constraint that rules out the occurrence of the same element in more than one tuple in the same group (compare definition 1 and the surrounding text). Since KIF contains full first-order predicate logic with equality and sets, such constraints can be expressed in 'pure' KIF. Ontolingua allows inclusion of KIF statements in definitions, but the translation programs do not support them. As a result, portability is only ensured for other KIF applications.

The extension to cover implicit definition of taxonomies by means of `arbitrary` has not yet been realized. KIF has an operator for λ-abstraction, so this extension appears feasible. However, this construct, too, is only portable to other KIF applications.

5.2 Prolog

Development of the Prolog version of the Plinius ontology is underway. When viewed as an exercise in logic programming, the Prolog version can be considered a representation in a particular subset of first-order predicate logic. Since this version can be run on a computer it can also be called an implementation, even though in the current version no measures have been taken to

81

improve efficiency. The background for this exercise has been provided largely by the approach taken by 29.

The Prolog version of the ontology now developed consists of so-called type predicates. Type predicates in the Prolog ontology are unary predicates that take a concept as argument and return true only if the concept is of a particular type. The full set of type predicates unambiguously defines the ontology concepts. An obvious extension, actually realized, introduces an additional predicate `type/2` that returns the type of a given concept. Mark that the same approach is in principle possible in Common Lisp. New types can be declared in Common Lisp by means of `declare` and `the` forms (28, chapters 4 and 9). Appropriate functions return true if they are given an argument of the intended type. The difference between an assertion that is true or false on the one hand, and a function that returns a Boolean value on the other is not that large.

In our Prolog version, the extensionally specified sets of atomic concepts become lists. For the sets of numbers, use has been made of the standard type predicates `integer/1` and `real/1` in a straightforward way.

Complex concepts are written using sets and tuples. Both can be written in Prolog as lists. In practice, it is beneficial to be able to distinguish between sets represented as lists and tuples represented as lists. This has been done by introducing each such list as the single argument of a functor `set(...)` or `tuple(...)`. The necessary operations are defined only for the lists that are arguments of the appropriate functors. Although many Prologs in use today have library predicates for sets, those predicates are not (yet) defined in the current proposal for standard Prolog. To ensure portability, we have written our own predicates that come with the ontology.

Predicates able to recognize subconcept constitute the Prolog version of the `arbitrary` function. This issue has not been addressed so far.

5.3 Classic

Finally, the CLASSIC implementation provides interesting comparisons. CLASSIC is a member of the KL-ONE family of representation systems. It offers a restricted set of inferences with the advantage that its worst-case complexity is polynomial. Background information on CLASSIC is given by [5]. The CLASSIC version has been used in a comparison with other KL-ONE-like systems to measure runtime performance in classification tasks involving thousands of concepts and tens of thousands of assertions [27]. The experience has underlined the importance of possessing an ontology when dealing with large knowledge bases.

The CLASSIC implementation differs substantially from the Ontolingua and Prolog versions discussed above. This is due partly to efficiency considerations, partly to the restrictions imposed by CLASSIC. The extensionally specified sets of atomic concepts are implemented in CLASSIC in a straightforward way, namely by means of the `cl-define-disjoint-primitive` construct.

In the present CLASSIC implementation, however, numbers are treated differently. Instead of having numbers as atomic concepts, they are used exclusively as cardinality restrictions on the `at-least` and `at-most` constructs. One advantageous side-effect is a great efficiency improvement. Only natural numbers are allowed, so the use of real numbers has to be simulated. This has been done by multiplying all reals by a large integer value. For instance, the fractions to be specified in a complex concept for a phase are then expressed as integers > 0 and, say, $< 10^6$. The value of the upper bound can be chosen such that the error introduced this way is smaller than the random error of the empirically determined values. An alternative would be to use TEST functions. This alternative, however, carries disadvantages: TEST functions can only be applied to individuals; part of the formalization becomes procedural; and portability to other KL-ONE-like systems is severely impaired.

The approach for complex concepts in the CLASSIC version can again be illustrated for concepts for groups. There is a parent role defined for the concept group, with a value restriction to chemical elements. There are exactly 103 child roles, each with a value restriction to a particular chemical element. Since chemical elements are defined as disjoint primitives, no chemical element can occur as filler of two roles of the same group. The role that relates any particular group to chemical elements in general has an `at-most` m cardinality restriction, where m is the number of occurrences of chemical elements in the group. The proportion n of each chemical element separately is specified by means of the cardinality restrictions `at-least` n and `at-most` n on subroles. The effect of the `at-most` m cardinality restriction is to disallow changes (such as addition of a chemical element or changing n) in groups once they are defined.

As an important side-effect, certain versions of `arbitrary` are easily accommodated. The corollary of `arbitrary` in CLASSIC amounts to leaving out cardinality restrictions on roles. CLASSIC then assumes that roles can be added (subject to constraints imposed by roles attached to the parent concept), which is another way of expressing what `arbitrary` means.

6 CONCLUDING REMARKS

In the present paper we have discussed a particular ontology intended for use with very large knowledge bases at some length. The practical success achieved in particular with the implementation in several KL-ONE-like systems has convinced us that we are on the right track. Here, we want to reiterate the more important lessons learned by us in the course of the research.

(1) An ontology has to serve as a limitative list of concepts into which all knowledge is to be expressed. With respect to representation, the ontology serves as a specification. It has to supply the meaning of every non-logical constant occurring in the representation. The ontology may thus influence the choice of representation language, which is a separate problem.

(2) As a corollary to the first point, an ontology has to developed independently from any *particular* representation language or implementation. However, the kind of ontologies we are discussing are designed for computational purposes. It makes sense to avoid constructions that we know will be hard or impossible to represent at all.

(3) Ontology development currently is a craft rather than a science. This situation is unwanted. We have identified some issues that may contribute to more systematic ways of ontology development. These include: the use of implicit definitions for the majority of concepts (not supported by systems that require explicit, unique names for concepts) and the conceptualization of the domain as being concerned with assertions about entities, including a partitioning of the set of properties into defining and non-defining properties.

(4) We have also found that developing an ontology for a mature scientific or engineering domain takes expertise at an advanced level. In fact, such ontologies are best designed by researchers who are at home both in AI and in the domain in question. Very many decisions at a small scale depend on trade-offs between doing full justice to the domain on the one hand and wishing to introduce certain restrictions for computational purposes on the other. The ontology developer has to be aware of both.

REFERENCES

[1] P.W. Atkins, *Physical chemistry*, Oxford University Press, Oxford, 1982, 2nd edition.

[2] Bernd Bachmann & Markus Steffens, "An ontology of materials," in *Comparison of implemented ontologies. Proceedings of the ECAI'94 workshop, August 9, 1994, Amsterdam*, Nicolaas J.I. Mars, Thomas R. Gruber & Otto Kühn, eds., 1994, 17–34.

[3] Ronald J. Brachman, "'I lied about the trees', or defaults and definitions in knowledge representation," *AI Magazine* 6 (1985), 80–93.

[4] Ronald J. Brachman & Hector J. Levesque, "Competence in knowledge representation," in *Proceedings National Conference on Artificial Intelligence, Pittsburgh, PE, 18–20 August 1982*, American Association for Artificial Intelligence, 1982, 189–192.

[5] Ronald J. Brachman, Deborah L. McGuiness, Peter F. Patel-Schneider, Lori Alperin Resnick & Alexander Borgida, "Living with CLASSIC: when and how to use a KL-ONE-like language," in *Principles of semantic networks. Explorations in the representation of knowledge*, John F. Sowa, ed., Morgan Kaufmann, San Mateo CA, 1991, 401–456.

[6] M.L. Farinacci, I. Hulthage & M.A. Przystupa, "Acquiring and representing knowledge about material design," in *Knowledge based expert systems in engineering: planning and design*, D. Sriram & R.A. Adey, eds., Computational Mechanics Publications, Southampton, 1987, 99–114.

[7] Herbert Gelernter, J. Royce Rose & Chyouhwa Chen, "Building and refining a knowledge base for synthetic organic chemistry via the methodology of inductive and deductive machine learning," *Journal of Chemical Information and Computer Sciences* 30 (1990), 492–504.

[8] Michael R. Genesereth & Nils J. Nilsson, *Logical foundations of artificial intelligence*, Morgan Kaufmann, Palo Alto CA, 1987.

[9] Thomas R. Gruber, "The role of common ontology in achieving sharable, reusable knowledge bases," in *Proceedings of the Second International Conference on Principles of Knowledge Representation and Reasoning (KR'91), Cambridge, MA, April 22-25, 1991*, James Allen, Richard Fikes & Erik Sandewall, eds., 1991, 601–602.

[10] Thomas R. Gruber, "A translation approach to portable ontology specifications," *Knowledge Acquisition* 5 (1993), 199–220.

[11] Thomas R. Gruber & Gregory R. Olsen, "An ontology for engineering mathematics," in *Principles of knowledge representation and reasoning: proceedings of the fourth international conference (KR'94)*, Jon Doyle, Erik Sandewall & Pietro Torasso, eds., Morgan Kaufmann, San Francisco CA, 1994, 258–269.

[12] Nicola Guarino, "Formal ontology, knowledge acquisition and knowledge representation," in *Formal ontology in conceptual analysis and knowledge representation*, Nicola Guarino & Roberto Poli, eds., 1995, to appear.

[13] I. Hulthage, M.A. Przystupa, M.L. Farinacci & M.D. Rychener, "The representation of metallurgical knowledge for alloy design," *Artificial Intelligence for Engineering Design, Analysis, and Manufacturing (AI EDAM)* 1 (1988), 159–168.

[14] Ingemar A.E. Hulthage, Mark S. Fox, Michael D. Rychener & Martha L. Farinacci, "The architecture of ALADIN: a knowledge-based approach to alloy design," *IEEE Expert* 5 (August 1990), 56–73.

[15] W.D. Kingery, H.K. Bowen & D.R. Uhlmann, *Introduction to ceramics*, Wiley-Interscience, New York, NY, 1976, 2nd edition.

[16] Robert K. Lindsay, Bruce B. Buchanan, Edward A. Feigenbaum & Joshua Lederberg, "DENDRAL: a case study of the first expert system for scientific hypothesis formation," *Artificial Intelligence* 61 (1993), 209–261.

[17] Nicolaas J.I. Mars, "The role of ontologies in structuring large knowledge bases," in *Proceedings of the International Conference on Building and Sharing Very Large-Scale Knowledge Bases '93 (participant's edition)*, Japan Information Processing Development Center, Tokyo, 1993, 235–243.

[18] Nicolaas J.I. Mars, ed., *Comparison of implemented ontologies. Proceedings of the ECAI'94 workshop, August 9, 1994, Amsterdam*, 1994.

[19] Nicolaas J.I. Mars, "An ontology of measurement," in *Comparison of implemented ontologies. Proceedings of the ECAI'94 workshop, August 9, 1994, Amsterdam*, Nicolaas J.I. Mars, Thomas R. Gruber & Otto Kühn, eds., 1994, 153–162.

[20] Nicolaas J.I. Mars & A.T. Schreiber, "Direct access to knowledge in bibliographic databases," in *Proceedings of the ARTINT Workshop on Artificial Intelligence and Information Retrieval, Luxembourg, 13 September 1985*, Commission of the European Communities, Luxembourg, 1985, 83–86.

[21] Nicolaas J.I. Mars, Wilco G. ter Stal, Hidde de Jong, Paul E. van der Vet & Piet-Hein Speel, "Semi-automatic knowledge acquisition in Plinius: an engineering approach," in *Proceedings of the Eighth Banff Knowledge Acquisition for Knowledge-Based Systems Workshop, Banff, January 30 – February 4, 1994*, Brain Gaines & Mark Musen, eds., 1994, 4-1 – 4-15.

[22] Amedeo Napoli, "Subsumption and classification-based reasoning in object-based representations," in *Proceedings Tenth European Conference on Artificial Intelligence,3–7 August 1992, Vienna, Austria*, Bernd Neumann, ed., John Wiley, Chichester, UK, 1992, 425–429.

[23] Robert Neches, Richard Fikes, Tim Finin, Thomas Gruber, Ramesh Patil, Ted Senator & William R. Swartout, "Enabling technology for knowledge sharing," *AI Magazine* 12 (1991), 36–56.

[24] Dennis H. Rouvray, ed., *Computational chemical graph theory*, Nova Science Publishers, New York, 1990.

[25] M.D. Rychener, M.L. Farinacci, I. Hulthage & M.S. Fox, "Integration of multiple knowledge sources in ALADIN, an alloy design system," in *Proceedings Fifth National Conference on Artificial Intelligence, Philadelphia, PA, 11–15 August 1986*, Morgan Kaufmann Publishers, Los Altos, CA, 1986, 878–882.

[26] Piet-Hein Speel, *Selecting knowledge representation systems*, University of Twente, Enschede, the Netherlands, 1995, Ph.D. thesis.

[27] Piet-Hein Speel, Frank van Raalte, Paul E. van der Vet & Nicolaas J.I. Mars, "Scalability of the performance of knowledge representation systems," in *these proceedings*, 1995.

[28] Guy L. Steele, *Common Lisp: the language*, Digital Press, Bedford MA, 1990, second edition.

[29] Leon Sterling & Ehud Shapiro, *The art of Prolog. Advanced programming techniques*, MIT Press, Cambridge MA, 1994, second edition.

[30] Paul E. van der Vet, Hidde de Jong, Nicolaas J.I. Mars, Piet-Hein Speel & Wilco G. ter Stal, "Plinius intermediate report," University of Twente, Memoranda Informatica 94-35, Enschede, the Netherlands, 1994.

[31] Paul E. van der Vet & Nicolaas J.I. Mars, "Structured system of concepts for storing, retrieving, and manipulating chemical information," *Journal of Chemical Information and Computer Sciences* 33 (1993), 564–568.

[32] Paul E. van der Vet & Nicolaas J.I. Mars, "Concept systems as an aid for sharing and reuse of knowledge bases in materials science," in *Knowledge-based applications in materials science and engineering*, James K. McDowell & Kenneth J. Meltsner, eds., The Minerals, Metals & Materials Society, Warrendale PA, 1994, 43–55.

[33] Paul E. van der Vet, Piet-Hein Speel & Nicolaas J.I. Mars, "The Plinius ontology of ceramic materials," in *Comparison of implemented ontologies. Proceedings of the ECAI'94 workshop, August 9, 1994, Amsterdam*, Nicolaas J.I. Mars, Thomas R. Gruber & Otto Kühn, eds., 1994, 187–205.

Towards Very Large Knowledge Bases
N.J.I. Mars, Ed.
IOS Press, 1995

A Knowledge Media Approach to Ontology Development

Toyoaki Nishida, Hideaki Takeda, Kenji Iino and **Masanobu Nishiki**

Nara Institute of Science and Technology
Nara 630-01, Japan
nishida@is.aist-nara.ac.jp

ABSTRACT

In this paper, we propose a framework of *contextual media* which allows information to be weakly structured. *Contextual media* allow for data-driven ontology development, by accumulating almost raw data and incrementally creating the conceptual structure through human-computer collaboration.

The proposal is partly implemented and tested. Our preliminary experimental study on constructing an ontology-based knowledge media information base from existing knowledge sources has revealed that a data-driven knowledge media approach to ontology development is both feasible and effective.

1 INTRODUCTION

Large scale knowledge sharing is indispensable to put AI theories to work in the real world [6, 7, 14]. Ontologies, systems of vocabulary defining the terminology and underlying concepts used in knowledge based systems [10, 8], play a central role in achieving large scale knowledge sharing. They allow people and software agents to share a common vocabulary for exchanging information and indexing information resources.

Unfortunately, development of an ontology is often a quite painstaking and time consuming task. Generally, ontology development involves collection and selection of terms through task analysis, and formation of a system of term definitions. In addition, lots of discussions and negotiations are needed when ontology is developed by a group.

A promising approach would be to develop a system of knowledge media [18] that may facilitate effective computer support throughout the process of ontology development.

In this paper, we propose a framework of *contextual media* which allows for data-driven ontology development, by accumulating almost raw data and incrementally creating the conceptual structure through human-computer collaboration.

The proposal is partly implemented and tested. Our preliminary experimental study on construction of an ontology-based knowledge media information base from existing knowledge sources (*i.e.*, humans and natural language documents) has revealed that a data-driven knowledge media approach to ontology development is both feasible and effective.

In what follows, we first describe the role of ontologies in knowledge sharing with multi-agent system and discuss why ontology development is expensive. In section 3, we describe a preliminary work on construction of an ontology-based knowledge media information base from existing knowledge sources. In section 4, we describe the *contextual media* approach to ontology development, by introducing the framework of contextual media and its application to ontology development. Finally, we show a future perspective and compare our work with related work.

2 THE ROLE OF ONTOLOGIES IN KNOWLEDGE SHARING WITH MULTI-AGENT SYSTEM

It is natural to implement a large information space as a collection of interacting agents each of which conveys a relatively small piece of information. The initial step towards this direction was to develop a common language including message acts, syntax, semantics, and vocabulary through which agents can exchange information with each other [12, 15].

The role of ontology in the common language approach to knowledge sharing is twofold: (a) providing a pre-defined set of terms for exchanging information, and (b) indexing information resources dis-

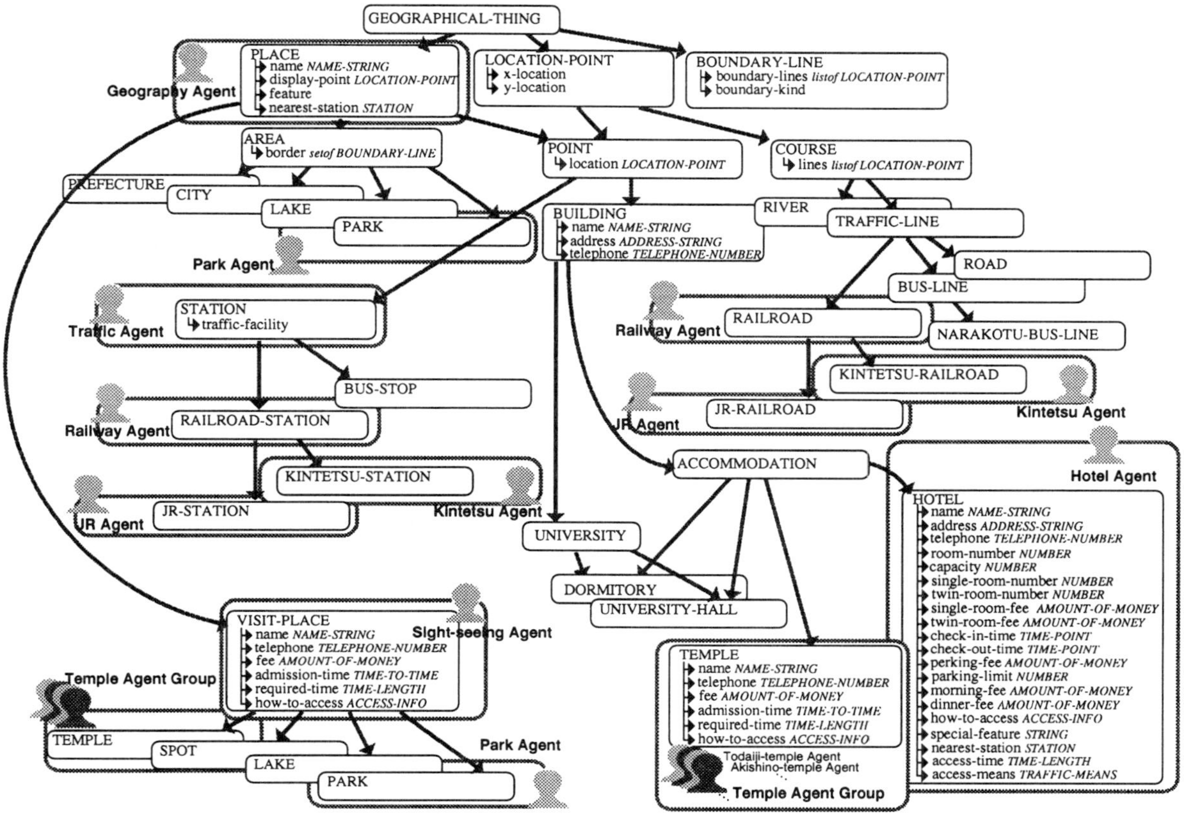
GEOGRAPHICAL-THING
PLACE
name NAME-STRING
display-point LOCATION-POINT
feature
nearest-station STATION
Geography Agent
LOCATION-POINT
x-location
y-location
BOUNDARY-LINE
boundary-lines listof LOCATION-POINT
boundary-kind
AREA
border setof BOUNDARY-LINE
POINT
location LOCATION-POINT
COURSE
lines listof LOCATION-POINT
PREFECTURE
CITY
LAKE
PARK
Park Agent
BUILDING
name NAME-STRING
address ADDRESS-STRING
telephone TELEPHONE-NUMBER
RIVER
TRAFFIC-LINE
ROAD
BUS-LINE
STATION
traffic-facility
Traffic Agent
RAILROAD
Railway Agent
NARAKOTU-BUS-LINE
KINTETSU-RAILROAD
BUS-STOP
RAILROAD-STATION
Railway Agent
JR-RAILROAD
JR Agent
Kintetsu Agent
ACCOMMODATION
Hotel Agent
KINTETSU-STATION
JR-STATION
JR Agent
Kintetsu Agent
UNIVERSITY
HOTEL
name NAME-STRING
address ADDRESS-STRING
telephone TELEPHONE-NUMBER
room-number NUMBER
capacity NUMBER
single-room-number NUMBER
twin-room-number NUMBER
single-room-fee AMOUNT-OF-MONEY
twin-room-fee AMOUNT-OF-MONEY
check-in-time TIME-POINT
check-out-time TIME-POINT
perking-fee AMOUNT-OF-MONEY
parking-limit NUMBER
morning-fee AMOUNT-OF-MONEY
dinner-fee AMOUNT-OF-MONEY
how-to-access ACCESS-INFO
special-feature STRING
nearest-station STATION
access-time TIME-LENGTH
access-means TRAFFIC-MEANS
DORMITORY
UNIVERSITY-HALL
VISIT-PLACE
name NAME-STRING
telephone TELEPHONE-NUMBER
fee AMOUNT-OF-MONEY
admission-time TIME-TO-TIME
required-time TIME-LENGTH
how-to-access ACCESS-INFO
Sight-seeing Agent
Temple Agent Group
TEMPLE
name NAME-STRING
telephone TELEPHONE-NUMBER
fee AMOUNT-OF-MONEY
admission-time TIME-TO-TIME
required-time TIME-LENGTH
how-to-access ACCESS-INFO
Todaiji-temple Agent
Akishino-temple Agent
Temple Agent Group
TEMPLE
SPOT
LAKE
PARK
Park Agent

Figure 1: The ontology in the Knowledgeable Community

tributed among agents. The former is mainly referred to by agent programmers at the agent system development stage, to make agreement on the usage of terms in messages. An extended first order predicate calculus or an object-centered frame language is often used to define concepts. In contrast, the latter is mainly referred to by software agents at the execution time, to look for the source of knowledge needed to pursue the task.

Knowledgeable Community [13] is a multi-agent system for knowledge sharing. In the Knowledgeable Community, ontological information is provided by a special agent called an *ontology server*.[1]

Figure 1 shows an ontology used in KC-Kansai, a travel arrangement system built on top of the Knowledgeable Community. A frame ontology is used which specifies conceptual terms referring to objects and relations in the travel arrangement domain. Agents are associated with the ontology according to the contents of information service they provide.

[1]Note that agent programmers can also access the ontology server and get appropriate information through her/his interface agent.

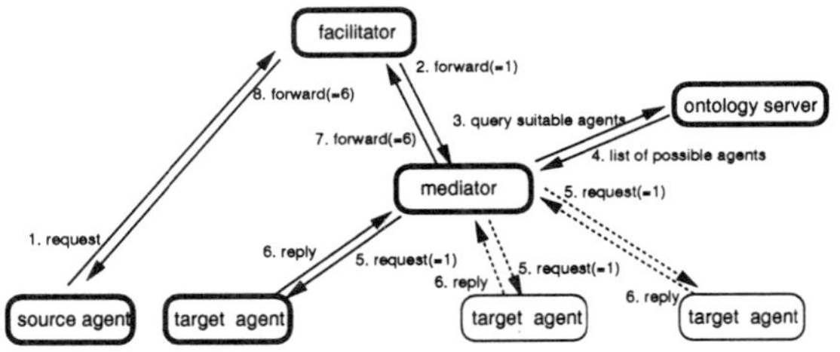
facilitator
2. forward(=1)
8. forward(=6)
3. query suitable agents
ontology server
7. forward(=6)
4. list of possible agents
mediator
5. request(=1)
1. request
6. reply
5. request(=1)
6. reply
5. request(=1)
6. reply
source agent
target agent
target agent
target agent

Numbers indicate the identifier of messages. The contents of messages 1 through 5 are shown in Figure 3.

Figure 2: Message passing for mediation

Figure 2 illustrates how an ontology is used to find an agent which can answer a given question. Agents ("`source agent`" in this case) are allowed to send messages without specifying the recipient. *Facilitators* take care of such messages. When a facilitator receives a message with empty recipient field (Message 1 in Figure 3a), it adds a broker request wrapper and sends the modified message to a *mediator* (Message 2 in Figure 3b). The mediator analyzes the content of the query, identifies the key terms for answering the give question, and asks an *ontology server* for the name of relevant agents (Message 3 in Figure 3c). Upon the request, the ontology server retrieves the name of the relevant agents if any ("`sight-seeing-agent`" in this case), by referring to term-agent associations in the ontology (Message 4 in Figure 3d). The mediator asks those agents a question on behalf of the client (Message 5 in Figure 3c). The response will be returned to "`source agent`", who originally asked for the information.

Unfortunately, the above approach turned out to be severely limited when we tried to scale up. The major bottleneck was a high cost for developing an ontology. Why is ontology development expensive?

The difficulty, as we believe, comes from three causes. First, the employed methodology, in effect, forces us to develop a relatively complete ontologies before developing agents, for making changes in ontologies involves rewriting codes of all the relevant agents and is quite expensive. However, this condition is hard to meet, for conceptualization in an ontology depends on the goal of the application and is difficult to make until a certain amount of experiences is obtained, say, with a prototype system. Thus, we have to repeat expensive cycles of scrap and build to scale up.

Second, the employed methodology assumes a top-down argumentation-based process in which ontology writers argue with each other to negotiate on terms and relations in an ontology. The process mostly relies on ontology writers' introspection, and is unreliable unless much time is spent on discussions.

Third, the employed ontology definition language is computer-oriented and is quite different from human-oriented media, such as natural language documents, images or movies. As human-oriented media are often ill-structured, ambiguous, indefinite, vague, unstructured, unorganized, inconsistent, and so forth, we need a tremendous amount of effort on translating human-oriented media into computer-oriented media.

In order to solve these problems, we propose a methodology that allows for building ontologies from human-oriented media in a data-driven fashion and facilitating elaboration and refinement of ontologies. Currently, we are working on two projects.

One is to develop a theory of multiple ontologies and mutual translation of messages in different ontologies. The *aspect theory* [19] allows us to concentrate on small tractable fragments of ontologies which may later be put together to cope with larger and more complex task domains.

Another is to develop a system of *knowledge media* [18] that may facilitate effective computer support throughout the process of ontology development, by allowing human-oriented information media to be ac-

(a) Message 1

```
(ask-one
   :content (and (hotel ?x)
                 (name ?x "Nara-hotel")
                 (nearest-station ?x ?y))
   :aspect ?y :language KIF
   :reply-with q1)
```

(b) Message 2

```
(broker-all :content
  (ask-one
     :content (and (hotel ?x)
                   (name ?x "Nara-hotel")
                   (nearest-station ?x ?y))
     :aspect ?y :language KIF
     :reply-with q1)
  :reply-with m1)
```

(c) Message 3

```
(recommend-all :content
  (ask-one
     :content (and (hotel ?x)
                   (name ?x "Nara-hotel")
                   (nearest-station ?x ?y))
     :aspect ?y :language KIF
     :reply-with q1)
  :reply-with m1)
```

(d) Message 4

```
(reply :content ("sight-seeing-agent")
       :reply-with m1)
```

(e) Message 5

```
(ask-one
   :content (and (hotel ?x)
                 (name ?x "Nara-hotel")
                 (nearest-station ?x ?y))
   :receiver sight-seeing-agent
   :aspect ?y :language KIF
   :reply-with q1)
```

Figure 3: The contents of messages in Figure 2

cumulated and enabling incremental, data-driven, inductive ontology development.

In the rest of this paper, we focus on the second approach. For the first approach, the reader is referred to [19].

3 CONSTRUCTION OF AN ONTOLOGY-BASED KNOWLEDGE MEDIA INFORMATION BASE

Human experts and natural language documents are the most valuable and ubiquitous knowledge sources. Natural language documents provide an explicit and formal knowledge. Some of them, handbooks and textbooks in particular, cover the subjects of a domain in a comprehensive fashion, contributing to the com-the more expensive will be information acquisition but the more useful will be the encoded information for information utilization. Accordingly, we need an inventory of knowledge representation languages with varying degrees of conceptualization and elaboration.

Let us call a linguistic facility of delimiting the scope of expression a *context mechanism*, and call a system of knowledge representation languages *contextual media*, if the system allows knowledge representation languages of different perspectives to co-exist and interact with each other through a context mechanism.

In what follows, we present a particular contextual medium, perhaps the simplest one, called CM-1. CM-1 provides a weakly structured way of representing information based on a simple semantics. As a human-oriented medium, CM-1 implies the ease of data acquisition and understanding. As a computer-oriented medium, CM-1 facilitates development of computational support for helping humans refine an information base as well as retrieve information.

4.1 Preliminaries

Information bases in CM-1 consist of entities of a single type, called *units*. Each unit can be referred to as a *concept* and can introduce a *context*. We introduce a *conceptual intersection operator* & to denote a concept $c_1 \& \ldots \& c_n$ resulting from intersecting a set of concepts $c_1, \ldots, c_n$ at the conceptual level. For example, a concept "Nara" & "temples" would denote temples in Nara.[2]

The semantics of CM-1 is based on Bayesian probabilities [16]. Given a concept $A_1 \& \ldots \& A_n$ and a concept c, we can think of conditional probability $P(c \mid A_1, \ldots, A_n)$ as specifying the degree of recalling c from $A_1, \ldots, A_n$.

In the current formalization, we introduce a hypothetical threshold θ and consider an information space made of concepts whose conditional probability is beyond θ:

$$C[A_1 \& \ldots \& A_n] = \{c \mid P(c) \geq \theta\},$$

and call it a *context* $A_1 \& \ldots \& A_n$.

For example, as the key words "Nara" and "temples" reminds us of "Todai-ji", "Kofuku-ji", and so on,[3] so

P("Todai-ji" | "Nara", "temples") = **High**

P("Kofuku-ji" | "Nara", "temples") = **High**

$$\cdots$$

and

C["Nara" & "temples"] = { "Todai-ji", "Kofuku-ji", ... }.

[2]In our formalization, $x \& (y \& z) \equiv (x \& y) \& z \equiv x \& y \& z$.

[3]We basically assume that information encoded into CM-1 is subjective.

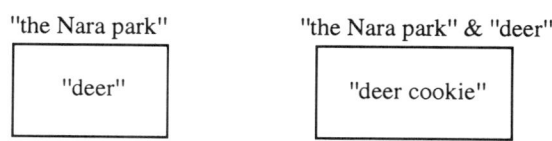

Figure 5: Pictorial representation in CM-1

In practice, it is quite often the case that actual quantitative values of conditional probabilities or the threshold may not be known and only qualitative judgments are given as to whether a concept belongs to a certain context or not. We interpret those qualitative information from the viewpoint of Bayesian probabilities.

For example, consider the following qualitative information:

"deer" ∈ C["the Nara park"]

; it is likely to recall deer given the Nara park,

"deer cookie" ∈ C["the Nara park", "deer"]

; it is likely to recall deer cookie given the Nara park and deer,

"deer cookie" ∉ C["the Nara park"]

; it may not be likely to recall deer cookie given the Nara park.

We pictorially illustrate the information above as shown in Figure 5. Boxes and symbols denote contexts and concepts, respectively. A symbol denoting a concept x is in a box denoting a context c iff $x \in C[c]$.

¿From the above information, we may be able to infer, for instance,

"deer" ∈ C["the Nara park", "deer cookie"]

; it is likely to recall deer given the Nara park and deer cookie.

for it follows from the Bayesian principle [16] that

P("deer" | "the Nara park", "deer cookie")
= P("deer cookie" | "deer", "the Nara park")
$$\cdot \frac{P(\text{"deer"} \mid \text{"the Nara park"})}{P(\text{"deer cookie"} \mid \text{"the Nara park"})}$$
= **High** $\cdot \dfrac{\textbf{High}}{\textbf{Low}}$
= **High**.

Instead of diving into the further formal analysis, we study the properties of contexts from practical points of view.

4.2 Weakly Structured Information Representation with CM-1

A typical representation in CM-1 is illustrated in Figure 6, which represents part of regional information concerning Nara, Japan.

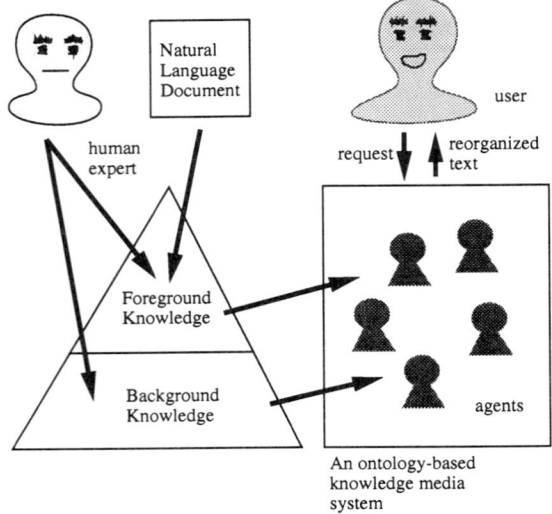

Figure 4: An ontology-based knowledge media system for investigating construction of ontologies from existing knowledge sources

pleteness of an ontology. On the other hand, human experts provide tacit background knowledge in interpreting natural language documents, contributing to the establishment of the soundness of an ontology. Information from those knowledge sources would be best captured by informal knowledge media such as multimedia documents, rather than formal languages.

In order to study empirical aspects of constructing ontologies from existing knowledge sources, we have developed an ontology-based knowledge media system, as shown in Figure 4. The most essential part of the system is an information base consisting of a collection of multi-media text pieces associated with an ontology. We employed a semantic network formalism as an ontology description language.

Given an information request, the system will collect relevant multi-media text pieces and organize them into a coherent discourse, so that it may be intelligible to the user. A multi-agent system architecture is employed.

Conceptually, the ontology is divided into foreground and background sub-ontologies. The purpose of the foreground sub-ontology is to capture the explicit conceptual structure observed in the natural language documents, as a table of contents or glossary for example. In contrast, the background sub-ontology is for capturing the tacit conceptual structure possessed by human experts. However, the distinction of the two sub-ontologies is not rigid in practice.

We took two sample documents and asked several students to handcraft an ontology along the following

procedure:

(step 1)   identify basic terms from a sample natural language document and classify them into pre-defined category types;

(step 2)   structure basic terms into the background sub-ontology using a set of pre-defined conceptual relations;

(step 3)   construct the foreground sub-ontology based on the table of contents of a given source document;

(step 4)   read through the body of sample documents and flesh out the ontology by supplementing terms and relations if necessary.

After an ontology was constructed, the sample document was partitioned into smaller pieces (consisting of a few paragraphs), which in turn were linked to appropriate terms in the ontology.

The result was quite encouraging, though not totally satisfactory. An ontology consisting of about four hundred conceptual items was built for one sample document. It provides a good coverage and characterization of the domain. For the other sample document, the resulting ontology contains about twelve hundred conceptual items and thirteen hundred conceptual relations. The total time required for the second work was about a hundred and twenty hours. The quality of the ontology is relatively good with respect to the scale of the ontology. On the other hand, we recognized as bad news a problem with predominance of pre-defined concept types and conceptual relations. Students had some difficulty in interpreting the definition of primitives to determine the primitive types for input. As a result, the usage of pre-defined concepts and conceptual relations is not uniform.

Another problem we recognized was the lack of computational support for helping people work together to build a large ontology. Tools for navigating through a large information space or maintaining consistency would be useful.

How can we avoid preoccupation and reduce cost at the initial phase of ontology development? The framework of contextual media, to be described in the next section, results from our attempt at answering the above question.

4   THE FRAMEWORK OF CONTEXTUAL MEDIA

Any knowledge representation language poses certain amount of prerequisites for information to be encoded. For example, in order to represent facts in predicate logic, one has to exploit logical aspects of information, by figuring out basic terms and relations adequate for characterizing the state of affairs and by making logical assertions. The more the amount of prerequisites,

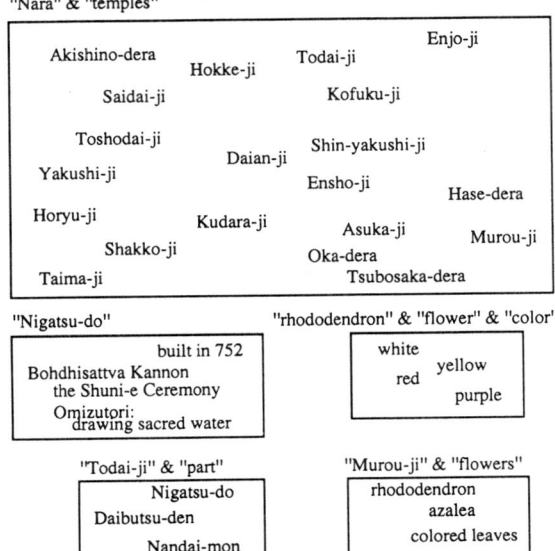

Figure 6: A typical representation with CM-1

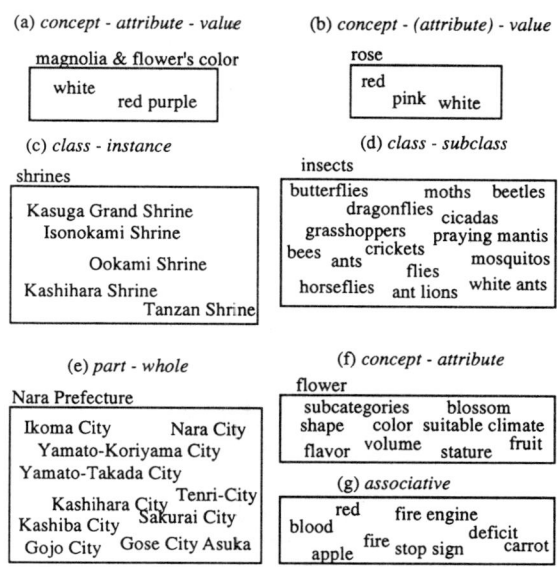

Figure 7: Information regression in CM-1

CM-1 is weakly structured in the sense that its representation only distinguishes whether a concept is contained in a context or not. In the single relationship, varieties of semantically different relations, such as concept-attribute-value, class-instance, superclass-subclass, part-whole, and so on, as shown in Figure 7. In addition, there is no clear separation between definitional and assertional statements. We call such a phenomenon *information regression*.

Information regression is good news in the sense that as it imposes very few prerequisites with respect to the formalization of data, it is quite easy to incorporate almost any raw data into contextual media.

As a trade-off, you may think that the contents of an information base are so ambiguous and ill-defined that it may be hard to use data without further formalization and refinement. This is true to some degree and the data refinement task is not easy. However, various computer-supported techniques are available for retrieving and refining information. In addition, the source of information is already there. The benefit of availability of information source and reliability of data-driven ontology, as we believe, subsumes the cost of refining and formalizing the raw material, as opposed to the opposite approach, *i.e.*, a rigid ontology-first, deductive approach.

We have implemented an editor called COMMON-1[4] for manipulating information bases with CM-1. Figure 8 shows a typical window of COMMON-1.

---
[4]It stands for "COnceptually Mediated Media with ONtology".

In addition to various editing and display facilities, COMMON-1 provides a couple of basic context access operators:

search-downward	given a set of concepts A, it searches contexts $C[B]$ such that $A \subseteq B$;
search-upward	given a set of concepts A, it searches contexts $C[B]$ such that $A \supseteq B$.

The above two operations are quite simple, but useful especially when a given information base contains a lot of contexts. Figure 9 shows how a context concerning "the temples in Nara" is accessed using the search-downward operator.

A more sophisticated algorithm is path finding which allows to retrieve information even though what is contained in an information base is structurally different from the presupposition of a given query. Given a set of key concepts, the path finding algorithm searches for a minimal tree connecting them and if one is found, it returns a set of intermediate nodes as an answer. Figure 10 illustrates how the algorithm works to answer a question:

are there any places in Nara that are famous for beautiful rhododendron?

Roughly speaking, the question presupposes a context indexed by "Nara" and "rhododendron" (above the dashed line in Figure 10), which is structurally dif-

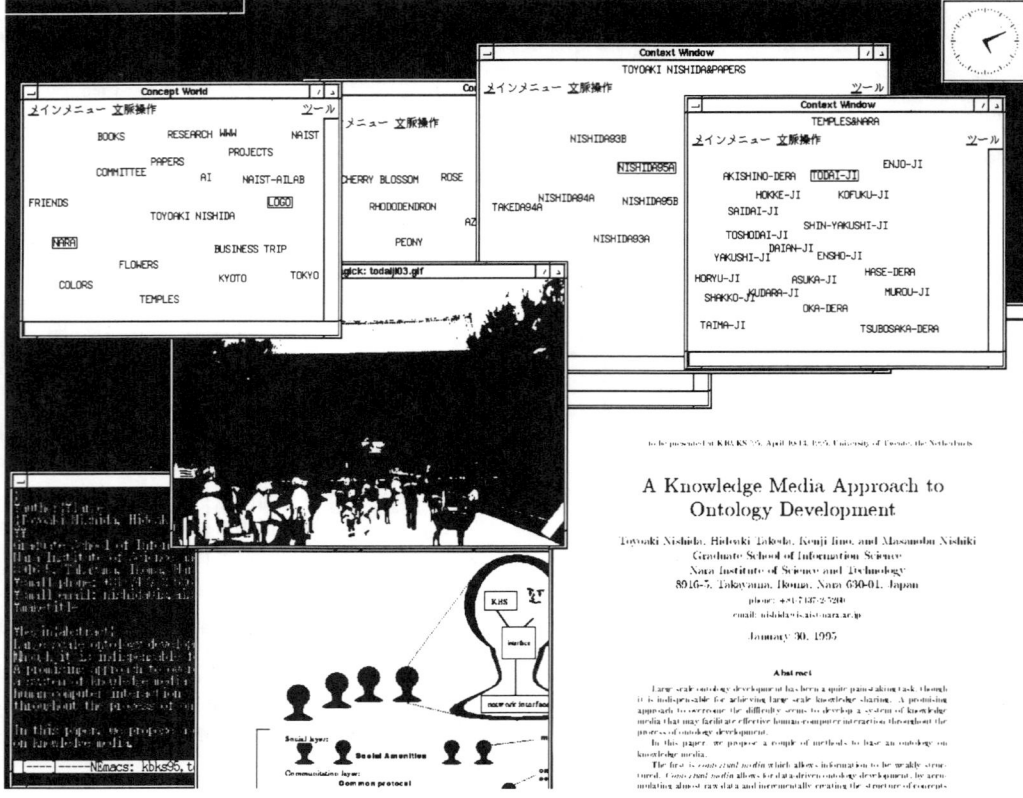

The current prototype (a Japanese version) is implemented using Common Lisp and tcl/tk. The upper windows display various contexts. The lower windows are image data and raw texts referred to by some contexts and are displayed upon user's request.

Figure 8: A typical window of COMMON-1

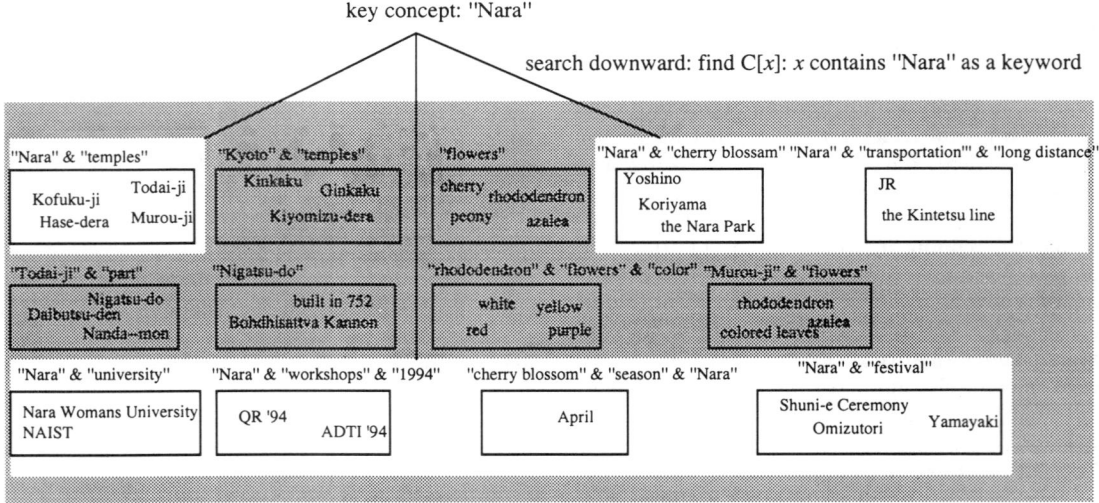

Figure 9: Retrieving a context concerning "the temples in Nara" by search-downward

Are there any places in Nara that are famous for rhododendron?

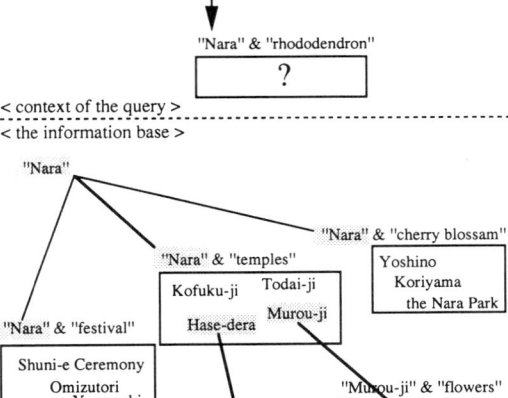

Even though structural mismatch exists between a query and the information base, a simple algorithm can produce answers which are appropriate in many cases. In this case, Hase-dera and Murou-ji are proposed as an answer, which is exactly what is expected in this case.

Figure 10: Intelligent retrieval of a context

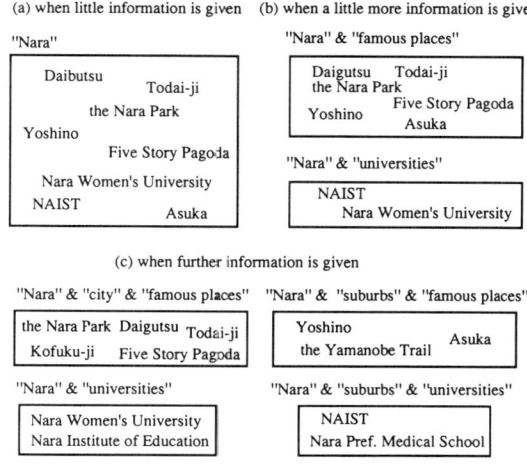

Figure 11: Incremental refinement and structuring of an information base

ferent from what is in the information base (below the dashed line in Figure 10).

The path finding algorithm seeks a minimal tree connecting the key concepts in the question, *i.e.*, "Nara" and "rhododendron", ending up with an answer:

$$\{\text{"Murou-ji", "Hase-dera"}\},$$

which is satisfactory in this case. However, note that the path finding algorithm may not always find an appropriate answer, for it does not take into account the semantics of the path. Extensive evaluation of the algorithm is left for future.

4.3 Incremental Refinement of CM-1 Information Base

We would like to refine and elaborate an information base as we obtain more insights about the task domain. We introduce computational support to refine the structure of an information base, incrementally making them more structured and consistent. The role of the computer is to generate hypotheses, evaluate each hypothesis, and maintain the consistency of the information base. The role of the human is to provide the system with new information and to choose an appropriate hypothesis.

We propose three techniques: base term identification, analogical information acquisition, and context merge.

Base term identification is a technique for recognizing and isolating *base terms*, which include attributes, general terms, and characteristic terms. Base terms are crucial for structuring the information base, as they specify viewpoints by which incoherent contexts can be partitioned into coherent contexts. The human identifies base terms and partitions the information base with the computer's support. Partitioning a context often contributes to shed light on tacit information in human's brain, promoting information acquisition.

Figure 11 illustrates how an information base might be refined and structured using the base term identification technique. In Figure 11a, no distinction is made about "Nara". In Figure 11b, the user identifies a couple of base terms "famous places" and "universities" as base terms, and partitions the context "Nara" into two contexts "Nara" & "famous places" and "Nara" & "universities". In Figure 11c, the user introduces two more base terms "city" and "suburbs" and further partitions the contexts. Note that the resulting partitioning has prompted the user to focus on finer contexts and add several new concepts such as "Kofuku-ji" and "Five Story Pagoda".

Analogical information acquisition is a technique for elaborating contexts by making cross products of contexts based on similarity. We heuristically measure the similarity between concepts A and B, by counting the number of occurrences of the following phenomena:

$$\exists X \ [\ A \in \mathrm{C}[X], B \in \mathrm{C}[X] \ ],$$
$$\exists X \ [X \in \mathrm{C}[A], X \in \mathrm{C}[B] \ ], \text{ and}$$
$$\exists \alpha \ [\ \mathrm{C}[A \cup \alpha] \neq \{\} \wedge \mathrm{C}[B \cup \alpha] \neq \{\} \ ].$$

If the measurement exceeds a certain threshold, we

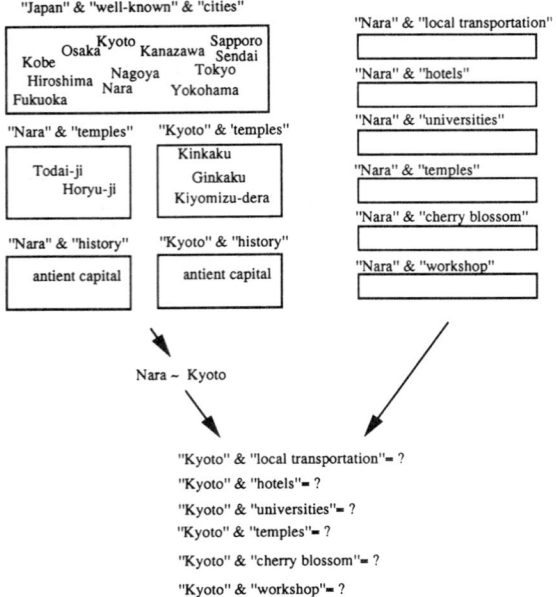

Figure 12: Power of analogical information acquisition

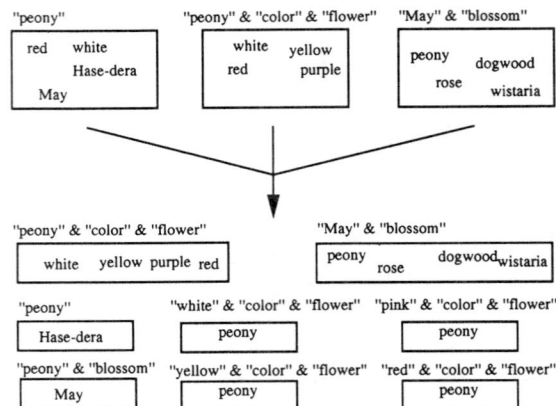

Figure 13: Applying heuristic rules to refine an information base

consider concept A and B are similar and denote $A \sim B$.

We use the following heuristic to ask humans for more information:

if $A \sim B$ and $\mathrm{C}[A \cup \alpha] \neq \{\}$ and $\mathrm{C}[B \cup \alpha] = \{\}$
then ask the user for what is in $\mathrm{C}[B \cup \alpha]$.

Analogical information acquisition is a powerful data-driven information refinement and elaboration technique. Figure 12 illustrates how it works: similarity between "Nara" and "Kyoto" is inferred from assertions made so far, and questions are asked about several conceptual intersections whose contexts have not been given for "Kyoto" but are given for "Nara".

Context merge is a technique for refining an information base by putting together information from several contexts. Currently, we use a few simple heuristics:

$$x \in \mathrm{C}[A] \land x \in \mathrm{C}[B] \land A \subseteq B \;\rightarrow\; \text{remove } x \in \mathrm{C}[A]$$
$$x \in \mathrm{C}[A] \land A \in \mathrm{C}[x \& y] \;\rightarrow\; \text{add } x \in \mathrm{C}[A \& y]$$
$$x \in \mathrm{C}[y \& z] \land y \notin \mathrm{C}[x \& z] \;\rightarrow\; \text{add } y \in \mathrm{C}[x \& z],$$

for merging information from contexts A and B. Figure 13 illustrates how they work: as "red" $\in$ C["peony"] and "red" $\in$ C["peony" & "color"], so only the latter is left; as "May" $\in$ C["peony"] and "peony" $\in$ C["May" & "blossom"], so "May" $\in$ C["peony" & "blossom"]; as "white" $\in$ C["peony" & "color" & "flower"], so "peony" $\in$ C["white" & "color" & "flower"]; and so on.

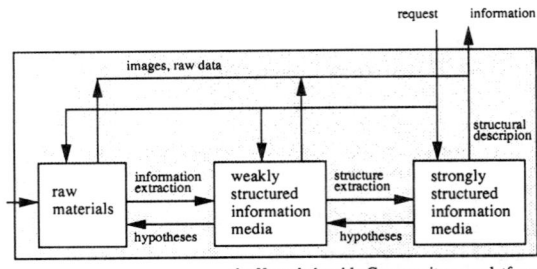

Figure 14: The architecture of an information base

The resulting version of the information base is conceptually more elaborate than the older version. Extensive evaluation of these rules and development of a more complex algorithm are left for future.

5 FUTURE WORK

We envision a whole picture of an information base with contextual media, as shown in Figure 14. The information base consists of annotated raw material, weakly structured information, and strongly structured information. Incremental conceptualization by human-computer collaboration takes place continually to transform annotated raw materials into weakly and strongly structured information. Strongly structured information is used to synthesize an efficient plan for answering questions, while annotated raw material and weakly structured information are used both to cope with questions that cannot be handled adequately with strongly structured information and to provide human-oriented intelligible information.

Interesting future research includes: extension for multiple media, information acquisition from natural language texts [1], elaboration in the context of creative concept formation [4], associative retrieval, allowing richer information structure for contexts [17], exploration for applications such as computer-aided language translation, incorporation of a more powerful mechanism for merging different contexts, implementation of fancy user interface, and extension for CSCW.

6 RELATED WORK

The role of contexts in Artificial Intelligence and knowledge sharing in particular are discussed by many authors [5, 11, 3, 9]. We share the common recognition that all knowledge representations have their own innate limitations in modeling the world, and argue for the necessity of a context mechanism. Guha and Mc-Carthy attempt at inventing a context mechanism on top of logical languages. In contrast, we incorporate a context mechanism in an informal language. Our ultimate goal is to characterize the context mechanism as a means of co-relating information across languages with different paradigms, ranging from informal languages to formal languages, or from declarative languages to procedural languages.

The notion of knowledge media originated with Stefik [18]. He argues for the information-centered approach. He discusses knowledge media mainly in the context of information flow among people and demonstrates his idea as a system for CSCW. By contrast our primary concern is the integration of human-oriented and computer-oriented knowledge representation.

Brachman [2] describes a method of allowing the user to view the raw data through the lens of knowledge representation. His approach is relevant to our work, for he also suggests a data-driven approach to knowledge representation and integration of data and knowledge. The difference is that he assumes that the chunk of raw data is given as a relational data base which provides a much more structured vehicle of knowledge representation and hence more prerequisites are required for information acquisition than CM-1.

7 CONCLUSION

In this paper, we have proposed a framework of contextual media for data-driven ontology development. This approach allows for accumulating almost raw data and incrementally creating the structure of concepts through human-computer collaboration.

8 REFERENCES

[1] Lawrence A. Bookman. Trajectories through knowledge space — a dynamic framework for medicine comprehension, 1994.

[2] Ronald J. Brachman. Viewing data through a knowledge representation lens. In *Proceedings International Conference on Building and Sharing of Very-Large Scale Knowledge Bases '93 (KB&KS '93)*, pages 117–120. Ohmsha, Ltd, 1993.

[3] Ramanathan V. Guha. *Contexts: A Formalization and Some Applications*. PhD thesis, Department of Computer Science, Stanford University, Stanford, CA, 1991. (Available as Report No. STAN-CS-91-1399-Thesis).

[4] Koichi Hori. A system for aiding creative concept formation. *IEEE Transactions on Systems, Man, and Cybernetics*, 24(5):882–894, 1994.

[5] Bob Jansen. Context: A real problem for large and sharable knowledge bases. In *Proceedings International Conference on Building and Sharing of Very-Large Scale Knowledge Bases '93 (KB&KS '93)*, pages 177–183. Ohmsha, Ltd, 1993.

[6] Douglas B. Lenat and Edward A. Feigenbaum. On the thresholds of knowledge. *Artificial Intelligence*, 47:185–230, 1990.

[7] Douglas B. Lenat and R. V. Guha. *Building Large Knowledge-based Systems*. Addison-Wesley, 1989.

[8] Nicolaas J.I. Mars. The role of ontologies in structuring large knowledge bases. In *Proceedings International Conference on Building and Sharing of Very-Large Scale Knowledge Bases '93 (KB&KS '93)*, pages 235–243. Ohmsha, Ltd, 1993.

[9] John McCarthy. Notes on formalizing context. In *Proceedings of IJCAI-93*, pages 555–560, 1994.

[10] Riichiro Mizoguchi. Knowledge acquisition and ontology. In *Proceedings International Conference on Building and Sharing of Very-Large Scale Knowledge Bases '93 (KB&KS '93)*, pages 121–128. Ohmsha, Ltd, 1993.

[11] Hideyuki Nakashima. Context reflection for flexible knowledge representation. In *Proceedings International Conference on Building and Sharing of Very-Large Scale Knowledge Bases '93 (KB&KS '93)*, pages 227–233. Ohmsha, Ltd, 1993.

[12] Robert Neches, Richard Fikes, Tim Finin, Thomas Gruber, Ramesh Patil, Ted Senator, and William R. Swartout. Enabling technology for knowledge sharing. *AI Magazine*, 12(3):36–56, 1991.

[13] Toyoaki Nishida and Hideaki Takeda. Towards the knowledgeable community. In *Proceedings International Conference on Building and Sharing of Very-Large Scale Knowledge Bases '93 (KB&KS '93)*, pages 157–166. Ohmsha, Ltd, 1993.

[14] Setsuo Ohsuga. How can people share large knowledge bases. In *Proceedings International Conference on Building and Sharing of Very-Large Scale Knowledge Bases '93 (KB&KS '93)*, pages 85–94. Ohmsha, Ltd, 1993.

[15] R. S. Patil, R. E. Fikes, P. F. Patel-Schneider, D. McKay, T. Finin, T. R. Gruber, and R. Neches. The DARPA knowledge sharing effort: Progress report. In Charles Rich, Bernhard Nebel, and William Swartout, editors, *Principles of Knowledge Representation and Reasoning: Proceedings of the Third International Conference*. Morgan Kaufmann, 1992.

[16] Judea Pearl. *Probabilistic Reasoning in Intelligent Systems*. Morgan-Kaufmann Pub. Inc., 1988.

[17] Mildred L.G. Shaw and Brian R. Gaines. Personal construct psychology foundations for knowledge acquisition and representation. In N. Aussenac, G. Boy, B. Gaines, M. Linter, J.-G. Ganascia, and Y. Kodratoff, editors, *Knowledge Acquisition for Knowledge-based Systems*, pages 256–276. Springer-Verlag, 1993.

[18] Mark Stefik. The next knowledge medium. *AI Magazine*, 7(1):34–46, 1986.

[19] Hideaki Takeda, Kenji Iino, and Toyoaki Nishida. Agent communication with multiple ontologies. In *FGCS '94 Workshop on Heterogeneous Cooperative Knowledge-Bases*, pages 111–124, 1994.

Part 3: Knowledge Acquisition

Steps Towards Automated Knowledge Acquisition

Yorick Wilks and **Sergei Nirenburg**
University of Sheffield
Sheffield, England

New Mexico State University
Las Cruces, NM, USA
yorick@dcs.shef.ac.uk

ABSTRACT

We argue that automating knowledge acquisition for natural language processing applications (such as machine translation, database query, dialog systems, etc.) must be considered as the central research direction of the 1990s for natural language processing (NLP). We have started a research program automating the acquisition of grammars; lexicons and ontologies (domain models).

An additional central concern is the shareability and reusability of both the acquisition methods and the results of the acquisition process. This paper discusses several possible directions for an initial effort, including a form for transputer-based massive parallel processing to speed acquisition. We propose a method for constructing meaning representations of text segments (under the constraints of an ontology) from text items deemed statistically significant. This can be seen as a top-down analogue to the bottom-up template items derived by an information extraction process. It is the fusion of these two sources that constitutes the heart of our method for deriving knowledge strutures automatically from existing corpora and MRD resources.

1 BACKGROUND

Building natural language processing systems requires static knowledge sources — grammars, lexicons, world models and auxiliary knowledge sources such as gazetteers and other proper name lists. Many realistic applications (especially those involving the processing of an entire text rather than its fragments) require sizable and very complex knowledge sources. The coverage of syntax must be more or less complete. The lexicon for even a limited domain must typically include tens of thousands of entries and, if semantic processing is necessary, a domain model of many thousands of variously interconnected nodes must be constructed. The creation of these knowledge sources is at present very expensive and the results are often brittle, difficult to reuse and even difficult to test.

NLP as a field has made significant progress in devising language processing techniques. However, almost all extant systems follow the so-called "demo" approach in which their capabilities are demonstrated on very limited lexicons and grammars. For NLP technology to break out into the world, it is necessary to make knowledge acquisition cheaper, more reliable and more abundant. It is therefore crucial to seek ways of automating this process.

1.1 Data Sources

There are two major types of data which can be used as sources for automatic knowledge acquisition — text corpora and machine-readable dictionaries. Transcribed corpora of spoken language could be used for spoken language applications. In this document, we are concerned primarily with knowledge acquisition for written text processing. A comprehensive knowledge acquisition environment will use a combination of corpora and dictionaries.

1.2 Analysis of Corpora

Large corpora are becoming increasingly available to researchers, in a large part through the efforts of ACL/DCI and LDC. What is more important, the corpora can be tagged with parts of speech and can also be bilingual (either aligned or not). A large set of programs for corpus processing has been developed, though not directly for the purpose of automating the acquisition of knowledge for NLP.

The great flowering of recent work on large text corpora can be conveniently divided into bilingual/parallel corpora-related efforts and monolingual corpora efforts. Work on bilingual corpora normally begins with algorithms to align the corresponding sentences across the languages and effective methods have been described and implemented based on the use of bilingual dictionaries and surveying words that appear opposed to a given word in a large number of sentences across the language boundary. Statistical methods for alignment based on number of characters in a region and on the number of words respectively have been described by Gale and Church [1] and Brown et al. [2].

After alignment methods have been described for obtaining matches of word strings between the languages based on cooccurrence between the pairs of language sentences, by those authors as well as Dagon and Itai [3]. There have also been projects based on word overlap (defined with respect to a bilingual dictionary) rather than statistics and due to suggestions of Kay (Catizone et al. [4]). All these methods result in a way of identifying polysemy in one language against different corresponding words in the other language (e.g. prendre as take or make, as in make a decision). In particular projects, as at IBM (Brown et al. [5]) have been extended to a full corpus-based MT system.

In the case of monolingual corpora, a substantial range of techniques has been defined for assigning syntactic tags automatically to corpora, most of them stemming from the the statistical techniques of Leech et al. [6] or the rule driven approach of Cherry et al. [7]; an example combining both methods would be Brill [8]. Attempts have been made to acquire subcategorisation information (e.g. typical subjects and objects of verbs) (Brent [9]) , sometimes done under the name of preferences (Lehnert [10]), as well as verb/preposition dependence information based on coocurrence or "mutual information" (Hindle [11]).

Attempts to derive semantically-related classes of words directly from corpora by coocurrence information based on on common neighborhoods have been done for syntagmic classes within the Pathfinder paradigm (McDonald et al. [12]) and for paradigmatic classes (of similar meaning) by IBM among others [13]). These classes at the bottom level are of striking semantic tightness (c.f. from IBM Christian Jew Buddhist Catholic Muslim; and Monday, Tuesday, Wednesday, Thursday etc.). Many of these willy-nilly are reimplementations of the early work of Sparck Jones [14] who did not have the computer power to apply her statistical algorithms twenty years ago. Large scale sense tagging of text remains an ideal and algorithms for doing it have been specified within the CRL lexical project [18], including a method due to Cowie that does not involve tagging with respect to an existing dictionary and is in that sense corpus driven). In addition there is a wide range of text-meaning extraction projects, usually a mixture of statistical and pattern matching approaches, within the US MUC and TIPSTER Projects [16].

1.3 MRD-Oriented Research

Machine-readable dictionaries (MRDs) contain substantial knowledge about language and the world essential for large-scale tasks in natural language processing (NLP), though an important empirical question remains whether they are sufficient for such tasks. This knowledge, however, collected and recorded by lexicographers for human readers, is not expressed in MRDs in a form that can be used directly as a tool for NLP tasks. What the NLP research community needs is machine tractable dictionaries (MTDs); that is, MRDs transformed into a format appropriate for NLP tasks.

Researchers, including those at NMSU CRL, have explored several large-scale computational methods for the transformation of MRDs into MTDs. A range of tools has been developed for extracting information from MRDs for specific NLP applications, including a hybrid SPIRAL methodology that combines elements from a number of numerical and non-numerical methods into a single coherent procedure to produce an MTD or a lexical knowledge base. The motivation behind the SPIRAL methodology is that, although each of the methods is incomplete in certain respects, and so a "weak" method in Newell's sense, the combination of them will yield better results than any individual method could. The chief difficulty with the MRD itself is that the defining items in the dictionary are themselves ambiguous, and it is this that the SPIRAL methodology has overcome by specifying effective procedures to "sense tag" dictionary definitions and general text [17, 18].

The result is an MTD that is an LKB, a Lexical Knowldge Base of unambiguous lexical facts, linked by a network of semantically-related word senses. At CRL a version of such a knowledge base has been derived from Longman's Dictionary of Contemporary English (LDOCE), though we are augmenting that from other MRDs such as COBUILD. Research on the structures contained within The Longman Dictionary of Contemporary English includes [19][20][21][22][23][17][24] and [18]. The innovation brought by MRDs is that, for the first time, both theoretical and practical concerns can be investigated using large-scale computational methods.

The next logical step for this ongoing research is to develop large-scale methods to extract both the syntactic and semantic information from MRD entries and present it in acceptable format as a data base for potential users. There are a number of ways one could construct such an MTD. One would be to extract the semantic information automatically and build the MTD, an approach we advocate; a second method would extract the semantic information manually and hand-code the entire MTD, as is being tried in the CYC Project (Lenat et al., [25] Feigenbaum, [26]). The main problem with the manual approach is the sheer amount of effort required. The CYC Project, for instance, which aims to hand-code a million entries from an encyclopedia, will take an estimated two person-centuries of work. We believe this to be a wasteful approach in terms of precious human resources that the approach itself is on shaky theoretical grounds (despite Lenat's claims that the project is "theory free").

2   WHAT MUST BE ACQUIRED?

Work on acquiring computational grammars, lexicons (MTDs) and ontologies can proceed in parallel. The program we outline here is an on-going cooperative research project between the University of Sheffield, Carnegie-Mellon University and New Mexico State University. Between them, these groups have constructed software in all these areas of grammar acquisition, automatic lexicon building, ontology construction and information extraction from text corpora. The basic research problem is how to combine the very specific, domain-dependent, factual information obtained from corpora by technologies like TIPSTER, with general, semantic, facts extracted from MRDs and corpora and organized by an ontology construction process.

2.1   Grammars

Syntactic markers in MRDs can supply some of the features for the syntactic parts of MTDs. Statistical processing of corpora can provide part of speech tagging and constituent boundary marking, thus "inducing" the grammar of a language. More advanced processing, such as establishment of syntactic dependency patterns (subcategorization information) should be attempted next.

Conventional approaches to NLP utilize a grammar which is created manually by encoding linguistic intuitions into a suitable formalism. The automatic acquisition of a grammar via statistical techniques is a challenging problem that is currently being investigated by a number of researchers in the field of NLP. Some of the most successful grammar inference techniques to date, have utilized finite-state language models such as N-gram models, Markov models, and Hidden Markov models (Levinson et al. [27]). Unfortunately such models are unable to capture long distance word associations or express the hierarchical structure of the language.

A stochastic context-free grammar (e.g. Baker [28]) is a hierarchical model introduced by Baker as a generalization of the parameter estimation methods for Hidden Markov models in the form of the inside-outside algorithm. Unfortunately, this model also suffers from

difficulties such as extreme computational costs and deterioration of convergence with increases in the number of non-terminals. Another effort directed at automatic phrase structure acquisition based on statistics gathered from corpora has been made by Marcus (Brill and Marcus [29]).

The Brill-Marcus distributional analysis method uses a technique from the days of structural linguistics (first proposed by Zellig Harris) that uses possible substitutions to determine phrase boundaries. The basic idea is that if two adjacent part of speech tags can be substituted for a single tag in many environments then the probability is high that the two tags form a constituent. This approach has been used to automatically induce English phrase structure using the their work the grammar rules are derived through a distributional analysis of the part of speech tags found in the Brown Corpus. Currently their work does not identify non-terminal labels nor is it applicable to more than simple sentences (A simple sentence is defined as a sentence with between 5 and 14 words containing no coordinates, quotations, or commas.). At CRL, Hargrave, Dunning and Wilks have designed and implemented an very effective tagger for Spanish, using the Penn Tree Bank tag-set that is about 96We are using this design as the basis for a grammar acquisition device at Sheffield for the acquisition of corpus-based grammars for English and Spanish.

2.2   Machine-tractable dictionaries

The non-syntactic information required in MTDs includes meaning, selectional restrictions, collocations and stylistic markers. Some of this information can be sought in MRDs, through available markers or through specialized automatic analysis of the texts of MRD entries. Candidates for collocations can be found by statistical search for cooccurrences in a corpus. Representation of meaning, however, centrally depends on an ontology which provides names and definitions of semantic primitives, including names of properties and their value sets.

CRL has completed a substantial part of its lexical program for the creation of a Lexical Knowledge Base (LKB), and would want to complete this program within the work described here in collaboration with the University of Sheffield: in particular a full treatment of automatic verb extraction of the kind that has been done for nouns; the establishment of techniques for merging and making consistent lexical information in the LKB from a range of MRD souces and corpora; and refining the method developed jointly between CRL and Brandeis University [18] lexical entries to the right form against particular corpora.

We would also like to implement a comprehensive treatment for the semantics and ontology of proper names, which can occupy up to half the text length of

100

some text types, and are of far more interest and complexity than simply items read off lists and gazeteers etc. We have detailed proposals for a comprehensive treatment of the semantics of unknown proper names based on inference from their surrounding context and spectrum of text appearances, which we believe to be how human readers are able to deal with unknown proper names in text by classifying them, pretty accurately, as companies, countries etc. on the basis of very general contextual knowledge.

2.3 Ontology

Efforts on acquiring unrestricted ontologies which are independent of particular applications (e.g., CYC) have proved unrealistic. On the other hand, it has proved very expensive to construct sufficiently detailed ontologies for realistic applications. Goals in creating ontologies include

I. establishing the vocabulary of primitive concepts in the domain (and a number of domain-independent concepts which appear in any kind of text) and connecting it through subsumption ("is-a") relations (thus, introducing inheritance in order to reduce the amount of work in both acquisition and maintenance as well as to provide a search space for inference-making for an application);

II. defining a set of basic properties (relations and attributes), their domains and ranges (the latter task can also involve defining concepts which are property values) with which to characterize the concepts in the ontology; this set includes, for instance, the definition of case roles as well as other general semantic properties (e.g., "part-of");

III. actually assigning properties and particular property values to the concepts in the network.

Work toward goal I above can be aided by "seeding" the ontology from an MRD, such as LDOCE and establishing at least partial hierarchical dependencies automatically by processing genus terms. Work toward goals II and III can be aided by statistical semantic "clustering" of words and phrases from a corpus, based on occurrence in similar contexts which serves as a weak heuristic for semantic affinity. Additionally, task III can be aided by the analysis of the text of MRD entries. We are also investigating the construction of meaning representations of text segments deemed "relevant" by some general selection system (in the spirit of [18]) by means of assembly of such structures (under the well-formedness constraints of the ontology) from items deemed statistically significant in the text.

This method can be seen as a top-down analogue to the bottom-up template items derived by the information extraction process. It is the fusion of these two sources that constitutes the heart of our method for deriving knowledge strutures automatically from existing corpora and MRD resources.

3 METHODOLOGY AND ASSUMPTIONS

We begin with a very general hypothesis about the organization of the ontology, which is a top-down description of events, objects and relations, based on our general knowledge about the world and which is further informed by our observations about the way in which particular languages choose to represent this knowledge (we acknowledge that the evidence will necessarily be partial at this stage, and limited by the languages with which we are acquainted).

We also stress strong methodological differences from both the contemporary COMLEX (at New York University under Grishman, supported by the Linguistic Data Consortium) and the long-term EC supported ACQUILEX enterprises. COMLEX is driven by a belief in the inessential nature of semantic and real-world information for lexicon building for text understanding, and it will be clear that we do not share that view for the reasons set out here.

Conversely, AQUILEX is a project whose aim is a high level of theoretical succinctness in the linguistic sense: it has no imperatives towards the provision of large-scale resources for text understanding and it will be clear from this paper and our track records that ours is essentially a practical approach to the provision of materials.

As to implementation, we propose to adopt the transputer-based IDIOMS data-base machine as a method for processing much larger volumes of text than is currently feasable at high speed. The IDIOMS project [30] has demonstrated the feasibility of building a large parallel database machine which can support relational database operations in which rows of tables are treated as objects and manipulated as such. The IDIOMS machine enabled both transaction processing and decision support queries on the same data at the same time. The decision support system generated SQL queries which accessed large volumes of data to undertake data mining and information extraction operations. Typically, the data sets exceed 200 Gbytes. The project also demonstrated that it is possible to build a scalable architecture with a low incremental cost.

This latter aspect was achieved by using a transputer based architecture to build a shared nothing database machine. Such a machine is inherently scalable but requires that new algorithms are developed for the operation and management of the machine. This has subsequently led to the design of a complete object based system which is to be developed as part of a European Commission funded project called IRISS. This machine separates the object storage subsystem from the processing system. This has the benefit of allowing each part of the system to be made fault tolerant in its own right. This will aid in the ease of scaling systems because each part will be individually fault tolerant reducing the need for a centralised fault control system. The IRISS machine is to be built using Inmos T9000 transputers because they provide the required communications infrastructure, in conjunction with the C104 communications chip. This communications infrastructure permits direct connection between the processes that make up the system without having to consider the underlying hardware topology, yet again easing the scalability of the system.

3.1 Concrete tasks to be carried out

Given a very general top level ontological specification, as described above, we are developing language-dependent world models (i.e., hierarchies or networks) for each of N languages in the chosen domain. The domain should be general enought that it exhibits cross-linguistic variation, but narrow enough that it focuses our research. The mergers and acquisitons domain would be a suitable point of departure, since certain types of business concepts vary across languages in more interesting ways than highly technical material. These models will be created by extracting information from domain-specific corpora, using automated techniques which we will develop as part of this project. We initially intend to select a minimum of 2 or 3 languages that are different enough so that the issues of language-independence which we ultimately wish to examine can truly be tested.

Taxonomies derived from a single language, such as WordNet or the Penman Upper Model, can provide a "baseline" for what the language-dependent models should look like. Note that WordNet and the Upper Model are handcrafted; one of the goals of this project would be to develop techniques for automating the process of extracting knowledge and constructing a Word-Net style model for a given language. We would start with domain specific extraction, and hope to generalize later to domain independent extraction.

Next, a methodology must be developed for comparing the various language-dependent models that are constructed using the automated techniques on the domain-specific corpora. A theoretical issue here is whether or not a method can be devised for measuring the distance between concepts extracted automatically in a language-specific environment.

Finally, a methodology must be developed for creating a language-independent world model that supports all N languages, constructing it from the language-dependent models, and basing it on the measurements of distance between concepts in the various hierarchies. How much of the "merging" process can be done automatically or semi-automatically?

REFERENCES

28 Baker, James K., (1975) "Stochastic modeling for automatic speech understanding" in D Raj Reddy (ed.) Speech recognition pp.521-542, Academic Press.

19 Binot, J. L., Jensen, K. (1987). A Semantic Expert Using an Online Standard Dictionary. In Proceedings of the 10th International Joint Conference on Artificial Intelligence. IJCAI-87 (Pub.). Milan, Italy. 709-714.

9 Brent, M., (1991). Automatic Semantic Classification of Verbs from their Syntactic Contexts: An Implemented Classifier for Stativity. In Proceedings of the 5th European Meeting of the Association for Computational Linguistics .

8 Brill, E., (1991). Discovering the Lexical Features of a Language. In Proceedings of the 29th Annual Meeting of the ACL, Berkeley, Ca.

29 Brill, E., and Marcus, M., (1992) "Automatically Acquiring Phrase Structure Using Distributional Analysis", Fifth DARPA Workshop on Speech and Natural Language, February 1992.

23 Boguraev,B., Briscoe, T. (1987). Large Lexicons for Natural Language Processing: Utilising the Grammar. In Computational Linguistics .

22 Boguraev, B. K., Briscoe, T., Carroll, J., Carter, D., Grover, C. (1987). The Derivation of a Grammatically Indexed Lexicon from the Longman Dictionary of Contemporary English. In Proceedings of the 25th Annual Meeting of the ACL . Stanford, CA. 193-200.

5 Brown, P., Cocke, J., Della Pietra, S., Della Pietra, V., Jelinek, F., Mercer, R., and Roosin, P. (1988) A statistical approach to language translation. In Proceedings of the International Congress on Computational Linguistics, Budapest, Hungary. 71-75.

2 Brown, P. et al. (1990). Class-based n-gram models of natural language. Proc. IBM NLP Workshop. Paris, France.

13 Brown, P. F. and others, (1991) "Word sense disambiguation using statistical methods", Proceedings of the 29th Annual Meeting of the ACL.

4 Catizone, R., Russell, G., Warwick, S. (1989). Deriving Translation Data from Bilingual Texts. In Zernik (Ed.) Lexical Acquisition:using on-line Resources to Build a Lexicon . Lawrence Erlbaum (Pub.).

7 Cherry, L., M. Fox, L. Frase, P. Gingrich, S. Keenan, and N. Macdonald, (1983) "Computer aids for text analysis" In Bell Laboratories Records, May/June, pp.10-16.

18 Cowie, J., Dunning, D., Guthrie, L., and Wilks, Y. 1993. Text Processing at CRL using multi-lingual resources. Literary & Linguistic Computing , vol. 8.

16 Cowie, J., and Lehnert, W., (in press) Information Extraction, In Y. Wilks (ed.) Special issue of the Communications of the ACM on Natural language Processing.

3 Dagon, Ido, and Alon Itai (1990). Processing Large Corpora for Reference Resolution. Proceedings of the 13th International Conference on Computational Linguistics (COLING-90) , Helsinki, Finland, 3, pp.330-332.

1 Gale, W. A. and Church, K. W., (1991), A Program for Aligning Sentences in Bilingual Corpora, Proceedings of the 29th Annual Meeting of the ACL.

24 Guthrie, L., B. Slator, Y. Wilks, and R. Bruce (1990). Is there content in Empty Heads? Proceedings of the 13th International Conference on Computational Linguistics (COLING-90) , Helsinki, Finland, 3, pp.138-143.

11 Hindle, D., (1989) "Acquiring Disambiguation Rules from Text", Proceedings of the 27th Annual Meeting of the Association for Computational Linguistics.

30 Kerridge, J. (1991) The Design of the IDIOMS Parallel Database Machine, In Jackson, R. and Robinson, A. (eds.) Aspects of Databases,

6 Leech, G., Garside,R., and Atwell E., (1983) "The Automatic Grammatical Tagging of the LOB Corpus" In

10 Lehnert, W., (1987). Automating the acquisition of semantic preferences. Department of Computer and Information Science, University of Massachusetts, Amherst.

25 Lenat, D. B., M. Prakash, and M. Shepherd (1986). CYC: Using Common Sense Knowledge to Overcome Brittleness and Knowledge Acquisition Bottlenecks. AI Magazine , 7, (4), pp.65-85.

26 Lenat, D. B., and E. A. Feigenbaum (1987). On The Thresholds of Knowledge. Proceedings of the 10th International Joint Conference on Artificial Intelligence (IJCAI-87) , Milan, Italy, pp.1173-1182.

12 McDonald, J.E., A.T. Plate, and R.W. Schvaneveldt (1990). Using Pathfinder to extract semantic information from text. In R. W. Schvaneveldt (ed.), Pathfinder Associative Networks: Studies in Knowledge Organization . Norwood, NJ: Ablex.

19 Michiels, A., Mullenders, J., Noel, J. (1980). Exploiting a Large Data Base by Longman. In Proceedings of the 8th International Conference on Computational Linguistics (COLING-80) . Tokyo, Japan. 374-382.

20 Michiels, A., Noel, J. (1982). Approaches to Thesaurus Production. In Proceedings of the 9th International Conference on Computational Linguistics (COLING-82) . Prauge, Czechoslovakia. 227-232.

27 Levinson, S. E., L. R. Rabiner, and M. M. Sonhi, (1983) "An introduction to the application of the theory of probabilistic functions of a Markov process to automatic speech recognition" in Bell Systems Technical Journal 62, pp.1035-1074.

14 Sparck Jones, K., (1989). Synonymy and Semantic Classification , Edinburgh: Edinburgh Univ. Press.

21 Walker, D.E., Amsler, R.A. (1986). The Use of Machine-Readable Dictionaries in Sublanguage Analysis. In Grishman, R., Kittredge, R. (Eds.) Analyzing Language in Restricted Domains . Hillsdale, NJ: Lawrence Erlbaum.

17 Wilks, Y.A., Fass, D. C., Guo, C.M., McDonald, J. E., Plate, T., Slator, B.M. (1987). A Tractable Machine Dictionary as a Resource for Computational Semantics. In Boguraev, B., Briscoe, T. (Eds.) Computational Lexicography for Natural Language Processing . Harlow, Essex, England: Longmans.

Knowledge Acquisition
from Natural Language Documents
for Large Knowledge Bases

Gian Piero Zarri
Centre National de la Recherche Scientifique EHESS - CAMS
Paris, France
zarri@cams.msh-paris.fr

ABSTRACT

This paper deals with the problem of producing a standard, formal representation of the semantic content (the "meaning") of complex natural language (NL) "narrative" documents (e.g., legal documents, unedited press releases, or intelligence messages). The resulting code can then be used to populate very large knowledge bases, which can, afterwards, provide support for all sorts of "expert" applications. After having presented briefly the Narrative Knowledge Representation Language (NKRL) that we employ as the target language, we illustrate the main phases of a "conceptual parsing" strategy able to produce, through a rule-based approach and in a (largely) automated way, an NKRL representation of the original natural language texts.

1   INTRODUCTION

This paper illustrates a strategy for automatically producing a standard, formal representation of the semantic content (the "meaning") of complex, natural language (NL) "narrative" texts ; the target language we use is called NKRL (Narrative Knowledge Representation Language), see [21, 24, 25]. The resulting code can then be utilised to populate very large knowledge bases, which can cater, afterwards, for all sorts of "expert" applications like case-based reasoning (CBR), intelligent information retrieval, temporal and causal reasoners, etc. In an industrial context, "narrative texts" may correspond to news stories, telex reports, corporate documentation, regulations and normative texts, intelligence messages, etc.

A full version of the strategy has been first implemented, from December 1990 to December 1992, in the framework of the European Commission (EC) Esprit Project 5330, NOMOS ("Knowledge Acquisition for Normative Reasoning Systems"). A (partially) new version has then been developed in the framework of another EC-granted project, COBALT ("Construction of Knowledge Bases from Natural Language Documents") ; COBALT is the LRE (Linguistic Research and Engineering) Project 61011. COBALT started in November 1992 and ended in January 1995.

The "narrative" textual documents examined in the two projects are fundamentally different. In NOMOS, they consisted essentially of regulations (in French) having a very general scope, like the French "General Taxation Law"; as a consequence, the NKRL code produced was a sort of "high-level" representation, that still included variables and constraints (see, *infra*, Section 4.2). This output was then used, in the context of some CBR-like, practical applications, to retrieve "low-level" NKRL code describing, now, particular, real-world events representing the "instances" of the abstract situations described in the original normative documents. In COBALT, on the contrary, the texts examined are essentially Reuters news stories in the financial domain: the NKRL code produced reflects this strictly "factual" nature of the input documents and does not include, normally, variables and constraints. COBALT's aim consists, mainly, in developing an advanced categorisation application by selecting, in a first phase, some *a priori* interesting documents, and by evidencing then their precise factual content through their translation into NKRL terms.

In the following, we will present briefly, in Section 2, the Narrative Knowledge Representation Language (NKRL).

In Section 3, we will discuss the general architecture which realises our "translation" strategy. Section 4 will be devoted to illustrating the "specialisation" procedures which allow the adaptation of the generic, predefined NKRL conceptual structures to the specific needs of the NL text actually processed. In Section 5, we will evoke briefly the new procedures recently added, in a COBALT context, to deal with the problem of the ambiguous prepositional phrases attachment. Section 6, "Conclusion", will supply, among other things, some technical details.

2 SOME INFORMATION ABOUT NKRL

NKRL — which bears some (superficial) resemblance to the well-known, canonical hybrid and terminological languages, see KL-ONE [5] or CLASSIC [6] — has been created to provide a *standard*, language-independent description of the content of narrative textual documents. Therefore, it can be seen, with respect to the description of the *semantic* characteristics of such documents, as the equivalent of the well-known standards, like SGML, used for the description of their *structural* characteristics. The Euroknowledge consortium — an industrial and academic working group supported by the European R&D authorities — has recently added NKRL to the list of knowledge representation tools they will promote to contribute to the creation of possible industrial standards.

The "conceptual coding" approach proper to NKRL differs strongly from some recent proposals (see, e.g., [20]) which advocate the direct utilisation of natural language (NL) as the best possible knowledge representation language ever created. Please note, however, that the two positions are not totally irreconcilable from a practical point of view. They share, in fact, the same exigency of making use of a complete, functional model for each given natural language. For the conceptual coding approach, this is necessary to accomplish the "conversion" operations into conceptual format. For the "pure NL approach", the existence of this model is a necessary (but not sufficient) condition to be able to exploit concretely the NL formulation of the original documents. A disadvantage of the conceptual coding approach concerns the unavoidable loss of original information which goes with the reduction to a canonical format. This is largely compensated, however, by the possibility of obtaining, thanks to the independence from any particular NL, a high degree of systems interoperability and information portability across a wide range of possible applications, and by the gain in efficiency of all the computer operations (e.g., inferencing) due, precisely, to the presence of a standardised (and, therefore, well-controlled) format.

Like the hybrid systems, NKRL consists of several integrated components (four in our case), each of which employs distinct, specialised representation languages which call, in turn, for their own, proper inference systems.

The "descriptive component" concerns the formal representation (called "predicative templates") of some general classes of narrative events, like "moving a physical object", "having a negative attitude towards someone", "having the control of some person or social body"; templates describe, therefore, the expected features of (a non-trivial set of) various ordinary events and human activities. All the legal templates are structured into a hierarchy, H_TEMP(lates). The NKRL objects built up in NOMOS were, essentially, "derived" templates, i.e., specialisations, according to the characteristics of the NL normative texts under examination, of the permanent, "basic" templates (independent from the domain) included in the H_TEMP hierarchy.

Templates' instances (called "occurrences"), i.e., the NKRL representations of single, specific events like "Lucy moves the wardrobe (this particular one)", "Mr. Smith has fired Mr. Brown", "Company X has taken the control of Company Y", etc., are in the domain of another NKRL component, the "factual component". Templates and occurrences are characterised by a threefold format, where the central piece is a (unique) "semantic predicate" (BEHAVE, EXPERIENCE, MOVE, EXIST). "Arguments" (role fillers) are introduced by "roles" as SUBJ(ect), OBJ(ect), SOURCE, etc.

The "definitional component" supplies the formal representation of the defining properties of all the general entities and notions, like "*physical_entity*", "*human_being_or_social_body*", "*control_power*", which can be used in the framework of the two components above. The corresponding NKRL structures are called "concepts" (basically, they can be equated to frames), and are grouped into a hierarchy which, for historical reasons, is called "H_CLASS(es)" — H_CLASS is, therefore, a hierarchy (more exactly, a lattice) of concepts. The instances of concepts, like "lucy_", "wardrobe_1", "company_x" are called "individuals", and pertain to the "enumerative component". Throughout this paper, we will use the italic type style to represent a "*concept_*", the roman style to represent an "individual_".

We can now supply (Fig. 1) a very simple example of NKRL code. It translates the NL sentence (a small fragment of COBALT's news) : "Milan, October 15, 1993. The financial daily Il Sole 24 Ore reported Mediobanca had called a special board meeting concerning plans for capital increase".

In Fig. 1, c1 and c2 are the symbolic names (OIDs, object identifiers) of two occurrences, instances of stan-

```
    c1)    MOVE         SUBJ       (SPECIF sole_24_ore financial_daily):(milan_)
                        OBJ        #c2
                        date-1:    15_october_93
                        date-2:

    c2)    PRODUCE      SUBJ       mediobanca_
                        OBJ        (SPECIF summoning_1 (SPECIF board_meeting_1
                                       special_))
                        TOPIC      (SPECIF plan_1 (SPECIF cardinality_ several_)
                                       capital_increase_1)
                        date-1:    circa_15_october_93
                        date-2:
```

Figure 1 - An example of NKRL coding.

dard NKRL templates. MOVE and PRODUCE are predicates; SUBJ, OBJ, TOPIC (the theme, "à propos of", of event(s) or situation(s) represented in the occurrence) are roles. With respect now to the arguments, sole_24_ore, milan_, mediobanca_ (an Italian merchant bank), summoning_1, etc. are individuals; financial_daily, special_, cardinality_ (which pertains to the property_ sub-tree of H_CLASS) and several_ (belonging, like some_, all_ etc., to the logical_quantifier sub-tree of H_CLASS) are concepts. The "attributive operator", "SPECIF(ication)", is one of the NKRL operators used to build up "structured arguments" (or "expansions"); the SPECIF lists are used to represent some of the properties which can be asserted about the first element of the list, e.g., sole_24_ore in occurrence c1, summoning_1 and plan_1 in occurrence c2. several_ is used within a SPECIF list having cardinality_ as first element to provide a standard way of representing the "plural number" mark, see occurrence c2.

The arguments, and the templates/occurrences as a whole, may be characterised by the addition of particular codes, "determiners" or "attributes", which give further details about their significant aspects. For example, the "location attributes" are associated with the arguments (role fillers) by using the "colon", ":", operator; they are represented always by using lists, see occurrence c1. For a recent paper on the NKRL representation of the temporal determiners, "date-1" and "date-2", see [22].

Please note that the MOVE template at the origin of the occurrence c1 is necessarily used to translate any event concerning the transmission of an information ("...Il Sole 24 Ore reported..."). It makes use of what is called a "completive construction". Accordingly, the filler of the OBJ(ect) slot in the occurrence (here, c1) which instantiates the transmission template is always an OID (here, #c2) which refers to another predicative occurrence, i.e., the occurrence bearing the information to be spread out ("Mediobanca has called a meeting..."). Please refer to [24, 25] for more on templates, their variables and constraints.

3 THE TRANSLATION PROCESS

Constructing (very large) knowledge bases of narrative, textual documents represented into NKRL format — they are sometimes called "metadocuments" — requires the existence of an "NL/NKRL translation system", in the style, e.g., of the (now so popular) "message understanding systems", see [3, 7, 19].

The two versions, NOMOS and COBALT, of our NL/NKRL translation system are both based on the use of independent "specialists". These are called in sequence, producing a progressive increment of the level of NKRL granularity. As is well known, this type of approach facilitates the achievement of a) the traditional goals concerning the "openness", "modularity" and "portability" of the global system; b) the insertion of additional processor into the architecture ("extendibility"); c) the "friendly interaction" with the user, who can easily intervene ("semi-automatic" processing) at each step of the procedure in order to choose, e.g., among multiple solutions — this is not applicable in a COBALT context (see, infra, Section 5.); d) the availability of partial, potentially useful results, also in the event of the impossibility of a full achievement of the translation process ("graceful degradation").

3.1 The common shared data structures

The specialists make use of permanent, common shared data structures (knowledge sources). Two of these data structures are reserved, e.g., for the storage of the H_CLASS ("concepts", definitional component) and H_TEMP ("templates", descriptive component) hierarchies.

The most important shared structure is, however, the "lexicon", which is a complex mechanism entailing that each of its NL lexical entries contains morpho-syntactic, semantic and pragmatic information (see also, in a similar vein, [14, 15]). The lexical entries represent, mainly, "rootforms" (infinitive for the verbs, etc.); each entry is a structured object including, normally, nine multivalued slots ("morphology-of", "morphological-features", "syntactic-category", "semantic-features", etc.); the entire lexicon is a hierarchy having the object "word" as root. Three particular slots, "ref-scenario", "ref-template" and "ref-concept", may contain pointers towards another category of conceptual data structures, i.e., the "conceptual" dictionaries (which include mainly pragmatic information).

A first conceptual dictionary concerns the "scenario references": it contains the "text grammar" rules allowing the quick focusing on a particular information to be extracted while ignoring irrelevant elements, see, e.g., [1, 13], etc. Scenario references have not been implemented in NOMOS owing, mainly, to the fact that the regulations to be "translated" were characterised by a semantic content which could be considered as totally pertinent. In COBALT, on the contrary, we make use of a commercial product, TCS (Text Categorisation System, by Carnegie Group, Pittsburgh, U.S.A.) to generate a first-level broad classification of the texts; TCS employs the standard H_CLASS hierarchy (concept hierarchy, definitional component) of NKRL instead of its own set of "concepts". The *a priori* interesting texts are then analysed in depth, using the usual NL/NKRL techniques, to produce a "second level" categorisation (content classification) of these texts.

The "template references" dictionary contains the "triggering rules" evoked by the lexical entry examined, i.e., rules allowing the activation of particular templates pertaining to the H_TEMP hierarchy (descriptive component) — the activated templates will supply the general framework of the final representation in NKRL terms of the input texts. Triggering rules are a sort of production rules, see also, *infra*, Section 4.1. The left hand side (antecedent part) is always a "syntactic condition", expressed under the form of a tree-like structure, to be unified with the results of the general parse tree produced by the syntactic specialist. If the unification succeeds, the right hand sides (consequents) are used to generate well-formed templates.

The last conceptual dictionary is the "conceptual references" dictionary, where we store the control structures ("substitution rules", similar to the "triggering rules") allowing the replacement, in the original NL text, of an NP (noun phrase group, NL domain), or part of NP, with the corresponding H_CLASS concept(s) or individual(s) (NKRL domain).

3.2 The specialists

With respect now to the specialists, the output of the first specialist of the sequence, the "pre-processing specialist", is a set of distinct sentences, to be separately processed, which have already been submitted to the morphological analysis.

In NOMOS, the syntactic analysis of each sentence was performed by a robust ATN compiler ("syntactic specialist") making use of a "*Grammaire Française de Surface*", GSF; syntactic ambiguity was handled a) by using "heuristics", see [11, 12]; b) by interacting with the user through a friendly interface. In COBALT, we use instead a morphosyntactic analyser for free texts based on an efficient implementation of Categorial Grammar with Unification, CGU. The output of the COBALT's "syntactic specialist" is, therefore, a quasi-logical form representing a shallow, under-specified analysis of the predicate-argument structures and the semantic features of the input text. For COBALT purposes, the output has been augmented with syntactic derivation trees to cater for the requirements of the subsequent specialists, already developed in a NOMOS context. Our translation procedures are, in fact, strongly syntax-controlled, and the topology of the parse tree(s) produced initially by the syntactic analyser is conserved until the end of the procedures.

The specialist called "separation into morpho-syntactic contexts" has been introduced for the purpose of modularity, robustness [12] and simplicity. It makes use of morpho-syntactic rules which are linked, e.g., with the presence of relative clauses, and which it applies, for each sentence, to the results of the syntactic analysis. For example, in a NL fragment pertaining to a NOMOS context, like: "In order to determine the income tax payable by companies which are under the authority of, or which exercise a control over, companies domiciled abroad...", a segmentation mark is introduced in correspondence of the first "which", and the fragment is split into two morpho-syntactic contexts which are processed separately.

The substitution procedures ("substitution specialist") constitute one of the fundamental steps of the translation process; they concern the terminal symbols (NL terms) of the syntactic tree, pertaining to the context at hand, which are part of a N(oun) P(hrase)'s head. For each one of these terms (NL domain), we must examine the substitution rules stored in the corresponding entries of the "conceptual references" dictionary, see the previous Section, to see if it is possible to replace it with the corresponding concept or individual (NKRL domain); see also [15]. A (unique) NKRL term may also replace the association of several terminal symbols (NL terms) : e.g., it may replace the entire NP group. The output of the substitution phase is, therefore, a context expressed as a fragment of parse tree where the leaves can be either NL or NKRL terms.

For example, after this phase, the context corresponding to the "Il Sole 24 Ore" NL fragment examined, *supra*, in Section 2, becomes equivalent, represented in linear form, to the mixed expression given in Figure 2, where "*financial_daily*", "*sole_24_ore*", "*mediobanca_*", "*special_*", etc. are NKRL terms (concepts or individuals). We do not dwell here on the formal characteristics of the substitution rules: they are handled in a way very similar to that used for the ."riggering rules", examined in some details, *infra*, in Section 4.1.

"The [*financial_daily*] [*sole_24_ore*] reported [*mediobanca_*] had called a [*special_*] [*board_meeting*] concerning [(SPECIF plan_1 (SPECIF *cardinality_ several_*))] for [*capital_increase_1*]."

Figure 2 - "Mixed" (NL/NKRL) formulation.

The following specialist, i.e., the "triggering — filling — merging" specialist ("specialisation specialist"), will be discussed in Section 4.

The last specialist of the sequence deals with the anaphoric phenomena and the calculation of the "inter-context" logical and semantic links. In the actual state of the "NL/NKRL translation system", only some simple cases of pronominal anaphora are dealt with, by making use of pure syntactic methods. The calculation of the inter-context links is based, mainly, on the search, on the syntactic tree, for the syntactic marks — e.g., co-ordination — which link together clauses having given rise to autonomous morpho-syntactic contexts. A set of rules associated with the identification of these syntactic marks will then allow the generation of the "binding structures" — binding templates and occurrences, see again [21, 24, 25] — which are proper to the NKRL language.

4 THE "SPECIALISATION" PROCEDURES

These procedures ("triggering — filling — merging" specialist) represent the core of our "NL/NKRL translation system". They are applied in sequence to the contexts obtained from the sentences of the NL texts under examination.

4.1 Triggering

For example, in the formulation of the "Il Sole 24 Ore" fragment, see Figure 2, which follows from the application of the substitution rules, the NL terms "said" and "called" are associated with specific subsets of the triggering rules stored in the template references dictionary.

We reproduce, in Figure 3, one of the several triggering rules to which the lexical entry "call" contains a pointer, i.e., one of the rules corresponding to the meaning "to issue a call to convene". This rule allows the activation of the template PRODUCE4.12 that can give rise, at a later stage, to the occurrence c2 of Figure 1, see, *supra*, Section 2; for clarity's sake, the syntactic condition (the antecedent) is expressed in indented form. Please note that "optional branches" under the form "(modifiers (adjs/noun x_n))" — see, in Fig. 3, the branch "(modifiers (adjs x_{31}))" — can be freely inserted in the "noun phrases" (np) of the syntactic condition to cater for the presence of optional modifiers, see also, e.g., [23].

We can also remark that the full template is not actually stored in the consequent, given that the H_TEMP hierarchy is already part of the "common shared data structures" mentioned before. Only the parameters relating to the specific triggering rule and strictly necessary to set up a "derived template" are, therefore, stored in the consequent. In Fig. 3 we indicate, e.g., that, to represent adequately the intended meaning, we require here the presence of SPECIF lists in the OBJ(ect) and TOPIC roles; the "+" symbol indicates the roles of the original H_TEMP template which become "mandatory". The list "constr" actualises the constraints on some of the variables, while others — e.g., the constraints on the variables x_1 (*human_being/social_body*) and x_3 (*assembly_*) — are, obviously, unchanged.

In our approach, variables are of paramount importance: the "expectations" mechanism which is central to the construction of any sort of "conceptual" parsers, see [17], etc., is realised here in a rigorous way by making use of variables and constraints. For clarity's sake, we distinguish between two sorts of variables.

"t", see the syntactic condition in Figure 3, are "triggering variables". Only one triggering variable can appear in a rule: it is defined in the syntactic condition part (antecedent) of the rule (i.e., the triggering variables are "antecedent variables", or "a-variables"), where it is immediately bound to the NL (or H_CLASS) term giving origin to a call to the triggering routines ("actualisation").

"$x_1 \ldots x_n$" are "template variables". Normally, they are first declared in the syntactic condition part (antecedent part) of the rules as a-variables, and then "echoed" in the consequent part of the same rules, where they appear under the form of arguments and constraints associated with the roles of the activated templates, see Figure 3. Please note that the triggering variables introduced before can be reused as template a-variables, see again Figure 3 before. The function of the template a-variables is that of "capturing" — during the match between the antecedent of the rule and the results of the general syntactic analysis per-

```
trigger : "call"

    syntactic condition :

    (s (subj (np (noun x1)))
        (vcl (voice active) (v t = x2 = call))
        (dir-obj
            (np (modifiers (adjs x31))
                (noun x3)
                (modifiers (pp (prep about | concerning | … )
                              (np (noun x4)
                                  (modifiers (pp (prep of  | for …)
                                                (np (noun x5))))))))))


    parameters for the template :

(PRODUCE4.12 (roles +subj x1 +obj (SPECIF x2 (SPECIF x3 x31)) +topic (specif x4
    x5)) (constr x2 summoning_ x31 quality_ x4 abstract_modality x5
    modification_procedures))
```

Figure 3 - An example of triggering rule.

formed by the syntax specialist — NL or H_CLASS terms to be then used as "specialisation terms" for the subsequent, filling operations. It is possible that some template variables — e.g., some "location" variables, see [23] and also, *infra*, Section 4.3 — appear only in the NKRL structures associated with the consequent parts of the triggering rules ("c-variables"). This means that, in such cases, the "specialisation values" to be bound to these variables cannot be derived in a simple way from the elements retrieved on the syntactic tree (i.e., from the original NL text): if really needed, they must be calculated at the end of the translation procedures, e.g., by inference or by asking for the intervention of the human operator. In Figure 3, all the template variables are a-variables.

With respect now to the match procedures between the syntactic conditions of the triggering rules and the general parse tree produced by the syntactic specialist, the unification algorithm works in a way which is partially different from that of an usual "Robinsonian" algorithm. The comparison is based here on the general principle of checking that each path (i.e., linear succession of nodes) linking the root of the syntactic condition subtree with a terminal symbol (a "leaf") of this subtree is "included" within the corresponding paths extracted from the general parse tree. "Inclusion" means here that a) all the nodes of the syntactic condition path must appear among the nodes of the general parse path ; b) no total coincidence is required (this allows, among other things, to cater for the "optional branches", see before; but c) identical nodes must be encountered in the same order when

traversing the paths. If the comparison returns "true", then the template a-variables contained in the syntactic conditions are bound to the corresponding nodes of the parse tree. In other words, the algorithm only checks a very general "topological" congruence of the two trees which excludes the "strict superimposition", i.e., it does not return systematically "false" when "numberof(u.subnodes) numberof(v.subnodes)", with "u" and "v" two generic nodes of the two trees.

In the "Il Sole 24 Ore" example, the antecedent of the triggering rule of Figure 3 effectively unifies the result produced by the syntactic specialist, thus authorising the instantiation of the template PRODUCE4.12 mentioned in the consequent. Moreover, its a-variables can "capture" on the parse tree, during the unification phase, NL or H_CLASS terms which can then be used as specialisation terms for the subsequent filling operations.

4.2 Filling

The "filling" operations include the two following, main steps :

1) We must verify that the values bound to the a-variables satisfy the constraints — see the consequent part of Figure 3 — associated with those variables. Verification is, mainly, a form of inheritance-based reasoning which makes use of the properties of the H_CLASS hierarchy (hierarchy of concepts). In the "Il Sole 24 Ore" example, from Figure 2 it is easy to see, e.g., that the values assumed by the a-variables x_4 and x_5

of Figure 3 are, respectively, "plan_1" and "capital_increase_1". These values satisfy, respectively, the constraints *abstract_modality* and *modification_procedures* indicated in Figure 3. Some additional operations can be performed in this phase. In our example, e.g., the NL value "call" associated with the triggering variable, t, will be replaced by an instance (individual) of the corresponding constraint, the concept *summoning_*.

2) If the constraints have been satisfied, the roles of the templates can be "filled". We must emphasise here that, for us, "filling the roles" has a meaning which is stronger than in other "conceptual" approaches: it contributes also to the adaptation of the abstract H_TEMP structures activated during the triggering phase to the particular needs of the NL texts under examination. This is particularly evident in a "regulations" context like that of NOMOS, where executing the filling operations must lead to the production of "derived" (specialised) templates, instead of giving rise to specific occurrences in the style of those of Figure 1. In the NOMOS application, therefore, "filling the roles" means replacing the very general constraints (concepts) originally associated, in H_TEMP, with the roles of the activated templates, by other concepts, i.e., their specialised "H_CLASS subtypes" corresponding to the values collected on the syntactic tree. In this way, the constraint *human_being/social_body* originally associated, in the template PRODUCE4.21, with the variable x_1, would be substituted by a more specific concept like, e.g., *merchant_bank*. See [36] for more details.

4.3 Merging

The merge of "semi-identical" NKRL syntactic structures, derived templates or occurrences, is the final step in the specialisation process. For each context, we try, in fact, to obtain the minimal, pertinent number of structures, where each one must able to supply the most complete description of an event or a category of events.

Our merging routines — which present some similarities with the "join" operations introduced by Sowa [18] — are based on the classical, "Robinsonian" unification procedures, given that, in the most complex case (i.e., in the presence of derived templates), explicit variables are ubiquitously present in all the structures we will try to merge. Unification is tried in a systematic way, i.e., if two structures t_i and t_j — included in the list l of (triggered and filled) NKRL structures obtained as output of the filling phase — unify, the resulting $t_{i,j}$ is added to l and submitted in turn to the unification procedures (but not merged again with its "parents" t_i and t_j). The unification of t_i and t_j is

successful under these general conditions:

a) t_i and t_j are characterised by the same predicate;

b) the intersection of their respective role sets is not empty (they have at least a role in common);

c) all the "corresponding" (same name) roles included in the intersection unify, meaning with this assertion that also their arguments (i.e., role fillers), determiners (e.g., location attributes, see, *supra*, Section 2) and, in case, constraints, must unify.

If these conditions hold, $t_{i,j}$ is automatically built up; it contains: a) the common predicate; b) all the roles (plus arguments etc.) of both t_i and t_j which do not appear in the intersection; c) the roles included in the intersection, associates with their new arguments, determiners and constraints resulting from the unification operations.

We will now comment briefly on the unification of two arguments, a_i and a_j. Let us suppose, as a simple example, that the list l contains the two "semi-identical", derived templates "à la NOMOS" represented in Fig. 4. t2 subsumes a set of possible occurrences, all relating the fact that a given company (x_4) exercises a control over another company (x_3) ; t1 says only that a company exercises some form of control. The two templates could have been obtained, after the filling phase, when dealing with the beginning of a simple normative text, article n. 57 of the French "General Taxation Law" we have already mentioned, *supra*, in Section 3.2: "In order to determine the income tax payable by companies which are under the authority of, or which exercise a control over, companies domiciled abroad." Let us suppose also that x_3, x_4 and x_5 are all "a-variables" (antecedent variables), i.e., that they have been bound to some values during the match between the antecedents and the syntactic tree; these values have then been used to specialise the constraints of the original OWN templates, see the previous Section. We suppose, moreover, that the "location" variables x_7 and x_{11} are both "c-variables" (consequent variables), i.e., they appeared in the original templates as stored in the H_TEMP hierarchy but not in the syntactic conditions of the triggering rules and, therefore, they have not assumed any value during the triggering phase.

As a first remark, we can note that arguments are, in general, structured arguments ("expansions") — see, *supra*, Section 2 and, more in detail, [24, 25]. They can, therefore, be represented under the form of a (forest of) tree(s). For example, the OBJ(ect) argument of t2 in Fig. 4 can be represented as a two-level tree where x_5 is the root and x_3 the left son; the explicit mention of the SPECIF(ication) operator disappears. The unification of a_i and a_j is then successful if:

```
t1)  OWN    SUBJ   x4  : x7
            OBJ    x5

            x4  =  company_
            x5  =  control_power
            x7  =  location_

t2)  OWN    SUBJ   x4  : x11
            OBJ    (SPECIF x5 x3 )

            x3  =  company_
            x11 =  location_
```

Figure 4 - Merging of templates.

1) The "less bushy" of the two trees corresponding to a_i and a_j — i.e., that including the minor number of elements and which, therefore, represents the less specific argument — is "totally included" in the "more bushy" (more specific) one. The more specific argument is then used for the resulting template. This condition stems from the fact that the merge is a specialisation operation, which gives then preference to the most informative elements: when unifying the OBJ(ect) arguments of t1 and t2 in Fig. 4, "(SPECIF x_5 x_3)" is the argument to be conserved because it retains more elements coming from the original text.

2) The "total inclusion" mentioned in the previous point is verified in a way similar to that used for the "match" of the triggering rules, i.e., by verifying the inclusion of the paths "root — terminal symbols", extracted from the bushless tree, within those extracted from the bushmost one. This total inclusion is now a strict Robinsonian inclusion, i.e., not only identical nodes must be met in the same order on the two paths, but also no node can be "omitted", with the possible exception of the last one (a leaf) of the longest (most specific) path, see the (successful) comparison between the path "x_5" (t1) and the path "x_5 x_3" (t2) in Fig. 4.

A last point about merging concerns the way of recognising that two variables x_i and x_j encountered on the previous "paths" may "unify". We can be confronted with three different situations:

a) x_i and x_j are both a-variables: in this case, they unify if they really coincide (i.e., if they are characterised by the same symbolic "name", $x_i = x_j$);

b) x_i and x_j are both c-variables: they unify if their constraints coincide, or if the constraints pertain to a same subtree of the H_CLASS hierarchy,

see [1]; in this last case, the variable linked with the most "specific" constraint is retained;

c) x_i and x_j are one a a-variable and the other an c-variable: they unify if the constraints coincide, or if the a-constraints are more specific than c-constraints; the a-variable is retained.

In our example, see Figure 4, the unification criteria are satisfied for both the SUBJ and OBJ arguments of t1 and t2: e.g., the OBJ argument of t1 is totally included in the OBJ argument of t2; x_7 and x_{11} are c-variables whose constraints coincide. t1 and t2 can, therefore, be merged into a single template having the same appearance of t2, i.e., including the expansion "(SPECIF x_5 x_3)" in the OBJ argument.

5 SOME REMARKS ON THE "PP-ATTACHMENT" PROBLEM

As already stated, the procedures expounded before, in Sections 3 and 4, are shared by the NOMOS and COBALT versions of the "NL/NKRL translation system". An important, novel contribution of the COBALT project concerns the set up of a specific module for handling the "PP-attachment problem".

In COBALT, the approach to syntactic analysis is fundamentally different from that followed in NOMOS. As we have already explained, an important assumption made by NOMOS was, in fact (see, *supra*, Section 3.2), that it was always possible to reduce to a minimum the number of solutions (parses) supplied by the syntactic specialist (ATN compiler), by making use of heuristics and, eventually, by asking for the intervention of an human operator. This strategy is inapplicable to COBALT. In this last system, the press releases which have passed the first, rough TCS filter, must be analysed "in real time" by the NL/NKRL translation system to extract their "deep meaning" and to allow their immediate classification and distribution. Halting the process to install a dialogue with the user and to perform "manual" adjustments is, therefore, definitely proscribed. Accordingly, see again, *supra*, Section 3.2, the syntactic specialist used in COBALT is now a "robust" parser which produces a "Quasi-Logical Form" (QLF) image of the original text.

"Robust" means, however, that the COBALT parser owes its computational efficiency and its aptitude to always produce a single result to an artifice consisting in deferring decisions when confronted with syntactic ambiguities (e.g., PP-attachment problems). Therefore, the result is often a fragmented analysis whose global coherence must then reconstructed later, at the semantic/conceptual level. For example, for a COBALT fragment like: "Sharp Corporation said it has shifted production of low value personal computers from Japan to companies in Taiwan and Korea", we obtain as output of the QLF syntactic parser a set of four syntactic sub-trees, i.e., a "forest" instead of a complete tree structure. The four sub-trees are due to the presence of four prepositions in the original fragment, "of", "from", "to", "in", all of which give rise to a PP-attachment ambiguity. We have been led, accordingly, to augment the "triggering — filling — merging" specialist of the NL/NKRL translation system, see Section 4, with a special, knowledge-based, "PP-attachment module".

Space limitations do not allow us to go into the details of the COBALT PP-attachment procedures — for more information, see, e.g., [26]. We will only say that our "attachment algorithm" employs a strategy based on two main principles :

1) The use of a "generate and test" procedure allowing us to construct all the possible semantic renderings, called "readings" in our approach, of the textual fragment examined: more specifically, a reading is a set of NKRL output structures that correspond to an identical semantic interpretation of the fragment.

2) The use, for each possible ambiguous preposition, of a set of "attachment rules" having the usual format: "syntactic condition (antecedent) — operations concerning the NKRL domain (consequent)", which are used to reduce to a minimum the number of readings. In each rule, the consequent specifies the conditions under which the NKRL term(s) corresponding to the head noun of an ambiguous PP (prepositional phrase) can fill a particular position in one or more of the NKRL structures produced by the usual triggering rules.

To give only an example, we reproduce in Figure 5 some of the (greatly simplified) "attachment rules" associated with three of the prepositions which appear in the COBALT "Sharp Corporation" fragment mentioned before: "from" ("from Japan"), "to" ("to companies"), and "in" ("in Taiwan and Korea"). The first PP-ambiguity in this fragment, which concerns the preposition "of", can be taken directly into account by a simple "heuristic syntactic post-processor" in the NOMOS style, see also [11]. The antecedent parts refer to the results of the syntactic analysis — here, the forest produced by the QLF parser. The SOURCE role refers to the animate entity (group of entities) who is responsible for the particular behaviour of the SUBJ(ect) of the template or occurrence; the DEST(ination) role — sometimes called "benefactive" in other knowledge representation systems — refers to the "addressee" of the activity of the SUBJ(ect). Please note the lack of precision of rule c), owing to the very ambiguous character of the preposition "in".

The new module is already producing some very encouraging results: it seems actually able to deal correctly with about 77% of the COBALT PPs which appear as "unattached" before the application of the PP-attachment algorithm, see again [26] for more details.

6 CONCLUSION

The NOMOS prototype of "NL/NKRL translation system" has been realised in COMMON LISP. All the NOMOS software is based on a three layers model, see the well-known Brachman classification [4]: a COMMON LISP layer ("implementation level"), a CRL, "Carnegie Representation Language", layer ("epistemological level"), a NOMOS-proper layer ("conceptual level"). This means that CRL — the frame- and object-oriented language included in the Knowledge Craft knowledge engineering environment developed and commercialised by the Carnegie Group — provides all the basic building primitives, independent from the domain (epistemological level), to be used to support the NKRL structures and the procedures of the NL/NKRL translator.

A (partial) re-implementation of the NOMOS prototype has been accomplished in the context of the COBALT project. This has consisted, among other things, in the replacement, at the epistemological level, of CRL by another object-oriented tool, QSL ("Quinary Semantic Language"); the general philosophy of the NOMOS implementation has been left unchanged. QSL has been developed by Quinary SpA, Milan, Italy, the COBALT co-ordinating partner. Another important characteristic of the COBALT implementation concerns its "robustness", see also the previous Section. A particular effort in this direction was, in fact, necessary to move from a NOMOS environment where relatively few (albeit complex) normative texts had to be examined, to a COBALT context where some hundreds Reuters news have been actually processed. The "standard" prototype of NL/NKRL translation system is a relatively fast system which, e.g., in a NOMOS context, takes 3 min 16s on Sun Sparc-Station 1 with 16Mb to process a full article of the French General Taxation Law (on average, 4 sentences and 150 wordforms) ; 1 min 06s for the longest sentence. The processing of one of this normative articles requires, typically, the use of 40 "substitution rules" and 25 "triggering rules".

The work expounded in this paper is obviously related to that accomplished in the context of many other "knowledge acquisition from natural language" projects. In this domain, the systems which share the greatest number of similarities with our NL/NKRL translation system are probably KERNEL [15] and its predecessor PUNDIT [9]. We can mention, here, the similarities which exist between NL/NKRL and KERNEL with respect to a) the way of distributing the work between syntactic and semantic/pragmatic processing, b) the use in KERNEL of "lexical semantic clauses" (LCCs) which operate in a very similar fash-

```
a)  "from" followed by an NKRL term pertaining to the
    H_CLASS <location_> sub-tree ("from" + <x₁ -
    location_>) ------> make use of the value bound to
    the a-variable x₁ to fill the "initial location"
    position of the "location attribute" linked with
    the OBJ argument of a MOVE3.2 ("move a method
    or process") template.

b)  1) "to" + <x₁ - human_being_or_social_body>  ------>
    make use of the value bound to the a-variable to fill
    the DEST slot of a MOVE3.2 template ;

    2) "to" + <x₁ - location_> ------> use the value bound
    to the a-variable to fill the "final location" position
    of the "location attribute" linked with the OBJ of a
    MOVE3.2 template.

c)  "in" + <x₁ - location_> ------> use the value bound
    to the variable to fill any generic
    "location attribute" linked with any possible
    SUBJ, OBJ, SOURCE or DEST argument.
```

Figure 5 - Attachment rules.

ion to that proper to our triggering/filling routines, c) some analogies in knowledge representation domain (see, e.g., the way of representing and structuring the concepts), etc. Similarities, with respect to, e.g., the organisation of the lexicon or the techniques for "template activation", can also be found with SCISOR, see [14, 16]. However, SCISOR seems more concerned with the implementation of (very powerful) "skimming techniques" in the tradition of the well-known work of De-Jong [8] than with an accurate and exhaustive conceptual representation of NL texts. Consequently, syntactic and semantic analysis are carried out in SCISOR by using options which could be considered as "shallower" than ours. See also, in a similar vein, the JASPER [1] and FAUSTUS [2] systems. A "PP-attachment system" which shares some similarities with our proposals is [10].

Finally, some of the advantages of the NKRL approach concern, e.g., the use of a "canonical" style of target representation, that can guarantee "reproducibility" and "shareability", the full integration of syntactic and semantic techniques, the realisation of the "expectations" mechanism (triggering, etc.) according to a simple and rigorous technique based on variables and constraints, the presence, in the COBALT version, of some promising tools for dealing with the difficult "PP-attachment" phenomenon. A considerable amount of work is, however, still necessary to transform the actual prototypes into something not too dissimilar from a pre-industrial product.

REFERENCES

1. Andersen, P.M., Hayes, P.J., Huettner, A.K., Schmandt, L.M., Nirenburg, I.B., Weinstein, S.P. (1992) "Automatic Extraction of Facts from Press Releases to Generate News Stories", in *Proceedings of the Third Conference on Applied Natural Language Processing*. Morristown (NJ): ACL.

2. Appelt, D.E., Hobbs, J.R., Bear, J., Israel, D., and Tyson, M. (1993) "FASTUS: A Finite-state Processor for Information Extraction from Real-world Text", in *Proceedings of the Thirteenth International Joint Conference on Artificial Intelligence - IJCAI/93*. San Mateo (CA): Morgan Kaufmann.

3. *ARPA Proceedings of the Fifth Message Understanding Conference (MUC-5)*. San Mateo (CA): Morgan Kaufmann.

4. Brachman, R.J. (1979) "On the Epistemological Status of Semantic Networks", in *Associative Networks*, Findler, N.V., ed. New York: Academic Press.

5. Brachman, R.J., and Schmolze, J.G. (1985) "An Overview of the KL-ONE Knowledge Representation System", *Cognitive Science*, 9, 171-216.

6. Brachman, R.J., Mc Guinness, D.L., Patel - Schneider, P.F., Resnick, L.A., and Borgida, A. (1991) "Living with CLASSIC : When and How to Use a KL-ONE-Like Language", in *Principles of Semantic Networks*, Sowa, J.F., ed. San Mateo (CA): Morgan Kaufmann.

7. Chinchor, N., Hirschman, L., and Lewis, D.D. (1993) "Evaluating Message Understanding Systems: An Analysis of the Third Message Understanding Conference (MUC-3)", *Computational Linguistics*, 19, 409-449.

8. DeJong, G.F. (1982) "An Overview of the FRUMP System", in *Strategies for Natural Language Processing*,

Lehnert, W.G., and Ringle, M.H., eds. Hillsdale (NJ): Lawrence Erlbaum Associates.

9. Grishman, R., and Hirschman, L. (1986) "PROTEUS and PUNDIT : Research in Text Understanding", *Computational Linguistics*, **12**, 141-145.

10. Hirst, G. (1984) "A Semantic Process for Syntactic Disambiguation", in *Proceedings of the Fourth National Conference on Artificial Intelligence - AAAI/84*. Cambridge (MA): AAAI Press/MIT Press.

11. Hobbs, J.R., and Bear, J. (1990) "Two Principles of Parse Preference", in *Proceedings of the 13th International Conference on Computational Linguistics - COLING 90*, Karlgren, H., ed. Helsinki: University Press.

12. Hobbs, J.R., Appelt, D.E., Bear, J., and Tyson, M. (1992) "Robust Processing of Real-World Natural-Language Texts", in *Proceedings of the Third Conference on Applied Natural Language Processing*. Morristown (NJ): ACL.

13. Jacobs, P.S., and Rau, L.F.(1990) "SCISOR : Extracting Information from On-line News", *Communications of the ACM*, **33**(11), 88-97.

14. Jacobs, P.S., and Rau, L.F. (1993) "Innovations in Text Interpretation", *Artificial Intelligence*, **63**, 143-191.

15. Palmer, M.S., Passonneau, R.J., Weir, C., and Finin, T. (1993) "The KERNEL Text Understanding System", *Artificial Intelligence*, **63**, 17-68.

16. Rau, L.F., and Jacobs, P.S. (1988) "Integrating Top-Down and Bottom-Up Strategies in a Text Processing System", in *Proceedings of the Second Conference on Applied Natural Language Processing*. Morristown (NJ): ACL.

17. Riesbeck, C.K. (1975) "Conceptual Analysis", in *Conceptual Information Processing*, Schank, R.C., ed. Amsterdam: North-Holland.

18. Sowa, J.F. (1984) *Conceptual Structures : Information Processing in Mind and Machine*. Reading (MA): Addison-Wesley.

19. Sundheim, B., ed. (1992) *Proceedings of the Fourth Message Understanding Conference - MUC/4*. San Mateo (CA): Morgan Kaufmann.

20. Yokoi, T. (1993) "Very Large-Scale Knowledge Bases : From Lexical Knowledge to World Knowledge", in *Proceedings of the Thirteenth International Joint Conference on Artificial Intelligence - IJCAI/93*. San Mateo (CA): Morgan Kaufmann.

21. Zarri, G.P. (1992) "The Descriptive Component of a Hybrid Knowledge Representation Language", in *Semantic Networks in Artificial Intelligence*, Lehmann, F., ed. Oxford: Pergamon Press.

22. Zarri, G.P. (1992) "Encoding the Temporal Characteristics of the Natural Language Descriptions of (Legal) Situations", in *Expert Systems in Law*, Martino, A., ed. Amsterdam: Elsevier Science Publishers.

23. Zarri, G.P. (1992) "Semantic Modeling of the Content of (Normative) Natural Language Documents", in *Avignon 92 - Proceedings of the Specialized Conference on Natural Language Processing and Its Applications*. Nanterre: EC2.

24. Zarri, G.P. (1993) *NKRL: A General Survey* (Technical Report COBALT/QUI/9/93). Milano: Quinary SpA.

25. Zarri, G.P. (1994) "A Glimpse of NKRL, the Narrative Knowledge Representation Language", in *Working Notes of the AAAI Fall Symposium on Knowledge Representation for Natural Language Processing in Implemented Systems*. Menlo Park (CA): American Association for Artificial Intelligence.

26. Zarri, G.P. (1995) "Knowledge Acquisition from Complex Narrative Texts Using the NKRL Technology", in *Pre-Proceedings of the 1995 Banff Knowledge Acquisition Workshop - KAW'95*. Calgary: Department of Computer Science of the University.

Towards Very Large Knowledge Bases
N.J.I. Mars, Ed.
IOS Press, 1995

Extracting Knowledge from Biological Descriptions

Andrew Taylor
University of New South Wales
Sydney, Australia
andrewt@cse.unsw.edu.au

ABSTRACT

We describe a system which performs biological identification on the basis of natural language descriptions. The system parses texts containing large sets of biological descriptions in restricted natural language and constructs a knowledge base. The system can semi-automatically adapt to a text by extending its lexicon and perhaps its grammar. The constructed knowledge bases are used to perform interactive identification of specimens. The system automatically constructs HTML forms to provide a World Wide Web identification interface which can be integrated with hypermedia resources. We describe the system's implementation and its performance on two large botany texts.

1 INTRODUCTION

This work addresses a very old problem - given a set of biological taxonomic descriptions how do we efficiently find the description corresponding to a specimen? As the first systematic biologists developed classifications they quickly realised they also needed to develop methods for finding the appropriate classification for a specimen. The obvious approach is a linear search of classifications. A good example of this is the common novice approach of leafing through a book until they find a picture they think matches their specimen. This, unfortunately, is unreliable and too time-consuming for all but the smallest sets of taxa.

The first remedy - construction of decision trees - appeared in the seventeenth century in the works of Morison and Ray [19] with classifications presented diagrammatically as trees. The great taxonomist Linnaeus [15] gave these trees the name *keys* by which biologists have known them since. The key as a method of identification was fully realised in Lamarck's Flora

Francoise [14]. The modern key in Figure 1 (paraphrased from [5]) differs little from the keys Lamarck constructed two centuries ago.

Not surprisingly given their long and widespread use, keys are effective tools but they have weaknesses. Some of the decision questions may be unanswerable for a particular specimen. For example, flower characters are commonly used in botanical keys but plants are often not in flower. This will make use of the key difficult or impossible but in many cases a diagnosis could quickly be made with characters present in the particular specimen but not employed in the key.

Occasionally specimens will be atypical in some character causing diagnosis to follow a fruitless path through the key. An error in determining whether a specimen meets a decision criterion produces the same result. In both cases backtracking is difficult when the user is uncertain at which node the diagnosis diverged from the correct path. Both these problems are exacerbated if the person attempting the diagnosis is inexpert.

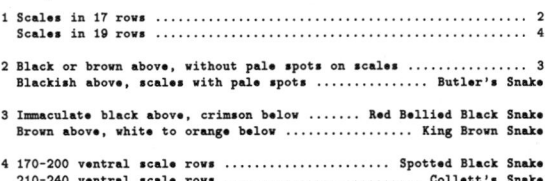

```
1 Scales in 17 rows .................................................... 2
  Scales in 19 rows .................................................... 4

2 Black or brown above, without pale spots on scales ................ 3
  Blackish above, scales with pale spots ............... Butler's Snake

3 Immaculate black above, crimson below ....... Red Bellied Black Snake
  Brown above, white to orange below ................. King Brown Snake

4 170-200 ventral scale rows ....................... Spotted Black Snake
  210-240 ventral scale rows ......................... Collett's Snake
```

Figure 1 - Key to Australian Snakes of Genus *Pseudechis*

2 COMPUTER-BASED IDENTIFICATION

Biologists' first attempts to construct more flexible identification methods which would allow the user to choose the characters used in a diagnosis were largely frustrated by the media available. Typically these methods were based on punched cards but other even more ingenious mechanical techniques were tried. Unfortunately all of these were expensive to produce and most suffered from a degree of clumsiness.

The arrival of computers brought a much more suitable medium which was quickly employed in the development of identification systems such as [12]. The most successful of current computer-based identification systems is DELTA [7]. The heart of DELTA is a language into which taxonomic descriptions must be encoded to use the system. One of the components of DELTA is INTKEY, an interactive identification program which given a set of descriptions in DELTA format can efficiently and flexibly perform identifications.

However DELTA's success depends more on its integration with traditional paper-based technology than on INTKEY's virtues for identification. DELTA can generate traditional keys and its language is also carefully designed to allow the DELTA descriptions to be converted to natural language if suitable care is taken in the construction of the DELTA descriptions. This has allowed large books to be generated from DELTA descriptions [23]. Biologists' reactions to DELTA and other computer-based identification systems are mixed. It is clear that natural language will dominate new taxonomic work for at least a short time to come and there is, of course, a vast existing body of such descriptions.

3 TAXONOMIC DESCRIPTIONS AS NATURAL LANGUAGE

Our approach is in an important sense the inverse of DELTA. We have built an identification system based on automatically building a knowledge base from natural language taxonomic descriptions. If you examine taxonomic descriptions, such as Figure 2 (taken from [13]), it is clear they are written in a distinctive sublanguage. The descriptions contain few verbs and are mainly a terse sequence of noun phrases which are rich in adjectives and adverbs. Many of the nouns and adjectives are peculiar to this domain; others may have a more specialised meaning within this domain.

Shrubs with few erect, slender, few-branched stems to 3 m high; glabrous except at apex of bracts or sparsely to moderately rusty-hairy on axes and lower surface of leaves. Adult leaves narrow-obovate to narrow-spathulate, 8-28 cm long, 20-65 mm wide, apex usually acute to truncate, margins rarely entire or more often toothed with 0–3 pairs of teeth in lower half, base very attenuate, leathery but usually not harsh, minutely granulate when dried; both surfaces with prominently raised veins. Conflorescences few, 90-250-flowered; basal flowers opening first; involucral bracts mostly 5-9 cm long, bright red.

Figure 2 - Taxonomic description of the Waratah

This sublanguage is clearly much more amenable to computer analysis than unrestricted English. Even so, many of the problems that make natural language understanding so difficult persist to some degree. Another important aspect is that our purpose of identification does not require complete understanding of the text. Our system can operate successfully even with incomplete knowledge extraction.

Although our system is intended to handle taxonomic descriptions of any group, so far our efforts have been restricted to two botany texts with usefully disparate characteristics. The Flora of New South Wales [13] is a four volume 2,000 page text containing descriptions of the over 6,000 plant species known from the state of New South Wales. There is great variety in the plants involved from tiny aquatic plants a few millimetres across to towering forest trees over 50 metres tall. There is a corresponding variety in the nature of the descriptions. This is compounded by the text having over twenty authors.

The Flora of Australia - Volume 19 [9] is a 540 page volume describing the almost 600 species in the genera Eucalyptus and Angophera. In contrast to the previous text the species described are closely related and quite similar and there is a single main author. The result is its descriptions are much more consistent in nature than those in [13].

4 ONTOLOGY

Taxonomists consider the essence of a taxonomic description to be a list of properties possessed by the taxon. Each property in the list is considered to be composed of a *character* and one or more *states*. A *character* describes the property that varies between taxa, for example - *petal colour* or *leaf width*. A *state* is the instance of the property for the taxon being described - for example *red* or *7cm*. Commonly multiple states of a character will occur in one taxon - for example, petal colour may be red or pink, leaf width may be between 8cm and 12cm. The terminology is not universal with some authors meaning by *character* the combination of what we have termed character and state [16].

A character may be an arbitrarily complicated statement with the possible states being true or false. This would require a very expressive knowledge representation. We however wanted a simple knowledge representation to make the identification process very efficient even if this was at the expense of some characters being unrepresentable. Fortunately most characters have a simple form just referring to a simple attribute such as colour, shape, length or hairiness of a particular part of the specimen. We have relied on this using a triple consisting of specimen part, attribute and value/s as the basis of our representation. The specimen part can be a simple name e.g. *petal* or a compound indicating a subpart, e.g. *leaf hairs* or subset of parts e.g. *female flowers*. Attributes are simple names. Values have a simple syntax allowing representation of sets and ranges. The syntax for values also allows qualifiers e.g. *usually, often, sometimes* and *rarely* to be represented.

Our intention was to extend this simple representation only as strictly necessary for overall system performance. The only extension that has so far been necessary is for relational characters. For example this allows the representation of *leaf length is more than twice leaf width*. There are certainly other forms of characters that can not be represented but this has not so far been important. In many cases these characters can not be easily employed in the identification process.

5 PARSING

The idiomatic nature of the taxonomic sublanguage and the relative simplicity of its structure have led us to construct a grammar rather than adopt an existing grammar. A particular concern was that a general-coverage parser would have an unacceptable error rate in determining the attachment of adjectives because of the dense nature of the sublanguage. This was certainly a problem in cursory trials of general-coverage parsers.

The sublanguage was sufficiently restricted that construction of a special purpose parser with useful coverage was not difficult. Several man-days were invested in constructing incrementally about 70 definite clause grammar rules [21]. These were combined with an initial phase which split a sentence into components allowing information to be obtained when only part of a sentence can be parsed. Unfortunately we found proceeding past an unparsed sentence component resulted in an unacceptable error rate but information from preceding components can be safely used.

The construction of the lexicon was more problematical than the grammar. A sizable fraction of the sublanguage is not even found in general dictionaries nor was a suitable on-line compilation of biological terms available. Instead as the basis of our lexicon we used Radford's textbook work on plant systematics [22]. This was more valuable than a dictionary because it provided an extensive listing of characters and their possible states. This is useful because the character is often partly or completely implicit in the text and must be inferred from its state and the context.

It was necessary to accommodate sloppiness in the texts in the definition of characters. Radford quite logically treats *two-dimensional shape* and *three-dimensional shape* as separate characters. However it is not uncommon for two-dimensional and three-dimensional terms to be used interchangeably or mixed improperly, but not ambiguously in the text. The eas-

iest way to accommodate this was to merge these two characters into a single character *shape*.

Radford's text provided 1500 entries for the lexicon which were supplemented by a further 500 words added manually as they were encountered during parses of the texts. These were mainly words which see wide use outside botany and thus were not present in the lists extracted from [20].

The base lexicon is supplemented by a number of lexical rules. Some of these implement general English morphology, for example almost all plurals of nouns are generated this way rather than by being explicitly included in the lexicon. Other rules are specific to the domain, for example botanists often use the prefix *sub-* to mean almost - for example using *subglobose* to mean almost globose. Botanists also commonly construct terms using Latin or Greek prefixes indicating size, number or symmetry and Latin or Greek suffixes indicating plant parts e.g *tri-foliate* or *micro-phyllous*.

6 COVERAGE

Our parsers provide a useful but far from complete coverage of the texts. It is difficult to provide a precise assessment of coverage because both texts contain varying amounts of information apart from plant descriptions such as details of a plant's commercial value. These sentences contain words that we are not interested in providing in the lexicon and often follow forms we do not need to parse. Furthermore, there is a tendency for the sentences containing the most important descriptive information to follow typical forms and thus they are more easily parsed. Thus raw statistics of sentence coverage which could be easily gathered are not useful.

Our manually constructed parser extracted from [13] 100,000 character/state pairs and 20,000 character/state pairs from [9]. Unfortunately we have no way to estimate how many character/state pairs are present in the text. Our only useful assessment method is manual examination of randomly sampled taxa. Our manually constructed parser typically yields between 60 to 80% of the character/state pairs we would like to extract from each description. This is sufficient for the system to function but overall system performance at identification fell short of desired levels.

If our objective was to only parse the two texts mentioned above then we would have continued extending our grammar and lexicon by hand. As we hope to parse many texts, we instead examined techniques to automatically assist in the extension of the lexicon and grammar.

7 EXTENDING THE LEXICON AND GRAMMAR

Categorising unknown words so they can be added to the lexicon appears to be tractable in many cases. It can be apparent even from a single occurrence of an unknown word. For example, suppose the word *puce* is unknown. If we encounter the phrase - *leaves puce to red* then it is likely *puce* should be in the same category as *red*, a state of the character *colour*.

The reversibility of Prolog DCG clauses means this can be implemented elegantly and trivially by leaving the category of the word uninstantiated and examining how it is instantiated by legal parses.

Useful negative information can also be discerned from single occurrences of unknown words. If we see the phrase - *circular puce leaves* then it is unlikely *puce* belongs in the same category as *circular*. We also exploit this but unfortunately the non-logical nature of negation in standard Prolog means it must be done less elegantly than in the positive case.

We also attempt to use definitions from a general dictionary, an on-line version of Collins English Dictionary [10], when available in classification of unknown words. Our system does not parse the definitions but rather examines them for words in our lexicon. For example, the dictionary definition for *puce* is *adj, a dark purplish brown* suggesting that *puce* might belong to the same category as *brown* and *purple*.

Thirdly we use statistical information for unknown words which occur a sufficient number of times. This is done by extracting bigrams from the text and looking for known words which have similar associations [8]. As yet the error rates on classification of unknown words using the above three methods is too high for the classifications to be used without manual checking, nonetheless they are useful.

More useful and unfortunately more difficult is automatically or semi-automatically adding grammar rules to improve the grammar's coverage. The results of Zelle and Mooney [24] using machine learning to construct parsers are very promising. Unfortunately their methods probably can not be directly applied in our context because of the difficulty in obtaining a training set. We are hopeful inductive logic programming techniques can at least be used to suggest possible new grammar rules.

8 IDENTIFICATION

The task of the identification engine is, for each taxon in the text, to determine the likelihood that the specimen the user has described belongs to this taxon. The identification engine has a knowledge base containing the list of character/state pairs extracted for each taxon. Similarly it is given a list of character/state pairs obtained from the user's description of the specimen. The engine compares the specimen to every taxon. This non-hierarchical approach is alien to biologists not only because they are accustomed to the hierarchical structure of keys but also because hierarchy is very important in taxonomy.

The user's description is compared to that of a taxon by comparing the states of characters which are known for both. The comparison of two states is not treated as a boolean operation. For example, suppose a taxon is described in the text as having leaves 10-15mm long and a specimen is described as having leaves 17mm long. This is only a minor discrepancy which could easily result from an aberrant specimen, an error in the text or an error in measurement of the specimen. If instead the specimen were described as having leaves 50mm long, this is a major discrepancy and it is much less likely that the specimen belongs to the described taxon. At least notionally when comparing states the identification engine produces the conditional probability that if the specimen belongs to the taxon the user would describe it as having the given state.

This concerns many biologists because identification is commonly viewed as a determinate rather than probabilistic process. This is fostered at least partly by specialists typically dealing with identifications made with a high degree of certainty. They not only have the skills and resources to make identifications with a high degree of certainty but they also often need such a degree of certainty. Although it is undeniable that a fraction of even specialists' identifications are incorrect, there is considerable resistance to viewing identification as a probabilistic process [20]. We believe accommodating the probabilistic nature of the process becomes more important when dealing with non-specialists who are both less skilled and demand less certainty. We hope, in future work, by instrumenting our system to demonstrate that a probabilistic approach has significant benefits. Certainly solid evidence will be needed to convince many biologists that a probabilistic approach is appropriate.

For numeric characters it is easy to develop a formula that estimates a conditional probability in some reasonable and well-behaved way. Non-numeric characters are more problematic. The only exception is colours where Euclidean distance between their coordinates in a metric space designed to match human perceptions can be used as an estimate of their similarity. For other non-numeric characters there is a facility to indicate some degree of similarity between states in the lexicon. For example, the lexicon indicates the shapes *hastiform* and *triangular* are similar. This similarity is applied transitively so if the lexicon indicates state X is similar to state Y and Z is similar to Z then the identification engine will assume there is a lesser degree of similarity between X and Z. In many cases states are not just similar but exact synonyms and this can be indicated using the same facility.

Synonyms also occur in the naming of specimen parts and this can be indicated in the lexicon. More problematic is where specimen parts can be easily confused. For example, non-expert users will often use the term *leaves* when describing Australian Acacias when the structure they are referring to is actually a phyllode and described as such in botanical texts. A solution in this case is easy because indicating that *phyllode* is a synonym for *leaf* does not cause other conflicts. Other cases are more difficult to handle. For example, non-experts will often confuse the green branchlets of a *Casuarina* with cylindrical leaves. Treating *branchlet* and *leaf* as synonyms will cause other problems. We do not have a good solution to this problem.

Our system can automatically obtain similarity information where two or more texts are available describing common taxa. For example, if one text describe as a taxon as having *fusiform* buds and another text describes it as *conical* then this suggests that these are similar terms. If this occurs in multiple cases then the assumption of similarity seems safe. Comparing the results for texts with common taxa is also valuable for detecting errors in the parser and in the texts. The combination of information from multiple texts may be useful in many situations.

The conditional probabilities obtained for each character common to the specimen description and taxon description are combined using Bayes' Rule to give, at least notionally, an overall probability that the specimen belongs to the taxon. In practice, the presence of unknown distributions and invalid assumptions of independence mean that the results are best viewed as ad-hoc estimates. Nonetheless, this method seems to perform well. There are some similarities with the ranking algorithms of information retrieval [11] and we hope to explore if these can offer better performance.

Taxonomists consider some characters more important than others. This can be because they are less variable, more easily determined correctly or better known. If giving all characters equal weight proves a weakness it may be possible to remedy this where a text contains keys by examining the keys to see which characters are preferred.

9 USER INTERFACE

Our identification system has been designed with users who have limited knowledge of the domain but are not experts. In the case of our two botanical texts, such users might include farmers, park rangers, gardeners, bush regenerators and biologists from other disciplines. We feel there is much more scope to improve the efficiency of the identification process for such users than for experts. We believe computer-based identification could also assist considerably users with no knowledge of the domain. However this will require considerable support at the interface level which is beyond the scope of our current work.

The identification process is not independent of the text which supplied the identification database. Rather we expect the user to supply information about the specimen until the set of likely candidates is sufficiently small, then the user will make a final determination by examining the textual descriptions of these candidates and any accompanying material such as figures or photographs.

We have explored several different user interfaces. As we have a parser for the sublanguage, it was easy to construct an interface where the user describes the specimen in similar natural language to that of the texts. This yields a very simple interface and it has the advantage that the user can choose which characters of the specimen to describe. This is not only convenient but if the user is aware that some of the specimen's character states are unusual they can narrow the candidate set very quickly. The primary disadvantage of this interface is that it provides no cues to the user about how to describe the specimen or which characters will be most useful in narrowing the specimen set.

Another possibility is to provide a menu for each non-numeric character with a menu entry for character state of that character and entry fields for numeric characters. This has the advantages of the natural language interface and it provides cues to the user for describing the specimen. Unfortunately it also can produce a very crowded interface. The diversity of the species described in [13] and the resulting number of characters and states make it difficult to provide such an interface. The much more homogeneous descriptions of [9] and the resulting smaller number of characters and character states make it more suitable but the resulting interface is still very crowded.

A third alternative is to mimic the use of a key incrementally querying the user for the state of characters. Some flexibility could be provided to avoid the disadvantages of keys described in the introduction. For example, the user could be able to refuse a query and a query based on another character would be provided. However when the user is aware that some character states are unusual then the previously described methods will narrow the candidate set much more quickly. Conversely when the user is left with a group of largely similar candidates and they are unaware of appropriate discriminating characters this alternative may be more efficient at obtaining the information necessary to reduce the set of candidates.

We believe our eventual interface will be a hybrid of all three approaches but so far integrating them has proved troublesome. We have implemented a natural language-based interface and a menu-based interface as HTML forms [1]. This allows identification of eucalypts using information extracted from [9] to be conducted via the World Wide Web [3]. Both interfaces display the current candidate set as hypertext links to an HTML version of the source text. Thus by clicking on a candidate taxon's name, the user can see the description of the species from the text complete with figures and links to distribution maps.

The centralisation of the knowledge base that this use of the World Wide Web provides offers a very important potential for on-going maintenance of the knowledge base. Although only published six years ago [9] is already seriously out of date because a hundred or more new taxa have since been described by taxonomists. It may be many years before this is remedied by a new edition. A central electronic knowledge base can be much more cheaply and frequently maintained than a paper text.

We have also implemented a natural language-based interface in X. This uses the tool Wafe [17] which allows the X windows calls to be embedded in a small external Tcl program [18]. This is an extremely convenient way to build an X interface into a Prolog program. This allows use of the system in the field on a notebook computer.

10 PERFORMANCE

The performance of our system is already surprisingly good. External users successfully employed even alpha versions of the system. We are currently obtaining quantitative performance statistics including speed and accuracy for identification made with our system and for identifications made with the original texts.

Our system when using the knowledge base extracted from [13] is dealing successfully with an order of magnitude more taxa than any computer-based identification system we are aware of. Perhaps more importantly it is also dealing successfully with taxa of far more disparate character than any computer-based identification system we are aware of.

11 IMPLEMENTATION

Some 3,000 lines of SICStus Prolog [4] make up almost the entirety of our system. Apart from the Prolog, 120 lines of Tcl are used to implement an X interface and a number of small shell scripts are used in the initial processing of texts and as wrappers for the HTML-based interfaces.

Many think that Prolog is well-suited for natural language parsing applications [6]. This also proved to be very much so in our case. Not only was the top-down backtracking approach of DCGs a comfortable formalism for our main grammar but their reversibility proved very useful when extending the lexicon automatically. It is impressive that Prolog was well-suited to implementation of not just part but the entirety of a system of diverse components. We feel that only other logic programming languages could match Prolog for its suitability for this system.

12 CONCLUSIONS AND FUTURE WORK

We believe we have more than established the viability of basing a biological identification on natural language.

In upcoming work we will build an identification system for amphipods (small crustaceans) based on [2]. The small degree of lexical overlap between this and our current texts and the grammatical differences should provide an interesting test of the generality of our methods.

ACKNOWLEDGEMENTS

I would like to thank Gwen Harden and the Royal Botanic Gardens Sydney for their vital cooperation. I would also to like to thank the Environmental Resources Information Network for making the [9] electronically available.

REFERENCES

1. M. Andreessen, "A HTML Primer", http://www.ncsa.uiuc.edu/demoweb/html-primer.html.

2. J. L. Barnard and G. S. Karaman, "The Families and Genera of Marine Gammaridean Amphipoda", *Records of the Australian Museum*, Supplement 13, 1991.

3. Berners-Lee, T.J, R. Cailliau and J.-F. Groff, "The World-Wide Web", *Computer Networks and ISDN Systems* 25 (1992) 454–459, North-Holland.

4. M. Carlsson and J. Widen, *SICStus Prolog Users Manual*, SICS Research Report R88007B, October 1988.

5. H. Cogger, *Reptiles and Amphibian of Australia*, Reed Books, 1992.

6. M. A. Covington, *Natural Language Processing for Prolog Programmer*, Prentice-Hall, 1994.

7. M. J. Dallwitz, "DELTA and INTKEY", *Advances in Computer Methods for Systematic Biology*, R. Fortuner (Ed.), Johns Hopkins University Press, 1993.

8. T. Dunning, "Accurate Methods for the Statistics of Surprise and Coincidence", *Computational Linguistics*, 19(1), March 1993.

9. *Flora of Australia Volume 19, Myrtaceae, Eucalyptus, Angophora*, Australian Government Publishing Service, Canberra, 1988.

10. E. A. Fox, "Development of the CODER system", *Information Processing and Management*, 23(4), 1987.

11. W. B. Frakes and R. Baeza-Yates (Eds), *Information Retrieval Data Structures and Algorithms*, Prentice-Hall, 1992.

12. H. G. Gyllenberg, "A General Method for Deriving Determination Schemes for Random Collections of Microbial Isolates", *Annals of the Finnish Academy of Sciences*, ser. A, IV Biology, 69, 1–23, 1963.

13. G. Harden (Ed.), *Flora of New South Wales*, University of New South Wales Press, 4 Volumes, 1991-1994.

14. J. B. P. Lamarck, *Flora Francoise*, 1st edition, Paris, Imprimerie Royale, 1778.

15. C. Linnaeus, *Clavis Classium in Systemate Phytologorum* in Bibliotheca Botanica, Amsterdam, 1736.

16. E. Mayr and P. D. Ashlock, *Principles of Systematic Zoology*, McGraw-Hill, 1991.

17. G. Neumann and S. Nusser, "Wafe - An X Toolkit Based Front end for Application Programs in Various Programming Languages", *USENIX Winter 1993 Technical Conference*, San Diego, California, January 25-29, 1993, see also ftp.wu-wien.ac.at:pub/src/X11/wafe.

18. J. K. Ousterhout, "Tcl: An Embeddable Command Language", *USENIX Winter 1990 Conference*, January 1990.

19. R. J. Pankhurst, *Biological Identification*, Edward Arnold, 1978.

20. R. J. Pankhurst, "Principles and Problems of Identifications", *Advances in Computer Methods for Systematic Biology*, R. Fortuner (Ed.), Johns Hopkins University Press, 1993.

21. F. C. N. Pereira and D. H. D. Warren, "Definite Clause Grammars for Language Analysis", *Artificial Intelligence*, 13:231-278, 1983.

22. A. E. Radford, *Fundamentals of Plant Systematics*, Harper & Row, 1986.

23. L. Watson and M. J. Dallwitz, *Grass Genera of the World*, C.A.B. International, Wallingford England, 1992.

24. J. M. Zelle and R. J. Mooney, "Inducing Deterministic Prolog Parsers from Treebanks: A Machine Learning Approach", AAAI-94.

Part 4: Large-Scale Applications

Towards Very Large Knowledge Bases
N.J.I. Mars, Ed.
IOS Press, 1995

A Very Large-Scale Knowledge Base for the Knowledge Intensive Engineering Framework

Masaki Ishii, Takayuki Sekiya and **Tetsuo Tomiyama**
The University of Tokyo
Tokyo, Japan
ishii@zzz.pe.u-tokyo.ac.jp

ABSTRACT

Model-based techniques are becoming essential for engineering applications, and the development of large-scale knowledge bases is required to support model-based engineering. In this paper, we discuss our idea of a knowledge intensive engineering framework (KIEF) and describe our project of developing a very large-scale knowledge base (VLKB) to support KIEF. We propose a new architecture of VLKB that can utilize various model representations and report the current status of collecting engineering knowledge.

1 INTRODUCTION

Building a very large-scale knowledge base (VLKB) of engineering knowledge is indispensable for the development of a knowledge intensive engineering framework (KIEF) that can assist engineers and designers in various engineering activities [11][10]. Knowledge intensive engineering is a new style of engineering in which engineering knowledge is used in a flexible and integrated manner and aims at generating more added-value. Figure 1 shows the concept of KIEF in which various engineering models play a crucial role to improve and innovate engineering activities over product life cycle including design, manufacturing, operation, maintenance, and recycling. Knowledge intensive engineering is, therefore, largely model-based engineering activities and its key concepts are model building, simulation, model-based reasoning, model validation, and model modification. The VLKB should contain a wide variety of engineering design knowledge, from commonsense knowledge about the physical world to domain specific knowledge systematized as physics theories.

In this paper, we focus on the knowledge intensive design stage, because design is the activity that gener-

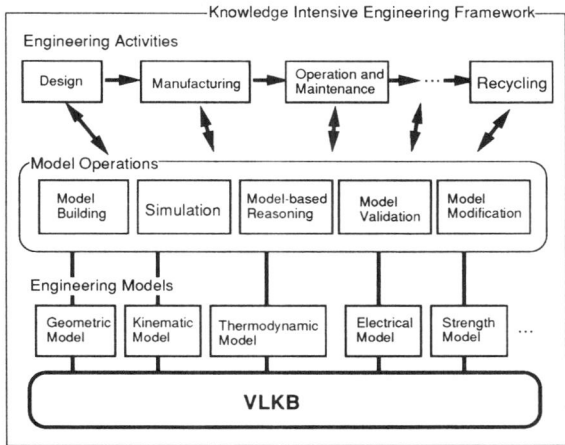

Figure 1: A Knowledge Intensive Engineering Framework

ates models used in later product life cycle stage. Typically, design requires knowledge to assist designers in deriving design solutions, building computational design object models, and analyzing the design solutions.

There are several projects conducted towards construction of VLKBs that can handle real-world problems. The Cyc Project [7] conducted at MCC and the How Things Work Project [2] at Stanford University are examples of such projects. The Cyc Project aims at first codifying the foundational knowledge, which is commonsense knowledge students have before learning specific domains, such as notions of time, space, and causality. Then, the knowledge base is expected to easily acquire domain specific knowledge based on the foundational knowledge. The How Things Work Project aims at collecting knowledge that explains how

124

physical mechanisms work in the real world, including knowledge about fundamental mechanisms that people have as commonsense.

At the University of Tokyo, we have been conducting a project called $o(10^4)$ project to build a VLKB to be installed in KIEF by collecting engineering knowledge including vocabulary of engineering and physical domain theories [5]. In the early stage of this project, we employed Qualitative Process Theory (QPT) [1] as the fundamental theory of knowledge representation, and attempted to collect engineering knowledge based on it. However, it soon turned out that we needed to extend QPT, because engineering knowledge deals with various kinds of ontology besides causality.

This paper describes our extended architecture of a VLKB for knowledge intensive engineering that deals with a variety of ontology based on a *metamodel mechanism* [9]. The metamodel mechanism integrates multiple design object models through a network of physical concepts such as concepts of physical phenomena.

In the rest of this paper, we discuss the fundamental architecture of the VLKB for knowledge intensive engineering and report our project to collect engineering knowledge. In Chapter 2, we discuss characteristics and backgrounds of the VLKB. Chapter 3 summarizes our early work to collect engineering knowledge based on QPT and discusses its limitations. In Chapter 4, we propose our extended architecture for representing engineering knowledge to deal with a variety of ontology. Chapter 5 concludes this paper.

2 CHARACTERISTICS OF A VLKB FOR KIEF

In this chapter, we discuss characteristics of a VLKB required for building KIEF. Such a VLKB should be different from those about commonsense knowledge, both in the vocabulary and in the structure of knowledge.

2.1 Physical Laws as a Background Theory

The ultimate goal of engineering design is to produce design objects that operate in the physical world. Therefore, the knowledge about physical laws should be included in the VLKB for engineering design. The knowledge about physical laws includes theories of physics and engineering, such as dynamics, thermodynamics, theories for electric circuits, and kinematics.

When a designer designs a new mechanism, she/he usually generates design object models that explain how the mechanism works. This model can be a rough sketch on a piece of paper or a computational model built on a computer system. No matter what medium the designer uses, the usefulness of the model depends on the consistency of the model with physical laws. In other words, a design object model contains a background theory created by selecting physical laws relevant to the design object.

KIEF enables designers to synthetically build models of mechanisms with descriptions of physical laws that are essential components to compose design object models. It further allows the designer to analyze the behavior of the model by simulation and model-based reasoning, to validate the design by testing the behavior against the specification, and to modify the model. Therefore, the VLKB for KIEF is required to contain a large number of descriptions of physical laws so that the designer can conduct various model operations.

2.2 Model Generation in Design

Generation of engineering models is one of the hardest task for designers. Figure 2 depicts a typical process of model generation in KIEF. The process of model generation can be roughly divided into two phases. The first phase is to specify aspects of the models, and the latter phase is to build up the models in modelers. To assist designers efficiently, KIEF should be involved from the first phase of the model generation process.

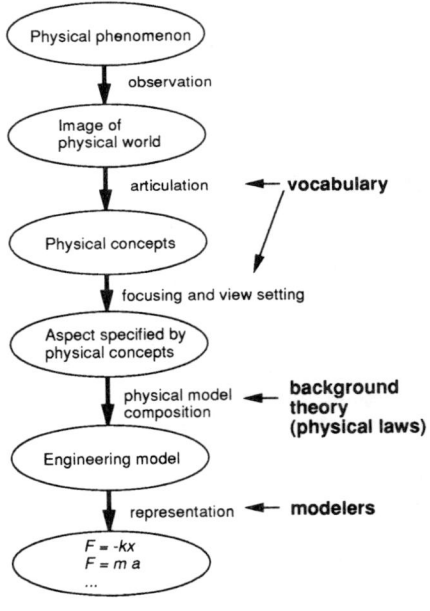

Figure 2: Model Generation Process

In the first phase, designers articulate their ambiguous image of the physical world obtained through observation, form into a number of physical concepts, and extract a part of the concepts by focusing and setting up views such as geometry, dynamic behaviors, materials, and electric properties. This phase is important to select appropriate background theories and modelers.

Vocabulary of physical concepts is required to describe such conceptual image and to manage the extracting operations of focusing and setting views. The VLKB for KIEF should store a large number of vocabulary to facilitate the operations in this phase.

In the second phase, engineering models are created by selecting background theories and represented in modelers. KIEF should provide descriptions of physical laws as discussed in the previous section. To select appropriate background theories, relationships among physical concepts and physical laws should be described in the VLKB for KIEF. In KIEF, vocabulary of physical phenomena is considered to be essential to derive physical laws. Furthermore, to compose engineering models in the corresponding modelers, the VLKB should provide fragments of models associated with physical laws.

3   A VLKB BASED ON QUALITATIVE PROCESS THEORY

In this chapter, we summarize our preliminary research [5] to build a VLKB for KIEF based on Qualitative Process Theory (QPT) by Forbus [1].

In Chapter 2, we stated that the VLKB for KIEF requires descriptions of both physical laws and vocabulary of physical concepts. QPT satisfies this requirement, because QPT includes both vocabulary of physical concepts as views and processes and a qualitative model of physical laws with which we can execute behavioral reasoning. We developed a QPT-based "physical feature" database to describe and collect knowledge of physical behaviors of mechanisms.

3.1   Knowledge Representation Based on QPT

In QPT, a notion of *process* is at the center of knowledge representation. A process is defined as "something that acts through time to change the parameters" in QPT. We employed this notion of process to represent a physical phenomenon in our framework. Examples of physical phenomena include motion, heat flow, evaporation, explosion, friction, and combustion.

Static structure of physical mechanisms is modeled as topological relations among the physical objects in QPT. We use entity and relation for modeling static structure. Entities include physical objects such as mechanical parts and electric devices and relations include such terms as "on," "above," "connected," and "fixed." The conceptual structure of a mechanism is represented as a network of the entities linked by the relations. Entities and relations have class hierarchies respectively. For example, a "helical gear" is a subclass of a "gear." This implies that physical phenomena that occur on a gear pair also occur on a helical gear pair.

On the other hand, physical laws are described as physical phenomena that have frame-type descriptions

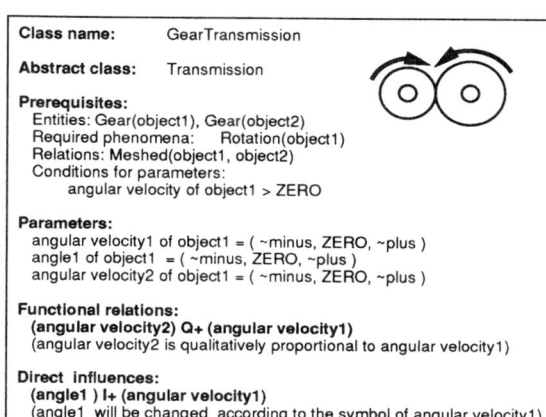

Figure 3: Description of Gear Transmission

(see Figure 3). A physical law has effects when a physical phenomenon that involves the law occurs. Physical phenomena have class hierarchies so that subclasses can inherit the physical laws of superclasses.

The frame of a physical phenomenon contains descriptions of;
(i) prerequisites for the occurrence of the physical phenomenon,
(ii) parameters required to describe behaviors of the entities, and
(iii) descriptions of physical laws.

The prerequisites of a physical phenomenon include required entities, relations, and other physical phenomena which need to occur. These descriptions constrain the environment in which the physical phenomenon should be considered. Prerequisites for the parameters are also described. For example, "boiling" occurs when the temperature of water is above the boiling point.

The required parameters attached to an entity indicate states of the entities, such as temperature. In QPT, parameters can have only discrete values, instead of continuous real numbers. Behaviors of mechanisms are modeled as changes in parameters.

The physical laws of a physical phenomenon are represented as influences which directly cause parameters to change and functional relations between the parameters which indirectly propagate changes from one parameter to another. Through the descriptions of physical laws, changes of the parameters are determined according to the current state of the parameters, so that the next states can be derived in behavioral simulation.

Figure 3 shows the description of a mechanical transmission with a pair of gears. The example shows that, when one of a pair is rotating, the phenomenon "gear transmission" occurs and causes rotation of the other gear. In the description, object1 is the driving gear and the prerequisites describe that rotation of object1 is required to cause the transmission. The influence states that if angular velocity of a gear is positive, then angle of the gear increases. The functional relation states that increase (decrease) of velocity of one gear causes increase (decrease) of velocity of the other.

3.2 Physical Features

With the concepts defined in the last section, we can build conceptual models of mechanisms to be used for design. We call the model a *physical feature*. Figure 4 illustrates some examples of physical features.

Figure 5 shows representation of a physical feature which includes the physical phenomenon of gear transmission. A physical feature is represented by a network of physical phenomena, entities, and relations. Links between a physical phenomenon and entities represent that the particular physical phenomenon occurs to a set of particular entities. Links among physical phenomena represent causal dependencies, which means that activation of one of the physical phenomena causes activation of others. Links between a relation and entities represent that the entities has the relation.

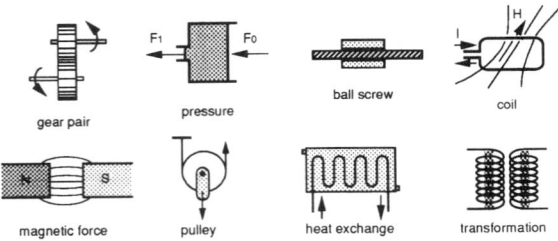

Figure 4: Examples of Physical Features

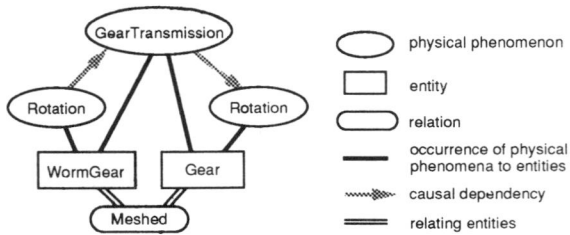

Figure 5: A Physical Feature of Gear Transmission

3.3 Preliminary Research on Knowledge Collection

We started a project to collect engineering knowledge consisting of physical concepts and qualitative descriptions of physical laws. There are two approaches for collecting the knowledge. One is to systematically obtain descriptions of domain knowledge from textbooks (e.g., [3][8]). The other is to select real mechanisms as examples and to obtain the knowledge needed to model the mechanism.

We tried both approaches. For collecting knowledge from textbooks, we chose the domains of kinematics, robotics, and classical physics. Examples of physical features include "guide," "slide," "fix," and "release" in kinematics; "open," "close," "put," and "hold" in robotics; and physical laws such as Newton's laws, Kirchhoff's law, and Faraday's law in classical physics. From these domains, we collected about 2,000 entities and about 300 physical phenomena. For collecting knowledge from mechanisms, we have modeled fundamental mechanisms such as a motor, a contactor which is a device to switch electric current, and a jumping machine which is a toy that jump up with a spring. The behaviors of the mechanisms could be reasoned out using the knowledge extracted from the model by a QPT-based reasoning system [5].

3.4 Limitations of the Framework

In collecting knowledge of engineering, we found out limitations of the QPT-based approach.

One limitation comes from that we used only one representation scheme (i.e., QPT) to describe design object models. Although QPT provides important vocabulary of physical concepts, the representation of physical laws using relations among qualitative parameters was too weak to cover everything. This is not a problem of QPT. However, as discussed in Chapter 2, since having multiple models from various aspects is essential to describe design objects, it is desirable to include, for instance, quantitative parameter representation.

This limitation became also apparent, when we failed to describe static phenomena such as "supporting." Such physical phenomena contain equilibrium of action and reaction forces as physical laws, and this was difficult to describe in QPT. The other type of examples we found difficulty to model was a physical phenomenon in a space with more than one dimension, such as movement of a mass that receive forces from different directions. This requires vector expressions. Furthermore, a physical phenomenon such as "slide" is characterized by the "contact" relation between a moving object and a guiding surface. However, the relation "contact" requires spatial representation and is difficult to model.

Another limitation of the representation comes from

inflexible descriptions of the prerequisites for entities in the physical phenomenon frame. This resulted in inefficiency of the knowledge base and very painful knowledge collection work. Consider a physical phenomenon "rotation." In definition, there must be an entity that can rotate. Unless there is an explicit description in the definition of a "shaft" that is a rotatable entity, we cannot reason out that a shaft can rotate. This requests to create a new abstract entity class "rotatable entity," and to declare that a shaft belongs to this "rotatable entity." However, deciding if a shaft belongs to this class requires the knowledge about rotation. This means that definitions of "rotation," "rotatable entities," and "shaft" are mutually dependent on each other, and consequently we tended to come up with an "integrated" physical phenomenon of "rotation of shaft." This sort of descriptions is needed for any rotatable entities, and we resulted in inefficient knowledge collection with numerous slightly different physical phenomena that have exactly the same physical rule.

Therefore, physical phenomena should not define entity classes as prerequisites. The knowledge of direct links between physical phenomena and entities should be considered in physical features defined in Section 3.2. A physical feature is a case in which physical phenomena occur. Instead of writing entity class names in the frames of physical phenomena, physical properties of the physical entities to be considered in the physical phenomena should be described. For example, physical properties such as "elastic" should be considered to think about a physical phenomenon "bending," rather than an "entity that can bend."

This problem is also associated with how a physical laws is described in QPT. In QPT, physical laws are independently described as relations and influences within each physical phenomenon. Consequently, it happened that the same physical laws are described differently in various physical phenomena without noticed. Names of the parameters and definitions of the parameter values for the same physical law were not consistently described. From a view point of knowledge collection, physical laws and parameters should be categorized and described in an integrated manner.

4   A NEW APPROACH TO BUILDING A VLKB

This chapter presents our extended architecture of a VLKB for KIEF to continue the project of collecting engineering knowledge. The extended architecture allows describing physical concepts more independently from particular models, so that, in the VLKB, descriptions of physical concepts become more reusable.

4.1   The Metamodel Mechanism

We have proposed the idea of a multiple modeling environment based on the *metamodel mechanism* [6] illustrated in Figure 6. The metamodel mechanism integrates various external models describing a design object from different aspects. We intend to plug in commercial modelers (e.g., solid modelers) as external modelers [12]. A metamodel is a higher level description that integrates concepts in the external models, from which "aspect" models are generated and through which information about the design object is shared. A metamodel is represented as a network of physical concepts which we will discuss in the next section. We have developed a prototype system of the metamodel mechanism on Objectworks\Smalltalk.

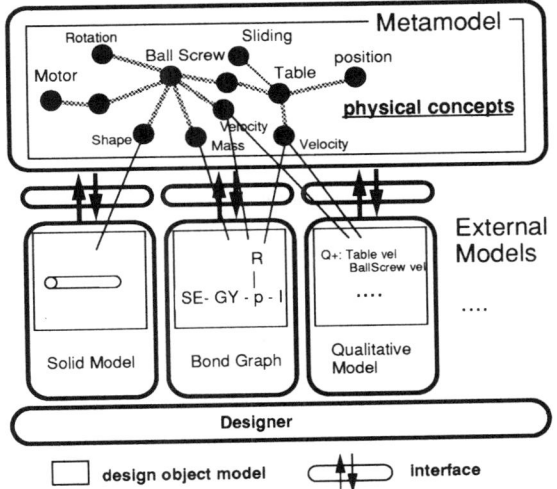

Figure 6: A Metamodel Mechanism

4.2   The New Architecture

As discussed in Chapter 3, the architecture based on QPT had limitations, and we needed to extend it as depicted in Figure 7. In this new architecture, the VLKB consists of three layers. In the middle layer, there is a *concept base* which contains concepts about entities, physical phenomena, relations, attributes, and physical properties. The upper layer contains physical features that are combinations of physical concepts. The lower layer contains physical laws that are used as model fragments for various design object models.

Entities, physical phenomena, and relations stored in the concept base are conceptually similar to those described in the previous chapter. An attribute is a concept attached to entities and takes a values to indicate the state of entities, such as "position," "temperature," and "mass." A physical property is a concept that describes generic characteristic of entities such as

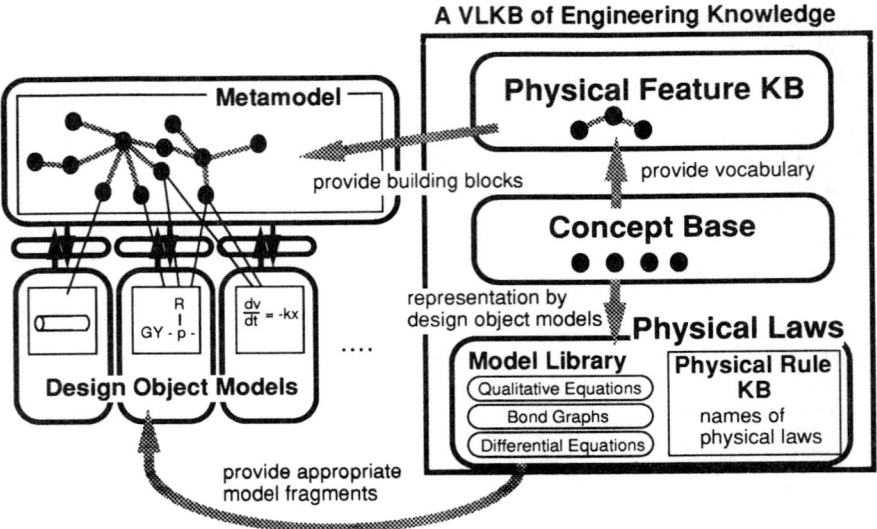

Figure 7: The Extended Architecture of a VLKB

"elastic" and "magnetized." A physical property is associated with a set of attributes that indicate degree of the physical property. For example, Young's modulus indicates elasticity.

The concept base contains names of physical concepts and relationships among physical concepts. The relationships include abstract-concrete hierarchy of physical concepts, differential relations between attributes, and "has" relations between entities and physical properties.

In this architecture, the frames of physical phenomena are different from the ones in the previous chapter. Instead of describing entity classes as prerequisites, the frame contains only pointers to link instances of entities for delegation when building physical features. The frame also describes the attributes and the physical properties required in the physical phenomenon. Physical laws are described by symbolic names which are managed by the physical rule KB in the lower layer.

In the upper layer, physical features presented in Section 3.2 are built and stored in the physical feature knowledge base. The concept base provides only vocabulary of physical concepts such as "burn," "fuel," "warm up," and "air," and physical features are the statements that describe physical situations such as "fuel burns, generates heat, and warms up air." The designer constructs a metamodel with physical features.

In the lower layer, physical laws are described. The same physical law can be differently represented in different design object models. The *physical rule knowledge base* contains the unique names of physical laws

and the attribute concepts used in the laws. The names of physical laws keeps track of the same physical law represented in different design object models.

The *model libraries* store typical model fragments of a design object model that relate physical concepts and design object models. For example, an equation "$f = ma$" is a fragment of a dynamics equation model that describes "Newton's second law." These fragments are used as building blocks to generate design object models. The parameters used in a fragment corresponds to attribute concepts, so that, after a design object model is generated, the metamodel mechanism can maintain relationships among the attribute concepts in the metamodel and the parameters in design object models for sharing information.

Figure 8 illustrates how the knowledge of gear transmission can be represented in KIEF. Because the frame of physical phenomenon is simplified and abstract physical phenomena such as "rotational transmission" can be described, we can describe "rotational transmission" instead of "gear transmission." The functional relation of gear's velocity are described in various representations in model libraries.

4.3 Collecting Knowledge for KIEF

We are currently working on collecting engineering knowledge on our new framework. Hayes roughly estimated the number of tokens of human knowledge about the physical world as 10^4 to 10^5 [4]. The Cyc project sets its goal at collecting entries of the order of 10^6 [7] or even beyond. From our experience of working with engineers, the engineers require to have a kernel of physical knowledge so that they can add their own vocabulary to the knowledge base easily. This kernel knowledge is fundamental theories and mechanisms which engineers should have learned. We believe at least 10000 physical concepts are required to provide the kernel knowledge, hence the $o(10^4)$ project.

We developed the knowledge base system on Objectworks\Smalltalk. Compared to the previous knowledge collection work, the extended architecture of KIEF allows collecting physical concepts more independently from particular design object models. In this approach, we intend to systematically collect vocabulary from documents such as engineering text books. Figure 9 shows a browser for collecting physical phenomena and Figure 10 shows a physical rule knowledge base collecting physical laws.

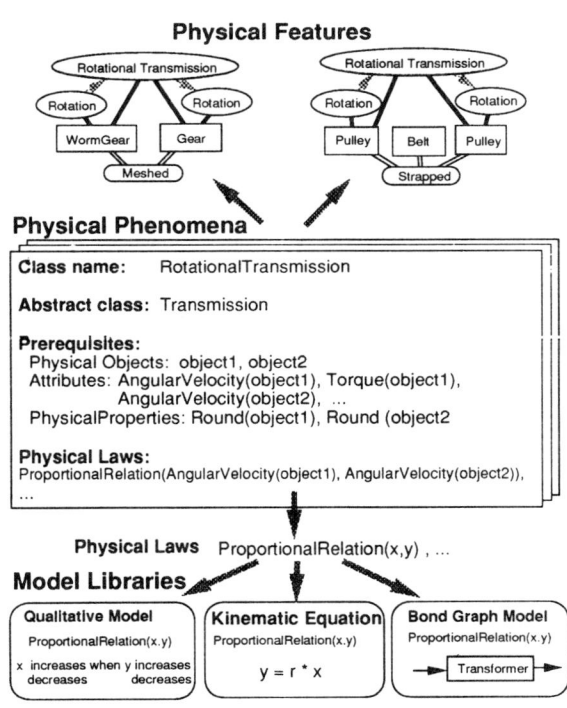

Physical Features

Physical Phenomena

Physical Laws ProportionalRelation(x,y) , ...

Model Libraries

Figure 8: Describing Gear Transmission in KIEF

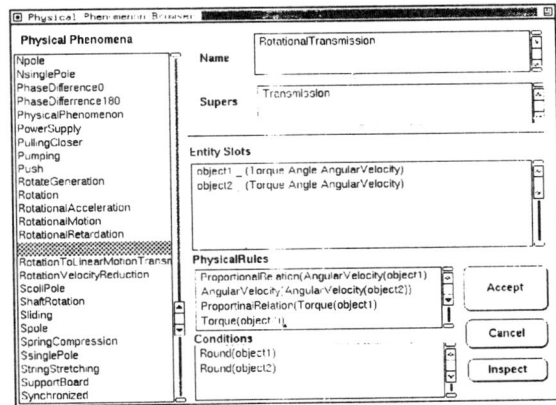

Figure 9: A Physical Phenomenon Browser

Table 1: Current Status of Knowledge Collection

Physical concepts	number
entities	200
relations	40
physical phenomena	150
attributes	280
physical properties	80
physical laws	300

The current status of knowledge collection is shown in Table 1. The physical concepts and the physical laws are collected mainly from engineering textbooks such as [3][8]. The collected knowledge covers basic theories of dynamics, heat dynamics, kinematics, and electric circuits. Using the vocabulary, we experimentally built 39 physical features of fundamental mechanisms

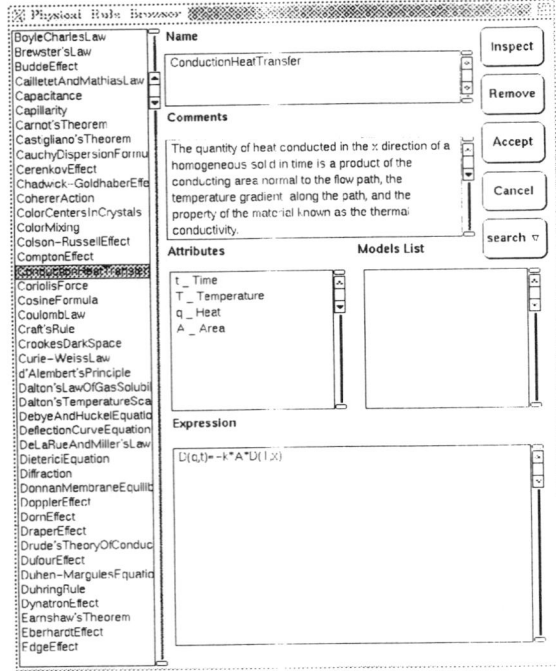

Figure 10: A Physical Rule Knowledge Base

5 CONCLUSIONS

In this paper, we discussed a fundamental architecture for building a VLKB for the knowledge intensive engineering framework, and reported our project of knowledge collection work. This fundamental architecture consists of three layers, i.e., physical features, physical concepts, and physical laws. The architecture can deal with various engineering models and can assist designers in generating models. This allows KIEF to generate the models used in the engineering activities such as manufacturing, operation, maintenance, and recycling and to intensively use knowledge through these activities.

Currently, we are working on collecting engineering knowledge based on the architecture. Future work includes implementing various engineering models plugged into the metamodel mechanism, so that the VLKB can use a variety of ontology to describe physical laws.

ACKNOWLEDGMENT

The authors would like to thank Dr. Takashi Kiriyama, Dr. Yasushi Umeda, Mr. Yoshiki Shimomura, Mr. Masaharu Yoshioka and other colleagues in our group of the University of Tokyo who helped us in the discussions and implementations of the ideas presented in this paper.

REFERENCES

1. K.D. Forbus, Qualitative process theory, *Artificial Intelligence*, Vol. 24, pp. 85–168, 1984.

2. T. Gruber, The development of large, shared knowledgebases: Collaborative activities at stanford, Technical Report KSL90-62, Stanford Knowledge Systems Laboratory, 1990.

3. C.F. Hix and R.P. Alley, *Physical Laws and Effects*. John Wiley & Sons, London, 1958.

4. P. Hayes, The second naive physics manifesto, In J. Hobbs and R. C. Moore, editors, *Formal Theories of the Commonsense World*, pp. 1–36. Ablex, 1985.

5. T. Kiriyama, T. Tomiyama, and H. Yoshikawa, Model generation in design, In *Fifth International Workshop on Qualitative Reasoning about Physical Systems*, pp. 93–108, 1991.

6. T. Kiriyama, T. Tomiyama, and H. Yoshikawa, The use of qualitative physics for integrated design object modeling, In J.R. Rnderle, editor, *Design Theory and Methodology –DTM'90–*, volume DE-Vol. 27, pp. 53–60. ASME, 1991.

7. D.B. Lenat and R.V. Guha, *Building Large Knowledge-Based Systems*, Addison-Wesley, Reading, MA, 1989.

8. K. Roth, *Konstruieren mit Konstruktionskatalogen*, Springer-Verlag, Berlin, 1982.

in mechanical design such as electromagnetic coils and spring damper. As we collect more knowledge, the numbers of physical features, entities, and relations grow, while the numbers of other concepts (physical phenomena attributes, physical properties, and physical laws) hopefully stay the same. Currently, the physical laws are modeled mainly by numerical equations and qualitative physics, so that the collected physical features can be simulated by numerical simulation or qualitative reasoning.

We are also working on other modeling methods besides qualitative physics and numerical equations, and developing model libraries. For instance, we developed a Bond graph system as an example case study to evaluate model generation in the new architecture. The Bond graph system is plugged into the metamodel mechanism. A Bond graph is a model of power flow in design objects and can numerically simulate behaviors. The designer can build a Bond graph model of the design object from a network of physical concept. Figure 11 shows a hardcopy of the system designing a table moving mechanism. The top left window shows the conceptual network, the bottom left window shows the bond graph, and the right window shows results of simulation which depict rotation of the motor and the movement of the table.

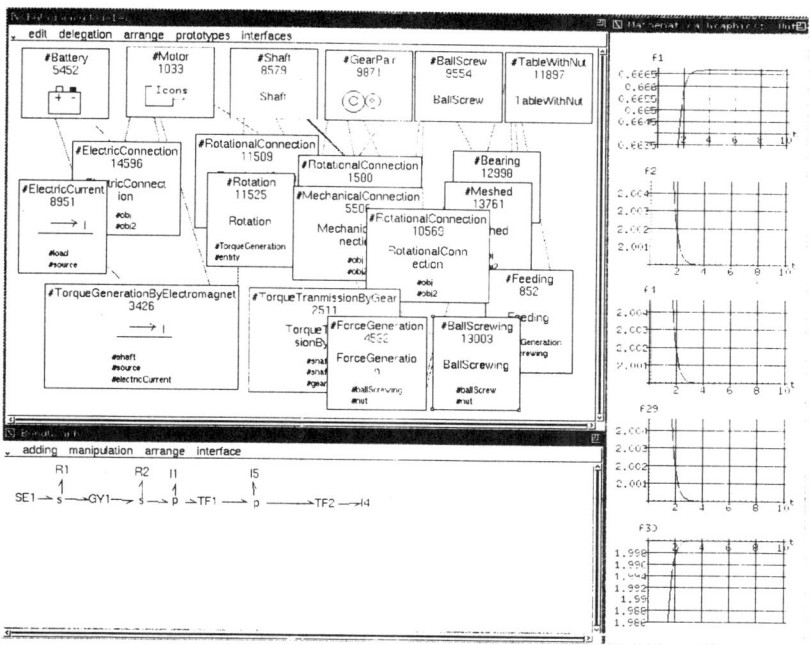

Figure 11: A Bond Graph Modeler

9. T. Tomiyama, T. Kiriyama, H. Takeda, D. Xue, and H. Yoshikawa, Metamodel: A key to intelligent cad systems, *Research in Engineering Design*, Vol. 1, No. 1, pp. 19–34, 1989.

10. T. Tomiyama, T. Kiriyama, and Y. Umeda, Toward knowledge intensive engineering, In K. Fuchi and T. Yokoi, editors, *Knowledge Building and Knowledge Sharing*. Ohmsha, Tokyo and Osaka and Kyoto, 1994.

11. T. Tomiyama, Y. Umeda, and T. Kiriyama, A framework for knowledge intensive engineering, In *Proceedings of the Fourth International Workshop on Computer Aided Systems Technology (CAST'94)*. University of Ottawa, Ont.,Canada, 1994.

12. M. Yoshioka, M. Nakamura, T. Tomiyama, and H. Yoshikawa, A process model with multiple design object models, In *Design Theory and Methodology – DTM'93–*, pp. 7–14. ASME, 1993.

Towards Very Large Knowledge Bases
N.J.I. Mars, Ed.
IOS Press, 1995

A Scientific Knowledge Base for Extracting and Justifying Scientific Hypotheses in Atmospheric Research

Epaminondas Kapetanios
Research Center Karlsruhe
Karlsruhe, Germany
nondas@iai.kfk.de

ABSTRACT

A scientific knowledge–based system design approach is presented in this paper which concerns scientific data analysis in terms of extracting and justifying scientific hypotheses about observed atmospheric phenomena. They will be extracted from the underlying data instances of measurements and observations with the help of metadata. Scientific hypotheses and metadata will constitute the declarative knowledge. Justification of hypotheses will be provided by connecting appropriate knowledge structures. The resultant justification structures will be regarded as the compiled procedural knowledge of the scientific knowledge base. Compiled knowledge is computationally efficient in the case of building very large–scale knowledge bases where knowledge must be provided in terms of justifications based on the relevant data instances from which observed phenomena or scientific hypotheses have been derived.

1 INTRODUCTION

Global climate change understanding requires interdisciplinary research efforts by bringing together scientists from different disciplines [44]. In particular, phenomena like the occurence of "ozone hole" or "earth heating" require an explanation based on the analysis and understanding of atmospheric chemistry. For this purpose, remote sensing instruments are being developed aiming at gathering emitted radiance data in the atmosphere on a global scale.

The limb sounder MIPAS (Michelson Interferometer for Passive Atmospheric Sounding) is an example of such a remote sensing instrument and will be installed on a satellite polar platform (ENVISAT–1 mission of the European Space Agency) collecting emitted radiance data from trace gases in the atmosphere [12, 13].

The study of atmospheric chemistry is not only a challenge to climate researchers but also to the computer science society [52, 47, 19]. Processing and analysis of scientific data should provide an insight into the atmospheric chemistry by relating atmospheric phenomena and the corresponding scientific hypotheses to observed parameters (e.g., temperature, pressure, NOy gases, etc.) and beyond that to the data instances (measurement and observation data) from which the observed phenomena have been derived.

For this purpose, a scientific information system (see figure 1) is being developed at the Research Center Karlsruhe – Technology and Environment, in order to cope not only with collecting and managing measurement and observation data but also with extracting and managing knowledge about chemical processes in the atmosphere. Hence, the most abstract level of the information to be provided by the system is strongly related to the scientific field of atmospheric chemistry. A global layout of the system is depicted in figure 1.

In particular, extracted or a–priori defined knowledge, concerning the scientific discipline and experiment under consideration, must be modelled and provided in terms of metadata. This will be interfaced with the underlying source data instances of measurements and observations made during the execution of the scientific experiment, and with the visualization system.

In this framework, a scientific knowledge base will be described in this paper. In the first section 2, the needed knowledge structures and the scientific activities to take place in accordance with these knowledge structures are presented. These activities take place in order to extract and justify observed atmospheric phenomena. In order to illustrate this, a validation scenario of long–living gases in the atmosphere will be used as a representative example.

In section 3, justification structures which connect

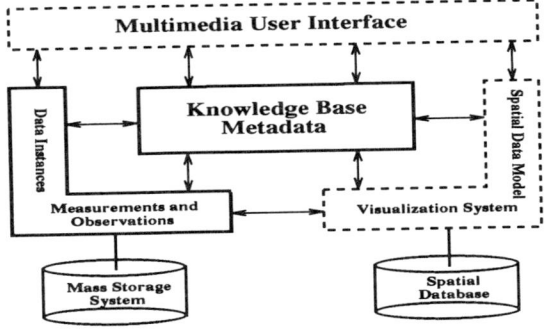

Figure 1: The scientific information system

knowledge elements that belong to various knowledge structures are defined as the inference mechanism in order to provide a justification for extracted scientific hypotheses concerning atmospheric phenomena. In section 4, the design approach of the knowledge-based system is presented in terms of its declarative and procedural knowledge. Symbolic and connectionism approaches are also discussed as potential knowledge representation formalisms due to their appropriateness for our problem solution strategy. The related work and state–of–the–art are given in section 5 as a summary of the work done in similar reasearch areas and application fields. Finally, a conclusion summarizes the main issues presented in this paper.

2 THE SCIENTIFIC KNOWLEDGE STRUCTURES AND ACTIVITIES

At first, a scenario is given in order to illustrate the way of extracting and using knowledge while validating scientific hypotheses. Consequently, we will give some definitions describing the needed knowledge in terms of *scientific knowledge structures* and the corresponding *scientific activities*. These definitions are closely related to those given in [48].

2.1 The scenario

The formalism used to describe the activities is a *flowchart* which is a labeled, finite directed graph where the arcs indicate causal relationships (the control flow) between activities represented by boxes and knowledge structures represented by parallelograms (see figure 2). They are considered to be the input/output of the activities.

The scenario of long–living gases. The group of the trace gases $N_2O, CFC - 12, CFC - 11$ is considered to be the **taxonomy** of long–living gases in the atmosphere. An **experimental law** gives an insight into the correlation quality. All trace gases that belong to the taxonomy of long–living gases must be correlated according to the **theory/hypothesis** of *dynamically dependent correlation for this group of trace gases*. If trace gases $N_2O, CFC - 12$ are not correlated, then an **anomaly** has occured. This anomaly has to be confirmed by addressing the source data instances (measurements or observations) from which the phenomenon has been derived, i.e., the relevant source data has to be addressed by tracing back the derivation (transformation) history.

If something went wrong during the transformation process of the relevant measurement and observation data, all affected data instances must be reprocessed according to an improved algorithm which will replace the old one. If the anomaly could be confirmed by the source data, then the theory/hypothesis must be modified which means that an unknown chemical process must be inserted into the theories/hypotheses. In parallel, the taxonomy of long–living gases must also be modified in that, for example, CFC–12 will be deleted from the taxonomy.

2.2 The scientific knowledge structures

According to the scenario described above, we will define the following knowledge structures:

- **Measurements and Observations.** They are objects addressing the relevant instances of measured or transformed into observation data, e.g., interferograms $\rightarrow$ calibrated spectra $\rightarrow$ trace gas distributions. These objects can be described by atomic or complex concepts. They enrich the semantics of the underlying scientific data and are considered to be equivalent to the database conceptual design of an information system. *This knowledge is a–priori definable and strongly related to the application domain (scientific experiment) under consideration.*

- **Transformation processes.** They are classes of objects representing atomic or complex concepts addressing the instances of transformation processes. They can take values by interactively changed parameters, versioning of specification and implementation of algorithms, etc., throughout the transformation processing chain of measurement data towards observations.

  The concepts of transformation processes enrich the semantics of processes and implemented algorithms and are considered to be equivalent to the *design issues of the software applications* as being addressed during the development of an information system. *This knowledge is a–priori definable and strongly related to the application domain (scientific experiment) under consideration.*

- **Generation histories.** They constitute the behavioral model of the information system in terms of event–condition–action triples. They are expressed

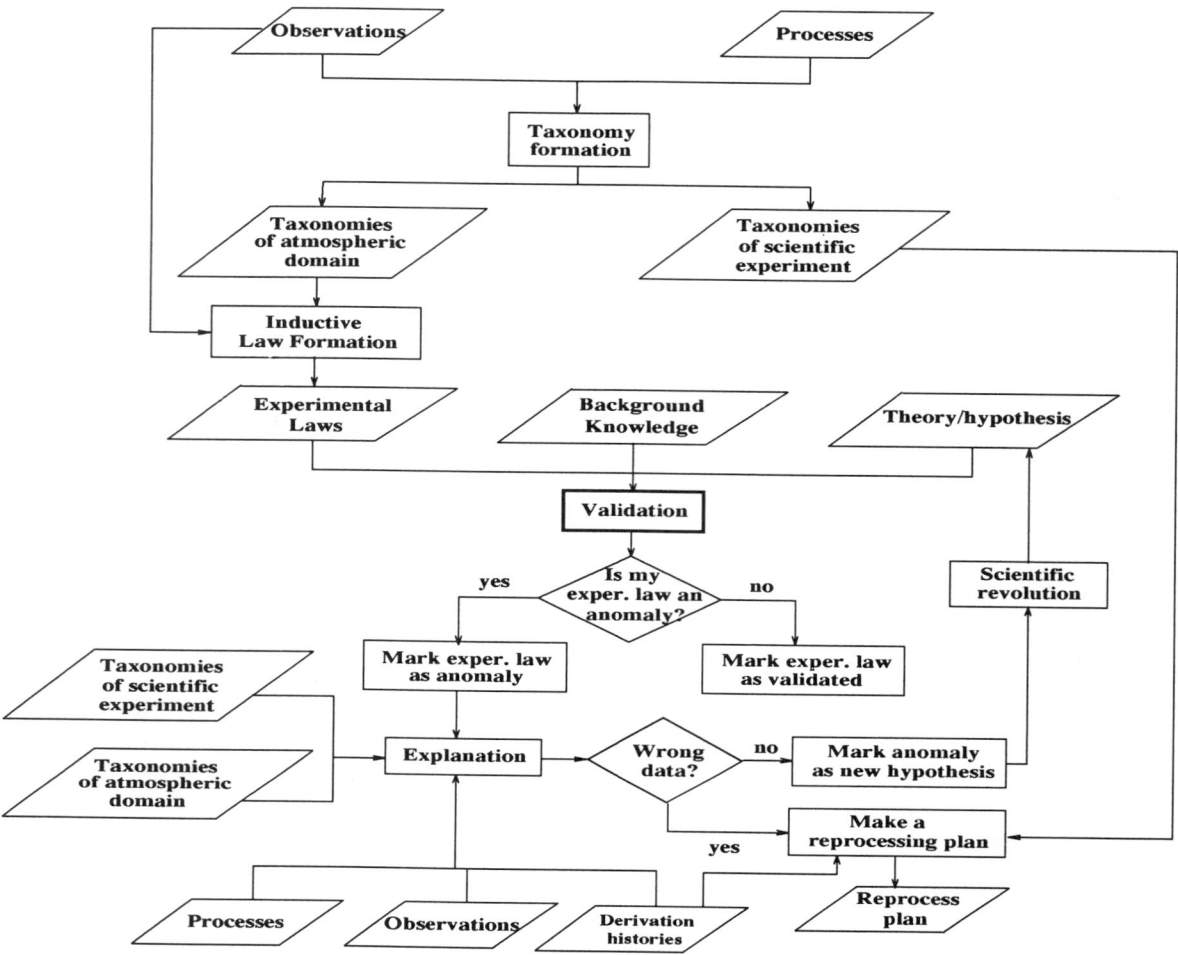

Figure 2: Flow chart of extracting and justifying scientific hypotheses in atmospheric research

by network concepts which are related to the data derivation history of the scientific data instances [53]. Based upon these network concepts, observations or measurements from which other observations have been derived can be traced back. *This knowledge is a–priori definable and strongly related to the application domain (scientific experiment) under consideration.*

Generation histories interrelate *transformation processes* with *measurements and observations* in that the latter are considered to be the inputs and outputs of the transformation processes. Bringing these two knowledge structures (data and process models of the information system) in conjunction, we will be able to give insight into the conditions under which observations have been transformed and/or generated.

- **Taxonomies.** They are links used to organize concepts into a hierarchy or some other partial ordering [50]. We must distinguish here between taxonomies and concepts in that the notion of a concept is primarily the notion of a *data structure*. Taxonomies are considered to be storing information at appriopriate levels of generality and automatically making it available to more specific concepts by means of a mechanism of inheritance.

From another perspective of view, taxonomies provide the *information* to steer the extraction of new knowledge through learning methods. Considering the taxonomies which deal with the concepts of the scientific discipline (e.g., trace gases), a connection point can be specified through the generation history between the concepts of the scientific experiment and discipline. *This knowledge is partly a–priori definable and is related to the application domain (scientific experiment and discipline) under consideration.*

- **Experimental laws.** They summarize relations among observed variables (e.g., NO_y, temperature, pressure), or atomic objects (e.g., trend of ozone concentration). They can be in qualitative or in quantitative form and must be inductively inferenced according to the underlying data. They are mostly related to a certain phenomenon of interest. *This knowledge cannot be defined a–priori.*

- **Theories/hypotheses.** They represent *scientific hypotheses* about chemical processes in the atmosphere. They differ from experimental laws in making reference to unobservable objects or mechanisms. Scientific hypotheses are statements that belong to the empirical sciences and have this status if and only if they are falsifiable [45]. These statements are falsifiable if and only if there exists at least one potential falsifier. Thus a logical relation exists between the scientific hypothesis and the class of potential falsifiers. *This knowledge can be partly defined a–priori.*

- **Anomalies.** They are experimental laws marked as potential falsifiers of a theory/hypothesis. It will be the output of a validation process of an experimental law and could demonstrably falsify a scientific hypothesis. *This knowledge cannot be defined a–priori.*

- **Background knowledge.** This is a set of beliefs or knowledge about the environment aside from those that are specifically under study. It differs from theories/hypotheses or experimental laws in that the scientist holds background knowledge with relative certainty rather than as the subject of active evaluation. Auxiliary data sets, like climatology or spectroscopic data (spectral lines of already known molecules) and/or data from other contemporary experimental campaigns, are mainly considered to form the background knowledge. *This knowledge can be defined a–priori.*

- **Experiment model.** They are descriptions of the environmental conditions for an experimental or observational setting. It indicates the manner in which an experimental law or theory/hypothesis applies according to a particular situation (specific experimental arrangement) or external conditions. Instrument and flight related data sets give an insight of these conditions and settings.

2.3 Scientific Activities

According to the scenario described above, we will also define the scientific activities [48] as considered to be essential in order to extract and organize scientific knowledge.

- **Taxonomy formation.** This activity involves the organization of observations and processes into classes and subclasses, along with the definition of those classes. This operation relates on existing taxonomies concerning both the domain of scientific experiment and discipline.

- **Inductive experimental law formation.** This involves the generation of experimental (qualitative or quantitative) laws that cover observation parameters. The experimental laws are stated using terms from the related taxonomy in the domain of scientific discipline and are constrained by the experiment's conditions.

- **Validation process.** This involves the validation of extracted experimental laws on the basis of theories and background knowledge (e.g., data from contemporary scientific campaigns or ancillary (climatological or spectroscopic data). The result of this activity is a possible demarcation of the experimental law as an anomaly.

- **Explanation process.** This activity will take place after identifying an anomaly. Explaning this anomaly requires the accessing of data instances of measurements and/or observations through the related taxonomies which are involved in the experimental law formation.

  The result of this activity will be either the confirmation of an unjustified experimental law (anomaly) or the identification of wrongly derived observations. In the first case, the anomaly must be accepted (experimental law to be marked as potential falsifier) and may lead to a revision of a scientific hypothesis and/or taxonomy. In the second case, a reprocessing plan for the affected data instances of measurements and/or observations involved in the anomaly formation must be elaborated on the basis of the data generation histories.

- **Connecting and/or disconnecting knowledge structures.** This activity is related to the construction of explanation or justification structures over knowledge elements which are instances of the knowledge structures. They connect a theory/hypothesis to experimental laws and/or anomalies, and these to the corresponding taxonomies, and consequently, to the instances of observations, processes and generation histories. In case of an anomaly as potential falsifier or as experimental law based on wrongly derived observations, the affected justification structures must be revised. We will return to this subject in the following section.

- **Experimental design.** This activity deals with the specification of transformation process chains by which observations are going to be generated.

136

New algorithms may be developed and tested on an experimental basis. Consequently, the behavioral model of the scientific experiment may be enhanced or modified. Furthermore, a reprocessing plan must be elaborated in case of an occuring anomaly which is based on wrongly derived observations.

- **Scientific revolution (theory/hypothesis revision).** This activity is related to empirical (experimental) laws as does law formation to observations. A new scientific hypothesis may be created by considering a justified anomaly in conjunction with a known theory/hypothesis modification. The theory/hypothesis is stated using terms from the domains' taxonomy of the scientific experiment and discipline. It is strongly related to the background knowledge and the experimental settings.

3 INFERENCE THROUGH JUSTIFICATION STRUCTURES

The extraction and justification of scientific hypotheses about atmospheric phenomena enable an *information oriented access* of the underlying scientific data instances (measurements and observations). In other words, information can be provided on the level of observed atmospheric phenomena and not only on catalogs of collected data instances. The explanation mechanism can be achieved by conceptual structures which will be called *justification or explanation structures* according to the definition given in [8]. They provide a connection of knowledge elements which belong to the various knowledge structures.

The justification structures are spread among the layers of the domains of scientific discipline, experiment and instances (see figure 3). The various knowledge structures are mapped onto the domain layers as follows: (a) the set of experimental laws, anomalies, theories/hypotheses, background knowledge and taxonomies on the domain of scientific discipline, (b) the set of experiment related taxonomies (data, process and behavioral models of the scientific information system) and the knowledge structure defined as experiment model on the domain of the scientific experiment, and (c) the set of measurements and observations, generation processes and histories on the domain of instances.

Each explanation or justification structure can be considered as a *case* on which reasoning about a particular phenomenon has been based. A *case-based* reasoning mode could follow from these structures delimiting the search space which will be very large [15]. Therefore, the process of searching for an explanation will be steered by the generic knowledge elements to be found in the domains of scientific discipline and experiment [54]. Reorganization of knowledge is confined to the formulation of new theories/hypotheses

and their relationships to experimental laws. Reorganization also affects the elimination of already extracted justification structures for experimental laws or anomalies in the case of wrongly derived observation data instances.

Considering the scientific knowledge to be represented in the knowledge base, we have distinguished between the knowledge of the outside world (domain of scientific discipline), and the knowledge of the system's structures and of how the system works (domains of scientific experiment and instances). The latter is essential in order to characterize the system as *intelligent*, according to the Knowledge Representation Hypothesis of Smith [6]. This also enables an introspection on the actions undertaken by the system.

4 THE DESIGN APPROACH OF THE SCIENTIFIC KNOWLEDGE BASE

Considering the distinction between symbolics and connectionism as top–down and bottom–up reasoning, respectively, and the various knowledge structures to be addressed, the design approach of the scientific knowledge base is presented in this section. At this point, the following definition is given [55] where *an agent is considered to be a computer program that operate independently, or perhaps as groups, possibly with human intervention, to solve a problem (either control or informational). An agent can be trying to solve a single problem or a subset of a problem, or something peripheral but necessary to another agent's solving of the problem.* With respect to the knowledge structures and activities, as they have been described in section 2, we will distinguish between *knowledge server agents* for the organization of the declarative knowledge and *knowledge processor agents* for the manipulation of the compiled procedural knowledge, respectively.

4.1 The declarative knowledge

Before going into the architectural design approach, we will give an insight into the knowledge structures and their representation issues. At this point, we have to examine the nature of the knowledge to be addressed in order to understand what is the appropriate knowledge representation formalism to be further considered. Consequently, the appropriate knowledge servers will be determined and presented (figure 4).

Starting with the knowledge structures of *measurements and observations*, a time–series oriented representation and addressing of data instances is mainly considered that can be sufficiently handled by a conventional relational database management system (data accessing profile in not based on complex structures). The mapping of knowledge representation to relations appears straightforward and relational queries can naturally express queries that one would pose to the underlying representation [29]. Thus

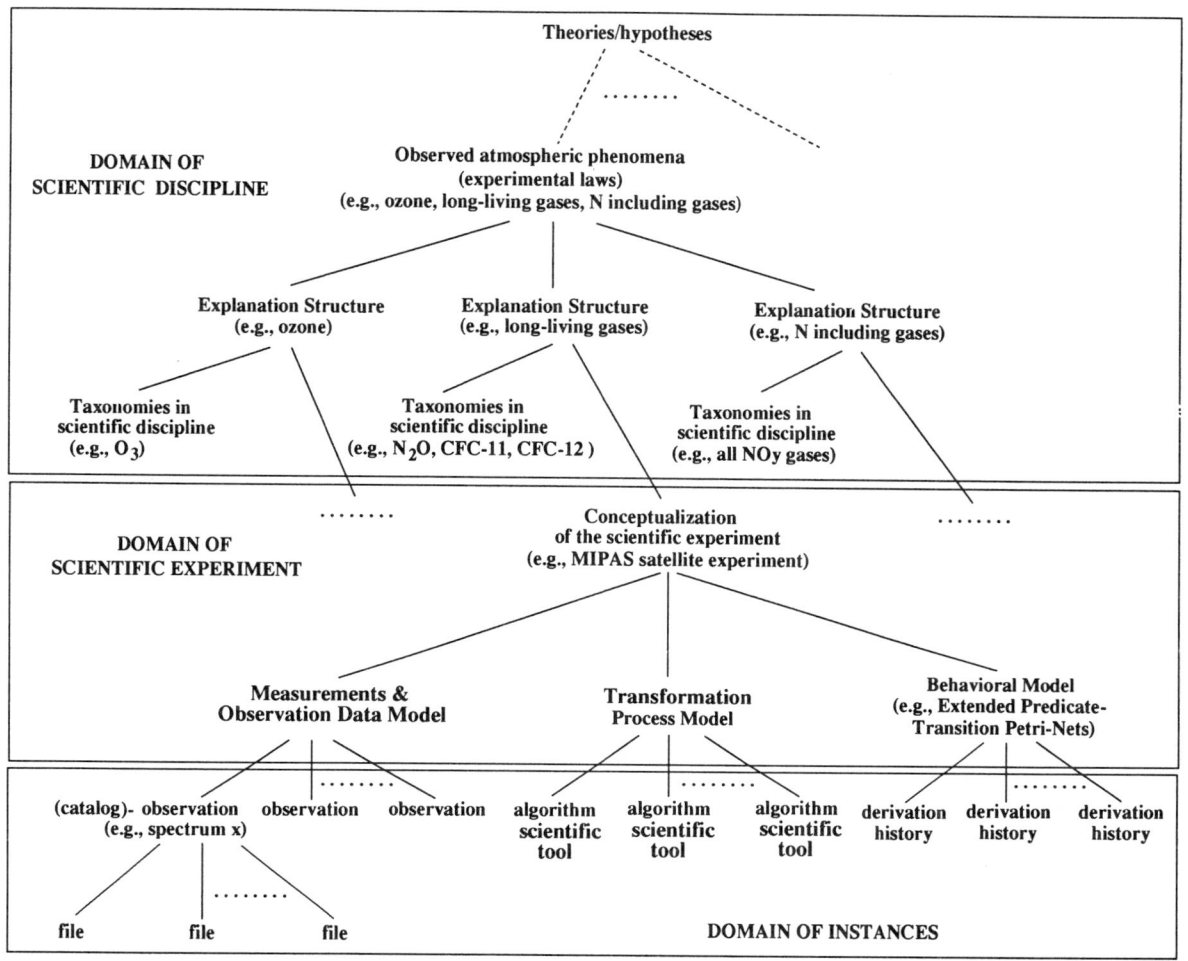

Figure 3: The justification or explanation structures for MIPAS scientific experiment

the RDBMS provides a suitable knowledge representation mechanism for this kind of knowledge structures. Therefore, the RDBMS will be further considered as the knowledge server to be known as MOS.

The knowledge structures of *transformation processes* and *taxonomies* as well as the concepts at the level of the conceptual database design for the measurement and observation data push the representation formalism as provided by a conventional RDBMS to its limits [5, 37, 18, 29]. The knowledge representation mechanism for these knowledge structures must be considered at the level of abstract conceptions which concern with real–world entities and actions. These conceptions are going to be referred as objects to be classified in categories or to change dynamically an assigned category, for instance, by modifying the taxonomy of long–living trace gases (see also scenario). These conceptions can also be regarded as *metadata*

for the description of the underlying data and processes [19]. The knowledge server dealing with these knowledge structures will be known as EXPER.

Accordingly, the modeling and derivation of the *generation histories* will be based on the conceptions of an extended predicate–transition network [53]. Places and transitions are also modelled as objects. Their instantiations are related to a certain algorithm version, or a certain processing path, or interactively instantiated process parameters. The corresponding knowledge server will be known as PETRI. The conceptions supported by the knowledge servers EXPER and PETRI are naturally represented by complex structures through which they will also be accessed. Therefore, these conceptions can be handled sufficiently by an object–oriented DBMS.

A part of the *background knowledge*, especially the knowledge which is referred to climatological or spectroscopic data of known molecules will be mapped onto a separate knowledge server. On the same server, the *experimental model* may also be mapped, and therefore, the knowledge structures which are regarded to affect the environment or conditions of the scientific experiment can be represented by the knowledge server EXTERN. The addressing mode of these knowledge structures must be further elaborated.

For the knowledge structures of *experimental laws*, *anomalies* and *scientific hypotheses*, a more powerful representation mechanism is needed in order to accomodate conceptions like the description of atmospheric phenomena, space–, time– and context depedency, incomplete data, qualitative reasoning, etc. For this purpose, a representation formalism on the basis of a semantic network will be further considered. This decision has been taken due to the powerful expression mechanism of describing natural phenomena [56], and to the structural properties (various kinds of associations) which are provided by semantic networks.

The description of a phenomenon and/or a scientific hypothesis will be made in terms of associations which are related to certain contexts and events, whereby the context is related to the space–time association, and the event to the association of subject–predicate. These associations will constitute a propositional representation of theories/hypotheses. Although there is an equivalent representation of a semantic network in logic [49], the structural properties provided by semantic networks are more closely related to natural language representation issues [51], and can be more easily handled than logic in order to construct justification structures which will be the subject of the next subsection.

Moreover, scientific knowledge is often based on knowledge that is contradictory (theories/hypotheses and background knowledge that cannot justify experimental laws). Trying to represent contradictory knowledge declaratively, e.g., in first order predicate logic, will result in contradictory conclusions. However, an inconsistent database can prove anything [25]. Using non–monotonic logic is an attempt to overcome this problem, but there are still some problems concerning the complexity and the undecidable nature of determining whether a formula is consistent with a theory [41].

Using knowledge structures can overcome the problem of representing contradictory knowledge by considering them as microtheories [16]. Hence, we are not obliged to have a standard point of inference. There is also a fundamental difference between human knowledge and declarative knowledge representation; it is the improved ability of human reasoning with more knowledge, whereas a theorem prover would quickly lead to a combinatorial explosion. Organizing scientific knowledge as human knowledge with microtheo-

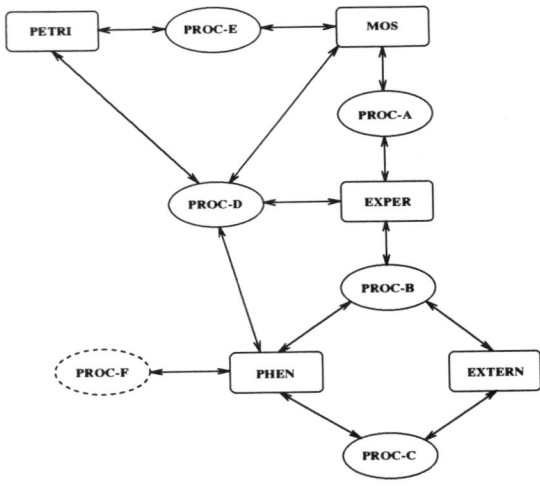

Figure 4: The design approach of the scientific knowledge–based system

ries and connections among them (justification structures), will also enable the addition or deletion of knowledge elements to a specific microtheory, in contrast to the general declarative knowledge base.

4.2 The procedural knowledge

Considering the extraction and justification of a scientific hypothesis, the knowledge of *how* (procedural knowledge) a scientific hypothesis has been created will be addressed in this subsection. This knowledge will be provided by the justification structures as they have been described in section 3. Therefore, the procedural knowledge is rather a *compiled* knowledge, in other words, a knowledge that will not be inferred in run–time. Therefore, a computational effectiveness can be achieved which is a crucial feature in case of building very large–scale knowledge bases.

The expensive process of inference (combinatorial explosion by declarative knowledge) can be prevented by making reference a matter of search. Searching will be done with the help of metadata (knowledge elements) which can guide search. Effective knowledge is only an organized knowledge as cases or beliefs, whereby priorities may be assigned. All inferences should be constructed before run–time and stored as compiled knowledge (justification structures).

The extraction of experimental laws and/or scientific hypotheses can be characterized as a bottom–up reasoning (data → information). At this point, machine learning methods [48, 40] for classification and/or the extraction of knowledge in terms of qualitative or quantitative description can be used. On the other side, providing a justification of an extracted hypothesis and/or modifying it, is rather a process of providing knowledge in terms of structures. Otherwise it is not possible to address the data instances on which the scientific hypotheses are based.

For this reason, approaches based on the connectionist paradigm as a counterpart of symbolics in artificial intelligence are not sufficient as a knowledge representation formalism in the case of providing knowledge based on explanations or justifications [17]. The most serious problem of neural nets is the *problem of opacity* [41, 36] which means that the knowledge embodied inside the network's numeric coefficients cannot be made accessible outside the net. This, in turn, makes it very difficult to form higher level knowledge concepts and structures.

The construction and revision of justification structure will be the subject of the suggested problem solution strategy which is based on knowledge processor agents. They must be specified in order to manipulate the corresponding knowledge servers, and consequently, the knowledge structures with their various representation formalisms. The mappings among knowledge processors and servers are depicted in figure 4. We have mainly distinguished among the following processors:

(a) PROC–A including the activity of *taxonomies formation and classification*, (b) PROC–B related to the activities of *inductive experimental law formation* and *construction of justification structures*, (c) PROC–C related to the activity of *taxonomies formation and classification*, (d) PROC–D related to the activity of *explanation process* and/or *revision of justification structures revision*, (e) PROC–E related to the activity of *experimental design*, and finally (f) PROC–F related to the activity of *theory/hypothesis revision*.

5 RELATED WORK AND STATE–OF–THE–ART

Extracting knowledge from data and providing explanations have been also addressed in other application areas found in the expert systems field, especially those dealing with the extraction of knowledge (facts) from data and not from users, and in the subfield of artificial intelligence concerning machine learning approaches related to knowledge or scientific discovery.

Expert systems. In the field of expert systems, diagnostic expert systems using model- or explanation-based reasoning methods [11], are strongly related to functional classification as a problem solution strategy [46]. Model–based diagnosis systems (MBD) use models of devices in order to find faults when observations of abnormal behavior are given. Explanation–based diagnosis systems provide a hybrid reasoning method that connects MBD with more traditional, associational (symptoms and diagnoses) components, in order

to overcome the combinatorial explosion of MBD when these systems cope with novel and multiple–faults.

The corresponding modeling approaches don't deal with structural properties that enable accessing of the source (instance) data from which an abnormal behavior has been derived, and nevertheless, the amount of data to be elaborated is not considered to be a problem at all. These approaches deal with the system description in terms of its structural and functional issues.

In particular, device functioning uses functional representation in terms of structure of constituents [22], or a framework for classifying knowledge is suggested [1, 4]. The knowledge classification is based on various abstraction levels which are defined as spaces (kernel domain, abstraction, use). In these spaces, the description of the system's functionality has been addressed only in terms of processes and not of data. In a similar way, a functional model based on abstraction levels has been suggested in [2], for the application domain of automatic debugging. Consequently, a representation strategy has been developed in [7] that uses both kinds of knowledge (structure, functional) by separating them from each other. Assumptions are also considered. This approach has been implemented in the DORIS system, but what is mainly missing, is an approach of organizing all this knowledge in order to provide an efficient knowledge pool for giving explanations and/or incremental knowledge creation (learning methods).

In the field of process engineering, diagnosis must be performed in real time through monitoring [32, 10, 3, 23, 30]. In all these cases, the knowledge representation model aims at the recognition of faults and their causalities, according to the functional and behavioral description of the processes and the observations which have been recorded by the operators. A suggestion has been made in [10] that continuous–variable dynamic systems (such as chemical refineries, nuclear power plants, waste incineration plants) should be modelled taking into account not only the current observations but also the mental model as a key cognitive skill of process operators. Thus the near–term behavior as well as the effect of possible control actions can be predicted. Monitoring advances the model's state due to the observations from the physical system. When observations disagree with the predictions, model–based diagnosis is used in order to determine the possible faults. These are injected into the current model so that predictions will continue to agree with observations.

There has also been an increasing research effort in the field of model–based diagnosis which is aiming at providing more abstract types of knowledge in order to increase the efficiency of model–based diagnosis by improving the cognitive coupling with the user of the diagnostic system [21]. In all these efforts, the focus has been mainly on the functional knowledge, and on multi–modeling approaches as a modeling and reasoning framework, in order to encourage cooperative problem–solving among different models of the same system. The complex data model in terms of an explanation or justification structure is not involved in this framework. The functional and behavioral knowledge is only the *connectionism knowledge* among the data with respect to their derivation history, and not the structural one.

A step towards structural knowledge has been made by building and maintaining a model for a particular domain [26], where frame–based representation schemes are introduced. The representation makes use of *event classes* (event model) and the component model which describes the kinds of components and subsystems of the plant to be diagnosed. But the coupling between structural knowledge and source data is still missing. Some approaches to this direction have been made in [26], whereby the diagnostic inference is based upon backward chaining using the causal rules, and forward chaining when hypotheses must be elaborated. Thus a rule–based inference mechanism must be provided with a formal semantics like the TELOS knowledge representation language [38], in which it has been implemented. In other words, the reasoner to be provided is an *abductive* one, and not an *empirical/inductive*.

Machine learning and artificial intelligence. In the subfield of *machine learning* in artificial intelligence, several approaches have been presented aiming at the extraction of knowledge by using various learning strategies [33, 24, 35]. Among these strategies, learning by induction, especially from observation and discovery [27, 57], deals with the extraction of knowledge from observation data (scientific discovery) [28], and/or from big amounts of already existing data (knowledge discovery from databases) [42].

There is a major trend in the last years for knowledge discovery in very large databases (relational databases), where manual analysis of all these data is almost impossible. This is the case especially in scientific, financial and manufacturing applications [43]. The learning strategies applied aim at elaborating data in order to discover dependencies and models which are mostly hidden behind the existing data. In particular, the main issue in knowledge discovery is not the data itself, but the interrelationships among dependent variables and their behavior in terms of space and time [9].

In the systems, which already exist, for knowledge discovery in databases [14, 31], the problem of an efficient accessing of the source data instances has not been elaborated. The focus was mainly on the direction of extracting knowledge and not on accessing

Tera(Peta)Bytes of source data using the extracting knowledge for a query formulation. In the field of scientific discovery, research on machine discovery aims at computational understanding of the processes that underlie scientific behavior [40]. The focus has been on empirical (quantitative and/or qualitative) discovery, taxonomy and theory formation, and generally, on the integration of manageable components in order to provide a framework for empirical discovery. But the problem of addressing terabytes of data through justification structures still remains.

Furthermore, multistrategy approaches have been taken in [34, 39, 20]. In [34], an intelligent multistrategy assistant for knowledge discovery from facts (INLEN) is described and illustrated by an exploratory application. It integrates a database, a knowledge base, and machine learning methods within a uniform-oriented framework. In [39], a model–based and incremental knowledge engineering method is presented based on a semiformal representation which serves as a basis for communication between the knowledge engineer and the expert through which the expert is integrated in the knowledge engineering process. In [20], the problems that arise in representing and analysing knowledge about metabolism are described. Emphasis has been put on the limits of existing techniques for qualitative reasoning, knowledge representation, machine learning, and on the challenges of building databases and knowledge bases which describe the structures and functions of engineered systems.

6 CONCLUSION

The design approach of a scientific knowledge base has been presented in this paper in order to support the extraction and justification of scientific hypotheses about atmospheric phenomena. The declarative knowledge will be provided by knowledge servers which can accomodate knowledge structures according to their most appropriate representation formalisms. The procedural knowledge will be based on justification structures (compiled knowledge) which will be extracted and/or modified by knowledge processors affecting the relevant knowledge servers.

At the moment, the knowledge server for the time–series oriented measurements and observations is being developed on the basis of a relational DBMS. Besides a prototype exists for the knowledge server (PETRI) concerning the generation histories on the basis of an object–oriented DBMS. In the future, the other knowledge servers will be implemented on the basis of an object–oriented DBMS and semantic networks. The knowledge processors as well as their interfaces to the corresponding knowledge servers will be further specified.

ACKNOWLEDGEMENTS

I am grateful to Prof. P. C. Lockemann, at the University of Karlsruhe - Faculty of Computer Science, for his suggestions and comments in order to improve the contents and the presentation of this paper.

I also want to express my thanks to Mr. Hermann Oelhaf, scientific employee at the Institute of Meteorology and Climate Research, for his time spent on the interesting discussions we had. My special thanks also to Mrs. Julia Breakspear for reading and improving the text of this paper as a native speaker of english.

REFERENCES

[1] Ameen Abu-Hanna, Richard Benjamins, and Wouter Jansweijer. Device Understanding and Modeling for Diagnosis. *IEEE Expert*, pages 26–32, April 1991.

[2] Dean Allemang. Using Functional Models in Automatic Debugging. *IEEE Expert*, pages 13–18, December 1991.

[3] Anton Beschta, Oskar Dressler, and Michael Montag. Modellbasierte Systemüberwachung. joint project BEHAVIOR 08–93, Siemens AG, München, 1993.

[4] C. Boettcher, O. Dressler, H. Freitag, M. Montag, and P. Struss. Architectural Design and Specification of GenDE. joint project BEHAVIOR 12–91, Fraunhofer Institute IITB Karlsruhe, February 1991.

[5] A. Borgida, M. Jarke, J. Mylopoulos, J. Schmidt, and Y. Vassiliou. The Software Development Environment as a Knowledge Base Management System. In J. Schmidt and C. Thanos, editors, *Foundations of Knowledge Base Management*, pages 411–439. Springer Verlag, 1989.

[6] R. J. Brachman and H. J. Levesque, editors. *Readings in Knowledge Representation*, chapter Proloque to Reflection and Semantics in a Procedural Language. Morgan Kaufmann, Los Altos, California, 1985.

[7] John A. Bradshaw and Richard M. Young. Evaluating Design Using Knowledge of Purpose and Knowledge of Structure. *IEEE Expert*, pages 33–40, April 1991.

[8] Hidde de Jong, Nicolaas J.I. Mars, and Paul E. van der Vet. Justification Structures in Scientific Knowledge Bases. draft paper, University of Twente, Dep. of Computer Science, The Netherlands, 1994. Submitted to the 11th European Conference on Artificial Intelligence (ECAI 1994).

[9] Dietrich Dörner. *Die Logik des Mißlingens: Strategisches Denken in komplexen Situationen*, chapter 5,6, pages 107–223. Rowohlt Taschenbuch Verlag GmbH, 1994.

[10] Daniel Dvorak and Benjamin Kuipers. Process Monitoring and Diagnosis. *IEEE Expert*, pages 67–74, June 1991.

[11] Yousri El Fattah and Paul O'Rorke. Explanation-Based Learning for Diagnosis. *Machine Learning*, 13:35–75, 1993.

[12] H. Fischer. Remote Sensing of Atmospheric Trace Gases. *Interdisciplinary Science Reviews*, 18(3):185–191, 1993.

[13] H. Fischer. Ozonveränderungen in der Stratosphäre: Dynamische und chemische Prozesse. *KfK Nachrichten*, 26(2):61–66, 1994.

[14] W. Frawley, G. Piatetsky-Shapiro, and C. Matheus. Knowledge Discovery in Databases: An Overview. *AI Magazine*, 13(3):57–70, 1992.

[15] Andreas Günter. Fallbasiertes Konfigurieren mit hybriden Expertensystemen. *KI*, (2):82–84, 1994. Zur Diskussion.

[16] C. Hewitt. Metacritique of McDermott and the Logistic Approach. *Computer Intelligence*, 3, 1987.

[17] G.E. Hinton. Preface to the Special Issue on Connectionist Symbol Processing. *Artificial Intelligence*, 46(1–2), 1990.

[18] Matthias Jarke. DAIDA - Conceptual Modelling and Knowledge-based Support of Information Systems Development Processes. *Technique et Science Informatiques*, 9, 1990.

[19] Epaminondas Kapetanios and Ralf Kramer. A Knowledge-based System Approach for Scientific Data Analysis and the Notion of Metadata. In *Proceedings of IEEE 14th (2nd International) Symposium on Mass Storage Systems*, Monterey, California, 1995. Computer Society Press. To appear.

[20] Peter D. Karp and Michael L. Mavrovouniotis. Representing, Analysing, and Synthesing Biochemical Pathways. *IEEE Expert*, pages 11–21, April 1994. AI in Molecular Biology.

[21] *Fourth International Workshop on Principles of Diagnosis*, volume DX–93, Univ. College of Wales, September 1993.

[22] Anne M. Keuneke. Device Representation. *IEEE Expert*, pages 22–25, April 1991.

[23] Sabine Kockskämper and Bernd Neumann. Vorgangserkennung - ein wissensbasiertes Verfahren zur überwachung technischer Prozesse. *Künstliche Intelligenz*, (2):19–27, 1994.

[24] Yves Kodratoff and Ryszard Michalski, editors. *Machine Learning: An Artificial Intelligence Approach*, volume 3. Morgan Kaufmann Publishers, Inc., 1990.

[25] R. A. Kowalski. Logic-Based Open Systems. In Jakob Höpelman, editor, *Representation and Reasoning: Proceedings of the Stuttgart Conference Workshop on Discourse Representation, Dialoque Tableaux and Logic Programming*, Tübingen, 1988. Max Niemeyer Verlag.

[26] Bryan M. Kramer. The Role of Event Classes in an Adbuctive Reasoner for Diagnosis of Continuous Processes. In *Fourth Inter. Workshop on Principles of Diagnosis*, pages 260–269, Univ. College of Wales, September 1993.

142

[27] Pat Langley. Editorial: Machine Learning and Discovery. *Machine Learning*, 1:363–366, 1986.

[28] Pat Langley, Herbert A. Simon, Gary L. Bradshaw, and Jan M. Zytkow. *Scientific Discovery*. MIT Press, Cambridge, Massachusetts London, England, 1987.

[29] Peter C. Lockemann, Hans-Hellmut Nagel, and Ingrid M. Walter. Databases for knowledge bases: empirical study of a knowledge base management system for a semantic network. *Data and knowledge engineering*, (7):115–154, 1991. North-Holland.

[30] Heinz Marburger. Monitoring und Diagnose. *KI*, (2):46–47, 1994.

[31] C. Matheus, P. Chan, and G. Piatetsky-Shapiro. Systems for Knowledge Discovery in Databases. *IEEE Transactions on Knowledge and Data Engineering*, 5(6):903–913, 1993.

[32] James K. McDowell, Mark A. Kramer, and James F. Davis. Knowledge-Based Diagnosis in Process Engineering. *IEEE Expert*, pages 65–66, June 1991.

[33] R. Michalski, J. Carbonell, and T. Mitchell, editors. *Machine Learning: An Artificial Intelligence Approach*, volume 2. Morgan Kaufmann Publishers, Inc., New York, 1986.

[34] R.S. Michalski, L. Kerschberg, and K.A. Kaufman. Mining for Knowledge in Databases: The INLEN Architecture, Initial Implementation and First Results. *Journal of Intelligent Information Systems*, (1):85–113, 1992.

[35] Ryszard Michalski and Gheorghe Tecuci, editors. *Machine Learning: A Multistrategy Approach*, volume 4. Morgan Kaufmann Publishers, Inc., 1994.

[36] M. Minsky. Logical versus Analogical or Symbolic Versus Connectionist or Neat Versus Scruffy. *AI Magazine*, 12(2), 1990.

[37] J. Mylopoulos, A. Borgida, M. Jarke, and M. Koubarakis. Telos: Representing Knowledge about Information Systems. *ACM Transactions on Information Systems*, 8(4):325–362, October 1990.

[38] John Mylopoulos, Alex Borgida, M. Jarke, and M. Koubarakis. Telos: A Language for Representing Knowledge About Information Systems. *ACM Transactions on Office Information Systems*, 1990.

[39] Susanne Neubert. Model Construction in MIKE (Model Based and Incremental Knowledge Engineering). Bericht 277, Institut für Angewandte Informatik und formale Beschreibungsverfahren, Univ. Karlsruhe, June 1993.

[40] Bernd Nordhausen and Pat Langley. An Integrated Framework for Empirical Discovery. *Machine Learning*, 12:17–47, 1993.

[41] Rosli Omar. Artificial Intelligence through Logic? *AI Communications*, 7(3–4):161–174, Sept–Dec 1994. The European Journal on Artificial Intelligence.

[42] G. Piatetsky-Shapiro and W. J. Frawley, editors. *Knowledge Discovery in Databases*. AAAI / MIT Press, California, 1991.

[43] G. Piatetsky-Shapiro, C. Matheus, P. Smyth, and R. Uthurusamy. KDD-93: Progress and Challenges in Knowledge Discovery in Databases. *AI Magazine*, pages 77–82, 1994.

[44] M. Popp and J. Hoffmann. Technologies for Sustained Development. *Interdisciplinary Science Reviews*, 18(3):180–184, 1993.

[45] Karl R. Popper. *Realism and the aim of science*. Hutchinson and Co. Ltd, 1983.

[46] Frank Puppe. *Problemlösungsmethoden in Expertensystemen*. Studienreihe Informatik. Springer-Verlag, 1990.

[47] F.J. Radermacher and W.-F. Riekert. Datenbankkonzepte und -Systeme in Umweltinformationssystemen (UIS). *it+ti*, 36(4/5):14–19, 1994.

[48] Jeff Schrager, editor. *Computational Models of Scientific Discovery and Theory Formation*, chapter Computational Approaches to Scientific Discovery, pages 1–25. San Mateo, California, 1990.

[49] Lenhart K. Schubert. Semantic Nets Are in the Eye of the Beholder. In John F. Sowa, editor, *Principles of Semantic Networks*, chapter 2, pages 95–108. Morgan Kaufmann Publishers, Inc., San Mateo, California, 1991.

[50] John F. Sowa, editor. *Principles of Semantic Networks - Explorations in the Representation of Knowledge*, chapter Understanding Subsumption and Taxonomy: A Framework for Progress, pages 45–94. Morgan Kaufmann Publishers Inc., 1991.

[51] John F. Sowa. Toward the Expressive Power of Natural Language. In John F. Sowa, editor, *Principles of Semantic Networks*, chapter 5, pages 157–190. Morgan Kaufmann, San Mateo, California, 1991.

[52] M. Stonebraker, James Frew, and Jeff Dozier. The Sequoia 2000 Architecture and Implementation Strategy. Technical Report CA 94720, University of California, Berkeley, 1993.

[53] G. v. Bültzingsloewen, R. Kramer, and E. Kapetanios. On modelling and controlling data derivation in a scientific information system. FZI Report 3/94, Forschungszentrum Informatik (FZI), Karlsruhe, Germany, April 1994.

[54] T. Vietze and A. Guenter. A Generalization Based Approach for Case-Based Configuration in Technical Domain. In *Proc. 2. World Congress Expert Systems*, Lissabon, 1994.

[55] J. Vittal, B. Silver, W. Frawley, G. Iba, T. Fawcett, S. Dusseault, and J. Doleac. Intelligent and Cooperative Information Systems Meet Machine Learning. *Inter. Journal of Intelligent and Cooperative Information Systems*, 1(2):347–361, 1992.

[56] Michael G Wessells. *Kognitive Psychologie*, chapter Wissen und Repräsentation, pages 249–293. UTB für Wissenschaften, 1994. Translated from the original: Cognitive psychology, J. Gerstenmaier, 1982,.

[57] Jan M. Zytkow. Introduction: Cognitive Autonomy in Machine Discovery. *Machine Learning*, 12:7–16, 1993.

Towards Very Large Knowledge Bases
N.J.I. Mars, Ed.
IOS Press, 1995

Building Consensual Knowledge Bases:
Context and Architecture

Jérôme Euzenat
INRIA Rhône-Alpes
Grenoble, France
Jerome.Euzenat@imag.fr

ABSTRACT

A protocol and architecture are presented in order to achieve consensual knowledge bases (i.e. bases in which knowledge is expressed in a formal language and which are considered as containing the state of the art in some research area). It assumes that the construction of the base must and can be achieved collectively. The architecture is based on individual workstations which provide support for developing a knowledge base: formal expression of knowledge through objects, tasks and qualitative equations annotated with hypertext nodes and links. It also provides tools for detecting similarities and inconsistencies between pieces of knowledge. These bases can be grouped together in order to constitute a new reference knowledge base. The process for constructing this last base mimics the submission of articles to peer-reviewed journals. This is achieved through a protocol for submitting knowledge to the group base, confronting it with the content of that base, amending it accordingly, reviewing it by the other knowledge bases and finally incorporating it. The system is to be used by researchers in the field of genome sequencing.

1 INTRODUCTION

Research activity is principally collaborative: available knowledge is increased by the work of many people in different disciplines and in many places. Collaboration is achieved through one main medium: written books and journals. Thus it takes months and years to be fruitful.

Nowadays, research in molecular genetics aims at understanding and comparing the information contained in genomes. The data involved has two important characteristics: it is growing so fast that it cannot be dealt with manually and it is expressed in such a way that formal computerised treatments can be applied. Thus, an important proportion of people involved in molecular genetics work in "collaboratories": the research teams are located in different laboratories and they use the computer as a medium. It is used for communicating informal text (by mail or ftp), but moreover for communicating the formal results of experiments (through the large general sequence data banks and small specialised ones [17, 24, 10]). We have already developed knowledge management tools which have been used in the building of knowledge bases in molecular genetics [19] and other fields [25]. We are currently involved in the development of a (software) workstation for molecular genetics research in close collaboration with two biology laboratories.

The "computer as medium" idea could be strengthened by extending it towards the knowledge itself. Hence, instead of merely reproducing the paper journals in computers, the principles of scientific journals must be applied to the knowledge formally expressed in a computer. The result should be a consensual knowledge base, i.e. which everybody in a group agrees to be a reasonable state of the art. It can be used for confronting new results and for learning new knowledge. A consensual knowledge base can also evolve with research results. For that purpose, a computer environment called Co4 (for collaborative construction of consensual knowledge) is presented here. Co4 is dedicated to the incremental and concurrent building of a knowledge base organised around formalised knowledge and a set of various annotations (text, bibliography, image, experimental data, etc.) from which this knowledge originates. It provides researchers with support for, on one hand, expressing, annotating and manipulating their knowledge, and on the other hand, submitting it to other people and achieving consensus.

The organisation of the paper is as follows: first

the features of a researcher workstation are presented. This is basically an extrapolation from what already exists in biology laboratories. Then, the organisation of a college whose aim — from the computer point of view — is the constitution of a consensual knowledge base is presented. It includes the protocols for consulting and submitting knowledge to the base. The fourth section takes a closer look at the software ground for such a system and fundamental problems which remain open. Finally, an extended discussion places Co4 in the many current trends of knowledge sharing and collaborative work.

2 THE RESEARCHER'S WORKSTATION

The aim of Co4 is the construction of a formalised knowledge base: this means that knowledge is expressed in a formal language carrying a precise semantics. The formal structure of the corpus enables the use of consistency checking or comparison tools for helping the process of integrating knowledge into the base and the process of revising the base when necessary. As anyone would agree, this is far too formal and restrictive, so the formal knowledge is connected to informal knowledge (mainly in terms of text and image) structured in a hypertext network. This informal knowledge has two purposes: recording the reasons for acceptance and changes in the knowledge base and adding annotations to the formal knowledge. This section describes the components of a knowledge base and their manipulation by a user. The next section describes how the knowledge bases can communicate with each other.

2.1 The knowledge model

Co4 comes from two experiences with knowledge bases in the domain of molecular genetics. The first one, ColiGene [18], describes the regulation mechanism of gene expression in the *E. coli* bacterial genome. The second one, MultiMap, allows to describe and to manipulate mammalian genomic maps at the cytogenetic, genetic and physical levels. The researcher's workstation is an assistant to the researcher. It helps the description of knowledge and also its discovery by automating the more repetitive tasks of genome research. The design of these two knowledge bases has led to the identification of four types of knowledge to be represented:

Descriptive knowledge on the biological entities involved is represented in an object-based knowledge representation system. This enables the representation of classes of objects (e.g. genes), subclasses (e.g. protein genes) and the identification of an object as belonging to such a class.

Methodological knowledge specifies the ways to select and link up methods for a given task. It is represented through a task management system able to integrate, represent, process and monitor the many computer programs for analysing the results of experiments.

Behavioural knowledge, which has not been introduced in these two knowledge bases, concerns the modelling of dynamic phenomena, such as the dynamics of gene inhibition or activation, through a qualitative modelling system. Such kind of knowledge has already been used for representing metabolism [10].

Textual annotations on the various objects and tasks involved are achieved through a hypertext system which connects hypertext nodes with the components of the descriptive and methodological knowledge. It allows browsing among texts, objects and tasks (see figure 1).

The knowledge, both formal and informal, is stored in an object-based knowledge representation system called TROPES [14]. It comes with a clear and simple formal semantics and tools for classification, constraint management and task processing. In particular, it is able to organise objects into multiple separated taxonomies and allows the user to work on a subset of these taxonomies. It thus answers to the need to express several viewpoints on object classifications [17, 10]. TROPES precursor, SHIRKA, has been connected to a hypertext management system [8] and it is planned that it will soon be the same for TROPES.

2.2 Software architecture

The architecture of the Co4 workstation is as described in figure 2. It is made up of three main layers:

- A user interface allowing the researchers to communicate with their knowledge bases and with other knowledge bases;

- The knowledge base itself which provides support for storing formal and informal knowledge, detecting inconsistencies in formal knowledge, returning possible modifications in the formal knowledge and managing the dialogue with other knowledge bases.

- The communication layer which provides software and hardware facilities for communicating with other knowledge bases.

For the sole manipulation of the knowledge base, the user only accesses the revision and negotiation controllers through the graphic interface (see figure 3). The other components are used in the cooperative process; they are included here for completeness. However, the knowledge management system is accessed through an application programming interface which enables queries and tentative modifications of the base

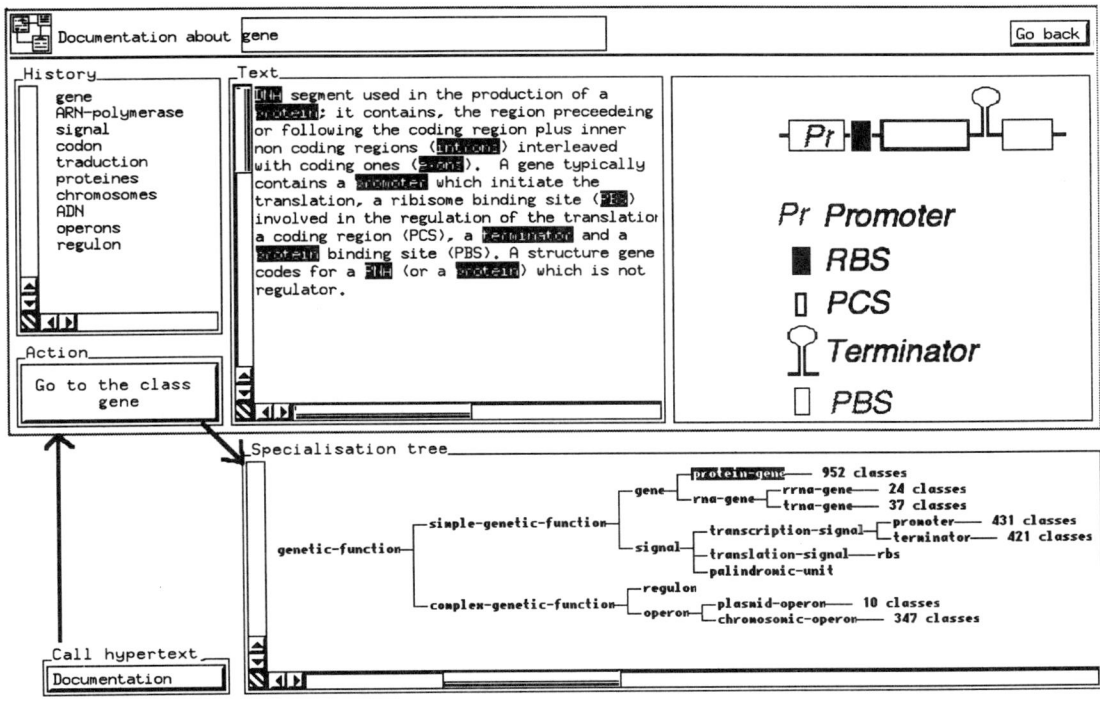

Figure 1: The navigational interface using hypertext. The user has selected a class in the class taxonomy (upper window) and has consulted the associated node of the hypertext (lower window). Some of the words of the text are links to other nodes. From a hypertext node, it is possible to come back to the entity it is attached to. The example is drawn from the ColiGene knowledge base, in which only the highest levels of the specialisation graph have been annotated, essentially for pedagogical purposes (adapted from [19]).

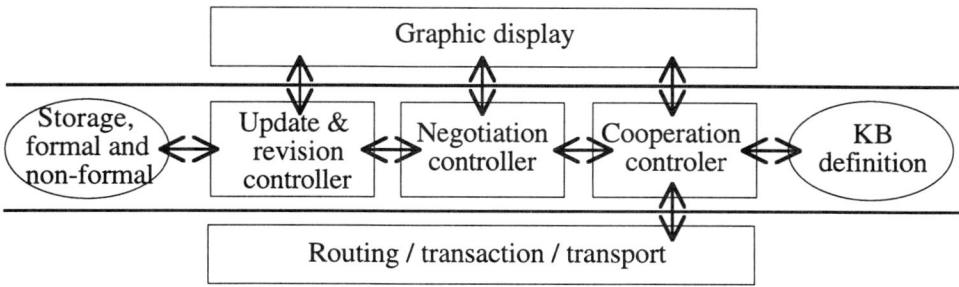

Figure 2: The three-layered software architecture. Each box represents a software module, each circled unit is a data/knowledge repository and each arrow represents the call of a program functionality.

146

from both the graphic interface and messages coming from other bases (see §3).

2.3 The user and the base

The present section shows how the user can interact with the knowledge base. It can seem obvious that the user can query and modify the base and that modifications must leave the base in a consistent state. However, the way this is achieved in Co$_4$ is particular since it must work when the researchers want to communicate a part of their bases to another base. Thus, the way individual stations work is useful for both the individual and the cooperative modes. The process is presented in figure 3.

The consultation or modification are ordered through the graphic interface and directly processed by the revision controller. However, in the usual mode, the modification is prepared by a confrontation query which asks for a comparison of a new piece of knowledge (made of objects, tasks, hypertext nodes and qualitative equations) and the knowledge base. The comparison of a corpus of knowledge with another results in a report about what is different, what is the same and what is contradictory. If the piece of knowledge does not contradict the knowledge base, it can be submitted for integration. If it contradicts it, the researcher can modify it in order to fit the group base. Concerning the informal documentation, if the user wants to create a hypertext node for instance, it is possible to detect if a node with the same name already exists and to negotiate its modification.

A first requirement for a formal knowledge base is consistency. Consistency is here defined with regard to what the system can deduce to be consistent or not: in typical object-based representation systems, a class whose extension is logically reduced to the empty set is inconsistent and an error is raised by the system. Apart from consistency checks, the system is able to deal with sophisticated queries asking if a piece of knowledge is redundant, subsumed or similar (w.r.t. some distance) to a part of the knowledge base. These queries are subject to limitations drawn by the expressiveness of the knowledge representation language and the expected degree of completeness of the answer.

When a change is attempted, it first goes through the update and revision controller which determines if the change does not introduce inconsistencies. The organisation of Co$_4$ is particular in that the revision controller, which is usually a part of the knowledge base management system, has been detached from the knowledge base itself. The revision controller should be able, given an operation on a knowledge base, to manage it in the most consistent way. If the proposal is consistent with the base, the change is committed and the knowledge base is simply modified. The controller also records all the modifications committed directly

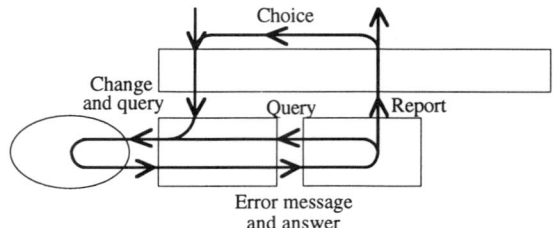

Figure 3: Interactions between the users and their bases. The arrows represent the flow of information: the user can query the knowledge base and get an answer or a report. The report can be made of a set of alternative changes to apply to the base in order for the user to achieve a modification of the base. This requires a dialogue between the revision and negotiation controllers for determining what are these possible changes.

by the user in order to be able to transmit them later to the group base (the modifications must be recorded together with their rationale, etc.).

When Co$_4$ detects some problem (misspelling, typo, inconsistency) it raises an error which is transmitted to the negotiation controller. The negotiation controller then opens a dialogue with the update controller in order to establish the putative causes of each error and the possible repairs. Then the negotiation controller is able to submit these diagnoses and repairs to the user through the graphic interface. It is up to the user to decide which one to apply (or to retract the tentative change).

The behaviour and decomposition of the architecture is directed by the wish to provide the most efficient response to a tentative change of the base. It is based on the idea that when users ask for a change, they express the will to see it committed. Thus if this change is not immediately possible, Co$_4$ must propose the best way to make it possible while preserving the majority of the base. This enforces the opportunities for the change to be accepted by the other partners when it is submitted to the consensual knowledge base. The same holds true for propositions of the system concerning similarity.

Moreover, in the context of the submission of knowledge to a collective base, the architecture allows to ask for a report and help from that base. This is presented below.

3 OVERALL ARCHITECTURE AND PROTOCOL

The primary aim of Co$_4$ is the construction of a consensual base. The principles underlying Co$_4$ are derived from those of peer-reviewed journals: before being introduced in a consensual knowledge base, the knowledge must be submitted and accepted by the community. This requires submitting knowledge to the base, letting it be reviewed by the other participants and accepting or amending it according to their reactions. The informal knowledge is also subject to submissions, reviewing and so on. At the end, it is intended that the knowledge stored in a consensual knowledge base be safe enough so that anybody can use it confidently and easily.

In this section we emphasise the collaborative facilities offered by Co$_4$. The organisation of a college of knowledge bases is first presented. Afterwards, the interaction of a workstation with the consensual group bases is detailed before turning to the protocol implemented for dealing with knowledge submission and negotiation.

3.1 The network of knowledge bases

Co$_4$ is made of a set of knowledge bases. Any co-operator is viewed by the system as a knowledge base. Knowledge bases are organised into a tree whose leaves are user knowledge bases and whose intermediate nodes are called group knowledge bases (see figure 4). Each group base represents the consensual knowledge shared by its sons (called subscriber knowledge bases). Each knowledge base can subscribe to only one group. However nothing prevents the human researcher from creating several knowledge bases (maybe subscribing to different group bases) representing different research trends, and nothing prevents anyone from transferring knowledge from one base to another. Also, nothing prevents several physical users from sharing the same base.

The knowledge bases are linked together in such a way that a particular knowledge base knows its subscribers and its group base. To its subscribers it mainly sends messages for broadcasting a change accepted by everyone and calls for comments in order to establish whether a change must be committed or not. To its group base it sends changes that it wants the group base to integrate. Of course, as a group base, it also receives changes to commit and as a knowledge base it also receives calls for comments and change broadcasts.

Each of these knowledge bases are made of the same structure and the same software. The main difference between group bases and researcher workstations is that the former are completely automated and only respond to the stimuli from other bases.

3.2 The user and the group

The user of a workstation can subscribe to a consensual knowledge base. This is achieved very simply through the knowledge base definition controller which manages the description of the group to which the knowl-

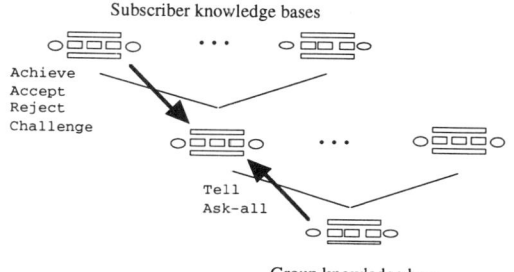

Figure 4: The hierarchical architecture and message flow. The knowledge bases are organised in a tree whose leaves are individual knowledge bases and nodes represent the consensual knowledge of connected individuals. The downward types of messages include the submission of a proposal and the reports of approval, rejection or alternate proposal about a submitted proposal. The upward messages include the broadcast of accepted proposals and the call for comments (ask-all) about a submitted proposal.

edge base subscribes (and for the group bases, the set of subscribers). This base definition enables the communication layer to route queries from one base to its group base and its subscribers. It is intended that it also describes the topics which the knowledge base is interested in, etc.

As soon as the base is part of a group base, it receives the complete content of that base (to which it is supposed to subscribe), it is entitled to give its opinion on all submissions currently under examination and is entitled to submit knowledge. The interesting point is the submission of knowledge, so let's see what happens.

When the researchers are confident enough with the specifics of their knowledge base corresponding to some research results, they can submit them to the group knowledge base to which they subscribe. This is achieved by circumscribing the submitted part (which can include hypertext annotations justifying them) through the graphic interface and calling the submission procedure of the negotiation controller. In order to complete the submission message, the negotiation controller collects the sets of differences between the consensual group base connected and the selected changes (they are logged in by the revision controller) and sends them to the group base. Usually, the group base, through its own revision and negotiation controllers issues a report describing how the submitted knowledge can be added to the group base. Thus, as usual, the user can choose a better (and consistent) way to achieve the submission. This proposal will be submitted to the other subscribers and committed if it reaches consensus.

As a subscriber of the group base, the user also receives the call for comments issued by the group base in response to the submission (by another user) of some material. The users can read the submission or play it in their own knowledge base by submitting it to the revision controller. This can result in a favourable report or an inconsistency detection that can be used by the user for issuing an alternate proposal. In response to the call for comments, the users must answer by one of the following: accepted when they consider that the knowledge must go in the consensual knowledge base, rejected when they do not, and alternate when they propose another change.

When the group base has gathered enough comments, it integrates, or not, the change in the base. The change being now consensual, it is broadcast to all subscribers. It may happen, however, that the research they are currently involved in contradicts what is in the group base. So the users can refuse the new knowledge (just as they can also modify parts of the group base knowledge in their local base) which is then stored in a change logbook for further change submission.

The fact that anyone can maintain a knowledge base as different from the consensus, allows obviously the exploration of alternate research paths. But on a more basic ground, it enables the communication, negotiation and acceptation to be asynchronous. This, in fact, reproduces the way papers are submitted, discussed and accepted or rejected in a scientific journal: the reviewer can take time for carefully examining a proposal since this will not stop the work of the base which issued it.

3.3 The submission protocol

The words consensus, message, etc. have been used freely so far. A protocol has been established for the communication between the knowledge bases. It is implemented in the cooperation controller of the knowledge bases. The protocol is very simple, since it only reproduces what happens for paper submission to journals plus the management of new subscriptions. The messages are expressed as a collection of speech acts: achieve (submit a proposal for inclusion into the consensual base), ask-all (ask for the acceptance of subscriber bases, call for comments), accept (accept the insertion of the piece of knowledge), reject (reject it), challenge (submit a concurrent proposal), deny (the submitter retracts the submission), tell (send an accepted proposal to each subscriber base). It seems quite general since the performatives can be found, for instance, in concurrent software engineering [15, 26].

The consensual aspect is dealt with through the acceptation of proposals which achieve acceptance by all of the subscribers and the rejection of other proposals (for instance, in the context of genome sequencing, a consensus map is a map that people involved in the research field think correct). Consensus could be replaced by some other definitions (like majority or intersection, see §4.1), but it has been retained for two reasons: (1) it enjoys interesting formal properties (if a consensual base contains only knowledge which is accepted by all the subscribers, this remains true if subscribers are added or retracted), and (2) it should lead to the discussion of proposals — not only conflicts — and thus the collaboration of the researchers.

In a first version of Co_4, the group base applies the non destructive modifications without discussion. These modifications are always possible in the group base, since they are in the subscriber's base which contains it. In the case of destructive modification, a call for comments, identified by a unique number (surrogate), is issued towards all the subscribers. Among the answers provided by the subscribers, three cases may happen:

- They all agree that the modification must be accepted, then the modification is committed into the group base and broadcast to all the subscriber knowledge bases;

- One of them rejects the proposal, then the changes are not committed and the comments provided by the rejecter are sent to the submitter (the call for comments is discarded in all the subscribers knowledge bases);

- One submitter sends an alternate proposal, then the call for comment is replaced by a call for comment about all the proposals available (those who already accepted the change, are asked to consider the new proposal and to answer again).

It also can happen that the submitter retracts the proposal thus leading to the retraction of the call for comments from all the knowledge bases.

The protocol is made of a set of rewrite rules which state what a knowledge base must do when it receives a particular message from another knowledge base. Each rule specifies what happens when some performative is received by a knowledge base, for instance:

$$\frac{s - reply(n, accept) \to g}{\begin{array}{c} C := C - \{(n, achieve(p), 1)\}, \\ K := K + p, \\ g - tell(p) \to S \end{array}} (n, achieve(p), 1) \in C$$

means that upon arrival of the last "accept" for a proposition with surrogate n, the group base discards the structure recording the calls for comments, adds p to its local knowledge base and broadcasts it to each subscriber. The group bases blindly apply these rules

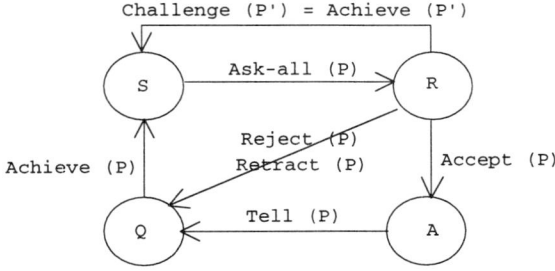

Figure 5: The automaton corresponding to the submission of proposal P at the scale of the whole system of group base plus subscribers. It reproduces four states of publication submission: initial state (Q), submitted (S), under review (R), accepted (A).

and the final decision comes from the researchers who are the holders of the leaves of the architecture. When a message is issued by a group base whose subscribers are also group bases, these last bases only dispatch the messages to their subscribers. The protocol is presented in figure 5 as a finite state automaton. It is worth noting that the protocol is (1) asynchronous, so that several proposals can be in different states concurrently, (2) parameterised by proposal p, so that the real situation in Co_4 is the Cartesian product of automata corresponding to all the proposals, and (3) abstracted from the status of each individual knowledge base with regard to the protocol. Some properties of the protocol can be proved (under additional assumptions): whenever a proposal is submitted, it reaches in a finite time the status of accepted or rejected, the protocol always takes into account the opinion of a reviewer (it never waits for a report when it is established that the proposal is to be rejected, etc. — see §4.3).

The protocol is handled by the cooperation controller which acts differently on an individual base and on a group base: in the first case it submits the changes to the user interface while in the second one it dispatches them to all of its subscribers. The cooperation controller is also in charge of the management of the negotiation for applying a change in a group knowledge base (emitting the call for comments, receiving the answers, managing the alternate proposals and committing or retracting the changes). The negociation requires the identification of the change by a unique number, the count of positive answers, the management of alternate proposals and retractions of a proposal. It also requires the recording of the process in order to recall the reasons why some change is made or not.

4   SOFTWARE TECHNOLOGY

The development of the platform presented above is not yet complete and the representation of genetic knowledge is not a simple task. However, the technology for object based-knowledge representation is well known, and similar experiences that we have had, lead us to be confident of its achievement. Thus, the present section focuses on the specific problems concerning the cooperation between distributed knowledge bases. To our knowledge, the technology is not already established for such a proposal; thus the Co_4 proposal is an occasion to explore solutions for two particular fundamental research areas: assisted revision in knowledge bases (§4.2) and cooperation protocols (§4.3). Problems and solutions are presented below, but keep in mind that they should meet acceptance from the users before being declared successful. So, the properties of the architecture enabling a smooth integration of facilities are first presented (§4.1).

4.1   Modularity and genericity

The knowledge base architecture presented above included two particularly interesting design choices: it is the same for all of the bases, so they can be made out of the same software packages, and it is described in a modular fashion, so that it can be used with a very raw system or a very complex one. This leaves the door open for a trade-off between the complexity and power of each algorithm. This is very precious during Co_4 development since it allows us to start with very simple components and to enhance them progressively.

For instance, the knowledge repository can be a simple hypertext system which identifies nodes by a reference and raises an error when two nodes have the same reference (the simplest system is a text repository with the UNIX "diff" and "patch" utilities). The *degré zéro* of change control consists in routing error messages to the user, in order to have the error corrected.

Such a system can be enhanced, for example, in the framework of a logic clause representation system (say Prolog) by a revision module able to abduct the reasons for the errors and to display them to the user who can take the corrections into account. Going further in this direction the revision module can be a knowledge base combining algorithm able to automatically propose corrections (e.g. [2]).

Finally, the protocol can be easily replaced by another one, based for instance on a vote of the majority of the subscribers, on the intersection of all of the knowledge base or on economic decision making (for determining the introduction or not of knowledge into the base). The protocol is also designed independently of the content and language of the knowledge base. This enables to use it for different pieces of knowledge (hypertext or classes as well as tasks or equations). One could imagine to refine the protocol for dealing specifically with these expressions. However, the specific aspect is actually assigned to the revision module which issues the reports.

So, the architecture and the protocol provided above are independent of the knowledge repository and the modules which manage it.

4.2 Assisted revision in object based knowledge bases

The aim of the update and revision controller is the modification of the knowledge base. It is usually a part of the knowledge base able to perform an authorised operation on a knowledge base or to raise an error. The revision controller should be able, given an operation on a knowledge base, to resolve it in the most consistent way (this covers truth maintenance or, when an error message is raised, finding the best way to achieve the operation). The aim of Co_4 will be to propose meaningful ways to realise it, the last word being that of the user or the subscribers.

Assisted revision of knowledge base — i.e. the ability of detecting error messages and proposing consistent changes — is related to the problematic of knowledge base revision. It is a real enhancement with regard to current knowledge base management systems and is required by the submission of the knowledge of a particular base to another.

Knowledge base revision has been introduced in [1]: from a set A of axioms which deductively leads to a theory $Th(A)$, let the operation $\perp$ be such that $A\perp p$ is the set of maximal subsets of A such that $p \notin Th(A)$. Retraction $(\dot{-})$ and revision $(\dot{+})$ operations are defined such that $A\dot{-}p \in A\perp p$ if $A\perp p \neq \emptyset$, and $A\dot{-}p = A$ otherwise. A set of eight postulates defines what are the possible retraction operators ($A\perp p$ is deductively closed, does not entail p, contains $Th(A)$ if $p \notin Th(A)$, etc.). These postulates can also be defined for revision.

Syntactically, existing knowledge representation systems are already capable of inference, consistency check and even revision since it is possible to add new objets (or classes or field values, etc.). Thus this framework can be applied to object-based systems: the set of axioms (A) is the content of a knowledge base communicated by the subscribers, the theory ($Th(A)$) is what is deducible from A.

The decision problem on what is deducible or what is inconsistent is computationally language dependent. In TROPES, it seems that it is decidable but that some predicates such as classifiability should be at least NP-complete. In object-based knowledge systems, the foreseen revision operators should have the following properties:

- They strongly take into account the syntactic structure of the object-based representations, which defines the revision rules for the syntactic operators

over objects (a class is less often modified than a simple instance for instance);

- They correspond semantically to the postulates for preferred revision — the model preference being defined by a relationship between them —allowing the definition of a relational revision operator [1].

TROPES is able to signal errors. This is the basis for update and revision. These errors are transmitted to the negotiation system (errors are not just messages, but structured objects enabling the identification of the error). This is systematically used in order to detect what are the causes of the error and then what are the possible alternative changes which may be issued. For instance, when an overly large domain is given to a field in a class, object-based systems issue errors such as "your domain includes values which are not possible for the field". However, the solution can be the restriction of the given domain or the enlargement of the domain for the super-classes of the class (there may be other errors: the class is not the right one, the field is not the right one, etc.). A system like TROPES must be able to find these simple causes for errors and to prepare a repair action.

More operationally, the aim of such operators is:

1. localising quickly all the sources of inconsistency;

2. finding repair solutions to these inconsistencies;

3. ordering these sources and solutions with regard to their syntactic nature;

4. presenting them to the user.

At least it is not intended that Co_4 applies the revision by itself, but rather that it helps the researchers to easily revise their knowledge when it is inconsistent. In the framework of such a system, there are strong constraints of speed and intelligibility. It seems that these constraints can be satisfied with the help of the use of interaction which allows fast feedback from the user and the constraining structure of objects (which limit the exploding character of abduction and can reduce the size of the search space).

Another promising idea is the revision operation based on what a the users know and what they are interested in. TROPES already supports, through viewpoints, the selection of a particular perspective on knowledge. Ordering the topics of interest has already been used for expressing the semantics of revision with several people involved (in the expression of knowledge) [3].

4.3 Cooperation protocol

The cooperation protocol is based on the architecture of the knowledge bases (which ones are the group base and which ones are the subscribers) and a complete set of behaviour rules [5]. This protocol has several properties:

- there is no need for human intervention in the group base;
- there is no message but from group base to subscribers and back;
- each decision has been approved by all the subscribers (recursively for a group of group bases).

The actual protocol is routed automatically (once a knowledge base has subscribed to another), the performative and content levels are interpreted automatically in the group bases and the performative level is automatically interpreted by the individual knowledge bases (however, the system asks the user before committing these performatives).

The set of messages sent from one base to another are expressed through a speech act (loosely inspired from "speech act theory"). Speech acts are used here for building a set of relevant "artificial" acts rather than trying to understand the "natural" speech acts occurring in ordinary conversation (the same way the idea of a grammar has been borrowed by computer science from linguistics). Thus each particular act carries a precise semantics (taken as the goal of the sender). The notion of a speech act has several advantages for the particular architecture presented here:

- It allows the separation of knowledge from what its use (add or retract it from a particular base, for instance);
- It is independent from the knowledge representation language and the protocol can thus be expressed abstractly and the library implementing it can be used with other systems;
- It allows a speech act to refer to another speech act (retracting a submission, for instance).

The inter-base communication uses KQML (Knowledge Query and Manipulation Language [6]) which has been chosen because, in its early stages, it clearly distinguished the three levels required by Co4:

Communication: to be used for the communication layer in order to route the message;

Performative: to be used by the negotiation and revision controllers in order to know what kind of action the message is intended to achieve;

Content: to be used by the knowledge base management system.

While building the protocol, some formal properties are required and ensured. For instance, under the following assumptions:

- there is always, in a finite amount of time, an answer to a query (to an individual base),
- there is not an infinite number of alternate-proposal for a proposal, and,
- different proposals are independent,

each submission reaches the accepted or rejected status in a finite amount of time and this status is such that a submission is accepted if and only if it agrees each subscriber. The two first assumptions are part of the fairness assumption of Co4 while the latter requires taking into account the interaction between proposals.

Difficulties with the cooperation protocol come from the fact that it must be closely suited to the needs of cooperative knowledge base building. Otherwise, subscribers would work around it. The ideal protocol should be mechanically interpretable (at least at the performative level) and rich enough for covering adequately all of the needs. The first requirement has been successfully achieved through the construction of an automatic group base protocol [5]. However, our present protocol is very simple (only 33 rules) and must be enhanced through experience and some assumptions may have to be relaxed. For instance, it does not take into account the demand from a reviewer to clarify some point (this is planned but informal communication is not very well taken into account by KQML).

5 DISCUSSION AND RELATED WORKS

So far, the Co4 system has been presented as an extension of existing systems and references to similar systems have been avoided. In this section, Co4 is first placed in the many taxonomies of collaborative systems. Then the system is compared with the many current works on knowledge sharing. Co4 is particular in several concerns for knowledge sharing and collaborative work, thus the third part is dedicated to the explaination of the principles governing Co4 and of why they make it close to some systems.

5.1 What is Co4?

Co4 can find its place among the many taxonomies of CSCW systems. With regard to [20] it has asynchronous indirect interaction, system based coordination, data hiding and is collaborative aware and technically non flexible. While cooperative, Co4 dictates the way the cooperation is achieved. This takes into account the usual context in which research is carried out (as opposed to "is a general purpose support for cooperative work") in order to deal with usual attitudes as advocated by [11].

152

Co_4 allows the coordination of people for publishing results they consider as achieved. So, as presented in [13], it is only tailored for the execution stage and enables information sharing and activity coordination. As such, it does not aim at supporting the organisation of collaboration on a precise topic by planning experiments and analysis. Extending Co_4 is possible, but would require a very different interaction protocol such as the contract net protocol [21].

According to Ellis [4], Co_4 would not be a groupware system *stricto sensu*, but could be classified under coordinated multi-user editor. By opposition to Gibb's definition of groupware, people do not really share a common environment since they work on their own knowledge base. But they share the goal and the content of the consensual knowledge base.

Co_4 shares many features with the coordinator [26]. The coordinator is a system which allows people to submit requests and offers to others who can answer by declining, accepting or proposing an alternative. The system is able to store these proposals and to manage the state of each proposal. The main differences lie in the goal of building a consensual knowledge base (common to each individual), the formal treatment that Co_4 can apply to knowledge and the hierarchical construction of knowledge bases (and hence of the communication) instead of peer-to-peer communication.

5.2 Co_4 and knowledge sharing

The knowledge sharing idea has been promoted as a way to avoid constructing multiple knowledge bases and multiple reasoning systems about the same domain. It defends, instead, the idea of sharing this achievement by either merging the knowledge of several bases into one (knowledge sharing approach [16]) or submitting the problems to several accessible knowledge based systems (software agent approach [7]).

There are some hints that knowledge sharing cannot be achieved without sharing the building of the knowledge base itself. Knowledge sharing requires not only the intelligibility of the knowledge description language semantics, but also the agreement on the meaning of concepts of the domain. A project for sharing the construction of a knowledge base has already been described in [19]: it aims at helping scientists to build a consensual knowledge base about their scientific research domain. In this context, shared with the knowledge medium idea [22], producing and maintaining the knowledge base constitutes an end in itself. Such a framework can also be used for huge scientific projects, distant collaborative works or knowledge elicitation in order, for instance, to achieve a corporate memory.

The Co_4 approach differs from the software agent approach because it considers a general architecture and the homogeneity of agents and from the knowledge

sharing approach because it assumes that knowledge cannot be shared unless the elaboration process has been shared. The fact that all agents share a common goal represented by their common knowledge base is another unusual characteristics. This led to the design of a very specific interaction protocol and the enforcement of consistency in Co_4.

However, the Co_4 principle is similar to that of the SHADE project [9] which has one foot in each world. The SHADE project builds a knowledge medium which aims at supporting the collaborative design of an artefact; in Co_4 the artefact is the knowledge base. Such a system must enforce both the consistency and the agreement of everyone (human or software agent) involved into the design process. However, there are several technical differences between both systems:

- The SHADE project uses pre-existing knowledge bases (in the knowledge sharing fashion). It thus puts less emphasis on knowledge base revision than Co_4.

- In SHADE, agents can be very different while in Co_4 all agents are equal (peers) and play different roles (submitter, reviewer, etc.) depending on the situation. The variety of agents constrains to take into account a variety of behaviours (which changes to notify, etc.) and requires tools for expressing how to deal with them (publication of interest) which have not been considered here.

The agents (bases) of Co_4 are very structured since they already share their goal (establishing of knowledge base) and a mode of organisation (subscription tree). The society as a whole has to process a contract (building a consensual base by submission) by opposition to establishing a plan for achieving the goal. It does not have resource allocation and coordination problems: the only problem is communication. This multi-agent architecture is like the federated systems of [7], in which agents communicate indirectly through facilitators. Here, each agent is connected to the other through its communication software which is a very specialised facilitator: only groups accept subscription and the communication is enabled only from one group to its subscribers and from the subscribers to the group. The group bases constitute the mediators between the actual users. Their routing level is like both a KQML router and a very simple KQML facilitator; as a consequence, each base has the same router and facilitator components (at the moment they have two: one for sending messages to the group base and one to send messages to its component bases). This is a divergence from the KQML facilitators which are considered as knowledge bases themselves able to dialogue with any other knowledge base.

In the scientific community metaphor [12], close to the software agent approach, the emphasis was on solving problems rather than sharing knowledge. So the aspects of the building process of a corpus of knowledge have not been considered. However, the basic properties of the system (commutativity, monotonicity, pluralism and parallelism) hold true for Co_4.

5.3 The Co_4 principles

Co_4 is here presented in terms of a set of principles which provide the background of the system. These principles allow us to stress the differences between Co_4 and other efforts concerning knowledge sharing or collaborative processes.

Uniformity

Co_4 is made up of a set of knowledge bases. Any co-operator is viewed by the system as a knowledge base. For simplicity, all the bases are equipped with the same software. Something interesting with regard to other cooperation schemes (and mainly the one used in the software agent trend) is that the knowledge bases have the same description language (this is to be contrasted with other approaches, in which the agents are seen as knowledge bases but their languages can be heterogeneous). This simplifies the implementation and use of the system by allowing to stress the collaborative aspects, but, above all, this ensures that people are talking about the same representation formula instead of a translated item. Of course, each base cannot have its own representation system. However, the use of a language independent from the knowledge representation language (KQML), preserves the possibility to use heterogeneous representation languages (but communication between bases expressed in different languages is, to our knowledge, far from achieved). One can easily imagine a particular agent able to translate the content of some sequence data bank into TROPES and able to submit it to Co_4.

Consistency

The knowledge stored in group knowledge bases must be correct, consistent and consensual. This is in great contrast with what is currently developed over the networks: databases available through WAIS, Gopher or WWW do not have to be consensual nor consistent. The data is provided as such, without any warranty of consistency from the provider, and the retrievers have to make it consistent before introducing it into their own databases. This is also different from other frameworks in this respect: neither the knowledge sharing (when the opportunity to modify the shared knowledge is considered) nor the software agents provide any warranty about the consistency of the knowledge they provide.

Moreover, the consistency is not only syntactic. The collaborative knowledge base building ensures that the collaborators agree on all of the details of the base and it is expected that they also agree on the meanings they

assign to the terms. At the opposite, the knowledge sharing view allows the sharing of "ontologies" and mechanisms without caring that the meaning of the components are agreed (see also [10] about ambiguous names).

Good will and fair use

Of course, a system such as Co_4 is not suited for just any purpose. It is designed for a community whose common interests lie in the results obtained by the community. In fact, Co_4 is firstly dedicated to the members of large groups of people sequencing genomes in different laboratories for which the better the results of the community, the better those of the subscribers. Thus Co_4 does assume from its users, their good will (they will submit their discovery and opposition to proposals) and a fair use (they will not delay some publication by not reviewing it, they will not consume more resources than necessary or submit proposals they know to be false). So, there is no place for financial refunding, quotas, deadlines or control on the queries emitted: it is assumed that the use of Co_4 will be fair enough (no systematic submission of unverified material, etc.).

However, this does not mean that there is no conflict: the conflicts are to be treated by negotiation upon a protocol a bit stronger than those used in scientific journals because it is more formal and it aims at reaching consensus. Co_4 includes an authentication of who proposed a modification and who issued an alternate proposal in such a way that the discoveries can be acknowledged. There is also the obligation of citing the sources in the hypertext annotations; this should be facilitated by the availability of a citation editor in Co_4.

Co_4 could be enhanced first by deadlines (for returning answers, etc. [26]) and second by punishments for those reviewers who take a very long time for reviewing (for instance, suspension of their submissions). There also could be, for reviewing, an anonymity management system which provides both independence and recognition [23].

Assuming good will and fair use from the agents of a distributed system is not unusual but not always explicitly stated.

The paper submission metaphor

Any system allowing the building of some artefact must have a particular change policy. The Co_4 protocol mimics that of scientific journals. To our knowledge, the scientific journal protocol has never been used for that purpose. The choice of such a protocol is not neutral: first it is well known within the community and, in the consensual version, it enforces the dialogue between people (rather than a simple majority or intersection protocol). The requirements of consistency and formality allow for more strictness concerning what is published and thus leads to a consensual rather than a review protocol.

6 CONCLUSION

An architecture able to support the proposal of [19] has been presented. This proposal is original in two respects: it allows for the sharing of knowledge instead of non formalised data and it emphasises the consistency and the global coherency of shared knowledge. In summary, it is a formalised peer-reviewed scientific journal rather than a *dazibao*. For achieving this, we propose a *knowledge base* system able to deal with formalised and non formalised knowledge, *consistent*, because the formalised knowledge constitutes a consistent corpus, *consensual*, because whatever is deposited in the base is agreed by everyone, whose aim is the sharing of the knowledge base elaboration process.

Co_4 has some limitations since the communication protocol is very restrictive (however, the same protocol does not prevent people from submitting to, reviewing for and reading scientific journals). However, it will have to be enhanced. The protocol itself is unable to account gracefully for the concurrent submission of mutually contradictory proposals. These major weaknesses are under consideration and will have to go through experimentation.

The framework presented here is not restricted to genome research but can be applied to other research fields, and to other activities such as the constitution of a corporate memory. Co_4 is based on deep experience with individual workstation design and use. A complete prototypical knowledge base management system has been designed and implemented along these ideas. It has been used, in various stages of achievement, for the development of ColiGene and MultiMap, and is now being used for the implementation of a complete cooperative computer system for genome sequence analysis. The collaborative part is in its beginning: a prototype system is currently developed in our team using the knowledge base management system TROPES and KQML as a communication support.

ACKNOWLEDGEMENTS

This research is being supported by GREG (Groupement de Recherches et d'Études sur les Génomes) and by GdR CNRS "Informatique et Gnomes" (CNRS: Centre National de la Recherche Scientifique). The author thanks François Rechenmann, Steve Jones and Jutta Willamowski for their help.

REFERENCES

1. Carlos Alchourrón, Peter Gärdenfors, David Makinson, "On the logic of theory change: partial meet contraction and revision functions", *Journal of symbolic logic* 50(2):510–530, 1985

2. Chitta Baral, Sarit Kraus, Jack Minker, V. Subramanian, "Combining knowledge bases consisting in first order theories", *Computational intelligence* 8(1):45–71 1992

3. Laurence Cholvy, Robert Demolombe, "Reasoning with information sources ordered by topics", Proc. 6th international conference on artificial intelligence: methodology, systems, applications, Sofia, BU, pp151–162, 1994

4. Clarence Ellis, Simon Gibbs, Gail Rein, "Groupware — some issues and experiences", *Communication of the ACM* 34(1):38–58, 1991

5. Jérôme Euzenat, "Building consensual knowledge bases: protocol", Internal report, INRIA Rhône-Alpes, Grenoble, FR, 1995

6. Tim Finin, Richard Fritzson, Donald MacKay, Robin MacEntire, "KQML as an agent communication language", Technical report CS-94-02, University of Maryland, Baltimore, ML US, 1994 (rep. in proc. 3rd CIKM, Gaithersburg, ML US, 1994) [ftp.cs.umbc.edu:/pub/ARPA/kqml/papers/cikm.ps]

7. Michael Genesereth, Steven Ketchpel, "Software agents", *Communication of the ACM* 37(7):48–53, 1994

8. Sylvain Grivaud, François Rechenmann, "Navigation dans les bases de connaissances associant objets et hypertextes", Actes 1er Représentation par objets, La Grande-Motte, FR, pp262–280, 1992

9. Thomas Gruber, Jay Tenenbaum, Jay Weber, "Toward a knowledge medium for collaborative product development", in John Gero (ed.), Proc. 2nd. international conference on artificial intelligence in design, Pittsburg, PA US, pp413–432, 1992 [ksl.stanford.edu:/pub/knowledge-sharing/papers/SHADE.ps]

10. Peter Karp, Michael Mavrovouniotis, "Representing, analyzing and synthesizing biochemical pathways", *IEEE Expert* 9(2):11–22, 1994

11. Rob Kling, "Cooperation, coordination and control in computer supported cooperative work", *Communication of the ACM* 34(12):83–88, 1991

12. William Kornfeld, Carl Hewitt, "The scientific community metaphor", *IEEE transactions on man, systems and cybernetics* 11(1):24–33 (rep. technical report AI-memo 641, MIT, Cambridge, MA US, 1981), 1981

13. Robert Kraut, Jolene Galegher, Carmen Egido, "Relationship and tasks in scientific research collaboration", *Human-computer interaction* 3(1):31–58, 1987

14. Olga Mariño, François Rechenmann, Patrice Uvietta, "Multiple perspectives and classification mechanism in Object-oriented Representation", Proc. 9th ECAI, Stockholm, SE, pp425–430, 1990

15. K. Narayanaswamy, Neil Goldman, "*Lazy* consistency: a basis for cooperative software development", Proc. 3rd CSCW, Toronto, CA, pp257–264, 1992

16. Robert Neches, Richard Fikes, Tim Finin, Thomas Gruber, Ramesh Patil, Ted Senator, William Swartout, "Enabling Technology for Knowledge Sharing", *AI Magazine* 12(3):36–56, 1991

17. G. Christian Overton, Kimberle Koile, Jon Pastor, "GeneSys: a knowledge management system for molecular biology", in G. Bells, T. Marr (eds.), *Computers and DNA*, pp213–239, Addison-Wesley, Reading, MA US, 1990

18. Guy Perrière, Christian Gautier, "ColiGene: object-centered representation for the study of *E. coli* gene expressivity by sequence analysis", *Biochimie* 75(5):415–422, 1993

19. François Rechenmann, "Building and sharing large knowledge bases in molecular genetics", Proc. KB&KS workshop (International Conference on Building and Sharing of Very Large-Scale Knowledge Bases), Tokyo, JP, pp291–301, 1993

20. Walter Reinhard, Jean Schweitzer, Gerd Völksen, "CSCW tools: concepts and architecture", *IEEE computer* 27(5):28–36, 1994

21. Reid Smith, "The contract net protocol: high level communication and control in a distributed problem solver", *IEEE transactions on computers* 29(12):1104–1113 (rep. in Alan Bond, Les Gasser (eds.), *Readings in distributed artificial intelligence*, pp357–366, Morgan Kauffman, San Mateo, CA US, 1988), 1980

22. Mark Stefik, "The next knowledge medium", *AI magazine* 7(1):34–46, 1986

23. David Stodolsky, "Consensus journals: invitational journals based upon peer consensus", *Datalogiske Skrifter* 29, 1990

24. Hidetoshi Takana, "A private knowledge base for molecular biological research", Technical report 811, ICOT, Tokyo, JP, 1992

25. Jutta Willamowski, François Chevenet, François Jean-Marie, "A development shell for cooperative problem-solving environments", *Mathematics and computers in simulation* 36(4-6):361–379, 1994

26. Terry Winograd, "A language/action perspective on the design of cooperative work", *Human-computer interaction* 3:3–30, 1987

A Case Study in the Use of Large-Scale Knowledge-Based Technology for An Environmental Application

Nabil B. Pinto, Larry M. Stephens and Ronald D. Bonnell
University of South Carolina
Columbia, SC, USA

ABSTRACT

This paper describes a project established to develop a representation schema for engineering and common-sense knowledge about the environmental and biological impacts arising from the operations of a nuclear weapons processing facility. The Cyc system was used as the testbed for the implementation of the knowledge base for this project. The primary motivation for the project was to evaluate large-scale knowledge bases as a technology for building reasoning systems and to obtain an understanding of the effort involved in scaling-up to real-world applications. The practical problems that were encountered in the development of the knowledge-base and integration with existing knowledge are highlighted.

1 LARGE-SCALE KNOWLEDGE BASES

Large-scale knowledge bases have been the focus of the AI community over the past few years. While size is one characteristic, it is difficult to provide a good definition of what constitutes a large-scale knowledge base. However, it is important to distinguish between large-scale knowledge based systems and related systems, specifically databases and expert systems.

Database systems are designed to store and retrieve large amounts of data efficiently [Date, 1990]. Two things distinguish a knowledge base from a database — (1) the nature of the data being stored, and (2) the reasoning capabilities of the associated systems. In a database, the data being stored pertains to an enterprise or application and consists primarily of basic computer data types, such as strings and integers. The modeling approach in a database is based upon identifying the entities in a domain and capturing their attributes and relationships with other entities [Batini

et al., 1992]. A knowledge base on the other hand contains more complex symbolic descriptions of a domain's prototypical entities, which may be organized in some ontological scheme. In addition, it contains knowledge that characterizes the inferences that can be drawn about the entities in that domain. This additional knowledge gives a knowledge base the capability to reason about its data an! d explain its inferences — a cap ability not easily achieved in a database.

Expert systems are designed for inferencing over a specific area of expertise in a narrow domain [Hayes-Roth et al., 1983]. A typical expert system consists of a knowledge base containing descriptions of the objects in the problem area and an inference engine that embodies a reasoning technique, such as backward-chaining. Expert systems are considered to be "brittle" because they cannot handle situations which are related to their problem areas but outside the scope of their knowledge. There are no mechanisms for an expert system to extend its knowledge base or to share it with other systems having knowledge of that domain.

In a large knowledge base, knowledge from several domains (or problem areas within a domain) is encoded within a framework of a top-level taxonomy. The contention is that a system built around a large-scale knowledge base might overcome the brittleness problem by sharing the knowledge and problem-solving techniques via the knowledge base's common ontology [Gruber, 1991], [Skuce and Monarch, 1990]. While there exist several large or "full size" expert systems [Silverman and Murray, 1991], such as XCON (over 10,000 rules), they are designed for a singular problem-solving task and lack the generality of large knowledge bases discussed here.

The Cyc project [Guha and Lenat, 1990] is perhaps the best example of an attempt to develop a large-scale multi-contextual knowledge base. It was begun as a ten-year research initiative in 1984 at the Microelectronics and Computer Technology Corporation (MCC) in Austin, Texas and is currently on-going. The primary task of the project is codifying a vast amount of knowledge that is considered as "consensus reality" — the background knowledge possessed by a typical person living in the United States today. In addition to the encoded "common-sense" knowledge, the Cyc system contains a wide range of reasoning mechanisms for the purpose of generalized deduction and inference. The researchers' hypothesis is that a system possessing a critical mass of common-sense knowledge and general reasoning techniques (independent of the specific domain knowledge entered) can overcome the brittleness problem and provide reasonable answers to queries that were not anticipated at the t! ime of knowledge entry. Additiona lly, the Cyc system could act as a knowledge server, enabling the sharing and reuse of knowledge between other reasoning systems.

Cyc is primarily a frame-based system. Assertions about a concept in the Cyc knowledge base are gathered in a single structure referred to as a "unit." The assertions on a frame appear as "predicates". A "slot" can be loosely interpreted as a binary relation or a binary predicate, but Cyc also supports higher-order relations, such as ternaries and quaternaries.

Every frame in Cyc is conceptually a member of at least one represented "collection" or class. Both classes and slots can be specialized and generalized. Assertions such as statements or rules of thumb are entered as "axioms" in Cyc. An assertion may be associated with one or more microtheories or "contexts" [Guha, 1991], which are related to some domain or area of knowledge representation. Mechanisms for interpreting and using information from different contexts for problem-solving are supported. Cyc is said to be self-describing because nearly everything — classes, slots and individual objects — must be represented by a unit. The only exceptions include numbers, character strings, and procedures. A discussion on the current status of the Cyc project can be found in [Guha & Lenat, 1994].

2 PROJECT DESCRIPTION

The Westinghouse Savannah River Company supported a project to develop a representation schema for engineering knowledge and common-sense knowledge about the environmental and biological impacts arising from the operations of the Savannah River Site (SRS), a nuclear weapons processing facility. The primary motivation for the project was to evaluate the potential of using large-scale knowledge base as a technology for building the next generation of reasoning systems and to gain an understanding of the effort involved in scaling up to real-world applications. Of particular interest was whether this technology could (1) serve as a means for providing a common-sense in-

terpretation of the information contained in databases supporting the Waste Management and Environmental Restoration at SRS, and (2) handle queries that are related to the content of the database but fall outside the scope or format of the database. The Cyc system was selected as the testbed for the implementat! ion of the knowledge base for this project.

Resource constraints restricted the project scope to representing knowledge required in understanding an individual's dose committment as a result of an inadvertent atmospheric release of tritium [Murphy et al., 1990], [Davis et al., 1989]. This value is estimated by using highly complicated computer models. The project began with an analysis of the underlying assumptions in the computer models. This analysis led to the development of a simplified qualitative model that captured the causal chain of events starting with the release of tritium into the atmosphere and ending with the subsequent ingestion of that tritium by humans. Qualitative models are useful for specifying processes and their effects in a way that (1) induces a natural qualitative representation for quantities and (2) allows both the deduction of what processes occur in a situation and how they might change [Forbus, 1985]. Rather than representing the processes of atmospheric transport with procedures in! volving mathematical or physical l aws, the model drew on the some of following common-sense notions of a smoke plume and its movement with the wind:

- Smoke travels downwind, and dissipates with distance.

- At a given downwind distance away from the source, the smoke concentration falls off in the crosswind direction.

- There is no smoke in a direction upwind of the source.

- Outside some region in the downwind direction, the smoke concentration is so low that it may be ignored.

The domain specific concepts in the resulting ontology included weapons plants and related features such as emission points (stacks and outfalls), releases (routine and episodic) of substances (tritiated water) as plumes (atmospheric and aquatic); and environmentally impacted regions (atmospheric and aquatic) surrounding SRS. In addition, the ontology contained general concepts such as geographical directions, weather conditions during a release (wind speed, wind stability, precipitation) and people. Portions of the resulting ontologies are shown in Appendix A. Causal knowledge about the entities in the model was implemented as axioms which were organized into appropriate microtheories. In addition, assertions in Cyc's naive microtheories were used to support the common-sense assumptions (e.g. "People breathe") that were implicit in the model.

An application was developed which produced a qualitative estimate of dose exposure based on a simple description of a person's location and weather conditions during a release. A qualitative model is useful in checking if the estimates from a simulation or mathematical model are reasonable — the validation notion of Forbus and Falkenhainer [1990]. Based on this notion, the application could verify it's estimate against the numerical estimate computed by the computer models. Beside the knowledge in Cyc, the application could draw on external sources (such as geographical and weather databases) to retrieve information that was then instantiated in Cyc. The application could also contrast the individual's dose with another (typically, the worst case) and offer comparisons to other sources of radiation, such as background radiation.

The expressive nature of the concepts that can be represented in a knowledge base was a salient feature. For instance, the notions of *upwind, downwind, within-plume, outside-plume* could not be naturally expressed in the computer models that predict the dispersal of a substance released from a stack. This feature was useful in supporting reasoning about qualitative differences. In everyday conversations, people tend to use qualitative measures, rather than numerical intervals, for comparative purposes. In the application, a five-valued scale — *Very-Low, Low, Medium, High, Very-High* — was useful for reasoning about distances, wind speeds, wind stability, and even dose commitments. These qualitative differences were used in providing simple common-sense explanations such as "your dose commitment is very much lower than the worst case because you were much further away downwind."

3 PROJECT EXPERIENCE

The project was undertaken to identify the problems encountered in developing applications using a large-scale knowledge base. The following sections address some of the general problems that were encountered in the project, in particular with regard to the methodologies for constructing ontologies, reuse of concepts in the knowledge base, and applicability to types of problem domains.

3.1 Approaches to Building Ontologies

At the start of the project (1991), there were no well-defined methodologies available for ontological engineering in Cyc or any other knowledge-based system. Since there were no formal guidelines, two intuitive approaches were examined in building the knowledge base.

The first approach undertaken could be described as ad hoc: the "scruffy" approach [Lenat and Guha,

1990]. The process consisted of identifying concepts in the problem domain and attempting to match those concepts with knowledge in Cyc. The knowledge-engineering process was informal consisting of periodic meetings with a domain expert. A list of concepts to be represented was determined from these discussions, along with the published technical reports [Murphy et al., 1990] and [Davis et al., 1989]. Only the knowledge needed to support explanations required by the qualitative model was represented. The first step was to examine the Cyc knowledge base for a matching concept based on a search of unit names or browse the top levels of the ontology to identify potential branches under which the concept might exist An existing concept was used as-is or augmented by the addition of new predicates. Due to the specialized nature of our application, a good amount of units ha! d to be created and integrated int o the top levels of the Cyc ontology.

The result of using this approach produced an ontology that embedded knowledge "specifics." The concepts and underlying ideas were not always explicated in detail. The ontology was a shallow one, i.e., the root and leaf nodes of the ontology were defined, but the interior nodes were seemingly missing. A consequence was the existence of "orphan" classes — classes whose only links are directly to the highest levels of the ontology, with minimal number of intervening taxonomic layers. In the project ontology, many classes were direct specializations of the root node *Thing* in the Cyc ontology — a condition leading to little semantic interpretation about the concept. Therefore, in developing applications for a large knowledge base, a problem ontology of this nature may be symptomatic of insufficient modeling and may point to gaps in the higher levels of the ontology. Consequently, there can be problems in reusing such concepts.

Since the ad hoc approach resulted in a shallow ontology, it was decided to try a more principled approach. The approach consisted of defining an initial set of primitive concepts (based on the idea of semantic primitives [Hayes, 1985]) and using these concepts to define new ones; thereby in effect developing a theory. The hypothesis was that this approach would force the explication (or at least consideration) of details surrounding a concept and reveal any underlying taxonomic layers.

The application required reasoning about distances and the relative geographical positions of individuals. These inferences were based on the following common-sense ideas used in interpreting a map:

- a city is viewed as a point whose location is expressed with latitude and longitude

- a resident of a city is understood to have the same location as the city

- distance between two locations is related to the straight line distance between two points

While the general concepts required were present in the Cyc taxonomy, the notions stated above were not fleshed out. Based on ideas used for spatial representations in GIS (geographical information systems) [Laurini and Thompson, 1992], a grounding for these concepts within the framework of the *Terrestrial Coordinate System* was developed. This grounding required the representation of the concept of Coordinate System from a geometrical standpoint and then specializing it to develop the concept of the *Terrestrial Coordinate System* [Maloney, 1978] from a geographical perspective. The primitive *Point* and other geometrical entities such as *Lines* and *Vectors* were used to define Coordinate System and its specializations — rectangular, cylindrical, and spherical. In a geographical context, the Terrestrial Coordinate System was asserted as an instance of *Spherical Coordinate Systems* with its origin located at the center of the Earth center! and a grid composed of Longitudes and Latitudes.

While this approach resulted in "grounded" ontology, it required the representation of a greater number of concepts and detail than was needed for the actual problem. The significant observation here is that the amount of background knowledge to be entered in relation to the problem-specific knowledge can be overwhelming.

3.2 Reuse of Knowledge Base Concepts

The utility of a large-scale knowledge base comes from the availability of domain-independent general concepts and the ability to reuse the concepts for applications developed in other domains [Mark, 1991]. While the specific nature of our domain required the definition of new concepts, we encountered the following general problems in trying to reuse concepts:

- **Semantic interpretation of concepts** A concept may be named, but nothing is articulated about the concept. This refers to "grounding" problem mentioned earlier where important relationships or interpretations are not represented. In other words, the concept is defined only in terms of where it fits in the ontology. The only assertions appearing on such concepts are those describing taxonomic properties such as class membership, generalization, and specialization. In other cases, the definition of a concept maybe too shallow or incomplete for use in other applications. For instance, the general concept of *North* was defined as an instance of *Geographical Direction*, but relationships in terms other geographical concepts (such as Earth and the North Pole) were missing.

- **Distinction between attributes and relations** An attribute is an inherent property of an entity. A relation is a physical or a conceptual association among entities. This distinction is important in a knowledge base because attributes are useful in defining a prototypical object, while relationships are useful in characterizing links between entities.

- **Multiple representation of the same concept** A common problem in developing large ontologies is the occurrence of differently named versions of a concept. For instance, the units *FrameOfReference* and *CoordinateSystem* were found to represent the notion of a coordinate system.

- **Overuse of concepts** It is usually easier to create a new concept than reuse or modify an existing one resulting in the creation of localized pockets of knowledge. In addition, there exists a problem with "widespread reification" [Elkan and Greiner, 1993] in that a new concepts may have to be instantiated for every aspect of an entity about which a fact is to be asserted.

The project also highlighted the larger problem in reusing a concept defined for one domain in another. For example, the application used the concept of *transpiration* to describe a pathway for intake of atmospheric tritium by people. The Cyc knowledge base contained the concept of transpiration under the Botany microtheory as a biological process carried out by plants. In order to apply to humans, the definition of the concept would require being (a) generalized to describe a process that exchanges gaseous substances through a permeable membrane, and (b) specialized as a human biological process that describes the passing of water vapor through the skin. This would have necessitated the development of additional anatomical and physical concepts — such as skin, membranes, and permeability — that were far removed from the problem domain. This issue brings up an open-ended question as to the exponential number of changes that may be required to reuse or modify a ! concept in a large-scale knowledge base.

3.3 Applicability of Problem Domains

One of the aims of the project was to determine the types of problem areas for which large-scale knowledge bases may be useful. Inherently, this technology is best suited to developing applications based on problems areas such as classification, which involve representing and inferencing over static ontological relationships.

On the other hand, dynamic events and phenomenon proved to be extremely difficult to represent. For instance, the phenomenon of *Rotation* and related concepts rely heavily on visual imagery and human experience. This phenomenon can be best described in terms of mathematical propositions that are outside the realm of common-sense knowledge. A qualitative representation typically results in leaving the nuances of the phenomenon implicit. A related issue in representing dynamic events is the difficulty in the representing the temporal state of an event or object over time. Cyc uses the concept of "sub-abstractions" [Lenat and Guha, 1990] to represent an event over time. Each sub-abstraction of a concept is a new frame that represents the concept at a particular instant or during a specified interval.

4 CONCLUSIONS

Large-scale knowledge bases and common-sense reasoning have been the topics of increasing attention as the basis for developing the next generation of larger and more competent AI systems. This is evidenced by the ongoing national initiatives aimed at developing technology and interchange formats for building large and reusable knowledge bases [Neches et al., 1991]. The interest stems from the fact that the field is now reaching beyond the building of small prototype systems and grappling with large-scale processes of knowledge creation and use [Stefik and Smoliar, 1993].

The project described in this paper was initiated to encode the engineering and common-sense knowledge about the environmental and biological impacts of SRS operations using Cyc as the testbed. The motivation of the project was to understand the effort and utility of creating a application that required knowledge from multiple domain areas. The observations from using a large-scale knowledge based system for this project are as follows:

- In developing such an application, one may find that the knowledge needed is missing, is represented in a manner that is not useful for the application, or conflicts with the ontology as viewed in the application.

- In adding to or integrating with an existing ontology, one has to first understand and navigate through the existing ontology. This can be a time-consuming and arduous task because of the sheer volume of the knowledge and the complexity of the underlying models and their assumptions. In addition, the amount of background knowledge that must be entered prior to entering application-specific knowledge can be overwhelming.

- One should be aware of the potentially large number of side effects resulting from the modification and reuse of an existing concept. This could lead to development of isolated ontologies that tie into the global ontology only at the highest levels; this over-generalized knowledge can require later redefinition and have diminished potential for reuse and sharing.

The preliminary conclusion from the project with regard to using large-scale knowledge bases is that the technology may not be mature enough for the purpose of developing robust industrial applications at the present time. Technical issues aside, it appears that the challenge lies in resolving the ontological principles and techniques behind the development of these knowledge bases. The project is currently focusing on developing related applications to investigate the potential for knowledge reuse and sharing. A lack of suitable metrics make it difficult to give quantifiable estimate of the effort involved in scaling-up to real-world applications. However, as the technology of large-scale knowledge bases is being developed, some key issues to consider with regards to application development in this environment are:

1. Multiple views or interpretations of the same phenomenon are supported. through use of microtheories or similar concepts.

2. Protocols and formats for exchange of information are developed for knowledge sharing and reuse. The KIF-related initiatives are addressing this issue [Genesereth and Fikes, 1992], [Gruber, 1992].

3. Applications should be layered on a substrate provided by the knowledge base. The notion of a knowledge server is advocated by several researchers [Silverman and Murray, 1991].

4. Large scale knowledge bases may be best deployed around large application domains with many sub-domains. In other words, the problems surrounding the construction of a single universal knowledge base may make the task insurmountable. However, developing a knowledge base for a large domain that supports a broad range of tasks appears feasible. An example is "Metathesaurus" [Tuttle, 1993], which is an attempt by the National Library of Medicine to build a uniform interface to the world's biomedical knowledge.

Critical to the deployment of this technology will be the development of tools and procedures for domain modeling, knowledge entry and classification, consistency checking and knowledge base maintenance. For example, developing metrics such as "semantic closeness" [Barnett et al., 1992] can be useful in evaluation of knowledge base and assist in knowledge entry. Work remains on uncovering techniques like analogical reasoning and knowledge mining that will enable applications to utilize the vast amount of knowledge contained in the system.

ACKNOWLEDGMENT

This work was supported in part by Westinghouse Savannah River Company under Task Order 43 for the South Carolina Universities Research and Education Foundation.

161

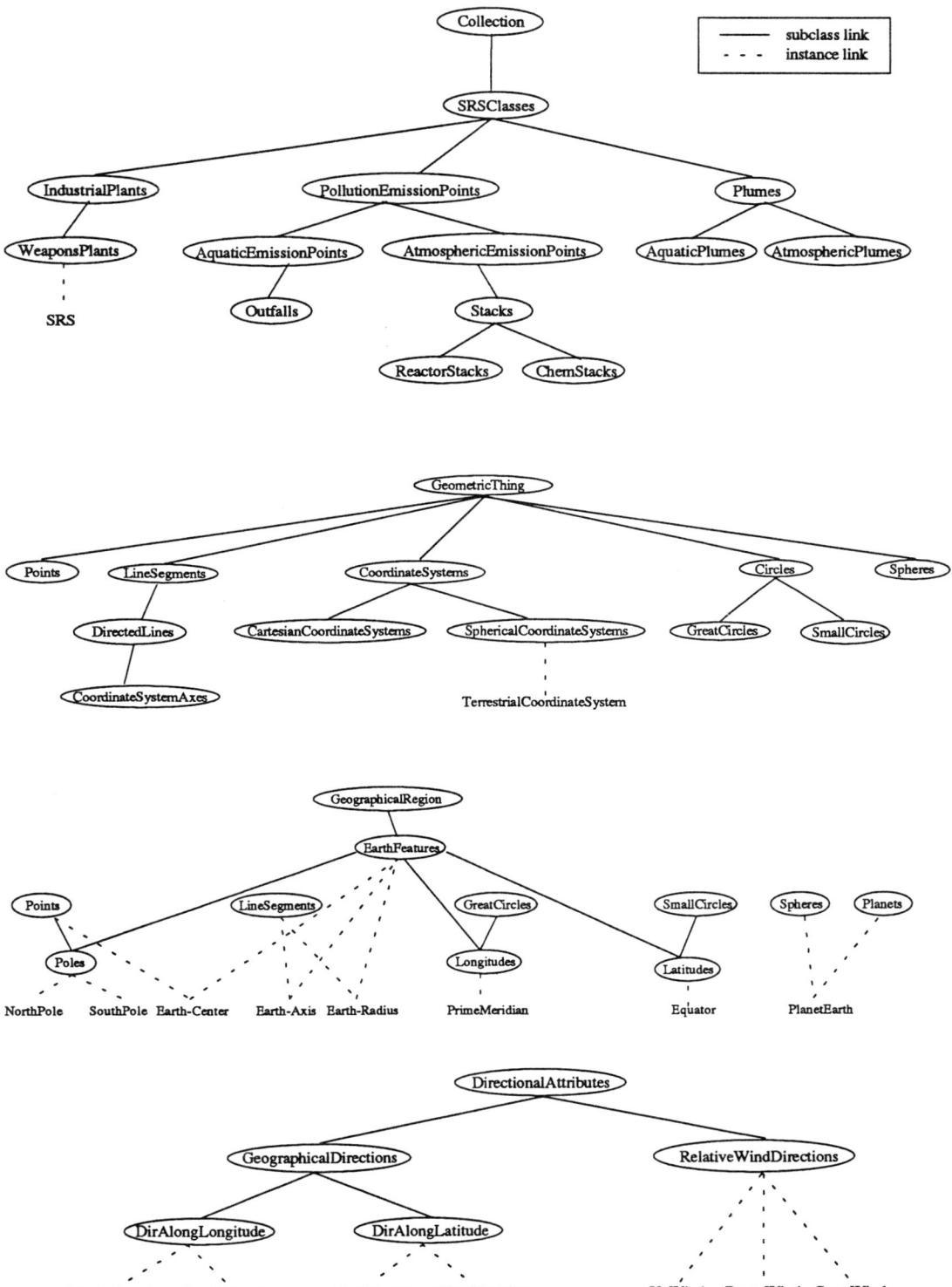

REFERENCES

[Barnett et al., 1992] J. Barnett, I. Mani, and E. Rich, "Reversible Machine Translation: What to Do When the Languages Don't Match Up," MCC Technical Report NL-068-91, MCC, 3500 West Balcones Center Drive, Austin, TX 78759, August 1992.

[Batini et al., 1992] C. Batini, S. Ceri and S. B. Navathe, *Conceptual Database Design: An Entity-Relationship Approach*, Benjamin Cummings Publishing Company, Inc., Redwood City, California, 1992.

[Date, 1990] C. J. Date, *An Introduction to Database Systems*, Addison-Wesley Publishing Company, Inc., Reading, Massachusetts, 1990.

[Davis et al., 1989] H. A. Davis, D. K. Martin, and J. L. Todd, Savannah River Site Environmental Report for 1988, Technical Report WSRC-RP-89-59-1, Volumes I and II, Westinghouse Savannah River Company, Savannah River Site, Aiken, SC, 1989.

[Elkan and Greiner, 1993] C. Elkan and R. Greiner, "Book Review of Building Large Knowledge-Based Systems: Representation and Inference in the Cyc project (D.B. Lenat and R.V. Guha)" in *Artificial Intelligence*, Vol. 61, No. 1, May 1993, pp. 41-52.

[Forbus, 1985] K. D. Forbus, "The Role of Qualitative Dynamics in Naive Physics," in *Formal Theories of the Commonsense World*, eds. Jerry R. Hobbs and Robert C. Moore, Ablex Publishing Corporation, Norwood, NJ, 1985, pp. 185-226.

[Forbus and Falkenhainer, 1990] K. D. Forbus and B. Falkenhainer, "Self-Explanatory Simulations: An Integration of qualitative and quantitative knowledge," *Proceedings AAAI-90*, Boston, MA, July-August 1990, pp. 380-387.

[Genesereth and Fikes, 1992] M. R. Genesereth and R. E. Fikes, "Knowledge Interchange Format: Version 3.0 Reference Manual," Computer Science Department, Stanford University, Stanford, CA 94305, June1992.

[Gruber, 1992] T. R. Gruber, "Ontolingua: A Mechanism to Support Portable Ontologies," Technical Report KSL-91-66, Stanford University, Knowledge Systems Laboratory, 1992.

[Gruber, 1991] T. R. Gruber, "The Role of Common Ontology in Achieving Sharable, Reusable Knowledge Bases," *Proceedings of the Second International Conference on Principles of Knowledge Representation and Reasoning (KR91)*, Morgan Kaufmann Publishers, Inc., San Mateo, California, 1991.

[Guha, 1991] R. V. Guha, "Contexts: A formalization and some applications," MCC Technical Report No. CYC-423-91," Microelectronics and Computer Technology Corporation, 3500 West Balcones Center Drive, Austin, TX 78759, March, 1991..

[Guha and Lenat, 1994] R.V. Guha and D.B. Lenat, "Enabling Agents to Work Together," *Communications of the ACM*, Vol. 37, No. 7, July 1994, pp. 127-142.

[Guha and Lenat, 1990] R.V. Guha and D.B. Lenat, "Cyc: A Midterm Report," *AI Magazine*, Vol. 11, No. 3, Fall 1990, pp. 32-59.

[Hayes, 1985] P. J. Hayes, "The Second Naive Physics Manifesto," in *Formal Theories of the Commonsense World*, eds. Jerry R. Hobbs and Robert C. Moore, Ablex Publishing Corporation, Norwood, NJ, 1985, pp. 1-36.

[Hayes-Roth et al., 1983] F. Hayes-Roth, D. Waterman, D. B. Lenat, *Building Expert Systems*, Addison-Wesley Publishing Company, Inc., Reading, Massachusetts, 1983.

[Laurini and Thompson, 1992] R. Laurini and D. Thompson, *Fundamentals of Spatial Information Systems*, Academic Press, 1992.

[Lenat and Guha, 1990] D. B. Lenat and R. V. Guha, *Building Large Knowledge-Based Systems: Representation and Inference in the Cyc Project*, Addison-Wesley Publishing Company, Inc., Reading, Massachusetts, 1990.

[Maloney, 1978] E. S. Maloney, *Dutton's Navigation and Piloting*, Naval Institute Press, Annapolis, Maryland, 1978.

[Mark, 1991] W. Mark, "Panel: Achieving Large Scale Knowledge Sharing," *Proceedings of the Second International Conference on Principles of Knowledge Representation and Reasoning (KR91)*, Morgan Kaufmann Publishers, Inc., San Mateo, California, 1991.

[Murphy et al., 1990] C. E. Murphy et al., "Tritium in the Savannah River Site Environment (U)," Westinghouse Savannah River Company Technical Report WSRC-RP-90-0424-1, May 1990.

[Neches et al., 1991] R. Neches, R. E. Fikes, T. Finin, T. Gruber, R. Patil, T. Senator, and W. R. Swartout, "Enabling Technology for Knowledge Sharing," *AI Magazine*, Vol. 12, No. 3, 1991, pp. 36-56.

[Silverman and Murray, 1991] B. G. Silverman and A. J. Murray, "Full-sized Knowledge-Based Systems Research Workshop," *AI Magazine*, Vol. 11, No. 5, January 1991, pp. 88-94.

[Skuce and Monarch, 1990] D. Skuce and I. Monarch, "Ontological Issues in Knowledge Base Design: Some Problems and Suggestions," in *Proceedings of the 5th Workshop on Knowledge Acquisition for Knowledge Based Systems*, Banff, Canada, 1990.

[Stefik and Smoliar, 1993] M. J. Stefik and S. W. Smoliar, "Editorial: The Common Sense Reviews," in *Artificial Intelligence*, Vol. 61, No. 1, May 1993, pp. 37-40.

[Tuttle, 1993] M. S. Tuttle, "Book Review of Representations of Commonsense Knowledge (E. Davis) and Building Large Knowledge-Based Systems: Representation and Inference in the Cyc project (D.B. Lenat and R.V. Guha)," in *Artificial Intelligence*, Vol. 61, No. 1, May 1993, pp. 121-148.

Part 5: Scaling Issues

Towards Very Large Knowledge Bases
N.J.I. Mars, Ed.
IOS Press, 1995

On the Integration of
Specialized and General Reasoning

Gerhard Wickler
Rutherford Appleton Laboratory
Chilton, United Kingdom
gw@inf.rl.ac.uk

ABSTRACT

One problem with large knowledge-bases is that reasoning over them can become extremely inefficient. This is true unless we can exploit specific characteristics of the knowledge-base. In this paper we will argue that there are usually large parts of knowledge-bases that have these desired characteristics. We will show how it is possible to integrate specific and general reasoning mechanisms to achieve the benefits of both: a general reasoning mechanism gives us the freedom to represent arbitrary knowledge without having to force it into a special representation formalism; a spezialized reasoning mechanism has the advantage that it is efficient. Finally we will argue that given the integration the main problem is to identify and formalize types of knowledge that can and should be extracted from the general representation.

1 INTRODUCTION

1.1 Knowledge Requirements of Explanation

It is widely agreed that knowledge-based systems should not only be able to solve a given problem but they should also be able to explain what they did or how they did it. It is this context that this paper grew out of. In the I- SEE project (cf. [16]) we are trying to build a generic explanation component that can be added to existing and new application systems. One of the problems in doing this is that it takes some knowledge to solve a problem, but for the purpose of explanation usually much more knowledge is necessary. The main reason for this can be seen as follows: To be able to explain something the explainer has to have an understanding of what he is explaining (cf. [1]). An understanding in this context means that the knowledge to be explained is grounded in other (more fundamental) knowledge, e.g. common sense knowledge.

Only if this knowledge is shared between explainer and explainee then the explanation will be successful. This means that a generic explanation component has to have enough knowledge to share a common ground with the explainee.

Furthermore, it also has to have knowledge in the area of expertise of the underlying application, preferably more than the application itself. As opposed to common sense knowledge this is specific to a given domain. Then there has to be knowledge about how the application works, how it performs its task, and knowledge about the reasoning the application has performed in the course of solving a specific problem. This knowledge is necessary to generate the according explanation (cf. [14] or [13]). In I-SEE we represent this knowledge in different modules that can be added to an application or share its knowledge as far as available in order to avoid inconsistencies. Figure 1 gives an overview of the architecture of I-SEE. The *domain model* holds the common sense knowledge that is not application specific and the domain specific expertise. The *system model* contains a model of the problem-solving method of the application system similar to the upper layers in KADS (cf. [18]). The *reasoning record* is basically a knowledge-level trace. In this paper we will be mainly concerned with the domain model.

The point here is that an explanation component requires a large amount of knowledge and thus has to reason over a large knowledge-base. Even worse, it has to do this in a short time because users can hardly be expected to wait long for the answers to their questions. Explanation is usually a dialogue (cf. [10]) and must not bore the user if it wants to be sucessful.

1.2 Specific Types of Knowledge

So what knowledge do knowledge-bases like, for example, our domain model usually contain? The first distinction we want to talk about here is between the

166

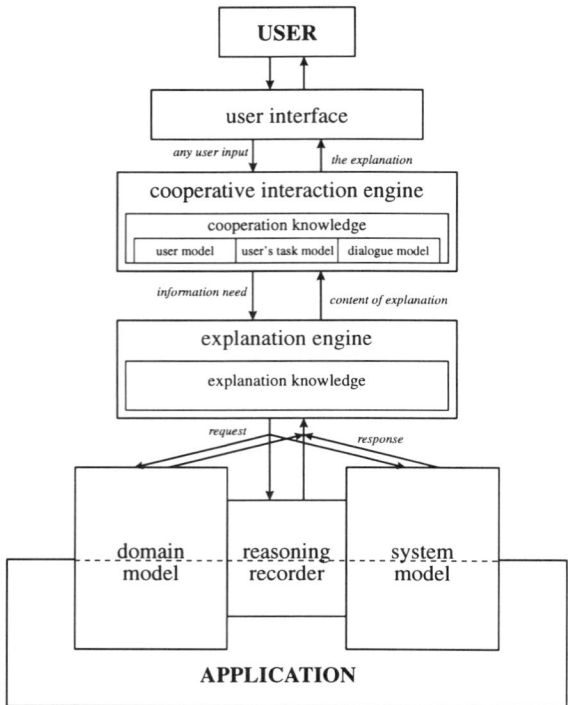

Figure 1: The Global Architecture of I-SEE

A-Box and the *T-Box* (cf. [2]). The T-Box can be seen as the ontology of the domain and defines the terminology we want to use. It describes the concepts (of the domain) in terms of how they are related to each other. While smaller knowledge-bases might get by without a defined ontology, it is not disputed that large knowledge-bases need one for various reasons. Most important for explanation, if we want to build a knowledgable system that has an understanding of the concepts it reasons about then it is necessary to provide it with some sort of semantics what the symbols that represent the concepts mean. In a computer that has only very limited means to interact with the outside world grounding the symbols in each other might be the best we can do to give this machine an understanding of the concepts represented (cf. [9]). Thus, a large knowledge-base almost by definition must contain an ontology.

On the other hand there is the A-Box that contains assertions about the domain we want to reason over. Some of these assertions must describe the actual instances of the concepts of the T-Box. The instances are the symbols that represent the individual objects that exist in our world. The objects might be of a physical or abstract nature and the world might be the real world or any other, that does not matter to the system. However, a knowledge-base has to contain

instances if it wants to represent an adequate model of some world. One can even assume that there will be far more instances than concepts in many domains. These instances will be described in terms of which concepts they belog to, the values of their attributes, and which other instances play given roles for them.

But instances are not all the A-Box contains. In general there will also be other types of knowledge (cf. [12]). For example, there could be knowledge about time if we want to reason about change over time. Or we might have to deal with spatial models and thus need knowledge about spatial relations and movements. A lot of knowledge-bases also contain knowledge about how objects can be decomposed, i.e. structural models. Another example of a specific kind of knowledge is a functional description of things in terms of their input and output. Not all of these different kinds of knowledge will be found in every knowledge-base, but if we are dealing with large knowledge- bases then it is quite likely that we will find that sort of *specialised knowledge*. Does that mean that we can just split our knowledge-base into a number of smaller knowledge-bases that have certain characteristics we can exploit to reason over them? Unfortunately this is not the case. Experience shows that there is always some knowledge that does not really fit into any of the categories described above. And it is for this comparatively small part of the knowledge-base that we need a general reasoning component.

2 REASONING OVER SPECIFIC TYPES OF KNOWLEDGE

In this section we will demonstrate that it is possible to reason efficieltly over specific parts of a knowledge-base by exploiting properties of the kind of knowledge represented. Queries to a knowledge-base hardly ever refer to just one specific kind of knowledge. Only if there is an integrating framework for the specific kinds of knowledge we want to reason over such queries can be dealt with. In the next section we are going to introduce such a framework. Thus, the knowledge-base will appear as one homogenus unit to the outside but contain several specialised reasoners internally. This distinction is similar to the distinction between the epistemological and heuristic level in Cyc (cf. [7]).

2.1 The General Representation Framework

Before we continue by describing types of knowledge that can be reasoned over efficiently we wnat to say a few words about the integrating framework that we envise. On the one hand we need a framework that does not impose restrictions on the knowledge we want to represent because this is exactly the knowledge that does not fit into any of the specialised frameworks. On the other hand it must be possible to reason over the knowledge represented in the general framework.

Thus, a compromise is unavoidable.

In order to restrict the representatioin framework of the knowledge-base as little as possible we will choose first order predicate logic (FOL) (cf. e.g. [8] or [4]) as the general knowledge representation formalism. Some will now claim that this is not general enough and that more powerful approaches like e.g. modal logics or even higher order logics are needed because real world knowledge can only be adequately represented in such formalism. Since reasoning over these logics is sometimes done by reducing them to the standard FOL, this is not really more powerful and since FOL is not decidable we believe that this is almost too complex to reason over it anyway. Others will want a more restricted framework for knowledge representation like e.g. FOL with Horn-clauses only or only propositional logic because reasoning over these logics is much simpler. However, since we want to be rather general here and since there exists a reasonable inference mechanism for FOL with resolution (cf. [11]), we believe that FOL is at least a good starting point for a general knowledge representation formalism. The complexity of FOL on the other hand makes it a completely unreasonable choice if we want to reason over large knowledge-bases.

Important here is that we have a unifying framework that allows the integration of specific reasoners. We will show that FOL with resolution provides such a framework. Note that the same techniques as described below can also be applied to other frameworks, e.g. Prolog. However, it is necessary to show soundness and completeness of the integrated solution. In this sense the choice of FOL and resolution can be seen as arbitrary.

2.2 Reasoning over Ontologies

Large ontologies are currently a very active field of research (cf. [5], [6]). What do these ontologies actually contain? The backbone of an ontology is usually the so-called *is-a*-hierarchy. Let us choose a specific FOL representation here that can represent this kind of knowledge:

$$\text{IsA}(C_1, C_2)$$
iff
C_1 is a subconcept of the concept C_2

The IsA-predicate allows us to represent a concept hierarchy in FOL. This plus a statement of the transitivity of the IsA-relation makes it possible to evaluate queries of the from $\text{IsA}(C_i, C_j)$ where C_i and C_j are concepts. If we really would represent the concept hierarchy in this form in FOL then evaluating the query with resolution would take roughly $\mathcal{O}(n*log_k(n))^1$ time where n is the number of concepts and k is the average

number of subconcepts of a concept. The $\mathcal{O}$-notation, of course, hides the fact that there is a rather large constant factor involved in unification. Futhermore, the factor n comes as the size of the knowledge-base and thus grows if we represent more than just the concept hierarchy.

The alternative to representing the concept hierarchy in FOL is to construct a tree[2] where the concepts are nodes and the IsA-relation is represented by the links, i.e. each concept has a pointer to its father. The time to evaluate the same query in this representation is $\mathcal{O}(log_k(n))$. Not surprisingly, it is much faster. And building this representation is simple: When a positive 1-clause without variables and the IsA-predicate is asserted we do not add it to the FOL-knowledge-base but to our special representation. Problems can come in if the representation contains redundant links in which case we have to compute the direct father for every concept which can be computationally expensive especially in the case of multiple inheritance. However, viewing this process as a compilation of the knowledge-base makes it appear reasonable.

In fact, exploiting the IsA-relation in a resolution framework is not new at all. In [15] it is shown how this can be done in sorted logics. But we do not want to restrict ourselves to the IsA-relation. In the remainder of this section we will describe further relations that have properties that can be exploited for more efficient reasoning.

2.3 Reasoning over Instances and Attributes

The next obvious step onwards from the IsA-relation is to introduce the InstanceOf-relation as:

$$\text{InstanceOf}(I, C)$$
iff
I is an instance of the concept C

Again, the evaluation of literals of this type can be done much more efficient if the knowledge is represented separately in a specific framework. The time needed is again $\mathcal{O}(log_k(n))$ compared to $\mathcal{O}(n*log_k(n))$ with pure resolution.

In an ontology concepts and instances of those will be described in terms of their properties, attributes, and roles, all of which can have values. To continue the method used in the examples above, we can introduce new predicates that express this knowledge and can be represented in a much more efficient framework. Query evaluation times will be even better relative to the general framework of FOL because inheritance of attributes, for example, involves the evaluation of the IsA-relation and thus the time advantage gained there will show up in relations based on a concept hierarchy as well. A precise description of the predicates that can

---

[1]$\mathcal{O}(n)$ to find a represented link in $n-1$ 1-clauses times the *distance* between two concepts: $\mathcal{O}(log_k(n))$

[2]This assumes single-inheritance. Multiple-inheritance would only effect both representations in the same way.

168

be used to represent this knowledge is given in [17]. The Is-relation defines mainly boolean properties of entities, the Has-relation asserts values for attributes of entities, and the HasA-relation describes entities that play given roles for another entities.

Earlier we were also talking about other types of specific knowledge that can be handeled more efficiently by applying specific methods, e.g. temporal models, spatial models, structural models, or functional model. Although we will not demonstrate it, we claim that using specific representation and reasoning mechanism will result in the same benefits as shown for the concept hierarchy.

The point here is that specific representations are possible and can be handled in a very efficient manner that allows the reasoning over large knowledge-bases of that sort of knowledge. However, a query involving several of these types of knowledge cannot be answered.

3 INTEGRATING THE SPECIFIC REASONERS WITH RESOLUTION

Up to now we have argued that there are specific types of knowledge in large knowledge-bases that can be extracted and reasoned about effieiently. In this section we will indroduce an algorithm that integrates these specific reasoners with a general resolution theorem prover. We will show that the integrated reasoner is still sound and complete and talk about its complexity. The following section will give examples how the algorithm is applied.

3.1 The Algorithm

Let us restate what exaclty the knowledge-base we are talking about looks like at this point. On the one hand we have a set of knowledge-bases that all have their specific internal representation and that can evaluate queries of the form $P(a_1, \ldots, a_n)$ in the simplest case. This does not represent a restriction since we can think of a specific reasoner that can handle different predicates as consisting of several reasoners that handle only one predicate. Futhermore, constructing a reasoner that takes e.g. a disjunction of literals as arguments only complicates the process of deciding where to send the query not the principle itself as we will see.

On the other hand there is some knowledge represented in FOL and we assume that the inference rule applied is resolution. We make no assumption about the resolution strategy itself here but as we will see this becomes important when we get to the completeness of the algorithm.

The basic algorthm looks like this[3]:

---

[3]A slightly more sophisticated version of the algorithm would check the query for clauses that contain literals that can be evaluated to true or false and then remove clause or literal respectively.

```
REPEAT

    select two clauses C1 and C2 for
    resolution;

    let R be the result of this
    resolution step;

    FOR all literals L in R;

        IF there is a specific reasoner that
        can evaluate L
        THEN

            IF L is true
                remove R from the clause base
            IF L is false
                remove L from R

UNTIL
    the empty clause has been generated
```

The exploitation of the specific reasoners comes in when a new clause is the result of a resolution step. If there is a literal in this new clause that we can evaluate with a specific reasoner then we know something about this new clause. If the literal is true then the whole clause is true since it is a disjunction of the literals. If the literal is false then the truth value of the whole clause does not change by deleting the literal. Notice that this might result in the empty clause. Now, if this literal is in the resulting clause, then why could we not remove one of its parent clauses because this literal must come from one of its parents. Simply because resolution involves unification which can bind variables and thus the literal will not be the same in the parent clause. Basically, the rules applied in the algorithm are similar rules applied in the Davis and Putnam procedure (cf. e.g. [8]).

Finally, the rule that is applied in the case where the resulting clause contains a literal we can evaluate to be false can be formally given as:

$$\frac{\neg Q(a) \quad \mathcal{M} \vee P(x) \vee Q(x) \quad \mathcal{N} \vee P(a)}{\mathcal{M} \vee \mathcal{N}}$$

The case where the resulting clause contains a literal we can evaluate to be true is not really a rule application. It is much more the prevention of applying the usual resolution step:

$$\frac{Q(a) \quad \mathcal{M} \vee P(x) \vee Q(x) \quad \mathcal{N} \vee P(a)}{-}$$

3.1.1 The Closed World Assumption

Woods (cf. [19]) pointed out that one problem with current knowledge- based systems is that they either assume a closed world or they do not. Another aspect of the framework described above is that we can choose whether we want to use the closed world assumption for each reasoner separately. For example, we might not want to assume it for the general part of the knowledge representation since we do not know what sort of knowledge we will find there. For the IsA-relation on the other hand it is clearly a good thing. How far this can be taken is not clear at present. The second example in the following section will illustrate the idea a bit further.

However, Woods reckoned that a system should be able to decide whether it wants to adopt the closed world assumption based on knowledge about its own competence. We agree with this and do not claim that adopting the closed world assumtion for specific reasoners solves the problem. It is only a way of exploiting the knowledge engineers knowledge about the competence of the system.

3.2 Soundness and Completeness

As can be shown easily, the algorithm is sound, i.e. if it derives the empty clause then the clause base is inconsistent. In other words, a query that has been negated and added to the clause base follows from the axioms in it and the knowledge represented in the specific representations.

To show that our extension of resolution is sound we can use that resolution is sound, i.e. that the new clause follows from its two parent clauses. If the new clause does not contain a literal that can be evaluated by the specific resoners then we add a clause to the clause base that is the result of standard resolution. If the evaluation of one of the literals is positive then we do not add anything to the clause base. The only case where we add a clause that is different from the standard resolution result is if it contained one or more literals we could evaluate to false. This, however, means that the specific reasoners hold knowledge that is exactly the negation of a literal in our new clause. Then we could remove this in another resolution step anyway. Thus, the algorithm described above is sound.

Completeness is a bit more suttle and depends on the resolution strategy chosen. The problem is the following: Assume we have a special reasoner that can has knowledge about the predicate IsA, e.g.:

1 IsA(car, vehicle)

Assume further that our FOL-knowledge-base contains the following knowledge:

2 Can(vehicle, drive)
3 -IsA(x, y), -Can(y, z), Can(x, z)

In the case of standard resolution we can resolve the clauses (2) and (3) in the knowledge-base and the result with (1) to:

4 -IsA(x, vehicle), Can(x, drive)
5 Can(car, drive)

If we now add the query 6 -Can(car, drive) this is directly contradicted by (5), i.e. Can(car, drive) follows from the theory.

In general the problem is this: The axioms in the knowledge-base are assumed to be true and consistent with the knowledge in the specific knowledge-bases. Thus, clauses that we derive from this knowledge must be true. If in the process of unification we generate literals that can be evaluated to true (which is quite likely since we know that the whole clause is true) then these clauses will be removed from the knowledge-base. It might however be necessary to generate exactly those clauses that are inconsistent with the query.

The solution to the problem is to choose input resolution as the strategy. Input resolution is complete. This strategy lets us to always choose one clause from the knowledge-base, i.e. the set of (true) axioms and one clause from the query or the clauses derived up to now. If the axioms together with the query are inconsistent then the falsehood must of couse come from the query. Thus, this strategy tries to derive a clause from the query that is inconsistent with the axioms. If such a derived clause contains a true literal, however, it can not be inconsistent with the axioms since all of those clauses are true. Therefore our extended resolution is complete.

Finally, it is now clear which resolution strategies could make the extended resolution incomplete. These are exactly those that are incomplete if combined with input resolution. However, since input resolution is only used to show the completeness of the method and not directly part of the algorithm, the completeness of some combined strategies might be preserved but can not be shown as above.

3.3 Complexity

As argued above it is much more efficient to extract knowledge with special characteristics from the FOL-knowledge-base in order to exploit these. But there is another source for the speed-up. While the complexity of the extended resolution is still the same as for standard resolution, the size of the underlying knowledge-base we apply resolution to is considerably smaller. If the original size of the clause base was n then the complexity to derive the empty clause was $\mathcal{O}(2^n)$. If we can reduce the size to mthe complexity will be $\mathcal{O}(2^m)$ and thus the speed-up is $\mathcal{O}(2^{n-m})$. This will result in a major gain inefficiency. The results of the experiments are not yet available.

As mentioned earlier, there are similar approaches, for example, sorted logics. A generalization of this ap-

170

proach that is also similar to what are proposing here
is contrained resolution (cf. [3]). The idea there is to
annotate clauses with contraints over their variables.
If one takes this to be the spzialised knowledge we want
to extract from the knowledge-base then the resulting
FOL-knowledge-base is the same. However, nothing is
mentioned there about the evaluation or form of the
constraints. Since we restrict the extracted knowledge
mainly to fully instantiated 1-clauses contrained logics are a more general approach. But they are also
more difficult to handle. To derive the empty clause
in constrained logics does not necessarily prove the inconsistency of the clause base. Only the unconstrained
empty clause does this, i.e. a set of empty clauses with
constraints the disjunction of which represent no constraints. It is also worth mentioning that constrained
resolution is sound and complete.

4   TWO EXAMPLES

We will now demonstrate where the algorithm described above restricts the search space of a conventional resolution theorem prover. There are, of course,
other resolution strategies that would exclude similar
steps to the ones given below. However, these strategies are not equivalent to our algorithm and do not
exploit features of predicates.

4.1   Example 1: Clause Elimination

The first example shows the kind of resolution steps
that are excluded by checking for knowledge about the
literals they contain. We have chosen arbitrary symbols with no semantics to keep the example as simple
as possible and still show our point. Consider a clause
set with the predicates P, Q, and R, all of which are
unary. Let a and b be two constant symbols of the
domain and let x be a variable. The following clauses
are now to be tested for inconsistency:

```
1  -P(a)
2  +R(b)
3  -P(b), -R(a)
4  -Q(b), -R(b)
5  +Q(x), +R(x)
6  +P(x), +Q(b), -R(x)
7  +P(x), -Q(a), -R(b)
8  +P(x), -Q(x), +R(x)
```

As can be shown, this clause set provides an inconsistent knowledge-base. One poosible proof for this is
the following:

```
 9  -P(b), +Q(a)          3+ 5
10  -Q(b)                 2+ 4
11  +P(x), -R(x)          6+10
12  +P(b)                 2+11
13  +Q(a)                 9+12
14  +P(x), -Q(a), +Q(b)   5+ 7
15  +P(x), -Q(a)          10+14
```

```
16  -Q(a)                 1+15
17  #                     13+16
```

As this is a proof in which every clause generated
is also used, this proof cannot be shortened and our
algorithm does not influence the proof. However, there
are inference steps that are excluded. Let us look at
all posible clauses that can be deduced by resolving
two clauses from (3) to (8), that is, from the original
clauses without the Ground-1-clauses:

```
3+5  -P(b) +Q(a)
3+6  +Q(b) -R(a) -R(b)
3+7  -Q(a) -R(a) -R(b)
3+8  -Q(b) -R(a) +R(b)
4+5  -R(b) +R(b)
4+5  -Q(b) +Q(b)
4+6  +P(x) -R(x) -R(b)
4+8  +P(b) -Q(b)
5+6  +P(x) +Q(b) +Q(x)
5+7  +P(x) +Q(b) -Q(a)
5+8  +P(x) +R(x)
6+8  +P(x) +P(b) +R(x) +R(b)
6+8  +P(x) +Q(b) -Q(x)
7+8  +P(x) +P(b) -Q(a) -Q(b)
```

A specialised reasoner that would eveluate the predicate R for us would know that R(b) must be true. Four
clauses in the above clause-set contain the literal -R(b)
which can be deleted from these clauses. Three of the
newly generated clauses contain +R(b) and can thus be
deleted completely. Of course, both versions of (4+5)
are tautologies anyway, but an algorithm for detecting
whether a clause contains two complementary literals
is expensive compared to evaluating single literals in
frameworks that are specialized on the predicate. Furthermore, the methods do not exclude each other.

4.2   Example 2: Specific Reasoning

The second example is geared towards demonstrating
how the exploitation of specific properties of relations
can speed up the inference process. While the elimination of clauses can be seen as yet another resolution
strategy, the idea here is best seen as compiling parts of
the knowledge-base into more efficient representations.
Let us assume the following simple concept hierarchy:

```
 1  +IsA(Train, Vehicle)
 2  +IsA(InterCity, Train)
 3  +IsA(Bus, Vehicle)
 4  +IsA(Car, Vehicle)
 5  +IsA(VW, Car)
 6  +IsA(VWGolf, VW)
 7  +IsA(Plane, Vehicle)
 8  +IsA(Jet, Plane)
 9  +IsA(Jumbo, Plane)
10  +IsA(Boeing747, Jumbo)
```

What we also know is that the IsA-relation is tran-
sitve, which results in one further clause:

11 -IsA(x, y), -IsA(y, z), +IsA(x, z)

Furthermore we want to assert a few properties of these ojects, namely that trains, busses, and cars can drive while planes can fly:

12 Can(Train, Drive)
13 Can(Bus, Drive)
14 Can(Car, Drive)
15 Can(Plane, Fly)

Finally we want these capabilities of the different vehicles to be inheritable:

16 -Can(y, z), -IsA(x, y), +Can(x, z)

Now, let the query we have to evaluate be whether a VW Golf can drive:

17 -Can(VWGolf, Drive)

With conventional resolution we could unify this query with the inheritance rule and then use the transitivity rule to prove the inconsistency:

18 (16+17)   -Can(y, Drive), -IsA(VWGolf, y)
19 (14+18)   -IsA(VWGolf, Car)
20 (11+19)   -IsA(VWGolf, y), -IsA(y, Car)
21 (5+20)   -IsA(VWGolf, VW)
22 (6+21)   #

Note that this is the shortest possible proof and that no superflous resolution steps are done. If, on the other hand, the concept hierarchy would be left to a specific reasoner then the situation would change as follows. The knowledge-base would be much smaller because the clauses (1) to (11) would not be represented in clause form. Note that this includes the transitivity rule. The resulting proof would look like this:

18 (16+17)   -Can(y, Drive), -IsA(VWGolf, y)
19 (14+18)   #

The first step is the same as in ordinary resolution. However, after resolving (14) and (18) to -IsA(VWGolf, Car) we eliminate this literal and the result is the empty clause. As mentioned above evaluating such a query against an efficient representation can be done in $\mathcal{O}(log_k(n))$ time, i.e. much quicker then resolution or unification.

We have also indicated above that this framework can be extended by introducing the closed world assumption for the specific reasoners. If we would make this assumption for the whole knowledge-base we could, for example, deduce that planes cannot drive. In fact, this piece of knowledge has been left out of the knowledge-base intensionally because whether a plane can drive clearly depends on the definition of drive. Thus, making the closed world assumption would be like asserting that planes cannot drive. However, we would like to be able to infer that a VW is not a train, i.e. we would like to exploit the closed world assumption with respect to the IsA-relation. Evaluating this predicate within a specific reasoner makes this possible.

5 CONCLUSIONS

We have argued that explanation requires fast reasoning over large knowledge- bases. To achieve this we have proposed to extract knowledge that has certain characteristics that allow efficient reasoning into spezialised representations with spezialised reasoning mechanisms. We have then shown how these can be integrated into a general, resolution-based knowledge representation and reasoning framework. The latter we believe gives us a reasonable flexibility for representing arbitrary knowledge.

However, there are problems. The examples given heavily rely on the fact knowledge can be extracted and reasoned over efficiently elsewhere. The queries to the spezialised reasoner were in the form of a singlr literal and this might be too restrictive. While one can see how this can be done for concept hierarchies and the IsA-relation, it is quite different to try to do the same for temporal knowledge. Does this mean that the algorithm above is in fact superfluous? It is certainly true that concept hierarchies are well understood and representations are similar in all systems that use them. This is not true for temporal reasoning to that degree. Our hypothesis is that the better a spcific kind of knowledge is understood, the easier it can be inegrated in the framework described in this paper. Thus, we can achieve more not by trying to improve the basic reasing mechanism (resolution here), but by better understanding specific types of knowledge and inventing representations that can be combined with general reasoners.

REFERENCES

[1] P. Achinstein. *The Nature of Explanation*. Oxford University Press, New York, USA, 1983.

[2] R.J. Brachman and J.G. Schmolze. An Overview of the KL-ONE Knowledge Representation System. *Cognitive Science*, 9(2):171–216, 1985.

[3] Hans-Jürgen Bürckert. A Resolution Principle for Constrained Logics. *Artificial Intelligence*, 66(2):235–271, April 1994.

[4] Jean H. Gallier. *Logic for Computer Science*. Harper and Row, New York, 1986.

[5] Thomas R. Gruber. Toward Principles for the Design of Ontologies Used for Knowledge Sharing. Technical Report KSL 93-04, Knowledge Systems Laboratory, Stanford University, Palo Alto, CA, August 1993.

[6] Nicola Guarino. The Ontological Level. In R. Casati, B. Smith, and G. White, editors, *Philosophy and the Cognitive Sciences*. Hölder-Pichler-Tempsky, Vienna, 1994.

[7] R. V. Guha and D. B. Lenat. Cyc: A Midterm Report. *AI Magazine*, pages 32–59, Fall 1990.

[8] Donald W. Loveland, editor. *Automated Theorem Proving: A Logical Basis*. North-Holland, Amsterdam, 1978.

[9] George A. Miller and Philip N. Johnson-Laird. *Language and Perception*. Cambridge University Press, Cambridge, UK, 1976.

[10] Johanna D. Moore and William R. Swartout. A Reactive Approach to Explanation. In *Proceedings of the eleventh IJCAI*, 1989.

[11] J. A. Robinson. A Machine-Oriented Logic Based on the Resolution Principle. *Journal of the ACM*, 12(1):23–41, January 1965.

[12] Luc Steels. Components of Expertise. *AI Magazine*, 11(2):28–49, Summer 1990.

[13] W. Swartout, C. Paris, and J. Moore. Design for Explainable Expert Systems. *IEEE Expert*, 6(3):58–64, June 1991.

[14] William R. Swartout. Knowledge Needed for Expert System Explanation. *Future Computing Systems*, 1(2):99–114, 1986.

[15] Christoph Walther. A Mnay-sorted Calculus Based on Resolution and Paramodulation. In *Proceedings of the IJCAI 83*, pages 882–891, 1983.

[16] Gerhard Wickler, Helen Chappel, and Simon Lambert. An Architecture for a Generic Explanation Component. In Michael R. Wick, editor, *The IJCAI Workshop on Explanation and Problem Solving*, pages 53–64, University of Wisconsin – Eau Claire, WI, August 1993.

[17] Gerhard Wickler and Myles Chippendale. Representing conceptual structure in predicate logic. In *Conceptual Structures Workshop*, Armidale, Australia, November 1994.

[18] Bob Wielinga and Joost Breuker. Models of Expertise. In *Proceedings of the 7th ECAI*, pages 306–318, Brighton, 1986.

[19] William A. Woods. Beyond Ignorance-Based Systems (invited talk). In J. Doyle, E. Sandewall, and P. Torasso, editors, *Principles of Knowledge Representation and Reasoning*, page 646. Morgan Kaufmann, May 1994.

Scalability of the Performance
of Knowledge Representation Systems

Piet-Hein Speel,* **Frank van Raalte**, **Paul E. van der Vet** and **Nicolaas J.I. Mars**

University of Twente
Enschede, the Netherlands
{speel,vraalte,vet,mars}@cs.utwente.nl

ABSTRACT

We have experimentally compared runtime and memory usage performance as a function of size of the knowledge base for four knowledge representation systems of the KL-ONE family: BACK, BACK++, CLASSIC, and LOOM. We have measured performance for loading and classifying progressively larger synthetic knowledge bases. The knowledge bases have been prepared automatically following a pattern identified for a particular application. Terminological knowledge bases in isolation, combined terminological/assertional knowledge bases, and mainly assertional knowledge bases have been studied up to hitherto unrivalled sizes. The results show that BACK++ performs well for terminological knowledge bases, and LOOM and CLASSIC perform well for mainly assertional knowledge bases. None of the systems studied is able to load and classify combined terminological/assertional knowledge bases with sizes corresponding to about 400 input documents for the knowledge extraction application.

1 SETTING AND SCOPE

We have carried out experiments aimed at finding out how certain knowledge representation systems of the KL-ONE family perform in terms of runtime and memory usage when the knowledge bases get large. It gives experimentally determined figures for runtime and memory usage performance of four knowledge representation systems as a function of the sizes of the knowledge bases involved. The four systems are: BACK version 5.1.3; BACK++ version November 1993; CLAS-

SIC version 2.2; and LOOM version 2.1. This investigation is part of a Ph.D. thesis project done by one of us. It is aimed at developing systematic ways for selecting a knowledge representation system given a specification of the knowledge of the application domain in the form of a conceptualisation, *i.e.*, at the knowledge level [28].

In the following sections we will provide background on KL-ONE-like knowledge representation systems, complexity analysis, and the aim of the present experiment. Subsequent sections describe the experiment itself and its results.

2 KL-ONE-LIKE KNOWLEDGE REPRESENTATION SYSTEMS

KL-ONE stands for a large family of knowledge representation languages, often called *description logics* (hence DLs), and associated implementations, called knowledge representation systems (hence KRSs) here. The languages combine the structured, graphical representations of semantic nets and the formal properties of logics. KL-ONE-like KRSs have become increasingly popular in recent years and many small-scale applications have been built. Detailed descriptions of DLs and the associated KRSs are given in [4], [22], [23], and [33]; see also the special issue of the *SIGART Bulletin* (vol. 2, no. 3, 1991) on implemented knowledge representation and reasoning systems. For background information on the KRSs studied here, see [26] on BACK; [7] on CLASSIC; and [15] and [16] on LOOM. BACK++ is largely a C++ implementation of BACK (which is implemented in Prolog).

KRSs based on the KL-ONE paradigm as described in [8] store knowledge in an object-centered and declarative way. Central notions are *individuals*, *concepts*, standing for classes of individuals, and *roles*, standing for properties (relations between individuals). A compositional semantics is assigned to the terms of

---

* Beginning April 1, 1995, Piet-Hein Speel works for Unilever Research Laboratory, Vlaardingen, the Netherlands.

these languages in a standard model-theoretic way [1, 25]. Subsumption of concepts, determination of the concept of which an individual is an instance, and inheritance of properties can be computed on the basis of structured descriptions of concepts and individuals. KRSs based on DLs are able to automatically classify descriptions of concepts and individuals in a taxonomy.

In the KL-ONE tradition, the knowledge base is divided into a *terminological part* that stores concepts and roles and an *assertional part* that stores knowledge in the form of assertions about individuals. The ability to distinguish between terminological knowledge (concerned with correct usage of technical terms) and assertional knowledge (concerned with correct theories about the domain) has been an important incentive for developing KL-ONE [5].

3 COMPUTATIONAL COMPLEXITY ANALYSIS

Computational complexity analysis is concerned with estimating a system's performance in terms of runtime and memory usage. Often, the estimate is given as a function of the size of the problem space so that scalability can be judged. For general discussions, see for instance [9] and [13].

There are many ways to arrive at an estimate of performance. An important distinction, not often made, is that between performance of an algorithm and that of a program.

One method, usually called *worst-case analysis*, analytically investigates the problem to yield an expression for the performance of the best algorithm on the worst case. This gives rise to the well-known classification of problems into decidable and undecidable problems, and, if decidable, into the complexity classes $\mathcal{P}$ (polynomial), $\mathcal{E}$ (exponential), and $\mathcal{NP}$ (non-deterministic polynomial). The class $\mathcal{P}$ is commonly called that of *tractable* problems; the other problems are called *intractable*.

For many practical applications, however, worst-case analysis does not produce a fair estimate. Apart from the fact that it gives results for algorithms rather than programs, it is also very often found that worst cases occur either not at all or very seldom. A telling example is the Simplex algorithm in linear programming ([13], pp. 172–173). The algorithm can be shown to have a worst-case runtime complexity of $O(n^m)$, with n the number of variables and $m - 1$ the number of constraint equations. In actual practice, even with problems as large $n = 40,000$ and $m = 1000$, runtime complexity has never exceeded $O(n^3)$. Similarly, the satisfiability problem is known to be in $\mathcal{NP}$-complete. This means that, assuming $\mathcal{P} \neq \mathcal{NP}$, the best algorithm has exponential complexity. However, in actual fact exponential cases are sparse and most cases run in polynomial time [10].

Instead of worst cases, *normal cases* can be considered.[1] These normal cases are created by the formulation of particular assumptions which exclude *abnormal* cases. Within these assumptions, then, worst-case analysis can be performed. If adequate assumptions are formulated, the actual performance for applications is closely related to the normal-case performance, and will not exceed the normal-case performance. In CLASSIC, for example, normal-case analysis has been used, based on the assumptions that expanding concepts does not significantly increase the size of a KB, and that the size of role hierarchies are small.

Average-case performance estimates can be obtained analytically or empirically. Analytical methods might try to characterise average cases and add this knowledge to the problem formulation. Then, complexity measures can be calculated by employing statistics to average over a number of cases. The alternative is empirical determination: select a system, implement the application, and run it. The empirical evaluation constitutes the only way to arrive at an unadulterated estimate of a program's performance. One of the problems of empirical studies is that it is often hard to tell how representative the application is.

There is consensus that analytical and empirical studies complement each other, and that many empirical studies are needed to arrive at a satisfactory picture.

4 PERFORMANCE OF KL-ONE-LIKE KRSS

Worst-case analyses of KL-ONE-like KRSs have a tradition that goes back to the early work on KL-ONE itself [6]. On the basis of such work, Brachman and Levesque [14] formulated the meanwhile well-known conjecture that runtime increases as expressiveness increases. The worst-case runtime performance of the main algorithm of KL-ONEs, the subsumption determination algorithm, depends on the expressiveness of the language. It is undecidable for certain variants [24,27] and intractable for others [21]. As a result of these analyses, systems have been realised with restricted expressive power and tractable subsumption. CLASSIC largely follows this approach [2,3] and is among the KRSs studied here.

However, the apparent attraction of worst-case analyses has not led to an equally voluminous literature on average-case analysis. In particular, there is to date only one empirical study of performance of KL-ONEs. We will refer to this study as the DFKI experiment; see [11] and [12] for details. This experiment measured runtime performance of six real terminological knowledge bases that were offered by their developers, with sizes ranging from 100 to 400 concepts and

---

[1]This information has been obtained via personal communications with Peter F. Patel-Schneider.

expressed in six different DLs. Additionally, the experiment measured runtime performance for synthetic terminological knowledge bases with up to 5,000 concepts that were constructed by random generation of concepts, using guidelines obtained by analysis of the real knowledge bases. The researchers found that size and structure of the knowledge base can significantly influence performance and that there can be considerable differences between different KRSs. In fact, on occasion the difference between the slowest and fastest systems became approximately a factor 1,000.

There are various reasons to perform an experiment resembling the DFKI experiment anew:

1. There is the simple reason that, pending a good method to determine how representative any particular application is, we learn from measuring performance for many different cases.

2. The largest KB studied in the DFKI experiment is still quite small compared to what certain applications require in practice.

3. The DFKI experiment only studied terminological KBs, while assertional KBs will be at least as important for applications.

4. The DFKI experiment did not measure memory usage. Memory usage may become a problem when the knowledge bases get large.

5. The DFKI experiment did not measure time needed for answering queries.

6. Many KRSs studied in the DFKI experiment have been superseded by newer versions.

For these reasons, we have performed a variant on the DFKI experiment.

5 CONTEXT OF THE EXPERIMENT

The experiments reported here have been carried out in the context of the Plinius research project. Plinius aims at developing a semi-automatic system for knowledge extraction from natural-language texts. The texts involved are abstracts of primary literature on mechanical properties of ceramic materials. They are collected in a pre-determined corpus. An ontology for the domain was available. Details on the Plinius project in general [19,20,29] and on the ontology [17,18,30,31,32] are given elsewhere. The knowledge bases used for the present experiment mimic the output of the Plinius system in a way that will be described below. If the output is stored in a KRS of the KL-ONE family, it will be an assertional knowledge base with an associated terminological knowledge base that can be considered the representation of the ontology.

One of the problems that has to be addressed in the context of Plinius is the choice of a KRS to hold

the output. Runtime and memory usage performance are among the factors to be considered. The output is expected to become voluminous when the Plinius system is able to process the whole corpus, and it will become even larger when (as we intend to do in the future) supersets of the corpus are processed.

The conceptual structures defined by the ontology and subsequently represented in the knowledge representation languages considered here are such, that an estimate of the sizes of Plinius output cannot be produced by simple multiplication of the counts for a small sample. Redundancy occurs in a number of ways. We have to go into some detail about the ontology here; see also [28] for details on the way these concepts are represented in DLs.

The Plinius ontology consists of atomic concepts and construction rules for all other concepts. These other concepts are called complex concepts in the present context. Where the ontology defines every complex concept implicitly, a complex concept has to occur explicitly in the terminological knowledge base if the concept or an individual that is an instance of the concept has to be stored in the assertional knowledge base. The first form of redundancy occurs when individuals generated by processing one or more abstracts are instances of the same concept. The second form of redundancy is a consequence of the way the ontology is organised. Complex concepts are defined in terms of atomic concepts and/or other complex concepts. Redundancies occur when a particular concept is used to define a number of other concepts.

For obvious reasons we have not attempted to exhaustively count all concepts and individuals that occur in the Plinius corpus. Instead, we have analysed a sample of ten documents and manually constructed the output Plinius is required to generate if it processes these documents. We counted 355 concepts, of which 137 occurrences are unique. The output consists of 173 assertions (many of which serve to introduce individuals). The results have been used to establish what will be called a *redundancy pattern* for the corpus as a whole. The sizes of the output knowledge bases estimated on the basis of this redundancy pattern are smaller than those obtained by simple multiplication. On the other hand, redundancy will occur more often in larger samples. Therefore, the estimates based on the redundancy pattern are pessimistic.

Sizes of the knowledge bases have been expressed in two ways. The primary measure is number of terms, where 'terms' embrace concepts, roles and auxiliary individuals for terminological knowledge bases, and individuals for assertional knowledge bases. The other measure is number of documents. The (non-linear) relation between the two is given by the redundancy pattern. To give an example, the whole current corpus of 400 documents is expected to lead to a terminological knowledge base containing 14,000 terms and additionally an assertional knowledge base with 7,000 terms.

6 OVERVIEW OF THE EXPERIMENT

The experiment was designed to find out the runtime and memory usage performance as a function of the size of the knowledge bases in a comparison between four KRSs: BACK, BACK++, CLASSIC, and LOOM. Both terminological knowledge bases on their own and combinations of terminological and assertional knowledge bases have been tested. The knowledge bases involved have been made progressively larger. Runtime and memory usage have been measured each time in absolute quantities (seconds and kilobytes).

Performance has been measured for one tell operation and for three ask operations. The tell operation was 'load'. All KRSs studied here perform classification when they load a knowledge base. Therefore, the 'load' experiments measure performance of loading and classifying the knowledge base. These measurements are the subject of the rest of this paper.

The results for the ask operations can be summarised here. They queried: (i) the subconcepts of a given concept; (ii) the instances of a concept; and (iii) the fillers of a role of an individual. Memory usage has not been determined for ask operations as they assume the presence of a loaded knowledge base. All KRSs studied answered queries within a few hundreds of seconds with the exception of LOOM that on occasion took over a minute to retrieve all instances of a given concept from a knowledge base containing about 13,000 terms. Ask operations are not discussed further here.

The knowledge bases have been constructed synthetically in a way that will be explained below. The representations in the various KRSs have been chosen such that they only use constructions that are available in each of the systems. This ensures a good comparison, but each individual system might have performed better if optimal descriptions (using locally available constructions) had been used.

7 SETUP OF THE EXPERIMENT

7.1 Preparation of the knowledge bases

The Plinius project has not progressed to the point that large output knowledge bases are actually available. Moreover, we want the present research to help us select an appropriate KRS for holding that knowledge; we want to prevent problems rather than fix them as they occur.

Since the actual knowledge bases were not available, they had to be constructed. This has been done in three steps, of which the first two are common to every experiment. The first step consisted of manual implementation of a common core. In the sec-

ond step, a number of manually constructed auxiliary terms needed for representing the terminological knowledge bases was added.

In the report of results and their discussion below, we have collected the first and second steps under the heading of "Preparatory actions".

For the third step, the redundancy pattern has been used to automatically generate synthetic knowledge bases on top of the core ontology and auxiliary concepts. At this stage, all concepts, roles, individuals, and (where applicable) assertions are generated randomly but obeying the redundancy pattern. Since runtime performance does not depend on the actual concepts but rather on matters such as structure and the redundancy pattern, synthetic knowledge bases provide adequate objects for experimental investigation.

Three series of synthetic knowledge bases have been generated.

Series A Terminological knowledge bases.

Series B Terminological knowledge bases and assertional knowledge bases combined.

Series C Assertional knowledge bases that use a terminological knowledge base generated for the equivalent of 20 documents.

Each series consists of a number of knowledge bases with sizes that grow in discrete steps. Performance was measured for each knowledge base. The synthetic knowledge bases have in fact been generated and subjected to the experiments by a program that also collected the data and stored them in a file. In this manner, a whole suit could be performed in batch mode.

7.2 Technical setup

The four KRSs used were run on a single Sun SPARCsystem 10, Model 40, with 64 MB RAM. The operating system used was SunOS 4.1.3. The size of virtual memory was 137 MB. In cases where memory limits were reached, the virtual memory was extended by 100 Mb by using the operating system facility to swap on regular files. This extension, however, slightly influenced the runtime performance negatively. All knowledge bases were loaded from local disk to minimise influences from network loads caused by foreign processes.

BACK version 5.1.3 was received as Prolog code. It was run under Quintus Prolog version 3.1.4. The `statistics` predicate of Quintus Prolog was used to measure both runtime and memory usage. Runtime is that used by Prolog. Memory embraces program space and global and local stack memory. The represented knowledge is stored in program space.

The BACK++ system, version November 1993, consists of a core, originally written in C++, and a Prolog interface called PLBACK++. We received the core as an executable. PLBACK++ was run under Quintus Prolog version 3.1.4. The `statistics` predicate was used to measure runtime performance. It could not, however, be used to measure memory usage as it returns only memory used by Prolog processes. Since the represented knowledge in BACK++ is stored in C++ space, the C library function `mallinfo` (in particular `int uordbytes`) was used to measure allocated memory space (including overhead). The function `mallinfo` is part of the general-purpose memory allocation package `malloc`. The allocated memory space includes the storage of data structures.

CLASSIC version 2.2 and LOOM version 2.1 were both received as Common Lisp code. They were compiled with Sun Common Lisp (Lucid) version 4.1.1 in 'production mode'.[2] Production mode compiles slowly but produces very efficient code. For instance, efficiency gains of over 30% were achieved for CLASSIC.

The Common Lisp functions `time` and `room` have been used to measure runtime and memory usage in the CLASSIC and LOOM runs These functions are implementation-dependent. For Sun Common Lisp, `time` measures total CPU time, which is the sum of CPU time to execute the process and CPU time spent by the operating system. As regards memory usage, the Sun Common Lisp memory includes a dynamic area divided into two semi-spaces of equal size. One semi-space holds the data, the other is reserved for garbage collection. The Sun Common Lisp `room` function measures the size of the occupied semi-space holding the data, after calling both an ephemeral and a dynamic garbage collection.

In the CLASSIC and LOOM runs, the 137 MB virtual memory was controlled by issuing the Sun Common Lisp command `change-memory-management` to alter growth limit and growth rate. Only approximately 60 MB could be used for each semi-space of the dynamic area. Since the memory space available turned out to be too limited, the virtual memory was expanded by another 100 Mb when necessary. In this environment, a maximum of approximately 110 Mb was allocated for each semi-space of the dynamic area.

Loading and classifying a knowledge base is integrated in a single command for all KRSs. In the LOOM runs, a single `tellm` construct was added at the end of each knowledge base to update its state.

In each case except BACK++, preparation of the systems for the experiments uncovered bugs. Often, debugging and adaptation had to run over several cycles before the system was fit for experimentation. This shows that the systems in case are still somewhat unstable.

---

[2]This mode has been set by the command
`(proclaim '(optimize (speed 3) (safety 1) (compilation-speed 0)))`

7.3 Interpretation of the results

The technical setup of the experiments makes comparison of the results tricky. There are three reasons to approach the matter with caution.

(a) Comparability of actual measurement results. It is not clear that the time and memory usage statistics that have been collected indeed refer to the same quantities. In particular, it is doubtful whether the Prolog, Lisp and C++ results are directly comparable. Even the official system administrator's documentation is not completely clear on this matter.

Therefore, we performed a small experiment in which we compared these language-specific statistics with an unbiased judge: Unix. We loaded Plinius synthetic terminological and assertional knowledge bases for the equivalent of 10, 20, 60, 100 and 140 Plinius documents and measured the runtime and memory usage according to the previous descriptions. In addition, we used Unix commands `time` and `ps SZ` in this experiment for comparisons purposes.

We conclude that the Common Lisp runtime measures correspond to Unix measures within dozens of seconds and that Prolog measures correspond to the user time of the Unix measures. For BACK++, this is not a real problem since the system time does not exceed the dozens of seconds. In BACK, system time forms a substantial part of the overall runtime. Therefore, we conclude that runtime measures to load large knowledge bases in BACK++, CLASSIC and LOOM are comparable within minutes. Compared to these measures, one should be aware that substantial system time measures are *not* contained in the runtime measures of BACK presented in the following sections.

Since we are interested in *used* memory space and not in *allocated* memory space, we conclude that Unix command `ps SZ` is not useful. The Quintus Prolog `statistics` predicate and the Common Lisp `room` function are suitable for measuring used memory space in BACK, CLASSIC and LOOM. In BACK++, we measured allocated memory space. This means that actual used memory in BACK++ might be less than the measures presented in the following section. Note that due to our choice for measuring used memory space, the information for BACK, CLASSIC and LOOM presented in the following sections cannot be directly used to determine the required memory sizes of the computer to be used.

(b) Completeness of the inferences. Subsumption determination in BACK, BACK++ and LOOM is incomplete, while in CLASSIC, it is complete with respect to a variant semantics (3). One expects negative results for CLASSIC relative to a KRS with comparable computational complexity but incomplete subsumption. It probably takes more time and memory to compute and store all inferences rather than a subset of them.

Whether completeness matters, depends entirely on

the application. Any inference not computed by a KRS with incomplete subsumption may be immaterial for the application at hand or perhaps be computed at query time by the application program. This issue cannot be addressed here; it has to be taken into account when developing a concrete application.

(c) Soundness. The performance differences found by us might in part be attributed to erroneous behaviour. To give a drastic and fictitious example, a KRS may outperform all others on loading and classifying a terminological knowledge base because it simply subsumes each concept under the root concept and leaves it at that. Checking soundness of a program (as opposed to soundness of an algorithm), however, is a time-consuming activity. Worse, it can only guarantee soundness with respect to the test suites used to do the checking.

For these experiments, we have assumed that the KRS developers themselves have made sure that their programs are sufficiently sound. Just to be on the safe side, we have checked the correctness of the results of the three ask operations (see section 6). They are correct for all experiments, but this cannot be interpreted as a warrant for overall correctness.

8 PREPARATORY ACTIONS

8.1 Results

For each run, the core ontology and auxiliary terms had to be loaded first. As a result, many performance measurements could be carried out.

Ontology variant	concepts defined	primitive	roles	individuals
Ont.A	10	125	38	0
Ont.B	117	18	39	0

Table 1: Numbers of terms used to represent the core ontology using common constructions available in all four DLs. Two variants of the core ontology have been compared: "Ont.A" is the variant with primitive concepts for chemical elements, "Ont.B" the variant with defined concepts for chemical elements.

For the core ontology, two variants have been compared. One had primitive concepts for chemical elements, as in the ontology itself. For the other variant, chemical elements have been re-defined. The opportunity is in fact offered by consensus knowledge in chemistry, where a chemical element (or kind of atoms) can be characterised by its so-called atomic number (number of protons in the atomic nucleus). Pursuing this option turns chemical elements into defined concepts. In KL-ONE terms, the concept chemical element has a role atomic number that can be filled by exactly one natural number in the interval [1,106]. Each subconcept corresponds to a particular chemical element and has the atomic number-role filled.

DL	Ontology with def. CE		
	time (sec.)		mem (Kb)
BACK	39.2	(±0.8)	465
BACK++	61.04	(±0.06)	520
CLASSIC	2.6	(±0.12)	320
LOOM	13.5	(±0.6)	596
DL	Ontology with prim. CE		
	time (sec.)		mem (Kb)
BACK	109	(±1)	857
BACK++	12.82	(±0.09)	1048
CLASSIC	1.9	(±0.1)	304
LOOM	6.0	(±0.3)	403

Table 2: Time and space used to load and classify the core ontology knowledge base. The two variants are as described in the main text. The deviation of the memory usage was 0 Kb in all cases.

See table 1 for the sizes of the two variants. Table 2 gives performance results, averaged over all runs with standard deviation specified. For all other experiments, the variant with defined concepts for chemical elements has been used.

DL	Auxiliary terms		
	time (sec.)		mem (Kb)
BACK	203	(±3)	1138
BACK++	2.91	(±0.03)	150
CLASSIC	0.31	(±0.01)	25
LOOM	4.9	(±0.4)	203

Table 3: Performance of loading and classifying the auxiliary terms (second step). The deviation of the memory usage was 0 Kb in all cases.

For the second step, a knowledge base of 124 auxiliary terms (7 defined concepts, 108 roles, and 9 individuals) was loaded. The performance results, again averaged over all runs with standard deviation specified, are collected in table 3.

8.2 Discussion

Most of the results speak for themselves. The deviant behaviour of BACK++ for the core ontology with defined chemical element concepts (61 seconds) is probably due to the fact that it inefficiently handles concrete individuals used as fillers of the atomic number role. One indication that supports this is that BACK++ needs less than two seconds to load and classify a core ontology without chemical elements.

The large difference between BACK's performance for the core ontology with primitive chemical element concepts (109 seconds) can be attributed to the fact that the system uses concept negation constructs to represent disjointness between primitive concepts. As a result, primitively defined chemical elements have to be introduced using progressively larger negation constructs, for 106 elements a total of $\sum_{n=1}^{105} n = 5565$. BACK++ in fact has the same problem, but it is apparently able to process the negations in ten seconds.

For the second step, only the disappointing performance of BACK is remarkable. We found that BACK needs about 14 seconds to load and classify the auxiliary terms without certain subroles. It is therefore probable that BACK's performance is caused by inefficient manipulation of subroles.

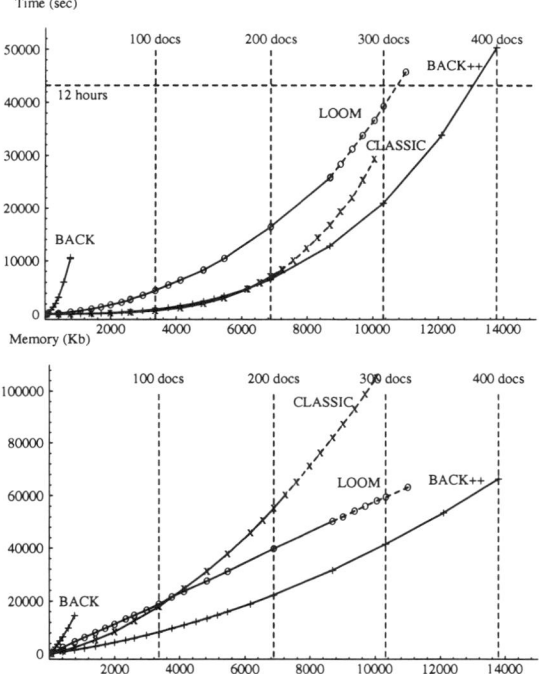

Figure 1: Performance for loading and classifying synthetic terminological knowledge bases up to 14,000 terms (series A). Solid lines indicate results obtained with the original 137 MB virtual memory. The dashed lines indicate continuation of the experiments with additional 100 MB virtual memory, see the main text.

9 SERIES A: TERMINOLOGICAL KNOWLEDGE BASES

9.1 Results

A series of progressively larger synthetic terminological knowledge bases was loaded and classified on top of the core ontology and auxiliary terms. The results of

this series are distributed over two figures for clarity. Figure 1 gives all results, while figure 2 (giving the results for sizes up to 5,000 terms) is included to make certain details in that region visible.

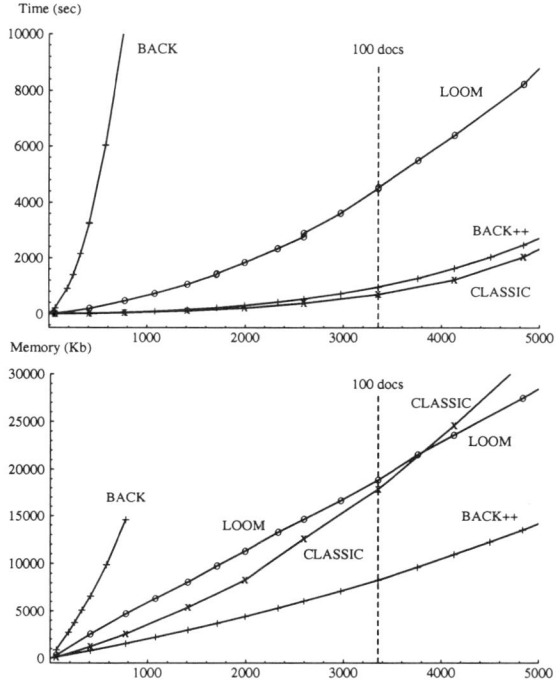

Figure 2: Detailed view of the first range included in figure 1 (series A). This figure shows performance for loading and classifying synthetic terminological knowledge bases up to 5,000 terms.

We intended to stop increasing the knowledge bases at the limit of 14,000 terms (which is the estimated equivalent of 400 documents). This worked for BACK++, but for the other KRSs we had to stop earlier for various reasons.

At sizes of > 500 terms, BACK's behaviour became unpredictable. It sometimes stopped with the Prolog answer read_stopped and ran on in other cases. We have not been able to find out what went wrong. Whatever the cause, the BACK experiments have been discontinued at that point.

For CLASSIC and LOOM the 60 MB virtual memory available for data was insufficient to continue the experiments. CLASSIC reached the limit for knowledge bases of about 7,000 terms, LOOM for those of about 8,500 terms. We were able to continue the experiments with CLASSIC by making an extra 100 MB virtual memory available. Under those conditions, the CLASSIC experiments could then be continued to sizes of about 10,000 terms, when the new limit was reached. For

LOOM, knowledge bases of about 11,000 terms could be loaded in about 12 hours. Then we were forced to stop experimenting due to local problems. Since swapping on files is somewhat slower than swapping on block devices, extending virtual memory this way will negatively affect runtime performance. The results for these extended experiments have been marked as such in the figures.

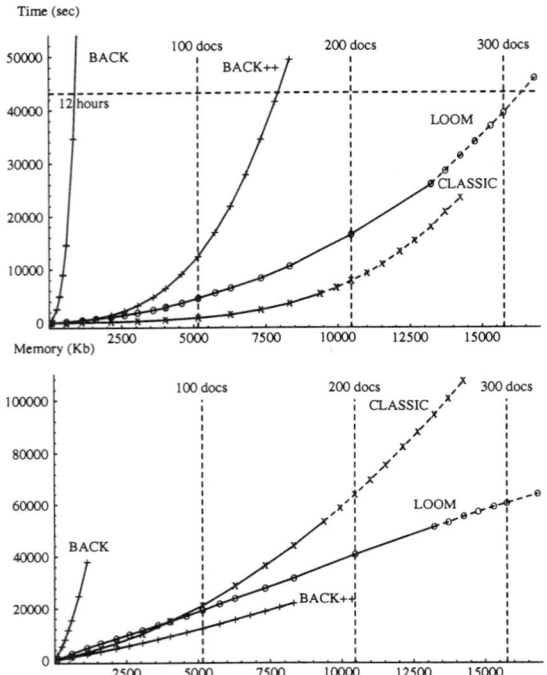

Figure 3: Performance results for loading and classifying combined terminological/assertional knowledge bases (series B). The dashed lines indicate continuation of the experiments with additional 100 MB virtual memory.

9.2 Discussion

As stated above, BACK's performance became unpredictable when the size of the knowledge base exceeded about 500 terms. The results show that, even if performance could have been determined above that limit, BACK is decidedly outperformed by all other KRSs. As regards runtime, CLASSIC is the winner until about 6,000 terms, while BACK++ is faster for larger knowledge bases. The memory usage performance results indicate that CLASSIC runs into memory trouble for larger knowledge bases. For experiments with CLASSIC loading and classifying knowledge bases $> 7,000$ terms we had to extend the original virtual memory of 137 MB as described above. Very quickly, even this

proved insufficient. Memory usage of LOOM showed a satisfactory development. BACK++ in fact shows outstanding memory usage performance.

10 SERIES B: COMBINED TERMINOLOGICAL AND ASSERTIONAL KNOWLEDGE BASES

10.1 Results

A series of progressively larger synthetic knowledge bases composed of combined terminological and assertional parts was loaded and classified on top of the core ontology and auxiliary terms. The sizes have been increased until about 17,000 terms. The results are given in figure 3.

The limit of 17,000 terms is lower than the size of the estimated equivalent of 400 documents, which is 20,000 terms. As in series A, we have used enlarged virtual memory for CLASSIC and LOOM. The BACK experiments had to be stopped because the unpredictability found in series A showed up here, too. The BACK++ experiments were stopped when the trend was obvious.

10.2 Discussion

None of the KRSs studies proved able to load and classify the estimated equivalent of 400 documents within system limits. BACK's performance is similar to that for series A. CLASSIC again runs into memory problems, while LOOM's memory usage is an almost linear function of the number of terms (at least, for the range studied). In contrast to what was seen for series A, BACK++ is outperformed by both CLASSIC and LOOM in terms of runtime. Apparently, some construction present in assertions but absent or sparse in terminological knowledge is responsible. We suspect concrete individuals to be the culprit; they caused trouble in the preparatory actions, too, and occur very frequently in assertions. In contrast, BACK++ outperformed both CLASSIC and LOOM in terms of memory usage.

11 SERIES C: ASSERTIONAL KNOWLEDGE BASES WITH SMALL TERMINOLOGICAL COUNTERPARTS

11.1 Results

For the final series, we wanted to take a closer look at the performance for assertional knowledge bases. We generated a synthetic terminological knowledge base for the estimated equivalent of 20 documents (a bit under 800 terms). We then generated progressively larger synthetic assertional knowledge bases on top of the core ontology, the auxiliary terms, and the small terminological knowledge base. We stopped the CLASSIC experiments at the point where the program crashed

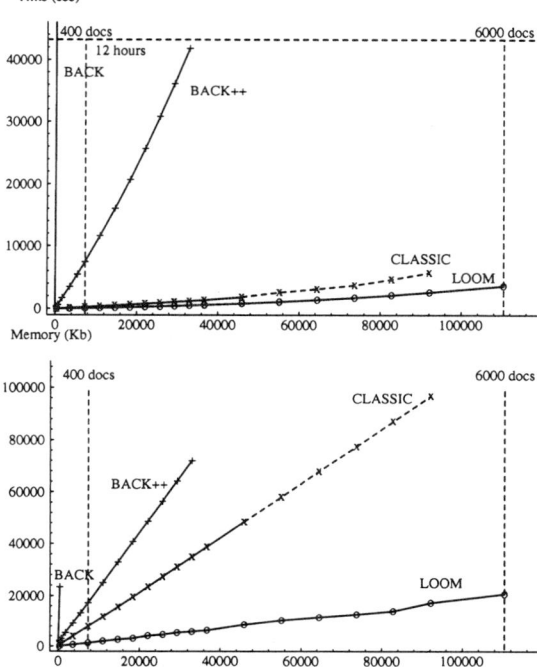

Figure 4: Performance results for combinations of a fixed, small terminological knowledge base and progressively larger assertional knowledge bases (series C). The dashed lines indicate continuation of the experiments with additional 100 MB virtual memory.

due to memory problems, and the BACK++ experiments at the point where the trend became obvious. The LOOM experiments could be continued to sizes up to 110,000 terms in the assertional knowledge base, which is the estimated equivalent of 6,000 documents. We probably could have gone even further. BACK's performance is similar to that for series A and B. The results are given in figure 4.

11.2 Discussion

The results of series B, where BACK++ was outperformed by CLASSIC and LOOM in terms of runtime, are found repeated here. In addition, also in terms of memory usage, BACK++ was outperformed by CLASSIC and LOOM. CLASSIC again runs into memory problems but is able to handle assertional knowledge bases > 90,000 terms in the system environment used by us. LOOM's behaviour is remarkably constant in the range studied here. Both runtime and memory usage are slowly rising and approximately linear functions of the number of terms. It takes LOOM a bit over an hour and about 20 MB of memory to load and classify an assertional knowledge base of 110,000 terms, a result that can be

called outstanding.

12   CONCLUDING REMARKS

In a series of experiments we have compared runtime and memory usage performance of four KL-ONE-like KRSs, BACK, BACK++, CLASSIC, and LOOM. None of the KRSs proved able to load and classify a combined terminological/assertional knowledge base with a size that is the estimated equivalent of 400 documents. BACK runs into trouble even for relatively small knowledge bases and appears unsuitable for large knowledge bases. BACK++ performs very well for terminological knowledge bases, but is outperformed by others when assertions are to be stored as well. For the remaining two KRSs, CLASSIC's memory problems make it appear unsuitable in the system environment used here for applications that require more than 14,000 terms in a combined terminological/assertional knowledge base or more than 90,000 terms for a mainly assertional knowledge base. Where CLASSIC can be used, it outperforms LOOM as regards runtime for combined terminological/assertional knowledge bases. LOOM is the better of the two for mainly assertional knowledge bases, where it in fact shows outstanding performance.

The inability of all KRSs studied here to load and classify large combined terminological/assertional knowledge bases is a point of concern not only for the Plinius application but also for other applications that require large combined knowledge bases. We expect that most knowledge bases in scientific and engineering domains fall in this category. Evidently, something needs to be done to make the KRSs studied here suitable for such applications. Two options can be pursued.

One option is to pay attention to the internal working of the systems to increase performance. For example, the comparison of CLASSIC and LOOM can be interpreted as showing that CLASSIC's memory performance might be significantly increased. Another example is BACK++. Our tentative diagnosis of its disappointing performance in series B and C blames inefficient handling of concrete individuals. If this is fixed, BACK++ might outperform the other KRSs studied by us.

Another option in fact abandons the idea of storing all knowledge into a single knowledge base altogether. The alternative would be to investigate control structures able to make use of several knowledge bases. This option might be preferable for the very large knowledge bases that may be needed for or produced by particular applications. Take knowledge extraction systems. The knowledge bases built in the course of the experiments of series B constitute a fair approximation of the knowledge bases generated by such systems. The results of series B indicate that storing the output of knowledge extraction from whole volumes of bibliographic databases might pose insurmountable problems. We had to stop the experiments of series B at a point way just over 300 documents. For comparison, the bibliographic database from which we have taken our corpus grows by 20,000 documents descriptions annually, and must be called small. There are bibliographic databases that grow by a quarter million documents descriptions each year.

ACKNOWLEDGMENT

We would like to thank the developers of the KL-ONE knowledge representation systems BACK, BACK++, CLASSIC, and LOOM for providing us their systems and for their support. In addition, we would like to thank Wim Vossebelt for developing the generators creating the Plinius synthetic knowledge bases.

REFERENCES

[1] Franz Baader, Hans-Jürgen Bürckert, Jochen Heinsohn, Bernhard Hollunder, Jürgen Müller, Bernhard Nebel, Werner Nutt & Hans-Jürgen Profitlich, "Terminological knowledge representation: a proposal for a terminological logic," in *Proceedings of the International Workshop on Terminological Logics, SchloßDagstuhl, Germany, May 6–8, 1991*, Institut für Wissensbasierte Systeme, Wissenschaftliches Zentrum, IBM Deutschland, Stuttgart, Germany, 1991, 120–128, also appeared as KIT-Report 89, Technische Universität Berlin, Berlin, Germany.

[2] Alexander Borgida, Ronald J. Brachman, Deborah L. McGuinness & Lori Alperin Resnick, "CLASSIC: a structural data model for objects," in *Proceedings of ACM-SIGMOD 1989 International Conference on Management of Data, Portland, OR, May 31–June 2, 1989*, James Clifford, Bruce Lindsay & David Maier, eds., ACM Press, New York, NY, 1989, 58–67, (also appeared as ACM SIGMOD Record, 18, 2, June, 1989).

[3] Alexander Borgida & Peter F. Patel-Schneider, "A semantics and complete algorithm for subsumption in the CLASSIC description logic," *Journal of Artificial Intelligence Research* 1 (1994), 277–308.

[4] Ronald J. Brachman, "A structural paradigm for representing knowledge," Bolt Beranek and Newman Inc., BBN Report No. 3605, Cambridge, MA, 1978, revised version of Brachman's Ph.D. thesis, Harvard University, 1977.

[5] Ronald J. Brachman & Hector J. Levesque, "Competence in knowledge representation," in *Proceedings National Conference on Artificial Intelligence, Pittsburgh, PE, 18–20 August 1982*, American Association for Artificial Intelligence, 1982, 189–192.

[6] Ronald J. Brachman & Hector J. Levesque, "The tractability of subsumption in frame-based description languages," in *Proceedings National Conference on Artificial Intelligence, Austin, TX, 6–10 August 1984*, William Kaufmann, Los Altos, CA, 1984, 34–37.

[7] Ronald J. Brachman, Deborah L. McGuinness, Peter F. Patel-Schneider, Lori Alperin Resnick & Alexander Borgida, "Living with CLASSIC: when and how to use a KL-ONE-like language," in *Principles of semantic networks: explorations in the representation of knowledge*, John F. Sowa, ed., The Morgan Kaufmann series in representation and reasoning, Morgan Kaufmann Publishers, Inc., San Mateo, CA, 1991, 401–456.

[8] Ronald J. Brachman & James G. Schmolze, "An overview of the KL-ONE knowledge representation system," *Cognitive Science* 9 (1985), 171–216.

[9] Michael R. Garey & David S. Johnson, *Computers and intractability: a guide to the theory of NP-completeness*, A series of books in the mathematical sciences, W. H. Freeman and Company, New York, 1979.

[10] A. Goldberg, "Average complexity of the satisfiability problem," in *Proceedings of the Fourth Workshop on Automated Deduction*, W.S. Joyner, ed., Austin, TX, 1979, 1–6.

[11] Jochen Heinsohn, Daniel Kudenko, Bernhard Nebel & Hans-Jürgen Profitlich, "An empirical analysis of terminological representation systems," in *Proceedings Tenth National Conference on Artificial Intelligence, July 12–16, 1992*, AAAI Press/MIT Press, Menlo Park, CA, 1992, 767–773, also as DFKI Research Report RR-92-16.

[12] Jochen Heinsohn, Daniel Kudenko, Bernhard Nebel & Hans-Jürgen Profitlich, "An empirical analysis of terminological representation systems," *Artificial Intelligence* 68 (1994), 367–397.

[13] Jean-Louis Laurière, *Problem solving and artificial intelligence*, Prentice-Hall International, London, England, 1990.

[14] Hector J. Levesque & Ronald J. Brachman, "A fundamental tradeoff in knowledge representation and reasoning," in *Readings in knowledge representation*, Ronald J. Brachman & Hector J. Levesque, eds., Morgan Kaufmann Publishers, Inc., Los Altos, CA, 1985, 41–70, (revised version).

[15] Robert M. MacGregor, "Inside the LOOM description classifier," *SIGART Bulletin* 2 (1991), 88–92, special issue on implemented knowledge representation and reasoning systems.

[16] Robert M. MacGregor & David Brill, "Recognition algorithms for the LOOM classifier," in *Proceedings Tenth National Conference on Artificial Intelligence, 12–16 July 1992, San Jose, CA*, AAAI Press/MIT Press, Menlo Park, CA, 1992, 774–779.

[17] Nicolaas J.I. Mars, "The role of ontologies in structuring large knowledge bases," in *Proceedings of the International Conference on Building and Sharing Very Large-Scale Knowledge Bases '93*, Japan Information Processing Development Center, Tokyo, 1993, 235–243.

[18] Nicolaas J.I. Mars, "An ontology of measurement," in *Proceedings of the ECAI'94 Workshop Comparison of Implemented Ontologies, Amsterdam, The Netherlands, August 9, 1994*, Nicolaas J.I. Mars, ed., 1994, 153–162.

[19] Nicolaas J.I. Mars, Hidde de Jong, Piet-Hein Speel, Wilco G. ter Stal & Paul E. van der Vet, "Semi-automatic knowledge acquisition in Plinius: an engineering approach," in *Proceedings of the 8th BANFF Knowledge Acquisition for Knowledge-Based Systems Workshop, Alberta, Canada, January 30–February 4, 1994*, Brian R. Gaines & Mark Musen, eds., 1994, 4-1-4-15.

[20] Nicolaas J.I. Mars & A.T. Schreiber, "Direct access to knowledge in bibliographic databases," in *Proceedings of the ARTINT Workshop on Artificial Intelligence and Information Retrieval, Luxembourg, 13 September 1985*, Commission of the European Communities, Luxembourg, 1985, 83–86.

[21] Bernhard Nebel, "Computational complexity of terminological reasoning in BACK," *Artificial Intelligence* 34 (1988), 371–383.

[22] Bernhard Nebel, *Reasoning and revision in hybrid representation systems*, Lecture notes in artificial intelligence; subseries of lecture notes in computer science; edited by Jörg Siekmann; volume 422, Springer-Verlag, Berlin, 1990, revised version of Nebel's Ph.D. thesis, Universität des Saarlandes, Saarbrücken, Germany, 1989.

[23] Peter F. Patel-Schneider, "Decidable, logic-based knowledge representation," Palo Alto Research, Technical Report No. 56, Palo Alto, CA, 1987, modified version of Patel-Schneider's Ph.D. thesis, University of Toronto, 1987.

[24] Peter F. Patel-Schneider, "Undecidability of subsumption in NIKL," *Artificial Intelligence* 39 (1989), 263–272.

[25] Peter F. Patel-Schneider & William R. Swartout, *Description-logic knowledge representation system specification*, Available from AI Principles Research Department, AT&T Bell Laboratories, Murray Hill, NJ, 1993.

[26] Christof Peltason, "The BACK system – an overview," *SIGART Bulletin* 2 (1991), 114–119, special issue on implemented knowledge representation and reasoning systems.

[27] Manfred Schmidt-Schauß, "Subsumption in KL-ONE is undecidable," in *Proceedings of the First International Conference on Principles of Knowledge Representation and Reasoning (KR'89), Toronto, Ontario, Canada, May 15-18, 1989*, Ronald J. Brachman, Hector J. Levesque & Raymond Reiter, eds., Morgan Kaufmann Publishers, Inc., San Mateo, CA, 1989, 421–431.

[28] Piet-Hein Speel, "Selecting knowledge representation systems," University of Twente, Ph.D. thesis, Enschede, The Netherlands, 1995, to be published.

[29] Paul E. van der Vet, Hidde de Jong, Nicolaas J.I. Mars, Piet-Hein Speel & Wilco G. ter Stal, "Plinius intermediate report," University of Twente, Memorandum UT-KBS-94-10, Memoranda Informatica 94-35, Enschede, the Netherlands, 1994.

[30] Paul E. van der Vet & Nicolaas J.I. Mars, "Structured system of concepts for storing, retrieving, and manipulating chemical information," *Journal of Chemical Information and Computer Sciences* 33 (1993), 564–568.

[31] Paul E. van der Vet & Nicolaas J.I. Mars, "Concept systems as an aid for sharing and reuse of knowledge bases in materials science," in *Knowledge-based applications in materials science and engineering*, James K. McDowell & Kenneth J. Meltsner, eds., The Minerals, Metals & Materials Society, Warrendale PA, 1994, 43–55.

[32] Paul E. van der Vet, Piet-Hein Speel & Nicolaas J.I. Mars, "Ontologies for very large knowledge bases in materials science: a case study," in *this proceedings*, 1995.

[33] William A. Woods & James G. Schmolze, "The KL-ONE family," in *Semantic networks in artificial intelligence*, Fritz Lehmann, ed., Modern applied mathematics and computer science; edited by Ervin Y. Rodin; Volume 24, Pergamon Press, Oxford, England, 1992, 133–177, published as a special issue of the journal *Computers & Mathematics with Applications* 23.

Part 6: Supporting Technology

Towards Very Large Knowledge Bases
N.J.I. Mars, Ed.
IOS Press, 1995

Structuring Methods for Nonmonotonic Knowledge Bases

Grigoris Antoniou
University of Newcastle
Callaghan, NSW, Australia
mgga@alinga.newcastle.edu.au

ABSTRACT

Complete information is difficult to come by and generally not available even in simple applications. Nonmonotonic reasoning is an important method of knowledge representation because it allows reasoning from incomplete information. One of the problems, though, is an increased computational complexity compared to classical logic. We propose and discuss structuring as a means of overcoming this limitation, thus contributing to an increased applicability in practice. Apart from this specific aspect, structuring bears also the usual benefits known from software engineering.

1 INTRODUCTION

Complete knowledge is difficult to come by and generally not available, not only in everyday situations but even in simple database applications. Consequently, an intelligent reasoning system must be capable of making plausible conjectures, which may be rejected when found to be incorrect according to new information that becomes available. Nonmonotonic Reasoning (NMR) provides a mechanism for an intelligent reasoning system to make such conjectures when its knowledge is incomplete. Many nonmonotonic logics have been presented, default logic [9], autoepistemic logic [7], and circumscription [6] being perhaps the most prominent.

One of the main problems of nonmonotonic formalisms is that they are computationally complex; situation is far worse than in classical logic. Two natural way of coping with this problem are

- parallelization, and

- structuring.

Structuring and modules are one of the lessons learned from the software crisis end of the 60es. The idea is to decompose a system into smaller, ideally self-contained, manageable parts. The benefits reported include comprehensibility, easy maintenance, and reuse. It should be noted that most of these benefits are addressing humans, i.e. they try to overcome human limitations.

The same needs arise in the area of knowledge systems, but here there are additional benefits in terms of increased efficiency. This is due to a resulting reduced search space. There is much work being done on structuring knowledge systems, e.g. [5,8,11].

The aim of this paper is to present some approaches of structuring nonmonotonic knowledge and reasoning, a subject that has not yet been addressed in a satisfactory way, although there are statements by pioneers of nonmonotonic logic that NMR should be carried out "in a local way". Indeed, we think that *nonmonotonic reasoning in the small combined with a modular design* is a promising solution to overcome the current limitations that have essentially restricted application to toy problems. We shall also show that structuring even supports parallelization, thus enabling us to dramatically increase efficiency by using new computing technology.

Some words on why we shall present *some* approaches to structuring are in order. This is because we believe that there is not *the* structuring principle, but rather the most suitable depending on the application at hand. In this sense, the best solution is to provide a toolkit of structuring mechanisms.

The methods we shall present are generic paradigms rather than formalisms ready to be used in applications. We believe that only practical work on real applications will enable us to carry out the "fine tuning" that is necessary in order to have applicable methods. Nevertheless, the ideas we present can serve as the starting point for such practical investigations. Since the intuitions underlying some of the notions are quite different, it is impossible to use the same examples for all of them; rather we have to use different examples for different methods (in particular for those in sections 3 and 4).

2 NONMONOTONIC LOGIC

In everyday life, people have to reason under incomplete knowledge by making conjectures which may turn out to be wrong when new information becomes available. Their conclusions are thus not correct in an absolute sense, as say in mathematics. Nonmonotonic logics capture this intuitive idea. They are nonmonotonic in the sense that if a set of premises (available knowledge) grows, the set of possible conclusions does not necessarily grow, due to revisions of previous conjectures.

One of the main nonmonotonic formalisms is default logic. A *default theory* consists of a set T of *truths* (correct, indisputable knowledge), and a set D of defaults. A *default* is a string of the form $\frac{\varphi : \psi_1, \ldots, \psi_n}{\chi}$, where $\varphi, \psi_1, \ldots, \psi_n, \chi$ are predicate logic sentences. Its intuitive meaning is the following:

If φ is currently known, and if the current knowledge allows us to believe in each of ψ_k, then conclude χ.

We call φ the *prerequisite*, $\psi_1, \ldots, \psi_n$ the *justifications*, and χ the *consequent* of the default. A default is applicable to a set of formulae E with respect to belief set F iff its prerequisite follows from E and all its justifications are consistent with F.

The semantics (meaning) of a default theory is based on the concept of *extension*, a deductively closed set of formulae defining a "possible view" of the world based on the given theory. A default theory may have none, one, or several extensions.

Extensions are defined as fixed-points of an operator. On a more intuitive level (sufficient for this paper), an extension is obtained by applying as many defaults as possible in a particular order, taking care that no justification of a previously applied default is violated (i.e. inconsistent with the current knowledge).

As an example, consider the default theory containing the defaults

$$\frac{bird : flies}{flies}$$

$$\frac{penguin : \neg flies}{\neg flies}$$

and the truths *bird* and *penguin*. Then there are two extensions, one containing *flies* (plus the truths), and one containing $\neg flies$.

The following discussion can be considered as being generic in the sense that it may be applied to several nonmonotonic formalisms. When referring to more

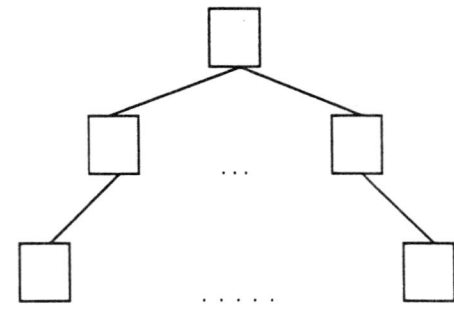

Figure 1: A structured knowledge base

technical questions or when presenting examples, we shall use only default logic because it is the method outlined above. It is also the most promising as far as applications are concerned, since defaults naturally occur in many domains (like diagnosis or law); this means that it is easy for "users" (experts and knowledge engineers) to think in terms of defaults.

3 SIMPLE STRUCTURING MECHANISMS

The basic idea here is to decompose a knowledge base, in particular a default theory, into smaller, manageable parts. A structured knowledge base is thus a collection of partial knowledge bases we call *modules*. These are combined in a hierarchical, partial order $<$ with one top module. Figure 1 illustrates the situation.

Lower modules are supposed to contain more specific information, which is interpreted as being more reliable than more general knowledge. The idea is that each module includes knowledge items that naturally fit together or concern one specific aspect of the problem domain. For example, a module in a legal knowledge system on Australian visas could include knowledge about expelling foreigners from Australia, another about conditions of providing political asylum. The knowledge of the latter module can be of great importance for the former, since there are severe restrictions to expelling a political refugee.

Before we consider an example, let us take a look at the semantics of a structured knowledge base. First we say informally what the semantics of a single module is: it imports some information from its environment (that is from other modules) and treats it as truths. Then the module computes an extension based on the knowledge it comprises plus the imported information. This extension is passed to its environment (that means to the modules that are connected to it and higher in the hierarchy $<$). The semantics of the entire structured knowledge base is the set of exten-

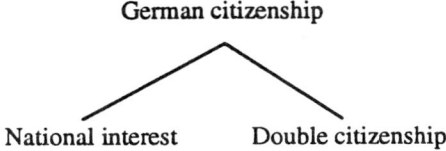

German citizenship

National interest   Double citizenship

Figure 2: Module structure for Example 1

sions of its top module. A formal definition will be given later on.

Example 1

The German law on how to obtain the German citizenship can be roughly described as follows. The main rule is that somebody who has lived for sufficiently many years in Germany, has no criminal record, and abandons their current citizenships of other countries, usually obtains the German citizenship, unless a national interest speaks against this; the latter could be the case for activists in extremist political groups, or students from developing countries. Exceptions to the general rule exist for people of German origin who usually get the citizenship automatically, and for persons whom the German state decides to offer its citizenship (for example famous athletes). Also, if someone tries to give up their citizenship but is unsuccessful for reasons they are not responsible for (as is the case with Greeks), then double citizenship is allowed.

Let us see how a structured knowledge base in default logic can represent this information. There are three modules: One for "National interest" (pro or contra an application), one for "Double citizenship", and "German citizenship" that makes the final decision (see Figure 2).

National interest

$$\frac{true : \neg nationalInterestPro}{\neg nationalInterestPro}$$

$$\frac{true : \neg nationalInterestContra}{\neg nationalInterestContra}$$

$$politicalExtremist \rightarrow nationalInterestContra$$
$$famousAthlet \rightarrow nationalInterestPro$$

Double citizenship
$$giveUpCurrent \rightarrow doubleCitCleared$$

$$\frac{\neg giveUpCurrent : \neg doubleCitCleared}{\neg doubleCitCleared}$$

$$triedGiveUp \wedge \neg responsible \rightarrow doubleCitCleared$$

German Citizenship
$$\frac{\neg criminal \wedge longInGermany \wedge doubleCitCleared : giveCitizenship}{giveCitizenship}$$

$$nationalInterestPro \rightarrow giveCitizenship$$
$$nationalInterestContra \rightarrow \neg giveCitizenship$$
$$germanOrigin \rightarrow giveCitizenship$$

Let us now see what happens given the following case: The applicant will give up her current citizenship, has no criminal record, but has not lived long enough in Germany:

$$giveUpCurrent$$
$$\neg criminal$$
$$\neg longInGermany$$

"National interest" computes $\neg nationalInterestPro$ and $\neg nationalInterestContra$. Unit "Double citizenship" computes $doubleCitCleared$. The top module uses this information but cannot derive a positive answer ($giveCitizenship$ is not included in the extension computed) since the main default is not applicable due to the missing information $longInGermany$.

But then the applicant informs the authorities that she is a famous athlete. Now we are faced with a different situation: the module "National interest" computes $\neg nationalInterestContra$ but $nationalInterestPro$, which allows the top module to deduce $giveCitizenship$!

We have not been very specific about the treatment of truths and defaults in the discussion above. There are two conceivable alternatives leading to two different structuring mechanisms. As already stated in the introduction, we do not believe that there is the *right* mechanism, so we describe both variants.

- In the first alternative, all truths (non-default knowledge) are treated as being more reliable than any defaults. This is technically achieved by considering the set of truths as the lowest module, that is imported by all others.

  The extensions obtained this way are also extensions of the unstructured default theory (the union of all knowledge items). But since defaults in lower modules are preferred to those in higher ones, some extensions of the unstructured theory may get lost.

  This model is essentially the same as Brewka's *preferred subtheories* [3], only translated to the default framework. Bu the focus is different: whereas Brewka was only interested in resolving conflicts among defaults, here we are concerned about structuring. So, the modifications to the model proposed in the next sections lead to completely new approaches.

- The alternative is to decompose the truths of the theory, too. This was the case with the example above! The rules on the national interest are included together with the corresponding defaults in

190

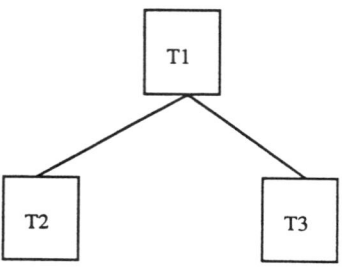

Figure 3: The effect of splitting the truths

module "National interest". We think that this approach seems more promising in practice, as it reflects the main underlying intuition of structuring: *determine the knowledge items solving a subtask, and put them together*.

Here is the formal presentation: let the knowledge base be decomposed in modules which are pairs $T = (W, D)$ of a set of formulae W and a set of defaults D. Let T be a module; the set $Ext(T)$ is defined as follows: let $\{T_1, \ldots, T_n\}$ be the set of parts T' such that $T' < T$. Let $E_i \in Ext(T_i)$ (for all $i \in \{1, \ldots, n\}$). Then $E \in Ext(T)$ if, and only if, E is an extension of the default theory $(W \cup E_1 \cup \ldots \cup E_n, D)$. The semantics of the entire structured knowledge base is the set $Ext(T')$ where T' is the top module in the hierarchy $<$.

Let us note that the approach adopted here can lead to a situation where truths of a higher module do not prevent application of a default in a lower module. Consider, for example, the schema of Figure 3.

Suppose that a default in T_2 has justification ψ and can be applied within T_2. This application of the default cannot be rejected a posteriori, even if a fact $\neg\psi$ is included in the truths of T_1. Obviously, we have an inconsistency here. We argue that this situation is an indication of bad decomposition of knowledge into modules. In such cases, application of *verification and validation techniques* seems to be appropriate to resolve the problem, for example by reporting to a knowledge engineer. A *correctness postulate* here would require some kind of *conservativity* stating that imported knowledge should not be modified in any module; conservativity is a well-known principle in the area of algebraic specification and formal software engineering [4]. In simple cases, it suffices to prevent usage of some predicates on

the right hand sides of rules or in consequents of defaults.

In computer science, the reasons for structuring are aiming at humans and not at execution necessities; by this we mean that comprehensibility, maintainability etc. are intended to help humans who are involved in program development, maintenance or usage, whereas there is no improvement in the program's running behavior. In the case of knowledge systems in general, and nonmonotonic systems in particular, structuring has still the effect of helping humans, but also computational implications.

Let us illustrate this point by referring to default logic. The complexity of determining the extensions of a default theory is exponential in the number of defaults, say 2^n. If we split the set of defaults to k modules (equal modules for the sake of this argument), then the complexity is reduced to $k \times 2^k$, which is dramatically lower! In our concrete example above, this would mean $2^3 + 1 + 1 = 10$ instead of $2^5 = 32$.

Of course, we may no more obtain all extensions of the unstructured theory, but two arguments can be said on this: first, the "right" ones will be obtained, given that the structuring is meaningful. And second, in many cases the same extensions will be obtained with less operations: in the example above, no extension got lost due to structuring!

Another important benefit of structuring is that it supports parallelization in a natural way. The extension generation within a module may be carried out in parallel to others, provided that its children have delivered theirs. In other words, extensions may be computed on parallel branches of the hierarchy tree (corresponding to $<$), with necessary synchronization at non-leaf nodes.

The following sections will rely on what has been achieved so far, and will extend this model by further important features. The first one concerns *competing knowledge*. This is knowledge that cannot be used at the same time, be it for the sake of consistency, be it for domain reasons. For example, there is knowledge on how to drive when in Australia, and how to drive when being in Germany. When I am driving in Newcastle, the knowledge about specific rules concerning Germany are not needed. This leads to a further reduction of the search space.

The idea discussed in section 5 concerns *interfaces*. Interfaces are useful in order to make a module (more) independent from its environment. They can also lead to reduced search space. For example, if a global "visas" module needs information about political refugees, then the only relevant information to decide a visa case is whether the person asking for a visa is a refugee or not. The details that have led the lower "asylum" module to this decision are irrelevant and should be disregarded (*information hiding*).

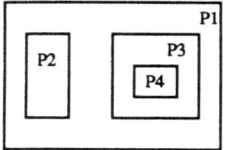 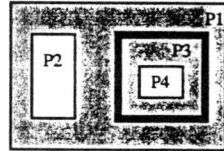

Figure 4: A packet structure

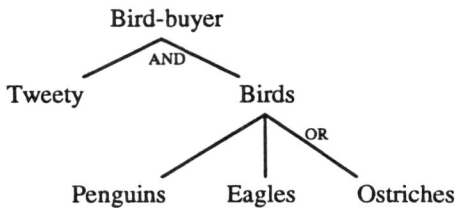

Figure 5: Knowledge base organization for Example 2

4 DISREGARDING IRRELEVANT KNOWLEDGE PORTIONS

It is quite obvious that humans are not acting and reasoning based on the entire knowledge they have about the world. We rather use only a small portion that seems relevant for the current activity. Should it turn out to be insufficient, other parts may be "consulted". Using this intuitively simple idea, the model of the previous section may be refined to allow restriction to "relevant" knowledge. Needless to say, such a restriction of focus has a great impact on efficiency issues.

As proposed in [1], the knowledge base may be decomposed into so-called *packets* that are organized as ordered by generality domains. A simple example of such a knowledge base is illustrated in Figure 4.

Inner packets contain more specific knowledge. For motivation, in the example above, P1 could contain information about English language, P2 about the idiom spoken in Australia, P3 about the language spoken at universities, and P4 information about specific vocabulary of the computer science community. Note that the outmost packet includes the knowledge that is useful for all problems of the application at hand. In contrast, P2 and P3 may comprise competitive knowledge to be used alternatively.

The semantics of this organization of knowledge is determined by the current *focus*, the most specific packet being "active" at the moment. Only knowledge in the focus or more general packets may be used (e.g. the dashed area in Figure 3). The main problem is, of course, how to determine the appropriate focus. This goes beyond the scope of this paper! Or, to say it in the KADS terminology [10], this belongs to higher layer that will make such decisions.

Combination of these ideas with the model presented in section 3 is straightforward: a module may choose to use the knowledge of *some* of its subordinate modules only. Instead of formally describing this approach (see [1] for more details, but not in a nonmonotonic setting), we will conclude this section with two illustrative examples.

Example 2

In the following theory we are using restricted knowledge from the birds domain. In particular, we model the representation and reasoning from a person's point of view who is expecting a bird named *tweety* he has bought but knows very little about (see Figure 5).

Tweety
$bird(tweety)$

Birds
$bird(X) \wedge flies(X) \rightarrow buyCage$

$$\frac{bird(X) : flies(X)}{flies(X)}$$

Ostriches
$ostrich(X) \rightarrow granivorous(X) \wedge bird(X) \wedge flies(X)$

Penguins
$penguin(X) \rightarrow carnivorous(X) \wedge bird(X) \wedge \neg flies(X)$

Eagles
$eagle(X) \rightarrow carnivorous(X) \wedge bird(X) \wedge flies(X)$

Buyer

$$\frac{true : \neg carnivorous(X) \wedge \neg outOfMoney}{buyCorn}$$

$$\frac{true : \neg granivorous(X) \wedge \neg outOfMoney}{buyMeat}$$

$buyCage \wedge buyMeat \wedge buyCorn \rightarrow outOfMoney$

Obviously, the buyer should not use all knowledge available about specific arts of birds, unless he knows that tweety is of the specific kind. And even then, only one of the many modules ("Eagles", "Penguins", "Ostriches" etc.) will be used; this is a situation of competing knowledge! Leaving out irrelevant information obviously reduces search space considerably.

Example 3

If we reconsider the domain of Example 1, the following organization of the knowledge base is also conceivable: in case no problem with double citizenship exists, the entire decision is made within the module "German Citizenship". Only in case there is a problem, the module "Double citizenship" is called, which carries out more involved reasoning and comes up with clearance or non–clearance. Thus "Double citizenship" is only called when required.

5 ADDING INTERFACES

Module interfaces play an important role in software engineering. They define the way a module communicates with its environment, and allows for *information hiding* by offering only some of the module's content to the public. The same ideas and benefits apply to knowledge systems, and in particular to nonmonotonic knowledge, too. Let us start with an example.

Example 4

We consider the Example 1 once again. The top module "National interest" might (and in reality is!) much more complicated, including far more detailed information which after all leads to a decision pro or contra an applicant. Now, this whole information that reflects the internal decision of the module is irrelevant for its environment; what the module above needs to know is only whether *national-interest-pro* or *national-interest-contra* holds. Thus, the export interface of the module "National interest" would filter out everything except the aforementioned two predicates.

In the above example, the interface contains only *syntactic information* that filters out knowledge that should not be exported; this idea is compatible with the main line of programming languages in computer science. There is, though, also the possibility that the interfaces include also *semantic information* in form of conditions that should be fulfilled. Conditions in the import interface specify what kind of knowledge is allowed to be imported, conditions in the export interface specify properties of the knowledge the module is offering to the public. Obviously, modules may only be combined if their interface information fit together. All these issues are fairly known in the area of algebraic specification, e.g. [4].

The semantics of a module T with interfaces is determined as follows:

- T imports a first order theory M in its import signature (M may be an extension of a subordinate module).

- An extension E (or all extensions) of $T \cup kb(T)$ is computed, where $kb(T)$ is the default theory in the "body" of T.

- The restriction of E to the export signature is offered to the public.

Again, the semantics of the top module is the semantics of the entire structured knowledge base.

Inclusion of formal interfaces also opens up the way for *verification* work. A module is considered as *correct* if all extensions computed satisfy the required conditions. It is beyond the scope of this paper discuss specification and verification of nonmonotonic knowledge.

6 DISCUSSION AND FUTURE WORK

Summary

In this paper, we argued that structuring is essential for a breakthrough of nonmonotonic knowledge systems in practical applications. The benefits outscore those known from computer science because a modular design helps to keep reasoning computationally manageable, which is especially crucial in NMR. Furthermore, structured decomposition supports parallel implementation.

We further argued that there is not *the* structuring principle, but rather methods that may be useful for some applications. We presented two approaches of structured nonmonotonic knowledge, and briefly described two possible refinements: competing knowledge, and addition of interfaces.

Formal versus informal presentation

Our presentation was partly kept on an informal level although some of the ideas in sections 3 and 5 were formalized. On one hand, we wanted to concentrate on the ideas and concepts. On the other hand, we wished to demonstrate that these ideas can be easily formalized and implemented, given a formal background of a nonmonotonic formalism, say a precise definition of default logic extensions. Indeed, the problem is *not* the formalization of the ideas – this is considerably simple. The real challenge is to identify the structuring mechanisms that fit to specific problems, as well as the 'fine tuning' (see below for more on this point).

How to decompose into parts

Sometimes there is an expectation that modularity concepts suggest how to actually decompose a system into parts. In our opinion, this is not necessarily the case. For example, given a programming language with a module concept, it is possible to decompose a program in a good way or in an inappropriate way. The same applies to knowledge bases as well, and to nonmonotonic knowledge in particular. The general (and therefore superficial) guideline we can give is that knowledge items belonging together (from the conceptual point of view) should be placed together. Apart from this general idea, a better feeling for appropriate decomposition can only be expected given a real application domain that has to be modeled. The question of how to obtain a good decomposition of knowledge is an open major research problem.

Approximative default reasoning

One way of overcoming the difficulties related to the high complexity of default reasoning is to allow for *approximative reasoning*, meaning that a default may be applied even if not all possible exceptions are taken into consideration. Instead, it can be only required that no reason for non-applicability of the default is readily apparent, that means in the "active part" of the knowledge base. Results from cognitive science show that humans often argue and act despite some knowledge they have to the contrary, given that this knowledge has been "forgotten"; humans are simply unaware of this part of their knowledge for the time being.

How can we put this intuitive idea to work? [2] proposes *knowledge base structuring mechanisms* as a natural means of defining concepts like "currently aware of" versus "forgotten", or "relevant parts of the knowledge". Clearly, a structured knowledge base supports restriction of the applicational focus to parts of the entire knowledge only.

Applications

We are planning to apply default logic in two areas: insurances, and legal reasoning. In each case, we shall attack real (instead of real–like) problems and will have to partition the knowledge into small, manageable parts. In the insurance project we shall study the possibilities of combining default reasoning with object–oriented techniques: apart from modules and interfaces, we shall investigate inheritance as well.

REFERENCES

1. G. Antoniou and I. Wachsmuth. Structuring and Modules for Knowledge Bases: Motivation for a New Model. *Knowledge-Based Systems* 1993

2. G. Antoniou. Efficient default reasoning through knowledge base structuring. (submitted to the *GW International Conference on Intelligent Systems* 1995)

3. G. Brewka. Preferred subtheories – an extended logical framework for default reasoning. In *Proc. IJCAI-89*

4. H. Ehrig and B. Mahr. *Fundamentals of algebraic specification Vol. 2*, Springer 1990

5. D. Landes and R. Studer. Mechanisms for structuring knowledge-based systems. *Proc. Database and Expert System Applications*, Springer 1994

6. J. McCarthy. Circumscription – a form of nonmonotonic reasoning. *Artificial Intelligence* 13, 1980

7. R.C. Moore. Semantical considerations on nonmonotonic logic. *Artificial Intelligence* 25, 1985

8. R. Neches, R. Fikes, T. Finin, T. Gruber, R. Patil, P. Senator and W.R. Swartout. Enabling Technology for Knowledge Sharing. *AI Magazine* 12, 3

9. R. Reiter. A logic for default reasoning. *Artificial Intelligence* 13, 1980

10. G. Schreiber, B. Wielinga and J. Breuker (eds.). *KADS – A Principled Approach to Knowledge-Based Systems Development*, Academic Press 1993

11. C. Sernadas, J. Fiadeiro and A. Sernadas. Modular construction of logic knowledge bases: an algebraic approach. *Information Systems* 15, 1990

Exceptions in Composition Graphs

Martine Magnan and **Chabane Oussalah**
LGI2P/EMA-EERIE
Nîmes, France
{magnan, oussalah}@eerie.fr

ABSTRACT

Unlike exceptions in inheritance graphs, exceptions in composition graphs have been the subject of little interest. Composite objects are structural aggregates of an object set, which represents the components of the related composite object. Each component may itself be a composite object. Using exceptions in composition graphs allows us to create new composite objects by reusing existing components without taking into account their own components. Indeed, like exceptions in inheritance graphs, exceptions in composition graphs favor reusability and incremental design.

1 INTRODUCTION

Data modeling, whether it be in the domains of Artificial Intelligence, Object-Oriented Databases or CAD/CAM, requires the representation of more complex objects than those used in conventional applications [36]. This has led to the development of more powerful data models allowing composite objects to be described [2] [6] [12] [14] [16] [20] [22] [37]. Composition hierarchies are a natural way for humans to organize and represent objects in order to manage and reason about the world [25].

The main advantage of systems providing inheritance and composition hierarchies is to favor the reusability of objects and incremental design. Reusability in inheritance systems generally means the reuse of existing objects thanks to the inheritance relationship which provides a way of sharing or factorizing information. Objects that are reused allow us either to design objects of the same type or to design more specific objects.

An object may also be reused as part of a new composite object. Reusing objects by composition consists in assembling in a variable way objects that are

themselves functionally invariant. The aim of this approach is to build objects by analogy with material components in order to use them as "building blocks" for software development [7] [35]. The reuse of components through the composition relationship starts from the principle that a component that is used often has already been debugged and improved. It is therefore better to reuse it instead of reprogramming a new one.

Nevertheless, most reusability requires the designer to modify the objects that are reused. Let us suppose that we have a library of objects for the edition of documents such as books, articles, novels, paperbacks, etc. This library contains in particular the composite object *chapter* composed of a *title* and *sections*, the sections being themselves composed of *paragraphs* and *figures*, the objects *table-of-contents*, *preface*, *first-page* and *bibliography*. If we want to model a *book*, we will design it by composing the objects previously defined. If we want to model a *novel*, we will declare that a novel is composed of a *preface*, a *first-page* and *chapters*. However, the chapters of a novel must not be composed of *figures*. We therefore want to reuse the component *chapter* without its component *figure*. In order to do that, we can declare an exception towards the link that references the component *figure* (Figure 1).

Another example is given by the domain of telecommunications networks and this corresponds to the application that we have developed in our laboratory [4]. In this application, there are libraries of network elements and in one of these libraries there is the object *switch-node* which is composed of three different types of components *ntcomp1*, *ntcomp2* and *ntcomp3*. We want to build a network of logical nodes. At the cable level, it is composed of the *switch-node* that must, however, not be composed of *ntcomp1*. On the contrary, at the system level, the *switch-node* must not be composed of *ntcomp3*. In order to reuse the compo-

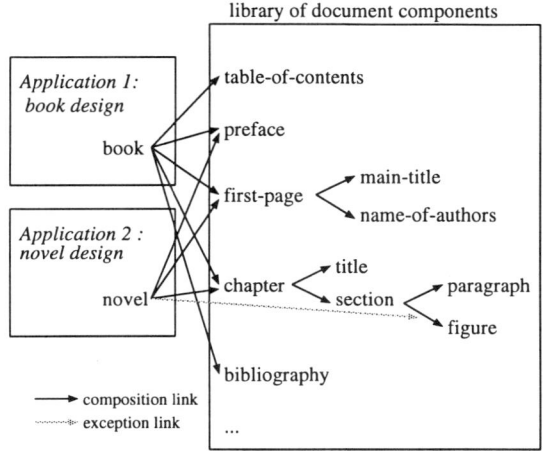

Figure 1: *Reusing document components*

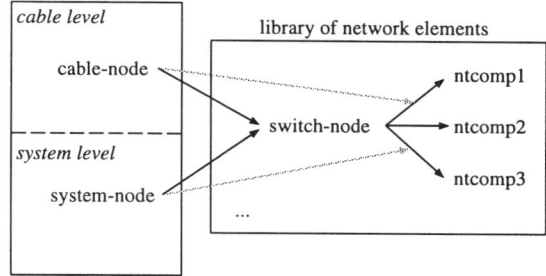

Figure 2: *Reusing network components*

nent *switch-node*, we declare exceptions in the objects being created (Figure 2).

Techniques for the representation of composite objects should therefore allow the customization of components, that is, allow a component to be reused without taking into account all its components. If there were no way of cancelling a component of the composite object that is reused, we would have to create a copy of the object that we wish to reuse and to remove from this copy the component that we do not want to take into account. This problem will be encountered frequently and will involve creating a large number of copies. Moreover, if these copies have been created only for the modeling of one composite object that contains an exception, these creations will involve the presence of objects which are not very useful. With a model of exceptions on the composition relationship, this problem may be solved.

The aim of our study is to propose a model for exceptions in composition graphs. The remainder of this paper is organized as follows. Section 2 gives a brief reminder of exceptions in inheritance hierarchies. Section 3 presents the notions of composition graphs and composition links. Section 4 is devoted to exceptions on composition links at a class level. In this section, we present the problematics of exceptions on composition links, the interpretation of composition graphs with exceptions and the algorithm to manage these exceptions.

2 RELATED WORK

2.1 Exceptions in inheritance graphs

Non-monotonic reasoning formalisms have been the subject of great interest in inheritance systems [8] [15] [18] [20] [29] 32]. They provide principles for representing and reasoning with rules that generally hold but they are nonetheless subject to exceptions [10]. Exceptions allow typicality to be dealt with, and this is essential for knowledge representation. For instance, all birds fly apart from ostriches and penguins; elephants are gray, except for royal elephants which are white, etc. If there were no way to cancel or override the application of a general statement that would otherwise be inherited, we would generally be faced with three very unattractive choices: remove the general statement and state it in each class concerned, or create classes for objects [1] that verify the general statement and classes for objects for which the statement does not hold, or remove the object which presents an exception from the class that represents the general statement and describe its general statement-like properties from scratch. As we accumulate large amounts of information in our knowledge base, this dilemma is encountered more frequently [11]. Without an adequate mechanism to represent exceptions in the knowledge base, the system is denied any ability to learn when exceptions are encountered [31]. Exceptions in inheritance graphs are therefore useful because they favor reusability and incremental design. On the one hand, exceptions allow the amount of redundant information

---

[1]The term *object* represents indifferently classes (or kinds, generic concepts, etc.) and instances (individuals, specific concepts, etc.).

196

to be decreased and, on the other hand, they allow new information to be taken into account without questioning the pre-existing hierarchy.

2.2 Existing techniques

The main problem regarding the management of exceptions in inheritance graphs consists in determining whether or not x inherits from y. Contradictions appear when there are simultaneously different paths allowing x to inherit or not to inherit from y. In inheritance graphs, several methods have been proposed depending on whether default or terminological logic [1] [3] [24] 30], semantic networks [27] [32] [34] or object-oriented languages [9] [18] are involved. Among the different approaches proposed in semantic networks, we can distinguish the shortest-path algorithm [11], the on-path or off-path preemption [26] [33] and the skeptical or credulous attitude [13] [33]. Refinements to these different notions have also been proposed [28]. In object-oriented languages, masking is applied on the inheritability property [23]. The main problem of the management of exceptions in inheritance graphs is that there is no common method allowing all the contradictions to be solved. This is certainly due to the fact that each methods gives its own semantics to exceptions in inheritance graphs and no common semantics has been defined. Moreover, algorithms that are used are often extremely complex [27].

As far as exceptions in composition graphs are concerned, to our knowledge, no research has been done on this subject.

3 COMPOSITION GRAPHS

A composite object is a structural aggregate of an object set which represents the components of the composite object. Each component describes a part of the composite object. Each component may itself be a composite object.

3.1 The composition relationship and composition links

In this section, we present some basic concepts of composite objects and composition graphs which will be used throughout the paper. If there is a composition relationship defined between the objects *vehicle* and *engine*, then vehicle is a composite object and engine is a component. A composition relationship between a class X and a class Y indicates that each instance x of class X is composed of an instance y of class Y.

The composition relationship is represented by composition links. A composition graph is defined as an acyclic-directed labelled multi-graph in which edges stand for composition links and labels for the name of composition links. The names of composition links represent the name under which the components are

known. Figure 3 gives an example of a composition graph.

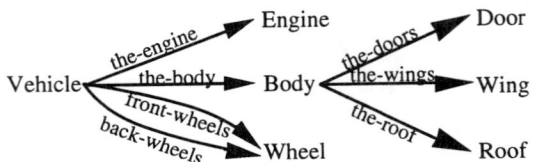

Figure 3: *The composition graph of the class Vehicle*

3.2 Composition graphs at class and instance levels

The composition graph of an instance is not necessarily isomorphic to that of its class. Whereas the composition graph of the class Vehicle is a multi-graph, the composition graph of the instance *my-vehicle* is a simple graph since a vehicle is composed of four different wheels (Figure 4).

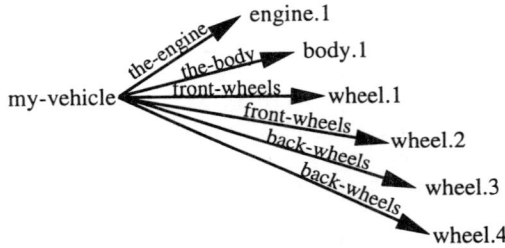

Figure 4: *A part of the composition graph of the instance my-vehicle*

Let us now consider the example given in Figure 5. In this example, the composition graph of the class Camping-equipment is a simple graph and the composition graph of the instance *camping-equipment.1* of this class is a multi-graph (we suppose that Swiss-army-knife.1 is an instance of the class Swiss-army-knife, which is a subclass of Knife, Corkscrew and Can-opener).

There may also be cases where the composition graph of a class has cycles and the composition graph of an instance of this class has no cycle, or vice-versa (example of the Swiss army knife) .

3.3 Explicit transitivity links

The composition relationship has a transitive semantics. If x is composed of y and y is composed of z, then x is composed of z. Nevertheless, if the composition link from x to z is explicitly indicated, this link is not redundant even if it is a transitivity link. It brings with it the information that x has two direct components y and z, y being itself composed of z. Figure 6 gives an illustration of a composition graph with explicit transitivity

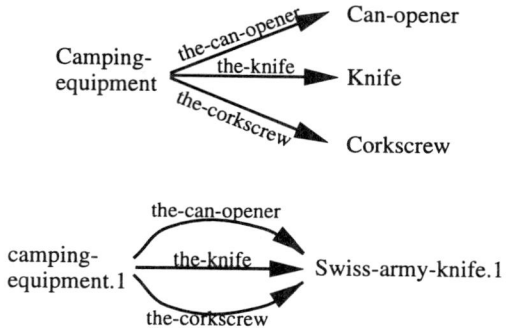

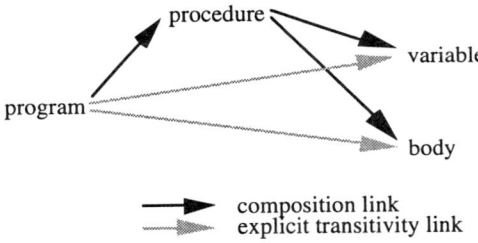

Figure 5: *The composition graph of the class camping-equipment and of an instance of this class*

links. A program is composed of variables, procedures and a body, procedures being themselves composed of variables and of a body.

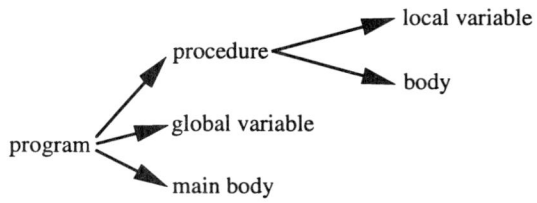

Figure 6: *A composition graph with explicit transitivity links*

If we had considered transitivity links as redundant, we would have had to differentiate between global and local variables (Figure 7) which is not the case when not considering transitivity links as redundant. In a more general way, all objects that appeared at the different composition levels of a composite object had to be duplicated if transitivity links were considered as redundant.

4   EXCEPTIONS ON COMPOSITION LINKS

Reusing components consists in allowing the programmer to design an object having components that already exist and which can also be components of some other objects. The reused components are stocked in libraries. For instance, if the object *body* exists and is a component of the object *vehicle*, it may be reused to design the object *convertible-vehicle*.

Components that are reused may themselves be composite objects. We may sometimes want to reuse a component without wishing to take into account all

Figure 7: *Composition graph of the class Program if transitivity links were considered as redundant*

its components. In the case of the convertible-vehicle, it is effectively composed of a body but the body must not be composed of a roof. Instead of defining a new component and therefore going against the reusability principle, an exception model is proposed which allows a component to be reused while excepting some of its components. These exceptions are exceptions on composition links.

Exceptions on composition links may occur at two levels: at the class and instance levels [19]. Exceptions on composition links at the class level are called class-level exceptions whereas exceptions on composition links at the instance level are called instance-level exceptions. In this paper, we are only concerned with class-level exceptions. Instance-level exceptions may be dealt with without explicitly defining an exception model but by using the notion of cardinality of composition links [19].

4.1   Exception links

An exception link has at its origin a composite class X and at its extremity a composition link L that is declared in a component class Z of X. The result of an exception link is to cancel the composition link that is referenced. Therefore, all instances of Z that are part of instances of X must not reference any components with the composition link L.

For example, a convertible vehicle is composed of an engine, a body and wheels and excepts the component roof of body (Figure 8). The composition link *the-roof* is excepted by the composite class Convertible-vehicle. Instances of the class Body that are components of the instances of the class Convertible-vehicle are composed neither of a roof nor of components of a roof. Nevertheless, instances of the class Body that are not part of the instances of the class Convertible-vehicle are composed of a roof (in particular, the instances of Body that are components of the instances of Vehicle).

There may be two nodes that are linked with more than one composition link. An exception link has at its extremity only one composition link and therefore cancels only this composition link. If there are other composition links having the same origin and extrem-

198

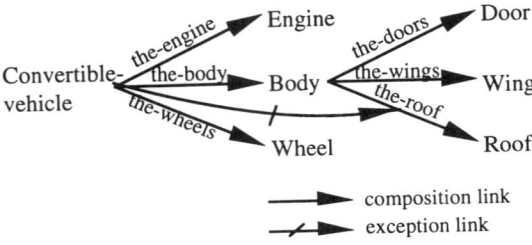

composition link
exception link

Figure 8: *The exception link in the composition graph of the class Convertible-vehicle*

ity of the excepted composition link, these links are not cancelled. For instance (Figure 9), the exception link which is declared in the class Function cancels only the composition link output-parameters (noted as output-para).

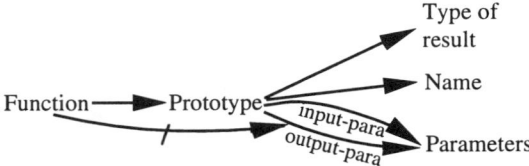

Figure 9: *An exception link in the multi-graph of the class Function*

An exception link indicates that a composite object must not be composed through a given composition link of a component. Conversely, it indicates that the component cannot be part of the composite object through this composition link.

In order to represent exceptions, we use a specific attribute, the value of which is a list of excepted composition links. This attribute can therefore be inherited or masked. This latter case allows exceptions to be cancelled.

4.2 Problematics

Let X and Y be two classes. The main problem regarding the management of composition graphs with exceptions consists in determining whether or not X is composed of Y.

A path of the composition graph is a sequence of composition links. The construction of compound paths is performed by a forward chaining process. A compound path $X \to ... \to Z \to Y$ is constructed by adding the direct link $Z \to Y$ to its permitted initial segment $X \to ... \to Z$.

Notation:

A path between X_0 and X_n is noted $X_0 l_1 X_1 l_2 ... l_n X_n$ where $X_0 ... X_n$ and $l_1 ... l_n$ stand respectively for nodes and composition links of a composition graph.

The paths between X and Y that are allowed must be determined in order to conclude that X is composed of Y. If there is no exception, we conclude that X is composed of Y as soon as there is a path between X and Y. On the contrary, a contradiction appears if there are one or more paths between X and Y and if at least one of these paths crosses a node that excepts a link of this path.

More precisely:
an exception link from X_i to l_j contradicts all paths σ such that $\sigma = X_0 l_1 X_1 l_2 ... l_n X_n$ and $X_i \in \sigma$ ($0 \le i \le n - 1$) and $l_j \in \sigma (1 \le j \le n)$.

As for contradictions in inheritance systems [19], we have identified five types of contradictions. These types of contradictions correspond to the basic structures of a composition graph which bring about a contradiction. The first contradiction is such that the exception link and the excepted composition link are declared in the same class (type 0). In the other contradictions, compound paths are involved. If we suppose that we have to determine if a class X is composed of a class Y, we can distinguish three cases: all vertices of the paths between X and Y may be compared by the composition relationship (type 1), only certain vertices may be compared (types 2 and 3) and, finally, none of the vertices may be compared (type 4).

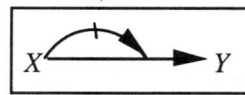

Type 0: This structure corresponds to the simplest case of contradiction: the exception link and the excepted composition link are declared in the same class. We consider this case as being inconsistent since consistent conclusions cannot be drawn from inconsistent information [13].

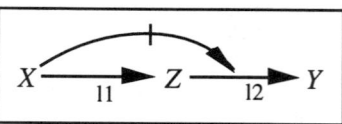

Type 1a: In this case, an exception is introduced in X towards the composition link l_2.

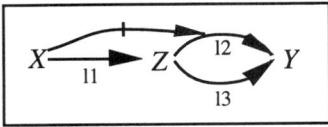

Type 1b: There are two composition links between Z and Y but X excepts only one of these two links.

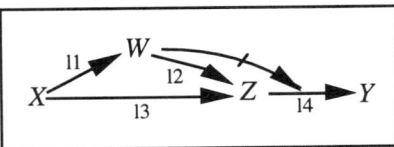

Type 2: There is a path from X to Y that follows an explicit transitivity link Xl_3Z. Explicit transitivity links in composition graphs are not considered as redundant, unlike transitivity links in inheritance graphs.

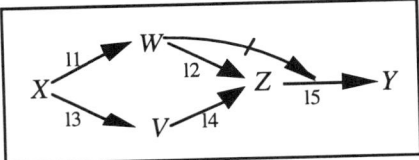

Type 3: The transitivity link is interrupted by the node V.

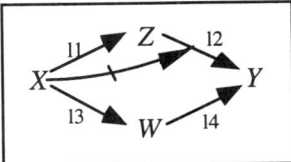

Type 4: There are two paths between X and Y - only one is contradicted - which have no common vertices except their origin and extremity.

4.3 Interpretation of composition graphs with exception links

If a class X declares an exception link towards a composition link L, the result of this exception is to cancel the composition link L. L is a *forbidden link* for X. For instance, the composition link *the-roof* is forbidden for the class Convertible-vehicle.

A composition path between X and Y is a path of the composition graph which allows us to conclude that X is of Y. This path must not therefore follow forbidden links for X. More generally, a composition path between X and Y must not follow forbidden links for a node of this path. It should be remembered that a same class cannot declare and except a same composition link (a contradiction of type 0 is forbidden).

> A path $\sigma = X_0l_1X_1l_2...l_nX_n$ is a composition path if there is no link $l_i \in \sigma$ $(1 < i \leq n)$ that is forbidden for a node $X_j \in \sigma$ $(0 \leq j < n - 1)$.

We conclude that X is composed of Y if there is a composition path between X and Y. All composition paths are therefore allowed. This interpretation is justified by the semantics of the composition links. If the composition path between X and Y is reduced to a composition link, this means that X is "directly" composed of Y. Otherwise, the composition path has the form $X...Z...Y$, which means that there is a component of X (Z) which is composed of Y: Y is a component of X because it is a component of Z.

In the example of the Convertible-vehicle, there is no composition path between Convertible-vehicle and Roof. The only path between these two classes follows a forbidden link for the class Convertible-vehicle. We can therefore conclude that a convertible vehicle is not composed of roof.

Let us apply this result to the basic structures of composition graphs with contradictions. We conclude, in the case of a contradiction of type 1a, that X is not composed of Y since the path Xl_1Zl_2Y follows a forbidden link for X. In all other cases, there is always a composition path between X and Y which allows us to conclude that X is composed of Y. These composition paths are Xl_1Zl_3Y in the contradiction of type 1b, Xl_3Zl_4Y in the contradiction of type 2, $Xl_3Vl_4Zl_5Y$ in the contradiction of type 3 and Xl_3Wl_4Y in the contradiction of type 4.

4.4 Instance composition graphs

We have seen in the previous section that the composition graph of an instance is not necessarily isomorphic to that of its class. We will now consider the impact of exception links on instance composition graphs. In order to do this, we will look at the four types of contradictions.

Let us first consider the contradiction of type 1a. According to the definition of an exception link, if X excepts a composition link l_2 of a component class Z of X, the instances of Z that are components of the instances of X do not reference instances through the composition link l_2. On the contrary, the instances of Z that are not part of instances of X are composed of instances of Y (Figure 10).

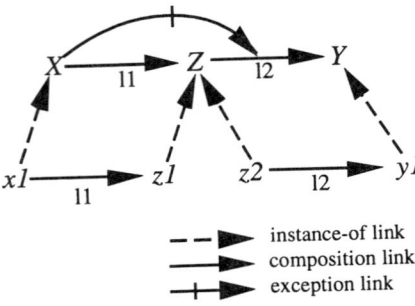

```
- - - ▶   instance-of link
  ——▶     composition link
 —|—▶     exception link
```

Figure 10: *The instance composition graph in the case of a contradiction of type 1a*

Let us now consider contradictions of types 1b and 4. In these two cases, the exception is defined in the class X and there is a composition path between X and Y. For the contradiction of type 1b (Figure 11), the instances of Z that are components of the instances of X must not reference the instances of Y through the composition link l_2 but only through the composition link l_3. The composition graph of an instance of X is therefore isomorphic to that of x_1. In the example given in Figure 12, the instances of Y are components of the instances of X only as components of the instances of W.

In the contradictions of types 2 and 3, the exception is not defined in the class X but rather in a component class (W) of X. Moreover, there are several paths between X and Y, none of which pass through W. Only paths that do not pass through W are composition paths. The instances of Z must not reference components through the composition link l_4 (type 2) or l_5 (type 3) only in the case where they are compo-

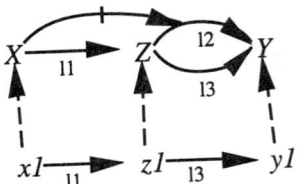

Figure 11: *The instance composition graphs in the case of contradictions of types 1b.*

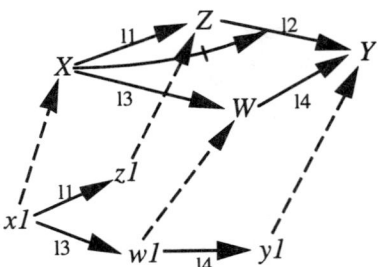

Figure 12: *The instance composition graphs in the case of contradictions of types 4.*

nents of the instances of W. Since a same instance of Z cannot at the same time reference and not reference a component through a given composition link, the composition graph of an instance of X necessarily contains two instances of Z (Figures 13 and 14).

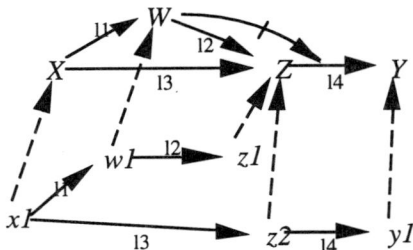

Figure 13: *The instance composition graphs in the case of contradictions of types 2.*

4.5 Algorithm for processing exception links

As for exceptions in inheritance graphs where we have to compute the set of inheritable objects, when exception links are present in composition graphs, we have to compute, for a given class X, the set of its components, denoted by $\mathrm{Comp}(X)$.

The algorithm that allows us to compute the set of components of a given class X is based on a depth-first search strategy. Its principle is to memorize vertices that declare exception links and the list of exceptions (that is, for each exception, we memorize the excepted composition link as well as the class that defines this

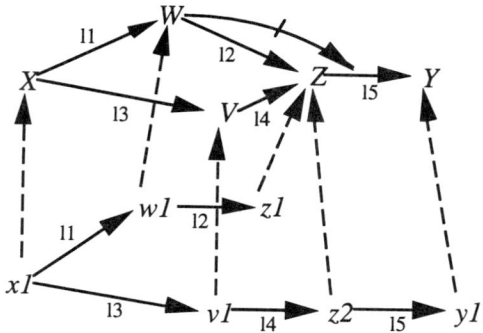

Figure 14: *The instance composition graphs in the case of contradictions of types 3.*

composition link). Since an exception between a class X and a composition link L implies that all the components of X cannot reference components through the composition link L, the exception declared in the class X is memorized while the exploration of vertices Z such that there is a path between X and Z has not been completed. A composition link may be followed only if it does not belong to the current list of excepted composition links. All vertices that are referenced by a composition link that could be followed are components of the class from which the algorithm has started.

Algorithm
Input : a class X and a composition graph with exception
    links.
Result : Comp, list of classes that are components of X.

Let
    Comp : list of components of X;
    P : stack of vertices that declare exceptions;
    PileE : stack of lists of pairs (excepted link,
        class having this link);
Begin
    Comp= empty list;
    P = PileE= empty stack;
    If *X declares exception links*
    Then
        push (X, P);
        push (list of exceptions declared by X, PileE);
    End If
    For each *composition link Li of X* Do
        Succ(Li);
    End For
End

Function *Succ(L : composition link)*
Let x : the class that is referenced by L;
Begin
    Comp = Comp + x; (set union)
    If *x declares exception links*
    Then
        push (x, P);
        push (list of exceptions declared by x, PileE);
    End If
    For each *composition link Li of x* Do
        If *(Li x)* ∉ *PileE* Then *Succ(Li);*

        End If
    End For
    If *head(P)=x* Then *pull (P);*
                    pull (PileE);
        End If
End

For more information concerning the proof of this algorithm, refer to [19]. The complexity of this algorithm is polynomial.

Different algorithms are based on the algorithm which has been defined above. For instance, the instantiation algorithm which has to determine classes that must be instantiated is based on this algorithm. Moreover, we have also defined a process of property sharing allowing a composite object to propagate its properties towards its components selectively. Therefore, we have to determine if a component is part of a composite object before propagating a property.

4.6 Discussion

We may wonder why exceptions in composition graphs are used instead of exceptions in inheritance graphs. Different reasons may be given.

If we use exceptions in inheritance graphs to customize the object that is reused, we have to:
- create a subclass of the class that possesses the composition link to be excepted
- declare an exception in the subclass towards the composition link (this exception must be an exception on the inheritance of the composition link [19])
- create subclasses of components appearing between the composite object we are creating and the subclass mentioned above
- and declare that the composite object we are creating is composed of this subclass.

In the example given in Figure 1, for the representation of a *novel*, we want to reuse the component *chapter* without taking into account the component *figure*. If we use exceptions in inheritance graphs (Figure 15), we first have to create a subclass of *section* and to declare an exception in this subclass towards the composition link not to be inherited. Then we create a subclass of *chapter* and declare that this subclass is composed of the new subclass of *section*. The class *chapter-of-novels* therefore inherits the composition link towards *title*, the component *section* being specialized by the component section-without-figure. Finally, we declare that a novel is composed of *chapter-of-novels*.

The creation of these subclasses may be useful if they are often reused, otherwise it is useless.

On the other hand, if we use exceptions on composition links to customize an object, we only have to:
- declare that the composite object being created is

202

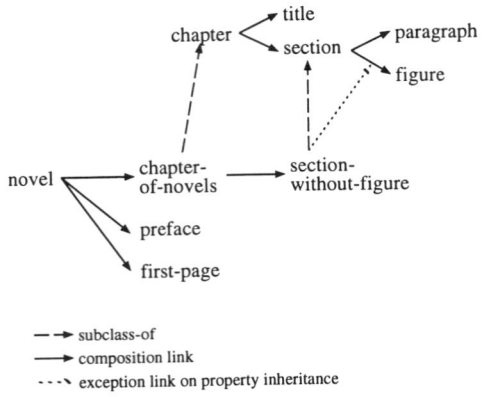

Figure 15: *Definition of the object novel by using exceptions on property inheritance*

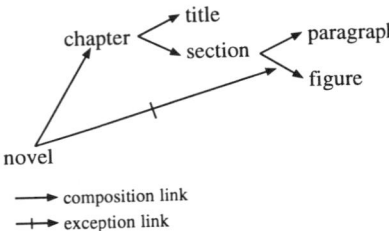

Figure 16: *Definition of the object novel by using exceptions on composition links*

composed of the object that is reused
- declare an exception towards the composition link to be excepted.

As the exception on composition may reference a component of any level of composition, no subclass has to be created. For instance, in order to represent a *novel*, we state that a *novel* is composed of the component *chapter* and we add an exception link towards the composition link that references the component *figure* (Figure 16).

Consequently, if a direct component has to be cancelled, exceptions on property inheritance may be used. Otherwise, it seems to be more interesting to use exceptions on composition links when indirect components have to be excepted. Moreover, as we have previously seen, the algorithm for the management of exceptions in composition graphs always has a polynomial complexity.

5   CONCLUSION

In this paper, we have proposed a model of exceptions on composition links. The aim of this model is to favor object reusability by allowing a composite object to be reused without taking into account all its own components.

Exceptions on composition links are applied at class level and are used to cancel a composition link declared in a component class of the class that declares the exception. As in the case of exceptions in inheritance graphs, the main problem of the management of exceptions in composition graphs is the management of contradictions. Five types of contradictions have been identified. Nevertheless, as a clear and well-defined semantics of exceptions in composition graphs has been outlined, all these contradictions may be resolved, except the contradiction of type 0 that is considered as inconsistent.

Exceptions in composition graphs also favor object evolution that consists in dynamically changing inheritance and composition graphs [17]. Our future work will therefore consist in extending the model of object evolution by introducing exceptions on composition links. Moreover, although exceptions may be very useful to customize objects that are reused, there must never be too many exceptions in composition graphs. Otherwise, this means that the composition graph has to be reorganized [5]. Therefore, we will also study a mechanism for the reorganization of inheritance and composition graphs with exceptions.

REFERENCES

1. F. Baader *et al.*, "How to Prefer More Specific Defaults in Terminological Default Logic", In Proceedings of *the 13th International Joint Conference on Artificial Intelligence*, Chambéry, France, 1993, 669–674.

2. E. Blake *et al.*, "On Including Part Hierarchies in Object-Oriented Languages, with an Implementation in Smalltalk", In Proceedings of *ECOOP'87*, AFCET, Paris, 1987.

3. G. Brewka, *Nonmonotonic Reasoning: Logical Foundations of Commonsense*, Cambridge University Press, Cambridge, 1991.

4. A. Caminada, *Presage, un Environnement de modélisation multi-vue/multi-niveau pour la construction et l'utilisation d'applications de planification des réseaux de télécommunications*, PhD Thesis, University of Montpellier II, 1992.

5. E. Casais, *Managing Evolution in Object-Oriented Environments: An Algorithmic Approach*, PhD Thesis, University de Geneva, 1991.

6. F. Civello, "Roles for Composite Objects in Object-Oriented Analysis and Design" In Proceedings of *OOPSLA'93*, 1993, 376–393.

7. B. J. Cox *et al.*, *Object-Oriented Programming: an Evolutionary Approach*, 2nd Edition, Addison-Wesley Publishing Company, 1991.

8. F.M. Donini et al., "Nonmonotonic Reasoning", *Artificial Intelligence Review* 4, 1990, 163–210.

9. R. Ducournau et al., "Masking and Conflicts; or To Inherit is not to Own!", *Inheritance Hierarchies in Knowledge Representation and Programming Languages*, M. Lenzerini, D. Nardi, M. Simi (Eds), John Wiley & Sons, 1991, 223–244.

10. D. W. Etherington, "More on Inheritance Hierarchies with Exceptions: Default Theories and Inferential Distance", In Proceedings of the *AAAI*, Morgan Kaufmann, Los Altos, Californie, 1987, 352–357.

11. S. E. Fahlman et al., "Cancellation in a Parallel Semantic Network", In Proceedings of the *7th IJCAI*, Vancouver, Canada, 1981, 257–263.

12. M. Halper et al., "An OODB "Part" Relationship Model", *Proceedings of the 1st International Conference on Information and Knowledge Management*, CIKM'92, 1992, 602–611.

13. J. F. Horty et al., "A Skeptical Theory of Inheritance in Nonmonotonic Semantic Networks", *Artificial Intelligence* 42, 1990, 311–348.

14. W. Kim, *Introduction to Object-Oriented Databases*, MIT Press, Cambridge, Massachusetts, 1990.

15. M. Lenzerini, D. Nardi, M. Simi (Eds), "Inheritance Hierarchies in Knowledge Representation and Programming Languages", In Proceedings of the *Viareggio Workshop on Inheritance Hierarchies (1989)*, John Wiley & Sons, London, 1991.

16. M.E.S. Loomis et al., "An Object Modeling Technique for Conceptual Design", In Proceedingsof *ECOOP'87*, 1987, pp. 325–335.

17. M. Magnan et al., "Object Evolution", In Proceedings of the *5th International Conference on Software Engineering and Knowledge Engineering*, San Francisco, California, 1993.

18. M. Magnan et al., "Inheritance Systems with Exceptions", *Artificial Intelligence Review* 7(6), 1994, 421–443.

19. M. Magnan, *Reutilisability of Components: Exceptions in composition graphs*, PhD Thesis, University of Montpellier II, France, 1994.

20. E. Neufeld, "Notes on "A Clash of Intuitions"", *Artificial Intelligence*, 48, 1991, 225–240.

21. G.T. Nguyen et al., "Representing Design Objects", *AI in Design'91*, Butterworth Heinemann Ltd, 1991, 367–386.

22. J.J. Odell, "Managing Object Complexity, Part II: Composition", *Journal of Object-Oriented Programming* 5(6), October 1992, 17–20.

23. C. Oussalah et al., "Exceptions in Multiple Inheritance Systems", *Artificial Intelligence and Cognitive Science'92*, K. Ryan & R. F. E. Sutcliffe (Eds.), Springer Verlag, 1992, 338–341.

24. L. Padgham et al., 'Combining Classification and Nonmonotonic Inheritance Reasoning: A First Step", *7th International Symposium on Methodologies for Intelligent Systems*, Trondheim, Sweden, 1993, 132–141.

25. L. Padgham et al., "A Framework for Part-of Hierarchies in Terminological Logics", In Proceedings of the *4th International Conference on Principles of Knowledge Representation and Reasoning*, Bonn, Germany, May 1994.

26. E. Sandewall, "Nonmonotonic Inference Rules for Multiple Inheritance with Exceptions", In Proceedings of the *IEEE* 74(10), October 1986, 1345–1353.

27. B. Selman et al., "The Tractability of Path-based Inheritance", *Inheritance Hierarchies in Knowledge Representation and Programming Languages*, M. Lenzerini, D. Nardi & M. Simi (Eds.), John Wiley, 1991, 83–95.

28. G. Simonet, 'RS Theory: a Really Skeptical Theory of Inheritance with Exceptions", In Proceedings of the *Conference on Knowledge Representation*, 1994, 615–626.

29. L.A. Stein, 'Resolving Ambiguity in non-momotonic hierarchies", *Artificial Intelligence* 55, 1992, 259–310.

30. U. Straccia, "Default Inheritance Reasoning in Hybrid KL-ONE-style Logics", *Proceedings of the 13th International Joint Conference on Artificial Intelligence*, Chambéry, France, 1993, 676–681.

31. P.L. Tan et al., "Modelling Exceptions in Semantic Database and Knowledge-based Systems", In Proceedings of *Knowledge Based Computer Systems*, Bombay, India, 1989, 120–132.

32. R. H. Thomason, "NETL and subsequent path-based inheritance theories", *Computers Math. Applic.*, 23(2-5), 1992, 179–204.

33. D. S. Touretzky et al., "A Clash of Intuitions: The Current State of Nonmonotonic Multiple Inheritance Systems", In Proceedings of the *10th IJCAI*, Milan, Italy, 1987, 476–482.

34. D. S. Touretzky et al., "A Skeptic's Menagerie: Conflictors, Preemptors, Reinstaters, and Zombies in Nonmonotonic Inheritance", In Prooceedings of the *12th IJCAI*, 1991, 478–483.

35. P. Wegner, "Concepts and Paragdims of Object-oriented Programming", *OOPS Messenger* 1(1), 1990.

36. W. Wilkes et al., "Complex and Composite Objects in CAD/CAM Databases", In Proceedings of the *5th International Conference on Data Engineering*, 1989, 443–450.

37. M.E. Winston et al., "A Taxonomy of Part-Whole Relations", *Cognitive Science*, 11, 1987, 417–444.

C$\underset{\smile}{\text{O}}$LOR-$\mathcal{X}$: Object Modeling Profits from Linguistics

J.F.M. Burg* and **R.P. van de Riet**
Vrije Universiteit
Amsterdam, The Netherlands
{jfmburg,vdriet}@cs.vu.nl

ABSTRACT

This paper describes a linguistically based object modeling technique for modeling Information and Communication Systems. This technique is a combination of a linguistically based, formal conceptual modeling language and a high-level graphical analysis and design method. The process of modeling Information and Communication Systems is interactively supported by a Lexicon, which delivers correct information that the analyst and designer use as a base for their final models. Our modeling technique and the supporting lexicon facilitates the modeling process and results in models that are consistent and complete.
Keywords: Object Model, Linguistics, CPL, Information and Communication Systems, Lexicon

1 INTRODUCTION

This paper, which is based on [4], describes a linguistically based object modeling technique to model Information and Communication Systems. This modeling process will be supported by a lexicon by means of linguistic information. In a previous project we have developed a structure for such a lexicon, and we have incorporated its implementation in a commercial data-dictionary environment [6].

The name of our current project, COLOR-X, is an acronym for the **CO**nceptual **L**inguistically based **O**bject oriented **R**epresentation Language for Information and Communication Systems (ICS abbreviated to **X**). In the COLOR-X project we are combining the formal conceptual modeling technique

*Supported by the Foundation for Computer Science in the Netherlands (SION) with financial support from the Dutch Organization for Scientific Research (NWO), project 612-123-309

CPL (Conceptual Prototyping Language) [8], which is linguistically based, with existing graphical modeling techniques. This approach is chosen to facilitate the process of conceptual modeling and which leads to more consistent and complete models that are linguistically correct. COLOR-X is the first phase of a larger project which has as objective the generation of object-oriented programming code from a natural language based modeling technique, which brings, as a side-effect, the conceptual models closer to programming code. In addition, by using a modeling technique based on linguistic notions, we are narrowing the gap between requirements documents, written in natural language, and conceptual models as well.

This project is part of the LICS-project (Linguistically based Information and Communication Systems), in which we investigate how linguistic knowledge could be used when building Information and Communication Systems (ICS for short). In our view, the problem of controlling the *meaning* of words is becoming a key issue in ICSs, like Database Management Systems, Communication Systems, Office Automation, etc. The ICSs offer highly sophisticated tools for efficient storage, processing and transmission of data. However, transmission of data is only useful when the sender and the receiver agree on the meaning of the words. Database retrieval is only successful when the user knows where to look and what words (s)he should use. Although Data Dictionaries already exist for decades, and the best among them do contain meaning definitions of terms [6], they are of limited help, for several reasons worth noting. First, they lack any linguistic knowledge, which makes it difficult to sort out semantic and morpho-syntactic aspects. Secondly, they lack a formal basis, hence making it impossible for the system itself to reason with the meaning descriptions. Thirdly, they are usually *closed systems*, and not integrated with the user interface, the CASE design environment, or other applications.

LICS itself is a subproject of the LIKE-project (Linguistic Instruments in Knowledge Engineering) which is a consortium of researchers of three disciplines: Linguistics, Business Administrators and Computer Science. The LIKE-project is focusing research around the theme: how linguistic instruments can be used profitably in the area of Knowledge Engineering, see [15].

In order to develop COLOR-X we started with Dignum's CPL, because

1. it is based on a linguistic theory, called Functional Grammar [10]

2. it is formally consistent because it is founded in several logics [8] and [9] and

3. it already contains some conceptual modeling features.

We have added some additional features and a graphical layer on top of CPL, so that the resulting models are easier to work with, to discuss and to reuse. We have tried to find a set of aspects a conceptual modeling technique should contain, by examining some existing techniques. We have chosen Rumbaughs OMT (Object Modeling Technique) [17], because, firstly, it supports three different models of an ICS, which is according to us a necessary aspect of every modeling technique. The second reason is that it relates closely to other well-known and accepted methods and, finally, we have chosen OMT, because it is also widely accepted in the object-oriented community as being effective and efficient.

In this paper we will describe the COLOR-X *static object model (*CSOM*)*, which shows the objects and classes of objects in an ICS and the relationships between them. The static model is of course the central model because it defines the overall structure of the system to be built. CPL gives the opportunity to model the static part as well, but focuses on specifying constraints (static and dynamic). This has led to a very awkward notation when CPL is used to model just the static description of the system. In order to overcome this problem we have used CPL as an internal representation language and we have defined a (graphical) layer on top of it. This graphical layer uses some OMT **object model** notations, because they are well-known and easy to use. As a matter of fact, OMT considers this object model also as the fundamental base of the modeling process, so the knowledge represented in the models will often overlap, but exactly at the points where the linguistic knowledge is necessary or more effective our COLOR-X model will differ from the OMT one.

One of the main reasons to use linguistic knowledge is to make the use of words appearing in the models consistent. Among the obvious rules are: *"class names should be nouns"* and *"relationship names should be verbs"*. Less trivial, but more interesting and important, are the rules between the meaning of words used in the model: *"certain relationship-types require certain class-types"* and *"certain class-types can not be related in some systems"*. An example of the first rule constrains the type of class required in the *buy*-relationship to be (a descendant in the is-a hierarchy of) *person*. An example of the other rule forbids a *marry*-relationship between two persons of the same sex.

Another reason to use linguistic knowledge in modeling techniques is to give more expressive power to those techniques. It will be shown further on in this paper that adding the *roles* objects play in a relation, such as *agent* or *instrument*, will make the model easier to understand and to use. The addition of modalities, like *must* and *permit*, clarifies the status of the used relationships.

An additional nice feature of a linguistically based modeling technique is that it is relatively easy to generate natural language sentences from it, in order to give some feedback to the system designers and to the end-users as well. This feedback consists of generated sentences during the modeling phase, in order to check if the model is consistent with the requirements ([7] and [14]) and on the other hand this feedback consists of explanation facilities, like Gulla defines and uses in his PPP-case tool [11]. The first kind of feedback is the subject of research in another LIKE-project.

Now that we know *why* to use linguistic knowledge, we need to know *how* to use it. We will use a lexicon as a source containing this knowledge. This lexicon could be used during the modeling process in two ways:

First, it could be used *after* the models are finished to check whether these models are correct and consistent. We have followed this approach in a fruitful experiment [3], in which Entity-Relationship-diagrams (ERD) were translated into formal, linguistically based specifications (CPL) which were verified for correctness by consulting a lexicon.

It would be more useful and efficient, however, to use the lexicon *interactively during* the modeling process by *giving* structures, types and constraints to the designer instead of *checking* them, because then the models are always linguistically correct. We have opted for this latter approach in this paper. Another difference with the before mentioned ERD-project is the choice of modeling technique. We will introduce a technique which has more expressive power than ER-Diagrams, by including linguistic notions.

In the following section we will give a short introduction to CPL. In section 3 we will introduce the static model of COLOR-X. Section 4 will treat the use of a lexicon during the process of creating such a static model and it will show an experiment which demonstrates the usefulness of this approach. We will conclude this paper by listing some conclusions and research that is still to do.

2 INTRODUCTION TO CPL

The language CPL has been developed as a specification language as close as possible to natural language, by basing it on **Functional Grammar** [10], but formal enough to specify the requirements of an ICS in a precise and unambiguous way. The formal semantics, as defined in [8] and [9], is based on predicate, modal, deontic and temporal logic. Each CPL construct is translated into some combination of these logics. The general form of a CPL specification language is as follows:

Mode : Tense : Predication $T_1 \cdots T_n$
      (**id:** $\cdots$)
      (**sit:** $\cdots$)

Mode	= **FACTUAL|MUST|NEC|PERMIT**
Tense	= **ACTION|DONE|**
	PROSP|PERF|PRET
Predication	= a relation between n terms $T_1 \cdots T_n$,
T_i	= a term denotes a (set of) object(s). Each object occurs in a specific role.
id	= identification of the objects
sit	= situation in which this CPL specification is supposed to hold
term	= [~] Verb [([< $Card[, Distr]$ >] **Role** = [Var **in**] Noun)] +

For example, the following specification says that *When a company has sold a car to a customer, it has to send a bill to this customer within a week.*:

MUST: ACTION:
send(**ag**=C in company) (**go**=bill)
      (**rec**=C2 in customer) (**temp**=T2 in time)
      (**id:** T2 = T1 + 1*week)
      (**sit: PERF:** sell(**ag**=C in company) (**go**=car)
      (**rec**=C2 in customer) (**temp**=T1 in time))

A *role* corresponds with the FG notions *semantic function* and *satellite*. Table 1 shows the most frequently used semantic functions and satellites.

The following CPL specification (*The thief broke the window with a brick*) demonstrates the use of roles:

FACTUAL: PERF:
break(**ag** = thief) (**go** = window) (**instr** = brick)

This example also shows the (linguistic) difference between semantic functions and satellites: satellites give additional information about some SoA, whereas the semantic functions can not be left out without loosing the intended meaning of the verb.

Modality and *Tense* are also linguistic oriented notions which clarify the status of the specific relationship, the corresponding CPL specification and natural language sentence. Table 2 shows the their meaning.

CPL gives the possibility to express the cardinality of relationships, as Figure 1 shows.

In addition to these cardinalities CPL specifies the *distributivity* of the cardinalities, which defines the difference between the following two sentences:

Two companies order **together** *three products*

Two companies order **each** *three products*

which both have the following underlying CPL (without distributivity) specification:

FACTUAL:
order(< 2 > **ag** = company) (< 3 > **go** = product)

but by adding distributivity the results are, respectively:

FACTUAL:
order(< 2, c > **ag**=company) (< 3, c > **go**=product)
FACTUAL:
order(< 2, d > **ag**=company) (< 3, c > **go**=product)

The distributivity is either **collective** or **distributive**. The exact meaning of the used modalities, tenses, semantic functions and cardinalities can be found in [8].

Role	Meaning
Semantic Functions	
agent	entity controlling an action
goal	entity effected by the operation of agent or force
recipient	entity into whose possession something is transferred
source	entity from which something moves/is moved
Satellites	
instrument	tool with which an action is carried out or a position maintained
beneficiary	animate for whose benefit the SoA is affected
time	point in time at/from/until which SoA takes place

Table 1: FG's Semantic Functions and Satellites

3 STATIC OBJECT MODEL

In this section we will treat the static object model of COLOR-X (CSOM). We will do this by defining each modeling concept (*classes, objects, relationships* and *constraints*) in a separate section.

Modality	Meaning	Corresponding Logical operator
MUST	should be	deontic obligation
NEC	has to be	modal necessity
PERMIT	allowed to be	deontic permission
FACTUAL	happens to be	– (FOL)

Tense	Meaning	Consequence
PRET	past tense	relation is dead
PERF	perfect tense	relation exists but action has died
DONE	perfect tense	same as PERF but action was last action
ACTION	present tense	the actual action and birth of relation
PROSP	future tense	future relation

Table 2: The Meaning of Modalities and Tenses

Cardinalities	Mathematical	Graphical
Exactly one	1	
Exactly n	n	n
Zero or more/less	0+ / 0-	●
n or more/less	n+ / n-	n+
zero or one	0,1	○
Interval n-m	n-m	n-m
Set of Disconnected Intervals	n,m-m2,k,...,l	n,m-m2,k,...,l

Figure 1: Cardinalities of Relations

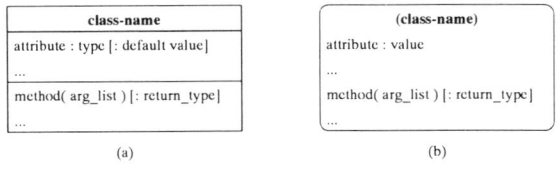

Figure 2: Class Notation, (a) Class, (b) Object

3.1 Classes

A **class** in the static model is denoted by a noun. It contains the usual *methods* and *attributes*, which are of a certain *type*, and could have some *default value*. An **object** is an instance of a certain class and its attributes have certain *values*. This information is depicted using the graphical notations found in Figure 2.

As said before, linguistically class-names and attributes should be nouns. The corresponding and underlying CPL specifications are listed below:

(a) **FACTUAL:** has(class-name) (A in attribute)
   (**id:** value-of(A) (type))
   (**id:** A = default-value)

(b) **FACTUAL:** exists(< 1 > class-name)
   FACTUAL: has(class-name) (A in attribute)
   (**id:** A = value)

3.2 Relationships

Relationships are denoted by verbs, and the designer can retrieve most of them by examining the verbs occurring in the requirements document. Traditionally, no designer made a distinction between different *types* of verbs. There are several (linguistic) dimensions in which verbs can be different:

1. features of the verb, like: *dynamism, control, telic,* etc.

2. arity of the verb, like: *intransitive, transitive, ditransitive*

3. semantic category of the verb, like: *SPEAK, MOVE, TRANSFER, etc.* defined by Schank and also used in [18]

We have used these dimensions as well, but we have distinguished the verbs mainly on their use as a relationship in a conceptual model. The three different kinds of relationships, *standard (conceptual), intra-SoA (State of Affairs)* and *inter-SoA relationships*, will be discussed in the next section. The remaining sections about relationships will treat the common structures of relationships and their correspondence with associations and links, as used in traditional modeling techniques, such as OMT.

3.2.1 Conceptual Categories of Verbs

During the modeling process, two kinds of relationships are used: *standard conceptual modeling relationships* and *user-relationships*. The first kind corresponds roughly to the *rhetorical relationships* which are defined in [12] and used in [11]. We have divided this set into two subsets:

- **Standard Static Relationships**, which is a set containing CPL's *special relations*, such as the **is_a-**, **has_a-**, **exists-**, **value-of**-relations, etc. This set is completed with other, sometimes overlapping, traditional relationships like *aggregation*, *generalization* and *attributes*.

- **Inter-SoA Relationships**, which is a set of relationships that relate two states of affairs to each other. Among the relationships contained in this set are: *cause, result, reason* and *concurrent*.

The third set of relationships we distinguish contains **Intra-SoA** or **User-Defined Relationships**. These relationships are defined by the user because they are directly retrieved from the requirements document. In a library environment common intra-SoA relationships would be *borrow* and *return*, [2] and [3].

We consider the inter-SoA relationships to be necessary especially for explanation facilities and the dynamic part of the conceptual model. Therefore we will not discuss it here but we will treat it in a separate paper [5]. Briefly, we are using this kind of relationships to inter-relate dynamic aspects with static or other dynamic aspects of an ICS. An example would be the causal relationship between *"borrow a book"* and *"possessing a book"*.

Figure 3 shows the graphical notation for the standard relationships we use. The underlying and equivalent CPL-specifications are listed below:

(a) **Generalization/Specialization**
NEC : is-a(sub-class1) (superclass)
NEC : is-a(sub-class2) (superclass)

(b) **Generalization/Specialization**
The subclasses cover the superclass fully. This is an extension of the generalization mentioned in the previous point. The additional CPL-statement is:
NEC : cover(superclass) (sub-class1) (sub-class2)

(c) **Non-disjoint Generalization**
Members of the subclass may overlap.
NEC : is-a(sub-class1) (superclass)
NEC : is-a(sub-class2) (superclass)
NEC : nexclude(sub-class1) (sub-class2)

(d) **Aggregation**
FACTUAL :
has-a(**zero** = class) (**pat** = part-class1)
FACTUAL :
has-a(**zero** = class) (**pat** = part-class2)
NEC : exclude(part-class1) (part-class2)

(e) **Instantiation**
FACTUAL : exists($< x[+|-] >$ class)
There exists x, x or more (x+) or x or less (x-) instances of the class

In the next section we will concentrate on intra-SoA relationships and the related CPL specifications.

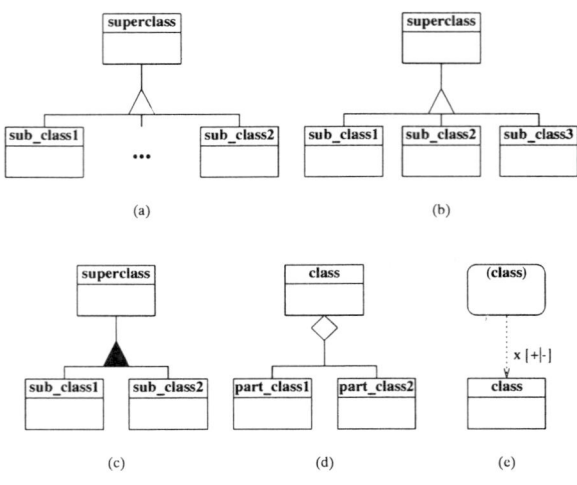

Figure 3: Standard Relationships, (a) Generalization, (b) Generalization (cover), (c) Non-disjoint Generalization, (d) Aggregation, (e) Instantiation (exists)

3.2.2 Syntax and Semantics of Intra-SoA Relationships

We have incorporated the notions of roles, modalities and tenses into the graphical conceptual model, as Figure 4 shows. The linguistically motivated roles, that specify which object is the agent, object, goal, etc. of the relationship, are sometimes found in modeling techniques, but not as a fundamental part of the technique. Mostly, they are just added as some sort of comment, like OMT's *role names*, which have some meaning for the (human) user of the model, but which are not theoretically founded and can, therefore, not be used in automatic model translation processes. We will use FG's *semantic functions* and *satellites* as defined in [10] and as used in [21] and [8]. Both CPL and OMT have the possibility to use *cardinalities* in conceptual models.

noun	$<card,distr>$	**Modality:Tense:**
	role	**[NOT:] verb**

Figure 4: Graphical Notations of Relations

The mapping from the graphical notation to CPL is one-to-one and very straightforward :
Modality: Tense: [not: | $\sim$]

$$\text{verb} (\underbrace{[< card, distr > \textbf{role} = noun])}_{\forall \text{ object}}$$

3.2.3 Associations and Links

In the OMT method a difference is made between *associations* and *links* analogous to the difference between classes and objects. In CSOM we do not introduce two similar concepts, but stick to one: *relationships*. Relationships relate classes as well their instances. The bidirectional nature of relationships (a person *works for* a company and that company *employs* that person) is abandoned in CSOM, due to the introduction of semantic functions. This ambiguity reduction is appreciated during the feedback in natural language, because now the generated sentences match with the original ones from the requirements document.

Another difference between CSOM and OMT's object modeling is the absence in CSOM of link attributes and the possibility to model associations as classes. The reason for this absence is:

- there is no linguistic equivalent to these concepts, which means that they are not translatable to CPL specifications nor to natural language sentences.

- the information modeled by these concepts can easily be captured by other constructs available in CSOM. An example should clarify this point: association attributes contain mostly some temporal or spatial information, which is modeled in CSOM by using the semantic functions *time* and *location*.

3.3 Constraints

One of the main objectives for developing CPL was to specify constraints in an easy, natural language based manner. Dignum, [8], mentions five categories of constraints which cover all constraints necessary to model a Universe of Discourse. These constraints, however, are mainly based on *inter-SoA* relationships, which are not treated in this paper. Because of this fact, we will focus on *static constraints* on classes, objects and relationships, which are not influenced or determined by other relationships. There are four of those constraints possible:

1. the *cardinality* of a certain relationship constrains the number of objects allowed in that relationship. The *distributivity* says something more about the distribution of objects over that relationship.

2. the **MUST** and **NEC** modalities specify whether a certain relationship should hold, and if it doesn't, whether it causes some reaction or inconsistent state, respectively.

3. constraints on values of attributes. These attributes can either belong to one or to several objects. The following general CPL specification shows this, where the $\mathcal{R}$ means some (mostly mathematical, like '=' or '<') relation:

has(class) (A_1 in *attribute$_1$*)
has(class) (A_2 in *attribute$_2$*)

(**id:** A_1 $\mathcal{R}$ A_2)

verb($role_1 = C_1$ in *class$_1$*) ($role_2 = C_2$ in *class$_2$*)
    (**id:** has(C_1) (A_1 in *attribute$_1$*)
    (**id:** has(C_2) (A_2 in *attribute$_2$*)
    (**id:** A_1 $\mathcal{R}$ A_2)

4. constraints between relationships or between classes. Examples of this kind are *subset* and *contain*.

The graphical notations for expressing these kinds of constraints are adopted from OMT. This means that they are textually added to the model between braces. They are formalized however in the underlying CPL specifications.

3.3.1 Consistency Checks

The introduction of a linguistic foundation makes the resulting models more consistent and correct. The following consistency checks take care of this:

- syntactic correctness:
  - relationships are denoted by verbs
  - classes and attributes are denoted by nouns

- semantic correctness:
  - classes can only be involved in a certain relationship when they are some descendant of the rootclasses appearing in the verb-frames of that relationship. Each verb requires some kinds of nouns
  - some standard relationships between classes are prohibited (a *person* can never occur as an attribute of a certain class, but should be connected to this class by some relationship) and other are obligated by the lexicon, because it contains already some aggregation-, generalization-, attribute- and other relationships between classes

- consistency:
  - among specifications:
    One of the biggest drawbacks of formal conceptual modeling techniques is the size of the specifications list. Having all those specifications it is very difficult to maintain the consistency between nouns, verbs and constraints that appear in different specifications (probably separated by an enormous amount of other specifications). The introduction of a graphical layer on top of the formal CPL method has reduced the complexity considerably.
  - between models and requirements document:
    The consistency between the models and the information from the requirements document is established by the combination of generated basediagrams from a lexicon, interactive use of this

210

lexicon, one-to-one correspondence between the graphical model and the CPL-specifications and the feedback through generated natural language sentences.

Our CPL2NL tool generates natural language sentences out of CPL specifications. We will list some aspects of the CPL specifications that have their impact on the generated sentences. First, the modality determines the auxiliary verb of the sentence as follows: **NEC**, **MUST** and **PERMIT** trigger *obliged to*, *should* and *permitted to* respectively. Secondly, the cardinality of the subject (agent or zero) of the relationship determines the singular or plural form of the related verb. The identification of the objects is added as a subordinate clause, starting with *where....* Finally, the satellites of the CPL specification are translated into adjuncts of place or time.

3.4 Example

In this section we will present a very simplistic example of the static object modeling technique, which is, however, big enough to contain a variety of modeling notions and which shows roughly the advantages our approach yields. The example consists of four stages:

1. **Requirements Document**:
   Company XYZ sells cars of type ABC to customers for the price of 20,000. A car consists of an engine, a break and an accelerator. Cars have to cost less than 30,000. The company employs 15 persons. A person has a name and a social security number. The required system keeps track of these facts.

2. **Final Model**: Figure 5

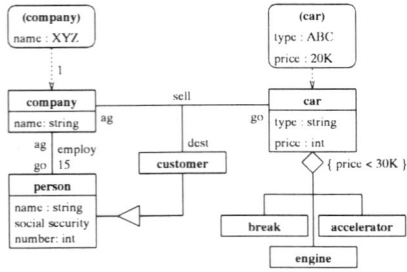

Figure 5: Example: Company XYZ

3. **(Some) Corresponding CPL specification**:
   - sell(ag=company) (go=car) (rec=customer)
   - employ(ag = company) (<15> go = person)
   - **NEC:** is_a(customer) (person)
   - **NEC:** exists(<1> zero = company)
     (**id:** has_a(company) (N in name)
       (**id:** N = 'XYZ'))

- **FACTUAL:** has_a(person) (name)
- **MUST:** has_a(car) (P in price)
     (**id:** P < 30K)

4. **(Some) Generated NL Sentences:** [1]
   - [a,company,sells,a,car,to,a,customer]
   - [There,exists,one,company,
     and,a,company,has,a,name,p,
     where,p,is,xyz]
   - [a,customer,is,obliged to,be,a,person]
   - [a,person,has,a,name]
   - [a,car,should,have,a,price,p,
     where,p,is smaller than,30k]

4 USING A LEXICON

As said before, we use a lexicon *during* the modeling process in order to obtain a correct and consistent model. By using a lexicon in such a way we get the following advantages:

1. the *base*-diagram, i.e. the relationship with its required classes, is generated directly from the lexicon, which saves the designer a lot of time (e.g. Figure 11)

2. the classes involved in a certain relationship are
   - syntactically correct, because every class is denoted by a certain noun
   - semantically correct, because every class is some descendant of the *base*-class connected to the specific verb (constructions like *"the building runs"* are prohibited because *building* is not a descendant of *living*, the class required by *run*)

3. the *base*-diagram is automatically extended with relevant relationships from the lexicon. Relevant relationships are: generalization, aggregation and attribute, but could also be: antonymy and hyponymy in certain universes of discourse

4. other extensions to the *base*-diagram contain linguistic notions, like semantic functions and satellites, which we have included in our modeling technique

Using our modeling technique and a lexicon during the modeling process leads to a syntactically and semantically correct model, which describes the static aspects of the universe of discourse in an adequate way. Additional advantages of this approach include the underlying linguistic method, which gives the possibility to generate sentences from the models and to use explanation facilities. Another advantage is the logic foundation of those models, which gives the opportunity to reason with models, to derive new knowledge from them and to prove the consistency of them.

---

[1]Automatically generated by our *CPL2NL* generator.

To show these advantages, we have implemented a demo-program, called VERP (Verb to Entity-Relationship Prototype), which generates models from a single verb by using a lexicon interactively. To show the usability and universality of this approach we have used existing, well-known tools, like WordNet [13] and the CASE-tool Software through Pictures (STP, [20]). The next section will describe this experiment. The last section of this chapter describes the future possibilities of this approach when our own CSOM-method and lexicon is used.

4.1 Experiment

Globally, VERP, which is implemented in C++, reads in a verb, retrieves information from WordNet about this verb and its required nouns and generates ER-diagrams readable by STP. The figures 6 till 10 show the graphical user interface of VERP.

During these steps the user has the possibility to direct the outcome to the required result, by:

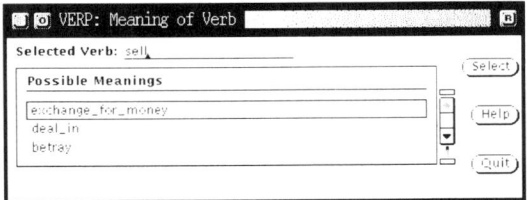

Figure 6: VERP: Specifying the meaning of 'sell'

- selecting meanings of words. This possibility is created by the fact that WordNet contains multiple meanings (concepts) of a certain word (6 and 9).

- selecting the arity and use of the verb. WordNet connects to each verb a set of sample sentences in which this verb could occur. By choosing such a sentence the number of nouns and their semantic function is determined. This choice is made easier by generating the underlying CPL specifications as well (7).

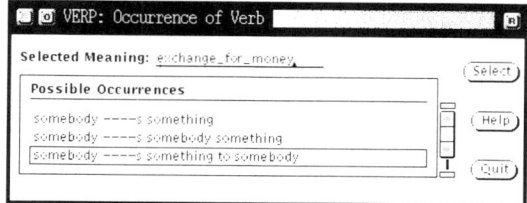

Figure 7: VERP: Specifying the occurrence of 'sell'

- specifying noun-classes retrieved from WordNet. When the noun *something* is found, the user could

specify this, for example, to *car*. This specification-process verifies if the new specific noun is a descendant of the original one, in order to preserve the semantics of the relationship (8).

- selecting meronymy-sets connected to a certain noun. Dependent on the universe of discourse different sets are of interest (10).

The before-mentioned *base*-diagram of *sell* in the meaning *exchange for money* with three roles is shown in Figure 11.

Figure 8: VERP: Specifying a noun

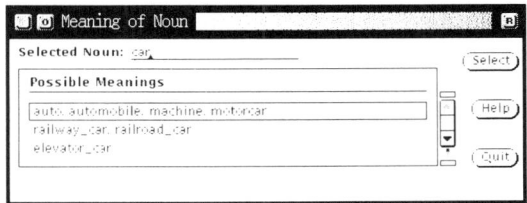

Figure 9: VERP: Specifying the meaning of 'car'

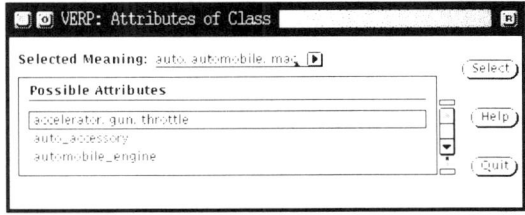

Figure 10: VERP: Specifying the attributes of 'car'

During the rest of the generation process, the nouns, i.e. classes, used are specified, some attributes are added and there is found a *generalization*-relationship between two classes entered: *person* and *boss*. The result of this process is shown in Figure 12. As an addition to the graphical model, we have attached the CPL-specification to this model in the form of an annotation of the global model, which is shown in the *View*-window of Figure 12.

4.2 Future Possibilities

As stated before, VERP is just a demo-environment that is meant to show the possibilities of our approach,

212

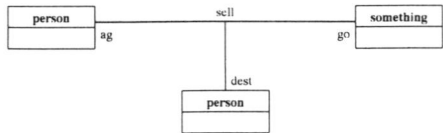

Figure 11: Csom Base Diagram

but that is limited to the capabilities of the tools used. At the moment, we are developing our own environment, which has led to the deliverance of the first version of the Csom graphical editor Tsod (Tool for Static Object Models). The generated *sell* relationship is also depicted using this tool in Figure 13. When we compare Tsod with the results of Verp, we notice the natural integration of information in Tsod versus the artificial look of the Er-diagrams (e.g. the textual inclusion of the semantic functions into the labels) in Figure 12.

In two earlier projects we have defined lexicon structures, based on the theory of Dik [10], and we filled them with a small set of words, in order to interpret Er-diagrams by generating CPL specifications from them [3] and to check the consistency of term defining information systems and generating natural language sentences from the internal formalisms [6]. The results of these projects were very promising and the structures defined appeared to be useful. Among the additions, found in our own lexicon, to the information in WordNet are *semantic functions* attached to verbs, more *common knowledge*, for example as attributes of nouns, and possibilities to add *specific knowledge* interactively, and more *types of relationships* between verbs. An example of this last category is the causal relation between *borrow* and *return*. These additions lead to a more complete generated diagram, and to a stronger relationship between the model and the underlying CPL specification.

5 CONCLUSIONS AND FURTHER RESEARCH

We have described in this paper the first part of the COLOR-X project, which consists of the definition of the static model. This graphical layer on top of CPL is similar to the object model of OMT but has some important linguistic additions. Another aspect of this model is the underlying CPL specifications, which are linguistically and logically founded. In order to facilitate the modeling process and to make the resulting model complete, correct and consistent we use (linguistic) knowledge from a lexicon. The advantages of this approach are demonstrated by the Verp-demo. Indirect advantages of our approach can be found in the fields of: *explanation facilities*, e.g. by generating natural language sentences, *code generation*, e.g. dependencies and constraints between components are cap-

tured in a better and more complete way, and *reusability issues*, e.g. a lexicon could be the base of reusable conceptual models.

At the moment we are focusing on the *dynamic* part of conceptual modeling by using COLOR-X Event Models [5], which show mainly the sequence of actions and events that take place in a particular UoD. Again, we are using CPL-specifications as a formal and linguistic foundation of these models. Nice features of these event models are the possibility to generate natural sentences and State-Transition Diagrams from it and the existence of standard building blocks to let the modeling process result in correct models. This process is also supported by a lexicon.

Another necessary addition to the static as well as the dynamic modeling techniques are the so-called *Inter-SoA Relationships*, which connect different States of Affairs for example by causal or result relationships.

In addition to these COLOR-X related extensions we are designing a supporting environment for our method, which includes of course a lexicon. This future environment will also contain an object-oriented code generator, which will interpret the static and dynamic COLOR-X diagrams.

Our participation in the LIKE-project has yielded some results in the area of communication analysis, in which useful UoD information is elicited from business conversations using a supporting lexicon. Research in this area is still going on.

ACKNOWLEDGMENT

We would like to thank Frank Dehne for his time and effort, which has led to the nice and useful Tool for Static Object Models.

REFERENCES

1. W.J. Black. "Acquisition of conceptual data models from natural language descriptions", In *Proceedings of the 2nd Conference of the European Chapter of the ACL*, Copenhagen, 1987.

2. P. Buitelaar and R.P. van de Riet. "The structure and use of a lexicon in conceptual modelling: A LIKE project", Technical report, Vrije Universiteit, 1992.

3. P. Buitelaar and R.P. van de Riet. "The use of a lexicon to interpret er diagrams: a LIKE project", In *Proceedings of the ER Conference*, Karlsruhe, 1992.

4. J.F.M. Burg and R.P. van de Riet. "COLOR-X: Object modeling profits from linguistics", Technical Report IR-365, Vrije Universiteit, Amsterdam, 1994.

5. J.F.M. Burg and R.P. van de Riet. "COLOR-X: Linguistically-based event modeling: A general approach to dynamic modeling", To appear in J. Iivari, K. Lyytinen and M. Rossi, *The Proceedings of the Seventh International Conference on Advanced Information System Engineering*, Jyvaskyla, Finland, Springer-Verlag's Lecture Notes in Computer Science, 1995.

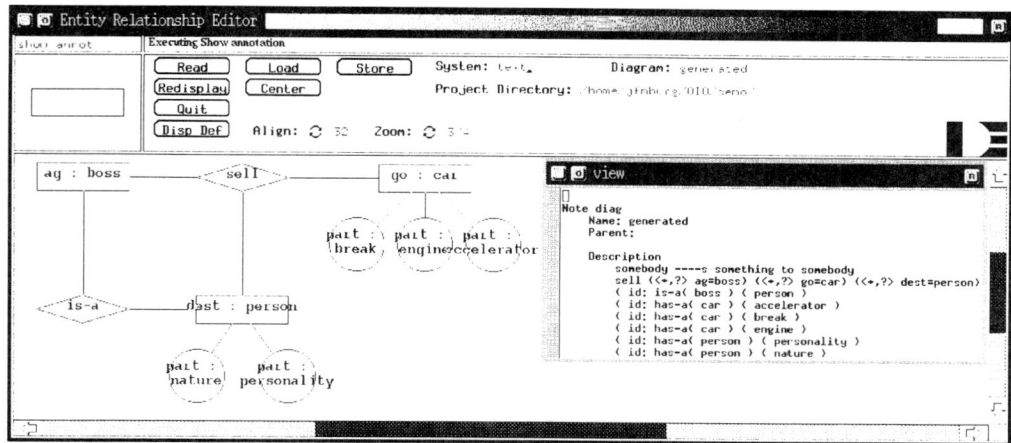

Figure 12: The 'sell' Relation, using STP's ER-editor

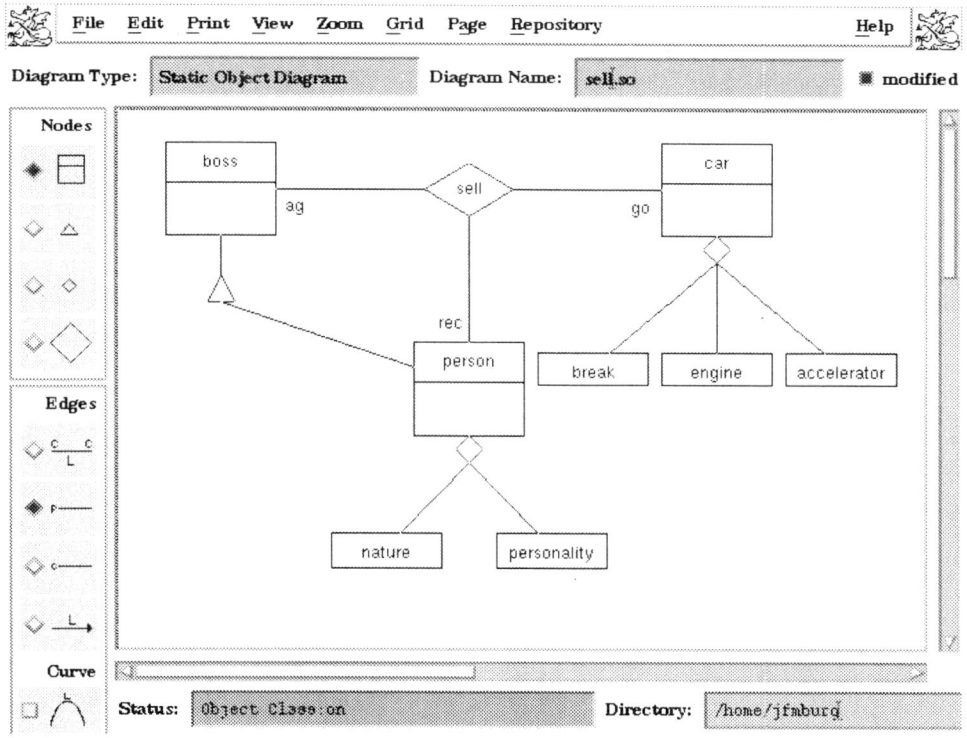

Figure 13: The 'sell' Relation, using CQOR-𝒳 Static Object Model Editor

214

6. J.F.M. Burg, R.P. van de Riet, and S.C. Chang. "A data-dictionary as a lexicon: An application of linguistics in information systems", In B.Bhargava, T.Finin, and Y.Yesha (Eds), *Proceedings of the 2nd International Conference on Information and Knowledge Management*, 114–123, 1993.

7. H. Dalianis. "A method for validating a conceptual model by natural language discourse generation", In *Proceedings of the 4th International Conference on Advanced Information Systems Engineering*, 1992.

8. F.P.M. Dignum. *A Language for Modelling Knowledge Bases. Based on Linguistics, Founded in Logic*. PhD thesis, Vrije Universiteit, Amsterdam, 1989.

9. F.P.M. Dignum and R.P. van de Riet. "How the modelling of knowledge bases can be based on linguistics and founded in logic", In *Data and Knowledge Engineering Journal*, 7:1–34, 1991.

10. S.C. Dik. *The Theory of Functional Grammar. Part I: The Structure of the Clause*. Floris Publications, Dordrecht, 1989.

11. J.A. Gulla. *Deep Explanation Generation in Conceptual Modeling Environments*. PhD thesis, University of Trondheim, Trondheim, 1993.

12. W.C. Mann and S.A. Thompson. "Rhetorical structure theory: Description and construction of text structures", In G. Kempen (Ed), *Natural Language Generation: New Results in Artificial Intelligence, Psychology and Linguistics*, 85–95. Martinus Nijhoff Publishers, 1987.

13. G.A. Miller, R. Beckwith, C. Fellbaum, D. Gross, K. Miller, and R. Tengi. "Five papers on wordnet", Technical report, Cognitive Science Laboratory, Princeton University, 1993.

14. G.M. Nijssen and T.A. Halpin. *Conceptual Schema and Relational Database Design : A Fact Oriented Approach*. Prentice Hall, 1989.

15. R.P. van de Riet. "Linguistic instruments in knowledge engineering, a research proposal and some experiments", In K. Fuchi and T. Yokoi (Eds), *Knowledge Building and Knowledge Sharing*, 200–207. Ohmsha (Tokyo) and IOS Press (Amsterdam), 1994.

16. C. Rolland and C. Proix. "A natural language approach for requirements engineering", In P. Loucopoulos (Ed), *Proceedings of the 4th International Conference on Advanced Information Systems Engineering*, 1992.

17. J. Rumbaugh, M. Blaha, W. Premerlani, F. Eddy, and W. Lorensen. *Object-Oriented Modeling and Design*. Prentice-Hall International, Inc., Englewood Cliffs, New Yersey, 1991.

18. J.F. Sowa. *Conceptual Structures*. Addison-Wesley, New York, 1984.

19. F.S.C. Tseng, A.L.P. Chen, and W-P. Yang. "On mapping natural language constructs into relational algebra through E-R representation", In *Data and Knowledge Engineering*, (9):97–118, 1992.

20. A.I. Wasserman and P.A. Pirchner. "A graphical extensible integrated environment for software development", In P. Henderson (Ed), *Proceedings of the ACM SIGSOFT/SIGPLAN Software Engineering Symposium on Practical Software Development Environments*, 131–142. ACM, ACM Press, March 1986.

21. H. Weigand. *Linguistically Motivated Principles of Knowledge Base Systems*. PhD thesis, Vrije Universiteit, Amsterdam, 1989.

Part 7: Knowledge Bases and Data Bases

OSIRIS: an Object-Oriented System Unifying Databases and Knowledge Bases

Ana Simonet and **Michel Simonet**
Faculté de Médecine de Grenoble
La Tronche, France
{Ana, Michel}.Simonet@imag.fr

ABSTRACT

The OSIRIS system implements an object model which was originally designed to answer modelling and manipulation needs in databases. Views are central to the model, both conceptually and technically. Automatic determination of the actual view(s) of an instance is the very process of classification in knowledge bases, hence the ability of the model to satisfy knowledge base requirements. A view is a class characterized by the classes it specializes and its own attributes and/or assertions.

Assertions express integrity constraints as well as production rules and behave either way according to the situation in which they are used, database type or knowledge base type. Both roles are unified through the declarative nature of assertions. The innovative features of the system are due to the definition of a classification space and its use as a pivot for the main operations : classification, procedural attachment, object indexing, query evaluation etc. The classification space is obtained by a partitioning of the object space from the assertions.

Physical object management is delegated to an independent object manager, ensuring time and space characteristics suitable for large databases and/or knowledge bases.

1 INTRODUCTION

Enabling a knowledge base to store a large amount of data raises several problems well known in databases : efficient storage and retrieval, data sharing, confidentiality, concurrent access, security, etc., along with problems specific to knowledge bases such as learning,

knowledge acquisition, schema evolution, efficient classification, explanation, reasoning guided by users information, hypothetical reasoning, etc. First generation knowledge representation systems were not designed to handle large quantities of data. At best, the number of concepts and classes could be fairly high, but their size bears no relation to the amount of data that can be handled by a DBMS. The question is therefore posed to design a knowledge base management system (hereafter KBMS) which may support a large amount of data with the same security as that of database technology and also provides concurrency control, distribution, etc. Brachman reminds us that "we certainly do not need to reinvent this" [5]. The derivation of the Telos KBMS from the OODBMS ORION [15] illustrates this opinion. In this paper we present an approach based on an original object model which enables unification of the database and knowledge base paradigms, and its implementation by the OSIRIS system.

OSIRIS's answer to these problems is mainly based on two elements : the P-type[1] concept and the classification space associated with a P-type. The classification space is built from the assertions of the P-type : domain assertions and inter attribute dependencies. Most functionalities expected from a KBMS (classification, explanation, procedural attachment), and a DBMS (efficient storage, query optimization, concurrency, confidentiality) rely on the equivalence classes of the classification space.

The P-type concept was originally designed in a database context [18]. This concept has been defined in the paradigm of algebraic data types [16] [13] and it proved later to be an object concept in its own right, providing data abstraction, classes, inheritance and en-

---

[1]P stands for the french word "partage" which means "shared". P-types were designed to ensure that its instances may be shared by several users who can see them according to different views.

capsulation, although we did not adopt all the choices of programming languages and current OODBMSs. P-types embody views as a primitive notion, in the very sense in which views are defined and used in relational databases [25]. Moreover, it provides automatic view determination from the values of the attributes of a given instance, which is in fact classification as dealt with in knowledge bases [9] [17]. The same approach applies to database and knowledge base contexts, through a declarative expression level, the OSIRIS language.

At the time the P-type concept was elaborated, most practical knowledge bases were still frame-based and did not attempt to deal with persistency, even less with large numbers of objects. OODBMSs did not deal with views, nor with classification, and the recent proposal for an OODBMS standard [8] does not even mention views. We should like to mention however the recently expressed opinion of a person active in relational databases, C. J. Date, "When a given row r is presented for insertion into a database, the DBMS should be able to decide for itself which table (if any) row r belongs to. In other words, the process of inserting a row can be regarded as a process of inserting that row into the database (rather than into some specific table) ..." [10]. In an OO context, a table roughly corresponds to a class[2], a row to an instance, and the process of deciding which class an instance belongs to is called classification.

Based on the P-type concept, we have designed and are implementing the OSIRIS system which is intended to provide knowledge base and database possibilities. However, some specific, and crucial, aspects of databases, such as transaction management, security, etc., are delegated to the object manager, which is used to deal with both user's objects and meta schemas objects. We use the YOODA object manager [1] which is particularly efficient and has a capacity which satisfies normal requirements for DBMSs. A relational implementation of the OSIRIS kernel is also under development and will provide transaction management, concurrency and security through existing DBMS technology.

We first present the main aspects of the object model and a sample OSIRIS program. We then present the building up of the classification space through the static analysis of the assertions associated with the classes. Finally we present the use of the classification space for the classification process as well as for runtime object management.

---

[2]In practice, a class "generates" one or several relations. An instance of a class is therefore represented by one or several rows in a relational database.

2 THE OBJECT MODEL

The main concept of the OSIRIS system is that of P-types [18][19]. It has been designed within the algebraic data type paradigm, with in mind the "oneness" of the physical objects of the real world which is modelled. Schematically, a P-type is designed to denote a family of objects which can be considered according to different points of view, possibly by distinct categories of users. It is defined from a set of views which are organized in a class-subclass hierarchy. Views may be seen as subclasses in the classic sense, although we prefer the term "view" because it corresponds to views in relational DBMSs; moreover, views have some properties which differ from those of usual subclasses. A given object belongs to one and only one P-type; it may belong to several views.

2.1 P-types and Views

It is commonly recognized that object modelling eliminated the need for view definition, because of the higher expressive power of object concepts compared with relational ones. We do not fully agree with this opinion and the resulting choices. For example, when using the sole notions of class and inheritance to create classes that are used to play the role of views, one has to build artificial classes if the object model does not support multi-instanciation.

Such classes clutter up the object model; their sole objective is to guarantee that a given object is intanciated in only one class. Moreover, these additional classes gives the user access to information of their superclasses. The user may thus access information which is non-pertinent to him from the point of view by which he is concerned. Moreover, when an object evolves and changes its class, it must be moved explicitly to its new class. This, in many OODBMSs, also implies changing its OID, which means suppressing the object and creating a new one in the new class, hence changing the object identity. This poses the problem of updating all objects of the base which referenced this object.

Multi-instantiation is not an easy-to-manage solution when large quantites of persistent data have to be shared. In such situation the system has to guarantee the consistent evolution of the many instances which represent the same object. The same kind of problems occurred when trying to make relational views persistent [2]. This is still an open problem.

The proposed solution consists in considering the set of entities (persons) as a type (*PERSON*), and views as subtypes in the algebraic sense [16] [13]. A P-type is defined as an algebraic data type $< S, F, E >$ where S is a set of sorts $\{s_1, ..., s_n\}$, the carrier of the type, F a set of functions $s_i \times s_j \times ... \times s_k \rightarrow sl$ and E a set of equations [19].

One sort, T, called the set of interest of the type,

is central, in that the aim of the type definition is to establish the elements of the type and define their behaviour. In general, the type is given the name of its set of interest : T. Among all possible functions, we call attributes those of the form $T \rightarrow s, s \in S$. Other functions are called methods.

To specify a P-type one first gives its minimal view then its other views by simple or multiple strict specialization, adding attributes and/or assertions. The minimal view is the root of the hierarchy of views of a P-type. Thus, a P-type is defined from its views. Such a top-down approach is contrary to that of relational systems where views are defined as restrictions of a set of existing relations, and may themselves be used as relations in order to define other views.

The algebraic type of the P-type is derived from the views declarations (including the minimal view). The type *PERSON* contains all the attributes and methods which appear in its views. The domain of an attribute in type *PERSON* is the union of its domains in the views where it is declared.

Let $t_{min}\ :\ <S, Fmin, Emin>$, $t_1\ :\ <S, F_1, E_1>$, $t_2\ :\ <S, F_2, E_2>$, ... be the views of a P-type T. T is defined as $<S, F, E>$ where :

- S is the support set of T ;

- $F = \bigcup_i F_i$;

- $E = E_{min}$

To express that a person may be seen as a student, a teacher, a sportsman, one will create the views PERSON, STUDENT, TEACHER, SPORTSMAN, ... as subtypes of the P-type *PERSON*.

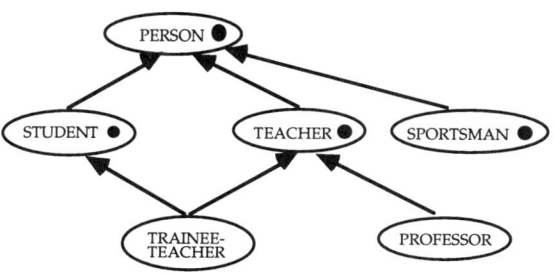

Figure 1: Graph of P-type *PERSON*

The set of interest (domain) of the minimal view person is identical to that of the P-type *PERSON*. The domain of another view is a subset of the domain of the view it specializes, or of the intersection of the domains of the views it specializes in case of multiple specialization.

In OSIRIS, the P-type is given the name of its minimal view. All the objects of a P-type are models of its

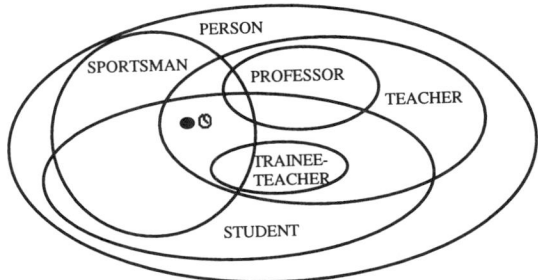

Figure 2: Inclusion set of P-type *PERSON*

minimal view. Access to the minimal view of an object only provides its attributes and methods. Access to the P-type provides the whole set of attributes and methods of the type; such access is necessary for the database administrator.

An object belongs to the P-type *PERSON* iff it satisfies the requirements of its minimal view. This means that the attributes of the external key[3] must be valued, and its assertions are valid. The criteria for an object to belong to a type (resp. subtype) is that the instance which represents it be a model of the equations of the type (resp. subtype).

Multiple inheritance is used only to specify a strict subset of the views intersection, or to give an explicit name to such an intersection. The object O in the above diagram belongs to the views PERSON (all objects of the type satisfy the minimal view), STUDENT, TEACHER and SPORTSMAN but not to the view TRAINEE-TEACHER, although it belongs to its two super-classes (super-views).

In OSIRIS the class/subclass hierarchy is that deduced from constraint restriction and/or introduction of new attributes. In [6] [7] subtypes *PERSON, STUDENT, TEACHER*, ... would be considered as distinct types, therefore different algebras (consequently disjoint OID domains), related by the subtyping relation. This corresponds to the programming approach, where the main objective of building a class hierarchy is to economize on the writing of methods, not to represent the real world entities. As types are the logical unit for static checking and implementation issues, an attribute, say IncomeTax, might be implemented in two different manners (by method overloading) in "types" *STUDENT* and *TEACHER*. This leads to the famous inheritance problem, where the system or the user has

---

[3]In order to enable the system to determine whether the object under creation corresponds or not to some other existing object, one needs an external key which is a cartesian product of some attributes of the minimal view. Thanks to the existence of an oid (non-modifiable internal object identifier), the external key may be modified during the lifetime of the object.

to decide which implementation of the attribute IncomeTax the TRAINEE-TEACHER class inherits. In OSIRIS, the implementation of methods is defined at the P-type level, independently from the class hierarchy. The procedure which may implement a method is chosen according to preconditions similar to the assertions.

2.2 The OSIRIS Language

A base schema is made up of several P-type definitions. In general, these P-types are not independent. In OSIRIS the interrelationships between different P-types of a schema are expressed by Inter-Object Dependencies (IODs).

We present the main features of the P-type description language and of the Inter-Object Dependencies through a very simple OSIRIS example. The universe modelled is that of persons and vehicles. Persons may be and/or students, teachers, trainee-teachers, professors, sportsmen. A given person is a model of the minimal view and may belong to none, any or several other views. The view TRAINEE-TEACHER, which inherits STUDENT and TEACHER, is not necessary to express that a person can be a student and a teacher at the same time. It has been created to designate a subset of their intersection, characterized by some more assertions, which restrict its domain.

```
class PERSON – Minimal view of P-type PERSON
attr
  Name : P_NAME; – P_NAME is declared elsewhere
  Children : setof PERSON;
  Sex : CHAR;
  Age : INT;
  MilitaryService : STRING;
  MaritalStatus : STRING;
  IncomeTax : REAL calc; – procedural attachment
  CarsOwned : setof CAR;
             – CAR is a view of a P-type VEHICLE
key  Name – External key
methods – other functions specification
assertions
– Domain Assertions
    Sex in { "f", "m" };
    0 ≤ Age ≤ 120
    MilitaryService in
      { "yes", "no", "deferred", "exempt" };
    MaritalStatus in
      { "single", "married", "divorced", "separated" };
– Inter-Attribute Dependencies
    Age < 18 ⇒ MilitaryService = "no";
    Age ≥ 18 ⇒ MilitaryService in
      { "yes", "deferred", "exempt" };
    Sex = 'f' ⇒ MilitaryService = "no";
end;
```

The minimal view automatically contains a private attribute OID : t_{oid}.

```
view STUDENT : PERSON
         – STUDENT specializes PERSON
attr
Studies : STRING in
    { "graduate", "postgraduate ", "doctorate"};
Year : INT ;
end;

view TEACHER : PERSON
attr
Diplomas : setof STRING in
    { "degree", "B.A.", "BSc" ,"M.A.","MSc",
      "PhD"};
Status : STRING in
    { "trainee", "lecturer", "professor", "instructor",
      "doctor" };
end;

view PROFESSOR : TEACHER
         – PROFESSOR specializes TEACHER
assertions
  Diplomas contain  "PhD";
  Status = "professor";
end;

view TRAINEE-TEACHER : STUDENT , TEACHER
         – specializes STUDENT and TEACHER
assertions
  Age ≤ 27;
  Status = "trainee";
  Studies = "graduate";
  Diplomas contain  "degree";
end;
⋮
implementation PERSON

  – stored attributes

  – body of methods

end;
```

The attributes of the type *PERSON* are those of the minimal view, PERSON, plus those defined in other views : Studies, Year, Status, Diplomas. Within a given view, the user may only access the attributes inherited from its super-views and the attributes proper to the view, if any. Thus, in the minimal view, the attributes Studies, Year, Status and Diplomas cannot be accessed.

Objects which are instances of the P-type *PERSON* may satisfy one or several views, among which only the minimal view is mandatory.

A part of the description of the P-type *VEHICLE* migh be :

```
class VEHICLE
attr
  Type : STRING;
  Year : DATE;
  . . .
assertions
  Type in { "car", "truck", "bus", "tractor"};
end;

view CAR : VEHICLE
attr
  Owner : PERSON;
  . . .
assertions
  Type = "car";
end;
```

Within the scope of the definition of P-type *PERSON* and view CAR of P-type *VEHICLE*, the interrelationships between cars and persons are expressed through the attributes CarOwner and Owner of the P-types *PERSON* and *VEHICLE* respectively. To express that these two attributes are reciprocal, one writes an Inter Object Dependency :

PERSON.CarsOwned reverse CAR.Owner

CarsOwned in P-type *PERSON* being declared as the reverse function of Owner in P-type *VEHICLE*, the OSIRIS system ensures integrity maintenance. In particular, every car whose owner is a person X must belong to the set of cars of X. For example, suppressing a car Y with owner X implies that Y no longer belongs to the set of cars owned by X. Similarly, adding a car Y with Owner X would trigger the checking that Y belongs to the set of cars owned by X, and adding it if necessary.

Thus referential integrity is checked and automatically maintained if necessary. This deductive aspect (deducing a new CarsOwned value from the insertion of a new car) is also present in Inter Attribute Dependencies (e.g. value "no" for MilitaryService can be deduced from an Age less than 18).

3 THE CLASSIFICATION SPACE

Most innovative features of the system come from the use of a classification space different from the original set of user classes. The classification space is a partitioning of the object space into equivalence classes named Eq-classes, according to the relation "have the same truth values according to the (entire set of) Domain Predicates of the type". As a consequence all objects of a given Eq-class are models of the same assertions (Domain Assertions and Inter-Attribute Dependencies).

They constitute a classification space in that classification of a given instance is equivalent to the determination of its Eq-class (or of its set of possible Eq-classes when the object is uncompletely known). By definition, all the objects belonging to the same Eq-class at a given moment are either valid or not valid for a given view; the valididity may be different for different views, but all the objects of the Eq-class have the same behaviour. Moreover, the validity of an Eq-class for each view may be determined at compile time.

3.1 Domain Constraints

Domain Assertions and Inter Attribute Dependencies play a dominant role in that they govern the partitioning of the object space[4] which leads to the classification space. These two categories of assertions, called Domain Constraints, are based on Domain Predicates, i.e. predicates of the form $Attr_i(X) \in Di$, where $Attr_i$ is some attribute of the type and Di some subdomain of its definition domain.

Domain Assertions are used to restrict the domain of an attribute. They can be written in the assertion part of the language, as well as in the declaration of the attribute. Their general form is a disjunction of Domain Predicates on the same attribute. Examples of Domain assertions are :

Age = 18   – strict form : Age in [18, 18]
$0 < Age \leq 120$ – Age in]0, 120]
Age in]0, 18[[65, 120]   – Age in [0, 18[or Age in [65, 120]

Inter Attribute Dependencies (IADs) are Horn clauses (first-order formulas), whose literals are Domain assertions.

3.2 Eq-classes

The building up of the classification space is based on the property that a domain predicate of the form $Attr_i(X) \in SubDomain_{ij}$ defines a partition of the domain of definition of the attribute $Attr_i$ into two blocks : $SubDomain_{ij}$ and its complement Domain $(Attr_i)$ - $SubDomain_{ij}$ [24] [20].

The partitioning of an attribute domain Domain $(Attr_i)$ is defined as the product of the partitions defined by all the domains predicates on $Attr_i$ present in the assertions of the P-type. The blocks of the partition are called the Stable-Subdomains (SSDs) of $Attr_i$.

In the context of the definition of the P-type *PERSON*, given the following domain constraints on attributes Age, MilitaryService and Sex :

a1: $0 \leq Age \leq 120$
a2: MilitaryService $\in$
     {"yes", "no", "deferred", "exempt"};
a3: Sex $\in$ { "f", "m" }
a4: $Age < 18 \Rightarrow$ MilitaryService = "no"
a5: $Age \geq 18 \Rightarrow$ MilitaryService $\in$

---

[4]Preconditions of methods are also used to determine this partition.

{"yes", "deferred", "exempt"}

a6: Sex = "f" $\Rightarrow$ MilitaryService = "no"

a7: Age ≤ 27

Considering the domain predicates in these assertions leads for each attribute to the partitioning :

SSDs of attribute Age :

$d11 = [0, 18[, d_{12} = [18, 27], d_{13} =]27, 120]$

SSDs of attribute MilitaryService :

$d_{21} = \{\text{"no"}\}$,

$d_{22} = \{\text{"yes", "deferred", "exempt"}\}$

SSDs of attribute Sex :

$d_{31} = \{\text{"m"}\}, d_{32} = \{\text{"f"}\}$

The domain of each attribute may be expressed in terms of its SSDs :

$$\text{Domain (Age)} = d_{11} \bigcup d_{12} \bigcup d_{13}$$
$$\text{Domain (MilitaryService)} = d_{21} \bigcup d_{22}$$
$$\text{Domain (Sex)} = d_{31} \bigcup d_{32}$$

By definition, each subdomain d_{ij} has the following property: when the value of attribute $Attr_i$ changes within the subdomain d_{ij}, all domain predicates maintain their truth value and consequently the assertions do likewise. Divisions d_{ij} are therefore stability zones for the assertions, hence their name : Stable Subdomains (SSDs). Domain Predicates are transformed into elementary predicates of the form $Attr_i \in d_{ij}$, where the d_{ij} are the SSDs of $Attr_i$. Introducing a new assertion with predicate Age > 40 would cause the splitting of d_{13} into $]27, 40]$ and $]40, 120]$, and the corresponding internal rewriting of the concerned assertions.

Classifying attributes are attributes whose domain is partitioned in at least two SSDs.

The classification space of a P-type is the cartesian product of the sets of Stable Subdomains of its classifying attributes. Elements of the classification space are called Eq-classes. For a P-type with n classifying attributes, Eq-classes are n-tuples $(d_{1i}, d_{2j}, \ldots d_{nl})$.

The classification space can be illustrated in a 3-dimensional space by the figure shown figure 3, obtained by considering only attributes Age, Military-Service and Sex, and the domain constraints above, leading to a partitioning into 3x2x2 = 12 Eq-classes.

A view may be represented by the set of Eq-classes whose objects are models of its assertions. For example, a hypothetical view V1 defined by the assertion MilitaryService "no" would be represented by the shaded set of Eq-classes shown figure 4. Such a set of Eq-classes is denoted by the tuple (*, d22, *) and is called a semi-domain, where * represents all possible SSDs of the corresponding attribute place.

In fact the semi-domain (*, d_{22}, *) does not represent the actual valid Eq-classes of the view V1 because of the properties of specialization : V1 necessarily specializes at least the minimal view PERSON. The assertions of PERSON would be inher-

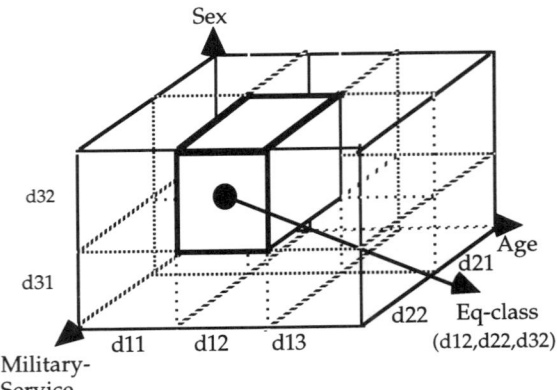

Figure 3: Space partitionning

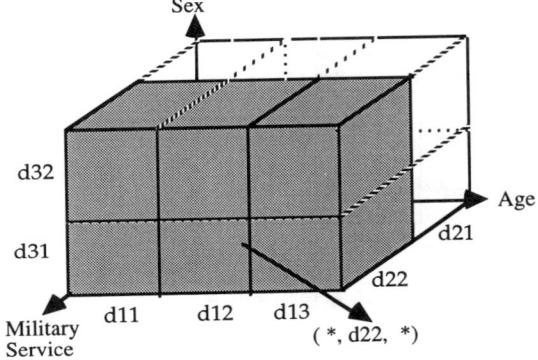

Figure 4: Semi-domain.

ited, leading to a set of Eq-classes defined as the intersection of the semi-domain (*, d_{22}, *) and of $(d_{11}, d_{21}, *) \bigcup (d_{12}, d_{22}, d_{31}) \bigcup (d_{13}, d_{22}, d_{31})$, the latter representing the valid Eq-classes of the minimal view.

3.3 View Determination

Within a given Eq-class, all the objects are either valid or invalid with respect to the set of assertions of a given view. Thus, one can speak of the validity of an Eq-class according to a view. The validity of each Eq-class for each view can be determined statically just by assessing the assertions of the view for any object of the Eq-class. Each view can then be associated with a map of Valid Eq-classes.

An object where all the attributes are known belongs to one Eq-class at a time; thus the knowledge of the Eq-class of an object determines which views are valid.

3.4 Dealing with Incomplete Information

At a given moment, the information on an object may be incomplete, e.g. the object has been created

223

by a user who is allowed a limited number of views (database context), or the user's knowledge of some instance he wants to identify more precisely is limited. Reasoning with incomplete knowledge obeys the same rules. The known values will determine several Eq-classes instead of a single one.

It may happen that incomplete information leads to an absolutely certain conclusion, without having to make hypotheses about unknown values of attributes. In some way, all possible hypotheses have been "compiled" through the Eq-classes.

A semi-domain representing a partially known object can be valid, invalid, or potential for a given view. If all the Eq-classes of a semi-domain are valid/invalid for a given view, the semi-domain is valid/invalid for that view. When the Eq-classes of a semi-domain are of a mixed sort (valid and invalid ones), the semi-domain is potential for the considered view. According to further instanciation of the unknown attributes, which will lead to the determination of one SSD for each attribute, and consequently one Eq-class for the object, the object will be known as certainly valid or invalid.

3.5 Consistency Checking

The consistency of the base is ensured by the integrity constraints expressed by the assertions. Integrity constraints verification is a by-product of the classification process. In effect, classifying an object in a given view means that the object is a model of its assertions. When the user assigns an object to a given view, which is the usual situation in databases, checking the integrity constraints of that view is performed by checking that this view belongs to the objects views.

Other consistency aspects may be considered in a knowledge base context : class validity and assertion contradiction. We also define Domain-inconsistency which is weaker than logical inconsistency and indicates a probable distortion between several assertions (possibly written by several users).

- Coherence of views.

  Within a P-type a view may be defined with assertions which make it inconsistent, i.e. no object instance of the P-type can be a model of its assertions (inherited and proper assertions). This is detected by an empty set of valid Eq-classes for the view.

- Assertion contradiction.

  Assertions can be checked for logical inconsistency, which is possible in spite of their first order general form, because the static process enables their transformation into an equivalent set of propositional formulas. Assertions :
  a1: Age< 18 $\Rightarrow$ MilitaryService = "no"
  a2: Age $\geq$ 18 $\Rightarrow$ MilitaryService $\in$

{"yes", "deferred", "exempt"}
a3: Sex = "f" $\Rightarrow$ MilitaryService = "no"

may be transformed into a propositional system where attributes are implicitly universally quantified, and where p_{ij} is the proposition expressing that attribute $Attr_i$ is in SSD d_{ij} :

al': $p_{11} \Rightarrow p_{21}$
a2': $p_{12} \bigvee p_{13} \Rightarrow p_{22}$
a3': $p_{32} \Rightarrow p_{21}$

along with propositions of the form

$$p_{ij} \Rightarrow \text{not } p_{ik} \text{ for all k} \neq \text{j}$$

expressing the mutual exclusion of stable subdomains for the same attribute :

$$(\forall i)d_{ij} \bigcap d_{ik} = \emptyset \text{ for all } k \neq j.$$

- Domain inconsistency.

  An assertion is said to be domain-inconsistent when its antecedent is always invalidated by other assertions of the type. In the context of the above example, the assertion 'Sex = "f" and $Age > 30 \Rightarrow$ some conclusion' is always valid, whatever its conclusion, because its antecedent is always false, being contradictory to assertions a1-a3, which impose that there cannot be any female aged over 18 in the base[5]. One can assume that such Domain-inconsistent assertions are not written deliberately and their detection is essential to the designer. Once they have been detected, it is up to the user to decide whether to maintain them or not. Domain-inconsistencies may be intended by the programmer; they may be harmless, but they may have unwanted hidden consequences, hence the interest of their detection.

4 THE CLASSIFICATION PROCESS

Given an instance of a P-type, the classification process consists in determining its views from the values of its attributes. This process is performed by a neural network whose input are the attribute values and output the valid views for that instance.

There is no intrinsic need to use a neural network, since algorithmic programming would achieve this task as well. Neural programming is used because it fits the problem and can later be optimised through parallel implementation. Contrary to neural networks usually used in classification and in most hybrid systems [12], this network needs no learning in that it is completely determined from the analysis of the type structure and the assertions [21] [22].

---

[5]This is due to assertion $Age \geq 18 \Rightarrow$ $MilitaryService \in \{$"yes", "deferred", "exempt"$\}$, which should have been written : $Age \geq 18$ and $Sex = 'm' \Rightarrow$ $MilitaryService \in \{$"yes", "deferred", "exempt"$\}$.

4.1 The Classification Network

The network which is presented figure 5 is a proto-type network which has been implemented at an early stage of the OSIRIS project. As the size of the Eq-class layer grows exponentially with the number of classifying attributes, this network has been since replaced by a four-layer network whose size is polynomial. Nevertheless we present the initial network because it is simpler and more directly related to the classification space whereas the latter is structured around assertions.

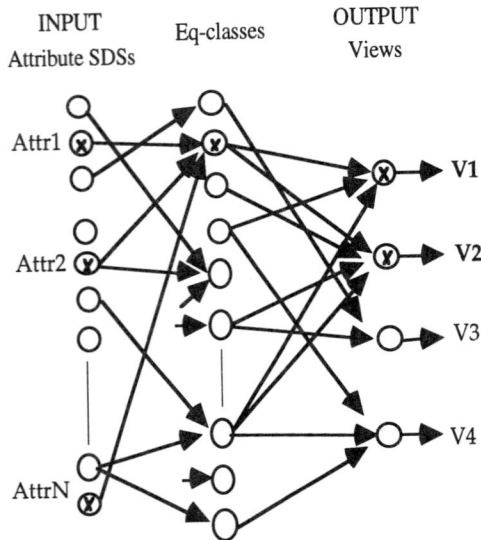

INPUT
Attribute SDSs

Eq-classes

OUTPUT
Views

Figure 5: The Classification Network

The neural net has three layers : the input cells represent the SSDs of attributes, the medium ones Eq-classes and the output ones Views. Cells of the input layer are logically grouped by attribute. From the partitioning of each attribute domain, only one cell is active for each attribute group : its output is 1 whereas the output of others is 0.

Each cell of the medium layer represents an Eq-class, which is defined as a vector of SSDs. There are as many Eq-classes as the cartesian product of SSDs. Each Eq-class cell is connected to n SSDs cells (one for each attribute). Not all connections are figured in the diagram. View cells are connected to all the Eq-classes for which they are valid. A view is valid if and only if at least one of its validating Eq-classes is valid. In the above diagram, views V1 and V2 are valid for input $(d_{12}, d_{22}, ..., d_{n2})$. Views which are not connected to the valid Eq-class have 0 output and therefore are not valid.

Given a P-type with N classifying attributes, n_i Sta-

ble Subdomains for attribute i and n_v views, the number of cells of this network is :

$$\sum_{i=1}^{N} n_i + \prod_{i=1}^{N} n_i + n_V$$

The actual network has the same input and output layers but the Eq-class layer is replaced by two layers structured according to the assertions [4]. For a P-type with n_a domain constraints (domain assertions and Inter-Attribute Dependencies), its size is :

$$\sum_{i=1}^{N} n_i + (N+1)n_a + n_V$$

Neither network needs learning and its architecture (cells, arcs and weights) is fully determined from the SSDs, the Eq-classes and the Views of the P-type.

4.2 Uncertainty Management

The network has been adapted to take into account the uncertainty associated with the values of unknown attributes and determine the probability a given view is valid for an incompletely known object [3]. This is done by assigning to each SSD of an attribute a probability value.

The output of an Eq-class cell is equal to the product of its input values, and the ouput of a view cell is the sum of its input values.

Let p_{ij} be the probability that attribute i belongs to the Stable subdomain dij. One has $\sum_{j=1}^{n_i} p_{ij} = 1$. Given an Eq-class E= $(d_{1k_1}, d_{2k_2}, ..., d_{nk_n})$ the probability that an object o belongs to E is $P(o \in E) = \prod_{i=1}^{N} p_{ik_i}$ where pij is the probability associated with the Stable subdomain dij. Let E_v be the set of Eq-classes which validate a view V. The probability that an object o belongs to this view is $P(o \in E) = \sum P(o \in V)$ with $E \in E_v$ The output value of a view cell is the probability that an object belongs to that view, given the probabilities associated with the SSDs of unknown attributes, and under the assumption that attribute values are independent. Views with value 1 are certain, 0 invalid and otherwise potential. When the probabilities associated with the SSDs of an attribute have only 1 or 0 values, we are in the case where the value of the attribute is known.

4.3 Hypothesis Management

When dealing with an incompletely known object, its potential Eq-classes implicitly encompasses all possible hypotheses. For example, given an animal with *Colour = grey* and *HasTrunk = true* OSIRIS classification process would determine that its potential Eq-classes can only satisfy terminal views ELEPHANT and FLY. Of course, any expert system dealing with hypotheses would have reached the same conclusion in the absence of further information.

However, in classical systems, a class can be valid only if its parent classes are valid. Therefore the system has to examine the classes in a top-down manner. When attributes have unknown values, the system questions the user and stacks hypotheses when the user cannot answer. In the case of the given example, the user would be asked questions about the VERTEBRATE/INVERTEBRATE status of the animal, then in the VERTEBRATE hypothesis, about its MAMMAL qualities, etc. Not only is this classification process annoying for the user but it is also time consuming.

In OSIRIS no question is necessary to reach the ELEPHANT-OR-FLY conclusion. The analysis of attributes of the final candidate classes enables the system to ask more pertinent questions. For example, comparing the Weight ranges of the candidate classes might lead to a decision, even without knowing the exact weight. It suffices to know that the weight of the animal is in the order of grams or hundreds of kilograms.

5 OBJECT MANAGEMENT

5.1 Meta Schema

The runtime structure is governed by a meta schema, an instance of which is built at compile time for a given application. It contains the informations about the base schema (attributes, user assertions, P-types, views, relationships, etc.) as well as the information resulting from schema compilation (SSDs, elementary predicates and assertions, etc.). The interrelationships between these two categories of informations are maintained in order to make possible schema updates and explanations.

The objects of the meta schema are managed by the same object manager as that used for the users' objects, thus providing a better homogeneity of storage management and ensuring the same performance in time and size.

5.2 Runtime Structure

The runtime structure is centered around a kernel which contains the set of methods giving access to the objects. All the modules have to communicate with the objects through the kernel. Only the kernel communicates with the object manager, ensuring a maximal independency from the chosen physical storage system. This independency has enabled the representation of objects in the main memory during the first phase of the project before the YOODA object manager was transported onto the DEC Alpha computer. A relational implementation is also being put into operation. It will provide a support for transaction management and concurrency control, until such a time as these features become available in the YOODA object manager.

The classification module contains the neural network described above. It is implemented as a C++ program but it could easily be transferred onto a specialized (e.g. parallel) computer. Communication with

an external language (C++ in this version) is performed through a server of methods. This architecture was necessary to ensure minimal recompilation in the case of method modification and also to isolate the OSIRIS kernel from the user's programs.

5.3 Memory Organization

The implementation unit is the P-type, and not the view. The record which is stored contains all the attributes of the P-type defined as "stored" in the implementation part of the P-type definition, not only those of its minimal view. Inner optimization may enable storing only attributes with a known value. An indexing structure (hereafter ISD) is defined for each P-type. Its main fields are :

- an array of stable subdomains (SSD), representing the semi-domain indexing a family of objects. Specific SSDs have been created to represent unknown values,

- a view vector whose elements are real values in $[0,1]$ representing the probability of each view of the P-type,

- a pointer to the first object indexed by the semi-domain of this ISD.

An object belongs to one (and only one) ISD because an ISD encompass all possible Eq-classes of a partially known object. Objects belonging to the same ISD are chained together.

5.4 Updating of Objects

Updating an object entails the determination of its new ISD, if and only if at least one modified attribute changes its SSD. When updating the object does not change any SSD, the object remains in the same ISD. Object updating is a much straightforward process than in classical sytems where all integrity constraints containing a modified attribute have to be dynamically checked. In OSIRIS this consists in SSD determination for modified attributes. If no SSD has changed, the constraints are known to be satisfied; if one SSD at least has changed, the object has to be reclassified, and its validity is known directly from its actual Eq-class(es).

6 CONCLUSION

We would like to recall Brachman's statement that "we must take seriously the notion of KB's that have huge numbers of individual objects in them - not just KB's with very large numbers of concepts or classes" [5]. He also emphasized the importance of being able to use in a knowledge base context, existing data contained in a relational database, and that it was likely there were several architectures to answer this problem. He himself proposed a solution which consists in interfacing an existing KB system, classic, with a relational database, transferring data periodically, bearing in mind that such a transfer is a time consuming task. Telos [15] is an example of an integrated system, built on an existing DBMS architecture by the addition of rules and constraints.

OSIRIS' answer consists in implementing an object model which enables the unification of database and knowledge base needs. The first version of the OSIRIS system is being implemented on a DEC Alpha computer. It contains the main features presented in this paper : classification as view determination through an (simulated) neural network, object indexing according to the classification space structure. Queries are "limited" to OSIRIS' assertions and are currently being extended to a full query language more or less similar to that defined in [8], although it is view-centered (a query defines a dynamic view).

The analysis of assertions and the construction of the neural network have been performed in a modular way such that when modifying, adding or suppressing assertions or views, consequences on the network and the indexing structure remain local. On introducing a view V with its assertions, only the Eq-classes (and ISDs) containing the concerned SSDs are modified and divided into further Eq-classes. Among them only those which were valid before the modification are liable to become invalid Eq-classes; Eq-classes which were invalid will remain invalid and therefore do not have to be checked for validity. The ISD structure has been designed to support schema evolution (adding or suppressing attributes, views, assertions ...) without necessitating a systematic restructuring of secondary storage.

Other work in progress concerns the use of a relational DBMS for the physical management of objects, implementation of Inter Object Dependencies, and the communication with an external language, C++. This communication is achieved through a client/server architecture enabling mutual calls of C++ and OSIRIS methods, while guaranteeing full adequation with the OSIRIS object model.

Amongst current research projects we would like to mention the following :

- Explanation, which is as important as the classification result in a KB context. Full mastery of the building up of the neural network enables the establishment of a sophisticated explanation system.

- Linear constraints are being introduced as assertions to characterize a view. Their treatment is optimized through the existing classification space.

- Deductive aspects will be extended to the use of recursive rules (e.g. to define the set of ancestors of a person).

- Parallelization, of the classification network on the one hand, and of Eq-classes access and storage, on the other.

- Definition of an interface with an existing relational database, thus enabling KB possibilities on existing relational data, without having to transfer it.

OSIRIS is currently being evaluated on an expert system for protein identification in molecular biology. The existing prototype, written with the KEE expert system tool [11], has 120 rules and is going to expand by a factor of 300, which will lead to significant consistency and efficiency problems [14]. Through this application, we are able to examine whether or not our model is adequate for classical expert system writing. The whole system of rules is much simplified : a single structure replaces two structures which are very similar, that of the objects and that of the rules. Moreover, most "expert" rules are reduced to attribute domain restrictions, which corresponds more directly to their initial expression by the expert [23].

A point we also want to emphasize is the adaptation to users knowledge. A major criticism which is levied against expert systems is their need to ask many questions, necessary for their internal deductions but not at all applicable in the current user situation. In OSIRIS, any information given by the user is used to determine the possible Eq-classes of the current object. Further questions can then be asked, but only in the context of the restricted set of classes which are valid for these Eq-classes, thus reducing the risk of irrelevant questions.

Bringing together separate domains has been a fruitful experience. The P-type model was conceived within the database and algebraic abstract data type paradigms; it proved later to tackle some knowledge base questions, even bringing some original answers. The database, knowledge bases and programming language fields may have much benefit in sharing their concepts, methods and techniques.

REFERENCES

1. E. Abecassis, *YOODA user's guide*, APIC systeme Arcueil, France, 1994.

2. S. Abiteboul, A. Bonner, *Objects and Views*, ACM SIGMOD, Denver, Colorado 29-31 May 1991.

3. C.-G.Bassolet, *Couplage a un modele objet d'une memoire associative basee sur la partition de l'espace des objets par des regles* , DEA informatique fondamentale, Univ. Claude Bernard - Ecole Normale Suprieure de Lyon, France, Juin 1993.

4. C.-G.Bassolet, *Reseaux de Neurones de Classement dans le modele des P-types*, Rapport de Recherche IMAG, GRENOBLE, to appear.

5. R.Brachman, *Viewing Data through a Knowledge Representation Lens*, KB&KS '93, Tokyo, 1993.

6. K. Bruce, P. Wegner, *An Algebraic Model of Subtypes in Object-Oriented Languages*, SIGPLAN Notices V21 #10, Oct 1986.

7. L. Cardelli, P.Wegner, *On understanding Types, Data Abstractions, and Polymorphism.*, ACM Computing Surveys, vol17, 1985.

8. R. G. G. Cattell, T. Atwood, J. Duhl, G. Ferran, M. Loomis, D. Wade, *Object Database Standard : ODMG-93*, Morgan Kaufmann Publishers, 1994.

9. W. J.Clancey, *Heuristic Classification*, Artificial Intelligence 27 (1985), pages 289-350.

10. C. J. Date and David McGoveran. *A New Database Design Principle*, In database Programming and Design, July 1994.

11. R. Fikes, T. Keller, *The role of Frame-based Representation in Reasoning*, CACM 85, 28(9) : pages 904-920, 1985.

12. A. Giacometti, *Modeles hybrides de l'expertise,* These Telecom Paris 1992.

13. J. Guttag, J. Horning, *The Algebraic Specification of Abstract Data Types*, Acta Informatica, 1978.

14. E. Langevin, *Prototype de systeme expert a base de connaissances dedie a l'identification de fonctions cellulaires portees par la sequence proteique*, DEA GBM, Univ. Cl. Bernard, Lyon, France 1993.

15. J. Mylopoulos, V. K. Chaudhri, D. Plexousakis, T. Topaloglou, *Adapting Database implementation techniques to manage very large Knowledge Bases*, KB&KS'93, Tokyo, Japan, 1993.

16. B. Liskov, B. Zilles, *Programming with Abstract Data Types*, Proc. of a Symp. on Very High Level Language, Sigplan Notices 9, 4, April 74.

17. A. Napoli, *Representation a objets et Raisonnement par classification en IA*, These Docteur Es -Sciences, Universite Nancy 1, France, 1992.

18. A. Sales-Simonet, *Types Abstraits et Bases de Donnees: formalisation du concept de partage et analyse statique de contraintes d'integrite* , These Docteur Ingenieur, Universite Scientifique et Medicale de Grenoble, France, Avril 1984.

19. A. Simonet, *Les P-TYPES: un modele pour la definition de bases de connaissances centrees-objets coherentes* , R.R. 751-I, laboratoire Artemis, Grenoble, France, Novembre 1988.

20. A. Simonet, M. Simonet, *Les classes d'equivalence induites par des dependances inter-attributs: fondements pour une representation des objets partages dans les bases de connaissances* - R. R. 769-I, laboratoire Artemis, Grenoble, France, Fevrier 89.

21. A. Simonet, M. Simonet, OSIRIS :*An Assertion-based Hybrid Object-Connexionist Knowledge Base System* , 14th International Conference on Artificial Intelligence, KBS, Expert-Systems and Natural Language, Avignon, France, may 30-june 3, 1994.

22. A. Simonet, M. Simonet, C-G. Bassolet, J. Demongeot, *Une architecture connexionniste pour un systeme hybride de representation de connaissances oriente objet*, Colloque sur le Neuromimetisme, Lyon, France, June 1994.

23. A. Simonet, M. Simonet, *Objects with Views and Constraints : from Databases to Knowledge Bases*, OOIS'94, London, Dec. 1994.

24. D. Stanat, D. McAllister., *Discrete Mathematics in Computer Science*, Prentice Hall 1977.

25. M. Stonebraker et al.,*On rules, procedures caching and views*, ACM SIGMOD conference on management of data, Atlantic City, June 1990.

Towards Very Large Knowledge Bases
N.J.I. Mars, Ed.
IOS Press, 1995

Interfacing of Object-Oriented Databases and Knowledge-Based Engineering Systems Using Views

Kari Tanskanen, Anne Aaltonen, Pasi Paasiala and **Asko Riitahuhta**
Tampere University of Technology
Tampere, Finland
ktanskan@me.tut.fi

ABSTRACT

Interfacing knowledge based engineering systems and object-oriented databases allows utilization of the best features of the both worlds. Methods of object-oriented databases enable storing, in addition to simple technical data, e.g. large part of component specific knowledge into the database. In this paper we present object-oriented views, which allow powerful interaction between the two systems. Features of the proposed system include object selection beyond the capabilities of normal query languages, accessing properties through object hierarchies and receiving results from parameterized calculation methods.

1   INTRODUCTION

The trend in modern production is to produce smaller quantities of goods which more accurately reflect the specifications of customer. This shift has caused an increase in the design cost, as design costs are now absorbed over fewer units than in the past. To reduce costs companies must take advantage of modern computerized methods, standardization and design paradigms. By using computerized methods it is possible to let the computer make more of the decisions relating to the design, speeding up the design process and reducing effort.

In different phases of design work, knowledge based engineering systems (KBES) are used for managing design knowledge e.g. product structure, component selection rules and various relationships between components and assemblies. However, rather than KBES, a database management system is a better tool for storing large amounts of factual data required in engineering design. Thus, the best results can probably be achieved with a tight cooperation between the KBES and the database [6].

Object-oriented database management systems (ODBMS) provide a better model than traditional relational databases for complicated data involved in engineering tasks. For example, each component in a product can be represented as an object in ODBMS. Class hierarchies and inheritance help in classifying objects and decrease redundancy, since common properties of different subclasses can be defined in a common superclass. In addition to simple data, object-oriented database can contain complex data structures and methods to describe behavior of the data.

Unfortunately, commercial ODBMSs are still rather new on the market and while the research and product development effort has concerned the novel ideas on database field e.g. version handling and long transactions, not much has been done on the topics related to user-friendliness, such as user defined views, which are more or less standard on an average relational DBMS.

In this paper we first discuss different roles of databases and knowledge based systems and show how to divide engineering knowledge into the two systems. After that we concentrate on the interface which makes these systems cooperative. In chapter 4 we define object view system and demonstrate its features with a simple example database. Finally we review optional ways of implementation and suggest some enhancements in the perspective of related research.

2   DIVISION OF TASKS

Database systems are designed to manage large bodies of information. Methods in object-oriented databases allow also large part of the engineering knowledge to be stored in the database. Better integration of data and knowledge is achieved when technical data and functional knowledge, e.g. calculation rules for the engine performance, can be stored in the same place. Also product and application independent part of the component selection knowledge can be stored in the

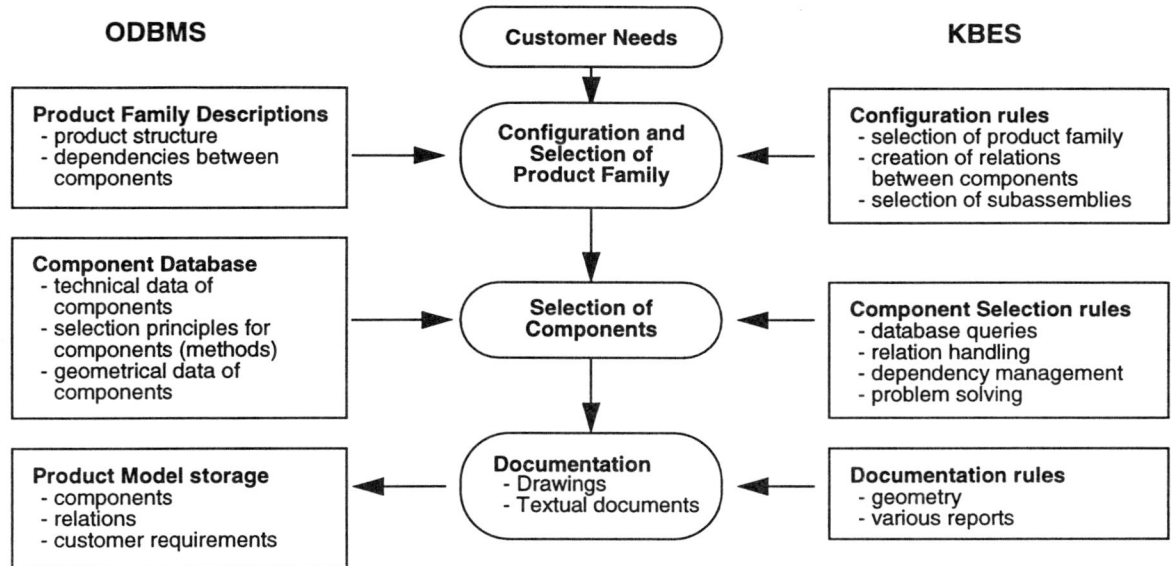

Figure 1: Design flow [1].

database.

In Fig. 1 we present design flow in a project where a configurable product is designed for a customer. Although the result is unique, it is assembled mainly from standard components, and general knowledge as well as experiences from previous projects can be used. Design knowledge is divided between the two tools, KBES and ODBMS. The division criterion is mainly the domain of the knowledge; whole product or an individual component. Knowledge stored in KBES concerns the whole product. Knowledge is stored into component or assembly classes and their attributes' rules. Data about individual components are stored in the ODBMS. [1]

In this kind of design project, the work starts with the selection of the product family upon the customer requirements, i.e. choosing a kind of template to start with more detailed design. The next phase is to create the basic product structure by selecting the subassemblies and component types. Also in this phase, different kinds of relationships are specified. The most obvious relationships are part-of relationships between assemblies and their components. Other relationships can be e.g. fuel-flow, power-chain, geometry and identical-to relationships [9]. Parts of these structures may be readily specified in the product family descriptions.

The next phase involves selection of individual components. To choose a specific part both the KBES and the ODBMS are used. Information regarding what kinds of requirements the component needs to ful-

fill is decided in the component selection rules of the KBES, which sends a query to the ODBMS. A component selection method can include more or less complicated calculations, references to other classes in the database, and other criteria. The ODBMS chooses either one component or a list of suitable components. In the latter case, further calculations may be performed in the knowledge based system, or the user may be prompted to make the final decision.

Once the product has been configured and the components are selected, it is possible to automate a large part of the document generation. This can be done by connecting the KBES to a CAD system for creating drawings and by producing pieces of text e.g. in SGML format. The documentation contains normally drawings, manuals, reports and bills of materials. The product model itself can be stored in the ODBMS for archival purposes and as a framework for other design disciplines. For example, the mechanical and electrical design can be done by different applications. Support for multidisciplinary design using object-oriented databases is discussed in [8].

3   INTERFACING THE SYSTEMS

A good interface is clearly defined and concise. When the interface between KBES and ODBMS is built in this way, only a small number of functions is required on both ends for handling the major part of the information transfer between the two systems. While the tasks of product model save and retrieval are left to special methods and rules, the components selection queries as well as different design instruction and standard table queries can be done through a standard interface.

When the systems are large, and especially when the KBES and ODBMS parts reside in different computers, it is important that the bandwidth is not wasted by passing unnecessary or insufficient information from one system to another. Thus the queries from the KBES have to be expressive enough to be able to describe what kind of information is required. On the database side, the system must be able to filter out insufficient information, e.g. those components, which are not able to fulfill the required function. It is also desirable, that those attribute data, which are not relevant for the application or are in a bad format would be omitted from the packet returned as a query result. On the other hand, the database should be able to return derived data, such as calculation results.

Database views are a normal solution for providing data in an appropriate format. In the next chapter we make a proposal for a view system, which is implementable on top of modern commercial object-oriented database management systems, and which is tuned to fit in engineering applications. Requirements for this kind of implementation include complicated selection beyond the capabilities of SQL, accessing properties of composite objects, as well as passing parameters to and receiving results from calculation methods.

4   CREATING VIEWS FOR ODBMS

4.1   Features of a view system

Views in databases are used for providing appropriately selected and structured data for user applications. The usual way to realize views is to make them to imitate tables in RDBMSs or classes in ODBMSs. We have, however, chosen a different approach.

Let us consider a normal view definition in SQL:

CREATE VIEW *viewname* AS SELECT *what* FROM *tables* WHERE *condition*

This definition creates a view, which can be used like any real table. Realizing views correspondingly on top of commercially available object-oriented database causes troubles.

Firstly, it may be impossible to create views that look like classes without changing the program code of the database management system. Secondly we think that it is good to remember that views are not classes. For example, problems of updating database through views are widely discussed in the literature on RDBMSs and lately also on ODBMSs [7],[10],[11].

Thirdly, relational view queries always return a relation as a result. Analogously class imitating object-oriented views should always return a set of objects. Often however, this is not what the user wants. The querying application has little use for data in the form of set of objects (or more technically, set of object identifiers). At least extra queries and thus extra data transfer between the systems would be required to gain meaningful information of objects' properties. Moreover, the object systems may differ or the querying application may not be object-oriented at all.

For these reasons we want, somewhat regressively, that our view system would be able to return results in the form of relation. By the term relation we here mean a set of rows (tuples) where each column (property) has a label. However, we allow the properties to be of complex types such as objects, sets of objects or lists. Using relations also help parallel usage of RDBMSs and ODBMSs. Both kinds of databases can be used in the same application and the same functions can handle data acquired from the both of them.

How should these views be defined? In the SQL example, "*tables*" part defines the tables used in the view. In our view model each view has one base class and properties of related classes are accessed by navigating through hierarchies (aggregation paths) where classes reference other classes in some attribute domain. Defining a base class for each view makes it possible to use the same names of views (analogous to "*viewname*") in different classes. This is beneficial when we want to use general terms like "Default" as a view name or classify the views by user group ("Administrator") or technical discipline ("Mechanical"). Views are also inherited from the base class to its subclasses.

Again in our SQL example, "*condition*" defines which objects to retrieve and "*what*" defines the properties to be viewed. We have decided to handle these view aspects, *selection* and *projection* [3] separately.[1] Questions about what to retrieve and how to present the results are basically orthogonal. The way to present properties does not depend on the set of objects you want to present. By making this separation, more flexibility is gained since the user can combine selection and projection views without restrictions. Besides, the nature of these aspects is different.

Question about which instances to select, requires often a procedural solution. This is not apparent when we think about simple cases, which SQL is capable of handling. However, we want our selection views to manage complex problems, which are typical in engineering applications. For example we may want to select components, which are able to fulfill a required function with given parameters. For this reason we have decided to define our select views as class methods i.e. methods which are associated with a class object, not instance object. These selection methods

---

[1]Barclay and Kennedy have also *join* views. In our model, using aggregation paths makes explicit joins unnecessary.

may have multiple arguments and they return a set of objects, usually instances of the class for which the method is defined, or its subclasses.

For specifying projection views, we have a more declarative solution. Of each view, we have to know its base class, name, the properties we want to present and the order of them. In addition to these minimum requirements, we have defined two additional features. Field labels rename each presented property, and sorting information allows the view to rearrange the presented tuples to some logical order.

We have defined a new class called VIEW for describing projection views. Each instance of this class defines one view, and its properties are presented in the instance attributes. This class has a set of defined methods, which realize the mapping from a set of objects to a desired relation. Attributes of this class are defined in Table 1. The domains of the attributes are in the style of LISP. Other systems may use string instead of symbol, vector instead of list and boolean instead of T.

There are two essential class methods in VIEW. **Present-view** makes the mapping from a set of objects to a relation defined by a view instance. **Present-all** realizes a kind of default view for each class by presenting all attribute values of each object and using attribute names as labels. The arguments and the behavior of these methods are described later with examples.

4.2 Information flow inside a database

Now we have defined the means to realize selection and projection views in ODBMS environment. In Fig. 2 we present the information flow in the database from the point where it receives the service request until some kind of result is achieved. The process is managed by a master method, which we call **Instance-data**. This method can be defined for the superclass on top of the class hierarchy, usually called CLASS. If it is not possible or desired to make additions to system-defined classes, **Instance-data** can be defined for some other high-level superclass.

First the request goes through an optional authorization phase. Access control data is gathered on the class called RIGHTS. Authorization checking method gets as arguments the base class of the query and the names of the selection and projection views. Each user is either granted or denied to use a named view, default view or a standard query of a certain class.

Unless authorization check causes service rejection, the next phase is selection of the appropriate objects. This is done either by the standard query facilities of the ODBMS or by a special purpose selection view. If the user wants, the selected objects can now be returned. Otherwise, the information is next filtered through the projection phase.

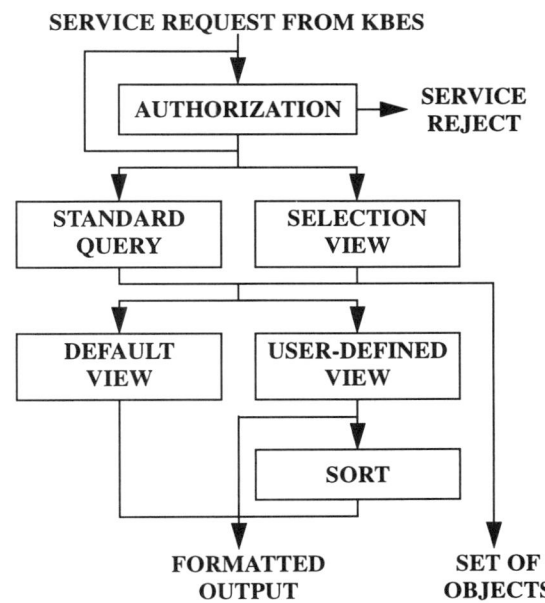

Figure 2: Information flow inside a database.

If the user has not given the view name, **Present-all** returns the default view of the class. If a named view is used, the desired relation is constructed. Sorting part is optional. Some database systems may be able to automatically return data sorted by an index. If however, the user wants to receive the data ordered by results of a method, explicit sorting is always necessary.

4.3 Sample database

In this section we define a miniature sample database for demonstrating the features of our view system. In a diesel power plant, electricity is generated by a generator set, which consists of diesel engine, generator and some accessories. The database has classes GENERATOR_SET, ENGINE and its subclasses SMALL_ENGINE and BIG_ENGINE. Example data and relating methods are imaginary and have nothing to do with real generators and engines.

The nominal power of each engine depends on the engine's rotational speed, which depends on the desired output frequency. The maximum power depends on the frequency and the usage type of the power plant. In our example 10more than nominal power can be used in emergency situations. To calculate these powers both SMALL_ENGINE and BIG_ENGINE have methods **Nominal_power** and **Max_power**. The contents of the database are described in Table 2.

Next we need to define some views. For generator set selection views we could have **Basic_selection**, which selects all generator sets of a given frequency,

ATTRIBUTE	DOMAIN	DESCRIPTION
VIEW-CLASS	CLASS	Base class of the view
NAME	SYMBOL	Name of the view
FIELDS	LIST	Ordered list of the the properties in the view
FIELD-LABELS	LIST	Ordered list of the property labels in the view
INDEX-FIELDS	LIST	Ordered list of the properties by which the tuples are sorted
ASCENDING	T	Ascending or descending sorting order

Table 1: ATTRIBUTES OF THE CLASS VIEW

GENERATOR_SET

OID	G_CODE	G_MANUFACTURER	VOLTAGE	FREQUENCY	ENGINE
G1	SRS470EU	SIEVERS	6.0	50	S1
G2	SRS570EU	SIEVERS	6.0	50	S2
G3	SRS1070EU	SIEVERS	11.0	50	S3
G4	SRS1170EU	SIEVERS	11.0	50	B1
G5	SRS470US	SIEVERS	6.6	60	S1
G6	SRS570US	SIEVERS	6.6	60	S2
G7	SRS1070US	SIEVERS	13.8	60	S3
G8	SRS1170US	SIEVERS	13.8	60	B1
G9	ASF50200	ABSOLUTE	11.0	50	B1
G10	ASF50210	ABSOLUTE	11.0	50	B2
G11	ASF50220	ABSOLUTE	11.0	50	B3
G12	ASF50230	ABSOLUTE	11.0	50	B4
G13	ASF60200	ABSOLUTE	13.8	60	S4
G14	ASF60210	ABSOLUTE	13.8	60	B2
G15	ASF60220	ABSOLUTE	13.8	60	B3
G16	ASF60230	ABSOLUTE	13.8	60	B4

SMALL_ENGINE					BIG_ENGINE				
OID	CODE	CYL	P720RPM	P750RPM	OID	CODE	CYL	P500RPM	P520RPM
S1	30SR6	6	1920	2070	B1	40BR6	6	5280	5460
S2	30SR8	8	2560	2760	B2	40BR8	8	7040	7280
S3	30SV12	12	3840	4140	B3	40BV12	12	10560	10900
S4	30SV16	16	5120	5520	B4	40BV16	16	14100	14500

Table 2: A sample database

and **Manuf_selection**, which returns generator sets of given frequency and desired generator manufacturer. In real applications these selection methods would probably be more complicated.

As projection views we define "Basic" for general information and "Engine-related" for usage concerning more about engine properties. The attribute values of these views are described in Tables 3 and 4. If one field is a list, it means that the property is searched through an aggregation path. For example in the basic view, (ENGINE NOMINAL_POWER) corresponds to nominal power of the engine of the generator set.

All service calls that use views, call the method **Instance-data**. In our implementation on top of ITASCA ODBMS, the call is of form:

(**Instance-data** base-class selection-view [args]

[projection-view] [view-method-args])

If the name of the selection-view is Select or Select*[2], a standard query is used.

Args includes arguments for selection view or query. Argument for a standard query can be a relational expression. Possible options naturally depend on the particular query language.

Projection-view tells the desired projection view. If it is omitted, default view is constructed. We have reserved view name "Oids" for returning data in the form of object identifiers.

View-method-arguments are used for passing arguments for methods involved in a projection view. For example, the method **Nominal-power** in the view "Basic" requires frequency as an argument. View

---

[2]Select* in the query language of ITASCA means selecting from base class and its subclasses.

ATTRIBUTE	VALUE
VIEW-CLASS	#[CLASS GENERATOR_SET]
NAME	BASIC
FIELDS	(G_CODE G_MANUFACTURER VOLTAGE (ENGINE NOMINAL_POWER))
FIELD-LABELS	(GENERATOR MANUFACTURER VOLTAGE POWER)
INDEX-FIELDS	(MANUFACTURER GENERATOR)
ASCENDING	T

Table 3: BASIC VIEW

ATTRIBUTE	VALUE
VIEW-CLASS	#[CLASS GENERATOR_SET]
NAME	ENGINE-RELATED
FIELDS	(G_CODE (ENGINE CODE) (ENGINE CYL) (ENGINE MAX-POWER))
FIELD-LABELS	(GENERATOR ENGINE CYLINDERS POWER)
INDEX-FIELDS	(POWER)
ASCENDING	T

Table 4: ENGINE RELATED VIEW

method arguments are expressed as pairs of method labels and arguments or argument lists as can be seen in the examples below.

During the execution of the **Instance-data**, the authorization checking method receives *base-class*, *selection-view* and *projection-view* as arguments. The method with a name of *selection-view* is next evaluated with *args* as arguments. Finally method **Present-view** creates the resulting relation with arguments *projection-view*, *view-method-args* and the instance list received as a result from *selection-view*.

The actual representation of the query results is system-dependent. The implementation with ITASCA returns the relation as a list of lists in the following format:

```
((label1 label2 ... labeln)
 ((inst1_attr1 inst1_attr2 ...inst1_attrn)
  (inst2_attr1 inst2_attr2 ...inst2_attrn)
  ...
  (instn_attr1 instn_attr2 ...instn_attrn)))
```

The following examples illustrate possible service calls and responses with our sample database. Here the results are presented in table format for clarity.

Example 1. Basic view

```
(Instance-data (class-object 'generator_set)
               'basic_selection '(50)
               :view 'Basic
               :view-method-args '(power 50))
```

GENE-RATOR	MANUFAC-TURER	VOL-TAGE	PO-WER
ASF50200	ABSOLUTE	11.0	5460
ASF50210	ABSOLUTE	11.0	7280
ASF50220	ABSOLUTE	11.0	10900
ASF50230	ABSOLUTE	11.0	14550
SRS1070EU	SIEVERS	11.0	4140
SRS1170EU	SIEVERS	11.0	5460
SRS470EU	SIEVERS	6.0	2070
SRS570EU	SIEVERS	6.0	2760

Results are returned in the order of manufacturer name and generator code. Note that view method arguments are associated with the label, not with the real name of the method. In this view, power means nominal power of the engine.

Example 2. Engine related view of a selected manufacturer

```
(Instance-data (class-object 'generator\_set)
               'manuf\_selection '(60 "SIEVERS")
               :view 'Engine-related
               :view-method-args
                 '(power (60 "Emergency")))
```

GENE-RATOR	ENGINE	CYLIN-DERS	PO-WER
SRS470US	30SR6	6	2112
SRS570US	30SR8	8	2816
SRS1070US	30SV12	12	4224
SRS1170US	40BR6	6	5808

Generator sets of Sievers with frequency of 60 Hz are presented in the order of power. Here power means calculated maximum power in emergency conditions.

Example 3. Standard query with a default view

```
(Instance-data (class-object 'engine)
               'select* '(< cyl 10))
```

CODE	CYL
30SR6	6
30SR8	8
40BR6	6
40BR8	8

Last example uses standard query and standard view. Only the attributes defined in the superclass Engine are presented.

5 DISCUSSION

This study has suggested a view system as a tool for interfacing knowledge based systems and object-oriented databases. Objects are selected by selection methods and the results are formatted by projection views. This system was designed for an application where configurable products are designed using Design^{++} of Design Power, Inc. as an engineering software and ITASCA of Itasca Systems, inc. as a database management system. The view system can be implemented on top of various ODBMS fulfilling requirements of complex objects, object hierarchies and methods for instances and classes. We believe that the proposed methodology is applicable on a wide range of science and engineering applications.

The described view system is just one possible implementation where the basic idea of separating selection views and projection views is used. The way to implement selection as class methods and projection as instances of a class VIEW has turned out to be practical, but the details may vary upon the underlying database system and the nature of applications.

One interesting issue is, how different views interact. Most proposed systems which treat views as classes allow a view to be defined using other views [3],[4],[5],[10]. Obviously it would be messy in our implementation. This kind of systems also usually allow building of view hierarchies where subviews inherit properties from superviews [2],[3],[4]. Since our project views are instances, not classes, this kind of behavior is not natural, but still possible to implement. In applications where there is a need for large number of views, some kind of hierarchical views may be desirable.

Another kind of view interaction is cascading. A set of objects may be selected with one selection view. These can be further passed to another selection view for filtration by different criteria. Since a class is a collection instances, as is the result of a selection view, this kind of enhancement would require only minor changes to our system. On the other hand, projection views are not cascadable because there is a significant change in the data format.

One possible way to handle updating through views is that when a single argument is passed to an instance attribute, the attribute is updated to this argument value. A prototype of view updating system has been constructed using this approach. Here the method, which is able to update attributes is of different name, Update-through-view instead of Present-view, to make the intention of updating more obvious. This kind of simple way may be chosen, if the need for updates is frequent, or random by nature.

If encapsulation properties are emphasized, it is probably better to handle updating through specialized methods. It is also desirable to handle data retrieve and update differently in the authorization phase. Inserting and deleting objects is beyond the scope of this system, although objects to be removed can be selected with a selection view.

ACKNOWLEDGMENTS

This research is part of the project called "Automatic Component Selection System" in Tampere University of Technology funded by Technology Development Centre of Finland. We wish to thank Wärtsilä Diesel Power Plants for providing an interesting test case, design knowledge and technical data. Thanks to Paavo Nevalainen for LaTeX help.

REFERENCES

1. A. Aaltonen, P. Paasiala, K. Tanskanen, A. Riitahuhta, "Configuration of Wärtsilä Diesel Power Plants' Fuel System." To be published in *10th. Int. Conf. Eng. Design ICED 95*, Praha, August 22.-25. 1995.

2. S. Abitebou, A. Bonner, "Objects and views." *SIGMOD Record*, Vol. 20, No 2, 1991, 238-247.

3. P.J. Barclay, J.B. Kennedy, "Viewing objects." *Advances in Databases*. (Eds. M. Worboys, A.F.Grundy) Springer-Verlag, Berlin, 1993, 93-110.

4. E. Bertino, "A view mechanism for object-oriented databases." *Advances in Database technology - EDBT '92* (Eds. A. Protte, C. Delobel, G. Gottlob), Springer-Verlag, Berlin, 1992, 136-151.

5. S. Heiler, S. Zdonik, "Object views: Extending the vision." *6th Int. Conf. on Data Eng.*, Los Angeles, CA, 86-93.

6. K. Higa, M. Morrison, J. Morrison, O. Sheng, "Object-Oriented Methodology for Knowledge Base/Database Coupling." *Comm. ACM*, 1992, Vol 35, No. 6, 99-113.

7. Y. Kimura, K. Tsuruoka, "A view class mechanism for object-oriented database systems." *Proc. 2nd Int. Symp. on Database Systems for Advanced Applications*, Tokyo, 1991, 269-273.

8. P. Paasiala, A. Aaltonen, K. Tanskanen, A. Riitahuhta, "Managing multidisciplinary design projects." *Proc. ICMA'94*, Tampere Univ. of Technology, Tampere, Finland, 1994. 659-670.

9. P. Paasiala, A. Aaltonen, K. Tanskanen, A. Riitahuhta, "Relationship modeling in design of diesel power plants." *Proc. 1st European Conf. on Product and Process Modelling in the Building Industry*, Dresden, Germany, 1994.

10. M.H. Scholl, C. Laasch, M. Tresch, "Updatable views in object-oriented Databases." *Proc. 2nd Int. Conf. on Deductive and Object-Oriented Databases*, Munich, 1991, 189-207.

11. S.D. Urban, K. Chalmers, "An investigation of the view update problem for object-oriented views." *11th Annual Int. Phoenix Conf. on Computers and Communications*, Scottsdale, AZ, USA, 1992, 156-163.

Why and How to Define a Similarity Measure for Object-Based Representation Systems

Gilles Bisson
INRIA Rhône-Alpes
Grenoble, France
gilles.bisson@imag.fr

ABSTRACT

Currently, in Objects-Based Representation Systems, both classification and categorization are based on the subsumption criterion. In practice, this criterion seems too strong as soon as we need to deal with incomplete or incoherent knowledge. The notion of similarity has been successfully used in many domains such as Data Analysis, Pattern Recognition, or Machine Learning to compare and to structure noisy knowledge. In this paper we present preliminary work aiming at demonstrating the advantage of using a similarity measure instead of a subsumption criterion in object-based representations.

1 MOTIVATIONS

The aims of Object-Based Representation Systems (OBRS) are twofold: on the one hand they allow to store and to organize a domain knowledge; on the other hand, they allow to answer some users queries through several inference mechanisms. Among the set of inference mechanisms, two of them are particularly important: the *classification* and the *categorization*. In the OBRS that distinguish between classes and instances, the classification process of these two kinds of objects has a different goal. The classification of an instance into a Knowledge Base, expressed as a hierarchy of classes, aims at finding the set of the most specific classes whose definition *subsumes* the slot values of the instances. Practically, the classification of instances aims at *identifying* the studied instances and allows to *deduce* some new information about these instances. The classification of a class aims at *placing* a class into a Knowledge Base by finding the two sets of the most specific classes (respectively most general ones) whose definitions subsume (respectively is subsumed by) the definition of the studied class. This

operation can be used to build a KB incrementally, or to compare two KB.

The categorization aims at building automatically a hierarchy of classes from a set of instances describing the different objects found in the application domain. The categorization process has been extensively studied from a *Numerical Standpoint* in Data Analysis [2],[32],[12] or more recently, from a *Symbolical Standpoint* in Conceptual Clustering [24],[15],[4]. However, it is worth noting that classification and categorization operations are not totally independent since some categorization processes are based on the classification of instances [13] or the classification of classes [11].

Currently, in the OBRS framework the inference processes of classification and categorization are based on the subsumption criterion. This criterion allows the system to compare the degree of generality between any two concepts A and B. In this way, the relation "A subsumes B" means that the set of individuals described by A, namely the extension of A, includes the set of individuals described by B. Here we propose to replace the subsumption criterion by a similarity criterion during the inference processes[1]. Now, the classification and the categorization will be based on a numerical measure allowing to quantify the similarities and the differences between any pair of objects.

The notion of similarity measure has been used and studied in many domains, such as Data Analysis, Pattern Recognition, Machine Learning or Cognitive Sciences. However, the measures defined in these domains are often unable to deal with representation languages as complex as those used in the OBRS framework. In the framework of OBRS, few publications dealing with the similarity notion are to be found, among which we can cite the work of [11] about the building (by categorization) of concept hierarchies for the knowl-

---

[1]However, the classes in the KB are classically organized hierarchically according to a strict subsumption criterion.

edge representation system TROPES [22],[23] or the work of [30],[29],[18] concerning the fuzzy classification of objects. In the neighboring domain of Conceptual Graphs some work has also been done by [25],[21]. Nevertheless, all of these similarity measures are based on the comparison of the attribute-value expressing the *local structure* of the objects; however, they hardly deal with the *relational structure* existing between the objects. By relational structure, we mean the graph of links between the objects. This paper proposes an approach allowing to deal with both local and relational structure.

However, before defining such a similarity measure between objects, we have to answer two questions: first, what relations exist between similarity and subsumption; secondly, what kind of advantages does the similarity bring with respect to the subsumption?

Let's consider the function SUB (O1, O2) testing during the classification if the description of the object O1 *strictly subsumes* the description of the object O2. This function takes its values from the set {true, false}. Now, let's consider the function SIM (O1, O2) that allows to evaluate the degree of similarity between the objects O1 and O2. We must note that such a similarity function is obviously *asymmetrical*[2]. As a matter of fact, the meaning of SIM (O1, O2) is: "What is the degree of inclusion between the definition of object O1 and the definition of object O2". Thus, the similarity function takes its values from the continuous interval [0..1]; the value 1 means a perfect inclusion of the first object within the second. In this way, the similarity function can be seen as an extension of the subsumption function because it provides a more precise information about the degree of generality between the objects. These functions verify the following implications [3].

$$SIM(O1, O2) = 1 \quad \Rightarrow \quad SUB(O1, O2) = true$$
$$SIM(O1, O2) \in [0..1[\quad \Leftarrow \quad SUB(O1, O2) = false$$

Henceforth, by using a similarity criterion the classification does not return the list of the most specific classes whose definitions strictly subsumes the definition of the object to classify, but it returns a list of classes ordered by decreasing degree of subsumption.

---

[2]It is worth noting that from the mathematical point of view a similarity function is always symmetrical $Sim(x, y) = Sim(y, x)$. However, in this paper we use the word similarity in a more general meaning, which is closely related to the one used in Cognitive Sciences [33]. In the classification problem, this function is clearly not symmetrical because each argument of the function plays a very different role: we compare a target object O1 with a reference object O2

[3]We don't have a full equivalence because the similarity computation described in this paper is based on some heuristics. However, these heuristics allow us to compute the similarity in a polynomial-time.

This capacity to deal with "weak" subsumption is interesting for several reasons.

On the one hand, a large Knowledge Base is never built in one step and in the course of its use, one always needs to refine some definitions of classes. Therefore, at a given moment a KB can be partially incomplete or incoherent. For instance, the definition of classes can be incorrect (some attributes are missing or irrelevant) or the slot definitions contain some errors (the ranges of the intervals are not correct). Clearly, the subsumption criterion can help the developers of the KB to detect such problems. But at the same time this criterion prevents us from using this KB because the classification process always stops as soon as it meets with a contradiction. By using a similarity criterion this problem disappears and the user can try to classify an object in the KB even if the definition of this object is partially incoherent with respect to the information contained in this KB.

On the other hand, when a user classifies an object, the relevance of the attributes is determined by his work and his goal. For instance, when a biologist and an ethologist want to compare two animals they obviously use a very different set of features. The system TROPES [22],[23] proposes an interesting modeling of this problem through the notion of Viewpoints. In TROPES, each concept can be described following different *viewpoints* that correspond to a specific hierarchy of classes; each viewpoint uses a subset of the attributes of the concept. In practice, the vocabulary (attributes) used in a viewpoint is defined by a Boolean vector $[A_1, \ldots, A_n]$ where each Boolean A_i corresponds to an attribute of the concept. Thus, A_i equals true when the corresponding attribute is used in the classes of the viewpoint and A_i equals false otherwise. Again, the notion of similarity allows to go further by associating a relevance value to each attribute. In this way, we can express the fact an attribute is used or not in the viewpoints (0 meaning not used), but we also can express a *relevance scale* between the attributes.

Finally, the possibility of having a similarity measure between the instances is very interesting for the categorization problem. As a matter of fact, there are many efficient methods able to build a taxonomy from a similarity[4] matrix. For instance, we can use some techniques coming from Data Analysis as in the system T-TREE [11]. Machine Learning approach also provides some methods allowing to build a hierarchy of concepts from a set of instances and a similarity measure; we could cite the system ADECLU [8] and KBG [4] or the work of [20]. This paper is composed of four parts. First, we describe (section 2) the Object

---

[4]Here, the similarity is a symmetrical function because during the categorization process each instance plays the same role. Thus, there is no reference object nor target object.

Based Representation and the terminology used in this paper. Next, we present (section 3) a rapid state of the art of the similarity measures in domains such as Data Analysis, Cognitive Sciences and Machine Learning and we propose a method allowing to evaluate the degree of similarity between two items in the classification and categorization contexts. In section 4 we apply the method previously defined in the frame of OBRS. Finally, we examine how our similarity can be used in the classification and categorization processes.

2 REPRESENTATION AND TERMINOLOGY

As in an OBRS like SHIRKA [28], we make a distinction between the notion of class (defining a concept) and the notion of instance (example of concept). A class is composed of a set of pairs attribute/facet with the following properties. First, we associate a numerical weight to each attribute (positive number) expressing the degree of relevance of this attribute in the class[5]. Secondly, we distinguish between two general kinds of facets: the facets that express a value (such that $default or $value) and the facets that define a type of data (such that $type, $range, $interval or $cardinality). When the type of an attribute is another object, we use the term relation to speak about this attribute. Finally, we do not consider the facets expressing a method or an action. We distinguish between two kinds of objects: the simple objects, which are objects without relation, and the complex objects, which correspond to a set of objects linked together by a set of relationship. In this paper, when we speak about the attributes (or properties) of an object we speak about all of its properties, including the inherited ones.

A Knowledge Base can be described as a graph whose each node expresses an object (class). In this graph, we can distinguish between a horizontal structure and a vertical structure (figure 1). The horizontal structure is correlated with the inheritance links (AKO) expressing the hierarchy of classes, the vertical structure is made of the binary relations existing between two classes[6]. Clearly, if the inheritance links always constitute an acyclic graph, that is not always true for the graph of relations.

Therefore, both classification and categorization processes are equivalent to a graph matching problem. As a matter of fact, the problem of classifying a complex object (class or instance) into a Knowledge Base comes down to find an optimal matching (figure 2) between the components of this object and the components of the KB. By optimal matching, we mean the

---

[5]We will not discuss in this paper the way this relevance scale has been established.

[6]In a complex instance, we just have a horizontal structure between the objects.

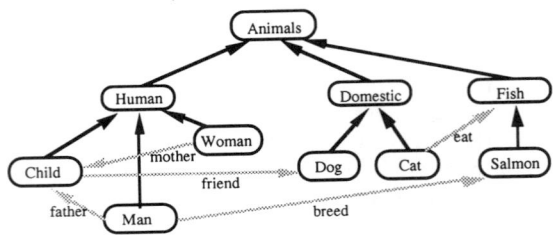

Figure 1: Vertical and horizontal structures.

matching that maximizes the value of the similarity function. In the same way, to compute the similarity between two instances we need to finding the optimal matching between the simple objects that compose these instances.

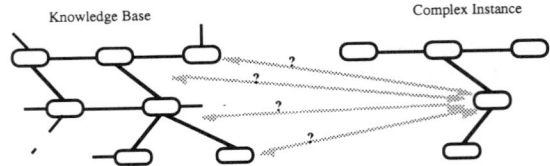

Figure 2: Matching problem during the classification.

As detailed in section 3.2, to be relevant the similarity measure must be able to take into account both local and relational structures of the matched objects. By local structure, we mean that the measure must evaluate the degree of likeness between the matched objects, that is to say the similarity between the shared attributes. By relational structure, we mean that the measure also must evaluate the degree of relationship between the matched objects, that is to say the similarity between the shared horizontal structures.

3 WORK ABOUT SIMILARITY

3.1 Similarity between attributes

The notion of distance has been extensively studied in the frame of Data Analysis (DA). Classically, a distance is defined as follow: Let Ω the set of individuals of the domain and let the metric $\mathcal{D}$ that is an application from $\Omega \times \Omega$ to R^+. $\forall a, b, c \in \Omega$:

$$
\begin{array}{lll}
\mathcal{D}(a, a) & = & 0 \qquad\qquad\qquad \text{(minimality property)} \\
\mathcal{D}(a, b) & = & \mathcal{D}(b, a) \qquad\quad \text{(symmetry property)} \\
\mathcal{D}(a, b) & = & 0 \Rightarrow a = b \quad \text{(identity property)} \\
\mathcal{D}(a, c) & \geq & \mathcal{D}(a, b) + \mathcal{D}(b, c) \quad \text{(triangular inequality)}
\end{array}
$$

A distance must verify these four properties. It is worth noting that the individuals of Ω, as described in Data Analysis, are closely related to simple objects described by a set of attributes. Currently, many distances have been developed according to the type of attributes, such as χ_2 or Manahalobis [9]. However, as soon as we are working with real values, the most used (and simplest) metric is the Minkowski measure:

$$\mathcal{D}_p(x,y) = [\sum_{i=1}^{K} W_i \times |x_i - y_i|^p]^{\frac{1}{p}} \text{ with } p \geq 0 \quad (1)$$

In this measure, x_i and y_i express the value of the ith attribute describing the individual x and y. W_i expresses the numerical weight correlated with this attribute. According to the value of the parameter P, we retrieve some well-known distances such as Manhattan distance ($P = 1$) and Euclidean distance ($P = 2$). To transform the Minkowski distance (1) into a similarity measure we just need to introduce a value D_i corresponding to the difference between the upper and the lower bounds of the range of the ith attribute:

$$\mathcal{S}_p(x,y) = [\sum_{i=1}^{K} W_i \times (\frac{D_i - |x_i - y_i|}{D_i})^p]^{\frac{1}{p}} \text{ with } p \geq 0 \quad (2)$$

The notion of distance between individuals has been also studied in Cognitive Sciences. From this point of view, [33] emphasizes that the mathematical properties defined in Data Analysis (minimality, symmetry and triangular inequality) are generally not verified when one analyses the way people feel and deal with the notion of similarity. In other respect, the individuals to compare are often described by different sets of attributes. Therefore, Tversky proposes to evaluate the degree of similarity $\mathcal{S}(x,y)$ between two individuals x and y, respectively described by a set of attributes A and B, by combining the four terms $A \cap B$, $A \cup B$, $A - B$ et $B - A$ into the formula:

$$\mathcal{S}(x,y) = \frac{f(A \cap B)}{f(A \cup B) + \alpha f(A - B) + \beta f(B - A)}$$

According to the way the parameters f, α et β are instantiated, we can express different kinds of cognitive models of similarity. For instance, if we want to compare a pair of individuals described by a set of numerical attributes, we can combine the definitions proposed by Tversky and Minkowski into two different similarity measures $\mathcal{S}\dagger\updownarrow$ and $\mathcal{A}\int\dagger$ that can be respectively used in the frame of classification and categorization. In these measures, we use the Tversky's model to compare the two set of attributes describing the individuals; the function f of this model is the Minkowski's formula as rewritten in the equation (2). The parameter P of this formula equals 1 since in the Tversky's model the

function f corresponds to a linear combination of the features.

The function $\mathcal{S}\dagger\updownarrow$ is a symmetrical similarity measure that is usable in a categorization process. The parameters of the Tversky's model are instantiated to the values $\alpha = \beta = 0$, leading to a measure like $f(A \cap B)/f(A \cup B)$. The function $\mathcal{A}\int\dagger$ is an asymmetrical similarity measure that is usable in a classification process. Here, the parameters of the Tversky's model are instantiated to the values $\alpha = 0$ et $\beta = -1$, leading to a measure like $f(A \cap B)/f(A)$. Hence, $\mathcal{A}\int\dagger$ allows to evaluate the degree of inclusion between the first argument (reference) into the second argument (target). In other words, $\mathcal{A}\int\dagger$ allows to quantify the degree of subsumption between the individuals B and A.

- Let the function: $Att.similarity(i) = \frac{D_i - |x_i - y_i|}{D_i}$

$$\mathcal{S}\dagger\updownarrow(x,y) = \frac{\sum_{i}^{A \cap B} W_i \times Att.similarity(i)}{\sum_{i}^{A \cup B} W_i}$$

$$\mathcal{A}\int\dagger(x,y) = \frac{\sum_{i}^{A \cap B} W_i \times Att.similarity(i)}{\sum_{i}^{A} W_i}$$

Both measures return a value belonging to the interval [0..1]. Here is an example of use of $\mathcal{S}\dagger\updownarrow$ and $\mathcal{A}\int\dagger$ with two individuals I_1 and I_2 described by a set of four attributes:

Attribute	W	I_1	I_2	D	$Att.similarity$
high	1	10	20	[0..99]	90%
length	2	2	2	[0..9]	100%
weight	1	8	-	[0..59]	-
strength	2	-	10	[-5..5]	-

Thus, we obtain:
$$\mathcal{S}\dagger\updownarrow(I_1, I_2) = 48\%$$
$$\mathcal{A}\int\dagger(I_1, I_2) = 73\%$$
$$\mathcal{A}\int\dagger(I_2, I_1) = 58\%$$

3.2 Similarity between relations

As soon as we work with a knowledge representation dealing with the notion of relations between the individuals (such that first order logic or object oriented modeling), the approach proposed in the previous section 3.1 becomes too rough since we need to compare two graphs of individuals. Moreover, in our approach we consider that all the individuals in the graphs are relevant for the similarity computation. Therefore, when we compare any two individuals A and B, the similarity measure between these individuals must express the similarity between their attributes, but also the similarity between the individuals that are connected to A and B through the medium of the relations.

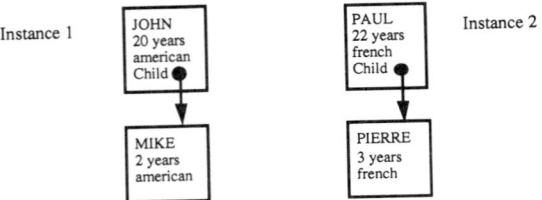

Figure 3: Example of connected individuals

Thus, in the previous example (figure 3) to compare together the individual JOHN in the first instance and the individual PAUL in the second one, we need to evaluate the similarity between the common attributes (age and nationality), but we also need to take into account the similarity between their children MIKE and PIERRE. Intuitively, the closer MIKE and PIERRE are, the closer JOHN and PAUL are too. If we consider the relation CHILD as symmetrical, the problem is the equivalent when we compare the children: we must take into account the degree of similarity between their parents.

Many researches have been done to define a relevant and efficient similarity measure to compare any graphs of individuals. We can cite Pattern Recognition [31],[35], Cognitive Sciences [14],[17],[19] and Machine Learning [10],[3]. A detailed comparison between these approaches is beyond the scope of this paper, however we can emphasize some salient features. In Pattern Recognition people use informed tree search methods, such as *branch and bound* search, to explore the space of matchings. This method allows the system to find the optimal matching, nevertheless the process can be very expensive if the cost function used in the branch and bound is not efficient. Moreover, these methods provide an evaluation of the similarity between the whole graphs and not between the individuals. The methods implemented in Cognitive Sciences aim generally at studying the notion of analogy. Thus, the algorithms are not very efficient since they use very weak hypothesis to constrain the search space; for instance, they allow the system to match individuals without common attribute. However, this work brings some interesting evidences about the way people feel the notion of similarity: on the one hand, these theories emphasize that it is crucial to take into account both attributes and relations during the comparison of two individuals; on the other hand, for human being the

soundness of a comparison increases when the matching choices preserves the relational structure between the individuals (the systematicity principle in [16]).

In the system KBG[7] [3],[4] we have defined a similarity measure having two advantages. First, the complexity of the similarity computation is quadratic in terms of the number of individuals involved in the graphs and linear in terms of common attributes between individuals. Secondly, the general behavior of this similarity measure is consistent with the cognitive theories previously evoked. Without detailing, we think this second point is crucial in the frame of the OBRS: when the system has an apparent comportment closely related to the human behavior, the user can understand more deeply the way the system is working and thus he can use more efficiently this system.

In practice, the method used in KBG is quite simple. To measure the similarity between a pair of individuals, two kinds of information must be considered: the attributes and the relations. In section 3.1 we have already proposed a simple approach allowing to evaluate the similarity between two sets of (numerical) attributes. Concerning the relations, the computation is based on the idea presented on the previous example (figure 3), that is to say: the result of the similarity evaluation between the relations CHILD of JOHN and PAUL depends on the similarity of MIKE with PIERRE, and reciprocally. More formally the similarity measure can be defined in the following way:

- Let X and Y a pair of individuals. These individuals are respectively described by two sets of the numerical attributes Ax and Ay and two sets of relations Rx and Ry.

1. Computation of the similarity between attributes.

   - Depending on whether we want to compute a symmetrical or asymmetrical similarity we use $\mathcal{S}\dagger\updownarrow(X,Y)$ or $\mathcal{A}f\dagger(X,Y)$ with Ax and Ay.

2. Computation of the similarity between relations.

   - Let the function $\mathcal{C}(R,X)$ returning the individual connected to X through of the relation R. For instance: $\mathcal{C}(Child, PAUL) \rightarrow PIERRE$
   - Let the function $Rel.similarity(i)$ computing the similarity between of the ith relations of the list $Rx \cap Ry$. This function plays the same role that the similarity function $Att.similarity(i)$ between attributes. Depending on whether we compute a symmetrical or asymmetrical similarity the function is slightly different:

---

[7]This tool was implemented in the frame of the MLT ESPRIT contract. It can be used to categorize a set of instances and to generate a diagnosis KB. The representation language is based on first-order logic.

Symmetrical:

$$Rel.similarity(i) = \frac{1 + \mathcal{FS}\!\int\!\dagger\!\updownarrow(\mathcal{C}(Ri,X),\mathcal{C}(Ri,Y))}{2}$$

Asymmetrical:

$$Rel.similarity(i) = \frac{1 + \mathcal{FS}\!\dashv\!\int\!\dagger(\mathcal{C}(Ri,X),\mathcal{C}(Ri,Y))}{2}$$

Here, the similarity between a common relation R_i between the individuals X and Y equals the average similarities between the individuals involved in this relation. The first term "1" expresses the similarity between X and Y with respect to the common relation. The second term ($\mathcal{FS}\!\int\!\dagger\!\updownarrow$ or $\mathcal{FS}\!\dashv\!\int\!\dagger$) expresses the Final Similarity (symmetrical or not) between the two[8] individuals connected to X and Y through the medium of the relation R_i.

- Let the function $\mathcal{R}\!\rceil\!\updownarrow\!\mathcal{S}\!\dagger\!\updownarrow$ and $\mathcal{R}\!\rceil\!\updownarrow\!\mathcal{A}\!\int\!\dagger$ computing the similarity (symmetrical or not) for all the common relations between X and Y. In practice, these functions are equivalent to the functions $\mathcal{S}\!\dagger\!\updownarrow$ et $\mathcal{A}\!\int\!\dagger$ defined for the attributes.

$$\mathcal{R}\!\rceil\!\updownarrow\!\mathcal{S}\!\dagger\!\updownarrow(x,y) = \frac{\displaystyle\sum_{i}^{Rx \cap Ry} W_i \times Rel.similarity(i)}{\displaystyle\sum_{i}^{Rx \cup Ry} W_i}$$

$$\mathcal{R}\!\rceil\!\updownarrow\!\mathcal{A}\!\int\!\dagger(x,y) = \frac{\displaystyle\sum_{i}^{Rx \cap Ry} W_i \times Rel.similarity(i)}{\displaystyle\sum_{i}^{Rx} W_i}$$

The final similarity ($\mathcal{FS}\!\int\!\dagger\!\updownarrow$ or $\mathcal{FS}\!\dashv\!\int\!\dagger$) between X and Y equals to the average similarities computed for the attributes and the relations.

$$\mathcal{FS}\!\int\!\dagger\!\updownarrow(X,Y) = \frac{\mathcal{S}\!\dagger\!\updownarrow(X,Y) + \mathcal{R}\!\rceil\!\updownarrow\!\mathcal{S}\!\dagger\!\updownarrow(X,Y)}{2} \in [0..1]$$

$$\mathcal{FS}\!\dashv\!\int\!\dagger(X,Y) = \frac{\mathcal{A}\!\int\!\dagger(X,Y) + \mathcal{R}\!\rceil\!\updownarrow\!\mathcal{A}\!\int\!\dagger(X,Y)}{2} \in [0..1]$$

By reading this definition we can easily notice the following phenomena: to compute the similarity between the common relations of X and Y ($\mathcal{R}\!\rceil\!\updownarrow\!\mathcal{S}\!\dagger\!\updownarrow$ or

---

[8]If the cardinality of the relation is higher than 1, we can have a list of individuals connected to X and Y rather than only one individual. We will detailed this point in the section 4.2. However, it is worth noting in this case the similarity measure keeps the properties previously evoked.

$\mathcal{R}\!\rceil\!\updownarrow\!\mathcal{A}\!\int\!\dagger$) one needs to know the overall similarity values ($\mathcal{FS}\!\int\!\dagger\!\updownarrow$ or $\mathcal{FS}\!\dashv\!\int\!\dagger$) between the individuals connected to X and Y. Obviously the situation is fully symmetrical and the individuals connected to X and Y also needs in their similarity computations the overall similarity value between X and Y. Therefore, the similarity computation between two graphs of individuals comes down to the problem of setting and solving a system of linear equations in several unknowns. In these equations the unknowns express the pairs of individuals whose we try to evaluate the similarity. This method allows to take into account the local and the relational structures simultaneously during the computation. In this way, the higher the similarity value between two individuals is, the closer their properties and their connected individuals are too. Finally, in this method no tree search is required to evaluate the quality of matching. Of course, as this approach is based on a heuristic, the similarity values found do not always correspond to an optimal matching.

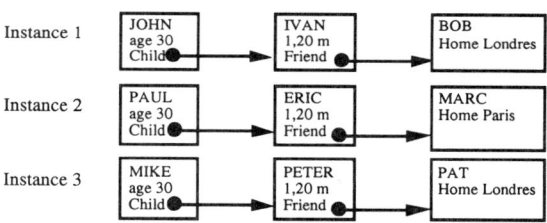

Figure 4: Propagation of the similarities

In figure 4, an example illustrates the advantages of our approach. If we compare the similarity between JOHN and PAUL and the similarity between JOHN and MIKE, we observe that $\mathcal{FS}\!\int\!\dagger\!\updownarrow(JOHN, PAUL)$ is smaller than $\mathcal{FS}\!\int\!\dagger\!\updownarrow(JOHN, MIKE)$. Indeed, although the fathers and their children are totally identical, there exist a difference concerning the place where the children's friends are living. With our method this difference is automatically taken into account in the similarity between the fathers. In practice, the scope of a piece of information (here, the attribute Home) into the graph is infinite. However, the influence an information has on the similarity between a pair of individuals decreases as a geometrical law according to the distance; namely, the number of relations between this information and the individuals (here, there are two relations: Friend and Child). Finally, we can demonstrate [3],[4] that the system of linear equations has always a solution even when they are some cycles between the relations.

3.3 Similarity between graphs of Individuals

We have evaluated the degree of similarity between all the pairs of individuals (sharing at least one common

242

property) occurring in a pair of graphs. Now, we need to study the way to compute the global similarity between these two graphs (figure 5).

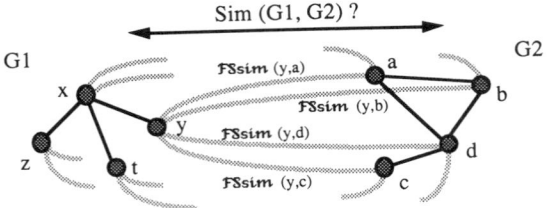

Figure 5: Computation of the similarity between two graphs of individuals.

Roughly speaking, we must search the 1-1 matching between the individuals of G1 and those of G2 that optimizes the global similarity. From a theoretical standpoint, this problem comes down to searching the optimal weighted assignment in a bipartite graph. Several polynomial algorithms have been developed [1] to deal with this problem. Moreover, [6] proposes a general discussion about this problem. Once the matching has been chosen, the global similarity between the two graphs can be evaluated by computing the average similarity between the matched individuals.

4 OBJECT AND SIMILARITY

Obviously, the work presented in the previous section can be easily reused in the framework of OBRS. As a matter of fact, the individuals described in the previous section can be seen as a kind of elementary objects. Thus, we are going to study how to redefine the functions *Rel.similarity* and *Att.similarity* described in section 3.2 in order to take into account the notion of facet. We split the discussion into two parts: the first part concerns the attributes (section 4.1) and the second part concerns the relations (section 4.2).

4.1 Similarity between attributes

Depending on the problem to solve, classification or categorization, the facets are compared in a different way. During categorization, we want to evaluate the likeness between two values (symmetrical similarity). During classification of instances or classes, we want to evaluate the degree a subsumption (asymmetrical similarity) that exists between a value and a type definition or between two type definitions. Although a facet definition can be rather complex, it seems possible to take into account the most part of the information it contains during the similarity evaluation. We are going to illustrate this point by defining such a measure

in the case of the numerical attributes[9] used in the system SHIRKA [28]. In this system an attribute (integer or real) can be defined either as mono-valued or multi-valued with cardinality constrains.

4.1.1 Similarity between two set of values (categorization of instances)

The comparison between a pair of values can be achieved with the help of a similarity measure (figure 6) denoted $\mathcal{SV}(x, y)$, which is identical to the one used in the section 3.1. However, when the attributes are multi-valued we have to deal with two sets of values. Thus, we need to introduce a new function denoted $\mathcal{BM}\dashv\sqcup\rfloor\langle(S1, S2, \mathcal{SV})$ that searches for the Best MATCHing between the values of $S1$ and the values of $S2$, that is to say, the matching that optimizes the global similarity between the two sets[10]. This function returns the average similarity between the matched values. Finally, we must take into account the fact that the cardinal of the two sets $S1$ and $S2$ can be different.

- Let two sets of values $S1 = (V_1, V_2, ..., V_n)$ and $S2 = (U_1, U_2, ..., U_m)$.

- Let D the difference between the bounds of the attribute domain.

- Let the similarity function $\mathcal{SV}(x, y) = \frac{D - |x - y|}{D}$

$$Att.similarity(S_1, S_2) = \frac{\mathcal{BM}\dashv\sqcup\rfloor\langle(S1, S2, \mathcal{SV})}{Max(n, m)}$$

4.1.2 Similarity between a set of values and a definition (classification of instances)

We have to evaluate the degree of inclusion between the values of the instance and the definition of the attribute (described in the form of an interval). The similarity measure must return 1 when all the values belong to the definition and a number between $[0..1[$ else. Thus, we introduce a function (figure 6) denoted $\mathcal{SI}$ allowing to evaluate the similarity between one value and an interval. Moreover, as the cardinality constraints on the multi-valued attributes are expressed in the form of an interval, the function $\mathcal{SI}$ is also used to evaluate if the number of values is coherent with the cardinality constraint.

- Let a set of values $S = (V_1, V_2, ..., V_n)$

- Let an attribute *Att* whose range is defined through the interval $Dom = [D1..D2]$ and its cardinality through the interval $Card = [C1..C2]$.

---

[9]We could also define a similarity measure on the other types such that: taxonomy or nominal value.

[10]As in section 3.3, the problem is to find the optimal weighted assignment in the bipartite graph

- Let the function:

$$\mathcal{SI}(x, [A..B]) = \text{If } x \in [A..B] \Rightarrow 1$$

$$\text{Else} \Rightarrow \frac{|A - B|}{|A - B| + Min(|x - A|, |x - B|)}$$

$$Att.similarity(Att, S) = \frac{\mathcal{SI}(n, Card)}{n} \times \sum_{i}^{n} \mathcal{SI}(V_i, Dom)$$

4.1.3 Similarity between two definitions of attributes (classification of classes)

We have to evaluate the degree of subsumption between the reference definition and the target definition. This comparison involves two intervals and is achieved with the help of the function denoted $\mathcal{SD}$. This function is quite similar to the function $\mathcal{SI}$.

- Let the reference attribute $A1$ (respectively the target attribute $A2$) whose domain is expressed by the interval $Dom1 = [D1..D2]$ and the cardinality by the interval $Card1 = [C1..C2]$ (respectively $Dom2 = [D3..D4]$ and $Card2 = [C3..C4]$).

- Let the function :

$$\mathcal{SD}([A..B], [C..D]) = \text{If } [A..B] \subset [C..D] \Rightarrow 1$$
$$\text{Elsif } A \subset [C..D] \Rightarrow \mathcal{SI}(B, [C..D])$$
$$\text{Elsif } B \subset [C..D] \Rightarrow \mathcal{SI}(A, [C..D])$$
$$\text{Elsif } [C..D] \subset [A..B] \Rightarrow \frac{|C - D|}{|A - B|}$$
$$\text{Else} \Rightarrow \frac{\mathcal{SI}(A, [C..D]) + \mathcal{SI}(B, [C..D])}{2}$$

$$Att.similarity(A_1, A_2) = \mathcal{SD}(Card2, Card1)$$
$$\times \ \mathcal{SD}(Dom2, Dom1)$$

Obviously, the similarity measures between numerical attributes that we described in this section are somewhat arbitrary. However, the user can easily modify these definitions without changing the properties of the general method described in section 3. Practically, the very advantage of using a similarity measure is to provide a flexible framework that the user can freely customize according to his application domain and to his needs. More generally, it seems important [7] in the OBSR to allow the users to define their own types of data with the corresponding similarity measures.

4.2 Similarity between relations

With respect to the method detailed in section 3.2 few modifications are needed to deal with relations in an object based representation. However, depending on the problem to solve, classification or categorization, the similarity measure Rel-similarity is different.

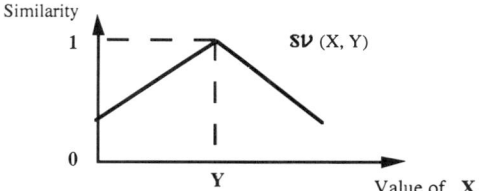

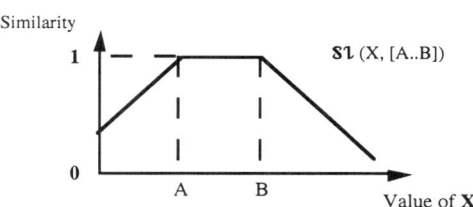

Figure 6: Behavior of the functions $\mathcal{SV}$ and $\mathcal{SI}$.

4.2.1 Similarity between two lists of objects (categorization)

In the section 3.2 we did not take into account the fact that an object can be connected to a set of objects (that is typically the case for the Children relation). This problem can be easily solved by using a function quite similar to $\mathcal{BM}\dashv\sqcup\rfloor\langle$ (see 4.1.1). The function $\mathcal{SBM}\dashv\sqcup\rfloor\langle(S1, S2, \mathcal{FS}\int\dagger\mathbb{1})$ searches for an optimal matching between the objects of the two sets S1 and S2. The only difference between $\mathcal{BM}\dashv\sqcup\rfloor\langle$ and $\mathcal{SBM}\dashv\sqcup\rfloor\langle$ is that the second function returns the summation of the similarity between the matched objects instead of the average of this summation. As the categorization process needs a symmetrical similarity, we use the function $\mathcal{FS}\int\dagger\mathbb{1}$ to evaluate each matching.

- Let two sets of objects $S1 = (O_1, O_2, ..., O_n)$ and $S2 = (P_1, P_2, ..., P_m)$.

$$Rel.similarity(S_1, S_2) = \frac{1 + \mathcal{SBM}\dashv\sqcup\rfloor\langle(S1, S2, \mathcal{FS}\int\dagger\mathbb{1})}{Max(n + 1, m + 1)}$$

4.2.2 Similarity between a list of objects and a definition (classification of instances)

During the classification of instances and for a given relation, we need to compare the set of objects (instances) in the slot value of the relation with the object (class) describe in the attribute definition. The final similarity equals the average similarity (computed with the asymmetrical function $\mathcal{FS}\dashv\int\dagger$) between each object of the slot value with the object of the attribute definition. The cardinality constraint is computed as in section 4.1.2.

- Let the set S of the objects in the slot value of the relation: $S = (O_1, ..., O_n)$.

- Let the object P (class) occurring in the definition of the studied relation. The cardinality of this relation is expressed in the form of an interval: $Card = [C1..C2]$.

$$Rel.similarity(P,S) = \frac{\mathcal{SI}(n,Card)}{n+1}$$
$$\times \quad (1 + \sum_{i}^{n} \mathcal{FS\dashv\!\!\int\dagger}(P,O_i))$$

4.2.3 Similarity between two definitions of relations (classification of classes)

In that case, we need to compare the objects (classes) occurring in the definition of the studied relation. The cardinality constraint is computed as in section 4.1.3.

- Let two objects (classes) $P1$ et $P2$ respectively occurring in the definitions of the relation R of the reference class $O1$ and the target class $O2$ we are studying. The cardinality of the relation R in $O1$ (respectively in $O2$) is expressed in the form of an interval $Card1 = [C1..C2]$ (respectively $Card2 = [C3..C4]$).

$$Rel.similarity(P_1,P_2) = \mathcal{SD}(Card2,Card1)$$
$$\times \quad \frac{1 + \mathcal{FS\dashv\!\!\int\dagger}(P1,P2)}{2}$$

Once the functions *Att.similarity* and *Rel.similarity* has been defined, the similarity between a pair of complex objects is evaluated with the method describes in sections 3.2 and 3.3.

5 USE OF THE SIMILARITY MEASURE

In the two previous sections we have defined a similarity measure allowing to evaluate the degree of similarity between two complex objects. Now we are going to see how such a similarity measure can be used to categorize and to classify a set of objects.

The categorization of a set of instances can be achieved by using a Conceptual Clustering approach [24]. Given a set of instances and some information about the domain, a Conceptual Clustering system aims at performing the following task:

- To find a set of relevant categories (class) grouping these instances.

- To provide a comprehensive symbolic definition of each cluster.

- To build a hierarchical organization of these clusters.

Currently, there are two kinds of Conceptual Clustering systems whose algorithms are based on a similarity measure. The system ADECLU [8] is representative of the Concept Formation approach [13] and it allows to build a hierarchy of classes in an incremental way. The system KBG [4] uses another method based on a non-incremental agglomerative clustering algorithm stemming from Data Analysis community. However, it is worth noting that most of these Conceptual Clustering systems use a representation language based on a logical framework. Nevertheless, it is possible to adapt the existing algorithms to an object representation framework: the system T-TREE [11] is a good example of such approach.

Concerning the classification tasks, the use of a similarity measure instead of the subsumption function involves some changes in the classification algorithms. As a matter of fact, the notion of impossible class (namely, a class that does not verify the subsumption criterion) disappears. Therefore, we lose the stopping criterion of the classification algorithms. The classification process can be controlled by using a kind of branch-and-bound algorithm: at each step, we explore the children of the classes having the higher score of similarity with the object to classify. However, the similarity measure proposed in this paper does not always monotonically increase during the specialization; eventually, we cannot guarantee to select the optimal classes in the Knowledge Base.

6 CONCLUSION

Currently, in the objects-based representation systems, both classification and categorization are based on a subsumption criterion. However, when we need to deal with incomplete or incoherent knowledge this criterion is difficult to use. In such a domain, the notion of similarity seems more relevant. In this paper we have proposed a general approach of the similarity combining some results stemming from Data Analysis, Cognitive Sciences and Machine Learning. Our measure allows to evaluate the degree of similarity between complex objects and this measure can be used both in the frame of classification and categorization. Moreover, the computational cost of this measure remains interesting since it is (at most) quadratic in terms of number of objects involved in the comparison and linear in terms of common attributes. However, this study must be pursued in order to define some new classification and categorization algorithms.

REFERENCES

1. AHUJA R.K, MAGNANTI T.L., ORLIN J.B. 1993. Network Flows: Theory, Algorithms and Applications. Prentice Hall.

2. ANDERBERG M. 1973. Cluster Analysis for Applications. Academic Press, New-York.

3. BISSON G. 1992a. Learning in FOL with a similarity measure. In Proceedings of 10th National Conference on Artificial Intelligence (AAAI) . San-Jose. 82-87.

4. BISSON G. 1992b. Conceptual Clustering in a First Order Logic Representation. Proceedings of 10th European Conference on Artificial Intelligence (ECAI). Vienna. 458-462.

5. BISSON G. 1993. KBG : Induction de bases de connaissances en logique des prédicats. Thèse de l'universit é de Paris-sud (number 2670) soutenue le 30 avril 1993.

6. BRISSAC O., LIQUIERE M. 1990. Un algorithme optimal pour l'association d'entités partir de leurs similarités. Actes des 9eme JFA. Strasbourg. B1-B14.

7. CAPPONI C. 1994. Exploitation des types dans un modèle de représentation des connaissances par objets. Actes 9e RFIA. 11-14 janvier. Paris. 171-183.

8. DECAESTECKER C. 1993. Apprentissage et outils statistiques en classification conceptuelle incrémentale. Revue d'Intelligence Artificielle. Volume 7. 33-71.

9. DIDAY E., LEMAIRE, J., POUGET J., TESTU F., 1982. Eléments d'analyse des données. Edition Dunod.

10. ESPOSITO F., MALERBA D., SEMERARO G. 1991. Flexible Matching for Noisy Structural Descriptions. In proceeding of 12th IJCAI, 658-664. Sydney.

11. EUZENAT J. 1993. Brief Overview of T-TREE : The TROPES Taxonomy Building Tool. Proceedings of the 4th ASIS SIG/CR Classification Research Workshop. 69-87.

12. EVERITT B. 1980. Cluster Analysis. Halsted press. New York.

13. FISHER D.H 1987. Knowledge Acquisition via Incremental Conceptual Clustering. Machine Learning Journal 2, 139-172.

14. FALKENHAINER B., FORBUS K., GENTNER D. 1989. The Structure-Mapping Engine: Algorithm and Examples. Artificial Intelligence Journal. Number 41. 1-63.

15. GENNARI J., LANGLEY P., FISHER D. 1989. Model of Incremental Concept Formation. Artificial Intelligence Journal, Volume 40, 11-61.

16. GENTNER D. 1983. Structure-Mapping: A Theoritical Framework for Analogy. In Readings in Cognitive Science. Morgan Kaufmann 1988. 303-310. (from Cognitive Science 7, 1983).

17. GENTNER D., RATTERMANN M., FORBUS K. 1993. The Roles of similarity in Transfer: Separating Retrievability from Inferential Soundness. Cognitive Psychology 25. 431-467.

18. GRANGER C. 1988. An application of possibility theory to object recognition. In Fuzzy Sets and Systems. Volume 28. 351-362.

19. HOLYOAK K., THAGARD P. 1989. Analogical Mapping by Constraint Satisfaction. In Cognitive Science Journal. number 13. 295-355.

20. LEBBE J., NICOLAS J., VIGNES R. 1991. From Knowledge to Similarity. In Proceedings of the International Conference Symbolic-Numeric, Data Analysis and Learning. 585- 597. Paris (France).

21. MAHER P. 1993. A Similarity Measure for Conceptual Graphs. International Journal of Intelligent Systems. Volume 8 Number 8. 819-837.

22. MARIÑO O. 1991. Classification d'objets composites dans un système de représentation de connaissances multi-points de vue. Actes de Reconnaissance des Formes et Intelligence Artificielle (RFIA). 233-242.

23. MARIÑO O., RECHENMANN F., UVIETTA P. 1990. Multiple Perspectives and Classification Mechanism in Object-Oriented Representation. Proceedings of 9th European Conference on Artificial Intelligence (ECAI). Stockholm. 425-430.

24. MICHALSKI R.S., STEPP E. 1983. Learning from Observation : Conceptual Clustering. In Machine Learning 1 an Artificial Intelligence Approach, Tioga, 331-363.

25. MYAENG S., LOPEZ-LOPEZ O. 1992. Conceptual graph matching: a flexible algorithm and experiments. Journal of Experimental and Theoritical Artificial Intelligence 4. 107- 126.

26. NAPOLI A. 1992. Représentations à objets et raisonnement par classification en intelligence artificielle. Thèse d'état de l'université Nancy I, soutenue le 31 janvier 1992.

27. NAPOLI A. 1994. Catégorisation, raisonnement par classification et raisonnement à partir de cas. Actes des 9eme JFA. E1-E14. Strasbourg 23-25 mars.

28. RECHENMANN F., UVIETTA P. 1991. SHIRKA - An object-centered knowledge base management system. In Artificial Intelligence in Numerical and Symbolic Simulation. ALEAS publisher. Lyon.

29. ROSSAZZA J.P 1990. Utilisation de hiérarchies de classes floues pour la représentation de connaissances imprécises et sujettes à exceptions : le systeme SORCIER. Thèse de l'université Paul Sabatier de Toulouse soutenue le 15 mai 1990.

30. SALOTTI S. 1992. Filtrage flou et représentation centrée objet pour raisonner par analogie : le systme FLORAN. Thèse de l'université Paris-sud (2339) soutenue le 4 décembre 1992.

31. SANFELIU A., FU K. 1983. A Distance Measure between Attributed Relational Graphs for Pattern Recognition. In IEEE Transactions on System, Man and Cybernetics. 13. 353-362.

32. SNEATH P.H.A., SOKAL R. 1973. Numerical Taxonomy. Freeman.

33. TVERSKY A. 1977. Features of similarity. In Readings in Cognitive Science. Morgan Kaufmann 1988. (from Psychological Review 84, 327-352, 1977).

34. VOSS (Ed) 1994. Similarity Concepts and Retreival Methods. FABEL project Technical Report number 13. Gesselschaft fr Mathematik und Datenverarbeitung (GMB). Sankt Augustin.

35. WONG A., YOU M. 1985. Entropy and Distance of Random Graphs with Application to Structural Pattern Recognition. In Transactions on Pattern Analysis and Machine Intelligence. 7. 599-609.

Towards Very Large Knowledge Bases
N.J.I. Mars, Ed.
IOS Press, 1995

Intelligent Caching in Heterogeneous Reasoning and Mediator Systems*

Sibel Adalı and **V.S. Subrahmanian**
University of Maryland
{sibel, vs}@cs.umd.edu

ABSTRACT

Heterogeneous Reasoning and Mediator Systems (HERMES), first proposed by Lu, Nerode and Subrahmanian, may be used to access and logically integrate information from external databases and/or software packages using functions already defined in those domains. When processing queries in HERMES, we need to execute these external programs, and this is often an expensive process, especially when these programs are located at remote sites on, say a network. Consequently, the problem of minimizing access to such external routines without compromising completeness is an important one. In this paper, we will present methods to cache the results of previous computations and use the knowledge about external programs to make intelligent use of the cached information to reduce calls to external programs.

1 INTRODUCTION

During the past few decades, the world has witnessed a spectacular explosion in the *quantity* of data available in one electronic form or another. This vast quantity of data has been gathered, organized, and stored by a small army of individuals, working for different organizations on varied problems in ways that were best suited to accomplish the task in question. To handle this increasing volume of data, Wiederhold [11] proposed the important concept of a *mediator*, which can be regarded as a program for performing semantic integration over multiple data sources. Intuitively, a mediator is a program that accesses and manipulates multiple databases and/or software packages. The user of a mediated system interacts directly with the mediator, which in turn passes along appropriate subqueries to different software packages and/or databases in the mediated system. Extending mediators coded using C-like languages requires understanding the program, and isolating and modifying parts of the program that express how to semantically integrate information, which is a very hard task.

In order to address these concerns, Lu, Nerode and Subrahmanian [8] have developed a formal theoretical framework called *Hybrid Knowledge Bases* that provides a rule-based framework for expressing mediators. Subsequently, Subrahmanian et. al. [10] have developed a system called HERMES (HEterogeneous Reasoning and MEdiator System) that can be used for developing mediators in. HERMES currently runs on both the Sparc/Unix/X platform as well as the PC/Windows platform. HERMES currently integrates the following systems: PARADOX, DBASE V.0, and INGRES (all commercially available relational DBMSs), a face recognition system, a path planning system developed by the US Army, a multimedia system, a text database system and a spatial database management system. It has been used to develop mediators for robotic applications at the National Institute of Standards and Technology [5], for federal law enforcement applications [9], and for missile siting problems [4]. All these applications involve processing several Gigabytes of widely varying forms of data, using widely varying data representation and reasoning techniques.

The primary aim of this paper is to investigate ways to make the processing of queries in heterogeneous reasoning systems more efficient. We advocate the intelligent use of high-speed caches to avoid computations

*This work was supported by the Army Research Office under Grant Nr. DAAL-03-92-G-0225, by the Air Force Office of Scientific Research under Grant Nr. F49620-93-1-0065, by ARPA Order Nr. A716, by Rome Labs contract F30602-93-C-0241, and by NSF Young Investigator award IRI-93-57756.

whenever possible. To accomplish this we introduce the concept of an "invariant", i.e. an expression about the known input/output relationships of a program that can be processed by the mediator. In this paper, we will describe how such caches may be maintained, and how the query processing procedure can make better use of these caches, given the knowledge about different packages, to reduce the complexity of query execution. Our methods are sound and complete, and apply to real-life implemented examples [4, 5, 9].

2 AN OVERVIEW OF HERMES

In our framework, a mediator is a ruled based program written in a special syntax and it operates on information coming from different sources of data. The clauses of the mediator specify how this information should be integrated in order to answer a specific query. These sources of data can be as different as relational, deductive, object oriented, text, spatial and temporal databases, problem solving domains such as spread sheets, data stored in different data structures as well as application programs written on top of such programs. Lu, Nerode and Subrahmanian proved that [8] these programs can be viewed as constraint domains and executing these programs can be viewed as solving a constraint in a given domain. We will refer to these domains as external programs.

HERMES syntax is an extension of generalized annotated programs (GAPs) introduced by Kifer and Subrahmanian [6]. Annotated logic is an extension of logic programming where atoms are marked explicitly with values which may be viewed as confidence factors, degrees of belief, or truth values. We will refer to these values as simply truth values. The set of possible truth values form a complete lattice under a given ordering, for example for the real values we can choose the $\leq$ ordering. The atom $A : 0.7$ can be read as: "the atom A is true with certainty of at least 0.7". The GAP framework has been studied extensively, and it has been shown that it is possible to express uncertainty, temporal information, etc. in this framework.

The lattice used in this paper is that of uncertainty and time points which is defined as the set of all functions $f : \mathbf{R}^+ \to [0,1]$. In other words, an atom of the form: $\texttt{temperature(obj,high)} : [0.7, \{1,3\}]$ can be read as: the temperature of $\texttt{obj}$ is $\texttt{high}$ with certainty of at least 0.7 at both time points 1 and 3. Hence, the annotation $[0.7, \{1,3\}]$ denotes the function f where $f(i)=0.7$ for $i=1,3$ and $f(i)=0$ otherwise. The ordering on this lattice is given as follows: $f_1 \preceq f_2$ iff for all $r \in \mathbf{R}^+$, $f_1(r) \leq f_2(r)$ where $\leq$ is the usual less-than-or-equal-to ordering on the reals.

Adalı and Emery [1] have shown that constraints can be viewed as proving that the output of an external program has certain characteristics when different parameters are input. In other words, we assume that

for each external program, we have a different set of functions that return a set of objects, each of which is an answer returned by that function call. Hence, we can link these functions in each program to HERMES, and specify their input and output types in the mediator. For example, in the relational database domain, the $\texttt{select}_=$ function returns a set of tuples for which the value of a given field is equal to the input value. We introduce special predicates to execute external functions, and access the answers returned by these functions. These special predicates are:

$$\texttt{in(Ans, Dom : Func(A1, \ldots, Am))}$$

which executes the (implementation of the) function $\texttt{Func}$ on arguments $\texttt{A1},\ldots,\texttt{Am}$ on domain $\texttt{Dom}$. This function will return a set of answers back to the mediator. $\texttt{Ans}$ is instantiated to one of these answers. This predicate will succeed as many times as the number of answers returned by the function $\texttt{Dom:Func}$. Every time this predicate is reevaluated, $\texttt{Ans}$ will be instantiated to a different answer from the set answers returned by $\texttt{Dom:Func}$. Here, typically $\texttt{Ans}$ is a complex object with different fields.

$$= \texttt{(Ans.F1\ldots Fn, Var)}$$

This predicate succeeds whenever the field $\texttt{F1}\ldots\texttt{Fn}$ of $\texttt{Ans}$ is equal to the value of $\texttt{Var}$, or if $\texttt{Var}$ is a variable, then its value is set to the value of $\texttt{Ans.F1}\ldots\texttt{Fn}$. Similar conditional predicates are implemented in the mediator such as $<, \geq, >, \leq$ and etc.

Consider the following constraint: "John Smith" is an employee of the company "Widget Co." in the table "Companies" over domain "$\texttt{relation}$". This can be written in the mediator as:

```
in(Emp,relation:select=(''Companies'',
             name,''John Smith'')) &
= (Emp.company,''Widget Co.'').
```

Now, we will give an example of a mediatory clause and show how it is executed.

Example 2.1 Suppose, a robot is placed in a room with several objects. The objects are stored in a spatial database with two different index structures: spatial and relational. The spatial index can perform range queries and it returns tuple ids (tids) corresponding to objects in the database. In addition to this, there are some sensors in the system which sense the temperature of the objects. This information is stored in a deductive database and combined using certain rules in the mediator. The temperature data for each object (stored according to the name) contains uncertainty factors and temporal information associated with it. Finally, the location of the robot is stored in the mediator. The layout of the room and the current temperature information is shown in figure 1.

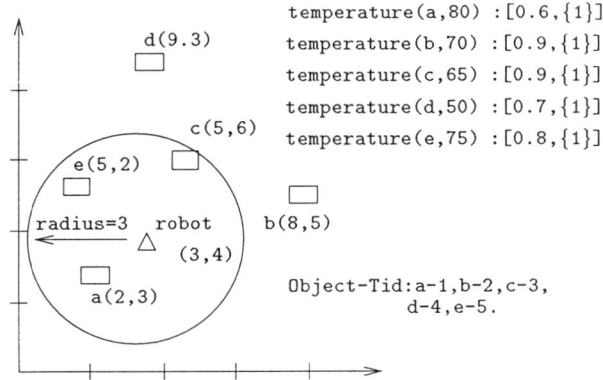

temperature(a,80) :[0.6,{1}].
temperature(b,70) :[0.9,{1}].
temperature(c,65) :[0.9,{1}].
temperature(d,50) :[0.7,{1}].
temperature(e,75) :[0.8,{1}].

Object-Tid:a-1,b-2,c-3,
d-4,e-5.

Figure 1: The layout of the room

We want to write a clause which will tell the robot to spray coolant on one of the hot objects close to the robot. For this reason, at any given time point (in some time unit used by the robot), we will search all the objects that are inside a circle of radius 3 (units) from the robot. Then, we will check if their temperature is recorded for this time point and if it is greater than 70 degrees with certainty of at least 0.8.

```
spray_coolant(Xpos,Ypos):[1,{Vt}] ←
    robot(X1,Y1):[1,{Vt}] &
    in(Tid,spatial:range(''Locations'',
                         X1,Y1,3)) &
    in(Object,relational:select_=("Objects",
                         tid,Tid)) &
    =(Object.name,Oname) &
    in(true,deductive:query(''Sensors'',
        temperature(Oname,Temp):[0.8,{Vt}])) &
    Temp ≥ 70 & =(Object.xpos,Xpos) &
    =(Object.ypos,Ypos).
```

Suppose we ask the query:
← spray_coolant(X,Y):[1,{1}]. Part of the processing of this query is shown in figure 2 using resolution as the inference rule. The resolution rule used in this example is given in [8]. Note that the queue for the outputs of functions relational:select_= and deductive:query are not shown in the figure since they contain only one item. The atom spray_coolant(Xpos,Ypos):[1,{1}-{1}] and the constraint 1 ≥ 1 are removed since {1}-{1}=∅ and 1 ≥ 1 is true.

2.1 Processing of queries in the mediator

As explained above, external programs are accessed by executing functions whose input and output types are specified in the mediator. These functions are referred to as external functions to indicate that their execution

```
← spray_coolant(X,Y):[1,{1}].
    ↓ {X=Xpos,Y=Ypos,Vt=1}
← robot(X1,Y1):[1,{1}] & ....
    ↓ {X1=3,Y1=4}
← in(Tid,spatial:range(''Locations'',
                       3,4,3)) & ...
           spatial:range(''Locations'',3,4,3)
  {Tid=1}  ↳ ☐→ ☐→ ☐ ⟍
    ↓       1   3   5
← in(Object,relational:select_=(''Objects'',
                       tid,1))&...
           spatial:range(''Locations'',
                         3,4,3)
  {Object=[1-a,2,3]} ↳ ☐→ ☐ ⟍
                        3   5
← =([1-a,2,3].name,Oname) & ....
    ↓ {Oname=a}
← in(true,deductive:query(''Sensors'',
        temperature(a,Temp):[0.8,{1}]))&...
    ↓                spatial:range(''Locations'',
  FAILS                            3,4,3)
    ↓               ↳ ☐ ⟍
    ↓ {Tid=3}          5
← in(Object,relational:select_=(''Objects'',
                       tid,3)) &...
    ↓ {Object=[3-c,5,6],Oname=c,Temp=65}
← 65 ≥ 70 & ....
    ↓
  FAILS
    ↓ {Tid=5}
← in(Object,relational:select_=(''Objects'',
                       ,tid,3)) & ....
    ↓ {Object=[5-e,5,2],Oname=e,Temp=75}
← 75 ≥ 70 & =([5-e,5,2].xpos,Xpos) &
                 =([5-e,5,2].ypos,Ypos).
    ↓ {Xpos=5,Ypos=2}
EMPTY CLAUSE
```

Figure 2: The processing of query ← spray_coolant(X,Y):[1,{1}] in the mediator.

takes place outside the mediator (though the invocation of the external routines is from inside the mediator). Below, we give the general query processing procedure for mediators.

Definition 2.1 (Query Processing in the Mediator (QPM)) Let M be a mediator, Q_0 an initial query. A *deduction* from Q_0 in the mediator is a sequence of distinct queries $Q_0, \ldots, Q_m$ such that Q_i is obtained from a query Q_j $(j < i)$ in the sequence in one of the following ways:

1. Q_i is obtained from Q_j by solving an annotated atom A using an appropriate resolution rule. (Many such resolution rules have been defined in the literature, e.g. Kifer and Subrahmanian [6], Adalı and Subrahmanian [3] and Lu, Murray and Rosenthal [7]. Which of these is used does not matter, as long as the one picked is sound and complete.)

2. Q_i is obtained from Q_j by solving an in(Ans, d:f(Args)) predicate, hence invoking the function d:f. In this case, if $\text{Ans}\vartheta$ is a solution to the instance $\text{d}:\text{f}(\text{Args}\vartheta)$ of the original function (hence making $(\text{in}(\text{Ans}, \text{d}:\text{f}(\text{Args})))\vartheta$ true), then $Q_i = (Q_j - \text{in}(\text{Ans}, \text{d}:\text{f}(\text{Args})))\vartheta$ where $Q_j - \text{in}(\text{Ans}, \text{d}:\text{f}(\text{Args}))$ is the query obtained by deleting the given in predicate from Q_j.

3. Q_i is obtained from Q_j by solving an equality predicate =(A,B) or similar conditional predicates for processing complex objects. In this case, if θ is the substitution that makes =(A,B)θ true, then $Q_i = (Q_j - =(\text{A},\text{B}))\theta$.

A *"refutation"* from an initial query Q_0 is a deduction $Q_0, \ldots, Q_m$ of queries produced by the mediatory query processor where Q_m is the empty clause. Completeness in mediated systems is defined a bit differently than the normal logic programs. The definition is given below:

Definition 2.2 (Completeness) Suppose M is a mediator that possesses the fixpoint reachability property and $\leftarrow Q$ is a query. Let M_d be an instance of M where $M_d \models Q$ and all the predicates in M_d of the form: in(Ans, d:f(Args)) have the property that d:f(Args) is evaluable and terminates. Then, there is a refutation of $\leftarrow Q$ from M_d.

Intuitively, a mediator M is said to possess the fixpoint reachability property (cf. Kifer and Subrahmanian [6]) iff whenever there is a infinite refutation for a query Q in M (i.e. involving an infinite sequence of queries produced by the mediatory query processor), then it is possible to find a finite refutation for Q in M. The fixpoint reachability property is critical for completeness because otherwise, we need to take recourse to infinitary proofs. *In [8], Lu, Nerode and Subrahmanian have proved that the above strategy is sound and complete, as long as the resolution rule used in step 1 of the above definition is sound and complete for annotated logic.*

The above definition of query processing shows how special predicates are treated when solving queries. However, the interface between external function calls and the query processor needs further explanation. We assume that there is an interface program for every external program (not necessarily different) that makes the actual calls, stores the output and fetches (different) answers from the output whenever they're needed by the mediator. Whenever the predicate in(Ans, d:f(Args)) needs to be solved, the query processor sends a request to this interface to fetch an answer. The function d:f(Args) is executed only once for every query Q_i in the query processing sequence, i.e. the first time the above predicate is chosen to be solved in Q_i. It is the interface's responsibility to fetch a new answer stored for this call and return it to the query processor. Similarly, whenever a refutation is found for a query the interface should terminate all the programs that are still running.

3 INVARIANTS

It is possible that in the processing of the rules in the mediator, "similar" function calls to external programs will need to be executed several times since the same kind of information may be requested over and over by different users. Backtracking is another reason for such a situation. Calling an external program is usually a costly operation because of the memory, CPU requirements and possible network delays [2]. Furthermore, actual packages may levy charges for accessing them. Suppose there is a way to guess "some" of the answers that will be returned by an external call. If a refutation is found by substituting one of these answers, then there is no need to execute the external domain call. This is accomplished by caching the answers returned by previous external calls and re-using them when needed. Similarly, if there is a way of knowing that a function is not defined for some inputs, whenever it is called for these inputs, we can terminate the search down a path of the search space.

The challenge of this approach lies in deciding which sets of answers are relevant, and in representing the input/output behavior of some external functions. This information is stored in the system with the help of some explicit rules which will be referred to as "invariants". Invariants are expressions specifying the relation between the set of answers returned by an external call, its arguments and other possible external calls.

As an example, consider the following invariant :

$$\text{T2} \geq \text{T1} \implies \text{f(T2)} \supseteq \text{f(T1)}$$

The above expression can be read as follows: if T2 $\geq$ T1, then all the solutions of f(T1) are also solutions of $\mathtt{f(T2)}$. Hence, if the set of answers for $\mathtt{f(T1)}$ were previously stored in a cache, then these answers can be re-used whenever the function $\mathtt{f(T2)}$ is called; if none of the answers to $\mathtt{f(T1)}$ satisfies the rest of the query then $\mathtt{f(T2)}$ needs to be computed. An example of such an invariant is given below:

Example 3.1 Suppose $\mathtt{relation}$ is a constant in the mediator which refers to a relational database with the usual selection operators. For example, $\mathtt{select}_{\leq}(\mathtt{R},\mathtt{F},\mathtt{V})$ selects all the tuples in table $\mathtt{R}$ such that the value of the field $\mathtt{F}$ is less than or equal to $\mathtt{V}$. Then, the following are possible invariants for different $\mathtt{select}$ functions.

$$\mathtt{T2} \leq \mathtt{T1} \Rightarrow \mathtt{relation}:\mathtt{select}_{\leq}(\mathtt{R},\mathtt{Field},\mathtt{T1}) \supseteq$$
$$\mathtt{relation}:\mathtt{select}_{\leq}(\mathtt{R},\mathtt{Field},\mathtt{T2}).$$
$$\mathtt{T2} \geq \mathtt{T1} \Rightarrow \mathtt{relation}:\mathtt{select}_{\geq}(\mathtt{R},\mathtt{Field},\mathtt{T2}) \supseteq$$
$$\mathtt{relation}:\mathtt{select}_{\geq}(\mathtt{R},\mathtt{Field},\mathtt{T1}).$$

The first invariant can be read as: For any given database $\mathtt{R}$ and field $\mathtt{Field}$ in the domain $\mathtt{relation}$, whenever $\mathtt{T2} \geq \mathtt{T1}$ is satisfied, all the tuples that are in $\mathtt{relation}:\mathtt{select}_{\geq}(\mathtt{R},\mathtt{Field},\mathtt{T2})$, are also in $\mathtt{relation}:\mathtt{select}_{\geq}(\mathtt{R},\mathtt{Field},\mathtt{T1})$.

Example 3.2 Suppose the domain $\mathtt{spatial}$ is a spatial data structure such as a point quadtree storing points in two-dimensional space. The function $\mathtt{vertical\_slice(File,X,Dist)}$ in this domain returns all the points that have X-coordinates between $\mathtt{X+Dist}$ and $\mathtt{X-Dist}$, in other words all the points that are in the vertical slice taken from $\mathtt{X-Dist}$ to $\mathtt{X+Dist}$. The following is an invariant about this function:

$$\mathtt{Dist1} \leq \mathtt{Dist2} \Rightarrow$$
$$\mathtt{spatial}:\mathtt{vertical\_slice(File,X,Dist2)} \supseteq$$
$$\mathtt{spatial}:\mathtt{vertical\_slice(File,X,Dist1)}.$$

which states that whenever the X-coordinate is fixed, the points in a vertical slice are contained in any of the bigger vertical slices. We can easily write similar invariants for other spatial functions. The invariant for the $\mathtt{horizontal\_slice}$ function is the same as $\mathtt{vertical\_slice}$. As for the $\mathtt{range(X,Y,Dist)}$ function which returns all the points that are at distance $\mathtt{Dist}$ from point $\mathtt{(X,Y)}$ (i.e. all points $\mathtt{(X1,Y1)}$ such that $(\mathtt{X}-\mathtt{X1})^2+(\mathtt{Y}-\mathtt{Y1})^2 \leq \mathtt{Dist}^2$ we can write the following invariants:

$$\mathtt{Dist1} \leq \mathtt{Dist2} \Rightarrow$$
$$\mathtt{spatial}:\mathtt{range(File,X,Y,Dist2)} \supseteq$$
$$\mathtt{spatial}:\mathtt{range(File,X,Y,Dist1)}.$$
$$|\mathtt{X1}-\mathtt{X2}| \leq |\mathtt{Dist1}-\mathtt{Dist2}| \Rightarrow$$
$$\mathtt{spatial}:\mathtt{range(File,X2,Y,Dist2)} \supseteq$$
$$\mathtt{spatial}:\mathtt{range(File,X1,Y,Dist1)}.$$

Example 3.3 Suppose $\mathtt{text}$ is a text database containing news articles. The function $\mathtt{heading(DB,Word)}$ returns all the articles from the database $\mathtt{DB}$ that contain $\mathtt{Word}$ in their heading. Suppose also that the function $\mathtt{Dict(Word)}$ returns true

when $\mathtt{Word}$ is in the local dictionary. (This function can be a call to a spelling check program.) Then, we can write the following invariant for the $\mathtt{heading}$ function:

$$\mathtt{Dict(Word)} = \mathtt{false} \Rightarrow \mathtt{text}:\mathtt{heading(DB,Word)} = \emptyset.$$

The above invariant enforces a spell-check before a more costly call is executed. Especially, if a special dictionary of keywords is available, searching in this dictionary before the whole text database is searched will avoid time consuming calls.

Finally, it is possible to have invariants with empty premises. These can be viewed as hard-coded information about the external program. Below we give such an example.

Example 3.4 Suppose the spatial data structure contains a function called $\mathtt{rectangle}$ which finds all the points within a rectangle specified by the $\mathtt{X,Y}$ coordinates of two opposite corners. Then, we have the following invariant:

$$\Rightarrow \mathtt{spatial}:\mathtt{rectangle(File,X1,Y1,X2,Y2)} =$$
$$\mathtt{spatial}:\mathtt{vertical\_slice(File,X1,X2)} \cap$$
$$\mathtt{spatial}:\mathtt{horizontal\_slice(File,Y1,Y2)}.$$

Now, we're ready to define some of the concepts used in the previous examples. We will first define what an external call is , then give the format of the invariants.

Definition 3.1 (External Call) Given a domain $\mathtt{d}$ and an n-ary ($\mathtt{n} \geq 0$) function $\mathtt{f}$ in domain $\mathtt{d}$, the expression $\mathtt{d}:\mathtt{f(A1,...,An)}$ is called an *external call* iff for all $\mathtt{i}$, $1 \leq \mathtt{i} \leq \mathtt{n}$, $\mathtt{Ai}$ is either a variable, an object of the same type as the the ith argument of $\mathtt{f}$ as specified in the mediator with some uniform specification language.

Suppose $\mathtt{d}:\mathtt{f(A1,...,An)}$ is an external call. An answer pair to this external call is a pair $(\mathtt{Ans},(\mathtt{d}:\mathtt{f(A1,...,An)})\vartheta)$ such that $\mathtt{Ans}$ is in the set returned by executing the function $\mathtt{f}$ in domain (program) $\mathtt{d}$ on arguments $\mathtt{A1}\vartheta,...,\mathtt{An}\vartheta$. The *type* of this external call is the type of $\mathtt{Ans}$. The *object space* of this external call is the set of all possible objects of the same type as $\mathtt{Ans}$.

Definition 3.2 (Invariant) An invariant is an expression of the form either

$$\mathtt{A_1} \& ... \& \mathtt{A_m} \Rightarrow \mathtt{E_0} \supseteq \mathtt{s(E_1,...,E_n)}$$

or,

$$\mathtt{A_1} \& ... \& \mathtt{A_m} \Rightarrow \mathtt{E_0} = \mathtt{s(E_1,...,E_n)}$$

where i) $\mathtt{E_0}$ is an external call (that is being evaluated as part of the query), ii) for all $1 \leq \mathtt{i} \leq \mathtt{n}$, $\mathtt{E_i}$ is either an external call or a set of objects, and if Obj is the object space of $\mathtt{E_i}$'s, then $\mathtt{s}$ is a function from Obj^n to Obj, and $\mathtt{A_k}, 1 \leq \mathtt{k} \leq \mathtt{m}$ are atoms in the mediator.

All the variables in the invariant are considered to be universally quantified. In the above invariant, the expression $A_1 \& \ldots \& A_m$ will be called the *premise*. The external call E_0 will be referred to as the *defined external call*, and the function $s(E_1, \ldots, E_n)$ is called the *substitute answer set* for E_0.

An example of the s function found in the conclusion of an invariant is the 0-ary function which returns the constant $\emptyset$ as given in example 3.3. Other examples of the s function are the following functions: the set intersection function $s(X,Y) = X \cap Y$ as given example 3.4, and the identity function $s(X) = X$ as given in example 3.2. The s functions can also be more complex, they may contain conditional operations and different set operators.

3.1 Query Processing with Invariant-Based Answer Caching

The query processing procedure discussed in section 2.1 uses only the program clauses, an inference rule and calls to external programs to process queries. In many cases, external calls made during query processing may bear a close relationship to external calls made previously to the same external program. Invariants were introduced to reflect the possible relationships between the previous calls to an external function and the current call. In this section, we will discuss how invariants can be used to avoid making costly calls to external programs. First, we will define a cache table that will store the answers obtained from an external call. Then, we will define how these cached answers are used in conjunction with invariants to speed up query execution.

Definition 3.3 (External Call Cache) is a table which stores pairs of the form $(call, answers)$ where $call$ is an external call of the form $\texttt{domain:function(A1,...,An)}$ and $answers$ is the complete set of answers returned by this call.

As an example, an external call to the selection function in a relational database will contain a set of tuples as the answers.

Definition 3.4 (Substitute Answer Pair) Suppose $\texttt{domain:function(A1,...,An)}$ is an external call and

$$I \equiv P \Rightarrow E_0 \; \mathcal{R} \; s(E_1, \ldots, E_m)$$

is an invariant associated with the mediator$\Phi\Phi$ed system M where $\mathcal{R} \in \{\supseteq, =\}$. Let ϑ be the most general substitution such that $M \models P\vartheta$ and

$$P\vartheta \Rightarrow E_0\vartheta \; \mathcal{R} \; s(E_1\vartheta, \ldots, E_m\vartheta)$$

is an instance of I where

- $E_0\vartheta$ is an instance of $\texttt{domain:function(A1,..}$ $\texttt{..,An)}$,

- for all $E_i\vartheta (1 \leq i \leq m)$, $\texttt{Ans}_i$ is the union of all set of answers in the cache for external calls E'_i that are instances of $E_i\vartheta$. If there are no such entries, then $\texttt{Ans}_i = \emptyset$. ($\mathcal{R}$ is changed internally to $\subseteq$ iff any one of $E_i\vartheta$ is not in the cache.)

Then $(\texttt{Ans}\vartheta, E_0\vartheta)$ is a *substitute answer pair* for the external call $\texttt{domain:function(A1,...,An)}$ according to invariant I and the cache where $\texttt{Ans}\vartheta = s(\texttt{Ans}_1, \ldots, \texttt{Ans}_m)$

Intuitively, the following definition can be interpreted as follows: Whenever the set of answers to an external call $\texttt{domain:function(A1,...,An)}$ needs to be determined, choose an invariant such that $\texttt{domain:function(A1,...,An)}$ is the defined external call (i.e. the first component of the consequent of an invariant). Moreover, suppose the appropriate instance of the premise is true in the mediated system, and the substitute answer set contains external calls which are cached. Then, the substitute answer set will replace the "real" call to $\texttt{domain}$. Note that the processing of invariants doesn't change according to the relation between defined call and its substitute (i.e. "$\supseteq$" vs. "$=$".) However, it will make a difference in the implementation, since the relation "$\supseteq$" states that different answers may be obtained the real external call and in such a case the real call should be made if none of the substitute answers leads to a refutation.

Example 3.5 Recall the query processing example shown in figure 2. The external call $\texttt{spatial}$ $\texttt{:range (``Locations'',3,4,3)}$ was executed, and the set of tuple-ids $\{1,3,5\}$ was obtained. Suppose this is cached in the table as the pair: $(\texttt{spatial:range(``Locations'',3,4,3),\{1,3,6\}})$. Now, recall the following invariant given for the $\texttt{range}$ function:

$$I \equiv \texttt{Dist1} \leq \texttt{Dist2} \Rightarrow$$
$$\texttt{spatial:range(File, X, Y, Dist2)} \supseteq$$
$$\texttt{spatial:range(File, X, Y, Dist1)}.$$

Now, suppose we are executing the external call $\texttt{spatial:range(``Locations'',3,4,6)}$. Substitute answer pairs for this call according to the above invariant are obtained as follows:

- Let $\vartheta = \{X = 3, Y = 4, \texttt{Dist1} = 3, \texttt{Dist2} = 6, \texttt{File=``Locations''}\}$.

- Clearly the premise of the invariant is satisfied, i.e. $3 \leq 6$ is true in the mediator.

- The cache contains the set of answers for the call $\texttt{spatial:range(``Locations'',3,4,3)}$.

- Then, the substitute answer set of the above invariant for substitution ϑ contains the answers $1, 3, 5$. Then, all the following are substitute answer pairs according to the given invariant and the cache:

```
(1,spatial:range(''Locations'',3,4,6)),
(3,spatial:range(''Locations'',3,4,6)),
(5,spatial:range(''Locations'',3,4,6)).
```

Note that, if the call was executed on the spatial domain, object b will also be found to be in the 6 units range to the robot. Hence its id 4 should be in the answer queue to this call. This is expected, since the relation in the invariant was partial (given by $\supseteq$).

Substitute answer pairs can be used to access cached answers for external calls as well. To do this we can write the invariant $\Rightarrow$ d:t(Args) = d:t(Args) for all the external calls d:t(Args) that are cached in the mediator. Hence, all the answers stored for an instance of an external call d:t(Args) will be used to obtain substitute answer pairs. Now, we're ready to define a query processing procedure which will make use of the cache and the invariants.

Definition 3.5 (Query Processing with Invariants and Answer Caching (QPIAC)) Suppose M is a mediator, M_I is a set of invariants and Q_0 is a query. Then, a query computation of Q_0 with invariant-based answer caching is a sequence of pairs:

$$\langle Q_0, \Sigma_0 \rangle, \ldots, \langle Q_p, \Sigma_p \rangle.$$

where $\Sigma_0, \ldots, \Sigma_p$ are distinct external call caches, and $Q_0, \ldots, Q_p$ are distinct queries such that $\ldots Q_{p+1}, \Sigma_{p+1} \rangle$ is obtained either using rules 1 and 2 in definition 2.1, or the following rule:

3. Suppose Q_{i+1} is obtained from Q_j for some $j \leq i$, by solving an in(Ans,Xcall) predicate. In this case, there are three cases to consider:

(a) (Cache Use) Suppose there exists an entry (Xcallϑ, Answers) in the cache such that Ans$\vartheta \in$ Answers. Then, $Q_{i+1} = (Q_j -$ in(Ans,Xcall))ϑ and $\Sigma_{p+1} = \Sigma_p$.

(b) (Use of Invariants) There exists a substitute answer pair (Ansϑ, Xcallϑ) for Xcall according to some invariant I in M_I and the cache Σ_p: Then, $Q_{i+1} = (Q_j -$ in(Ans,Xcall))ϑ and $\Sigma_{p+1} = \Sigma_p$.

(c) (External Function Call and Cache Update) Let (Ansϑ, Xcallϑ) be an answer pair for the (real) external call (i.e. make the actual external call and get one of the answers returned by it.) Then, $Q_{i+1} = (Q_j -$ in(Ans,Xcall))ϑ and the new answer pair ((Ansϑ, Xcallϑ)) is inserted into Σ_p to obtain Σ_{p+1}.

As can be seen from the above definition, in this new query processing procedure the cache is used both directly (step 3(a)) and indirectly (step 3(b)) with the help of invariants to answer a query. In the new procedure all results of previous function calls are cached. It is possible to make use of a function which determines

which external functions are cached, and the invariants and cache will be used only for those functions. Furthermore, QPIAC doesn't specify in which order steps 3(a,b,c) must be executed. In practice, the cache will be consulted first (step 3(a)), then the invariants will be evaluated against the cache (step 3(b)), and if both of these fail, then the actual external call will be executed (step 3(c).) To be able to prove the soundness and completeness of the QPIAC query processing procedure we must make sure that the invariants are correct statements about their respective domains. In other words, a substitute answer is guaranteed to be an actual answer pair.

Definition 3.6 (Well-formed Invariants) An invariant I is said to be well-formed iff for all possible caches Σ, and mediators M with the same domain as I, if (Ans,Xcall) is a substitute answer pair according to invariant I, mediator M, and cache Σ, then it is also an answer pair (i.e. Ans is an answer for the external call Xcall.)

Below, we prove that mediatory query processing procedure and QPIAC are equivalent.

Theorem 3.1 (Soundness and Completeness of QPIAC) Suppose M is a mediator and M_I is a set of invariants all of which are well-formed. Then, Q_0 has a refutation (i.e. without answer caches and/or invariants) iff Q_0 has a QPIAC-refutation (i.e. with answer caching and invariants). □

In particular, this means that as long as a sound and complete query processing procedure for annotated logic is used, the strategy of caching answers and using invariants to optimize external calls is sound and complete when used in conjunction with the annotated logic query processing procedure.

3.2 Cache and Invariant Management

In this section, we will define a new external program called "*Cache and Invariant Manager* (CIM)". This program will store the cache, process the invariants and mediate between the external call interfaces in the mediator and the external programs. We will then show that the original query processing procedure can simulate QPIAC using the cache and invariant manager (CIM) as an additional external program. As a side effect, we will show that it is possible to cache only the answers obtained for a set of domains and/or a set of selected functions for each domain.

Definition 3.7 (Answer Pairs returned by CIM) Suppose CIM is the cache and invariant manager, M_I is a set of invariants processed by the CIM and d:f(Args) is an external call cached in CIM. Then, (Ansϑ, d:f(Args)ϑ) is an answer pair for CIM iff one of the following is true:

- Ansϑ is stored in the cache as an answer for d:f(Args)ϑ, or

- $(\text{Ans}\vartheta, \mathtt{d} : \mathtt{f}(\text{Args})\vartheta)$ is a substitute answer pair for $\mathtt{d:f}(\text{Args})$ according to an invariant $I \in M_I$ and the cache, or

- $(\text{Ans}\vartheta, \mathtt{d} : \mathtt{f}(\text{Args})\vartheta)$ is an answer (of the real external call) $\mathtt{d:f}(\text{Args})$.

Next, we will give a transformation procedure which takes a mediator and a set of invariants as its input and produces another mediator with the extra external program CIM.

Definition 3.8 (CIM Transformation) Suppose M is a mediator, M_I is a set of invariants. Then, the CIM transformed program M' is obtained as follows:

1. Add CIM as an extra external program to the mediator.

2. For each external function $\mathtt{f}$ called for program $\mathtt{d}$, do the following: Create a new function $\mathtt{d|f}$ for program CIM and copy the input and output types of $\mathtt{d:f}$ to $\mathtt{CIM:d|f}$.

3. Change each external call $\mathtt{d:f}(\text{Args})$ in the mediator to the call $\mathtt{CIM:d|f}(\text{Args})$.

4. Store all the invariants in M_I in CIM.

As a result of the transformation, whenever an external call $\mathtt{d:f}(\text{Args})$ needs to be executed in the mediator, the call $\mathtt{CIM:d|f}(\text{Args})$ will be initiated. CIM will use the cache and the invariants to find the answers to an external call. Below, we define a new query processing procedure (QPCIM) which uses the QPM query processing algorithm together with the cache and invariant manager as a new domain.

Definition 3.9 (Query Processing with Cache and Invariant Manager (QPCIM)) Suppose M is a mediator and M_I is a set of invariants. If M' is the CIM transformation of M and M_I then QPCIM uses the mediatory query processing function (QPM, see section 2.1) on M' to execute queries.

Theorem 3.2 (Soundness and Completeness of QPCIM)) Suppose M is a mediator and M_I is a set of invariants. Then a query Q_0 has a QPCIM-refutation iff Q_0 has a QPIAC-refutation. □

3.2.1 Comparison of QPIAC and QPCIM Query Processing Procedures

Although QPIAC and QPCIM compute the same answers, they provide two different solutions to the same problem with their respective advantages and disadvantages. QPCIM has the advantage of providing for many different special purpose caches while the query processor remains general purpose. On the other hand, since the query processor has no control over how the caches are used and the external calls are made, some unnecessary calls cannot be avoided. Although,

QPIAC eliminates these disadvantages of QPCIM, it leads to the modification of the query processor as well as the specification language. Moreover, changing caching services provided by the query processor becomes harder and harder.

In the next section, we introduce a new concept, viz. invariant products. We show how invariants can be combined to produce new and more specific invariants. We will then introduce a new query processing function which makes use of invariant products as well as the invariants.

3.3 Invariant Products

Suppose, the mediator wants to avoid making external function calls as much as possible. Hence, whenever an "in" predicate needs to be executed, the mediator will check if there is some other function call stored in the cache which can be substituted for this call. Invariants are used for this purpose. It is possible to process invariants to obtain other possible ways of constructing the answer to an external function call. The following example illustrates this informal intuition.

Example 3.6 Recall the following invariants given for the spatial data structures:

$\Rightarrow$ `spatial:rectangle(File,X1,Y1,X2,Y2)` =
    `spatial:vertical_slice(File,X1,X2)` $\cap$
    `spatial:horizontal_slice(File,Y1,Y2)`.

$\text{Dist1} \leq \text{Dist2} \Rightarrow$
    `spatial : vertical_slice(File1,X,Dist2)` $\supseteq$
    `spatial : vertical_slice(File1,X,Dist1)`.

Now, we have two inequalities in the conclusions of the above invariants of the form $\mathtt{A} = \mathtt{B_1}$ and $\mathtt{B_2} \supseteq \mathtt{C}$. If $\mathtt{B_1} = \mathtt{B_2}$ then, from these two, we can conclude $\mathtt{A} \supseteq \mathtt{C}$. Hence, we will perform a special type of inference which we will call "Invariant Production". Notice that $\mathtt{B_1}\vartheta = \mathtt{B_2}\vartheta$ where $\vartheta = \{\mathtt{File1} = \mathtt{File}, \mathtt{X} = \mathtt{X1}, \mathtt{Dist2} = \mathtt{X2}\}$. Hence, the result of this production (which will be called the "invariant product" of the two invariants) is given as:

$\text{Dist1} \leq \text{X2} \Rightarrow$
    `spatial:rectangle(File,X1,Y1,X2,Y2)` $\supseteq$
    `spatial : vertical_slice(File,X1,Dist1)`$\cap$
    `spatial:horizontal_slice(File,Y1,Y2)`.

The advantage of having this new invariant is that, given an external call `spatial:rectangle(File,X1, Y1,X2,Y2)`, it may not be possible to find a cached call to `vertical_slice` with `X1,X2` as arguments. But, it may possible to find calls that are cached in the table for smaller values of `X2`. Similar invariants exist for `horizontal_slice` and for different values of `X1` and `Y1`. Note that it may not be possible to compare two external calls beforehand as in the above example. As an example, we cannot compare the external function calls `d:f(a)` with `d:f(b)` to obtain a product as above without knowing the output of these two functions. Since the cache provides this opportunity, we may be able to combine two invariants in a radically different way. Below, we will give such an example of invariant production which makes use of the cache.

Example 3.7 Recall the following two invariants which were presented earlier in the paper (variables are renamed to standardize the invariants apart).

```
Dist11 ≤ Dist21 ⇒
  spatial : vertical_slice(File11,X1,Dist21) ⊇
  spatial:vertical_slice(File11,X1,Dist11).
Dist12 ≤ Dist22 ⇒
  spatial : range(File2,X2,Y2,Dist22) ⊇
  spatial:range(File2,X2,Y2,Dist12).
```

Now, suppose the cache contains the following pairs: (spatial:vertical_slice(''qtree'',2,3), {a,b,c,d,e}), (spatial:range(''qtree'',3,1,5), {a,b,d}). Then, since $\{a,b,d\} \subseteq \{a,b,c,d,e\}$, we can write the following invariant product from the two invariants above by using the cached information:

```
3 ≤Dist21 & Dist12 ≤ 5 ⇒
  spatial:vertical_slice(''qtree'',2,Dist21)⊇
  spatial:range(''qtree'',3,1,Dist12).
```

which indicates that as long as we shrunk the circle of the range query and enlarge the area of the vertical slice, the relation stated in the invariant will hold. In this way we related two different functions of the same type that had no connection to each other according to the invariants stated for them by using the dynamic cache.

Definition 3.10 (Invariant Production) Suppose I_1 and I_2 given below are invariants in the mediator and Σ is an external call cache:

$$I_1 \equiv P_1 \Rightarrow E_{1_0} R_1 s_1(E_{1_1},\dots,E_{1_m}).$$
$$I_2 \equiv P_2 \Rightarrow E_{2_0} R_2 s_2(E_{2_1},\dots,E_{2_n}).$$

where $R_1, R_2 \in \{=, \supseteq\}$, E_{1_0}, E_{2_0} are external calls, and for all $1 \leq i \leq m$, and all $1 \leq j \leq n$, E_{1_i} and E_{2_j}'s are external calls or expressions denoting sets of objects, and P_1, P_2 are conjunctions of atoms in the mediatory language.

1. Suppose, there exists a substitution ϑ such that $E_{2_0}\vartheta = E_{1_p}\vartheta$ for some $1 \leq p \leq m$. Then, the following expression is an "invariant product" of I_1 with I_2 according to cache Σ:

$$(P_1 \& P_2)\vartheta \Rightarrow E_{1_0}\vartheta\ (R_1 \Diamond R_2)\ s_1(E_{1_1},\dots,E_{1_{p-1}},$$
$$s_2(E_{2_1},\dots,E_{2_n}),E_{1_{p+1}},\dots,E_{1_m})\vartheta.$$

2. Suppose, there exist substitutions ϑ_1, ϑ_2 such that there exist entries $(E_{2_0}\vartheta_1, \text{Ans}_{2_0})$ and $(E_{1_p}\vartheta_2, \text{Ans}_{1_p})$

in the cache and that $\text{Ans}_{1_p} \supseteq \text{Ans}_{2_0}$[1], then the following expression is an "invariant product" of I_1 with I_2 according to cache Σ:

$$P_1\vartheta_1 \& P_2\vartheta_2 \Rightarrow E_{1_0}\vartheta_1\ (R_1 \Diamond R_2)$$
$$s_1(E_{1_1}\vartheta_1,\dots,E_{1_{p-1}}\vartheta_1, s_2(E_{2_1},\dots$$
$$\dots,E_{2_n})\vartheta_2, E_{1_{p+1}}\vartheta_1,\dots,E_{1_m}\vartheta_1).$$

The operation $\Diamond$ is defined as:

$\Diamond$	$=$	$\supseteq$
$=$	$=$	$\supseteq$
$\supseteq$	$\supseteq$	$\supseteq$

We now define the set of invariants that can be generated using the cache and the invariant production rule.

Definition 3.11 Suppose M_I is a set of invariants and Σ is an external call cache. Then, the set of all possible invariant products for M_I and Σ denoted by $IP(M_I, \Sigma)$ is the set of all invariants I where either (1) $I \in M_I$, or (2) I is an invariant product of I_1 and I_2 according to cache Σ and $I_1, I_2 \in IP(M_I, \Sigma)$.

Suppose s is a function that takes sets of objects as its arguments and produces a set as output. Then, s is said to be *monotonic in its arguments* for all $1 \leq i \leq m$ $E_i \subseteq E_i'$ implies that $s(E_1,\dots,E_i,\dots,E_m) \subseteq s(E_1,\dots,E_i',\dots,E_m)$. For example, if the function s is computed by any combination of union and intersections $(\cup,\cap)$ only, then s is monotonic in its arguments.

Theorem 3.3 Suppose I_1 and I_2 are invariants where

$$I_1 \equiv P_1 \Rightarrow E_{1_0} R_1 s_1(E_{1_1},\dots,E_{1_m}).$$

If s_1 is monotonic in its arguments then the invariant product of I_1 with I_2 is well-formed whenever I_1 and I_2 are both well-formed. □

Now, we are ready to define a query processing procedure which makes use of the invariant products as well as the invariants to re-use the information stored in the cache.

Definition 3.12 (Query Processing Invariant Production (QPIP)) Suppose M is a mediator, M_I is a set of invariants and Q_0 is a query. Then, a query computation of Q_0 with invariant production is a sequence of pairs:

$$\langle Q_0, \Sigma_0 \rangle, \dots, \langle Q_p, \Sigma_p \rangle.$$

$\Sigma_0, \dots, \Sigma_p$ are distinct external call caches, $Q_0, \dots, Q_p$ are distinct queries such that $\langle Q_{p+1}, \Sigma_{p+1}\rangle$ is obtained in the same way as in the QPIAC query processing procedure as given in definition 3.5 with the exception that condition 3(b) ("There exists a substitute answer

---

[1]Note that for this to hold, both E_{1_p} and E_{2_0} must denote objects of the same type

256

pair ($\text{Ans}\vartheta$, $\text{Xcall}\vartheta$) for Xcall according to some invariant in M_I.") is changed to:

"There exists a substitute answer pair($\text{Ans}\vartheta$, $\text{Xcall}\vartheta$) for Xcall according to some invariant in $IP(M_I, \Sigma_p)$."

Theorem 3.4 (Soundness and Completeness of QPIP) Suppose M is a mediator and M_I is a set of invariants all of which are well-formed. Then, Q_0 has a QPIAC-refutation iff Q_0 has a QPIP-refutation. $\square$

4 CONCLUSIONS

The HERMES ("HEterogeneous Reasoning and MEdiator System") system provides a uniform way of expressing how information from existing programs can be semantically integrated to answer complicated questions that none of the component programs can on its own. Since uniform statistics/estimates of how long a query will take in a given program may not be readily available, choosing an appropriate execution plan for a mediator poses an important problem. In this paper, we have shown that query processors of the HERMES system can take advantage of caching techniques as well as the semantic information about each program to intelligently plan the execution of queries. Moreover, we have examined different methods with varying "intelligence" and compared the trade-offs of these methods.

REFERENCES

[1] S. Adalı and R. Emery. (1994) *A Uniform Framework For Integrating Knowledge In Heterogeneous Knowledge Systems*, To appear in Proc. of the Eleventh International Conference on Data Engineering. (http://www.cs.umd.edu/projects/hermes/publications/postscripts/cons.ps)

[2] S. Adalı and V.S. Subrahmanian. (1994) Amalgamating Knowledge Bases, II: Distributed Mediators, accepted for publication in: Intl. Journal of Intelligent Cooperative Information Systems. (ftp://ftp.cs.umd.edu/pub/papers/TRs/3124.ps.Z)

[3] S. Adalı and V.S. Subrahmanian. (1994) Amalgamating Knowledge Bases, III: Algorithms, data structures and query processing. Technical Report CS-TR-3124, Computer Science Department, University of Maryland, Aug 1993. Submitted for publication. (http://www.cs.umd.edu/projects/hermes/publications/postscripts/akbiii.ps)

[4] J. Benton and V.S. Subrahmanian. (1993) *Using Hybrid Knowledge Bases for Missile Siting Problems*, Proc. 1994 Conf. on Artificial Intelligence Applications, IEEE Computer Society.

[5] J. Horst, E. Kent, H. Rifky and V.S. Subrahmanian. (1994) *Hybrid Knowledge Bases for Real-Time Robotic Reasoning*, Proc. IVth Intl. Workshop on Pattern Recognition in Practice (eds. E. Gelsema and L. Kanal), N. Holland/Elsevier.

[6] M. Kifer and V.S. Subrahmanian. (1989) *Theory of Generalized Annotated Logic Programming and its Applications*, Journal of Logic Programming, 12, 4, pps 335–368, 1992. Preliminary version in: Proc. 1989 North American Conf. on Logic Programming, MIT Press. (http://www.cs.umd.edu/projects/hermes/publications/postscripts/galp.ps)

[7] J. Lu, N. Murray and E. Rosenthal. (1993) *Signed Formulas and Annotated Logics*, draft manuscript. Preliminary version in: Proceedings of the International Symposium on Multiple-Valued Logic, IEEE Computer Society Press, 1993, 48-53.

[8] J. Lu, A. Nerode and V.S. Subrahmanian. (1993) *Hybrid Knowledge Bases*, Accepted for publication in: IEEE Trans. on Knowledge and Data Engineering. (http://www.cs.umd.edu/projects/hermes/publications/postscripts/hkb.ps)

[9] V.S. Subrahmanian. (1994) *Hybrid Knowledge Bases for Integrating Symbolic, Numeric and Image Data*, Proc. 1994 SPIE Conf. on Applied Imagery and Pattern Recognition.

[10] V.S. Subrahmanian, S. Adalı, A. Brink, R. Emery, J. Lu, A. Rajput, T.J. Rogers, R. Ross. (1994) HERMES: A Heterogeneous Reasoning and Mediator System, submitted for publication. (http://www.cs.umd.edu/projects/hermes/overview/paper)

[11] G. Wiederhold. (1992) *Mediators in the Architecture of Future Information Systems*, IEEE Computer, March 1992, pps 38–49.

[12] G. Wiederhold. (1993) *Intelligent Integration of Information*, Proc. 1993 ACM SIGMOD Conf. on Management of Data, pps 434–437.

Part 8: Knowledge Sharing and Reuse

Towards Very Large Knowledge Bases
N.J.I. Mars, Ed.
IOS Press, 1995

An Agent Based Approach to Spacecraft Mission Operations

M Jones and **J Wheadon**
European Space Operations Centre, Darmstadt, Germany

D Whitgift
Logica UK Ltd., London, UK

M Niezette and **R Timmermans**
Space Applications Services, Brussels, Belgium

I Rodriguez and **R Romero**
GMV, Madrid, Spain.

ABSTRACT

Advanced Technology Operations Systems (ATOS) is a programme of work sponsored by the European Space Agency to integrate advanced applications, especially knowledge based applications, with ground systems for spacecraft mission operations. This paper describes the ATOS approach to sharing knowledge and the infrastructure which supports this approach. The approach builds upon the work of the ARPA Knowledge Sharing Effort [9] to meet specific requirements of spacecraft operations: applications are collaborating agents, each with its own knowledge base, which commit to a shared ontology and which are coordinated by the infrastructure. The paper summarises practical experience to date, and concludes with an outline of future work in the ATOS programme.

1 INTRODUCTION

As spacecraft become increasingly complex, and mission goals become increasingly ambitious, so the problems of planning and performing mission operations become greater. The Advanced Technology Operations System (ATOS) programme recognises that advances in information technology, especially in Knowledge Based Systems (KBS), can help to solve these problems. The benefits offered by these advances include cost savings, both in development and in operation, while enhancing operations reliability and keeping pace with the advancing state-of-the-art in spacecraft design technology and mission demands.

At the European Space Operations Centre (ESOC), several studies have applied

KBS to specific areas of spacecraft operations; for example, planning, modelling, anomaly detection and diagnosis. These studies have produced independent prototypes, each with its own large knowledge base and its own approach to structuring knowledge.

ATOS seeks to integrate these applications into a Spacecraft Mission Operations System (SMOS) in such a way that the applications (conventional as well as knowledge based) can share knowledge effectively but are not required to use a particular approach to structuring knowledge.

Section 2 summarises the domain of spacecraft operations, the knowledge with

which it is concerned and the issues it raises. Section 3 describes the federated, agent-based approach to knowledge sharing which has been adopted by ATOS. Section 4 illustrates how applications benefit from this approach by describing the way in which they communicate with each other. Section 5 describes the prototypes developed to date, both of the ATOS infrastructure and of applications which use the infrastructure, and highlights the lessons learnt by their development and use. Section 6 outlines the next stages of the ATOS programme.

2 THE PROBLEM DOMAIN: SPACECRAFT MISSION OPERATIONS SYSTEMS

2.1 Mission Operations Activities

A Spacecraft Mission Operations System (SMOS) comprises the set of facilities which carry out all aspects of mission operations. Mission operations can be divided into three areas:

- *Mission Preparation.* The preparation and configuration of the mission control system prior to the start of the mission, as well as the initialisation and subsequent maintenance of the basic reference mission knowledge (spacecraft databases, mission schedules etc) during the mission.

- *Mission Planning.* The planning and scheduling of mission operations activities.

- *Mission Operations.* All tasks involved in monitoring, control and reporting of the mission.

In general, independently developed applications, possibly running on different platforms support each of these areas. The areas are, however, far from independent: mission preparation produces the database for operations, mission planning produces the plan of operations to be executed by mission operations, and the progress of mission operations conditions the plan.

The development, integration and use of such applications raises the following issues, which the ATOS programme addresses:

- A SMOS is complex and expensive to develop *ab initio*. It is therefore essential that software components are reused both between missions and within a mission wherever possible.

- The required capabilities of the SMOS may change during its working life. For example, users' needs may change, or the spacecraft performance characteristics may change (in the case of a permanent malfunction, quite radically), or, for a long mission, the underlying supporting technology (platforms, networks) may change.

- The various mission-specific applications within current SMOS are typically inflexible; for example, a typical planning system in current use operates on the basis of generating a schedule of operations for a period of several hours; its rigid interface with the control system makes it very difficult to replace it by an enhanced planned system which performs realtime reactive replanning.

- SMOS applications make use of knowledge about the spacecraft, the ground systems and the operational procedures. Some of this knowledge is held centrally, but a significant amount is isolated locally within individual applications, each of which may use its own representations and conventions. This leads to potential duplication and inconsistency of knowledge and associated maintenance problems.

2.2 Mission Operations Knowledge

The applications which support the activities discussed above require extensive knowledge which covers many aspects of mission operations and is structured in widely different ways. This knowledge includes:

- *Flight Operation Plans (FOP)*, including timelines (a scheme of mission operations activities for a particular mission phase or scenario) and Flight Control Procedures.

- *Documents*, including text and graphics, for example the Spacecraft Users Manual.

- *Design information*, including the behaviour of components of the spacecraft.

- *Traditional spacecraft databases*, for example parameter characteristics and telecommand characteristics.

- *Rules and operational constraints* of the mission; for example, if the spacecraft is in eclipse then the payload is on stand-by.

It is the objective and challenge of ATOS to integrate and share these large knowledge bases between SMOS applications.

3 AN AGENT-BASED APPROACH TO KNOWLEDGE SHARING

Some of the issues raised above are addressed, at least in part, by the object-oriented approach of developing generic applications which are specialised for a particular mission. ATOS takes the object-oriented approach a stage further by using the principles of federation to integrate heterogeneous applications and their knowledge bases. ATOS provides the languages which the applications use to exchange messages, a mechanism for defining the meaning of these messages, and an infrastructure with a wide range of services for routing messages and for sharing knowledge.

ATOS draws heavily on recent work on intelligent agents and federated databases and especially on the ARPA Knowledge Sharing Effort [9].

3.1 The Mission Information Base

Each application in the ATOS environment is called an ATOS Application Module (AAM). AAMs communicate with each other via the ATOS infrastructure. In the language of [4], an AAM is an agent and the ATOS infrastructure is a facilitator.

Figure 1 depicts (hypothetical) AAMs communicating using the ATOS infrastructure. The MIB is defined to be the union of all data and knowledge bases in an SMOS. The scope of the MIB is thus very broad and encompasses all the knowledge mentioned in section 2.2.

As figure 1 illustrates, the MIB is federated: each AAM has its own knowledge base, which forms a component of the MIB.

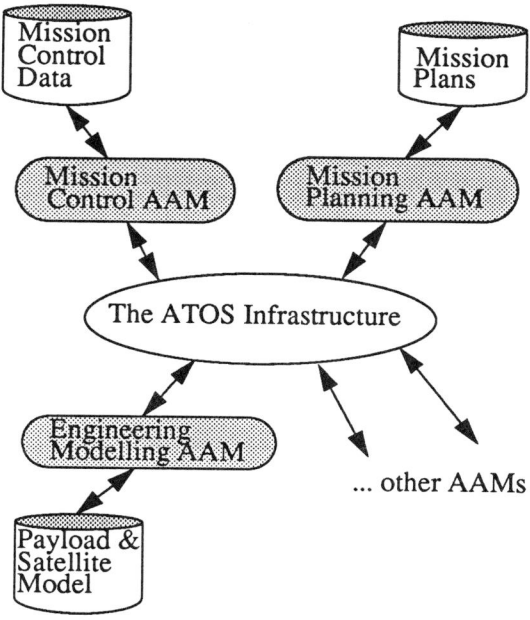

Figure 1: AAMs and the ATOS Infrastructure

3.2 The Ontology of Shared Knowledge

AAMs must be able to share knowledge. For example, the results of mission planning are inputs to mission execution; details of a detected anomaly are the basis of fault diagnosis. [7] includes a detailed discussion of the importance of knowledge sharing in spacecraft operations.

To share knowledge, AAMs must have a common understanding of concepts and terms. This is provided by the ontology.

The most basic use of the ontology is as a paper standard to which AAMs comply. Thus if there is a standard definition the terms 'resource', 'schedule' and 'activity' then AAMs which comply with the standard are guaranteed to use these terms in the same way.

A second use of the ontology is to derive an AAM's knowledge structures. The
ontology is written in a formal language (rather than, for example, English); it can therefore be translated into the tool-specific knowledge structures used by an AAM. This approach gives greater assurance that the AAM complies with the
ontology and it can also reduce the effort of developing the AAM.

3.3 The Functions of the Infrastructure

The ATOS infrastructure is the glue which integrates AAMs. The infrastructure "facilitates" the integration of AAMs by:

- *Maintaining links* between information items in different components of the MIB.

- *Detecting significant changes* in the state of the MIB and informing AAMs accordingly.

- *Routing a message* to an AAM which provides the information or service required by the message.

- *Controlling access* to the information and services provided by AAMs.

- *Maintaining a timetable* that describes which AAMs can use which services of other AAMs and when; this timetable is updated by a mission planning AAM.

- *Logging messages*, as requested.

- *Buffering messages* before they are read.

Clearly some of these services are more innovative and interesting than others. Later sections of this paper concentrate on link management, detection of change in the MIB, and message routing.

3.4 Links between MIB Components

As discussed in section 3.1, the MIB is distributed among AAMs. The infrastructure provides a way of maintaining links between information items in different components of the MIB which allow AAMs to navigate the MIB. Such links cannot be stored by any one AAM which only knows about its own component of the MIB.

To achieve this, the infrastructure maintains a metabase in which it records the classes of information in the MIB (as defined by the ontology), the AAMs that manage these classes of information, and identifiers of the objects to link. To link objects, AAMs export to the infrastructure identifiers of the objects and create a link between them in the metabase.

Link types are defined in the ontology and have different properties. For example, a link type might be defined to be many-to-one, or to be acyclic.

Figure 2 depicts three example AAMs which each manage part of the MIB. One AAM uses a relational database, one uses a hierarchical database and one stores documents. The existence of certain MIB objects is recorded in the metabase;
this is shown in the figure by a dashed line from the MIB object to its metabase image. The figure also shows links in the metabase between objects which are
managed by different AAMs. For example, a tuple in the relational database might be described by a document to which it is linked.

3.5 Detecting Changes

Another role of the infrastructure is in detecting significant changes in the state of the MIB. One AAM can request a second AAM to perform a specified action

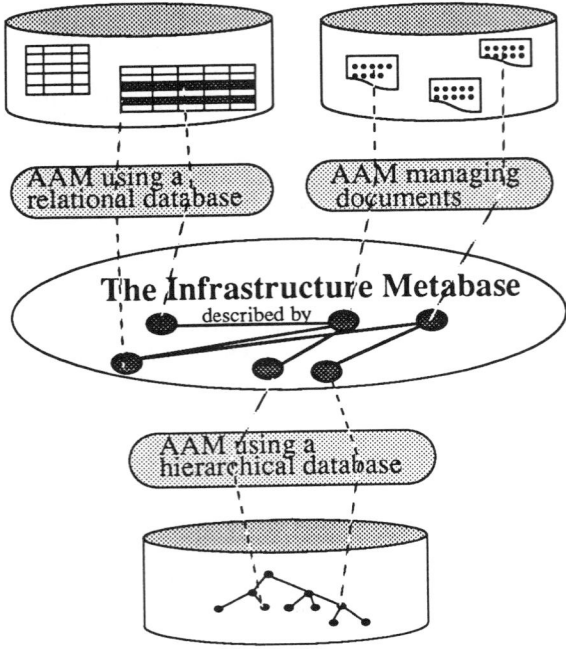

Figure 2: The Infrastructure Metabase

when a specified trigger fires. For example, an AAM may ask to be notified when the voltage of a battery falls below a certain level. A trigger is expressed in terms of the state of the MIB; more precisely, a trigger is a query over the MIB which evaluates to true or false; the trigger fires when the value of the query changes from false to true.

Unfortunately, this approach to detecting change has two limitations. The first is that not all AAMs are sufficiently sophisticated to detect changes expressed as arbitrary triggers. The second is that an AAM can only monitor its own component of the MIB for change; no single AAM can effectively monitor a trigger which involves two or more components of the MIB.

To address these limitations, the infrastructure can detect significant changes in its metabase; this allows monitoring of changes on the whole MIB, providing the AAMs export the appropriate local changes to the metabase. As the metabase is a global view of the MIB, the scope of the trigger is not limited to one component of the MIB.

When the infrastructure receives a request for notification it first determines the AAMs which manage the knowledge to be monitored; the infrastructure then requests that these AAMs collaborate in the notification process by exporting this knowledge to the metabase.

This role of the metabase allows dependencies between components of the MIB to be managed. Imagine, for example, two AAMs one of which plans a mis-

sion and the other of which maintains information describing the design of the spacecraft. The metabase holds an abstraction of the plan and the spacecraft design, as well as links corresponding to dependencies of the plan upon the design. The

planning AAM instructs the infrastructure to inform it when there is a change or correction to the design which requires the mission to be replanned. The planning AAM then obtains details of the change by querying the design AAM directly. This approach to managing dependencies is similar to that described in [8].

3.6 Message Routing

When an AAM sends a message, it can specify explicitly the AAM which is to receive the message. In this case, the infrastructure simply routes the message directly to its receiver.

In addition to this direct routing, the infrastructure provides the AAMs with a mechanism to access services of other AAMs of on the basis of the service itself. In this case the AAM instructs the infrastructure to send the message to the AAM which can best provide the required service or information. This is called content-based routing: AAMs first advertise their abilities to process messages, then the infrastructure routes messages on the basis of these advertisements.

As a simple example of content-based routing, an AAM might advertise its ability to provide the voltage of all batteries. The infrastructure can then route a message which asks the voltage of a specified battery to this AAM.

This section describes the theory of how the infrastructure routes messages. Section 4 gives examples of how this theory works in practice.

The matching criterion between required and provided services is based on a logical dependency between the advertised and routed messages. This logical dependency can be expressed as a formula α of logic for knowledge, and the matching algorithm is then reduced to proving $\models \alpha$.

To prove this, the ATOS infrastructure makes use of its knowledge of the MIB, in particular, the ontology (which defines the structure of the metabase) and objects that have been exported to the metabase (as discussed in sections 3.4 and 3.5). If this knowledge is represented by the set of formulas σ, the criterion $\models \alpha$ above can be rewritten as $\sigma \models \alpha$

Suppose, for example, an AAM advertises its ability to provide information about the power supply subsystem. The infrastructure can then route to this AAM a message which queries the current from the solar array if it knows from its metabase that the solar array is part of the power supply.

Two types of message can be routed by content-based routing: capabilities of processing queries and interests in assertions. The criterion for matching is different in each case.

3.6.1 Routing queries

The capability of answering queries can be expressed as the knowledge an AAM

has of the bindings of the free variables of a first order formula $\phi(x)$ representing the query which makes the formula true or false.

This property of the advertising AAM can be formalised in logic for knowledge [2] as

$$\forall x (K_A \phi(x) \vee K_A \neg \phi(x))$$

which expresses that, whatever x is, AAM A knows whether $\phi(x)$ is true or false.

An AAM which needs to access a query service on a formula $\psi(y)$ is looking for an AAM X whose property would be

$$\forall y (K_X \psi(y) \vee K_X \neg \psi(y))$$

AAM A is selected to provide the service if

$$\sigma \models \forall x (K_A \phi(x) \vee K_A \neg \phi(x)) \supset$$

$$\forall y (K_A \psi(y) \vee K_A \neg \psi(y))$$

3.6.2 Routing assertions

The interests in assertions can be expressed as the interests of an AAM in the knowledge about some kind of information propagated by other AAMs. Once again, if this information is described by a first order formula $\phi(x)$, the property of other AAMs the advertising AAM looks for can be formalised as

$$\exists x K_X \phi(x)$$

which expresses that AAM X knows that $\phi(x)$ is true for at least one binding of the free variables x appearing in ϕ.

If AAM B propagates information represented by a formula $\psi(y)$, this information is sent to all the AAMs for which

$$\sigma \models \exists y K_B \psi(y) \supset \exists x K_B \phi(x)$$

4 MESSAGES AND THEIR STRUCTURE

4.1 The ARPA Knowledge Sharing Effort

The Agent Communication Language (ACL) used in ATOS is derived from the language defined as part of the ARPA Knowledge Sharing Effort. In this approach, the meaning of the messages exchanged by the AAMs and the infrastructure is defined at three levels.

- A *vocabulary* of the terms and concepts of spacecraft operations. This vocabulary is provided by the ontology, as described in section 3.2.

The ontology is written in a declarative, formally defined language called Ontolingua [5], which is expressive enough to allow the sharing of rules and behavioural knowledge between AAMs, and which is independent of any particular approach to structuring knowledge.

- A *language*, called Knowledge Interchange Format (KIF) [3], to express knowledge using the terms and concepts of the ontology.

KIF expresses first order predicate calculus in a LISP-like syntax. It is not expected that AAMs use KIF internally; indeed, it is important that AAMs are not constrained to use a particular representation format. AAMs must therefore translate shared knowledge to and from KIF.

- A *protocol*, called Knowledge Manipulation Language (KQML) [1], which AAMs use to communicate at run time.

KQML provides performatives, i.e. message types, which define the intent of a message. The KQML performatives used by ATOS are adapted from those described in the draft KQML standard and include performatives in the following areas:

- Asking and replying to a question. Multiple answers to a question can be sent as one long reply or as a stream of replies each containing one answer.
- Asserting a fact to be added to the receiver's knowledge base.
- Advertising the sender's capability to perform a service.
- Instructing the infrastructure to route a message to the AAM best able to process it.
- Instructing the receiver to perform an action when a condition arises.

The following sections gives examples of how the ACL is used in the ATOS environment.

4.2 Directly Routed Messages between AAMs

AAMs use the ACL to communicate with each other via the infrastructure. For example, AAM 1 can query AAM 2 for the value of the voltage of the object bat7 by sending the message.

```
(ask-one :content (voltage bat7 ?x)
         :receiver "AAM 2")
```

AAM 2 receives this message as it is sent by AAM 1, except that the infrastructure adds an argument to the message to indicate its sender. AAM 2 may then reply to the query by sending the message

264

```
(reply :content (voltage bat7 280)
       :receiver "AAM 1")
```

AAMs can also directly exchange information using the `tell` performative. AAM 2 informs AAM 1 that the battery `bat7` is an `electrical-device` by sending the message

```
(tell :content (electrical-device bat7)
      :receiver "AAM 1")
```

In direct routing, the only restriction on the use of KIF by the AAMs is imposed by the subsets of KIF they can handle; the infrastructure does not restrict the use of KIF in any way.

The ACL is also used by AAMs to access services provided by the ATOS infrastructure. To provide services such as notification or content-based routing, the infrastructure interprets the KIF content of certain messages; in this case the content is restricted to be a subset of the full KIF language.

4.3 Link Management

To provide the link management service, the infrastructure enables information to be inserted in the metabase using the `achieve` performative.

For example, consider the link type `powers` that connects a battery to the motor which this battery powers, batteries and motors being managed by AAM 5 and AAM 7 respectively. To create a link between a given battery `bat1`, and a given motor `mot234`, identifiers for both objects must first be exported to the metabase. AAM 5 exports the identifier of `bat1` to the infrastructure metabase by sending the following message:

```
(achieve  :content (battery bat1))
```

(Note that this message does not have a `:receiver` argument; such messages are not routed directly to an AAM but are interpreted by the infrastructure.) Similarly, AAM 7 exports the motor `mot234` with a similar message.

Any AAM can now create the link by creating a relation between these two identifiers in the metabase:

```
(achieve :content (powers bat1 mot234))
```

4.4 Content-Based Routing

Content-based routing is supported by the performatives `advertise` for the declaration of a service, and `broker-one` and `broker-all` for the access to the service.

For example, an AAM 23 advertises its capability to answer queries about the voltage of electrical devices by sending to the infrastructure the message

```
(advertise :content (ask-all
    :content (and (electrical-device ?x)
            (voltage ?x ?y))))
```

This advertise contains a prototype of the messages that can be handled by the advertising AAM. Other AAMs can then access the advertised service by sending queries using the `broker-one` performative (if only one AAM is required to process the query) or the `broker-all` performative (if all AAMs able to process the query are required to do so). The content of a message like

```
(broker-one :content (ask-all
    :content (and (electrical-device B1)
            (voltage B1 ?y))))
```

is therefore routed by the infrastructure to an AAM that provides the service of answering queries on electrical devices' voltage.

As mentioned in section 3.6, the matching of the service provided with the service requested is based upon the logical dependency between these services. The matching takes into account equivalence of queries and subsumption of assertions. For example, the service advertised by the message

```
(advertise :content (ask-all
    :content (and (electrical-device ?x)
    (not (battery ?x))(voltage ?x ?y))))
```

that corresponds to the capability of answering queries about the voltage of electrical devices that are not batteries, matches the brokered message

```
(broker-one :content (ask-all :content
        (and (not (or (battery ?x)
        (not (electrical-device ?x))))
        (voltage ?x ?y)))
    :sender "AAM 10")
```

In addition, the infrastructure ensures that the syntax of the message actually forwarded to the AAM providing the service corresponds to the syntax of the advertised message, and instructs, by means of an :aspect argument, the receiving AAM to answer this message with the syntax of the brokered message. In the case of our example, the message forwarded by the content-based routing process is

```
(ask-all :content (and
          (electrical-device ?x)
          (not (battery ?x))(voltage ?x ?y)))
      :aspect (and (not (or (battery ?x)
          (not (electrical-device ?x))))
          (voltage ?x ?y))
      :sender "AAM 10" :receiver "AAM 9")
```

In effect, this provides a translation service between AAMs, and makes easier the development of interfaces between AAMs by reducing the semantic analysis of KIF queries and answers to a straightforward matching of variables in logical expressions.

This translation is also applied when brokering assertions. Suppose that AAM 10 has advertised its interest in knowing the identifiers of electrical-device with the message

```
(advertise :content (tell
          :content (electrical-device ?x))
      :sender "AAM 10")
```

The interpretation by the infrastructure of the message

```
(broker-all :content (tell :content
          (and (electrical-device bat1)
          (voltage bat1 622))))
```

results in the generation of the message

```
(tell :content (electrical-device bat1)
      :sender "AAM 11" :receiver "AAM 10")
```

to AAM 10. Furthermore, the infrastructure can make use of the ontology to broker messages. With the same advertised message as above, brokering the message

```
(broker-all :content (tell
          :content (and (battery bat1)
          (voltage bat1 622))))
```

causes the identical tell message to be sent to AAM 10 because the infrastructure knows that a battery is an electrical-device.

Furthermore, the infrastructure can use for content-based routing the information held in the metabase for link or notification purposes. For example, the message

```
(broker-all :content (tell
          :content (voltage bat1 266)))
```

is brokered to an AAM that has advertised

```
(advertise :content (tell
          :content (and (battery ?x)
          (voltage ?x ?y))))
```

if bat1 is known to be a battery in the metabase.

4.5 Notification of Change

An AAM uses the notify performative to specify those changes in the state of the MIB which the infrastructure should monitor, as discussed in section 3.5. The arguments of the notify performative specify a trigger-condition-action rule to be applied to the metabase. These rules are evaluated after each update to the metabase. The trigger of a notification is expressed as a list of KIF formulae, the condition is a single KIF formula, and the action is a set of messages to be sent by the infrastructure when the notification fires. An update of the metabase fires the notification if all KIF formulae of the trigger were false before the update and are true after the update, and the condition is true after the update. For example, the notification

```
(notify         :trigger ((battery ?x))
:condition (and (voltage ?x ?y) (> ?y 200))
:action ((tell :content (battery ?x)
          :receiver "AAM 2")))
```

results in the sending of a message to AAM 2 when a battery which has voltage greater than 200 is exported to the metabase.

5 PROTOTYPES

5.1 Infrastructure Prototype

A prototype of the ATOS infrastructure has been developed, which implements all the features described above (with some restriction on the way the notification mechanism constraints the AAMs to manage the consistency between their beliefs and the information they manage in the metabase).

Some of the features of the prototype are as follows:

- The infrastructure prototype has been developed in Common Lisp on Sun UNIX workstations. AAMs connect to the infrastructure using a simple API built on top of TCP/IP.

266

- The infrastructure database, which comprises the metabase and the internal database of the infrastructure, is implemented on top of the Oracle7 RDBMS. A compiler from Ontolingua definitions to SQL DDL has been developed, so that the schema of the metabase is derived from the definition of the ontology in Ontolingua. At runtime, a KQML/KIF to SQL DML compiler translates queries and assertions to the metabase so that they can be processed by Oracle.

- The evaluation of the matching conditions described in section 3.6, which is the core of the content-based routing mechanism, is performed by a theorem prover based on a restricted implementation of the linear resolution algorithm. To make the proof possible, matching conditions are rewritten as first order logic formula.

5.2 AAM Prototypes

As well as the infrastructure prototype, the ATOS programme has developed prototype AAMs. The objective of this development is to validate the ATOS approach and the infrastructure prototype, and to gain experience in integrating AAMs.

[7] describes a prototype tool called AMFESYS which maintains a model of a payload: a microprocessor controlled remotely programmable Automatic Mirror Furnace (AMF) for growing crystals in zero gravity.

The AMFESYS tool has been decomposed into three AAMs as shown in Figure 3. The Modelling AAM maintains a model of the AMF which the Monitoring AAM compares with telemetry from a simulation of the spacecraft. If a significant discrepancy is detected the Diagnostic AAM performs a rule-based diagnosis of the fault and suggests adaptations to the model to restore its consistency with the telemetered reality.

The three AAMs use different approaches to representing knowledge (C++, CLOS and Kappa) and interact with each other via the ATOS infrastructure.

5.2.1 The Automatic Mirror Furnace ontology

The meaning of terms which occur in messages exchanged between the AAMs, is defined by the AMF ontology. The following is a fragment of the AMF ontology which specifies a subclass of disks called AMF-Carrier-Disk and specifies that each AMF-Carrier-Disk has a Carrier-Disk-Position. The fragment also identifies an instance of the class Carrier-Disk in the AMF: SampleAMFDisk.

```
(define-class AMF-Carrier-Disk (?x)

'Carrier-Disks in the Automatic Mirror
 Furnace carry objects and can be
 rotated, lifted and lowered'

  :def (disks ?x))

(define-relation
          Carrier-Disk-Position(?x ?y)

'The position of a Carrier Disk is defined
relative to the Automatic Mirror Furnace,
which represents position 0, and the
lowermost position in which the carrier-disk
can rotate to select another sample, which
represents position 250. The position is
expressed in mm.'

:axiom-def (and (single-valued
                 Carrier-Disk-Position)
        (range Carrier-Disk-Position number)
(domain
   Carrier-Disk-Position AMF-Carrier-Disk)))

(define-instance
   SampleAMFDisk (AMF-Carrier-Disk))
```

AAMs which commit to this ontology can converse meaningfully about the Carrier-Disk-Position of AMF-Carrier-Disk's.

The AMF ontology has been automatically translated into the CLOS data structures used by the Diagnostic AAM, following the approach outlined in section 3.2.

5.2.2 Cooperation and coordination control

For the AAMs to cooperate, three problems must be solved: how can the problem be decomposed into subtasks, which the AAMs can handle; which AAMs will handle which subtask; and how is the coordination between AAMs organised?

The answers to the first two questions are straightforward for the prototype AAMs. Firstly, a basic modelling, monitoring and diagnosis task were identified. Secondly, a static attribution of tasks is applied: the AAMs have fixed roles (for example, the Monitoring AAM monitors the model, its responsibility does not evolve) and there is no overlap of responsibility. Note, however, that the ATOS infrastructure allows the dynamic restructuring of roles of AAMs via advertisements, see section 3.6.

The coordination of AAMs is organized at two levels: the macro level, where AAMs cooperate to perform a major task, and the micro level, where data exchange between the AAMs is handled. One major interaction

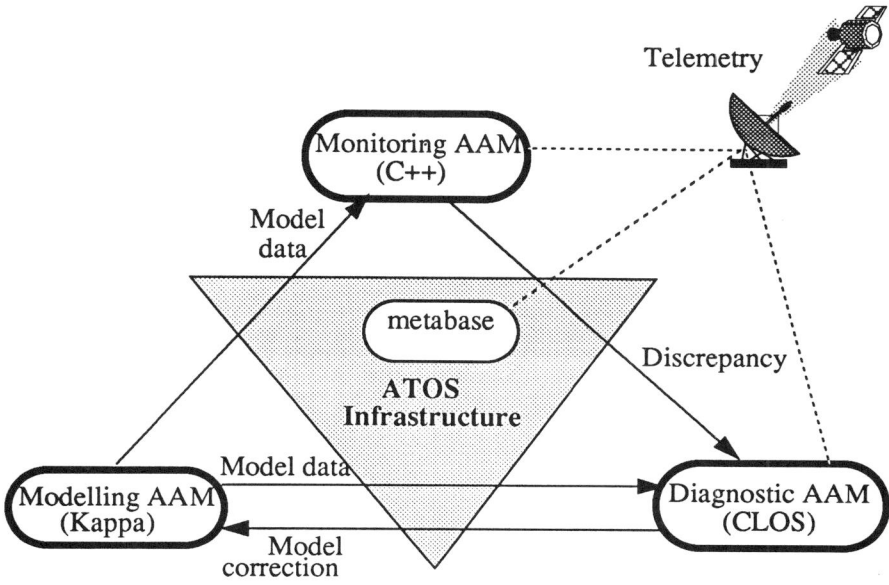

Figure 3: AAMs derived from AMFESYS

at the macro level can involve several dialogues (query-answer exchanges) between AAMs at the micro level.

At the macro level two mechanisms are used to coordinate the prototype AAMs:

consistent reactions to events and coordination by communication.

Firstly, AAMs demonstrate dynamic behaviour with respect to (events in) time; the coordination of their time-varying behaviour is partly based upon their consistent reactions in response to events. Using the change detection supported by the notification performative (see sections 3.5 and 4.5), AAMs can ask the infrastructure to be notified every time a certain event occurs. Since these events are of interest to multiple AAMs, the metabase is the appropriate mechanism to manage and detect them.

For example, in the prototype AAMs, the arrival of new telemetry data is recorded in the metabase (see Figure 3). The Monitoring AAM is notified of this event and starts a comparison of these telemetry data with synchronized model data. On the other hand, the Modelling AAM also knows that new telemetry data have arrived, and it stops modelling until the consistency of its model with the newly arrived telemetry data is confirmed by the Monitoring AAM. The arrival of new telemetry data is used as a control point for AAM co-ordination.

Secondly, AAMs can manage coordination control by themselves, by exchanging coordination information. In the AAM prototype configuration, the Modelling AAM tells the Diagnostic AAM

```
(tell :content (deviation model 1)
      :receiver "DAAM")
```

that a serious deviation between the model and telemetry has been detected by the Monitoring AAM, which means that the Diagnostic AAM should perform a diagnosis. The meaning of the content of this `tell` message is, of course, defined in the ontology.

At the micro level, KQML defines the protocol for conversations between AAMs. For example, an AAM that receives an

```
(ask-one :content (Carrier-Disk-Position
         SampleAMFDisk ?pos)
         :reply-with telemetry_data)
```

message must reply with a

```
(reply :content (Carrier-Disk-Position
       SampleAMFDisk 23)
       :in-reply-to telemetry_data)
```

message.

5.2.3 Lessons learnt from prototype AAM development

Decomposing AMFESYS gives AAMs that are potentially reusable. Whereas the dynamic model of the AMF is buried in the monolithic AMFESYS application, the Modelling AAM described above can be

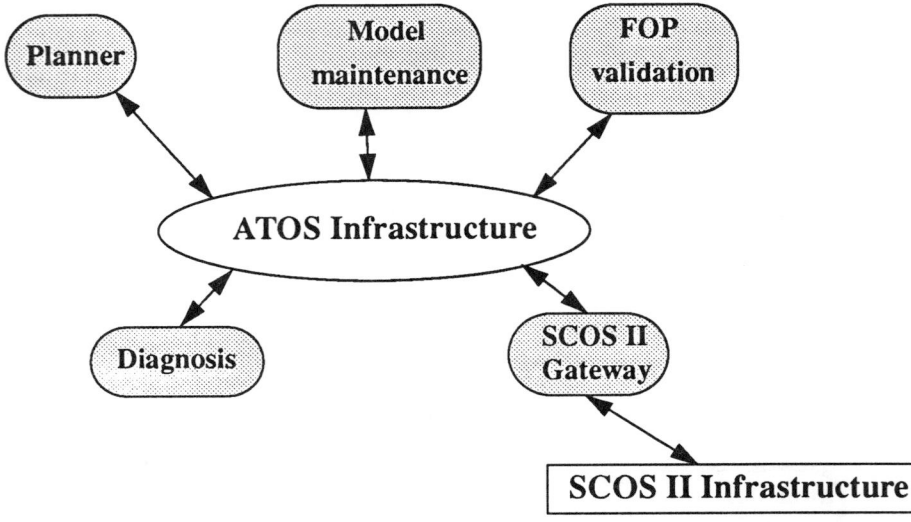

Figure 4: A SMOS based on ATOS

reused by other AAMs; for example, an AAM which calculates power consumption on the spacecraft or an AAM which validates flight operation plans. Thus, the environment of AAMs is easier to extend and adapt.

Other significant lessons learnt from prototyping the three AAMs include that:

- KIF and KQML are expressive and neutral enough to allow heterogeneous AAMs to communicate and cooperate

- Ontologies of shared knowledge are important, and seem to become more important as the size and complexity of the problem domain increases. However, it is overambitious and unnecessary to develop a complete ontology of, say, spacecraft operations; the ontologies can be developed as needed when AAMs which wish to share knowledge.

- Experts in the domain of spacecraft operations find it difficult to develop and review ontologies written in Ontolingua. A graphical tool is desirable to assist such experts. The ATOS programme has investigated the requirements for such a tool, and has considered how it should be developed.

- The ATOS infrastructure provides valuable services for coordinating AAMs: the notification service is useful for detecting events and changes acros s federated database; content-based routing relieves AAMs of the burden of reasoning about the beliefs and capabilities of other AAMs and therefore also enhances AAM independence.

6   CONCLUSIONS AND FUTURE WORK

The ATOS programme has got off to an excellent start. An approach to sharing

knowledge between the knowledge bases of a federation of intelligent agents (AAMs) has been identified, an infrastructure which supports this approach has been developed, and the approach has been validated by prototype AAMs which use the infrastructure.

The ATOS programme will now move towards the operational use of this technology. It is expected that AAMs will be developed for mission planning, maintaining a model of the spacecraft, validating flight operations plans and diagnosing anomalies and that a gateway AAM will be developed to ESOC's mission control system, SCOS II [6].

The interactions between the AAMs in this system will be complex, and a substantial ontology will be required. Extended trials of the system are planned, in parallel with real mission operations, using an ESOC simulator. Work is also envisaged to develop additional AAMs.

We confidently expect that the ATOS programme will continue to give insights

into the industrial application of the technology of knowledge sharing between federated agents and to support the development of advanced spacecraft mission operations systems.

ACKNOWLEDGEMENTS

This work was funded by ESA's Advanced Systems and Technology Programme (ASTP) which is managed by ESA's directorate of telecommunications. ASTP promotes the development of new technologies for the space domain, and supports European industry in implementing these in the form of marketable products.

The authors acknowledge the contributions of Herwig Laue (ESOC) and of Kevin Poulter and Howard Smith (Logica UK).

REFERENCES

1. Finin T., Fritzson R., Mc Kay D., McEntire R.; KQML as an Agent Communication Language, Proceedings of the Third International Conference on Information and Knowledge Management (CIKM '94), ACM Press, November 1994.

2. Genesereth, M.R. and Nilsson, N.J.; Logical Foundations of Artificial Intelligence, Morgan Kaufmann Publishers, 1987.

3. Genesereth, M.R., Fikes R. E., et al; Knowledge Interchange Format Version 3.0 Reference Manual, Stanford University Logic Group, Logic Report 92-1, June 1992.

4. Genesereth M.R., Ketchpel S.; Software Agents, Communications of the ACM, Vol. 37, No.7, July 1994.

5. Gruber T.; Ontolingua: A Mechanism to Support Portable Ontologies, Knowledge System Laboratory Technical Report, Stanford University, June 1992.

6. Jones, M., Head, N.C., Keyte, K., Symonds, M.; SCOS II: ESA's New Generation of Mission-Control System, ESA Bulletin No. 75, 1993.

7. Laue H., Kaufeler J-F, Poulter K., Smith H.; The Advanced Technology Operations System ATOS; Proc. 2nd Int. Sym. Ground Data Systems for Space Mission Operations. SPACEOPS 1992 Pasadena, California, USA. JPL Publication 93-5.

8. McGuire, J.G., Kuokka, D.R., Weber, J.C., Tenenbaum, J.M., Gruber, T.R. and Olsen, G.R.; SHADE: Technology for Knowledge-Based Collaborative Engineering, Concurrent Engineering: Research and Applications, Volume 1, Number 3, September 1993.

9. Patil R. et al; The DARPA Knowledge Sharing Effort: Progress Report, Proc. of the 3rd. Int. Conf. on the Principles of Knowledge Representation, Cambridge MA, Morgan Kaufman, 1992.

10. Wheadon, J.;AMFESYS: Modelling and Diagnosis Functions for Operations Support.; Proc. 2nd Int. Sym. Ground Data Systems for Space Mission Operations. SPACEOPS 1992 Pasadena, California, USA. JPL Publication 93.

Workplace-Adapted Behaviors:
Lessons Learned for Knowledge Reuse

Johan Vanwelkenhuysen and Riichiro Mizoguchi
Osaka University
Osaka, Japan
(johan, miz)@ei.sanken.osaka-u.ac.jp

ABSTRACT

Any problem solving behavior integrated in organized work practice is necessarily adapted to forces originating from characteristics of the workplace, organizational embedding, and social environment. An analysis and comparison of troubleshooting behaviors of *same* devices with access to the *same* technical information but performed in *different* workplaces teaches us that after integration, behaviors may be inadequate for other workplaces. Knowledge level models of the workplace-adapted behaviors showed significant differences. We investigate implications of this observation for the development and use of reusable problem solving components

1   INTRODUCTION

We focus on the development of knowledge based problem solvers for operation in a specific target workplace. We particularly scrutinize dimensions along which ontologies for reusable problem solving components should be defined to adequately support in the construction and maintenance of conceptual knowledge system designs.

Starting assumption of our discussion is that generic knowledge level models of problem solving behavior [14] (*generic models* for short) are a significant aid to create an initial conceptual design of the target knowledge system. There is a consensus that knowledge level models reach three dimensions useful to explore for the purpose of creating ontologies to share and reuse generic models: *task, domain,* and *methods* (or *inference*). We maintain this consensus.

Generic models are currently defined in a way that pretends context-independency. It is implicitly assumed that aspects not related to the three knowledge level dimensions (problem solving task, domain, and inference knowledge) have a minor effect on adequacy of behaviors: selection of generic models is typically driven by task and domain knowledge related concerns; tuning the generic model to the target workplace is reduced to translating and refining problem solving concepts.

We counter-argue this assumption. We have investigated in a bottom-up manner sources driving problem solving behaviors to realize the importance of the workplace context: A problem solver in any real workplace is exposed to forces which originate from characteristics about organizational processes, workplace resources, and social environment. Problem solving behaviors must adapt to these forces to acceptably integrate into on-going practice. Indeed, a tester of technical devices operating in a production plant is likely to adapt his hypothesis generation strategy as reliability of preceding assembly and testing processes change.

Justified by this study, we argue that reusable components to support in the development of knowledge systems should stress construction and adaptation next to reaching predefined conceptual knowledge system designs. This necessarily imposes the need for another dimension along which reusable ontologies should be defined, a workplace ontology.

Argumentation of our position is structured as follows. Section 2 makes explicit the starting hypothesis of our discussion. Section 3 motivates our focus on workplace adaptation by analysing a practical experience in knowledge system development. Section 4 proposes to create and integrate workplace ontologies in existing generic knowledge level models of problem solving behavior.

2   RESEARCH PREMISE

We are concerned with the construction of conceptual knowledge system designs. The line of research we adopt is that of defining and making available reusable (configurable) problem solving components. We support the construction and guide (re)use of problem solving components by creating generic expressive vocabularies (ontologies) which index and tie these reusable components. A knowledge system development team which can recognize relevance of ontologies in its situation is hinted at potential useful predefined problem solving components. This approach is detailed in [8,15] and shows similarities with [10,20].

Our research premise is that models of problem solving behavior (generic models) expressed in a knowledge level framework and encapsulated by ontologies make the construction of knowledge systems less costly. This benefit is due to the characteristic that generic models predefine boundaries of a class of solutions which can be accessed and explored early in the knowledge system's life-cycle. Ontologies guide to potential appropriate conceptual knowledge system designs.

This use of ontologies imposes the requirement that ontologies must capture aspects that drive and justify problem solving behaviors. Knowledge level research teaches us that problem solving behaviors are driven by [14]:

1. The need to satisfy aspects (goals/subgoals) of the problem solving task;

2. The problem solver's understanding of the domain theory;

3. The inferences that can be made by the problem solver;

We have created ontologies for problem solving components along two dimensions to capture these aspects.

Task ontology: necessary and sufficient vocabulary to describe problem solving goals and inferences for a particular class of tasks.

Domain ontology: necessary and sufficient vocabulary to describe a class of systems to be reasoned about (e.g., digital systems). We further differentiate two categories of domain ontologies dependent on their task (in)dependency:

  Model ontology: generic vocabulary to refer to statements about systems to be reasoned about independent of the problem solving task;

  Object ontology: necessary and sufficient vocabulary to describe a class of systems to be reasoned about in a manner suitable for a particular class of tasks.

Moreover, in knowledge level research it is recognized that interactions exist between task, domain, and inference knowledge. Indeed, domain knowledge cannot be adequately represented independent of the class of tasks it is designed for [3]; Task knowledge is

related to inferences through the competence of an inference structure to derive the required outputs from the task's inputs; Domain knowledge is related to inference knowledge through its ability to fill the inference's knowledge roles. Encapsulating problem solving behaviors in a justified manner requires that ontologies capture these interactions [19].

In contrast with the majority's line of ontology research, we maintain these important findings from knowledge level research: ontologies for problem solving components are only meaningful if their inherent interactions across the task, domain, and inference dimensions are maintained and made explicit.

3 BEHAVIOR ADAPTATION

In this section, we illustrate the intuitively known fact that contextual issues (i.e. issues outside the scope of task, domain, and method dimensions) govern problem solving behaviors. More importantly, we argue that leaving implicit certain of these contextual issues makes it difficult, if not impossible, for knowledge reusers

1. to assess and justify adequacy of behaviors defined by others;

2. to adapt reusable behaviors to the target workplace under focus.

Relevance of studying and sharing context to understand and design behaviors has been addressed by researchers including [2,4]. We add to this discussion an experience which triggered our interest in contextual issues in general and workplace characteristics in particular.

3.1 An experience in designing problem solving behaviors

We have developed a diagnostic knowledge system for digital processor boards for use in a telecommunications' production plant [16].

We closely interacted with testers to create a knowledge level model of their problem solving behavior following the model-based knowledge acquisition approach. We harmonized and refined our analysis to obtain a model to diagnose processor boards for which testers agreed that it reflects a way to understand their problem solving behavior. This knowledge level model was implemented and, as it reached a state of maturity, the resulting prototype and development team physically moved to the production plant. Through prototype demonstrations and by explaining prototype performances on test cases, testers, engineers, and other interest groups were encouraged to evaluate the prototype and to propose improvements. Refinements and new functionalities were developed and monitored.

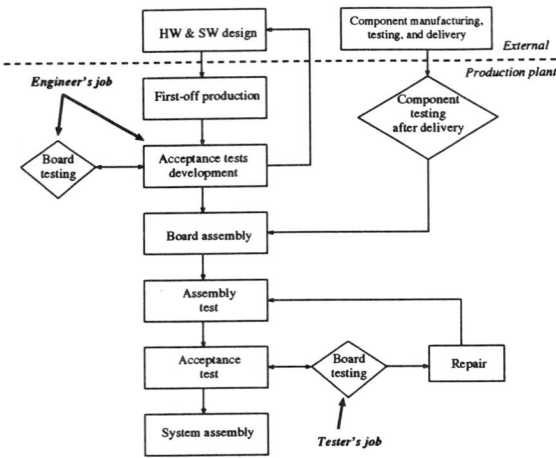

Figure 1: Tester and engineer engage in troubleshooting the same kind of processor boards. Because they diagnose a board at different life-cycle phases, their approaches are different and, apparently, incompatible.

Involvement of engineers increased. Up to that time, they had only played a minor role in the project. Because of their troubleshooting experiences (see figure 1 to situate an engineer's job) – and because they are a powerful group in the production plant – engineers became assigned to evaluate the knowledge system's performance and act as end-user representatives.

Engineers were less excited than testers about the prototype. They questioned adequacy of prototype behaviors, i.e. behaviors defined through cooperation with multiple testers. Testers disagreed with engineers. A confrontation between both experts in the field to directly discuss and resolve conflicting issues was discouraging. The engineer reproached the tester for having an insufficient understanding of performance of circuit boards; test results were insufficiently exploited resulting in a degradation of troubleshooting performance. Tester and engineer never came to an agreement.

3.2 Analysis

What went wrong in the confrontation between tester and engineer ?

Both had a long and well-appreciated experience in troubleshooting processor boards. They solved their diagnosis problems differently, each way being effective for routine problems in their workplace, but, apparently, inadequate for the other's.

We illustrate this "inadequacy" by analysing two observed differences. The analysis shows how, although both problem solvers have in principle access to the same technical information, their behaviors have adapted differently over time due to different forces

acting upon their work practice. It is the origin of these forces that need to be studied in more detail for knowledge reuse.

OBSERVATION 1

The tester generated impractical suspects. Recognizing this critique, he maintained his position that this behavior was sufficiently adequate for his work. Conflict between engineer and tester becomes intelligible if one understands differences of both workplaces.

As opposed to the tester's, the engineer's responsibility is critical with respect to the company's business goals (high product quality and low manufacturing cost). This imposes different priorities among troubleshooting performance requirements to which problem solving behaviors are necessarily adapted (to integrate in the company's work practice) as shown in figure 2.

An engineer comes into play after a first-off is produced[1]. He verifies hardware design for testing and manufacturing and he develops tests for device acceptance after manufacturing. After the engineer's work, the device hardware design is produced in large quantities.

An engineer thus operates early in the device's life-cycle. An inaccuracy in his work is likely to propagate through the manufacturing process with an exponential grow of cost to repair the inaccuracy. From the perspective maintain the low-cost business goal, troubleshooting fidelity and precision have higher priority than troubleshooting efficiency.

A tester can rely on stable hardware device designs. Less precise and faithful diagnoses result in higher manufacturing (in particular, repair) costs than actually necessary. However, because repair is a low-cost process and because incorrect diagnosis are quickly discovered as repaired boards are tested again, overall extra cost is marginal with respect to total manufacturing cost. Consequently, troubleshooting efficiency has higher priority than troubleshooting fidelity and precision. Moreover, final product quality can be maintained independent of the tester's troubleshooting performance because: (i) in case of less precise diagnosis, all hypothesized components are replaced, resolving the quality problem; (ii) an incorrect diagnosis is identified as the repaired board is tested again.

OBSERVATION 2

The tester's measurements and interpretations of device behaviors were sometimes too simplistic to be reliable for hypothesis discrimination. Sometimes, the tester verified through simple probes "aliveness" of signals while the engineer closely investigated timing relations between component behaviors.

---

[1]A "first-off production" refers to the production of a small series of devices to verify acceptability of the device design with respect to manufacturing and testing.

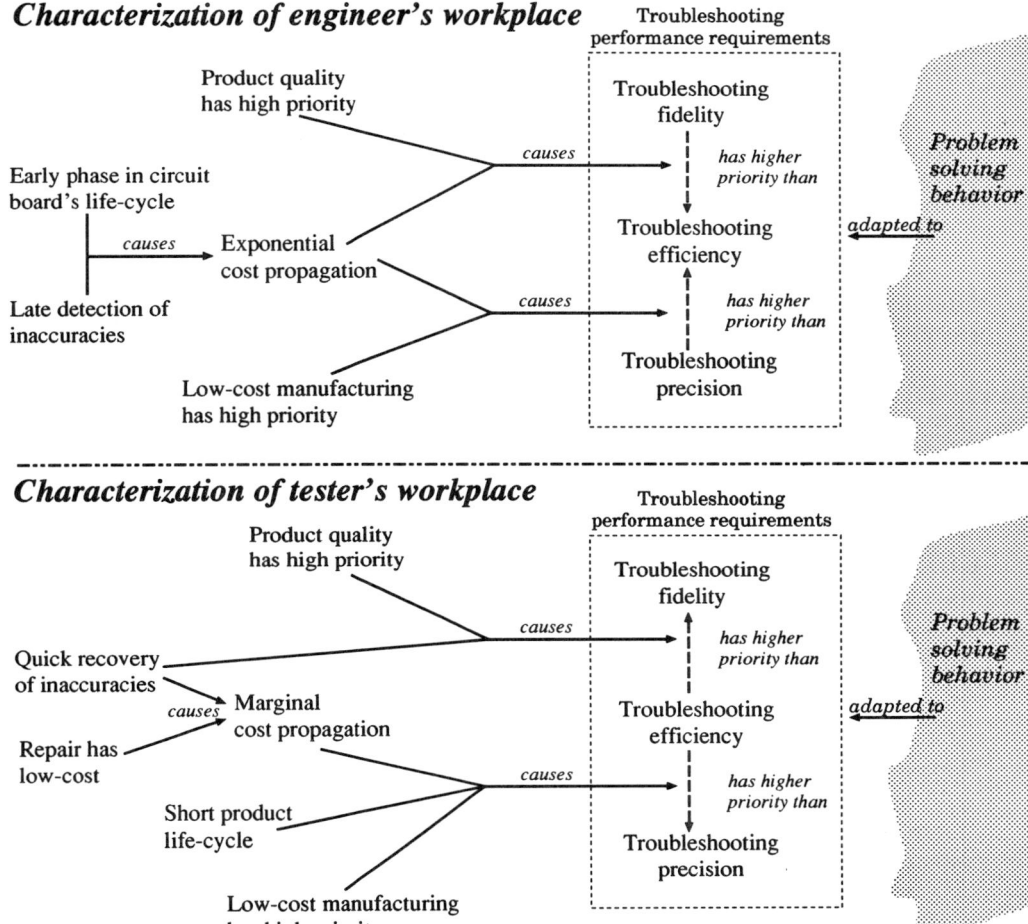

Figure 2: Engineer and tester behave differently because they are adapted to different characteristics of the workplace. One type of difference in workplace characteristics concerns priorities among troubleshooting performance requirements emerging from the same business goals.

274

Characterization of engineer's workplace

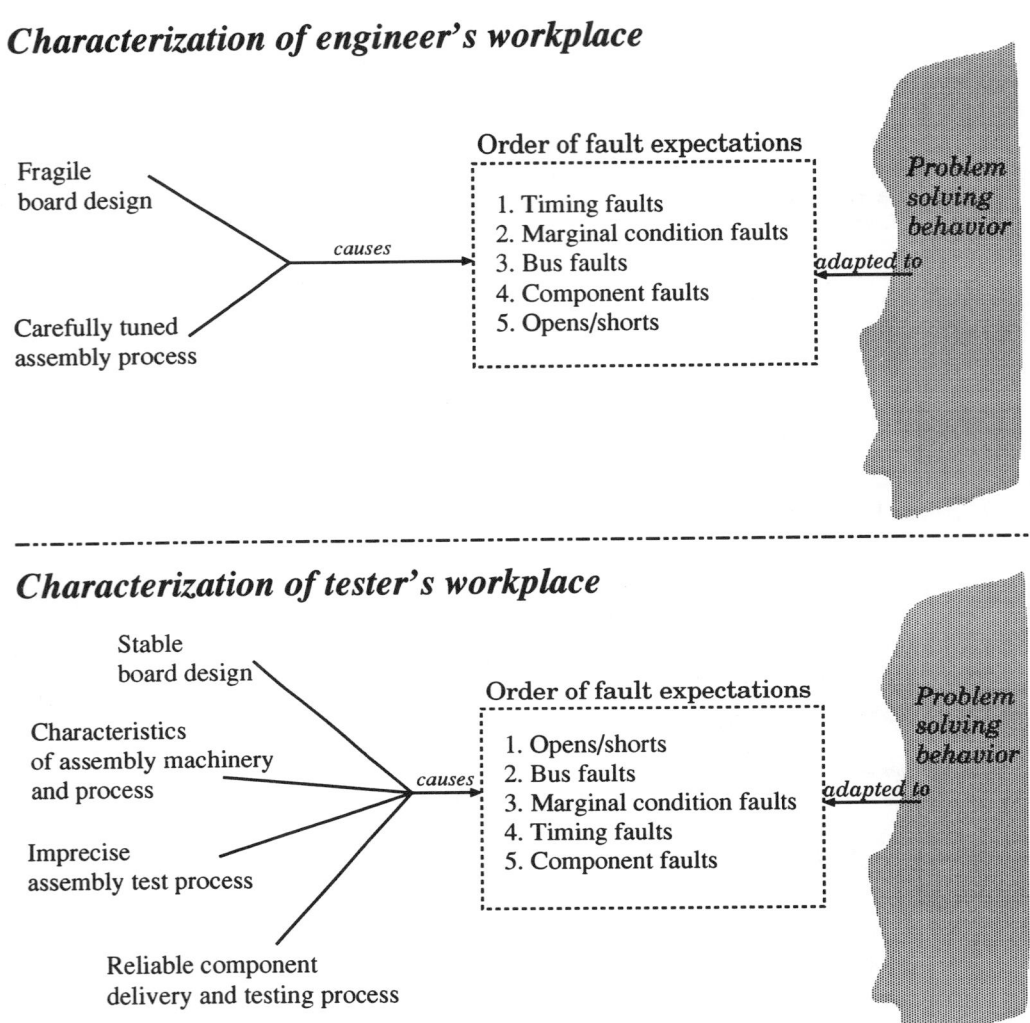

Characterization of tester's workplace

Figure 3: Another type of differences in workplace characteristics concerns characteristics of life-cycle processes and their effect on the type of problems expected.

An interplay of many factors underly this observed difference. A dominant factor was different expectations about the type of faults and fault characteristics in their workplace: engineers need to deal with board failures due to a fragile hardware design[2]. Such faults, often, emerge as timing or marginal condition faults. In a tester's workplace, timing faults do not occur frequently. Rather, opens or shorts make up the bulk of failures due to characteristics of the assembly process.

Purpose of the assembly test – a test preceding the tester's work (figure 1) – is to detect opens and shorts. Therefore, these type of faults should not be considered by the tester. However, in practice, it appears that the company's technique to detect assembly faults is not reliable. Failures slip through and are detected only during acceptance test. Moreover, components assembled on the hardware device are delivered by external suppliers and tested after delivery. This process is reliable, reducing the amount of failures due to broken components. Characteristics of these two life-cycle processes affect the fault distribution expected by the tester which, in turn, affects the kind of observations performed during troubleshooting.

Due to characteristics of life-cycle processes, the tester has expectations about the type of faults and their characteristics which differ from the engineer's. These expectations affect the kind of observations performed during troubleshooting (figure 3).

3.3 Lessons learned

The analysis and comparison of work practice of two troubleshooters performing at different stages in the life-cycle process of the same device illustrate how problem solving behaviors adapt over time to integrate into a workplace. Even though these behaviors may contribute to exactly the same task (whereby we take the definition of "task" as that one accepted in knowledge level research), if different forces act upon the workplaces, behaviors adapted to these forces may become inadequate for other workplaces.

The analysis convinces us that adapting the predefined problem solving behaviors to a particular workplace involves more than translating and refining the generic model (in the sense suggested in knowledge level research). It may involve significant re-representations of large parts of the task structures and domain knowledge. Problem solving methods may become inadequate and may need to be completely re-designed.

One lesson we learned is that selecting and adapting reusable problem solving components to the knowledge

system's target environment must (among others) be driven by a careful study of the workplace and its effects on behaviors defined by problem solving components.

This observation poses an important question how to proceed in knowledge reuse research[3]. One obvious line to pursue is to make explicit for each reusable problem solving component a characterization of the workplace for which the component is designed, the effect of these characteristics on the component, and guidelines how to change (re-represent) the reusable component as certain workplace characteristics do not apply or change. The next section gives an onset of this line of research.

4 KNOWLEDGE REUSE

This section discusses our proposal to augment previously constructed knowledge components with additional information structures to improve their competence for reuse. We envision two ways to achieve this:

- Make explicit the problem solving context for which the knowledge component was designed. Purpose is to enforce a more careful and justified selection of reusable components.

- Make explicit and rationalize design decisions behind previously constructed knowledge components to allow groups (other than the one who created the component) to appreciate the design and to decide upon its plausibility in new situations.

Making explicit problem solving context of a knowledge component intended at design time inherently restricts the component's scope of applicability. In fact, it turns out that the augmented knowledge components we propose are only reusable within the same class of task, domain, and workplace as the intended problem solving context (e.g. diagnosis of digital systems in production environments). It is known, however, that analyses in past design experiences can be pertinent to new system developments, even if the application task or domain differs. We will illustrate how the augmented knowledge components provide essential information to extract guidelines and allow for reuse of patterns of reasoning across task and domain environments.

4.1 Problem solving context

A *problem solving context*[4] defines boundaries of the problem for which a knowledge component was de-

---

[2]By "fragile design" we mean that circumstances in the production environment may interact with critical aspects of the hardware design frequently causing breakdowns.

[3]As argued in [13], recognizing the significance of context and behavior adaptation, some researchers take a more extreme position than we do. Some reduce the role of representations in system development (e.g., situated cognition) [4,11]. Others search for techniques towards knowledge evolution [6,12].

[4]See [9] for a more detailed definition of problem solving context.

signed. It captures all aspects that are (explicitly or implicitly) considered at design time. These aspects relate to problem solving task and subtasks, domain knowledge and pragmatics of the problem solving (sub)tasks. In this article, we have discussed pragmatics imposed by criticality of the workplace (with respect to business goals), relations between nonfunctional requirements, characteristics of life-cycle processes, and expectations about the type of faults and their characteristics.

We describe the problem solving context in terms of task, object, and workplace ontologies to capture aspects of the design problem related to (sub)tasks, domain and pragmatics respectively. Task and object ontologies have been defined in section 2. Note, however, that object ontologies are chosen above model ontologies to stress task-dependency of representations in domain models.

In a similar manner, workplace ontologies are task-dependent. We define a *workplace ontology* as a vocabulary to capture borderline issues (as defined in [2]) of the workplace in which problem solving is (to be) performed. These borderline issues lie outside the canonical knowledge level model defining the (observed/designed) problem solving behaviors but have a recognized effect on the behaviors.

Examples of expressions in a troubleshooting-in-production-plant workplace ontology are:

Expression: Low reliability of test and measurement equipment (resources)
Task affected: Behavior observation
Pragmatic affected: Fidelity of observations
Effect: Imposes symptom verification subtask

Expression: Intermittent faults are an expected type of fault
Task affected: Hypothesis discrimination
Pragmatic affected: Competence of hypothesis discrimination
Effect: Imposes the need for a problem solving method which can deal with inconsistent observations

Expression: High reliability of component testing process before assembly
Task affected: Hypothesis generation
Pragmatic affected: Competence of hypothesis generation
Effect: Reduces likelihood of failures inside physical components

Looking at some of these workplace characteristics, some researchers will disagree to label those characteristics as peripheral to troubleshooting (i.e. that they are not included in the knowledge level description of

troubleshooting behaviors). As argued in [2], borderline issues are not inherent in an artifact. Rather, they are the result of technical and social conventions in which a line is drawn about what is reasoned about explicitly and what remains peripheral. For example, the type of faults expected can be central to the reasoning pattern of some testers and, therefore, it may be decided to make it part of the domain representations in the knowledge level model. As in our design experience, this issue remained peripheral until new work practice was discussed: "... when attention, perspective, or practice changes, parts of the periphery may be swept to the center of attention and vice versa" [2, page 7].

4.2 Rationalized design decisions

We propose to make explicit key design decisions behind previously constructed knowledge components and to express their problem solving context.

Design decisions concern (i) selection or construction of a problem solving method decomposing the task under focus into subtasks, (ii) selection or construction of primitive inferences to realize the task under focus, (iii) representations of domain concepts.

For each key design decision, a rationalization is given. This *rationalization* expresses

- the *degree* to which the design decision satisfies aspects of the problem at hand (problem solving tasks and pragmatics)
- *plausibility* of the design decision (i.e. probability that the design decision is acceptable in the given situation).

We illustrate this idea by recapitulating a reasoning pattern from our experience in developing the diagnostic system [16]. Figure 4 represents this reasoning pattern in a semi-formal manner. Graphical objects denote formal concepts from the decision representation language, DRL [7]. Contents of the rectangles are natural language descriptions of expressions in problem solving and workplace ontologies.

4.2.1 Representation

We focus on how to design the hypothesis generation subtask of a diagnostic system for which, additionally, high priority requirements are defined about troubleshooting competence, efficiency, fidelity, and precision.

DRL does not differentiate aspects of the design problem. Anything which requires a decision is represented as a **decision problem**. **Goals**, although having the same graphical representation, are considered to be of a more general class in that they represent a desirable state or property for comparing alternative solutions. "How to design the hypothesis generation subtask" is represented in DRL as a

277

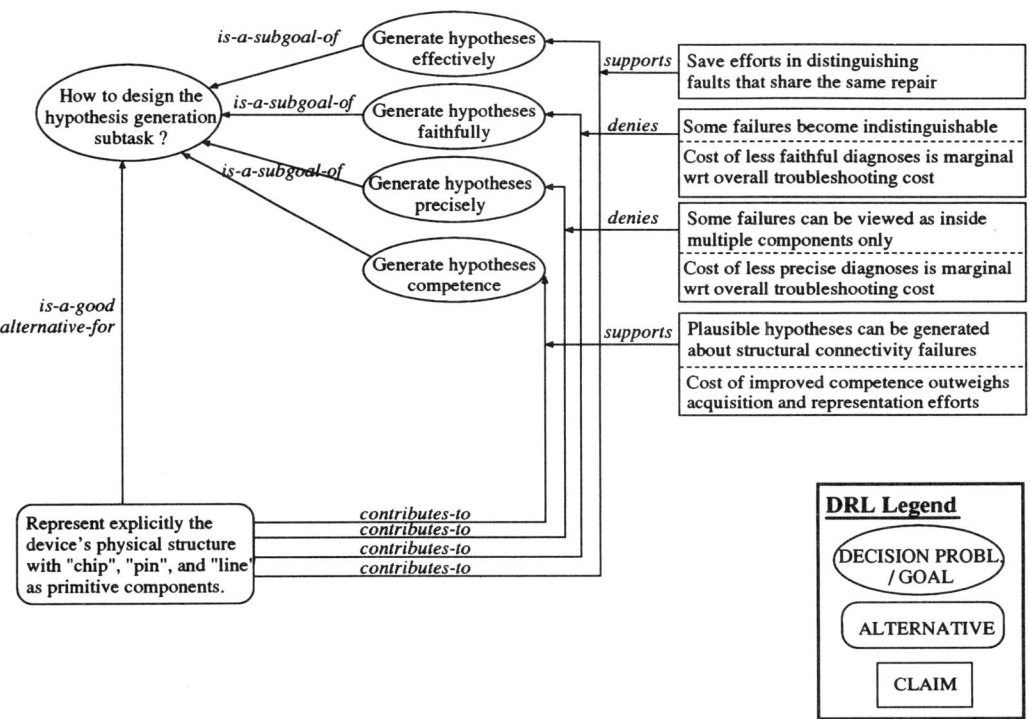

Figure 4: Illustration of a rationalized design decision represented in DRL [7].

decision problem while the non-functional requirements are defined as goals. The only relation between decision problem and goal available in DRL is is-a-subgoal-of.

We represent a *design decision* as a claim which states that an alternative achieves or contributes-to a decision problem while considering one or more goals. More precisely, it states that an alternative is-a-good-alternative because it fixes the decision problem while acceptably resolving conflicting goals.

For example, an alternative to contribute to the hypothesis generation decision problem is to "represent explicitly the physical structure of the device using as representational primitives *chip, pin,* and *line*". This alternative was fixed in our design experience because, next to contributing towards the hypothesis generation decision problem, it contributes in an acceptable manner to some high priority non-functional requirements (goals).

Arguments on which acceptability of an alternative are based are represented as claims that support or deny claims about the alternative. The set of supporting and denying claims constitute the *rationale* of the design decision. Each claim in a rationale is represented in terms of (i) the degree to which the alternative satisfies goals and

(ii) plausibility of the alternative.

For example, the alternative fixing the representational primitive of a physical domain model is supported by the claims (i) "competence of hypothesis generation is contributed to to the degree that hypotheses can be generated about failures due to structural connectivity (e.g., opens and shorts) and that these hypotheses are practically plausible and relevant" and (ii) "efficiency of hypothesis generation is contributed to to the degree that efforts are saved in distinguishing faults that share the same repair".

The alternative is denied by two claims: (i) "fidelity of hypothesis generation is sacrificed to the degree that some failures become indistinguishable" and (ii) "precision of hypothesis generation is sacrificed to the degree that some failures can be viewed as inside multiple components only" (e.g., a short-cut between lines causes all components connected to the line to incorrectly become suspect).

At present, formalizing descriptions about the degree of claims remains an open research issue. It appears that a formal vocabulary is needed expressing properties of representations such as "precision", "fidelity", and "efficiency" which can be related to nonfunctional requirements or other goals.

Plausibility that compromises established by the illustrated alternative are acceptable are described as (i) "the degree that the practical benefit of the improved hypothesis generation competence outweighs efforts involved in acquiring and representing the physical device structure" and (ii) "the degree that cost of less faithful and precise diagnosis (which is often the repair cost) is marginal with respect to overall troubleshooting cost".

The analysis in section 3.2 illustrated the reasoning that can be made explicit (figures 2 and 3) to arrive at a workplace characterization which can be used to assess plausibility of an alternative. We argue to maintain this reasoning by representing it using workplace ontologies.

4.2.2 Benefits for reuse

Improved benefit of knowledge components with rationalized design decisions with respect to reuse is multifold:

- Selection of reusable knowledge components can be driven by key design decisions, the extent to which and plausibility that high priority requirements are acceptably dealt with.

- Reuse of past design, workplace and requirements analyses is supported and patterns of reasoning can be reused within same task and domain environments.

- Guidance in maintaining the knowledge system design [17].

To illustrate the first benefit, consider the situation in which system adaptivity is a high priority requirement imposed upon a diagnostic system (i.e. the system must be easily adaptable to reason about new devices). The design team may wish to investigate key design decisions behind each reusable knowledge component to drive selection. A design decision behind Hamscher's XDE system mentions that system adaptivity is considered to the extent that the diagnostic engine is independent from the type of digital device it reasons about [5]. A side-effect of another design decision (the use of temporal abstractions) is that only people familiar with the XDE design can create and decide upon the appropriate level of temporal abstractions for each new type of device. This implies that adapting the system to new type of devices always requires the involvement of system designers. Acceptability of these key design decisions must be investigated and negotiated upon for each situation separately. Essential is that rationalized design decisions make explicit these interactions and reach arguments which allow groups other than the designers to discuss and decide upon acceptability of the compromises.

It appears that project interest groups can easily come up with a long list of requirements but deciding on the relative priorities among the requirements is difficult. A workplace characterization (as shown in figures 2 and 3) is useful to drive this analysis. Moreover, as these structures are related to problem solving tasks and pragmatics they affect, rationalized design decisions drive problem and requirements analysis through design synthesis [17].

4.3 Modification guidelines

The idea of modification guidelines is to support reuse of essential information about rationalized design decisions across tasks and domains.

The ontology research community typically creates *model ontologies* (section 2) to enable knowledge reuse and sharing across tasks and domains. The structural knowledge base of our diagnostic system would be encapsulated in model ontologies such as *components, connections, and sub-part relationships*. Indeed, that is a way to describe contents of the structural domain model free of any problem solving context. However, because these generic ontologies hide the representational primitives (*chips, pins,* and *lines*), this encapsulation necessarily loses the design decision and its rationalization we have discussed before.

While model ontologies are certainly useful to identify potential interesting knowledge components based on minimal constraints and across tasks and domains, isolated model ontologies itself capture little design knowledge useful for reuse.

We propose to filter out domain-dependent information from the rationalized design decisions and to extract guidelines which make design analyses reusable across domains but within the same class of tasks of the design decision's problem solving context.

For example, a guideline extracted from the design decision shown in figure 4 states in natural language the following:

If your problem solving task at hand requires hypothesis generation as subtask, competence, efficiency, fidelity, and precision are high priority requirements imposed upon the problem solver and two characteristics of the workplace are non-criticality and low-cost of repair

Then it may be useful to group the device's physical components and connections which share the same repair and to represent these groups as primitive components of the physical domain model.

The rationalization of the design decision can be reused to the extent that object ontologies in the problem solving context are replaced by their more abstract model ontologies. As a consequence, this guideline may be triggered by the need to create a more effective troubleshooting problem solver or to integrate a design into a non-critical workplace.

Another example of a modification guideline extracted from [19] is one which is triggered by the need to reduce knowledge acquisition and representation efforts involved in adapting the knowledge system design to new type of devices to be diagnosed.

If your problem solving task at hand requires behavior prediction as subtask, efficiency, precision, and system adaptivity are high priority requirements

Then it may be useful to group physical components into functional components based on the role of the combined behaviors in the device's hardware design.

These kind of functional components contribute to system adaptivity to the degree that the components are more transparent to hardware device designers and that the required representations are readily available after the hardware design process. Plausibility that this design guideline is useful depends on workplace characteristics including accuracy of the hardware device assembly process and the extra cost related to less precise diagnoses.

Advantage of these guidelines for reuse is that it facilitates the reverse construction from model ontologies to refined concepts and relationships tuned to certain task environments [19]. It suggests ways to modify knowledge components as non-functional requirement priorities or workplace characteristics change.

5 CONCLUSION

"The more designers struggle to attain freedom from context, the greater the tasks they set not only for themselves, but for the users of their designs" [2, page 6].

To integrate predefined problem solving behaviors in a workplace, they need to be adapted to forces originating from characteristics of organizational processes, workplaces, expectations, and so forth. Discovering what characteristics affect behaviors in the workplace under study is difficult, time-consuming, and hardly studied at all.

We believe that if we want to stick to reusable problem solving components of the same nature as currently offered, we need to study characteristics of classes of problem solving environments and their effect on problem solving behaviors. Results of these studies can be made of benefit to other teams by encapsulating the analysis in a problem solving and workplace ontology and by rationalizing design decisions behind problem solving components.

ACKNOWLEDGEMENT

The authors thank Dr. Kazuo Miyashita and Prof. Luc Steels for instructive discussions concerning issues treated in this article.

REFERENCES

1. Benjamins, R. and Jansweijer W., "Toward a Competence Theory of Diagnosis", *IEEE Expert*, pages 43–52, October, 1994.

2. Brown, J. and Duguid, P., "Borderline issues: Social and material aspects of design." *Human-Computer Interaction*, 9:3–36, 1994.

3. Chandrasekaran, B. and Johnson, T., "Generic tasks and task structures: History, critique and new directions". In David, J., Krivine, J., and Simmons, R., editors, *Second Generation Expert Systems*, pages 232–272. Springer-Verlag, Berlin, 1993.

4. Clancey, W., "The knowledge level reinterpreted: Modeling how systems interact." *Machine Learning*, 4(3/4):285–291, 1989.

5. Hamscher, W. "Modeling digital circuits for troubleshooting", *Artificial Intelligence*, 51:223–271, 1991.

6. Kang, B. *et al.*, "Multiple classification ripple down rules". In Mizoguchi, R., Motoda, H., Boose, J., Gaines, B., and Compton, P., editors, *Proceedings of the 3rd Japanese Knowledge Acquisition for Knowledge-Based Systems Workshop JKAW'94*, pages 197–211, Hatoyama, Japan, 1994.

7. Lee, J. and Lai, K., "What's in design rationale?" *Human-Computer Interaction*, 6(3-4):251–280, 1991.

8. Mizoguchi, R., "Knowledge acquisition and ontology". In *Proceedings International Conference on Building and Sharing of Very Large-Scaled Knowledge Bases '93*, pages 121–128, Tokyo, Japan, 1993.

9. Mizoguchi, R. *et al.*, "Task Ontology for Reuse of Problem Solving Knowledge", *Proceedings of Second International Conference on Building and Sharing of Very Large-Scaled Knowledge Bases*, IOS Press, Amsterdam, Netherlands, 1995.

10. Neches, R. *et al.*, "Enabling technology for knowledge sharing". *AI Magazine*, pages 36–56, 1991.

11. Pfeifer, R. and Rademakers, P., "Situated adaptive design: Toward a new methodology for knowledge systems development". In Brauer, W. and Hernandez, D., editors, *Verteilte kunstliche intelligenz und kooperatives arbeiten. Proceedings of the 4th international GI-congress on knowledge based systems*, pages 53–64, Berlin. Springer-Verlag, 1991.

12. Schmalhofer, F. *et al.*, "Beyond the knowledge level: Descriptions of rational behavior for sharing and reuse". In Steels, L., Schreiber, G., and de Velde, W. V., editors, *Proceedings of the Eight European Knowledge Acquisition Workshop (EKAW'94)*, Hoegaarden, Belgium. Springer-Verlag, 1994.

13. Steels, L., "How can we make further progress in knowledge acquisition ?" In Mizoguchi, R., Motoda, H., Boose, J., Gaines, B., and Compton, P., editors, *Proceedings of the 3rd Japanese Knowledge Acquisition for Knowledge-Based Systems Workshop JKAW'94*, pages 65–71, Hatoyama, Japan, 1994.

14. Steels, L. and McDermott, J., "*The knowledge-level in expert systems. Conversations and commentary*". Academic Press, Cambridge, MA, 1992.

15. Tijerino, Y. *et al.*, "Multis: A knowledge acquisition system based on problem solving primitives". *Intern'l Journal of Expert Systems*, 5(2), 1993.

16. Vanwelkenhuysen, J., "*Participative Conceptual System Design of Industrial Knowledge Systems*". PhD thesis, Vrije Universiteit Brussel, Artificial Intelligence Laboratory, Pleinlaan 2, 1050 Brussel, Belgium, 1993.

17. Vanwelkenhuysen, J., "Augmenting conceptual software designs with their rationales". *IEEE Expert* (forthcoming), 1995.

18. Vanwelkenhuysen, J. and Mizoguchi, R., "Maintaining the workplace context in a knowledge level analysis". In Mizoguchi, R., Motoda, H., Boose, J., Gaines, B., and Compton, P., editors, *Proceedings of the 3rd Japanese Knowledge Acquisition for Knowledge-Based Systems Workshop JKAW'94*, pages 33–47, Hatoyama, Japan, 1994.

19. Vanwelkenhuysen, J. and Mizoguchi, R., "Ontologies and guidelines for modeling digital systems". In *Proceedings of the Ninth Knowledge Acquisition for Knowledge-Based Systems Workshop*, Banff, Canada, 1995.

20. Wielinga, B. and Schreiber, A., "Reusable and shareable knowledge bases: A European perspective". In *Proceedings International Conference on Building and Sharing of Very Large-Scaled Knowledge Bases '93*, pages 103–115, Tokyo, Japan, 1993.

Knowledge Bases, Texts and Lexicon

Florence Lemaire
INRIA Rhône-Alpes
Grenoble, France
Florence.Lemaire@imag.fr

ABSTRACT

A knowledge base is a model and its sharing requires to document its content. In the context of a scientific knowledge base, the documentation is constituted of both the definition of the terminology employed in the base and the scientific publications justifying the validity of the knowledge. Thus, a structure allowing to store and to have an easy access to these documents must be found. Furthermore, this structure must support the access to the relevant documents associated to a piece of formal knowledge contained in the base.

We describe an environment made of three different structures of storage: a formal base, a base of texts and a lexicon. The lexicon does not only contain the definitions of the domain vocabulary but also provides a new type of access to the formal knowledge for a user. This one expresses his request by navigating in the lexicon from a general item to more specific ones. Consequently, he can access the formal base without being disturb by a lack of knowledge of the terminology.

We study here the roles of such a lexicon and its interactions with the other structures of the environment.

1 INTRODUCTION

Knowledge exchange is essential for major scientific achievements. In addition to enhancing access to raw data, it also implies sharing of complex knowledge such as hypotheses or models. Such chunks of knowledge are represented in knowledge bases but the sharing of these structures remains a problem. The way this problem is addressed depends on the meaning given to the *knowledge sharing* notion and principally on the scope assigned to a knowledge base.

The notions of *knowledge sharing* and reuse are often used in the same way. According to [8], *knowledge sharing* involves the use of a given knowledge base either at locations other than those at which the base has been developed or in the context of new computer programs. The term *knowledge reuse* denotes the reutilization of an existing knowledge base in significantly different contexts.

For us, *knowledge sharing* implicates the fact that the content of a knowledge base can be consulted or modified by someone who did not build it. In fact, we distinguish two kinds of users: the developers and the standard users. A developer has to integrate new information while he may not be a specialist in all the domains presented in the knowledge base. Thus, he must understand the entire content of the base in order to make modifications which are consistent with the other pieces of knowledge. A standard user may want to understand each piece of knowledge and their interrelationships in the base to complete his own knowledge. *Knowledge sharing* involves therefore that users find in the base the information required for understanding and to modifying its content.

A knowledge base is a structure which allows to store, organize and access a set of knowledge. Knowledge bases can be used as components of expert systems in order to solve problems but they are, above all, the result of a modeling process. Thus, when the language used is expressive enough, they can be seen as a model for a given field of knowledge. In this context, a knowledge base is used as a tool for increasing the knowledge of the user.

Since a knowledge base is a model, its sharing addresses several problems. In order to build it, the knowledge of a given field might have been simplified and abstractions might have been made. Furthermore, the modeling choices are implicit and all the information which have been used during the modeling process

282

are not represented in the knowledge base. Thus, the question here is how to help users to understand the knowledge base content and how to make clear the modeling process.

This search is carried out in the context of a team working on knowledge representation [10]. Our team defines new knowledge models whose descriptive capabilities allow to represent inter-related objects, methodological knowledge, and so on. These knowledge models are experimented for the development of several knowledge bases in molecular biology.

In section 2, we illustrate the problem of the legibility of the content of a knowledge base with an example taken from a knowledge base in molecular biology and then we identify requirements to improve knowledge exchange. In section 3, we study the ability and the inadequacies of a hypertext to document a knowledge base. Then, we propose an environment composed of three structures: a formal base, a lexicon and a textual base to remedy for these inadequacies. In section 4, we show that the lexicon is a structure which modifies notably the use of the knowledge base environment. In section 5, we give some characteristics of the lexicon and describe the perspectives of our work.

2 THE LEGIBILITY OF A KNOWLEDGE BASE

A knowledge base is the result of a modeling process. Thus, the knowledge base content depends on the developer's mental representation of the research field and on a set of simplifications and abstractions made on this representation to build the knowledge base. These transformations are not explicit in the knowledge base.

2.1 Understanding a knowledge base is not obvious

A developer or a user meets several difficulties when he wants to understand the content of a knowledge base. The study of a knowledge base in molecular biology will allow us to underline these difficulties. ColiGene is a knowledge base developed in collaboration with the "Laboratoire de Biométrie, Génétique et Biologie des Populations" of Claude Bernard University in Lyon and devoted to the analysis of gene expression in *E.coli* [9] [12]. ColiGene contains the description of all the entities known as implicated in the gene expression process: operons, regulation signals and so on.

This knowledge base uses an object-based representation in which knowledge is described as classes. Every class has a name and is composed by a list of attributes to which constraints on their values are attached. A class can be refined into sub-classes, this means that attribute descriptions can be added and/or refined. Thus, classes are organized in a hierarchical structure. The descriptions of elements

Lac-operon	
a-kind-of	chromosomic operon
map	?
repressor	lacI
gene1	lacZ
gene 2	lacY
gene 3	lacA

Figure 1: The operon lactose instance in ColiGene (a knowledge base in biology). An instance is described by a name (`lac-operon`) and a set of attributes (`repressor`, `gene1`...) with their associated values (`lacI`, ...).

of these classes are called instances (figure 1). The object-based knowledge model supports various inference mechanisms, such as default value inheritance, procedural attachment, and classification which determines the position of a given object in the specialization hierarchy.

During a consultation, the user of such a knowledge base may face three kinds of questions: questions about the meaning of a term, questions on the justifications of a piece of knowledge and questions about modeling choices. These questions concern different steps in the modeling process.

- *"What is a repressor"* is an example of question on the meaning of a name used to express a piece of formal knowledge. In an object-oriented representation, a piece of knowledge is an object or a set of inter-related objects. These objects are described using names (names of classes, instances, attributes) which are also words of a terminological language for some of them. Furthermore, in the formal base, these terms can be employed in a specific meaning that the developer accepts.

- The questions on justification of a piece of knowledge concern the validity of a scientific notion: what are the proofs that this affirmation is correct ? These questions also address the problem of the reasons why this notion is present in the knowledge base. This aspect concerns the relationship between a notion and the viewpoint presented in the knowledge base: is this piece of knowledge meaningful in the knowledge base? Is it at the right place in the base?

- The last kind of questions concerns the modeling choices made by the developer during the building of the knowledge base: why did the developer choose to represent a data an attribute and not as a class?

2.2 The user needs external information

The questions asked by a user show that external information is required to understand the content of a

Questions	Answers	Sources
On meaning		
What does the term repressor mean?	A repressor is a protein which binds to operator on DNA or RNA to prevent transcription or translation.	Glossary of "Genes IV", Benjamin Lewin
What is a repressor?	A multimeric DNA-binding protein interacts with polymerase.	Chapter 13, "Genes VI"
On justification		
Why is LacI a repressor?	Data resulting from mutations experiences	Jacob and Monod, Journal of Molecular Biology, 3:318-356, 1961.
Why are repressors represented in the base?	They are implicated in the expression of genes	
On modeling		
Why are 3 attributes "gene" distinguished in the description of an operon?	To allow the study of the expression of each gene	Guy Perrière PhD thesis, Claude Bernard University, Lyon, France.

Figure 2: Three kinds of questions, the users may ask about the content of a knowledge base with examples of answer and the sources used to answer. The sources are represented as references here, but the user needs the full text to answer his questions.

knowledge base. This external information is of different kinds (figure 2).

For example, the user needs the precise definition of a given term (its usual definition, and the developer's acceptance) to answer his questions on the meaning of the names used in the base. Furthermore, he needs more information on the concept expressed by this term, to be able to evaluate the place of the notion according to the peculiar point of view presented in the knowledge base.

To answer the knowledge validity questions, experimental data are required. For example, the repressor function of lacI has been established by mutant studies and enzymology experiments [6]. Furthermore, to justify the place of a piece of knowledge in the base, the developer's explanations or publications about this piece of knowledge related to the context of the base are required.

Finally, explaining the modeling choices requires a discussion with the developer or the consultation of documents in which some modeling decisions are made explicit such as in the PhD thesis of Guy Perrière in the case of ColiGene.

Thus, the information required is of three kinds: definitions, scientific justifications and modeling explanations, and it constitutes the "textual knowledge" in contrast to the "formal knowledge' contained in the knowledge base. This textual knowledge must be added to the formal base, in such a way that it really documents the content of the formal base

3 AN ENVIRONMENT FOR A DOCUMENTED KNOWLEDGE BASE

In the same way as in knowledge acquisition systems, where texts which allow to formalize knowledge are linked to the formal knowledge [5], we look for a structure that allows to link formal knowledge with a set of texts explaining and documenting the content of the base. During the consultation of a knowledge base, this textual knowledge must be available and easy to retrieve.

3.1 Documenting a knowledge base by means of a hypertext

A solution often chosen to document a knowledge base is to connect explanatory texts to the formal knowledge by using a hypertext structure. Thus, in expert systems, hypertext nodes are used to link textual explanations with rules [7] [3]. In the KASTLE project [11] for example, information given by the hypertext help the user to choose the right subroutine in a library of 900 FORTRAN subroutines.

Similarly, hypertext nodes have been connected to each class name and attribute of ColiGene, to improve its understandability (figure 3). Every new piece of text is turned into a hypertext automatically; this means that each text is searched for words which match class or attribute names. The node itself is named after the class or the attribute to which it is attached. Thus, navigating from a class to another, the user can read the associated text. Moreover, the user can choose to navigate among the objects or among the hypertext nodes, alternatively.

3.2 The inadequacy of the hypertext structure

A hypertext structure allows storage of textual information in a network of nodes and links. In such a case, it is only an implementation way of presenting textual information. Since all the nodes have the same level of importance, there is no conceptual organization and no way to look for a data concerning a specific question about a formal knowledge, whereas the explanation of a formal piece of knowledge may require numerous data and documents. For instance, the description of the regulation of the lactose operon by Jacob and Monod [6] refers to more than a hundred publications (in enzymology, genetics, molecular biology...); it is supported by a sum of experimental data and it requires the definition of several terms which are specific to regulation processes. The user may not be interested in all this information and may not want to browse it all. If a hypertext is used to represent information which explains the content of the formal base, the access to a piece of knowledge which matches the user's request is difficult.

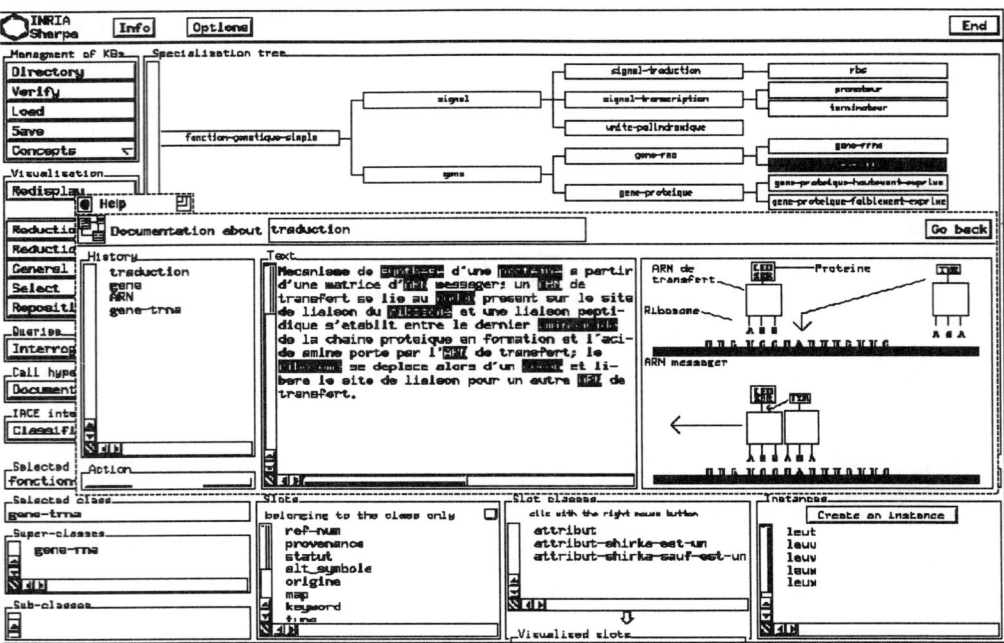

Figure 3: The hypertext in ColiGene. The user selects a class in the inheritance graph (upper window) and consults the associated node of the hypertext (lower window). Some words in the text are links to other nodes. From a hypertext node, it is possible to come back to the entity it is attached to. Only the highest levels of the specialization graph of ColiGene have been annotated, essentially for pedagogical purposes.

For this reason, the hypertext structure as it is used in ColiGene is insufficient to clarify the knowledge base contents. Thus, another way for documenting formal knowledge has to be found.

3.3 A formal base, a base of texts and a lexicon

To provide the user with some information relevant to his questions, i.e., terminological information and scientific documents, we propose an environment composed of three storage structures: a formal base, a textual base, and a lexicon.

- The **formal base** uses an object-based representation to model the knowledge about a specific phenomenon and supports various inference mechanisms as classification.

- The **textual base** contains texts extracted from publications or specifically written for the knowledge base. Each text is described by a set of keywords. These texts explain a specific aspect of a piece of knowledge, for example the value lacI of the attribute **repressor** of the instance **lac-operon** can be documented by texts about the constitutive mutation lacI or texts describing the interactions between lacI and the lactose. Furthermore, a developer can link together several pieces of texts using

hypertext links. The resulting hypertexts describe a specific notion from the point of view of a developer.

- The **lexicon** contains the terminological knowledge. It includes at least, the names used in the formal base (names of classes, attributes, names of instances) and a less specific vocabulary which allows to situate a term in a broader knowledge domain. It provides the definition of the formal terms. For example, an operon (name of a class in the formal base) can be defined in the lexicon as *"an unit of bacterial gene expression and regulation, including structural genes and control elements in DNA recognized by regulator gene products"*. The content of the lexicon is organized in different sub-domains. Its structure allows the user to navigate from term to term.

Thus, in this environment, each kind of information is stored and managed independently. Each structure provides the user with specific tools to find a piece of information. For example, the access to a definition is made by navigating in the lexicon structure whereas the access to a document is supported by keywords.

4 THE LEXICON IN A KNOWLEDGE BASE

In section 3, the lexicon has been described as the structure managing the definitions of the vocabulary used in the environment. But, the lexicon does not only provide the terminology knowledge, it also modifies the way a knowledge base is used. We will now describe the various roles played by the lexicon in a knowledge base environment.

4.1 A mediator for the knowledge of the base

On the one hand, the lexicon is the *repository* of all the terminology used in the knowledge base and of a part of the vocabulary of the domain. This terminology is organized according to conceptual criteria. Thus, the lexicon presents a model of the terminology used in the system. Consequently, the lexicon may help the user to understand the general organization of the knowledge domain to which belong the entities of the formal base.

On the other hand, Van de Riet [13] suggests to use a lexicon as a structure allowing the user to select the right term when he works with a computer tool or a database. For the point of view of Van de Riet, the lexicon will replace data dictionaries. In a knowledge base environment, the lexicon can be looked upon as a tool for connecting the terms employed in the formal base with the user vocabulary. The user is supposed to know some of the words belonging to the vocabulary of the domain treated in the knowledge base. In the lexicon, he can go from these words to more specific ones by browsing through a hierarchical graph of terms and so refine his request, furthermore he may navigate using topics different from the ones of the knowledge base (authors, type of methods...). At the end of his navigation, he reaches the relevant formal terms. Consequently, the lexicon is an *interface* between the user and the knowledge contained in the formal base.

4.2 A manager of the documents access

The lexicon may also contain the keywords associated to the documents of the base of texts and makes the structure of the indexing terms explicit and available to the user. Thus the lexicon provides a schema of concepts that describes the informative content of a document collection [1] [2]. Since, the formal terms and the keywords indexing the texts are put together and connected by semantic links, it is possible to browse between a piece of formal knowledge and a text, and to go back from a text to formal knowledge by using the lexicon. The lexicon plays the role of a *mediator* between the formal base and the textual knowledge.

4.3 How is the environment used: an example of consultation

We now illustrate how works a knowledge base environment in which the lexicon plays the different roles described above.

When the user consults the knowledge base, he has in mind a question expressed with his vocabulary and he wants to get a piece of formal knowledge that matches his request and probably several texts explaining and completing this piece of formal knowledge. In order to meet these requirements, the process of consulting is decomposed in different steps (figure 4).

- The first step consists in the conversion of the user question in a set of terms belonging to the formal terminology. The user makes this conversion by navigating through the lexicon. The terms in the lexicon are organized in a hierarchical graph in such a way that the user can refine his question. The leaves of the graph are the formal terms used in the formal base.

- Then, when the user has refined his request, he has access to a piece of formal knowledge. From this piece of knowledge, he can browse the content of the knowledge base by using the hierarchical graph or ask for more information on the formal knowledge.

- If the user wants more information on a formal piece of knowledge, he selects a term in the formal base. Then, he goes back to the lexicon, where the system provides the user with the list of keywords associated with this term during the indexing of the texts. The user may then compose a request of several keywords.

- When the user has chosen the relevant keywords, he has access to a specific piece of text or a hypertext explaining the notion he is looking for.

As shown by this scenario, the user uses the lexicon each time he is looking for more information. Thus, the lexicon is the interface with the user since it controls the interactions with the other structures. The definition of the different roles played by the lexicon in a consultation process allows to make some specifications on the environment.

5 SPECIFICATIONS AND PERSPECTIVES

The lexicon is a generic structure; its content and its organization depend on the content of the formal base, on the base of texts and on the developer needs. For example, a lexicon for a knowledge base as ColiGene must document 6,000 objects. This means that the lexicon must contains approximately 10,000 formal terms; we estimate that the description of an object requires two or three terms: one for the name of the object and one or two for the values of some attributes. Furthermore the same terms can be used in the description of several objects. The lexicon contains a number of keywords depending of the scale of the base of texts. The

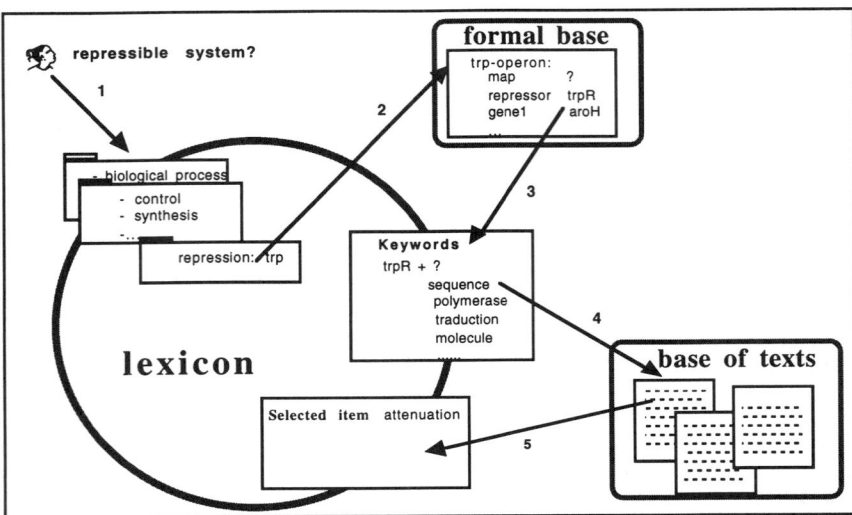

Figure 4: An example of consultation: (1)- A user has a question and convert it in a set of formal terms by navigating in the lexicon hierarchy. (2)-Then, he consults the part of the formal base content corresponding to his request. By selecting a term in the formal base, he goes back to the lexicon (3). Then, he can specify his request to access relevant documents by selecting a set of keywords in a list provided by the lexicon. This list groups together all the keywords associated with the selected term during the indexing of documents. The user selects several keywords and thus has access to a few number of documents relevant to his request (4). He can read these documents and if he wants more information, he can select a keyword in the index identifying the document he is reading. (5)- Thus, he goes back to the lexicon and can choose new keywords in the list associated with the new keyword he has selected.

number of context items depends upon the supposed knowledge of the future users.

Since the lexicon is an interface between a user and the environment, its design strongly depends on the point of view described in the formal base, and of the documents stored in the base of texts. However, some specifications on the lexicon and its connections to the other base can be made.

5.1 Specifications

The **lexicon content** is constituted of the terms used in the formal base, the keywords describing the documents of the base of texts and items (context items) used in order to define these two kinds of words. These words form several sub-domains in the lexicon : experimental methods, biological entities, biological functions, etc for a biological lexicon. The terms in a sub-domain are organized in a semantic graph. The context items are the roots of these graphs while the formal terms are the leaves. Thus the user refines his request by browsing through a graph. Furthermore, each term is defined by a set of features. These features are of three kinds: the *status of the term* i.e. formal term or keyword or context term, *derivative forms* i.e. synonyms, abbreviations and *semantic features* as composed-of, act-on and so on.

The **connections of the lexicon** with the formal base and the base of texts are realized by typed links so that the user can easily navigate from one base to another (figure 5). For example, the lexicon and the formal base are connected by a link `item-formal-term`. This means that when a user selects in the lexicon an item marked as being a formal term, he has access to the corresponding class or instance in the formal base. In the base of texts, every document is identified by a set of keywords. So, the connection between the lexicon and the base of texts is realized by the links set of `keywords-a-document` and links `keyword-keyword`.

5.2 Perspectives

We intend to achieve an implementation with an example in biology to see if the lexicon can really play the roles we have defined and whether its structure meets the users needs. The main problem met in the design of such an environment lies in the definition of the characteristics of the information which have to be in the lexicon and of those which have to be present in the knowledge base. The definition of these characteristics requires to clearly specify the role of each structure and then, their content. To simplify, the lexicon and the formal base can be seen as the result of two different analyses of a domain. In the knowledge base,

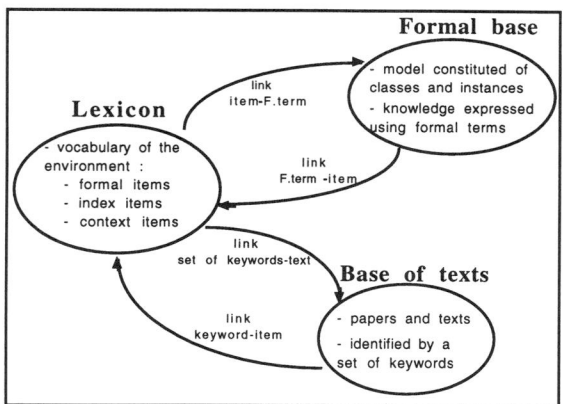

Figure 5: Structure of the knowledge base environment: the environment is constituted of three bases tightly connected by the mean of typed links. The lexicon supports the access to the content of the formal base and to the documents stored in the textual base. This access is made by selecting an item or a set of items in the lexicon.

only some domains of the knowledge are considered and knowledge is represented in order to allow inference mechanisms while the lexicon provides a general view of the domain and links various research domain. The lexicon can be seen as a didactic structure.

Furthermore, the contents of the formal base, of the lexicon and of the textual base can be modified during time, thus the system must maintain consistency between this three structures. This means that a name of the formal base must always been explained in the lexicon and whenever a document is deleted the keywords corresponding must also be deleted. A study of the modification process in such an environment must be made.

6   CONCLUSION

The improvement of knowledge exchange requires the development of powerful knowledge base environment in order to provide the user with documents and justifications related to the content of a formal base. Thus, we propose an environment containing three tightly connected structures: a formal base, a textual base and a lexicon. Each structure provides a different kind of information to the user; the formal base contains knowledge on which inferences mechanisms can be applied, the textual base provides all the information used in the modeling process and so explains the content of the base, the lexicon defines the terms used in the environment. Furthermore, the lexicon plays the role of an interface between the user and the knowledge base by connecting the user vocabulary with the terms used in the formal base and the documents of the textual base.   Such an environment provides a

generic structure allowing to document a formal base (object-oriented). The major difficulty of building such a knowledge base will be the elaboration of a consensual lexicon but this lexicon will improve the modeling process of the formal base.

The environment described above facilitates the understanding of the content of a base but a real sharing of knowledge also implies that anyone can model a new piece of knowledge. In this scope of sharing knowledge, structures as ontologies have been defined. An ontology is an explicit specification of a conceptualization. In our environment, the lexicon can be seen as an ontology which lack of formal axioms constraining the interpretation and well-formed use of the formal terms. These constraints are located in the object-oriented model in the form of a type system.

REFERENCES

1. Agosti M., Gradenigo G. and Marchetti P.G., *A Hypertext Environment for Interacting with Large Textual Databases*, Information Processing and management, 28(3):371-387, 1992.

2. Chen H., Lynch K.J., Basu K. and Dorbin T., *Generating, Integrating, and Activating Thesauri for Concept-Based Document Retrieval*, IEEE expert 8(2):25-34, 1993.

3. Gaines B.R. and Linster M., *Integrating a Knowledge Acquisition Tool, an Expert System Shell and a Hypermedia System*, International Journal of Expert Systems, vol 3 (2): 105-129, 1990.

4. Gruber T.R., *Toward Principles for the Design of Ontologies Used for Knowledge Sharing*, Technical Report KSL 93-04, Knowledge Systems Laboratory, Stanford University, 1993.

5. Hafner C.D., Baclawski K., Futrelle R.P., Fridman N. and Sampath S., *Creating a Knowledge Base of Biological Research Papers*, Second International Conference on Intelligent Systems for Molecular Biology. Standford, CA, August 14-17, 1994.

6. Jacob F. and Monod J., *Genetic Regulatory Mechanisms in the synthesis of proteins*, Journal of Molecular Biology,3:318-356, 1961.

7. Moia M., *Expert systems and Hypertext: a promising integration for training*, Computational Intelligence II, F. Gardin and G. Mauri (Eds), Elsevier Science Publishers B.V (North. Holland), pp 37-48, 1990.

8. Musen M.A., *Dimensions of Knowledge Sharing and Reuse*, Computers and Biomedical Research, 25:435-467,1992.

9. Perrière G., Dorkled F., Rechenmann F. and Gautier C., *Object-Oriented Knowledge Bases for the Analysis of Prokaryotic and Eukaryotic Genomes*, Proceedings of the First International Conference on Intelligent Systems for Molecular Biology. July 6-9, Bethesda, MD,1993.

10. Rechenmann F., *Building and Sharing Large Knowledge bases in Molecular Genetics*, Proceedings of International Conference on Building and Sharing of very

Large-Scale Knowledge Bases, Tokyo, Japan, december
93

11. Samuels P., *Hypertext for Computational Mathematics*,
In Artificial Intelligence in Mathematics. J.H. Johnson,
S. McKee and A. Velle(Eds), The institute of Mathemat-
ics and its applications. Oxford University Press,1994.

12. Schmeltzer O., Médigue C., Uvietta P., Rechenmann F.,
Dorkled F., Perrière G. and Gautier C., *Building Large
Knowledge Bases in Molecular Biology*, Proceedings of
the First International Conference on Intelligent Systems
for Molecular Biology. July 6-9, Bethesda, MD,1993.

13. Van de Riet R.P, *Linguistic Instruments in Knowledge
Engineering. A research proposal and some experiments*,
Proceedings of International Conference on Building and
Sharing of very Large-Scale Knowledge Bases, Tokyo,
Japan, dec 93.

Towards Very Large Knowledge Bases
N.J.I. Mars, Ed.
IOS Press, 1995

289

Evaluation and Assessment of the Knowledge Sharing Technology

Asunción Gómez-Pérez

Knowledge Systems Laboratory, Stanford University
Palo Alto, CA, 94304, USA
gomez@hpp.stanford.edu

Natalia Juristo and **Juan Pazos**
Laboratorio de Inteligencia Artificial
Madrid, Spain

ABSTRACT

There is no set of general guidelines for evaluating Knowledge Sharing Technology (KST) and specific ideas for evaluating user-independent ontologies. Instead of starting from the beginning, this paper discusses similarities and differences between knowledge bases (KB) and ontologies. The idea is to learn from Knowledge Base Systems' evaluation and assessment by picking up some successful ideas and adapting them to the domain of the ontologies. We also learn from its mistakes by avoiding them. The paper also describes how different agents that use ontologies with different aims have different concerns in the evaluation and assessment processes. Definitions and criteria for the terms: "Evaluation", "Verification", "Validation" and "Assessment" in the knowledge sharing domain are also given.

1 INTRODUCTION

Ontologies are essential for both building intelligent systems and enabling interoperation of agents. In this sense, judging an ontology is just as necessary for knowledge representation as getting a thorough inspection before purchasing a car. Just as one does not buy a car without first taking it to a mechanic for a checkup to ensure that the car is mechanically sound, it is unwise to publish your ontology, or to implement a software application that relies on ontologies written by others without first evaluating and assessing the definitions and axioms in the ontologies. The main problem appears to be: there is no set of general and specific ideas for judging user-independent ontologies in their own whole life cycle and when they are reused and shared. This gap is due to a vicious circle problem: almost anyone evaluates and assesses KST because of it is not still required; almost anyone asks for KST

evaluation and assessment because of nobody knows how to perform it; and, finally, nobody performs KST evaluation and assessment because of nobody did it before. This paper takes the following approach to break this vicious circle: if an ontology is like a KB, evaluation and assessment of the ontology should be done in the same way as Knowledge Based Systems (KBS) evaluation and assessment. However, if they are different, a conceptual framework should be created for their evaluation and assessment.

Since ontologies differ from KBs, the purpose of this paper is to take advantage of KBS evaluation, verification, validation and assessment in order to learn from successes and mistakes. The main idea is that it is not necessary to reinvent the wheel. We learn from KBSs's successes by picking up some successful ideas and adapting them to the domain of ontologies. We also learn from KBS mistakes by avoiding them. The following sections describe the outcome of this research:

- In section Two, we summarize the differences and similarities between ontologies and KBs.

- Section Three summarizes some KBS evaluation, verification, validation and assessment ideas.

- Section Four analyzes what can be learnt from KBSs's successes and mistakes.

- Section Five describes three kinds of agents dealing with the evaluation of the knowledge sharing technology. It also covers: what each agent should evaluate; when and where it should make the evaluation; and the benefits of the evaluation of the KST from different point of views.

- Finally, sections Six to Nine suggest definitions and criteria for the terms: "Evaluation", "Verification", "Validation" and "Assessment" in the knowledge sharing domain.

2 KNOWLEDGE BASES VERSUS ONTOLOGIES

The word ontology is a fashionable word in the artificial intelligence community. Sometimes the term is used with the meaning of a KB because both define, represent, and gather knowledge about concepts and their relations in a machine-readable language for an abstract or concrete domain. This section suggests definitions for these concepts as well as differences and similarities between them.

2.1 Definitions

A KB is the knowledge module of a KBS. It contains abstract and specific knowledge of a particular subject in a machine-readable format. The knowledge in the KB can be declarative or procedural, shallow or deep. The inference engine works with the information gathered in the knowledge module to create intelligent behavior.

As libraries of domain-independent and abstract definitions that can be used for different purposes in different applications, Gruber [8] defines ontologies as an explicit specification of a conceptualization. From the point of view of knowledge reusability, ontologies avoid the need to build a KB from scratch by allowing KBS developers to assemble reusable components [17]. Developing and implementing ontologies for reusing knowledge requires the development of methodologies, techniques and more powerful tools that coherently and consistently integrate their definitions into the entire life cycle of the KBS by developing technology that: (1) supports, checks and makes effective this integration; and (2) allows the integration of different solutions provided by different families of ontologies [5].

¿From the viewpoint of knowledge sharability, ontologies can be used by software agents [8, 10, 12, 17] that interoperate. From this point of view, there are many complementary definitions. Gruber [8] defines an ontology as the vocabulary with which queries and assertions are exchanged among agents; according to Gruber and Olsen [10], the ontology vocabulary defines the ontological commitments among agents that are agreements to use the shared vocabulary in a coherent and consistent manner; Guha and Lenat [12] view ontologies as foundational knowledge shared by agents to enable them to communicate their specialized knowledge; and Gómez-Pérez [5] sees ontologies as the platforms that reduce semantic differences among agents by establishing common vocabularies and semantic interpretations of terms.

2.2 Similarities and Differences

Ontologies and KBs have in common that both gather information that evolves over time. The term "knowl-edge" refers to the information in a KB, while "definition" refers to that of an ontology.

First, the generality of the information is the most important difference between ontologies and KBs. The definitions of ontologies should be more general than the knowledge of a KB, so that they can be shared among KBS. Definitions of ontologies must be independent of the agent (both KBS and software agent) that will reuse or share them.

Second, the KB of a KBS is separated from its inference engine. The inference engine decides when and how the information of the KB must be used to derive new conclusions. Ontologies differ from KBs because they don't usually have reasoning methods that take advantage of the ontologies' definitions and make them more understandable. However, ontologies written in CycL [16] can be used by a number of special-purpose inference schemas.

Third, the expressiveness and semantics of the target machine-readable language used in the formalization of a KB influence the quantity and quality of the knowledge in a KB. Ontologies should be written in an expressive, declarative, portable, domain-independent, and semantically well-defined machine-readable language that is independent of the final target machine-readable language of the application that will reuse or share the definitions in the application domain. Ontolingua's ontologies [8] written in KIF [4] provide these features, and Ontolingua also provides the software environment that transforms KIF definitions to many different target languages that can be used to build KBS.

Fourth, a KBS reasons with the knowledge stored in the KB to carry out tasks that are performed by experts in specific domains. The evaluation of KBS performance requires an understanding of how experts act and how their performance can be evaluated. How can we measure performance of ontologies without an inference engine to work with? A first approach consists of evaluating the performance of the ontologies in terms of the number of successful KBS that reuse their definitions, or by the amount of successful interoperation among agents. A set of competency questions [11] could be used for evaluating the performance of the ontologies used in different tasks in some domain.

Two important additional problems in KBS are the absence of a well-defined and well-structured set of requirements at the beginning of the development process, and the continuous changes in the requirements throughout the whole life cycle of the KBS. These problems are not as marked in ontologies because of a high level of abstraction about the useful vocabulary in the domain is required before building ontologies for a given domain. So, ontology requirements should be more complete and precise than KBS requirements are. For example, the first requirements for a domain-independent ontology about numbers could be: a list of kinds of numbers, a list of admissible operations on numbers, a list of comparisons between numbers, and constants used in this domain. Therefore, it would be easy to express these known requirements in a formal language, yielding a set of formal specifications for the ontology.

Finally, any engineering development requires the definition and standardization of a life cycle that goes from requirement definition to maintenance of the finished product. KBS has methodologies [14, 18, 22, 27, 28, 29] that guide its developments. Ontologies, as any engineering development, need the definition and standardization of a life cycle and methodologies and techniques that drive their development.

3 KBS: ASSESSMENT, EVALUATION, VERIFICATION, VALIDATION

A study [6] of the evaluation, verification, validation and assessment ideas in KBS preceded the evaluation, verification, validation and assessment of KST in order to learn from KBS successes and mistakes.

Technical evaluation "versus" user's evaluation. The majority of the authors [3, 13, 24, 26] consulted say that it is necessary to distinguish between evaluation of the intrinsic properties of a KBS and the evaluation of its actual use and utility within a given organization. O'Leary [21] and Guida and Mauri [13] call the former "Evaluation" and the latter "Assessment".

Related to Terminology and Definitions of terms, there are a set of terms related to the judge of a KBS, and they are: "Evaluation", "Verification", "Validation" and "Assessment". Although the set of common terms is identified, there is no consensus on their definitions. Hoppe and Meseguer [15] comment on several definitions and they make a proposal for a common terminology in this field.

In relation to the criteria for evaluating, verifying, validating and assessing, the majority of the authors consulted give criteria and methods to evaluate, verify, validate and assess KBS, some authors only offer criteria or methods (rather than both), and a few provide neither criteria nor methods. For authors who offer criteria attached to a term, there are a large number of qualitative and quantitative criteria to evaluate, verify, validate and assess KBS. The most of authors define these criteria as independence of the language used to formalize the KB and independence of the inference engine that works with this language. Others make definitions depending on the formalism used to express knowledge in the KB. The main dilemma is the absence of agreement on: (1) identification of the criteria attached to a given term; (2) definitions of the criteria; and (3) the phases of the KBS life cycle in which they should be applied.

With regards to the methods for evaluating, verify-ing, validating and assessing, for authors who provide methods attached to a given criterion, they often are complementary and independent of the formalism used to build the KB. However, the majority of the verification methods only work for KB formalized as rules.

Concerning methodologies [2, 13] and tools [19, 23], evaluation of a KBS is an iterative process [3, 13, 20, 24] that is performed throughout all the different stages of its life cycle. The lack of a complete, consistent, and precise definition of KBS requirements forces Knowledge Engineers (KE) to carry out evaluation from the start of KBS development until the maintenance of the finished product. For this reason, evaluation must follow an order, it has to be planned, and it must be controlled to reduce the cost (time and money) of the final system.

In relation to the measures of the results from empirical evaluation [24], KBS can be evaluated in an informal and qualitative manner, or by using quantitative methods [1, 20, 25].

4 WHAT CAN WE LEARN FROM KBS SUCCESSES AND MISTAKES?

Technical evaluation "versus" user's evaluation. A characterization of KST' users is needed in order to figure out what each one of them attempts to do with this technology. Section 5 identify three kind of agents dealing with KST: ontologies development team, KBS development team and software agent development team.

Terminology and Definitions. A set of terms need to be identified in the KST domain to provide a standard definition for these terms. As a starting point, Sections 6 to 9 provide definitions of the terms "Evaluation", "Verification", "Validation" and "Assessment".

Criteria to evaluate, verify, validate and assess. A set of criteria and definitions of these criteria will provide some guidance in the judge of KST. For each term identified, we offer some criteria that allow us to identify mistakes.

Methods to evaluate, verify, validate and assess. For each criterion, we recommend establish a set of methods that allow us to detect mistakes. Different methods should be provided for ontologies written in different languages.

Methodologies and Tools. For KST evaluators, the main idea to be taken from KBS is the need for developing and integrating methods and tools that allow one to judge KST during their whole life cycle.

Measures of the results. At the same time that KST is evaluated, measures of the results should be required to estimate the efficiency of the methods used.

5 WHO JUDGES KST?

Who evaluates KST is tightly related to what can be evaluated, when to evaluate and where the activity is carried out. While answering these questions, we discuss why it is important to evaluate this technology whatever its uses are.

5.1 Ontology development team evaluation

Before knowledge sharing technology leaves the academic or industrial lab, the ontology development team must guarantee to the end users some well-defined properties in the ontology definitions, software environments and documentation. In order to detect as soon as possible wrong, incomplete, or missed definitions or axioms, or wrong, incomplete, or missed functionalities in the software environments and in its documentation, development team evaluation should iteratively perform this technical evaluation during the products' life cycle. Evaluation of other expert development teams would help to ensure the quality, the abstraction and the domain-independence of the definitions and axioms.

5.2 Final users assessment

The knowledge factory idea allows different people (whether they are related or not to the development team) not only to build their own ontologies but to put them to work in real applications. The number of successful applications that use knowledge sharing technology will be the measure of the success of this technology.

The opinions of KBS and software agent development teams for or against the KST will be the key factor in companies' perception of that technology. Developing and implementing ontologies for reusing and sharing knowledge requires assessment by the final users: KBS development team and software agent development team.

5.2.1 KBS Development team Assessment

When KE decide to reuse components to build a KBS, they are looking for some definitions that simplify the development process of the new system and reduce its cost (in terms of time and money). Before reusing definitions and axioms from ontologies, the KE team assessment is focused on:

1. The understanding, usability, abstraction, quality, granularity, and portability of the definitions and axioms given by the ontology.

2. Features of the software environment that help the team to understand and locate the definitions in the set of ontologies. Software agents like Ontology Brokers may help the KE to find, understand and reuse a particular definition in the future.

3. Documentation (tutorial, case studies, etc.) that reduces the cost required to learn and assimilate this new technology.

4. Methodologies and tools that make possible the integration of the ontology definitions with the whole life cycle of the KBS.

5. Have the ontologies been technically evaluated?

So, although a technically well-evaluated ontology will not guarantee the absence of errors in the integration of its definitions with the KB of a KBS, it will make the process easier.

5.3 Software Agents Development Team Assessment

Since ontology definitions are the platforms that enable agents to share knowledge, inferences are always performed by the agent making the query and by the agent giving the answers. Given a technically well evaluated ontology, software agent development team assessment is focused on: (1) the correctness of the protocols used in the communication between agents and the ontologies; and (2) how the software used in the communication between agents and ontologies solves inconsistencies, ambiguities, omissions, and errors between human or agent requests/answers and ontology definitions.

6 EVALUATION OF KST

Evaluation means to make a technical judgment of the ontologies, their associated software environments, and documentation with respect to a frame of reference[1] during each phase and between phases of their life cycle. In this paper, the term "Evaluation" subsumes the terms "Verification" and "Validation", and it refers to the technical activity performed by the KST development team.

6.1 Evaluation of the ontologies

This activity is divided into evaluation of:

- Each individual definition and axiom.

- Collections of definitions and axioms that are stated explicitly in the definitions in the ontology.

- Definitions that are imported from other logical theories.

- Axioms that can be inferred using collections of definitions and axioms.

6.2 Evaluation of the Software Environments

It judges software used to build, reuse, and share ontologies such as: the graphic and text user interface used to browse and edit definitions, parsers that check the syntax of the definitions and some basic semantics, translators for some target knowledge representation languages, software required to install the environment, and so on.

---

[1]A frame of reference can be: requirements specifications, competency questions [11], and the real-world.

6.3 Evaluation of the Documentation

It is related to the judge of the documentation of the ontologies, software environments, tutorials and examples of real applications built by reusing and sharing this technology.

7 VERIFICATION OF KST

Verification refers to the technical process that guarantees the correctness of an ontology, its associated software environments, and documentation with respect to a frame of reference during each phase and between phases of the product's life cycle.

7.1 Verification of the Ontology

It refers to building the ontology correctly, that is, ensuring that its definitions correctly satisfy its requirements, its competence questions or perform correctly in the real world. Ontology verification is orthogonal to the use of the definitions by any KBS or software agent. To verify an ontology we have to determine: (1) the correctness of definitions and axioms by figuring out what the ontology explicitly defines, does not define or defines incorrectly, and (2) to determine the scope of definitions and axioms by figuring out what can be inferred, cannot be inferred, or can be inferred incorrectly. To guarantee that an ontology is well-verified, we have to verify its architecture, its lexis and syntax, and its content [7].

7.1.1 Verification of the Architecture

At this point, we look if the structure of an ontology has been developed following the principles of design of the environment in which the ontology is included. For example, ontologies built in the Ontolingua environment should satisfy the five design criteria given by Gruber [9].

7.1.2 Verification of the Lexis and syntax

The ontology definitions must be lexically and syntactically correct. The environment should provide a scanner to detect that the lexical structure of the expressions is correct, and a parser to detect that its syntactic structure is correct too. It is particularly important that the lexical and syntax analyzer components of the software environment rigorously implement the definitions of the lexis and grammar rules for the portable language. Failure to do this will allow the writing of non-portable definitions. As example we have the use of wrong keywords in formal definitions.

7.1.3 Verification of the Content

It is concerned with the analysis of completeness, consistency, conciseness, expandability, and robustness of the definitions and axioms that are explicitly stated in the ontology, and the inferences that can be drawn from those definitions and axioms. Since ontologies are developed incrementally by adding new definitions and modifying the old ones, one of the most important problems is to guarantee these criteria in the definitions from the start, during each stage and between stages of the development process.

Consistency refers to whether it is possible to get contradictory conclusions from valid input data. There are different ways in which inconsistencies appear in an ontology. You can find logically inconsistencies and semantically inconsistencies. Both kind of inconsistencies can be explicitly set out in the definitions of the ontology as well as they can be inferred by using other definitions or axioms belonging to the logical theory. An Ontology is semantically consistent if and only if its definitions are semantically consistent. A given definition in the ontology is semantically consistent [5] if and only if:

- It is individually consistent, that means, that: (1) the formal definition is itself consistent, (2) the meaning of the formal as well as the informal definition are consistent with the real world and consistent with each other.

- There is no inferred inconsistency, that is there are not contradictory sentences that may be inferred using other definitions and axioms.

Although ontologies differ from KBs, both have a common fundamental problem. Ontologies and KBs are often, by nature, incomplete, as it is impossible to capture all that it is known about the real world in a finite structure. What is more, even if an ontology of a particular domain can be complete in principle, it is usually impossible to prove that an ontology is complete; one can usually only prove it to be incomplete given certain testing criteria for completeness. An ontology is semantically complete [5] if and only if:

- All that is supposed to be in the ontology is explicitly set out in it, or can be inferred using other definitions and axioms.

- Each individual definition is complete.

Conciseness refers to if all the information gathered in the ontology is useful and precise. Conciseness doesn't imply absence of redundancies. Sometimes, some degree of controlled redundancy can be useful in the definitions. We can guarantee that a given definition in an ontology is concise if we avoid redundancies in its formal as well as informal definitions. Second, explicit redundancies don't exist among definitions. Third, redundancies cannot be derived using axioms attached to other definitions. Finally, the set of properties in the definition of a class are precisely and exactly defined. The natural language explanation of the definitions and examples are not considered redundant knowledge of the formal definitions.

Expandability refers to the effort required in adding new definitions to an ontology, as well as the effort needed to add new information to a definition, without altering the set of well-defined properties that are already guaranteed after the ontologies verification process.

Robustness relates how small changes in a given definition alter the set of well defined properties that are already guaranteed.

After modifying a definition, expandability and robustness must guarantee that: (1) the architecture of the ontology and definitions are still sound, (2) the definitions are lexically and syntactically correct, and (3) the ontology and its definitions are concise, consistent and complete.

7.2 Verification of the Software

It refers to building the software correctly. Software that can be shown to be able to build, reuse and share definitions and axioms correctly and completely implements its requirements is said to be verified. Software engineering methodologies, techniques and tools provide the appropriate framework to verify the KST software in each stage and between stages of its life cycle.

7.3 Verification of the Documentation

It refers to building the documents correctly. It seeks to guarantee that all the required documents have been written, that nothing has been overlooked in each document, and that the documents evolve in step with the knowledge and software environment in each phase and between phases of the product's life cycle. If WWW documents are indexed automatically by using a program, the verification of the documentation must guarantee that there are no semantic inconsistencies, context and morphological mistakes in the indexes.

8 VALIDATION OF KST

Validation guarantees that the ontologies, the software development environments, and the documentation correspond to the systems that they are supposed to represent. It is a technical evaluation performed by the ontology development team in each stage and between stages of the KST life cycle.

8.1 Validation of the Ontologies

It refers to whether the meaning of the ontology definitions really represent the real world for which it was created. The validation of the ontologies against the frame of reference provides information about whether the ontology definitions are necessary and sufficient to represent the tasks and their solutions for different uses.

8.2 Validation of the Software

It refers to whether the behavior of the software environment is adequate to perform the tasks given in its requirements with an acceptable level of accuracy. Software engineering methodologies, techniques and tools provide the appropriate framework to validate the KST software at each stage and between stages of its life cycle.

8.3 Validation of the Documentation

It refers to whether the natural language documentation of the ontologies and the natural language documentation of the software environment have the same meaning as the meaning of the ontologies and software environments. Validation of the documentation must be performed in step with validation of the definitions and validation of the software environments during their life cycles.

9 ASSESSMENT OF KST

Assessment judges the usability and utility of the ontologies, software environments, and their documentation when they are reused and shared.

9.1 Assessment of the Ontologies

It refers to the understanding, usability, generality, granularity, quality, portability, incrementalism, maintainability and uniformity of the definitions and axioms given by an ontology.

9.2 Assessment of the Software

It refers to the robustness, accuracy, portability or transferability, extendibility, reliability, computational efficiency of the software environments used to build, reuse and share ontologies.

9.3 Assessment of the Documentation

It refers to whether the natural language documents are self-explanatory, that is, if they provide precise and sufficient information to learn and use this technology efficiently.

10 CONCLUSIONS

The analysis of KBS evaluation and assessment enabled us to identify the main points in the evaluation and assessment of the knowledge sharing technology: technical evaluation versus user evaluation, the need to provide a terminology and definitions, the need to identify some criteria to perform the evaluation and assessment, the need to perform an iterative evaluation during the whole KST life cycle, and the need to build methods, methodologies and tools that support this process.

As KST is used by several agents, several evaluation types are required. This paper described three agents and how each agent has different concerns in the evaluation process; what should be evaluated by each agent; and when and where evaluation should be made.

We proposed definitions of the terms "Evaluation", "Verification", "Validation" and "Assessment" in the KST domain. We also provided some criteria for verifying the content of the ontologies.

The paper also points out some future work:

- A set of iterative methods that are integrated with the ontologies' life cycle are required to establish how and when evaluation activities should be performed during their life cycle. Although the iteration of the evaluation process is a key idea in order to detect mistakes as soon as possible, the main question is: how can an iterative evaluation be carried out throughout the whole ontologies life cycle if the ontology life cycle has not been yet defined?

- A set of evaluation tools is necessary to increase the performance of the evaluation process. We are developing now in Madrid a tool called ONE-T (ONtologies Evaluation Tool).

- There is a need for some recommendations and ontology-brokers to help end users to choose the best definitions for their systems. So, criteria that compare different definitions and axioms and characterize the end user are required before these recommendations.

ACKNOWLEDGMENT

This work was funded for the Spanish Ministry of Education and Science. Thanks to Bob Engelmore, James Rice and Lee Brownston for their comments.

REFERENCES

1. Adlassing, K.P. "The Application of ROC Curves to the Evaluation of Medical Expert Systems". In Proc. 7th International Conference of the European Federation for Medical Informatics. Rome. 1987. pp: 951-956.

2. Benbasat I; Dhaliwal, J.S. "A framework for the Validation of Knowledge Acquisition". Knowledge Acquisition. Vol. 1, No. 2, 1989, pp: 215-233.

3. Berry, C.D.; Hart, A. E. "Evaluating Expert Systems". Expert Systems. Vol. 7, No. 4, November , 1990, pp: 199-207.

4. Genesereth, M.R.; Fikes, R.E. "Knowledge Interchange Format". Version 3.0. Reference Manual. Report Logic-92-1. Computer Science Department. Stanford University. Stanford, CA, 94305. 1992.

5. Gómez-Pérez, "A. Some Ideas and Examples to Evaluate Ontologies". To appear in CAIA'95. The 11th IEEE Conference On Artificial Intelligence for Application. February. 1995.

6. Gómez-Pérez, A. "From Knowledge Based Systems to Knowledge Sharing Technology: Evaluation and Assessment". KSL-94-73. Knowledge Systems Laboratory. Stanford University. CA. 1994.

7. Gómez-Pérez, A. "Criteria to Verify Knowledge Sharing Technology". KSL-95-10. Knowledge Systems Laboratory. Stanford University. CA. 1994.

8. Gruber, T. "A Translation Approach to Portable Ontology Specifications". Knowledge Acquisition. Vol. 5. 1993. pp: 199-220.

9. Gruber, T. "Toward Principles for the Design of Ontologies Used for Knowledge Sharing". Technical Report KSL 93-04. Knowledge Systems Laboratory. Stanford University. CA. 1993.

10. Gruber, T; Olsen, G. "An Ontology for Engineering Mathematics". In Jon Doyle, Piero Torasso, & Erik Sandewall, Ed., Fourth International Conference on Principles of Knowledge Representation and Reasoning, Gustav Stresemann Institut, Bonn, Germany, Morgan Kaufmann, 1994.

11. Gruninger, M.; Fox, M.S. "The role of Competency Questions in Enterprise Engineering". IFIP WG5.7 Workshop on Benchmarking. Theory and Practice. Trondheim, Norway, 1994.

12. Guha, R.V.; Lenat, D. "Enabling Agents to work Together". Communications of the ACM. July 1994. Vol. 37. N0 7. pp: 127-142.

13. Guida, G.; Mauri, G. "Evaluating Performance and Quality of Knowledge-Based Systems: Foundation and Methodology". IEEE Transactions on Knowledge and Data Engineering. Vol. 5, No. 2, April, 1993. pp: 204-224.

14. Harmon, P.; King, D. "Expert Systems: Artificial Intelligence in Business and Industry". New York. NY. John Wiley & Sons. 1990.

15. Hope, T.; Meseguer, P. "VVT Terminology: A Proposal". IEEE Expert. Vol. 8, No. 3, June. 1993. pp: 48-55

16. Lenat, D.B., Guha, R.V.; "Building Large Knowledge-Based Systems: Representation and Inference in the Cyc Project". Addison-Wesley Publishing Company, Inc. CA. 1990.

17. Neches, R.; Fikes, R.; Finin, T.; Gruber, T.; Patil, R.; Senator, T.; Swartout, W.R. "Enabling Technology for Knowledge Sharing". AI Magazine. Winter 1991. pp: 36-56.

18. Mate, J.L.; Pazos, J. "Ingenieria del Conocimiento". Cordoba, Argentina. 1988.

19. Mengshoel, O.J.; Delab, S. "Knowledge Validation: Principles and Practice". IEEE Expert. Vol. 8, No. 3, June. 1993, pp: 62-68.

20. O'Keefe, R. M.; Balci, O.; Smith E.P. "Validating Expert System Performance". IEEE Expert. Winter. 1987. pp: 81-89.

21. O'Leary, D.E. "Validation of Expert Systems-With Applications to Auditing and Accounting Expert Systems. Decision Science". Vol. 18. No. 3. 1987. pp: 468-486.

22. Parsaye, K.; Chignell, M. "Expert Systems for Experts. In Measuring Expert Systems Performance". John Wiley. 1988. pp: 365-374.

23. Polat, F. Guvenir, H. A. "UVT: A Unification-Based Tool for Knowledge Base Verification". IEEE Expert. Vol. 8, No. 3, June. 1993, pp: 69-75.

24. Preece, A.D. "Towards a Methodology for Evaluation Expert Systems". Expert Systems. Vol. 7, No. 4, Nov. 1990, pp: 215-223.

25. Reggia, J.A. "Evaluation of Medical Expert Systems: A case of Study in Performance Assessment". In Proc. 9th Annual Symposium on Computer Applications in Medical Care. (SCAMC 85). 1985. pp: 287-291.

26. Sharma, R. S.; Conrath, D.W. "Evaluating Expert Systems: the Socio-Technical Dimension of Quality". Expert Systems, Vol. 9, No. 3, August, 1992. pp: 125-137.

27. Taki, I. "Expert Model for Knowledge Acquisition in the ICOT". Technical Presentation at Computer Science Department. Carnegie Mellon University, Pittsburgh, PA. 1986.

28. Waterman, D.A. "A Guide to Expert Systems". Reading MA: Addison-Wesley. 1986.

29. Wiellinga, B.J.; Schreiber, A.T.; Breuker, J.A. KADS: "A Modeling Approach to Knowledge Engineering". KADS-II/T1.1/PP/UVA/008/1.0.ESPRIT-KADSII. Amsterdam University. 1991.

Knowledge Dissemination = Digital Libraries + Collaboration Technology

Su-Shing Chen*
National Science Foundation
Arlington, VA, USA
schen@nsf.gov

ABSTRACT

In global information infrastructures, digital libraries will play an essential role in disseminating knowledge to the general public on the information superhighway. This paper describes a general framework for digital libraries and a specific model of knowledge dissemination using digital libraries and collaboration technology.

1 INTRODUCTION

In 1945, Vannevar Bush (President Roosevelt's Science Adviser) wrote an article in "Atlantic Monthly" about the need to develop and implement information systems — "memex" — which can manage and disseminate the vast amount of accumulated knowledge by humans [1]. After almost 50 years, his vision has not been fully realized, while the information age is generating an ever growing glut of information. In the US, several efforts are currently being made to advance the research and development of large information infrastructures and their applications [3]. The main objective is to provide knowledge dissemination for the general public of various kinds of information resources. The NSF/ARPA/NASA "Research on Digital Libraries" Initiative is one of such activities [7].

This paper describes a general framework for digital libraries and a specific model of knowledge dissemination using digital libraries and collaboration technology [10], [11]. Intuitively a digital library is defined as a collection of networked, distributed, and heterogeneous information bases, including databases, knowledge bases, information repositories, and bulletin boards, for access, dissemination, generation, storing,

---

The opinions expressed in this paper are those of the author and do not represent the views of the National Science Foundation.

processing, transmission, and receiving of information in general and knowledge in particular. Since traditional libraries have played a unique role in knowledge dissemination to the general public for ages, the future impact of digital libraries to education and learning will be significant and perhaps unprecedented [6].

Disseminating knowledge based on digital libraries expands traditional knowledge bases in significant ways. The first is the human-human, human-computer, and computer-computer interactions with the digital libraries as knowledge resources. The second is the shift of reasoning to humans from computers. Traditional knowledge bases are intelligent computer systems with automated reasoning schemes and knowledge resources which provide knowledge to queries of human users, who are not included in the reasoning process. On the contrary, the collaboration technology, e.g., CSCW (Computer-Supported Cooperative Work), supports a human user or a group of human users interactively in their access of knowledge with digital libraries. In this paradigm shift, artificial intelligence techniques are still essential to this model of knowledge dissemination. For examples, knowledge representation, automated reasoning, and knowledge base management are crucial to the ontology part of knowledge dissemination (See the section on a common ontology of information spaces).

2 WHAT IS KNOWLEDGE?

Why are very large-scale automated knowledge bases not the best model for knowledge dissemination? Some arguments have been made in the papers that appeared in [15]. There are two major difficulties with the knowledge base approach. First, the complexity of automated reasoning schemes is a major issue. Recently, several artificial intelligence problems have been proven to be NP-complete [13], [14]. Although NP-completeness has not been shown to directly cause the "scalability" problem of artificial intelligence, the "scalability" problem has been the main concern of automated reasoning in large-scale applications. Second, any fixed knowledge representation scheme imposes a brittle structure on knowledge in general, although this is necessary for automated reasoning by computers. But human knowledge should not be bounded by a fixed brittle knowledge representation scheme.

In a paper of [15], Fujisawa discussed human knowledge from a philosophical perspective. He was concerned that any knowledge representation scheme might not be adequate to encode human knowledge, because human knowledge might be broader and deeper than what existing knowledge representation schemes can encode. For example, we do not know exactly how human organizes and understands knowledge. This leads to the question: what is knowledge? Before considering this question, we may ask an easier question: what is information?

According to C. Shannon's information theory, information is the encoded data and messages in bits and bytes. Information is something that computers and communication channels can handle. But, it is something without semantic meanings attached. Knowledge is information with semantic meanings attached. Apparently, semantic meanings are the deep roots of human knowledge. And, different persons have different ways of organizing and understanding knowledge, and different interpretations in semantic meanings.

Knowledge dissemination must consider this human factor — semantic meanings. This paper proposes a more flexible approach, that is
knowledge dissemination = digital libraries + collaboration technology.
The human factor is treated by collaboration technology — a technology for human-human, human-computer, and computer-computer interactions (See the section on collaboration technology). And the information is provided by digital libraries. In order to support this human factor, digital libraries must have some capabilities of dealing with semantic meanings.

3 A KNOWLEDGE DISSEMINATION MODEL

Although Vannevar Bush's idea of "memex" did not yield practical value today, his vision has inspired the development of several disciplines: information retrieval, information science, and computer-supported cooperative work (CSCW). As early as the 1950s, research has been funded for handling scientific information by the NSF. From the 1950s to today, we have seen advances in high bandwidth communication networks, information retrieval, human-computer interface, knowledge representation, collaboration technology, database management systems, and multi-media computing. These technologies are mature enough so

that the realization of Vannevar Bush's vision seems to be quite feasible now. This knowledge dissemination model is a convergent form of these technologies.

This knowledge dissemination model consists of two components: digital libraries and collaboration technology (Detailed discussion will be given in the next two sections). The information space of digital libraries is the knowledge resources that human users access to. The computer-supported workspace of collaboration technology is where human users learn knowledge and solve problems. The interaction of these two spaces in a seamless fashion holds the key to this model. Preferably, a single user interface will connect the two spaces for human users. In digital libraries, the information retrieval and management system responds to user queries for information access and other user applications. In collaboration tools, accessed information is interleaved with user workspace for learning and problem solving. Since collaboration tools serve a group of users, retrieved information and collaborated work serve the whole group.

In digital libraries, information access requires distributed search of various heterogeneous information resources in the information space. From various resources, information needs to be integrated into a coherent piece. In collaboration tools, information is shared among a group of users. Often the retrieved information has to be tailored for different users, although they may be working on a common set of problems. In the sections on intelligent agents and common ontology, we shall describe how these can be achieved. This is where artificial intelligence techniques come in, including knowledge representation, automated reasoning, and knowledge base management.

4 A FRAMEWORK OF DIGITAL LIBRARIES

A digital library contains a collection of networked, heterogeneous information bases $\{I_n\}$ which may be databases, knowledge bases, information repositories, bulletin boards, and other information resources. The union $I = \cup I_n$ of all the information bases is called the information space of the information infrastructure. The users of the information infrastructure navigate through the information space I to access information and to solve problems.

An information base I_n contains information objects $\{o_{n_\alpha}\}$, (n_α is the enumeration index of objects in the n-th information base I_n) which are characterized by their names, types, fields, and contents. Names, types, and fields are used for identification and indexing. Contents include texts, images, graphics, charts, audio, video, tables, and etc.

To illustrate how information objects are indexed and retrieved, we consider a full text document or a book. The title, the author, key words, and subject classifications will provide the names, types, and identification and indexing fields of the document or the book. Moreover, text segmentation algorithms will divide a full text into objects, from words and phrases to sections and chapters. For search and retrieval, a word or a whole phrase is matched within text documents via boolean or weighted operators. Domain specific lexicons and thesauruses can be used to assist the search and retrieval. This relies on intelligent classification or categorization schemes. A well designed lexicon and thesaurus can reduce the number of search queries and improve the search precision.

The information space I has a set of basic functions $\{O_{mn...pqr\beta}\}$ (β is the enumeration index of functions involving the m-,n-,...,p-, q-, and r-th information bases) including the following categories:

1. information capture (digitization, authoring, composition),

2. information transmission (communication, transformation),

3. information organization (indexing, storing, global naming),

4. information access (query, search, retrieval, summarization),

5. information sharing and integration (collaboration tools).

These functions are applicable to various aspects of the information space I. While some functions, e.g., information composition, are functions on individual information objects, others, e.g., information global naming, are functions on the set of all objects.

Information composition uses for instance set theoretic operations on objects and hyperobjects in the information space. Information transformation is a parsing program which changes the format of an externally incoming information object into an information object of internal types. It changes the syntax and field names from the external object to an internal object. Information search and retrieval is based on indexing of names, types, and fields. Information browsing and navigation is conducted through links of objects and hyperobjects.

5 COLLABORATIVE TECHNOLOGY

Through various hardware and software tools, collaboration technology supports a group of users interactively writing articles, designing artifacts, and solving problems. Digital libraries provide the information objects to which these collaboration tools are applied. Therefore, these two technologies are complementary to each other. Digital libraries and collaboration technology expands traditional libraries and intellectual

work from a single user to a group of users. The expansion goes into time and space dimensions for all users.

Collaboration technology has been implemented by a suite of hardware (peripheral devices) and software tools on networked workstations and personal computers. Basically, CSCW (Computer-Supported Cooperative Work) is synonymous to collaboration technology. Recently, CSCW has been enhanced by DAI (Distributed AI). In fact, DAI provides some of the theoretical foundations of collaboration technology. In DAI, the computer-supported workspace S becomes the global state space which is the union of local state spaces $\{S_a\}$ belonging to users ($a \in A$, A is the set of all users). The local and global state spaces interact with the information space I. For example, global and local state spaces may be ingested into the global information space. If users only access and retrieve information from the global information space, those information objects retrieved become local state spaces. If users start to solve problems using the retrieved objects, then their local state spaces and the global state space will evolve.

Actually the combination of digital libraries and collaboration technology is what the ultimate digital library should be. There is a self-organizing ingest process of adding new objects into the information space. This leads also to the concept of self-organizing digital libraries. A digital library should be self-organizing to satisfy the need of changing environments and organizations.

6 INTELLIGENT AGENTS

The reliable, smooth, and stable operation of digital libraries depends on a collection of intelligent agents, each of which performs certain specific tasks at various levels in the complex hierarchy of digital libraries. Intelligent agents are intelligent software which are equipped with capabilities, such as planning, reasoning, clustering, sensing, and decision making. The agents should interact with the dynamic environment by receiving inputs and executing outputs through an I/O system. It understands and interacts with the environment, because it can reason, learn from experience, and make decisions to reach certain goals [4], [5].

The "glue" of digital libraries is to tie various system components together in a unified framework by system interface agents. System interface agents are necessary to assure interoperability among subsystems, which is the compatibility among subsystems at specified levels of interactions under a prescribed set of protocols. Interoperability allows diverse subsystems to communicate with each other so that any service will be transparent to the users. A system interface agent is the connection between two components which can be specified in logical (message format and exchange procedure) terms.

Also, user interface agents are needed to satisfy user-centered access to the information space I by the users ($a \in A$, A is the set of all users). Finally, mediator agents are needed to facilitate the mediation and meta control of components, system interface and user interface agents.

Some information agents have been studied by other researchers [12]. For example, the filtering agent, based on the user's interest, builds user profiles and filters incoming information, such as e-mail messages, to the user. The user profiles are extracted from local state spaces $\{S_a\}$. One may consider the user profile P_a for user a as a set of constraints defined on a set of variables in S_a. The filtering process is then reduced to a constraint-satisfaction problem on a dynamic set of incoming information objects. Such agents are considered as user-interface agents.

Mediator agents can be many kinds. They deal with more global and meta issues. One kind of mediator agents is for distributed search and resource discovery. Since resources $\{I_n\}$ are distributed, algorithms are needed to locate distributed resources and to perform network search strategies. A distributed search and resource discovery agent is needed for digital libraries. It has to resolve network protocol, resource allocation, and global naming issues. Another kind of mediator agents is for meta control of various user-interface agents. If a very large number of users ($a \in A, A$ is the set of all users) are on-line, a mediator agent as "traffic police" to manage the traffic of users becomes necessary.

7 A COMMON ONTOLOGY OF INFORMATION SPACE

Although human knowledge varies from individual to individual, knowledge dissemination using digital libraries and collaboration technology needs a common ontology and even a hierarchy of ontologies for semantic meanings of information.

In digital libraries, the distributed search of various heterogeneous information bases $\{I_n\}$ in the information space I has a common ontology. From various sources, information integration of retrieved objects depends on a common ontology. Even if one searches through a single information base, content-based or semantic-based search looks for the content of information objects with respect to a common ontology.

In collaboration tools, information sharing among a group of users requires a common ontology. The interaction among two user applications should include the application protocols that allow one application to communicate with another application. This requires automatic translation between two applications of messages, programs, images, graphics, and their

meanings with respect to a common ontology. The user interfaces must have a common ontology so that they can communicate with digital libraries, collaboration tools, and themselves.

A general approach to the construction of an ontology space is to extract features from information objects, hyperobjects, and agents. This returns to the question of categorization, learning, and knowledge acquisition of key ingredients of digital libraries. Only key ingredients are categorized, learned, and represented by artificial intelligence techniques. A large portion of digital libraries remains in general information format.

8 CONCLUSION

Digital libraries are networked, heterogeneous systems of information bases for education, research, engineering, business, and others. Its information space consists of a large collection of multi-media information bases, bulletin boards, and information services. Collaboration technology offers an additional dimension to the knowledge dissemination model. The scalability issue becomes more manageable, because of human-computer interaction and limited use of artificial intelligence techniques.

REFERENCES

1. V. Bush, "As we may think", *Atlantic Monthly*, 176(1), pp. 101-108, June 1945.

2. E. A. Fox (Ed.), *Source Book on Digital Libraries*, December 6, 1993.

3. *HPCC: Information Infrastructure Technology and Applications*, National Coordination Office for HPCC, 1994.

4. S. Chen, "Spatial mental models in cognitive systems", *Fundamenta Informaticae*, 18, pp. 183-192, 1993.

5. S. Chen, "Digital Libraries", in Critical Reviews: Defining the Information Infrastructure, SPIE, Boston MA, Nov. 2-4, 1994.

6. S. Chen, *Technologies for Digital Libraries*, Proc. of Digital Library Conference, Singapore, March 27-28, 1995.

7. S. Chen, "The NSF/ARPA/NASA "Research on Digital Libraries" Initiative", Proc. of Digital Library Conference, Singapore, March 27-28, 1995.

8. R. Pool, "Turning an info-glut into a library", *Science*, 266, pp. 20-22, Oct. 7, 1994.

9. *NSF News*, NSF PR 94-52, Sept. 27, 1994.

10. National Collaboratories: *Applying Information Technology for Scientific Research*, CSTB, NRC, Washington DC, 1993.

11. I. Greif (Ed.), *Computer-Supported Cooperative Work: A Book of Readings*, Morgan Kaufmann, 1988.

12. Special Issues on Intelligent Agents, *Comm. ACM*, 37(7), July 1994.

13. E. Ristad, *The Language Complexity Game*, MIT Press, Cambridge, 1993.

14. J. F. Canny, *The Complexity of Robot Motion Planning*, MIT Press, Cambridge, 1988.

15. *Proceedings of KB & KS '93*, Japan Information Processing Development Center, 1993.

Authors Index

Aaltonen, A.	228	Oussalah, C.	194
Adali, S.	274	Paasiala, P.	228
Antoniou, G.	187	Pazos, J.	289
Bateman, J.	60	Pinto, N.B.	156
Bisson, G.	236	Raalte, F. van	173
Bonnell, R.D.	156	Rechenmann, F.	7
Burg, J.F.M.	204	Riet, R.P. van de	204
Chen, S.-S.	297	Riitahuhta, A.	228
Dukes-Schlossberg, J.	33	Rodriguez, I.	259
Euzenat, J.	143	Romero, R.	259
Fabris, G.	60	Sekiya, T.	123
Giaretta, P.	25	Simonet, A.	217
Gómez-Pérez, A.	289	Simonet, M.	217
Guarino, N.	25	Speel, P.-H.	73, 173
Iino, K.	84	Stephens, L.M.	156
Ikeda, M.	46	Subrahmanian, V.S.	247
Ishii, M.	123	Takeda, H.	84
Jones, M.	259	Tanskanen, K.	228
Juristo, N.	289	Taylor, A.	114
Kapetanios, E.	132	Timmermans, R.	259
Kerber, R.	33	Tomiyama, T.	123
Lemaire, F.	281	Vanwelkenhuysen, J.	46, 270
Lenat, D.B.	3	Vet, P.E. van der	73, 173
Magnan, M.	194	Wheadon, J.	259
Magnini, B.	60	Whitgift, W.	259
Mark, W.	33	Wickler, G.	165
Mars, N.J.I.	73, 173	Wilks, Y.	97
Mizoguchi, R.	46, 270	Yokoi, T.	13
Niezette, M.	259	Zarri, G.P.	103
Nirenberg, S.	97		
Nishida, T.	84		
Nishiki, M.	84		

Addresses of Authors

Sibel Adalı
Department of Computer Science
Institute for Advanced Computer Studies
Institute for Systems Research
University of Maryland
College Park, MD 20742, USA
E-mail sibel@cs.umd.edu

Grigoris Antoniou
Department of Management
The University of Newcastle
University Drive
Callaghan, Newcastle, NSW 2308, Australia
E-mail mgga@alinga.newcastle.edu.au

John Bateman
GMD/Institut für Integrierte Publikations- und Infor-
mationssysteme (IPSI)
Dolivostr. 15
D-64293 Darmstadt, Germany
E-mail bateman@gmd.de

Gilles Bisson
INRIA Rhône-Alpes
IMAG-LIFIA, Project Sherpa
46, avenue Félix Viallet
38031 Grenoble cedex 1, France
E-mail gilles.bisson@imag.fr

Ronald D. Bonnell
Department of Electrical and Computer Engineering
University of South Carolina
Columbia, SC 29208, USA
E-mail bonnell@ece.scarolina.edu

J.F.M. Burg
Department of Mathematics and Computer Science
Free University
De Boelelaan 1081a
1081 HV Amsterdam, The Netherlands
E-mail jfmburg@cs.vu.nl

Su-Shing Chen
Information Technology & Organizations Program
National Science Foundation
Room 1115, 4201 Wilson Boulevard
Arlington, VA 22230, USA
E-mail schen@nsf.gov

Jérôme Euzenat
INRIA Rhône-Alpes
IMAG-LIFIA
46, avenue Félix Viallet
38031 Grenoble cedex 1, France
E-mail Jerome.Euzenat@imag.fr

Giovanni Fabris
Istituto per la Ricerca Scientifica e Tecnologica (IRST)
38050 Povo, Trento, Italy
E-mail fabris@irst.it

Asunción Gómez-Pérez
Knowledge Systems Laboratory
Stanford University
701 Welch Road, Building C
Palo Alto, CA 94304, USA
E-mail gomez@hpp.stanford.edu

Nicola Guarino
LADSEB-CNR
Corso Stati Uniti, 4
I-35020 Padova, Italy
E-mail guarino@ladseb.pd.cnr.it

---

*In same cases, only the name and address of the first
or corresponding author of a paper are included in this list.
Also, in case of multiple afiliations, only one is given here.

Masaki Ishii
Department of Precision Machinery Engineering
Faculty of Engineering
The University of Tokyo
Hongo 7-3-1, Bunkyo-ku
Tokyo 113, Japan
E-mail ishii@zzz.pe.u-tokyo.ac.jp

Natalia Juristo
Laboratorio de Inteligencia Artificial
Facultad de Informatica
Campus de Montegancedo sn
Boadilla del Monte 28660, Madrid, Spain
E-mail natalia@fi.upm.es

Epaminondas Kapetanios
Research Centre Karlsruhe
Institute of Applied Computer Science
P.O. Box 3640
D-76021 Karlsruhe, Germany
E-mail nondas@iai.kfk.de

Florence Lemaire
INRIA Rhône-Alpes
IMAG-LIFIA
46, avenue Félix Viallet
38031 Grenoble cedex 1, France
E-mail Florence.Lemaire@imag.fr

Douglas B. Lenat
CYCORP, Inc.
3500 West Balcones Center Drive
Austin, TX 78759, USA
E-mail doug@Cyc.com

Martine Magnan
LGI2P/EMA-EERIE
Parc Scientifique Georges Besse
30000 Nîmes, France
E-mail magnan@eerie.fr

Bernardo Magnini
Istituto per la Ricerca Scientifica e Tecnologica (IRST)
38050 Povo, Trento, Italy
E-mail magnini@irst.it

William Mark
Lockheed Artificial Intelligence Center
3251 Hanover Street O/96-20 B/254F
Palo Alto, CA 94304, USA
E-mail mark@aic.lockheed.com

Nicolaas J.I. Mars
Knowledge-based Systems Group
Department of Computer Science
University of Twente
P.O. Box 217
7500 AE Enschede, The Netherlands
E-mail mars@cs.utwente.nl

Riichiro Mizoguchi
Research Department of Electronics
The Institute of Scientific and Industrial Research
Osaka University
8-1 Mihogaoka
Ibaraki, Osaka 567, Japan
E-mail miz@ei.sanken.osaka-u.ac.jp

Toyoaki Nishida
Graduate School of Information Science
Nara Institute of Science and Technology (NAIST)
8916-5 Takayama-cho, Ikoma-shi
Nara 630-01, Japan
E-mail nishida@is.aist-nara.ac.jp

Chabane Oussalah
LGI2P/EMA-EERIE
Parc Scientifique Georges Besse
30000 Nîmes, France
E-mail oussalah@eerie.fr

Juan Pazos
Laboratorio de Inteligencia Artificial
Facultad de Informatica
Campus de Montegancedo sn
Boadilla del Monte 28660, Madrid, Spain
E-mail jpazos@fi.upm.es

Frank van Raalte
Knowledge-based Systems Group
Department of Computer Science
University of Twente
P.O. Box 217
7500 AE Enschede, The Netherlands
E-mail vraalte@cs.utwente.nl

Franqis Rechenmann
INRIA Rhone-Alpes & IMAG/LIFIA
46, Avenue Felix Viallet
38031 Grenoble cedex 1, France
E-mail Francois.Rechenmann@inria.fr

Reind van de Riet
Department of Mathematics and Computer Science
Free University
De Boelelaan 1081a
1081 HV Amsterdam, The Netherlands
E-mail vdriet@cs.vu.nl

Ana Simonet
Université Joseph Fourier–laboratoire TIMC IMAG
Faculté de médecine de Grenoble
38706 La Tronche cedex, France
E-mail Ana.Simonet@imag.fr

Michel Simonet
Université Joseph Fourier–laboratoire TIMC IMAG
Faculté de médecine de Grenoble
38706 La Tronche cedex, France
E-mail Michel.Simonet@imag.fr

Piet-Hein Speel
Unilever Research Laboratory, Room B0140
P.O. Box 114
3130 AC Vlaardingen, The Netherlands
E-mail piet-hein.speel@2488taux.urlnl.sprint.com

V.S. Subrahmanian
Department of Computer Science
Institute for Advanced Computer Studies
Institute for Systems Research
University of Maryland
College Park, MD 20742, USA
E-mail vs@cs.umd.edu

Kari Tanskanen
Laboratory of Machine Design
Tampere University of Technology
P.O. Box 589
FIN-33101 Tampere, Finland
E-mail ktanskan@tappi.me.tut.fi

Andrew Taylor
Department of Computer Science and Engineering
University of New South Wales
Sydney, Australia
E-mail andrewt@cse.unsw.edu.au

Johan Vanwelkenhuysen
Institute of Scientific and Industrial Research (I.S.I.R.)
Osaka University
8-1 Mihogaoka, Ibaraki
Osaka 567, Japan
E-mail johan@ei.sanken.osaka-u.ac.jp

Paul E. van der Vet
Knowledge-based Systems Group
Department of Computer Science
University of Twente
P.O. Box 217
7500 AE Enschede, The Netherlands
E-mail vet@cs.utwente.nl

Joe Wheadon
European Space Operations Centre
Robert-Bosch Strasse 5
64293 Darmstadt, Germany
E-mail jwheadon@esoc.bitnet

David Whitgift
Logica UK Ltd.
Stephenson House
75 Hampstead Road
London NW1 2NT, United Kingdom
E-mail whitgiftd@logica.co.uk

Gerhard Wickler
Informatics Department
Rutherford Appleton Laboratory
Chilton, DIDCOT, OX11 0QX, United Kingdom
E-mail gw@inf.rl.ac.uk

Yorick Wilks
Computer Science Department
University of Sheffield
Sheffield S1 4DP, United Kingdom
E-mail yorick@dcs.shef.ac.uk

Toshio Yokoi
Japan Electronic Dictionary Research Institute, Ltd.
Mita-Kokusai-Building Annex
4-28, Mita 1-chome, Minato-ku
Tokyo 108, Japan
E-mail yokoi@edr.co.jp

Gian Piero Zarri
EHESS - CAMS
54, boulevard Raspail
75270 Paris cedex 06, France
E-mail zarri@cams.msh-paris.fr